THE ROUTLEDGE ATLAS OF THE SECONI WORLD WAR

THE COMPLETE VISUAL HISTORY OF THE SECOND WORLD WAR

'This really is a brilliantly useful book . . . All in all, this is an outstanding reference work that can also be enjoyed as an unusual graphic history of the Second World War and its many political, economic and military dimensions.'

Military Illustrated

'Of the greatest interest and originality.'

Sir John Keegan

'Sir Martin Gilbert's *Atlas of the Second World War* is a work of extraordinary scholarship . . . No university, library, historian – or anyone interested in World War II – will want to be without it.'

Henry Kissinger

In *The Routledge Atlas of the Second World War*, Martin Gilbert graphically charts the war's political, military, economic and social history through 257 illuminating maps. The atlas covers all the major events from the German invasion of Poland in September 1939 to the defeat of Japan in August 1945, including the Blitz; the Fall of France; Pearl Harbor; the naval Battles of the Atlantic, the Indian Ocean and the Pacific; Dieppe; Stalingrad; Midway; the Normandy Landings; the bombing of Warsaw, London, Coventry, Hamburg, Dresden, Tokyo, Hiroshima and Nagasaki; the Burma Railway; concentration camps and slave labour camps; and prisoner-of-war camps in Europe, the Americas and the Far East.

Focusing on the human – and inhuman – aspects of the war, *The Routledge Atlas of the Second World War* includes examination of:

- Military, naval and air campaigns on all the war fronts
- The war on land, at sea and in the air, and behind the lines
- The economic and social aspects of the war
- The global nature of the war, in armed combat and in suffering
- The impact of the war on civilians, both under occupation, and as deportees and refugees
- The aftermath of the war: post-war political and national boundaries; war graves; and the human cost of the war on every continent.

This new paperback edition includes several updates to existing maps, as well as ten new maps specially drawn for this edition. The new maps include studies of Japanese-American and African-American soldiers serving with the United States Army, British women special agents, Belgium at war, and the German occupation of the Channel Islands.

Sir Martin Gilbert is one of the leading historians of his generation. An Honorary Fellow of Merton College, Oxford – of which he was a fellow for thirty years – he is the official biographer of Churchill and the author of eighty-two books, among them *Churchill – A Life*; *The Second World War*; *D-Day*; *The Day the War Ended* and the three-volume *A History of the Twentieth Century*. For more information please visit www.martingilbert.com.

BOOKS BY MARTIN GILBERT

THE ROUTLEDGE ATLAS OF THE SECOND WORLD WAR

2nd Edition

Martin Gilbert

Routledge
Taylor & Francis Group

LONDON AND NEW YORK

First edition published 2008

Second edition published 2009
by Routledge
2 Park Square, Milton Park, Abingdon, Oxon OX14 4RN

Simultaneously published in the USA and Canada
by Routledge
270 Madison Ave, New York, NY 10016

Routledge is an imprint of the Taylor & Francis Group, an informa business

Typeset in Sabon by Keystroke, Tettenhall, Wolverhampton
Printed and bound in Great Britain by The Cromwell Press Group, Trowbridge, Wiltshire

British Library Cataloguing in Publication Data
A catalogue record for this book is available from the British Library

Library of Congress Cataloging in Publication Data
A catalog record for this book has been requested

ISBN10: 0-415-55289-3 (pbk)

ISBN13: 978-0-415-55289-9 (pbk)

Contents

Introduction to the First Edition

Forty years ago, while I was preparing my *Atlas of the First World War*, I asked Field Marshal Montgomery, who had been a young officer in that war – seeing action at Mons, the Somme, Arras and Passchendaele – if he would write the introduction. In it he wrote: 'It was an honour when my friend Martin Gilbert asked me to write an introduction to this atlas. I look forward eagerly to his atlas of the 1939–45 war in which I fought on the battlefields of Africa and Europe – but by then being somewhat more senior in rank than in 1914.'

The Field Marshal, whose grave had been dug on the Western Front in 1914 in expectation of his death – after he had been shot through the lung by a sniper – died in 1976 at the age of eighty-eight. I dedicate this atlas to his memory, and for his encouragement of my work; I trust he would have approved of these maps, on several of which he appears: commanding the Eighth Army in North Africa, from Egypt to Tunisia, and the 21st Army Group in northern Europe, from Normandy to Luneberg Heath, where on 4 May 1945 he received the German offer to surrender.

In the past four decades, my researches have introduced me to many aspects of the Second World War. The 247 maps in this atlas are the fruit of those researches. At the centre of the war were the battles that marked its course and ensured its outcome: battles that were fought in Europe, in Asia, in Africa, on land, on the seas and oceans, and in the skies.

In addition to the maps of the battles, other maps tell the story of prisoners of war who were so often killed after they had surrendered; of millions of victims of racial policies; of millions who lived under the shadow of the bomber; and of individual heroes and heroism in every walk of life: men and women who showed that, even amid horrific evil, some shafts of light and goodness could survive, and be effective.

Every author is influenced by personal experiences and memories. Among the themes I have mapped is that of prisoners of war. As a ten-year-old schoolboy in Britain, I was greatly affected by the distressing experiences of my father's cousin Simmy Gordon, who had been a prisoner of war of the Japanese. In the 1970s I was influenced by Victor West, who signed his books of poetry for me with the names of the prisoner-of-war camps in which he had been incarcerated in Germany between 1941 and 1945: he had been taken prisoner during the fighting in Greece, when the unit with which he was fighting ran out of ammunition.

In my travels through Europe, I met and befriended men and women who had taken part in the partisan war, choosing the dangerous path of resistance to occupation. They too influenced my work, as did the numerous wall plaques in so many European countries dedicated to those who had been shot down at street corners and in doorways for daring to challenge the occupying power. This atlas has several maps showing the range and nature of the resistance movements: including those in France, the Soviet Union, Yugoslavia, Greece and the Far East.

In the summer of 1940, as a three-and-a-half year old evacuee to Canada, I was on board a Canadian Pacific ocean liner, the *Duchess of Bedford*, then part of a large convoy, when German U-boats attacked. The *Duchess* had the speed to hurry away, her captain having ordered the lifeboats to be extended on their davits as he hurried westward. The slower merchant ships had no means of escape, and five were torpedoed. My memories of that voyage, and what I learned about it after the war, influenced me in my determination to give due weight to the merchant seamen who carried food and war supplies across the oceans at such great risk. Their fortitude and plight is an integral part of several of the maps.

Returning to Britain by troopship – the converted ocean liner *Mauretania* – from New York in April 1944, my seven-year-old eyes were shocked by the sight of the devastation of aerial bombing: the dock area of Liverpool, where the troopship bringing me home had docked. As a London schoolboy a few years later, travelling through Germany and central Europe, I saw the still-pulverised ruins of Cologne. So many of those with whom I later talked in the course of my historical researches recalled being under attack from the air. When, in 1962, I was preparing a volume of interwar political and protest poetry (as yet unpublished), Siegfried Sassoon sent me a copy of his poem – written thirty years earlier, three months before Hitler came to power in Germany – in which he forecast that, in the not too distant future, 'Fear will be synonymous with Flight.' Many of the maps relate to the bombing war.

Thirty-seven years ago, I went with my father to the Western Front, to visit the battlefields of the First World War. Then, as on each subsequent visit to the war cemeteries there, I was struck by how many graves there were of those killed in action in the Second World War. On a recent visit to Belgium, at the Commonwealth War Graves Commission cemetery at Heverlee, are the graves of twenty-nine soldiers killed in the First World War and more than eight hundred airmen shot down during the Second World War: Australians, Britons, Canadians and Poles among them. In other war cemeteries in Western Europe, I have stood by the graves of Belgians, Czechoslovaks, Dutchmen, Frenchmen, Germans, Indians, New Zealanders, South Africans, and soldiers, sailors and airmen of many other nationalities, as well as nurses killed as they tended the wounded, or – as in Hong Kong – murdered after capture.

At Pearl Harbor, I have seen the graves and memorials of those killed in that sudden attack on 7 December 1941 that expanded the war to the Pacific. In the Philippines, I have bowed my head at the vast field of American war graves on a hill on the outskirts of Manila. In Hong Kong, I paid my respects at the graves of soldiers and civilians, men, women and children. These graves are a stark reminder of the grim range of war: Buddhists, Hindus, Jews, Muslims, Parsees, Sikhs and Chinese each have their own cemeteries throughout Hong Kong, as do the British and Commonwealth soldiers. In Normandy, I have visited the American, Commonwealth, German and Polish cemeteries that now mark the course of the battle.

No visitor can fail to be deeply affected by the Commonwealth War Graves Commission cemeteries, so beautifully maintained, and with so much of the human saga of war incised upon the gravestones and printed in the cemetery registers. Several maps in this atlas show the location of the war graves of all the combatants, in Europe, Asia and the United States.

During one of my journeys through Europe, in 1953, while crossing from the Soviet to the British zone of Austria, at the Semmering Pass, I came across a Displaced Persons' camp, one of the last still in existence, eight years after the war had ended. Comfortable in my London boarding school, with parents to visit at the weekend, and summer holidays by the sea, I had no idea at that time of the harsh realities of displacement and dispossession. Later in my historical researches, I met many people who had been uprooted during the Second World War, and had become wanderers, until some country took them in. Many of the maps in this atlas relate to the many millions who have been expelled, driven out, and forced to seek a new country in which to live – a new homeland.

Ironically, I had reached that Displaced Persons' camp in Austria after hitchhiking from Vienna: the man who gave me a lift in his car was a former German soldier who had fought on the Eastern Front and been taken prisoner. Like most of his fellow German prisoners of war, he had remained in captivity in the Soviet Union for five years after the war had ended. I already knew at first hand about Axis prisoners of war, thought not about those in such harsh conditions. When the Second World War ended, I had been evacuated with my parents to the village of North Hinksey, just outside Oxford. Some hundred yards behind the house to which I had been evacuated was a prisoner-of-war camp, mostly with Italian soldiers. As an eight-year-old, I often spoke to them through the fence. We envied the Red Cross rations they received: fresh eggs, while we used powdered eggs. This atlas – which includes the North Hinksey prisoner-of-war camp – reflects the wide range of experience of prisoners of war: including those in German, Japanese, and Soviet captivity.

The war at sea was continuous and relentless. I have drawn maps to show the extent of German submarine sinkings in the Atlantic; German submarine activities in the Pacific; the Arctic convoys; the destruction of three of Germany's greatest warships, *Bismarck*, *Scharnhorst* and *Tirpitz*; the Pacific naval battles; the Japanese naval attacks in the Indian Ocean and in Australian waters; the deaths of Allied prisoners of war, mostly Americans, on board the Japanese 'Hellships' bombed by American warplanes; and the destruction of the Japanese merchant fleet – Japan's wartime raw material lifeline.

I also map the worst maritime disasters of the Second World War, starting with at least 3,500 Allied soldiers, sailors, airmen and civilians drowned on steamship *Lancastria* as she was bombed while off St Nazaire in 1940; and ending in 1945 with 16,600 German refugees drowned on three ships as they tried to make their way from the approaching Soviet forces in East Prussia to a safer German port further west. I also map the drowning, during a British bombing raid on what were thought to be German troopships in Lübeck harbour, of 2,750 Jewish concentration camp evacuees on board the *Thielbeck* and 3,500 on the *Cap Arcona*.

A British historian naturally sees events through the prism of a British education and British experiences, but I have done my utmost in this atlas, as in all my historical writing, to give as wide a perspective as the narrative demands. The maps take the reader into many lands and episodes. Maps on the war in the Far East and the Pacific include the Bataan 'March of Death', the first United States bombing raid on Tokyo – the 'Doolittle Raid', the Kamikaze pilots, the 'Comfort Women' forced into prostitution in lands under Japanese occupation, and the firebombing of Japanese cities. There are maps on Latin America's contribution to the Allied war effort, on India's contribution, on Australia's contribution, and on Poland's contribution. Several maps relate to the fate and fortitude of Greece.

Those who left their countries and fought with the British forces are represented here, among them the Czechoslovak airmen, their bases in Britain, and their contribution to the war long after Czechoslovakia had been dismembered in March 1939. Another map shows the French forces in action in Europe and Africa after the fall of France in June 1940. There are two maps portraying Norway's contribution to the Allied war effort after Norway had been overrun by Germany. There are maps of the German and American quests to build an atom bomb. There are maps of Christians throughout Europe who saved the lives of Jews at the risk of their own; of the fate of the Gypsies (Roma and Sinti); and of the liberation of the concentration camps.

I have mapped Hitler's headquarters, and the bomb plots against him; and the conferences that Churchill attended, in the Americas, Europe, Africa and Asia, at which war policy was determined.

Canada, alone of the nations at war, had an entirely volunteer army from the beginning to the final month of the war. Maps show the Canadians in action in Europe, the Canadians at Dieppe, the British Commonwealth air training facilities set up throughout Canada, Japanese-Canadians interned during the war, and German and Italian prisoner-of-war camps in Canada.

Plans that were made but never came to pass are also part of the story of the Second World War. As well as a map on the German plan to invade Britain, there are maps in this atlas on the German plan to partition and virtually eliminate the Soviet Union, the Soviet plan to liberate Denmark in the last weeks of the war in Europe, and the United States plan – before the atom bomb became a reality – to defeat Japan by invading the Japanese mainland.

In 1959, I made the first of many visits to Poland: visits that helped me understand the different national perspectives on the war, and Polish suspicions of Germany, just as a visit to Shanghai forty-five years later showed me the extent of Chinese bitterness against the Japanese. My first Polish visit began on 1 September, in Poznan. The city was illuminated with lights and torches, as a sombre procession made its way through the streets. It was the twentieth anniversary of the German invasion of Poland, an act of aggression that had led Britain and France to declare war on Germany two days later, making it more than a two-nation conflict.

Poland's suffering under German occupation was intense. The bravery of her soldiers, sailors and airmen was remarkable, first in the battles in Poland, and then – after Poland had been overrun and partitioned between Germany and the Soviet Union – as part of the Allied forces. My maps include the contribution of Poles to the Allied war effort after the German conquest; the Polish forces in action in Europe and Africa, the Polish contribution to the war of Signals Intelligence; the Soviet massacre of Polish prisoners of war in April and May 1940, more than six months after they had been captured; Polish civilian victims of German atrocities; and the Warsaw uprising in the summer of 1944.

As many as half of the maps relate to the Soviet Union and the United States. As well as the battles in which they both fought, diverse aspects of their respective wars are an integral part of the story. The Soviet-related maps include Soviet factories dismantled and sent eastward to Siberia and the Urals for safety, the Soviet deportation of Soviet national groups, the routes of Allied aid, the epic battles of Moscow and Stalingrad, the siege of Leningrad, the partisan war, Soviet women snipers, and the massive Soviet fighting efforts on the Eastern Front, drawing steadily closer to Germany, and to Berlin; and the Soviet invasion of Japanese-held Manchuria, two days after the atom bomb had been dropped on Hiroshima.

American-related maps show the Destroyers-for-Bases deal with Britain; the struggle for the Aleutian Islands; Japanese-Americans interned in the United States; German submarine sinkings off the East Coast of the United States; the Liberty Ships built in American shipyards on both the Atlantic and the Pacific coasts to enable Britain to maintain its Atlantic lifeline for food and war supplies; landing craft built in the United States for the Italian, Normandy and South of France landings; American air bases in Britain; American air raids against Germany and Japan; and Japanese, German and Italian prisoner-of-war camps in Oklahoma and elsewhere in the United States.

No country is too small to have its place. Luxembourg has a map to itself. The siege of Malta has a map. There is a collective map for the European neutrals. Estonian and Latvian volunteers fighting alongside the German Army on the Eastern Front have their place in the atlas, as they did on the battlefield; so does the Bosnian Muslim volunteer SS division.

Along with the battles, the Second World War abounds in episodes of valour and daring, in which the courage and endurance of soldiers, sailors and airmen in every army were tested, often at the highest cost. Among the episodes that I have mapped are the evacuations from Dunkirk (30 May – 6 June 1940), the Lofoten Islands raid (4 March 1941), the St Nazaire raid (28 March 1942), the Dieppe raid (19 August 1942), the Chindit expeditions behind Japanese lines in Burma (February 1943 and March 1944), the 'Dambusters' raid on the Ruhr dams (17 May 1943), the 'Jedburgh' teams behind German lines in France after the Normandy landings (June – December 1944), the parachute landings at Arnhem (17–26 September 1944), the final German air attack of the war (7 April 1945), and the local partisan movements active behind the lines throughout the Japanese-conquered regions (January 1942 – August 1945).

There is a section of maps that examine specific aspects of the global war: the question of oil resources, Germany's reliance on imported raw material, Japan's need for steel,

United States aid to all its allies, and women at war. The post-war section includes war crimes trials, deportees and refugees, and war graves.

Maps can also address questions that arise after the guns are silent, and when debates and controversy have begun. Several maps in this atlas try to do just that. How and where did Signals Intelligence help the Allies to defeat Germany and Japan? Why was Auschwitz never bombed? Why was Dresden bombed?

The Second World War generated many statistics, all of them disturbing to contemplate. Together with the stories of individuals, and of specific episodes of the war, I have given statistics their place on the maps, culminating in the three final maps, which summarise the number of military and civilian dead in all the countries caught up in the war. The total, if counted up, reaches more than 24 million soldiers, sailors and airmen, and more than 34 million civilians: a combined death toll of more than 58 million men, women and children across the globe.

The war that began with Japan's renewed attack on China in 1937, and came to Europe two years later with the German invasion of Poland in 1939, spread ruthlessly to many nations and to every continent. It led to the loss of far greater military and civilian life than any previous conflict, exceeding in intensity even the ravages of plague and famine of earlier centuries.

The maps in this atlas reflect the war both in its strategic aspects, and in its inhuman – and human – face.

11 July 2008   MARTIN GILBERT

Introduction to the Second Edition

The opportunity of a Second Edition has enabled me to prepare ten new maps. These are: Thirteen British Women Agents Executed After Capture, 1944–1945 (map 144); Deceiving the Germans: The Bogus Allied Army in Scotland, May 1944 (146); A United States Bombardment Squadron, January–July 1945 (194); Japanese Balloon-Bomb Attacks on North America, 1944–1945 (196); Japanese-American – *Nisei* – Soldiers in Action, 1943–1945 (211); African-American Soldiers in Action, 1944–1945 (212); Allied Conferences, 1941–1945 (221); Belgium at War, 1939–1945 (222); Britain's Art Treasures Evacuated, 1939–1945 (223); and The Channel Islands, 1940–1945 (224). I have updated the map Christians Who Saved Jews from Death, 1939–1945 (map 230), using the most recent figures available on 1 January 2009. I have also been able to revise the map of The German Concentration Camp System, 1939–1945 (map 103), using the comprehensive single-sheet map *Mitteleuropa in der ersten Hälfte des Jahres 1945* (Munich, 1968) by Edward Kossoy, who has located 789 concentration camps in Greater Germany. It is my good fortune to have been in correspondence with Edward Kossoy for many years. I would like to dedicate this Second Edition to him.

26 April 2009   MARTIN GILBERT

Acknowledgements

First and foremost I am grateful to Tim Aspden, who has transformed a hundred and fifty of my rough drafts and suggestions into maps of the highest quality. For more than twenty years he has been a main pillar of my historical atlas work. For this atlas, a hundred maps were also drawn – on the basis of my rough drafts – by Mike Shand, CartoGraphics Unit, Department of Geographical and Earth Sciences, University of Glasgow; and Neil Hanson of Nordicmaps; their help has been indispensable.

In my search for historical and geographic information, I would like to thank all those who answered my queries, or who sent me material for specific maps, among them Peter Brannan, Debby Busse, Terry Cameron, Ronald I. Cohen, Frank Fletcher, Richard S. Garber, Rob Greene (*After the Battle*), Professor Cameron Hazlehurst, Ben Helfgott, Professor Dr. Sigfrid Hoefert, Major and Mrs Holt, Dan Mailer, Dominic Brendan Mammola, Paul Morley, Shoshana Poznansky, John Radzilowski, Margaret Shannon, Ksenya Shergova, Pawel Szymanski, Tamara Vershitskaya, Dr Nissim Yosha, Matthew White and Enid Wurtman. Sir John Keegan gave me the full benefit of his considerable expertise.

Dr Derek Tully has been a font of creative suggestions and encouragement. Serena Woolrich, Allgenerations Inc., has given me access to important data from her website.

I am grateful to Lieutenant-Colonel (retired) Arnost Polak, and the Free Czechoslovak Air Force Association, for material on the Czechoslovaks who served in the Royal Air Force in the Second World War. For material on Japanese prisoner-of-war camps, I am indebted, as are all historians, to Roger Mansell, Director, Center for Research, Allied POWS Under the Japanese, and his website: www.mansell.com

The following institutions have given me access to their holdings and materials: the Australian War Memorial Library and Archives, the Commonwealth Air Training Plan Museum, Brandon, Manitoba, Canada; the Imperial War Museum, London; the National Archives, Washington DC; and the National Archives (formerly the Public Record Office), Kew, London.

Max Arthur, as always, has been a font of wise suggestions. Mirit Poznansky gave me good guidance about topics to be included. For help in sorting a mass of material – which I have been collecting since the publication of my First World War atlas in 1971 – Ela Czernecka has been patient and indefatigable. Kay Thomson has scrutinised the maps with a careful and critical eye, and has made many important suggestions as to form and style.

The encouragement of Routledge, the publishers of my historical atlases, has been particularly important with this atlas, the first that I have prepared especially for them; I would like to thank the Publisher, Claire L'Enfant, Vicky Peters, Eve Setch, Emma Langley, Elizabeth Clifford, Susan Dixon, and all those at Routledge who have supported me in the long process from idea to publication.

To my wife Esther, my thanks are due for the myriad ways in which she has advised and guided me towards ensuring that this atlas is my best endeavour.

Maps

Section 1

FROM THE GERMAN INVASION OF POLAND TO THE FALL OF FRANCE

We are fighting to save the world from the pestilence of Nazi tyranny and in defence of all that is most sacred to man.

This is no war of domination or imperial aggrandisement or material gain; no war to shut any country out of its sunlight and means of progress.

It is a war, viewed in its inherent quality, to establish, on impregnable rocks, the rights of the individual; and it is a war to establish and revive the stature of man.

WINSTON CHURCHILL
House of Commons
3 September 1939

GERMANY, 1919–1939

After Adolf Hitler came to power in Germany in January 1933, at the head of the Nazi Party, Germany began to rearm, violating the clauses of the Versailles Treaty of 1920, and embarking on a process of territorial expansion.

SWEDEN

LATVIA

LITHUANIA

North Sea

DENMARK ● Copenhagen

Baltic Sea

Memel

MEMELLAND

Danzig

Königsberg

EAST PRUSSIA

● Esterwegen ● Hamburg

Sachsenhausen ● Berlin

FREE CITY OF DANZIG (since 1920)

Vistula

Bug

THE NETHERLANDS

BELGIUM

GREATER

● Poznan

Warsaw ●

● Cologne

GERMANY

Leipzig

POLAND

RHINELAND

LUX

SUDETENLAND

Breslau

SAAR

● Frankfurt-on-Main

Rhine

Prague ●

CZECHOSLOVAKIA

Vistula

FRANCE

Strasbourg

Danube

Dachau ●● Munich

Heuberg

Bratislava ●

Bern ●

SWITZERLAND

AUSTRIA

Vienna

Budapest ●

HUNGARY

ROMANIA

ITALY

Milan ●

YUGOSLAVIA

| 0 | kilometres | 200 |
| 0 | miles | 100 |

Adriatic Sea

----- International borders, 1919–1935

Saar: regained by League of Nations plebiscite, March 1935

Rhineland: German sovereign territory, remilitarised March 1936

Austria: annexed, March 1938

Sudetenland: annexed, October 1938

Bohemia and Moravia: occupied, March 1939

Memelland: annexed, May 1939

Concentration camps established in 1933

Germany's border, June to September 1939

© Martin Gilbert 2008

1

THE DEFEAT AND PARTITION OF POLAND, 1 SEPTEMBER – 31 OCTOBER 1939

The German invasion of Poland on 1 September 1939 marked the start of the Second World War.

LATVIA

LITHUANIA

Kaunas

Baltic Sea

Danzig
Königsberg
EAST PRUSSIA
GERMANY

Vilna

Minsk

Suwalki

Augustow
Grodno
Lomza
Bialystok

Poznan

Warsaw

P O L A N D

Lodz

Lublin

Breslau

Lutsk
Sokal
Rovno

GERMANY

Tarnow
Cracow
Jaroslaw

Lvov

Przemysl
Tarnopol

Pinsk

Brest-Litovsk

Kamenets-Podolsk

SLOVAKIA

Bratislava

Stanislawow

HUNGARY

ROMANIA

	Dividing line between the German and Soviet zones of occupation, agreed upon in advance in the Nazi-Soviet Pact of 23 August 1939
⇨	German advance into Poland from 1 September 1939
←	Soviet advance into Poland from 17 September 1939
■	Annexed by the Soviet Union in October 1939
▨	Annexed by Germany in October 1939
▨	Annexed by Lithuania in October 1939

0	kilometres	150
0	miles	100

Following the German invasion of Poland on 1 September 1939, Britain and France activated their treaty alliances with Poland and declared war on Germany on 3 September 1939.

© Martin Gilbert 2008

2

SOVIET ANNEXATIONS, 1939–1940

The eastward advance of German rule and influence led to a westward advance of Soviet control. By June 1940 the Soviet Union had set up what Stalin hoped would be a territorial barrier against any further German advance eastward.

0   kilometres   300

0   miles   200

FINLAND

SWEDEN
neutral

GERMANY

POLAND

SLOVAKIA

AUSTRIA   **HUNGARY**

ROMANIA

SOVIET UNION

Petrozavodsk

Lake Onega

KARELIA

Lake Ladoga

Vyborg

Helsinki

Hangö

Gulf of Finland

Leningrad

Tallin (Reval)

Lake Peipus

Lake Pskov

Pskov

Gulf of Riga

Riga

Memel

Kaunas (Kovno)

Vilna

Minsk

Danzig

Königsberg

Grodno

Pinsk

Warsaw

Lublin

Kiev

Zhitomir

Tarnow

Lvov

Przemysl

Kamenets-Podolsk

Balta

Uzhgorod

Jassy

Kishinev

Odessa

Baltic Sea

Black Sea

PART OF FINLAND
Russian before 1917
Finnish 1918–1939

ESTONIA
Russian before 1917
Independent 1918–1939

LATVIA
Russian before 1914
Independent 1920–1939

LITHUANIA
Russian before 1914
Independent 1919–1939

EASTERN POLAND
Russian before 1914
Polish 1919–1939

EASTERN GALICIA
Austrian before 1918
Polish 1918–1939

BESSARABIA
Russian before 1917
Romanian 1918–1940

BUKOVINA
Austrian before 1918
Romanian 1918–1940

■ Occupied by the Soviet Union between October 1939 and December 1940

— The German Reich (Greater Germany) in December 1939

▨ Under German political control or influence by December 1940

© Martin Gilbert 2008

3

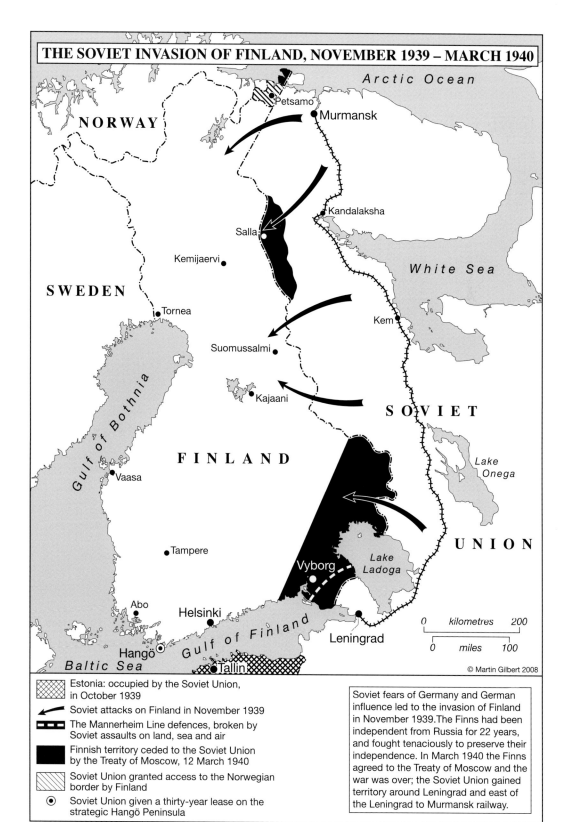

THE SOVIET INVASION OF FINLAND, NOVEMBER 1939 – MARCH 1940

Arctic Ocean

NORWAY

Petsamo

Murmansk

Kandalaksha

Salla

Kemijaervi

White Sea

SWEDEN

Tornea

Kem

Suomussalmi

SOVIET

Kajaani

FINLAND

Lake Onega

Vaasa

Gulf of Bothnia

UNION

Tampere

Vyborg

Lake Ladoga

Abo

Helsinki

Leningrad

Hangö

Gulf of Finland

Tallin

Baltic Sea

0   kilometres   200

0   miles   100

© Martin Gilbert 2008

Estonia: occupied by the Soviet Union, in October 1939

Soviet attacks on Finland in November 1939

The Mannerheim Line defences, broken by Soviet assaults on land, sea and air

Finnish territory ceded to the Soviet Union by the Treaty of Moscow, 12 March 1940

Soviet Union granted access to the Norwegian border by Finland

Soviet Union given a thirty-year lease on the strategic Hangö Peninsula

Soviet fears of Germany and German influence led to the invasion of Finland in November 1939. The Finns had been independent from Russia for 22 years, and fought tenaciously to preserve their independence. In March 1940 the Finns agreed to the Treaty of Moscow and the war was over; the Soviet Union gained territory around Leningrad and east of the Leningrad to Murmansk railway.

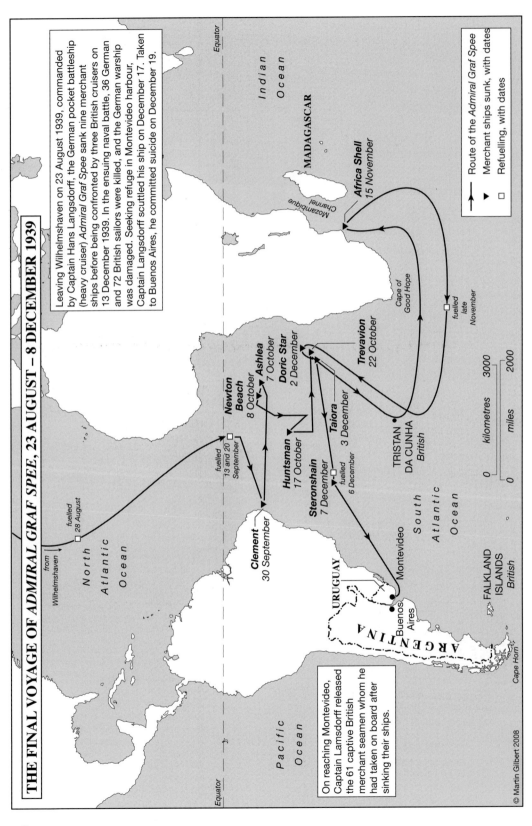

THE FINAL VOYAGE OF ADMIRAL GRAF SPEE, 23 AUGUST – 8 DECEMBER 1939

Leaving Wilhelmshaven on 23 August 1939, commanded by Captain Hans Langsdorff, the German pocket battleship (heavy cruiser) *Admiral Graf Spee* sank nine merchant ships before being confronted by three British cruisers on 13 December 1939. In the ensuing naval battle, 36 German and 72 British sailors were killed, and the German warship was damaged. Seeking refuge in Montevideo harbour, Captain Langsdorff scuttled his ship on December 17. Taken to Buenos Aires, he committed suicide on December 19.

On reaching Montevideo, Captain Lamsdorff released the 61 captive British merchant seamen whom he had taken on board after sinking their ships.

→ Route of the *Admiral Graf Spee*

▼ Merchant ships sunk, with dates

□ Refuelling, with dates

Equator

North Atlantic Ocean

Indian Ocean

MADAGASCAR

Mozambique Channel

Africa Shell
15 November

Cape of Good Hope

fuelled late November

fuelled 28 August

from Wilhelmshaven

fuelled 13 and 20 September

Newton Beach
8 October

Ashlea
7 October

Doric Star
2 December

Trevanion
22 October

Clement
30 September

Huntsman
17 October

Steronshain
7 December

Taiora
3 December

fuelled 6 December

TRISTAN DA CUNHA
British

South Atlantic Ocean

kilometres 0   2000   3000

miles 0   2000

Pacific Ocean

Equator

URUGUAY

Montevideo

Buenos Aires

ARGENTINA

FALKLAND ISLANDS
British

Cape Horn

© Martin Gilbert 2008

5

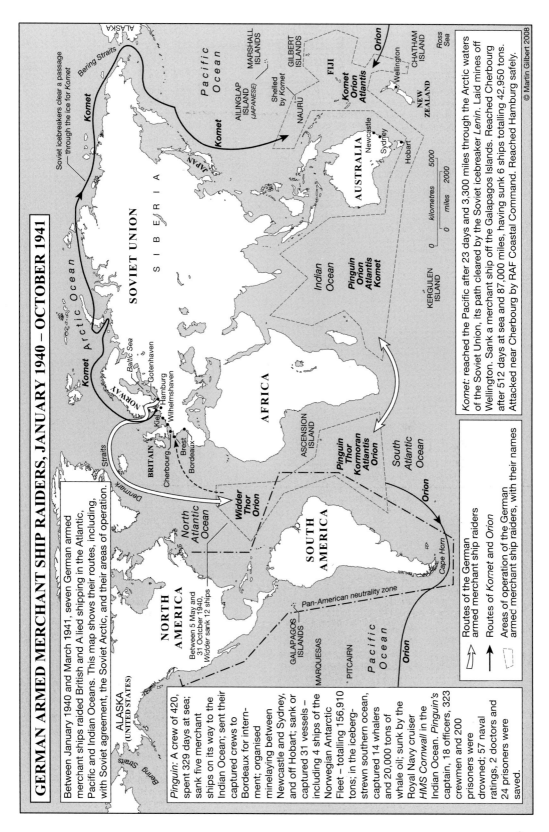

GERMAN ARMED MERCHANT SHIP RAIDERS, JANUARY 1940 – OCTOBER 1941

Between January 1940 and March 1941, seven German armed merchant ships raided British and Allied shipping in the Atlantic, Pacific and Indian Oceans. This map shows their routes, including, with Soviet agreement, the Soviet Arctic, and their areas of operation.

Pinguin: A crew of 420, spent 329 days at sea; sank five merchant ships on its way to the Indian Ocean; sent their captured crews to Bordeaux for internment; organised minelaying between Newcastle and Sydney, and off Hobart; sank or captured 31 vessels – including 4 ships of the Norwegian Antarctic Fleet – totalling 156,910 tons; in the iceberg-strewn southern ocean, captured 14 whalers and 20,000 tons of whale oil; sunk by the Royal Navy cruiser *HMS Cornwall* in the Indian Ocean. *Pinguin's* captain, 18 officers, 323 crewmen and 200 prisoners were drowned; 57 naval ratings, 2 doctors and 24 prisoners were saved.

Between 5 May and 31 October 1940, *Widder* sank 12 ships

Komet: reached the Pacific after 23 days and 3,300 miles through the Arctic waters of the Soviet Union, its path cleared by the Soviet icebreaker *Lenin*. Laid mines off Wellington. Sank a merchant ship off the Galapagos Islands. Reached Cherbourg after 512 days at sea and 87,000 miles, having sunk 6 ships totalling 42,950 tons. Attacked near Cherbourg by RAF Coastal Command. Reached Hamburg safely.

ALASKA (UNITED STATES)

NORTH AMERICA

Pacific Ocean

SOUTH AMERICA

Cape Horn

North Atlantic Ocean

South Atlantic Ocean

AFRICA

Indian Ocean

SOVIET UNION

S I B E R I A

Arctic Ocean

ALASKA

Bering Straits

Bering Straits

Soviet icebreakers clear a passage through the ice for *Komet*

Pacific Ocean

JAPAN

AUSTRALIA

Newcastle

Sydney

Hobart

NEW ZEALAND

Wellington

CHATHAM ISLAND

Ross Sea

FIJI

GILBERT ISLANDS

MARSHALL ISLANDS

AILINGLAP ISLAND (JAPANESE)

NAURU

Shelled by *Komet*

Komet
Orion
Atlantis

Pinguin
Orion
Atlantis
Komet

KERGUELEN ISLAND

Komet

Komet

Orion

NORWAY

BRITAIN

Denmark Straits

Baltic Sea

Gotenhaven

Kiel

Hamburg

Wilhelmshaven

Cherbourg

Brest

Bordeaux

Widder
Thor
Orion

Pinguin
Thor
Kormoran
Atlantis
Orion

ASCENSION ISLAND

Orion

Orion

GALAPAGOS ISLANDS

MARQUESAS

PITCAIRN

Pan-American neutrality zone

Bering Straits

kilometres
miles
0 2000 5000

→ Routes of the German armed merchant ship raiders

→ Routes of *Komet* and *Orion*

Areas of operation of the German armed merchant ship raiders, with their names

© Martin Gilbert 2008

6

SOVIET MASSACRES OF POLISH PRISONERS OF WAR, APRIL–MAY 1940

When the Soviet Union annexed Eastern Poland in October 1939, tens of thousands of Polish officers and intellectuals were arrested and taken to prison camps in the Soviet Union. Acting on Stalin's signed order of 5 March 1940, the Soviet secret police (the NKVD) began on 3 April 1940 executing 22,436 Polish prisoners of war and other Polish intellectuals. The killings took place in three separate locations: the Katyn Forest between the villages of Katyn and Gniezdovo in the Smolensk District, Kalinin Prison, and Kharkov Prison. The Katyn forest graves were discovered by the German Army on 13 April 1943.

Among those murdered in the Katyn Forest were one admiral, two generals, 24 colonels, 79 lieutenant colonels, 258 majors, 300 medical officers and physicians (many of them Jews), 654 army captains, 17 naval captains, 3,420 sergeants and corporals, 85 privates, seven army chaplains, 20 university professors, 200 pilots, more than 100 writers and journalists, and several hundred lawyers, engineers and teachers.

Gryazovets

Vologda

Baltic Sea

Stolbny Island
●NKVD camp

Ostachkov ○ ⟶ △ Kalinin Prison
7,305

S O V I E T   U N I O N

●Moscow

▲Vilna

Katyn
4,421 △
●Smolensk
●Gniezdovo

0   *kilometres* 200
0   *miles*   100

▲Bialystok

▲Slonim

Warsaw ▲

P O L A N D

Pinsk ▲

The figures on this map were those given by the KGB chief Alexander Shelepin to Nikita Khrushchev in 1956; they are widely considered to be at least 4,000 short.

G R E A T E R   G E R M A N Y

▲Lublin

Sarny ▲

28 September 1939. A secret supplementary protocol to the German-Soviet Boundary and Friendship Treaty stated: 'Both parties will tolerate in their territories no Polish agitation that affects the territories of the other party. They will suppress in their territories all beginnings of such agitation, and inform each other of suitable measures for this purpose.'

Rovno ▲

Kozelsk ○
Prisoner-of-War Camp

Lvov ▲

Kharkov Prison △
6,311

Starobielsk
Prisoner-of-War Camp

In the three mass murder sites, a total of 14 Polish generals and more than 40% of the Polish officer corps were killed, as well as many teachers, professors, physicians and writers: a deliberate attempt to destroy the potential future Polish governing and intellectual classes. The only survivors of at least 22,436 officer prisoners of war were 395 who had been sent to Gryazovets. 40,000 Polish privates, corporals and sergeants were interned, most in Siberia *(see map 38)*.

In 2005 the Russian State Prosecutor declared that the massacres, for which the Soviet Union had expressed 'profound regret' in 1990, were not genocide, a war crime, or a crime against humanity, but a military crime for which the fifty-year term of limitation had expired, and that in consequence 'there is absolutely no basis to talk about it in judicial terms.' Of the 183 volumes of files compiled by Russian investigators, 116 have been kept secret, despite assurances by President Putin that the truth could at last be told.

··········· The Polish frontier, 1919–1939

━━━ The German-Soviet partition line, October 1939

▲ Principal towns in eastern Poland, birthplaces of the victims of the April–May 1940 massacres

○ Some of the camps in which the Polish prisoners were held

⟶ Routes from the camps to the execution sites

△ Execution sites

© Martin Gilbert 2008

Black Sea

7

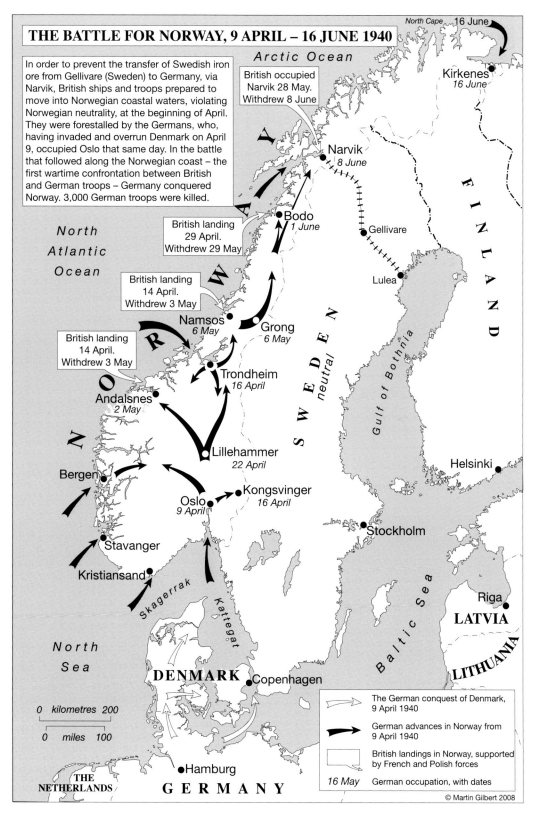

THE BATTLE FOR NORWAY, 9 APRIL – 16 JUNE 1940

In order to prevent the transfer of Swedish iron ore from Gellivare (Sweden) to Germany, via Narvik, British ships and troops prepared to move into Norwegian coastal waters, violating Norwegian neutrality, at the beginning of April. They were forestalled by the Germans, who, having invaded and overrun Denmark on April 9, occupied Oslo that same day. In the battle that followed along the Norwegian coast – the first wartime confrontation between British and German troops – Germany conquered Norway. 3,000 German troops were killed.

Arctic Ocean

North Cape — 16 June

Kirkenes
16 June

British occupied Narvik 28 May. Withdrew 8 June

Narvik
8 June

FINLAND

North Atlantic Ocean

British landing 29 April. Withdrew 29 May

Bodo
1 June

Gellivare

British landing 14 April. Withdrew 3 May

Lulea

S W E D E N *neutral*

British landing 14 April. Withdrew 3 May

Namsos
6 May

Grong
6 May

Trondheim
16 April

Andalsnes
2 May

Gulf of Bothnia

N O R W A Y

Lillehammer
22 April

Helsinki

Bergen

Oslo
9 April

Kongsvinger
16 April

Stockholm

Stavanger

Kristiansand

Baltic Sea

Riga

LATVIA

Skagerrak

Kattegat

LITHUANIA

North Sea

DENMARK

Copenhagen

	The German conquest of Denmark, 9 April 1940
	German advances in Norway from 9 April 1940
	British landings in Norway, supported by French and Polish forces
16 May	German occupation, with dates

THE NETHERLANDS

Hamburg

G E R M A N Y

0 kilometres 200

0 miles 100

© Martin Gilbert 2008

8

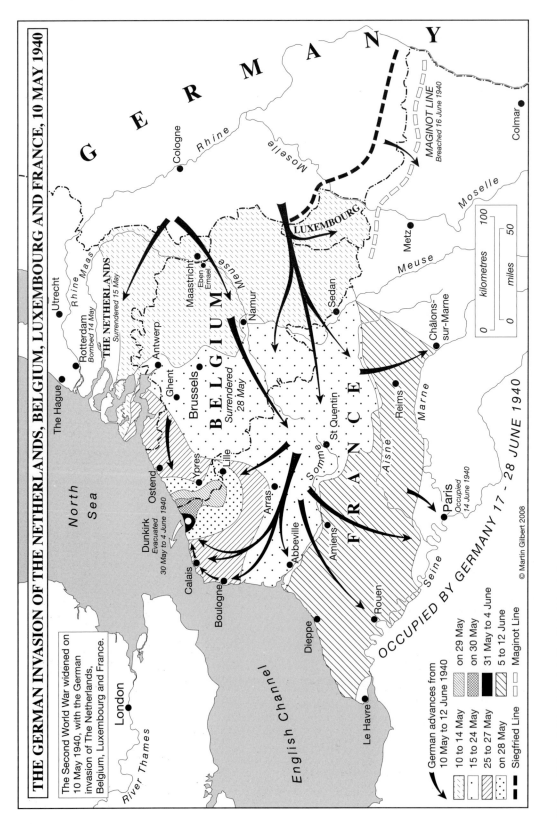

THE GERMAN INVASION OF THE NETHERLANDS, BELGIUM, LUXEMBOURG AND FRANCE, 10 MAY 1940

The Second World War widened on 10 May 1940, with the German invasion of The Netherlands, Belgium, Luxembourg and France.

G E R M A N Y

Cologne

Rhine

Moselle

MAGINOT LINE
Breached 16 June 1940

Colmar

Metz

Moselle

Meuse

LUXEMBOURG

Utrecht

Rhine

Maas

THE NETHERLANDS
Surrendered 15 May

Rotterdam
Bombed 14 May

Maastricht

Eben
Emael

Meuse

Namur

Sedan

Châlons-
sur-Marne

The Hague

Antwerp

Ghent

Brussels

B E L G I U M
Surrendered 28 May

St Quentin

Reims

Marne

100

50

kilometres

miles

0   0

North
Sea

Ostend

Ypres

Lille

Somme

Aisne

Paris
Occupied
14 June 1940

Dunkirk
Evacuated
30 May to 4 June 1940

Calais

Arras

Amiens

F R A N C E

Seine

Boulogne

Abbeville

Rouen

OCCUPIED BY GERMANY 17 – 28 JUNE 1940

Dieppe

Le Havre

English Channel

London

River Thames

© Martin Gilbert 2008

German advances from
10 May to 12 June 1940

10 to 14 May   on 29 May

15 to 24 May   on 30 May

25 to 27 May   31 May to 4 June

on 28 May   5 to 12 June

Siegfried Line   Maginot Line

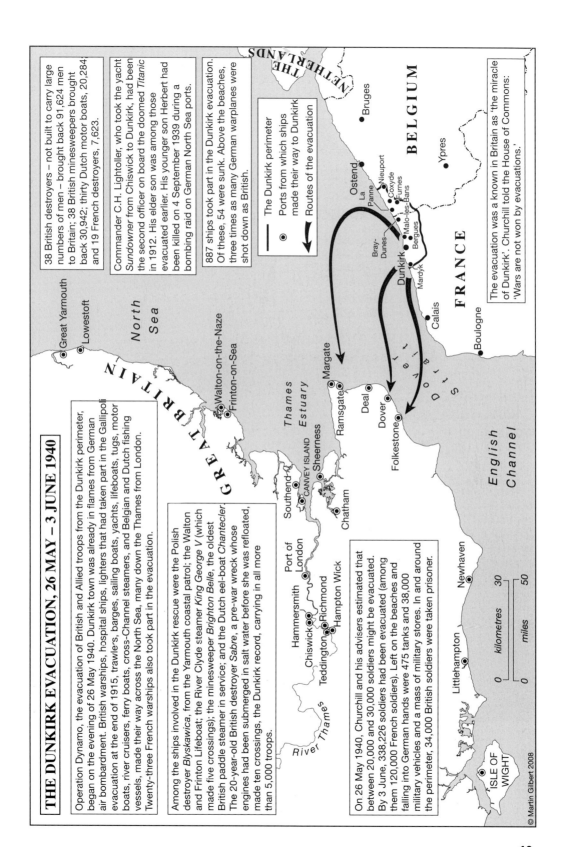

THE DUNKIRK EVACUATION, 26 MAY – 3 JUNE 1940

Operation Dynamo, the evacuation of British and Allied troops from the Dunkirk perimeter, began on the evening of 26 May 1940. Dunkirk town was already in flames from German air bombardment. British warships, hospital ships, lighters that had taken part in the Gallipoli evacuation at the end of 1915, trawlers, barges, sailing boats, yachts, lifeboats, tugs, motor boats, river cruisers, ferry boats, cross-Channel steamers, and Belgian and Dutch fishing vessels, made their way across the North Sea, many down the Thames from London. Twenty-three French warships also took part in the evacuation.

Among the ships involved in the Dunkirk rescue were the Polish destroyer *Blyskawica*, from the Yarmouth coastal patrol; the Walton and Frinton Lifeboat; the River Clyde steamer *King George V* (which made five crossings); the minesweeper *Brighton Belle*, the oldest British paddle steamer in service; and the Dutch eel-boat *Chantecler*. The 20-year-old British destroyer *Sabre*, a pre-war wreck whose engines had been submerged in salt water before she was refloated, made ten crossings, the Dunkirk record, carrying in all more than 5,000 troops.

On 26 May 1940, Churchill and his advisers estimated that between 20,000 and 30,000 soldiers might be evacuated. By 3 June, 338,226 soldiers had been evacuated (among them 120,000 French soldiers). Left on the beaches and falling into German hands were 475 tanks and 38,000 military vehicles and a mass of military stores. In and around the perimeter, 34,000 British soldiers were taken prisoner.

38 British destroyers – not built to carry large numbers of men – brought back 91,624 men to Britain; 38 British minesweepers brought back 30,942; thirty Dutch motor boats, 20,284; and 19 French destroyers, 7,623.

Commander C.H. Lightoller, who took the yacht *Sundowner* from Chiswick to Dunkirk, had been the second officer on board the doomed *Titanic* in 1912. His elder son was among those evacuated earlier. His younger son Herbert had been killed on 4 September 1939 during a bombing raid on German North Sea ports.

887 ships took part in the Dunkirk evacuation. Of these, 54 were sunk. Above the beaches, three times as many German warplanes were shot down as British.

The evacuation was a known in Britain as 'the miracle of Dunkirk'. Churchill told the House of Commons: 'Wars are not won by evacuations.'

--- The Dunkirk perimeter
⊙ Ports from which ships made their way to Dunkirk
➡ Routes of the evacuation

© Martin Gilbert 2008

10

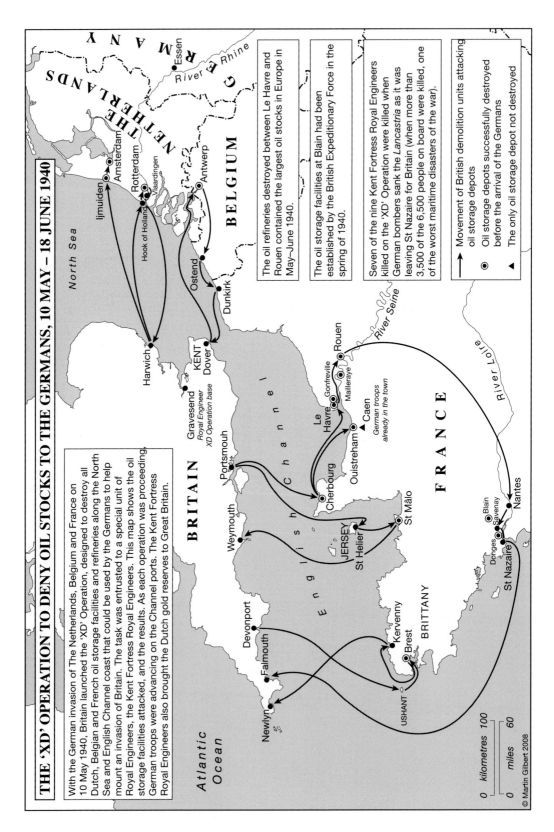

THE 'XD' OPERATION TO DENY OIL STOCKS TO THE GERMANS, 10 MAY – 18 JUNE 1940

With the German invasion of The Netherlands, Belgium and France on 10 May 1940, Britain launched the 'XD' Operation, designed to destroy all Dutch, Belgian and French oil storage facilities and refineries along the North Sea and English Channel coast that could be used by the Germans to help mount an invasion of Britain. The task was entrusted to a special unit of Royal Engineers, the Kent Fortress Royal Engineers. This map shows the oil storage facilities attacked, and the results. As each operation was proceeding, German troops were advancing on the Channel ports. The Kent Fortress Royal Engineers also brought the Dutch gold reserves to Great Britain.

The oil refineries destroyed between Le Havre and Rouen contained the largest oil stocks in Europe in May–June 1940.

The oil storage facilities at Blain had been established by the British Expeditionary Force in the spring of 1940.

Seven of the nine Kent Fortress Royal Engineers killed on the 'XD' Operation were killed when German bombers sank the *Lancastria* as it was leaving St Nazaire for Britain (when more than 3,500 of the 6,500 people on board were killed, one of the worst maritime disasters of the war).

→ Movement of British demolition units attacking oil storage depots

⊙ Oil storage depots successfully destroyed before the arrival of the Germans

▲ The only oil storage depot not destroyed

GERMANY

NETHERLANDS

BELGIUM

FRANCE

BRITAIN

North Sea

Atlantic Ocean

English Channel

River Rhine

River Seine

River Loire

Essen

Amsterdam

Ijmuiden

Rotterdam

Vlaardingen

Hook of Holland

Antwerp

Ostend

Dunkirk

Harwich

Gravesend
*Royal Engineer
XD Operation base*

Dover

KENT

Portsmouth

Weymouth

Devonport

Falmouth

Newlyn

Cherbourg

Ouistreham

Caen
*German troops
already in the town*

Le Havre

Gonfreville

Mailleraye

Rouen

St Malo

St Helier

JERSEY

Brest

Kervenny

USHANT

BRITTANY

Nantes

Blain

Savenay

Donges

St Nazaire

0   kilometres   100

0   miles   60

© Martin Gilbert 2008

11

BRITISH EVACUATION PLANS IN THE EVENT OF INVASION, 29 JUNE 1940

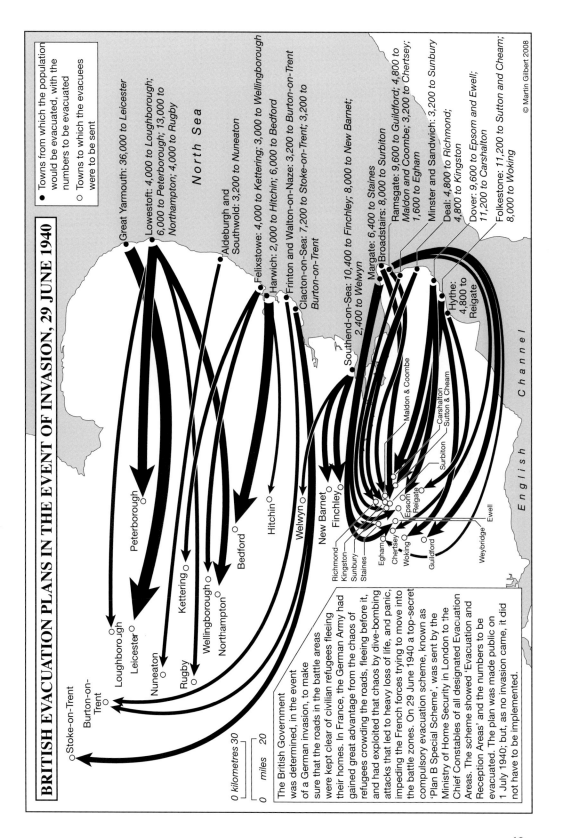

- Towns from which the population would be evacuated, with the numbers to be evacuated
- Towns to which the evacuees were to be sent

© Martin Gilbert 2008

North Sea

Great Yarmouth: 36,000 to Leicester

Lowestoft: 4,000 to Loughborough; 6,000 to Peterborough; 13,000 to Northampton; 4,000 to Rugby

Aldeburgh and Southwold: 3,200 to Nuneaton

Felixstowe: 4,000 to Kettering; 3,000 to Wellingborough

Harwich: 2,000 to Hitchin; 6,000 to Bedford

Frinton and Walton-on-Naze: 3,200 to Burton-on-Trent

Clacton-on-Sea: 7,200 to Stoke-on-Trent; 3,200 to Burton-on-Trent

Southend-on-Sea: 10,400 to Finchley; 8,000 to New Barnet; 2,400 to Welwyn

Margate: 6,400 to Staines

Broadstairs: 8,000 to Surbiton

Ramsgate: 9,600 to Guildford; 4,800 to Maldon and Coombe; 3,200 to Chertsey; 1,600 to Egham

Minster and Sandwich: 3,200 to Sunbury

Deal: 4,800 to Richmond; 4,800 to Kingston

Dover: 9,600 to Epsom and Ewell; 11,200 to Carshalton

Folkestone: 11,200 to Sutton and Cheam; 8,000 to Woking

Hythe: 4,800 to Reigate

English Channel

Stoke-on-Trent

Burton-on-Trent

Loughborough

Leicester

Peterborough

Nuneaton

Rugby

Kettering

Wellingborough

Northampton

Bedford

Hitchin

Welwyn

New Barnet

Finchley

Richmond
Kingston
Sunbury
Staines
Egham
Chertsey
Woking
Guildford
Weybridge
Ewell
Epsom
Reigate
Surbiton
Sutton & Cheam
Carshalton
Maldon & Coombe

0 kilometres 30

0 miles 20

The British Government was determined, in the event of a German invasion, to make sure that the roads in the battle areas were kept clear of civilian refugees fleeing their homes. In France, the German Army had gained great advantage from the chaos of refugees crowding the roads, fleeing before it, and had exploited that chaos by dive-bombing attacks that led to heavy loss of life, and panic, impeding the French forces trying to move into the battle zones. On 29 June 1940 a top-secret compulsory evacuation scheme, known as 'Plan B Special Scheme', was sent by the Ministry of Home Security in London to the Chief Constables of all designated Evacuation Areas. The scheme showed 'Evacuation and Reception Areas' and the numbers to be evacuated. The plan was made public on 1 July 1940; but, as no invasion came, it did not have to be implemented.

THE BATTLE FOR FRANCE, 1 – 25 JUNE 1940

Polish Government-in-exile arrived from Paris, 21 June. Met by King George VI at Paddington Station, London

North Sea

London

Southampton

Dunkirk

THE NETHERLANDS

Falmouth

English Channel

Cherbourg
30,630
18 June

Le Havre
11,000

BELGIUM

GERMANY

River Rhine

GUERNSEY
CHANNEL
ISLANDS
British

SARK

JERSEY

NORMANDY

River Seine

Brûly-de-Pesche
Hitler's Headquarters during the battle for France

LUXEMBOURG

Rethondes

River Marne

Verdun
15 June

Brest
32,584
19 June

St Mâlo
21,474

BRITTANY

Rennes
18 June

Vannes
18 June

Le Mans
18 June

Paris
14 June

River Seine

Epinal
22 June

Colmar
18 June

River Loire

St Nazaire
57,235

Nantes
19 June

Dijon
16 June

Nevers
18 June

Saône

Lake Geneva

SWITZERLAND
neutral

F R A N C E

Bay
of
Biscay

La Pallice
2,303

Villefranche
21 June

Lyon
24 June

Bordeaux

River Rhône

ITALY

River Garonne

0 kilometres 100

0 miles 50

Menton
22 June
occupied by the Italians

SPAIN
neutral

© Martin Gilbert 2008

Mediterranean Sea

Following their capture of the Dunkirk perimeter, German forces advanced rapidly southward. Paris was bombed on 3 June 1940, when 254 people were killed (195 were civilians). German troops entered Paris on 14 June. On 21 June the French Government signed an armistice at Rethondes. That day the Italian army attacked in the south. On June 25 the German army reached its southernmost line of advance. On 30 June German forces occupied the British Channel Islands.

On 14 June two scientists, Hans von Halban and Lew Kowarski, were taken from Bordeaux to Southampton with 26 cans (the world's supply) of heavy water.

Main evacuation ports from which 163,225 British, French, Canadian and Polish troops were evacuated, with numbers of troops taken off

22,656 British citizens evacuated, 19–24 June 1940

• Towns taken by the Germans, with dates

==== French Maginot Line

▽▽▽▽ German front line, 4 June 1940

▼▼▼▼ German front line, 17 June 1940

—— German and Italian front lines on the last day of fighting, 25 June 1940

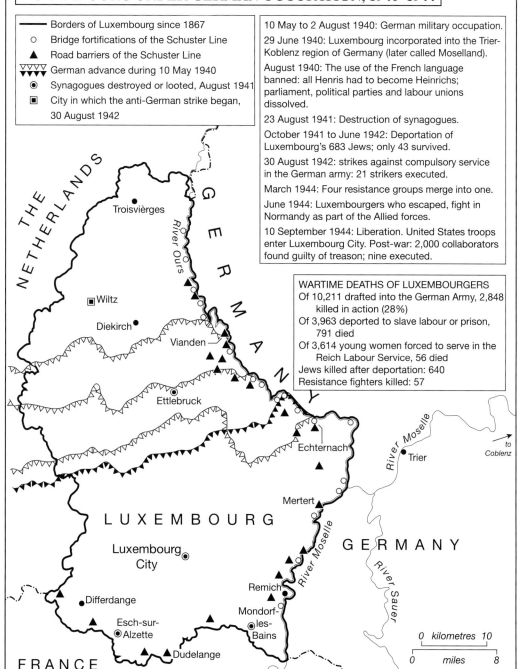

LUXEMBOURG UNDER GERMAN OCCUPATION, 1940–1944

Borders of Luxembourg since 1867

○ Bridge fortifications of the Schuster Line

▲ Road barriers of the Schuster Line

ⅤⅤⅤⅤ German advance during 10 May 1940

◉ Synagogues destroyed or looted, August 1941

▣ City in which the anti-German strike began, 30 August 1942

10 May to 2 August 1940: German military occupation.

29 June 1940: Luxembourg incorporated into the Trier-Koblenz region of Germany (later called Moselland).

August 1940: The use of the French language banned: all Henris had to become Heinrichs; parliament, political parties and labour unions dissolved.

23 August 1941: Destruction of synagogues.

October 1941 to June 1942: Deportation of Luxembourg's 683 Jews; only 43 survived.

30 August 1942: strikes against compulsory service in the German army: 21 strikers executed.

March 1944: Four resistance groups merge into one.

June 1944: Luxembourgers who escaped, fight in Normandy as part of the Allied forces.

10 September 1944: Liberation. United States troops enter Luxembourg City. Post-war: 2,000 collaborators found guilty of treason; nine executed.

WARTIME DEATHS OF LUXEMBOURGERS
Of 10,211 drafted into the German Army, 2,848 killed in action (28%)
Of 3,963 deported to slave labour or prison, 791 died
Of 3,614 young women forced to serve in the Reich Labour Service, 56 died
Jews killed after deportation: 640
Resistance fighters killed: 57

THE NETHERLANDS

GERMANY

Troisvièrges

River Ours

Wiltz

Diekirch

Vianden

Ettelbruck

Echternach

River Moselle

Trier

to Coblenz

Mertert

LUXEMBOURG

Luxembourg City

River Moselle

GERMANY

River Sauer

Remich

Differdange

Mondorf-les-Bains

Esch-sur-Alzette

Dudelange

FRANCE

0 kilometres 10

0 miles 8

© Martin Gilbert 2008

Luxembourg, neutral since 1867, had been occupied by Germany in the First World War. In 1939 its population was 300,000. Border defences (the Schuster Line) were in place by September 1939. On 10 May 1940, as part of its plan to conquer France, Germany prepared to invade Luxembourg for a second time in twenty-six years. At 3.15 a.m. on the morning of 10 May 1940, as German troops gathered on the river banks on the German side of the border, the steel barriers and gates of the Schuster Line were closed. At 4.35 a.m. the German invasion began. By evening, the northern half of the country had been overrun. The conquest was completed on 11 May.

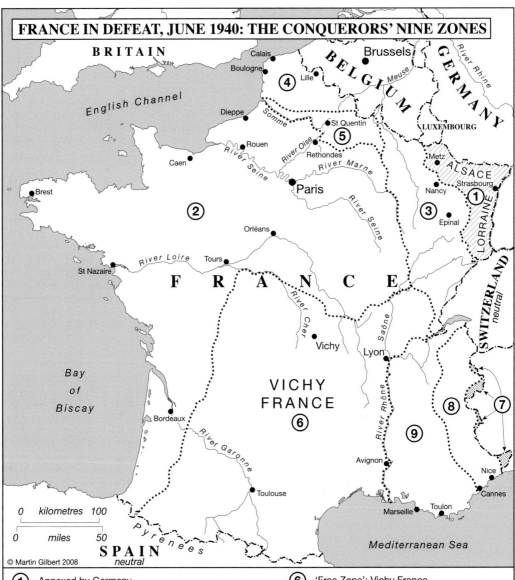

FRANCE IN DEFEAT, JUNE 1940: THE CONQUERORS' NINE ZONES

BRITAIN

BELGIUM

GERMANY

River Rhine

Brussels

Calais

Boulogne

Lille

Meuse

English Channel

LUXEMBOURG

Dieppe

Somme

St Quentin

(5)

Rouen

River Oise

Rethondes

Metz

ALSACE

River Seine

Caen

River Marne

Strasbourg

Nancy

(1)

Brest

(2)

Paris

(3)

Epinal

River Seine

LORRAINE

SWITZERLAND

neutral

Orléans

River Loire

Tours

St Nazaire

F R A N C E

River Cher

Vichy

Saône

Lyon

Bay
of
Biscay

Bordeaux

VICHY
FRANCE

(6)

River Rhône

(8)

(7)

River Garonne

(9)

Avignon

Nice

Toulouse

Cannes

0   kilometres   100

0   miles   50

Pyrenees

Marseille

Toulon

Mediterranean Sea

© Martin Gilbert 2008

SPAIN
neutral

(1) Annexed by Germany

(2) The Occupied Zone, administered by Vichy but subject to arbitrary German control

(3) Reserved Zone, intended for German settlement

(4) Incorporated Zone, administered from Brussels

(5) Prohibited Zone, no non-residents permitted

(6) 'Free Zone': Vichy France

(7) Annexed by Italy

(8) Demilitarized Zone under Italian control

(9) Under Italian supervision

Following the signing of the Franco-German Armistice at Rethondes, in the Forest of Compiègne, on 22 June 1940, France was divided into nine zones. The two principal parts were the Occupied Zone, with its capital in Paris, under German control, and the quasi-independent Free Zone, with its capital at Vichy. This map shows all nine zones.

ARTICLE THREE OF THE ARMISTICE TERMS (THE OCCUPIED ZONE):
'In the occupied parts of France the German Reich exercises all rights of an occupying power. The French Government obliges itself to support with every means the regulations resulting from the exercise of these rights and to carry them out with the aid of French administration. All French authorities and officials of the occupied territory, therefore, are to be promptly informed by the French Government to comply with the regulations of the German military commanders and to cooperate with them in a correct manner.'

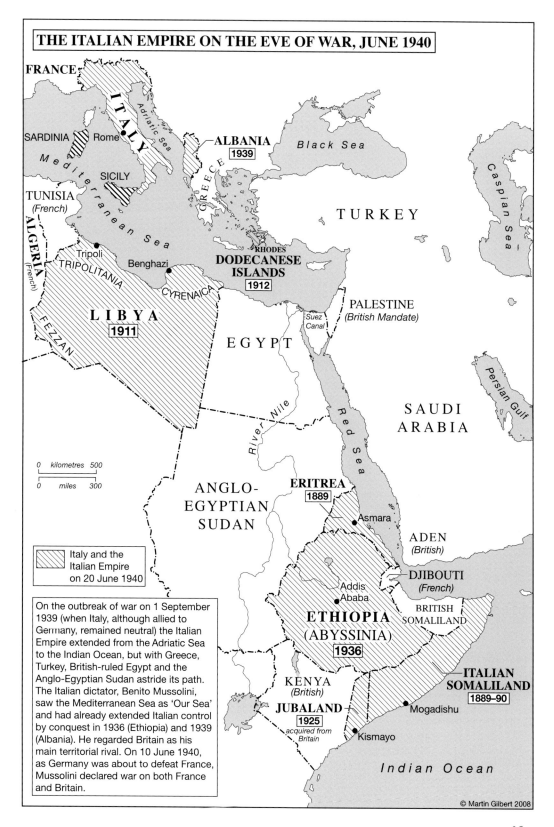

THE ITALIAN EMPIRE ON THE EVE OF WAR, JUNE 1940

FRANCE

ITALY

SARDINIA · Rome

SICILY

TUNISIA *(French)*

ALGERIA *(French)*

Tripoli

Benghazi

TRIPOLITANIA

CYRENAICA

FEZZAN

LIBYA
1911

Mediterranean Sea

Adriatic Sea

ALBANIA
1939

Black Sea

GREECE

RHODES

DODECANESE
ISLANDS
1912

TURKEY

Caspian Sea

PALESTINE
(British Mandate)

Suez Canal

EGYPT

River Nile

Red Sea

SAUDI
ARABIA

Persian Gulf

0   kilometres   500

0   miles   300

ANGLO-
EGYPTIAN
SUDAN

ERITREA
1889

· Asmara

ADEN
(British)

DJIBOUTI
(French)

BRITISH
SOMALILAND

Addis
Ababa

ETHIOPIA
(ABYSSINIA)
1936

ITALIAN
SOMALILAND
1889–90

KENYA
(British)

JUBALAND
1925
*acquired from
Britain*

· Mogadishu

Kismayo

Indian Ocean

	Italy and the Italian Empire on 20 June 1940

On the outbreak of war on 1 September 1939 (when Italy, although allied to Germany, remained neutral) the Italian Empire extended from the Adriatic Sea to the Indian Ocean, but with Greece, Turkey, British-ruled Egypt and the Anglo-Egyptian Sudan astride its path. The Italian dictator, Benito Mussolini, saw the Mediterranean Sea as 'Our Sea' and had already extended Italian control by conquest in 1936 (Ethiopia) and 1939 (Albania). He regarded Britain as his main territorial rival. On 10 June 1940, as Germany was about to defeat France, Mussolini declared war on both France and Britain.

© Martin Gilbert 2008

16

Section 2

BRITAIN ALONE AND ITS ALLIES

Silent Service

Now, multifold, let Britain's patent power
Be proven within us for the world to see.
None are exempt from service in this hour;
And vanquished in ourselves we dare not be.
Now, for a sunlit future, we can show
The clenched resolved endurance that defies
Daemons in dark, – and toward that future go
With earth's defended freedom in our eyes.
In separate soul let courage shine –
A kneeling angel holding faith's front-line.

SIEGFRIED SASSOON
23 May 1940

My estimate is that the war will be won in a fortnight.

CAPTAIN ERWIN ROMMEL
Letter to his wife
24 May 1940

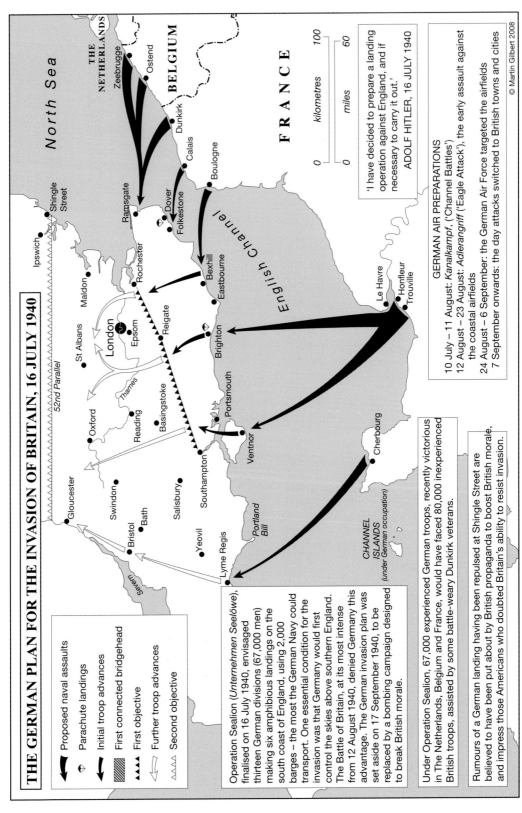

THE GERMAN PLAN FOR THE INVASION OF BRITAIN, 16 JULY 1940

Legend:
- Proposed naval assaults
- Parachute landings
- Initial troop advances
- First connected bridgehead
- First objective
- Further troop advances
- Second objective

Operation Sealion (*Unternehmen Seelöwe*), finalised on 16 July 1940, envisaged thirteen German divisions (67,000 men) making six amphibious landings on the south coast of England, using 2,000 barges – the most the German Navy could transport. One essential condition for the invasion was that Germany would first control the skies above southern England. The Battle of Britain, at its most intense from 12 August 1940, denied Germany this advantage. The German invasion plan was set aside on 17 September 1940, to be replaced by a bombing campaign designed to break British morale.

Under Operation Sealion, 67,000 experienced German troops, recently victorious in The Netherlands, Belgium and France, would have faced 80,000 inexperienced British troops, assisted by some battle-weary Dunkirk veterans.

Rumours of a German landing having been repulsed at Shingle Street are believed to have been put about by British propaganda to boost British morale, and impress those Americans who doubted Britain's ability to resist invasion.

GERMAN AIR PREPARATIONS

10 July – 11 August: *Kanalkampf*, ('Channel Battles')
12 August – 23 August: *Adlerangriff* ('Eagle Attack'), the early assault against the coastal airfields
24 August – 6 September: the German Air Force targeted the airfields
7 September onwards: the day attacks switched to British towns and cities

'I have decided to prepare a landing operation against England, and if necessary to carry it out.'
ADOLF HITLER, 16 JULY 1940

North Sea

English Channel

THE NETHERLANDS
BELGIUM
FRANCE

Zeebrugge
Ostend
Dunkirk
Calais
Boulogne
Le Havre
Honfleur
Trouville
Cherbourg

Ipswich
Shingle Street
Ramsgate
Dover
Folkestone
Bexhill
Eastbourne
Brighton
Rochester
Reigate
Maldon
St Albans
London
Epsom
Oxford
Reading
Basingstoke
Portsmouth
Ventnor
Southampton
Swindon
Salisbury
Bath
Bristol
Gloucester
Yeovil
Lyme Regis

Thames
Severn
Portland Bill

52nd Parallel

CHANNEL ISLANDS
(under German occupation)

0   kilometres   100
0   miles   60

© Martin Gilbert 2008

BRITISH AND GERMAN AIR BASES DURING THE BATTLE OF BRITAIN 12 AUGUST – 6 SEPTEMBER 1940

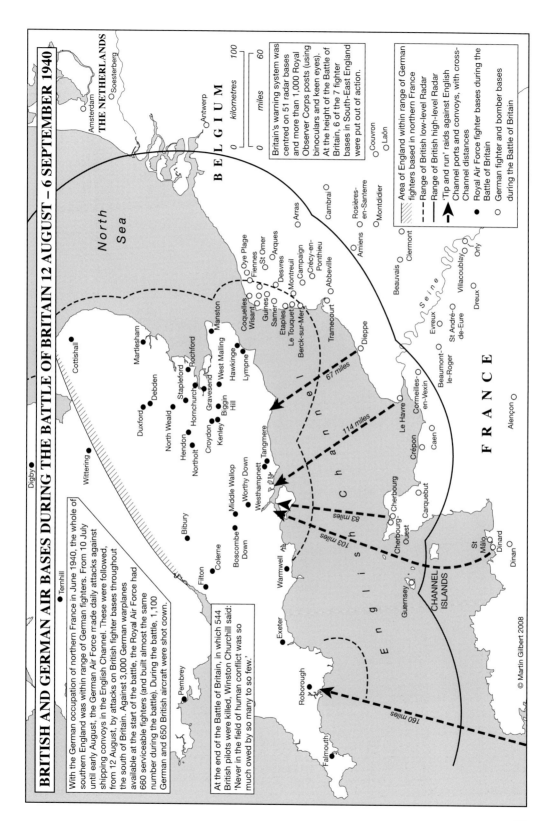

With the German occupation of northern France in June 1940, the whole of southern England was within range of German fighters. From 10 July until early August, the German Air Force made daily attacks against shipping convoys in the English Channel. These were followed, from 12 August, by attacks on British fighter bases throughout the south of Britain. Against 3,000 German warplanes available at the start of the battle, the Royal Air Force had 660 serviceable fighters (and built almost the same number during the battle). During the battle, 1,100 German and 650 British aircraft were shot down.

At the end of the Battle of Britain, in which 544 British pilots were killed, Winston Churchill said: 'Never in the field of human conflict was so much owed by so many to so few.'

Britain's warning system was centred on 51 radar bases and more than 1,000 Royal Observer Corps posts (using binoculars and keen eyes). At the height of the Battle of Britain, 6 of the 7 fighter bases in South-East England were put out of action.

////// Area of England within range of German fighters based in northern France

– – – Range of British low-level Radar

——— Range of British high-level Radar

→ 'Tip and run' raids against English Channel ports and convoys, with cross-Channel distances

● Royal Air Force fighter bases during the Battle of Britain

○ German fighter and bomber bases during the Battle of Britain

THE NETHERLANDS

BELGIUM

FRANCE

North Sea

English Channel

CHANNEL ISLANDS

Seine

0   kilometres   100
0   miles   60

67 miles
114 miles
83 miles
103 miles
160 miles

Ternhill ●
Digby ●
Cottishall ●
Wittering ●
Martlesham ●
Duxford ●
Debden ●
Stapleford ●
North Weald ●
Hendon ●
Northolt ●
Hornchurch ●
Croydon ●
Kenley ●
Biggin Hill ●
Gravesend ●
West Malling ●
Hawkinge ●
Lympne ●
Rochford ●
Manston ●
Tangmere ●
Westhampnett ●
Worthy Down ●
Middle Wallop ●
Boscombe Down ●
Bibury ●
Colerne ●
Filton ●
Pembrey ●
Warmwell ●
Exeter ●
Roborough ●
Falmouth ●

Amsterdam ○
Soesterberg ○
Antwerp ○
Arras ○
Cambrai ○
Rosières-en-Santerre ○
Montdidier ○
Amiens ○
Beauvais ○
Clermont ○
Couvron ○
Laón ○
Oye Plage ○
Fiennes ○
St Omer ○
Desvres ○
Arques ○
Coquelles ○
Wisant ○
Guines ○
Samer ○
Etaples ○
Le Touquet ○
Berck-sur-Mer ○
Montreuil ○
Campaign ○
Crécy-en-Ponthieu ○
Abbeville ○
Tramecourt ○
Dieppe ○
Le Havre ○
Crépon ○
Caen ○
Carquebut ○
Cherbourg ○
Cherbourg-Ouest ○
Beaumont-le-Roger ○
Cormeilles-en-Vexin ○
St André-de-Eure ○
Evreux ○
Dreux ○
Villacoublay ○
Orly ○
Alençon ○
Guernsey ○
St Malo ○
Dinard ○
Dinan ○

© Martin Gilbert 2008

18

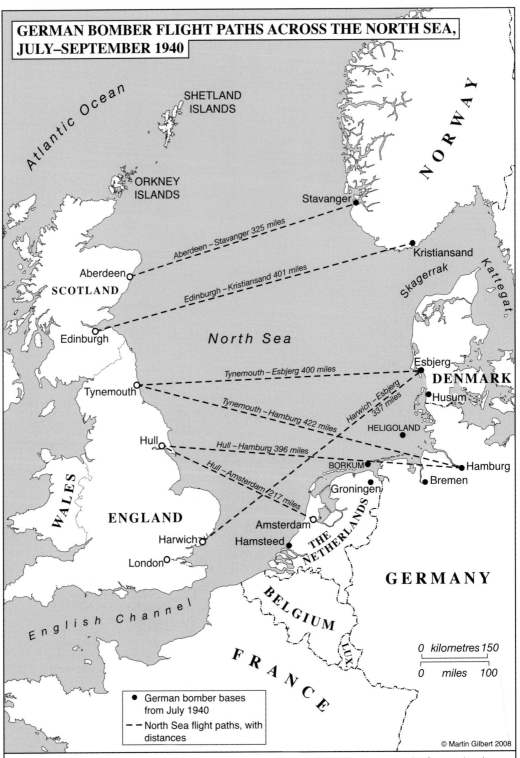

GERMAN BOMBER FLIGHT PATHS ACROSS THE NORTH SEA, JULY–SEPTEMBER 1940

Atlantic Ocean

SHETLAND ISLANDS

ORKNEY ISLANDS

NORWAY

Stavanger

Kristiansand

Aberdeen – Stavanger 325 miles

Aberdeen

SCOTLAND

Edinburgh – Kristiansand 401 miles

Skagerrak

Kattegat

Edinburgh

North Sea

Esbjerg

DENMARK

Tynemouth – Esbjerg 400 miles

Husum

Tynemouth

Harwich – Esbjerg 337 miles

Tynemouth – Hamburg 422 miles

HELIGOLAND

Hull

Hull – Hamburg 396 miles

BORKUM

Hamburg

Hull – Amsterdam 217 miles

Groningen

Bremen

WALES

ENGLAND

Amsterdam

THE NETHERLANDS

Harwich

Hamsteed

LUX.

London

GERMANY

BELGIUM

English Channel

0 kilometres 150

0 miles 100

FRANCE

● German bomber bases from July 1940

– – North Sea flight paths, with distances

© Martin Gilbert 2008

The German conquest of Denmark in April 1940 and Norway in June 1940 made it possible for German bombers to strike across the North Sea at northeast England and Scotland. This map shows the German airfields, and the distances to the British coast.

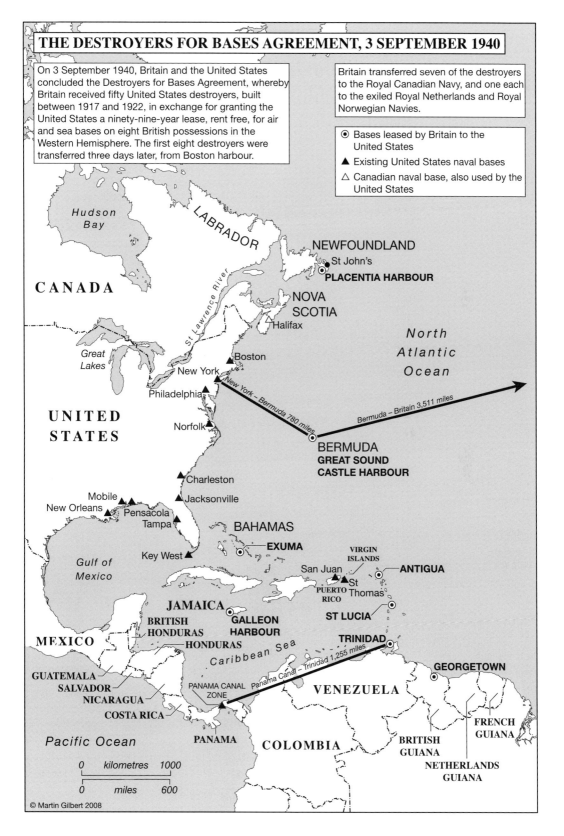

THE DESTROYERS FOR BASES AGREEMENT, 3 SEPTEMBER 1940

On 3 September 1940, Britain and the United States concluded the Destroyers for Bases Agreement, whereby Britain received fifty United States destroyers, built between 1917 and 1922, in exchange for granting the United States a ninety-nine-year lease, rent free, for air and sea bases on eight British possessions in the Western Hemisphere. The first eight destroyers were transferred three days later, from Boston harbour.

Britain transferred seven of the destroyers to the Royal Canadian Navy, and one each to the exiled Royal Netherlands and Royal Norwegian Navies.

- ⊙ Bases leased by Britain to the United States
- ▲ Existing United States naval bases
- △ Canadian naval base, also used by the United States

Hudson Bay

LABRADOR

NEWFOUNDLAND

St John's

PLACENTIA HARBOUR

CANADA

St Lawrence River

NOVA SCOTIA

△Halifax

Great Lakes

▲Boston

New York▲

North Atlantic Ocean

Philadelphia▲

UNITED STATES

Norfolk▲

New York – Bermuda 780 miles

Bermuda – Britain 3,511 miles

▲Charleston

Mobile

New Orleans ▲▲▲

▲Pensacola

Tampa▲

▲Jacksonville

BAHAMAS

⊙ **EXUMA**

BERMUDA
GREAT SOUND
CASTLE HARBOUR

Gulf of Mexico

Key West▲

San Juan

VIRGIN ISLANDS

⊙ **ANTIGUA**

▲St

PUERTO RICO

Thomas⊙

JAMAICA⊙

BRITISH HONDURAS

GALLEON HARBOUR

ST LUCIA⊙

MEXICO

HONDURAS

Caribbean Sea

TRINIDAD⊙

GEORGETOWN⊙

GUATEMALA

SALVADOR

NICARAGUA

COSTA RICA

PANAMA CANAL ZONE

Panama Canal – Trinidad 1,255 miles

VENEZUELA

Pacific Ocean

PANAMA

COLOMBIA

FRENCH GUIANA

BRITISH GUIANA

NETHERLANDS GUIANA

| 0 | kilometres | 1000 |

| 0 | miles | 600 |

© Martin Gilbert 2008

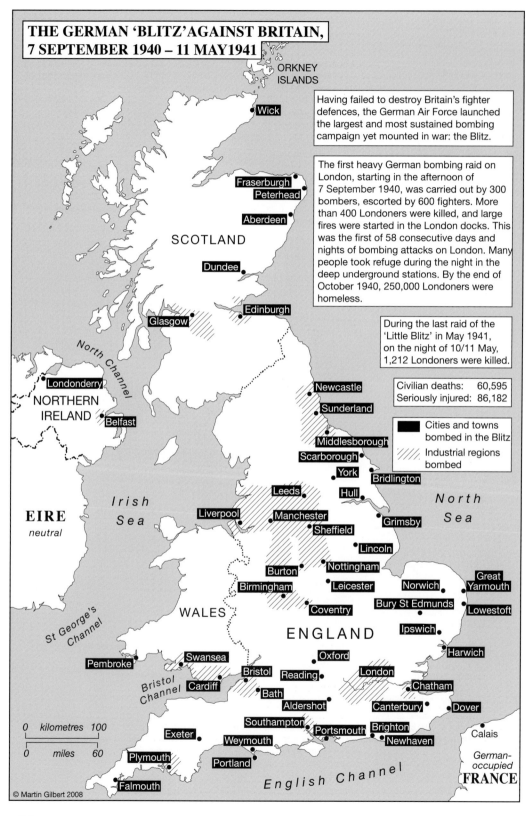

THE GERMAN 'BLITZ' AGAINST BRITAIN, 7 SEPTEMBER 1940 – 11 MAY 1941

ORKNEY ISLANDS

Wick

Having failed to destroy Britain's fighter defences, the German Air Force launched the largest and most sustained bombing campaign yet mounted in war: the Blitz.

The first heavy German bombing raid on London, starting in the afternoon of 7 September 1940, was carried out by 300 bombers, escorted by 600 fighters. More than 400 Londoners were killed, and large fires were started in the London docks. This was the first of 58 consecutive days and nights of bombing attacks on London. Many people took refuge during the night in the deep underground stations. By the end of October 1940, 250,000 Londoners were homeless.

During the last raid of the 'Little Blitz' in May 1941, on the night of 10/11 May, 1,212 Londoners were killed.

Civilian deaths: 60,595
Seriously injured: 86,182

■ Cities and towns bombed in the Blitz

⁄⁄⁄ Industrial regions bombed

Fraserburgh
Peterhead
Aberdeen

SCOTLAND

Dundee

Edinburgh

Glasgow

North Channel

Londonderry

NORTHERN IRELAND

Belfast

Newcastle
Sunderland
Middlesborough
Scarborough
York
Bridlington

EIRE
neutral

Irish Sea

Leeds
Hull

North Sea

Liverpool
Manchester
Sheffield
Grimsby

Lincoln

Burton
Nottingham
Birmingham
Leicester
Norwich
Great Yarmouth
Coventry
Bury St Edmunds
Lowestoft

WALES

ENGLAND

Ipswich

St George's Channel

Pembroke
Swansea
Cardiff

Bristol Channel

Bristol
Bath
Reading
Aldershot

Oxford

London
Chatham
Canterbury
Dover

Harwich

Southampton
Portsmouth
Brighton

Exeter
Weymouth
Plymouth
Portland

Newhaven

Calais

German-occupied
FRANCE

English Channel

0 kilometres 100
0 miles 60

© Martin Gilbert 2008

21

THE GERMAN BOMBING RAID ON COVENTRY, 14/15 NOVEMBER 1940

On 12 November 1940, Enigma decrypts read at the British Code and Cypher School at Bletchley revealed that a major German bombing raid was imminent. Its code name, Moonlight Sonata, was read in the decrypts, but not its target. Air Intelligence reported to Churchill that day that the latest Intelligence suggested the possible targets as Central London, Greater London, the Thames Valley, Kent, or the Essex coast. A German pilot shot down on 9 November suggested that Coventry and Birmingham would both be attacked in a 'colossal raid' between 15 and 20 November. The senior Air Intelligence Liaison Officer at Bletchley noted that this information was considered 'doubtful', as there was 'pretty definite information that the attack is to be against London and the Home Counties'.

Churchill was informed on the morning of 14 November that the target area would be 'probably in the vicinity of London', If, however, he was told 'further information were to indicate Coventry, Birmingham or elsewhere', it was hoped that the standard 'Cold Water' instructions for counter-measures – including fire engines and ambulances from a wide area around the target – could be got there in time.

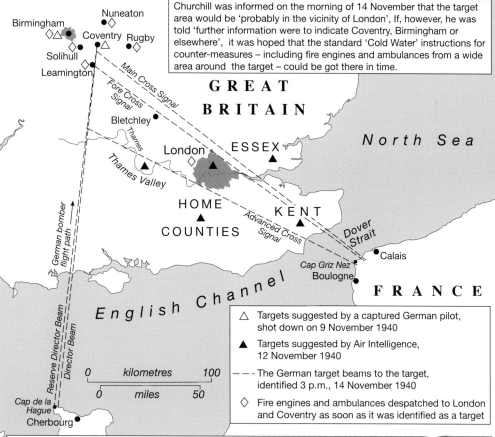

△ Targets suggested by a captured German pilot, shot down on 9 November 1940

▲ Targets suggested by Air Intelligence, 12 November 1940

‐ ‐ ‐ The German target beams to the target, identified 3 p.m., 14 November 1940

◇ Fire engines and ambulances despatched to London and Coventry as soon as it was identified as a target

As a result of three earlier German air raids on Coventry (25 August, 16 September and 14 October 1940), Churchill gave instructions on 7 November to strengthen Coventry's anti-aircraft defences. These instructions had been carried out by November 14.

At 3 p.m. on 14 November 1940, the Radio Counter-measures Organisation learned that German beams were intercepting just south of Coventry. The Air Ministry at once ordered British planes to bomb the aerodromes south of Cherbourg from which the attackers were expected to take off, authorized a continuous fighter patrol over Coventry itself, and activated the 'Cold Water' defence preparations.

On the night of 14/15 November 1940, German bombers dropped 33,000 incendiary bombs, 500 tons of high-explosive bombs, and more than 30 parachute mines on Coventry. The incendiary bombs were the first ones used in a bombing raid on a city; they contained phosphorus, causing a firestorm. Several hundred buildings, including St Michael's Cathedral, were burned out; 568 people were killed. A direct hit on the Coventry and Warwickshire Hospital killed 33 patients, 7 doctors and 2 nurses.

© Martin Gilbert 2008

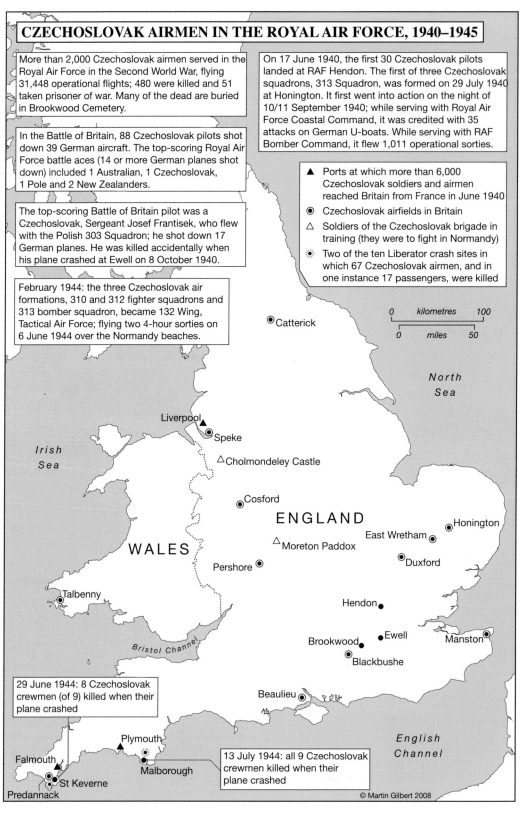

CZECHOSLOVAK AIRMEN IN THE ROYAL AIR FORCE, 1940–1945

More than 2,000 Czechoslovak airmen served in the Royal Air Force in the Second World War, flying 31,448 operational flights; 480 were killed and 51 taken prisoner of war. Many of the dead are buried in Brookwood Cemetery.

In the Battle of Britain, 88 Czechoslovak pilots shot down 39 German aircraft. The top-scoring Royal Air Force battle aces (14 or more German planes shot down) included 1 Australian, 1 Czechoslovak, 1 Pole and 2 New Zealanders.

The top-scoring Battle of Britain pilot was a Czechoslovak, Sergeant Josef Frantisek, who flew with the Polish 303 Squadron; he shot down 17 German planes. He was killed accidentally when his plane crashed at Ewell on 8 October 1940.

February 1944: the three Czechoslovak air formations, 310 and 312 fighter squadrons and 313 bomber squadron, became 132 Wing, Tactical Air Force; flying two 4-hour sorties on 6 June 1944 over the Normandy beaches.

On 17 June 1940, the first 30 Czechoslovak pilots landed at RAF Hendon. The first of three Czechoslovak squadrons, 313 Squadron, was formed on 29 July 1940 at Honington. It first went into action on the night of 10/11 September 1940; while serving with Royal Air Force Coastal Command, it was credited with 35 attacks on German U-boats. While serving with RAF Bomber Command, it flew 1,011 operational sorties.

▲   Ports at which more than 6,000 Czechoslovak soldiers and airmen reached Britain from France in June 1940

◉   Czechoslovak airfields in Britain

△   Soldiers of the Czechoslovak brigade in training (they were to fight in Normandy)

☀   Two of the ten Liberator crash sites in which 67 Czechoslovak airmen, and in one instance 17 passengers, were killed

0   kilometres   100
0   miles   50

North Sea

Irish Sea

◉ Catterick

Liverpool ▲
◉ Speke
△ Cholmondeley Castle

◉ Cosford

ENGLAND

△ Moreton Paddox

East Wretham ◉
◉ Honington

◉ Duxford

WALES

Pershore ◉

◉ Talbenny

Hendon ●

Brookwood ●
● Ewell
Manston ◉

◉ Blackbushe

Bristol Channel

29 June 1944: 8 Czechoslovak crewmen (of 9) killed when their plane crashed

Beaulieu ◉

English Channel

Plymouth ▲
☀
Falmouth ▲
Malborough
◉ St Keverne
Predannack

13 July 1944: all 9 Czechoslovak crewmen killed when their plane crashed

© Martin Gilbert 2008

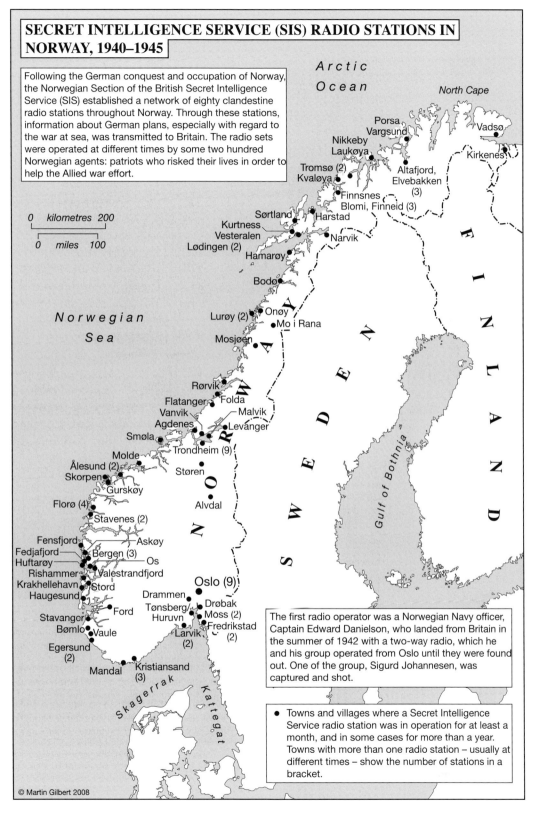

SECRET INTELLIGENCE SERVICE (SIS) RADIO STATIONS IN NORWAY, 1940–1945

Following the German conquest and occupation of Norway, the Norwegian Section of the British Secret Intelligence Service (SIS) established a network of eighty clandestine radio stations throughout Norway. Through these stations, information about German plans, especially with regard to the war at sea, was transmitted to Britain. The radio sets were operated at different times by some two hundred Norwegian agents: patriots who risked their lives in order to help the Allied war effort.

Arctic Ocean

North Cape

Porsa
Vargsund
Vadsø
Nikkeby
Laukøya
Kirkenes
Tromsø (2)
Kvaløya
Altafjord, Elvebakken (3)
Finnsnes
Blomi, Finneid (3)
Sørtland
Harstad
Kurtness
Vesteralen
Narvik
Lødingen (2)
Hamarøy
Bodø

Norwegian Sea

Lurøy (2)
Onøy
Mo i Rana
Mosjøen

Rørvik
Flatanger
Folda
Vanvik
Malvik
Agdenes
Levanger
Smøla
Trondheim (9)
Molde
Ålesund (2)
Støren
Skorpen
Florø (4)
Gurskøy
Alvdal
Stavenes (2)
Fensfjord
Askøy
Fedjafjord
Bergen (3)
Huftarøy
Os
Rishammer
Valestrandfjord
Krakhellehavn
Stord
Haugesund
Drammen
Drøbak
Stavanger
Ford
Tønsberg
Moss (2)
Huruvn
Fredrikstad
Bømlo
Vaule
Larvik
(2)
Egersund
(2)
Mandal
Kristiansand
(3)
Oslo (9)

Skagerrak
Kattegat

0   kilometres   200
0   miles   100

F I N L A N D

S W E D E N

N O R W A Y

Gulf of Bothnia

The first radio operator was a Norwegian Navy officer, Captain Edward Danielson, who landed from Britain in the summer of 1942 with a two-way radio, which he and his group operated from Oslo until they were found out. One of the group, Sigurd Johannesen, was captured and shot.

- Towns and villages where a Secret Intelligence Service radio station was in operation for at least a month, and in some cases for more than a year. Towns with more than one radio station – usually at different times – show the number of stations in a bracket.

© Martin Gilbert 2008

24

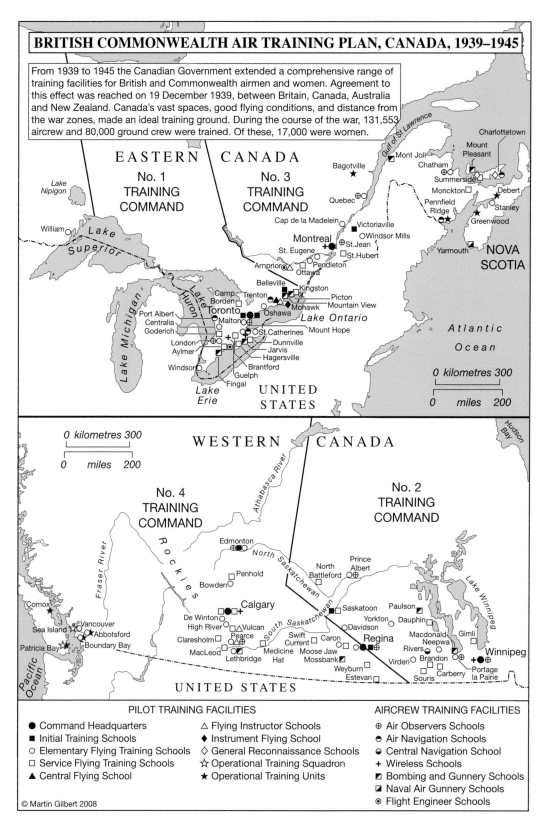

BRITISH COMMONWEALTH AIR TRAINING PLAN, CANADA, 1939–1945

From 1939 to 1945 the Canadian Government extended a comprehensive range of training facilities for British and Commonwealth airmen and women. Agreement to this effect was reached on 19 December 1939, between Britain, Canada, Australia and New Zealand. Canada's vast spaces, good flying conditions, and distance from the war zones, made an ideal training ground. During the course of the war, 131,553 aircrew and 80,000 ground crew were trained. Of these, 17,000 were women.

EASTERN CANADA

No. 1 TRAINING COMMAND

No. 3 TRAINING COMMAND

Lake Nipigon
Lake Superior
William
Charlottetown
Mount Pleasant
Gulf of St Lawrence
Mont Joli
Chatham
Bagotville
Summerside
Moncton
Quebec
Pennfield Ridge
Debert
Stanley
Cap de la Madelein
Greenwood
Victoriaville
Windsor Mills
NOVA SCOTIA
Montreal
St. Eugene
St.Jean
St.Hubert
Yarmouth
Arnprior
Pendleton
Ottawa
Belleville
Kingston
Camp Borden
Trenton
Picton
Mountain View
Toronto
Mohawk
Port Albert
Malton
Oshawa
Lake Ontario
Centralia
Goderich
St.Catherines
Mount Hope
London
Dunnville
Aylmer
Jarvis
Hagersville
Windsor
Brantford
Guelph
Fingal
Lake Erie
Lake Michigan
Lake Huron

Atlantic Ocean

0 kilometres 300
0 miles 200

UNITED STATES

WESTERN CANADA

0 kilometres 300
0 miles 200

No. 4 TRAINING COMMAND

No. 2 TRAINING COMMAND

Hudson Bay
Athabasca River
North Saskatchewan
Rockies
Fraser River
Edmonton
Penhold
Bowden
Prince Albert
North Battleford
Saskatoon
Paulson
Comox
Calgary
De Winton
Yorkton
Dauphin
Vancouver
High River
Vulcan
Davidson
Macdonald
Gimli
Sea Island
Abbotsford
Claresholm
Pearce
Swift Current
Caron
Regina
Neepwa
Patricia Bay
Boundary Bay
MacLeod
Medicine Hat
Moose Jaw
Rivers
Brandon
Winnipeg
Lethbridge
Mossbank
Virden
Portage la Pairie
Weyburn
Carberry
Estevan
Souris
South Saskatchewan
Lake Winnipeg
Pacific Ocean

UNITED STATES

PILOT TRAINING FACILITIES

- ● Command Headquarters
- ■ Initial Training Schools
- ○ Elementary Flying Training Schools
- □ Service Flying Training Schools
- ▲ Central Flying School
- △ Flying Instructor Schools
- ◆ Instrument Flying School
- ◇ General Reconnaissance Schools
- ☆ Operational Training Squadron
- ★ Operational Training Units

AIRCREW TRAINING FACILITIES

- ⊕ Air Observers Schools
- ◗ Air Navigation Schools
- ◖ Central Navigation School
- + Wireless Schools
- ◪ Bombing and Gunnery Schools
- ◣ Naval Air Gunnery Schools
- ◉ Flight Engineer Schools

© Martin Gilbert 2008

THE NORWEGIAN MERCHANT NAVY IN THE SECOND WORLD WAR

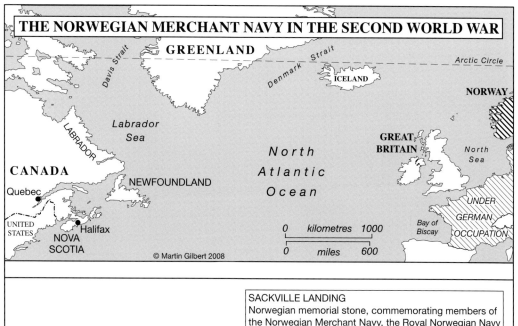

GREENLAND

Davis Strait

Denmark Strait

Arctic Circle

ICELAND

NORWAY

LABRADOR

Labrador
Sea

CANADA

NEWFOUNDLAND

North
Atlantic
Ocean

GREAT
BRITAIN

North
Sea

Quebec

UNITED
STATES

Halifax

NOVA
SCOTIA

© Martin Gilbert 2008

UNDER

GERMAN

Bay of
Biscay

OCCUPATION

| 0 | kilometres | 1000 |
| 0 | miles | 600 |

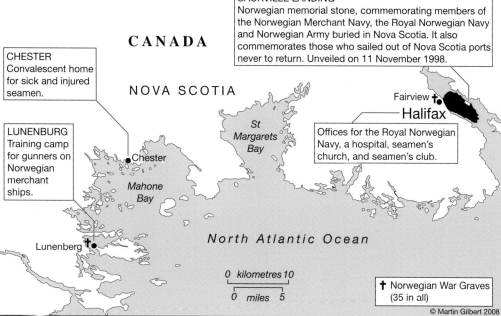

CANADA

NOVA SCOTIA

CHESTER
Convalescent home
for sick and injured
seamen.

LUNENBURG
Training camp
for gunners on
Norwegian
merchant
ships.

SACKVILLE LANDING
Norwegian memorial stone, commemorating members of
the Norwegian Merchant Navy, the Royal Norwegian Navy
and Norwegian Army buried in Nova Scotia. It also
commemorates those who sailed out of Nova Scotia ports
never to return. Unveiled on 11 November 1998.

Fairview ✝

Halifax

Offices for the Royal Norwegian
Navy, a hospital, seamen's
church, and seamen's club.

St
Margarets
Bay

Chester

Mahone
Bay

Lunenberg ✝

North Atlantic Ocean

| 0 | kilometres | 10 |
| 0 | miles | 5 |

✝ Norwegian War Graves
(35 in all)

© Martin Gilbert 2008

In 1940, Norway, with a population of three million, had the third largest ocean going merchant fleet in the world: 1,100 ships. When Germany invaded Norway on 9 April that year, 1,024 of those ships were at sea. King Haakon and his Government immediately ordered them to proceed to Allied ports. Not one refused, despite messages from the pro-German Quisling Government in Oslo, ordering them to return home. The distant Norwegian Antarctic whaling fleet, with about 2,000 men, also made its way to Halifax.

In Oslo on 11 May 1948, recalling 1940, Churchill said: '...at that time we had the Norwegian Merchant Navy, and that great enormous fleet of tankers, of other vessels too – but above all of tankers – carrying from all parts of the world that vital essence of war-making capacity. We did not feel entirely alone because we had that invaluable help from Norway, given at great cost for many. Many a good ship was sunk... We are very grateful for the sacrifices which were then made... the addition of many millions of tons of merchant shipping, manned by hardy and courageous men from Norway, played a very definite part in our existence.'

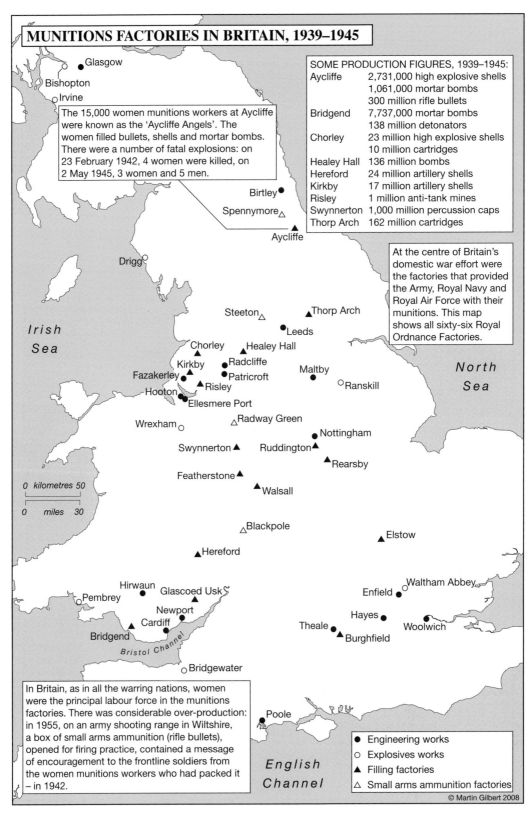

MUNITIONS FACTORIES IN BRITAIN, 1939–1945

Glasgow
Bishopton
Irvine

The 15,000 women munitions workers at Aycliffe were known as the 'Aycliffe Angels'. The women filled bullets, shells and mortar bombs. There were a number of fatal explosions: on 23 February 1942, 4 women were killed, on 2 May 1945, 3 women and 5 men.

SOME PRODUCTION FIGURES, 1939–1945:

Aycliffe	2,731,000 high explosive shells
	1,061,000 mortar bombs
	300 million rifle bullets
Bridgend	7,737,000 mortar bombs
	138 million detonators
Chorley	23 million high explosive shells
	10 million cartridges
Healey Hall	136 million bombs
Hereford	24 million artillery shells
Kirkby	17 million artillery shells
Risley	1 million anti-tank mines
Swynnerton	1,000 million percussion caps
Thorp Arch	162 million cartridges

Birtley
Spennymore
Aycliffe

At the centre of Britain's domestic war effort were the factories that provided the Army, Royal Navy and Royal Air Force with their munitions. This map shows all sixty-six Royal Ordnance Factories.

Drigg

Irish Sea

Steeton
Thorp Arch
Leeds
Chorley
Healey Hall
Kirkby
Radcliffe
Fazakerley
Patricroft
Maltby
Hooton
Risley
Ranskill
Ellesmere Port
Radway Green
Wrexham
Nottingham
Swynnerton
Ruddington
Rearsby
Featherstone
Walsall

North Sea

0 kilometres 50
0 miles 30

Blackpole
Elstow
Hereford

Hirwaun
Glascoed Usk
Waltham Abbey
Pembrey
Enfield
Newport
Hayes
Theale
Cardiff
Woolwich
Bridgend
Burghfield
Bristol Channel
Bridgewater

In Britain, as in all the warring nations, women were the principal labour force in the munitions factories. There was considerable over-production: in 1955, on an army shooting range in Wiltshire, a box of small arms ammunition (rifle bullets), opened for firing practice, contained a message of encouragement to the frontline soldiers from the women munitions workers who had packed it – in 1942.

Poole

English Channel

● Engineering works
○ Explosives works
▲ Filling factories
△ Small arms ammunition factories

© Martin Gilbert 2008

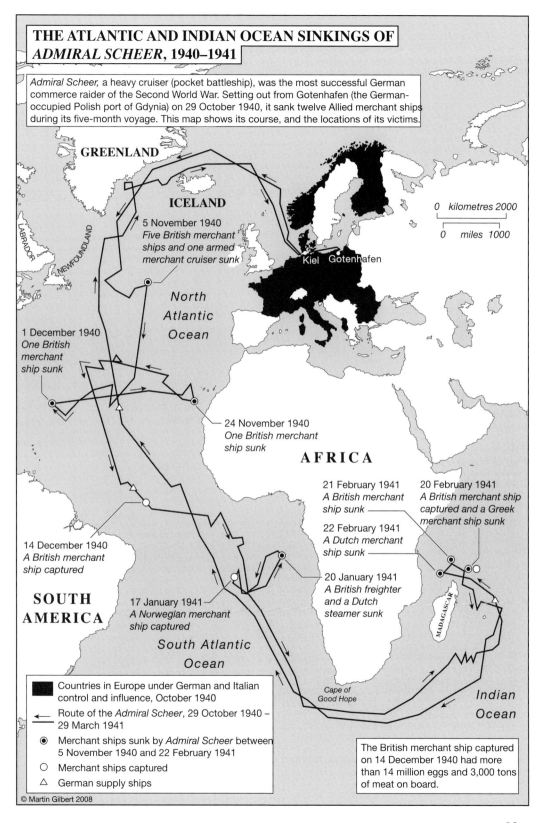

THE ATLANTIC AND INDIAN OCEAN SINKINGS OF *ADMIRAL SCHEER*, 1940–1941

Admiral Scheer, a heavy cruiser (pocket battleship), was the most successful German commerce raider of the Second World War. Setting out from Gotenhafen (the German-occupied Polish port of Gdynia) on 29 October 1940, it sank twelve Allied merchant ships during its five-month voyage. This map shows its course, and the locations of its victims.

GREENLAND

ICELAND

5 November 1940
Five British merchant ships and one armed merchant cruiser sunk

LABRADOR

NEWFOUNDLAND

Kiel   Gotenhafen

North Atlantic Ocean

1 December 1940
One British merchant ship sunk

24 November 1940
One British merchant ship sunk

AFRICA

21 February 1941
A British merchant ship sunk

20 February 1941
A British merchant ship captured and a Greek merchant ship sunk

22 February 1941
A Dutch merchant ship sunk

14 December 1940
A British merchant ship captured

20 January 1941
A British freighter and a Dutch steamer sunk

SOUTH AMERICA

17 January 1941
A Norwegian merchant ship captured

MADAGASCAR

South Atlantic Ocean

Indian Ocean

Cape of Good Hope

Countries in Europe under German and Italian control and influence, October 1940

Route of the *Admiral Scheer*, 29 October 1940 – 29 March 1941

⊙ Merchant ships sunk by *Admiral Scheer* between 5 November 1940 and 22 February 1941

○ Merchant ships captured

△ German supply ships

The British merchant ship captured on 14 December 1940 had more than 14 million eggs and 3,000 tons of meat on board.

© Martin Gilbert 2008

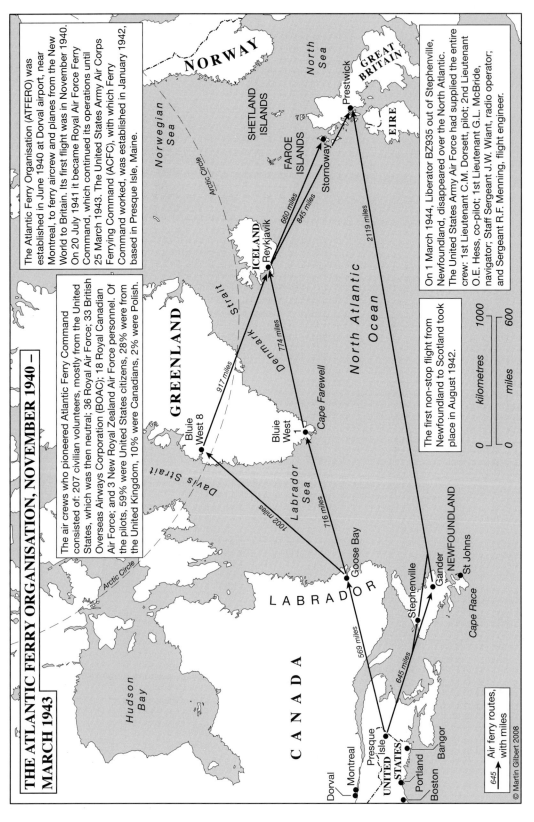

THE ATLANTIC FERRY ORGANISATION, NOVEMBER 1940 – MARCH 1943

The air crews who pioneered Atlantic Ferry Command consisted of: 207 civilian volunteers, mostly from the United States, which was then neutral; 36 Royal Air Force; 33 British Overseas Airways Corporation (BOAC); 18 Royal Canadian Air Force; and 3 New Royal Zealand Air Force personnel. Of the pilots, 59% were United States citizens, 28% were from the United Kingdom, 10% were Canadians, 2% were Polish.

The Atlantic Ferry Organisation (ATFERO) was established in June 1940 at Dorval airport, near Montreal, to ferry aircrew and planes from the New World to Britain. Its first flight was in November 1940. On 20 July 1941 it became Royal Air Force Ferry Command, which continued its operations until 25 March 1943. The United States Army Air Corps Ferrying Command (ACFC), with which Ferry Command worked, was established in January 1942, based in Presque Isle, Maine.

On 1 March 1944, Liberator BZ935 out of Stephenville, Newfoundland, disappeared over the North Atlantic. The United States Army Air Force had supplied the entire crew: 1st Lieutenant C.M. Dorsett, pilot; 2nd Lieutenant O.E. Hess, co-pilot; 1st Lieutenant G.L. McBride, navigator; Staff Sergeant J.W. Wiant, radio operator; and Sergeant R.F. Menning, flight engineer.

The first non-stop flight from Newfoundland to Scotland took place in August 1942.

NORWAY

North Sea

GREAT BRITAIN

SHETLAND ISLANDS

FAROE ISLANDS

EIRE

Prestwick

Stornoway

Norwegian Sea

Arctic Circle

ICELAND

Reykjavik

660 miles

845 miles

2119 miles

Denmark Strait

774 miles

North Atlantic Ocean

GREENLAND

917 miles

Bluie West 8

Bluie West 1

Cape Farewell

Labrador Sea

716 miles

Davis Strait

1002 miles

Goose Bay

Arctic Circle

LABRADOR

569 miles

Stephenville

Gander

NEWFOUNDLAND

St Johns

645 miles

Cape Race

Hudson Bay

C A N A D A

Dorval

Montreal

Presque Isle

UNITED STATES

Portland

Boston Bangor

| 0 | | | | 1000 |
kilometres

| 0 | | | 600 |
miles

645 → Air ferry routes, with miles

© Martin Gilbert 2008

29

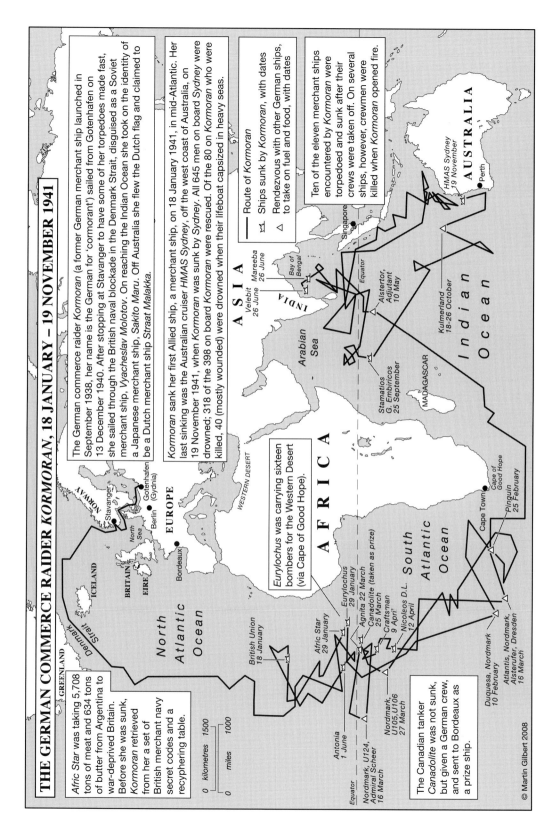

THE GERMAN COMMERCE RAIDER *KORMORAN*, 18 JANUARY – 19 NOVEMBER 1941

The German commerce raider *Kormoran* (a former German merchant ship launched in September 1938, her name is the German for 'cormorant') sailed from Gotenhafen on 13 December 1940. After stopping at Stavanger to have some of her torpedoes made fast, she sailed through the British naval blockade in the Denmark Strait, disguised as a Soviet merchant ship, *Vyacheslav Molotov*. On reaching the Indian Ocean she took on the identity of a Japanese merchant ship, *Sakito Maru*. Off Australia she flew the Dutch flag and claimed to be a Dutch merchant ship *Straat Malakka*.

Kormoran sank her first Allied ship, a merchant ship, on 18 January 1941, in mid-Atlantic. Her last sinking was the Australian cruiser *HMAS Sydney*, off the west coast of Australia, on 19 November 1941, when *Kormoran* was sunk by *Sydney*. All 645 men on board *Sydney* were drowned; 318 of the 398 on board *Kormoran* were rescued. Of the 80 on *Kormoran* who were killed, 40 (mostly wounded) were drowned when their lifeboat capsized in heavy seas.

Afric Star was taking 5,708 tons of meat and 634 tons of butter from Argentina to war-deprived Britain. Before she was sunk, *Kormoran* retrieved from her a set of British merchant navy secret codes and a recyphering table.

Eurylochus was carrying sixteen bombers for the Western Desert (via Cape of Good Hope).

The Canadian tanker *Canadolite* was not sunk, but given a German crew, and sent to Bordeaux as a prize ship.

Ten of the eleven merchant ships encountered by *Kormoran* were torpedoed and sunk after their crews were taken off. On several ships, however, crewmen were killed when *Kormoran* opened fire.

— Route of *Kormoran*
⋈ Ships sunk by *Kormoran*, with dates
△ Rendezvous with other German ships, to take on fuel and food, with dates

© Martin Gilbert 2008

0 kilometres 500 1000 1500
0 miles 1000

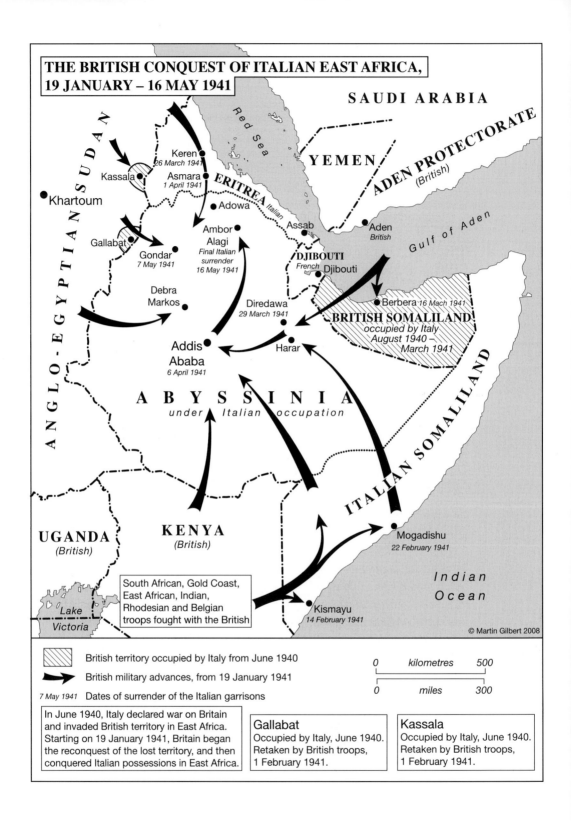

THE BRITISH CONQUEST OF ITALIAN EAST AFRICA, 19 JANUARY – 16 MAY 1941

SAUDI ARABIA

Red Sea

YEMEN

ADEN PROTECTORATE
(British)

ANGLO-EGYPTIAN SUDAN

Keren
26 March 1941

Kassala

Asmara
1 April 1941

ERITREA Italian

Khartoum

Adowa

Assab

Aden
British

Gulf of Aden

Gallabat

Ambor
Alagi
Final Italian
surrender
16 May 1941

Gondar
7 May 1941

DJIBOUTI
French Djibouti

Berbera 16 Mach 1941

Debra
Markos

Diredawa
29 March 1941

BRITISH SOMALILAND
occupied by Italy
August 1940 –
March 1941

Addis
Ababa
6 April 1941

Harar

A B Y S S I N I A
under Italian occupation

ITALIAN SOMALILAND

UGANDA
(British)

KENYA
(British)

Mogadishu
22 February 1941

Indian
Ocean

South African, Gold Coast,
East African, Indian,
Rhodesian and Belgian
troops fought with the British

Lake
Victoria

Kismayu
14 February 1941

© Martin Gilbert 2008

British territory occupied by Italy from June 1940

British military advances, from 19 January 1941

7 May 1941 Dates of surrender of the Italian garrisons

| 0 | kilometres | 500 |
| 0 | miles | 300 |

In June 1940, Italy declared war on Britain
and invaded British territory in East Africa.
Starting on 19 January 1941, Britain began
the reconquest of the lost territory, and then
conquered Italian possessions in East Africa.

Gallabat
Occupied by Italy, June 1940.
Retaken by British troops,
1 February 1941.

Kassala
Occupied by Italy, June 1940.
Retaken by British troops,
1 February 1941.

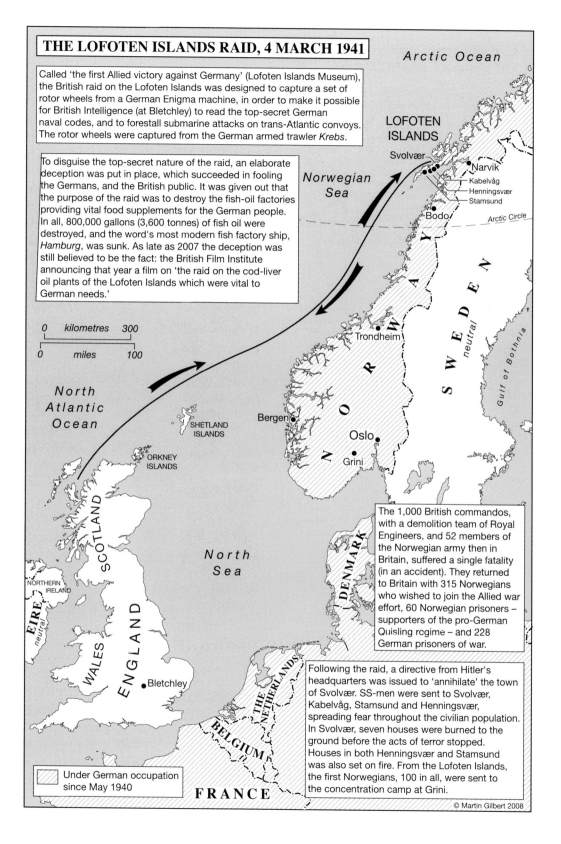

THE LOFOTEN ISLANDS RAID, 4 MARCH 1941

Called 'the first Allied victory against Germany' (Lofoten Islands Museum), the British raid on the Lofoten Islands was designed to capture a set of rotor wheels from a German Enigma machine, in order to make it possible for British Intelligence (at Bletchley) to read the top-secret German naval codes, and to forestall submarine attacks on trans-Atlantic convoys. The rotor wheels were captured from the German armed trawler *Krebs*.

To disguise the top-secret nature of the raid, an elaborate deception was put in place, which succeeded in fooling the Germans, and the British public. It was given out that the purpose of the raid was to destroy the fish-oil factories providing vital food supplements for the German people. In all, 800,000 gallons (3,600 tonnes) of fish oil were destroyed, and the word's most modern fish factory ship, *Hamburg*, was sunk. As late as 2007 the deception was still believed to be the fact: the British Film Institute announcing that year a film on 'the raid on the cod-liver oil plants of the Lofoten Islands which were vital to German needs.'

Arctic Ocean

LOFOTEN ISLANDS

Svolvær

Narvik
Kabelvåg
Henningsvær
Stamsund

Norwegian Sea

Bodo

Arctic Circle

| 0 | kilometres | 300 |
| 0 | miles | 100 |

North Atlantic Ocean

SHETLAND ISLANDS

Bergen

Trondheim

SWEDEN
neutral

Gulf of Bothnia

N O R W A Y

Oslo

Grini

ORKNEY ISLANDS

North Sea

SCOTLAND

NORTHERN IRELAND

EIRE
neutral

WALES

ENGLAND

• Bletchley

DENMARK

THE NETHERLANDS

BELGIUM

FRANCE

The 1,000 British commandos, with a demolition team of Royal Engineers, and 52 members of the Norwegian army then in Britain, suffered a single fatality (in an accident). They returned to Britain with 315 Norwegians who wished to join the Allied war effort, 60 Norwegian prisoners – supporters of the pro-German Quisling regime – and 228 German prisoners of war.

Following the raid, a directive from Hitler's headquarters was issued to 'annihilate' the town of Svolvær. SS-men were sent to Svolvær, Kabelvåg, Stamsund and Henningsvær, spreading fear throughout the civilian population. In Svolvær, seven houses were burned to the ground before the acts of terror stopped. Houses in both Henningsvær and Stamsund was also set on fire. From the Lofoten Islands, the first Norwegians, 100 in all, were sent to the concentration camp at Grini.

Under German occupation since May 1940

© Martin Gilbert 2008

THE GERMAN CONQUEST OF YUGOSLAVIA AND GREECE, 6–30 APRIL 1941

Legend:
- Axis Powers and their Allies
- Italian attacks and retreat October 1940
- Italian Albania, occupied by Greece (after Italian invasion repulsed)
- German advance, April 1941
- Italian advance
- Hungarian advance
- Bulgarian advance
- British, New Zealand and Australian troops

GERMANY

HUNGARY

HUNGARIAN TROOPS

GERMAN TROOPS

ROMANIA

Ljubljana

ITALIAN TROOPS

Zagreb
Occupied 10 April

Fiume

Y U G O S L A V I A

BULGARIA

Zara *Italian*

Split

Sarajevo
Occupied 15 April

Belgrade
Bombed 6 April
Occupied 12 April

Nish

Sofia

BULGARIAN TROOPS

Dubrovnik

Kotor

Skopje
Occupied 7 April

GERMAN TROOPS

A d r i a t i c   S e a

ALBANIA
Occupied by Italy

Durazzo   Tirana

ITALY

Brindisi

Valona

ITALIAN TROOPS

Klisura

Salonika
Occupied 9 April

BRITISH LINE 9 April

Aegean Sea

ITALIAN TROOPS

CORFU

Yannina

GREECE

Larissa

0   kilometres   150

0   miles   100

CEPHALONIA

I o n i a n   S e a

ZANTE

Thermopylae

BRITISH STAND 20–24 April

Patras

PELOPONNESE

Nauplia

Athens
Occupied 27 April

Piraeus
Bombed 6 April

Kalamata

Monemvasia

British evacuation
24–30 April
(to Crete)

Following the Yugoslav overthrow of the pro-German government in
Belgrade, Germany decided to bring Yugoslavia under Axis control,
and to complete its control of the Balkans by invading Greece.
Italian and Hungarian troops participated in the attack on Yugoslavia.
Italian troops, who had been driven out of northern Greece in
October 1940, also participated in the German invasion of Greece.
The Greeks were supported by British, Australian and New Zealand
troops. Yugoslavia and Greece were both conquered by 30 April 1941.

© Martin Gilbert 2008

GERMAN, ITALIAN AND BULGARIAN OCCUPATION ZONES OF GREECE, 1941–1943

YUGOSLAVIA

BULGARIA
allied to Germany

Black Sea

Tirana

YUGOSLAVIAN MACEDONIA
occupied by Germany

Lake Prespa

Lake Dojran

ALBANIA
occupied by Italy

THRACE

EASTERN THRACE

Sea of Marmora

GREEK MACEDONIA

THASOS

Salonika

SAMOTHRACE

TURKEY
neutral

G R E E C E

LEMNOS

STRATI

CORFU

PAXO

Arta

Volos

Aegean Sea

LESBOS

LEUCAS

CEPHALONIA

SKYROS

PSARA

CHIOS

SAMOS

Patras

PELOPONNESE

Athens

ANDROS

NICARIA

FURNI

ZANTE

CYCLADES

PATMOS

LEROS

Ionian Sea

KOS

MILOS

AMORGOS

DODECANESE

SIMI

Cape Matapan

SANTORINI

RHODES

KYTHERA

Mediterranean Sea

CRETE

Legend:
- Occupied by Germany
- Occupied by Italy
- Occupied by Bulgaria
- Italian sovereignty (conquered from Turkey in 1912)

© Martin Gilbert 2008

0 — kilometres — 150
0 — miles — 100

Following the evacuation of Athens and the Peloponnese by British forces on 30 April 1941, Greece was occupied by the three countries that had attacked her 24 days earlier: Germany, Italy and Bulgaria. Crete was divided between Germany and Italy after the final British evacuation on 31 May 1941. Germany insisted on control of the two largest Greek cities, Athens and Salonika, and of those Greek islands it considered of greatest strategic importance. When Italy surrendered in September 1943, Germany occupied all the Italian-controlled areas of Greece.

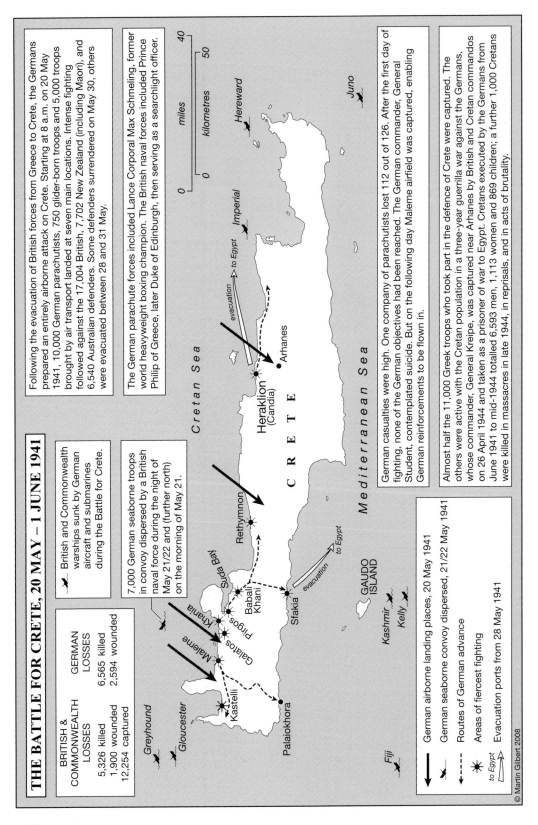

THE BATTLE FOR CRETE, 20 MAY – 1 JUNE 1941

BRITISH & COMMONWEALTH LOSSES

5,326 killed
1,900 wounded
12,254 captured

GERMAN LOSSES

6,565 killed
2,594 wounded

Following the evacuation of British forces from Greece to Crete, the Germans prepared an entirely airborne attack on Crete. Starting at 8 a.m. on 20 May 1941, 10,000 German parachutists, 750 glider-born troops and 5,000 troops brought by air transport landed at seven main locations. Intense fighting followed against the 17,004 British, 7,702 New Zealand (including Maori), and 6,540 Australian defenders. Some defenders surrendered on May 30, others were evacuated between 28 and 31 May.

The German parachute forces included Lance Corporal Max Schmeling, former world heavyweight boxing champion. The British naval forces included Prince Philip of Greece, later Duke of Edinburgh, then serving as a searchlight officer.

German casualties were high. One company of parachutists lost 112 out of 126. After the first day of fighting, none of the German objectives had been reached. The German commander, General Student, contemplated suicide. But on the following day Maleme airfield was captured, enabling German reinforcements to be flown in.

Almost half the 11,000 Greek troops who took part in the defence of Crete were captured. The others were active with the Cretan population in a three-year guerrilla war against the Germans, whose commander, General Kreipe, was captured near Arhanes by British and Cretan commandos on 26 April 1944 and taken as a prisoner of war to Egypt. Cretans executed by the Germans from June 1941 to mid-1944 totalled 6,593 men, 1,113 women and 869 children; a further 1,000 Cretans were killed in massacres in late 1944, in reprisals, and in acts of brutality.

British and Commonwealth warships sunk by German aircraft and submarines during the Battle for Crete.

7,000 German seaborne troops in convoy dispersed by a British naval force during the night of May 21/22 and (further north) on the morning of May 21.

Cretan Sea

Mediterranean Sea

Heraklion (Candia)

Arhanes

C R E T E

Rethymnon

Suda Bay

Khania

Galatos

Pirgos

Maleme

Kastelli

Babali Khani

Stakia

Palaiokhora

GAUDO ISLAND

to Egypt

evacuation to Egypt

evacuation

Greyhound

Gloucester

Fiji

Kashmir

Kelly

Imperial

Hereward

Juno

0   40 miles
0   50 kilometres

German airborne landing places, 20 May 1941

German seaborne convoy dispersed, 21/22 May 1941

Routes of German advance

Areas of fiercest fighting

to Egypt Evacuation ports from 28 May 1941

© Martin Gilbert 2008

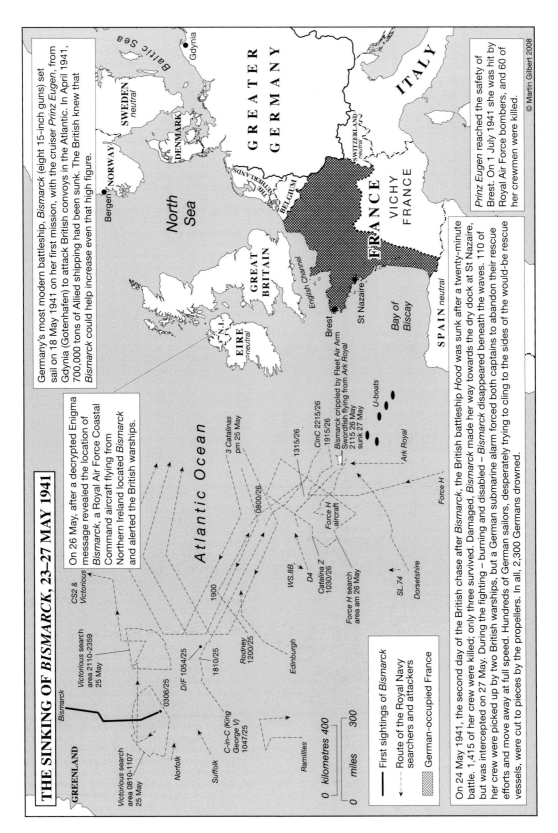

THE SINKING OF *BISMARCK*, 23–27 MAY 1941

Germany's most modern battleship, *Bismarck* (eight 15-inch guns) set sail on 18 May 1941 on her first mission, with the cruiser *Prinz Eugen*, from Gdynia (Gotenhafen) to attack British convoys in the Atlantic. In April 1941, 700,000 tons of Allied shipping had been sunk. The British knew that *Bismarck* could help increase even that high figure.

On 26 May, after a decrypted Enigma message revealed the location of *Bismarck*, a Royal Air Force Coastal Command aircraft flying from Northern Ireland located *Bismarck* and alerted the British warships.

Prinz Eugen reached the safety of Brest. On 1 July 1941 she was hit by Royal Air Force bombers, and 60 of her crewmen were killed.

Bismarck crippled by Fleet Air Arm Swordfish flying from *Ark Royal*
Bismarck 2115 26 May sunk 27 May

U-boats

Ark Royal

GREENLAND

Bismarck

Victorious search area 2110–2359 25 May

CS2 & *Victorious*

Victorious search area 0810–1107 25 May

0306/25

D/F 1054/25

1810/25

Rodney 1200/25

Edinburgh

Norfolk

Suffolk

C-in-C (King George V) 1047/25

Ramillies

1900

Atlantic Ocean

3 Catalinas pm 25 May

0800/26.

1315/26

CinC 2215/26
1915/26

WS.8B

D4

Catalina Z 1030/26

Force H search area am 26 May

Force H aircraft

SL.74

Dorsetshire

Force H

Baltic Sea

Gdynia

SWEDEN *neutral*

DENMARK

NORWAY
Bergen

GREATER GERMANY

North Sea

N.I.

EIRE *neutral*

GREAT BRITAIN

THE NETHERLANDS
BELGIUM
SWITZERLAND *neutral*

FRANCE

VICHY FRANCE

ITALY

English Channel

Brest

St Nazaire

Bay of Biscay

SPAIN *neutral*

© Martin Gilbert 2008

0 kilometres 400
0 miles 300

———— First sightings of *Bismarck*
- - - - - Route of the Royal Navy searchers and attackers

German-occupied France

On 24 May 1941, the second day of the British chase after *Bismarck*, the British battleship *Hood* was sunk after a twenty-minute battle. 1,415 of her crew were killed; only three survived. Damaged, *Bismarck* made her way towards the dry dock at St Nazaire, but was intercepted on 27 May. During the fighting – burning and disabled – *Bismarck* disappeared beneath the waves. 110 of her crew were picked up by two British warships, but a German submarine alarm forced both captains to abandon their rescue efforts and move away at full speed. Hundreds of German sailors, desperately trying to cling to the sides of the would-be rescue vessels, were cut to pieces by the propellers. In all, 2,300 Germans drowned.

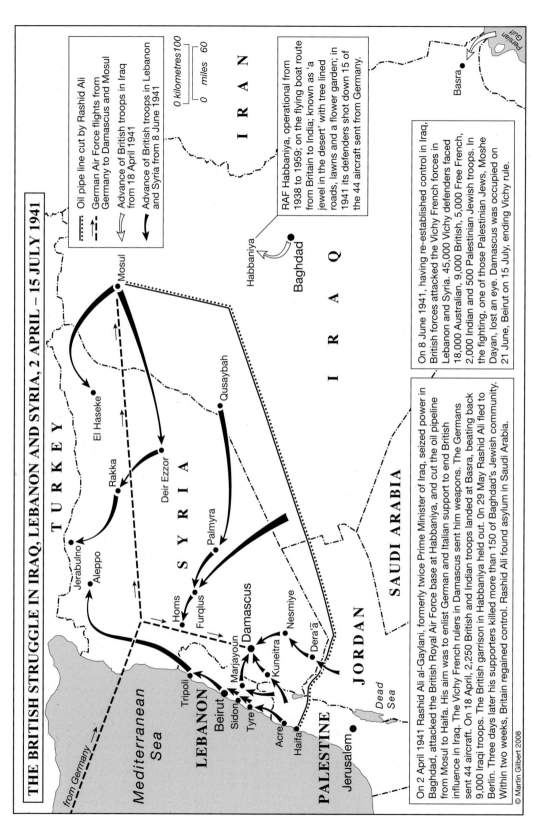

THE BRITISH STRUGGLE IN IRAQ, LEBANON AND SYRIA, 2 APRIL – 15 JULY 1941

············ Oil pipe line cut by Rashid Ali

–·–·–·– German Air Force flights from
Germany to Damascus and Mosul

⟨═ Advance of British troops in Iraq
from 18 April 1941

⬤➤ Advance of British troops in Lebanon
and Syria from 8 June 1941

```
0 kilometres 100
0      miles      60
```

RAF Habbaniya, operational from
1938 to 1959; on the flying boat route
from Britain to India; known as 'a
jewel in the desert' with tree lined
roads, lawns and a flower garden; in
1941 its defenders shot down 15 of
the 44 aircraft sent from Germany.

On 8 June 1941, having re-established control in Iraq,
British forces attacked the Vichy French forces in
Lebanon and Syria. 45,000 Vichy defenders faced
18,000 British, 9,000 Australian, 5,000 Free French,
2,000 Indian and 500 Palestinian Jewish troops. In
the fighting, one of those Palestinian Jews, Moshe
Dayan, lost an eye. Damascus was occupied on
21 June, Beirut on 15 July, ending Vichy rule.

On 2 April 1941 Rashid Ali al-Gaylani, formerly twice Prime Minister of Iraq, seized power in
Baghdad, attacked the British Royal Air Force base at Habbaniya, and cut the oil pipeline
from Mosul to Haifa. His aim was to enlist German and Italian support to end British
influence in Iraq. The Vichy French rulers in Damascus sent him weapons. The Germans
sent 44 aircraft. On 18 April, 2,250 British and Indian troops landed at Basra, beating back
9,000 Iraqi troops. The British garrison in Habbaniya held out. On 29 May Rashid Ali fled to
Berlin. Three days later his supporters killed more than 150 of Baghdad's Jewish community.
Within two weeks, Britain regained control. Rashid Ali found asylum in Saudi Arabia.

© Martin Gilbert 2008

Mediterranean Sea

from Germany

T U R K E Y

S Y R I A

I R A N

I R A Q

LEBANON

PALESTINE

JORDAN

SAUDI ARABIA

Dead Sea

Persian Gulf

Mosul

El Haseke

Rakka

Jerabulno

Aleppo

Deir Ezzor

Palmyra

Qusaybah

Homs

Furqlus

Damascus

Nesmiye

Kuneitra

Dera'a

Marjayoun

Tripoli

Beirut

Sidon

Tyre

Acre

Haifa

Jerusalem

Habbaniya

Baghdad

Basra

37

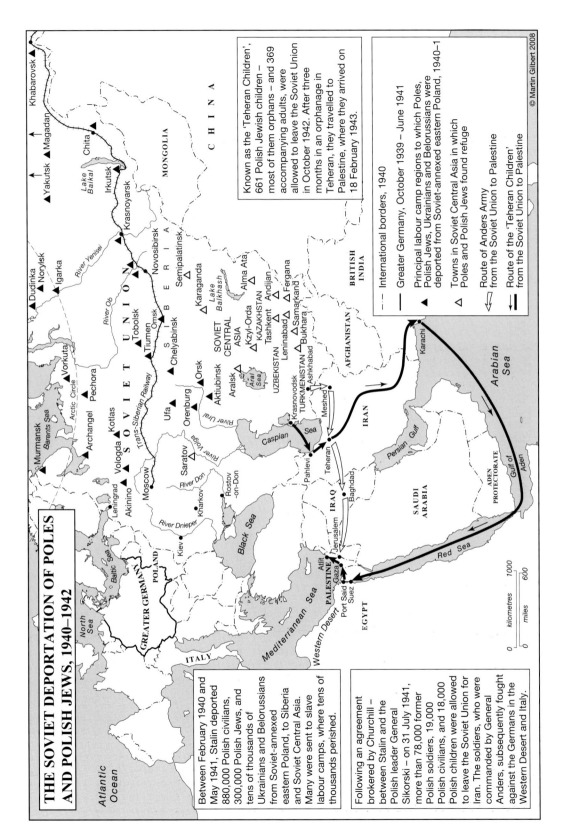

THE SOVIET DEPORTATION OF POLES AND POLISH JEWS, 1940–1942

Known as the 'Teheran Children', 661 Polish Jewish children – most of them orphans – and 369 accompanying adults, were allowed to leave the Soviet Union in October 1942. After three months in an orphanage in Teheran, they travelled to Palestine, where they arrived on 18 February 1943.

Between February 1940 and May 1941, Stalin deported 880,000 Polish civilians, 300,000 Polish Jews, and tens of thousands of Ukrainians and Belorussians from Soviet-annexed eastern Poland, to Siberia and Soviet Central Asia. Many were sent to slave labour camps, where tens of thousands perished.

Following an agreement brokered by Churchill – between Stalin and the Polish leader General Sikorski – on 31 July 1941, more than 78,000 former Polish soldiers, 19,000 Polish civilians, and 18,000 Polish children were allowed to leave the Soviet Union for Iran. The soldiers, who were commanded by General Anders, subsequently fought against the Germans in the Western Desert and Italy.

- - -   International borders, 1940

―――   Greater Germany, October 1939 – June 1941

▲   Principal labour camp regions to which Poles, Polish Jews, Ukrainians and Belorussians were deported from Soviet-annexed eastern Poland, 1940–1

△   Towns in Soviet Central Asia in which Poles and Polish Jews found refuge

⇨   Route of Anders Army from the Soviet Union to Palestine

➡   Route of the 'Teheran Children' from the Soviet Union to Palestine

© Martin Gilbert 2008

38

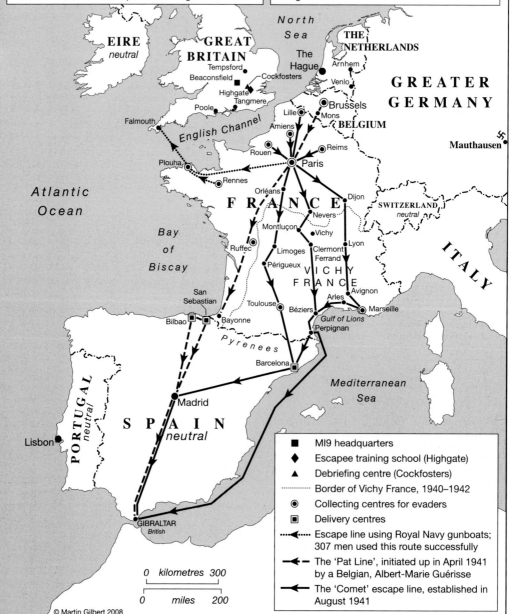

ALLIED ESCAPE AND EVASION ACROSS WESTERN EUROPE, 1940–1944

Allied airmen shot down over Germany, who managed to evade capture, could try to return to Britain by a series of escape routes set up and operated by the MI9 branch of British Military Intelligence, using local Dutch, Belgian and French helpers. Several helpers who were caught were executed by the Germans. Crossing the Pyrenees into neutral Spain, the route back led either through Gibraltar or through Lisbon, from where a flying boat service to Poole Harbour operated throughout the war.

Albert-Marie Guérisse, a Belgian army doctor who, after reaching England in May 1940, became a Lieutenant-Commander, Royal Navy, helped 600 evaders to return to Britain during the first year of the operation of his line. Using the name Patrick Albert O'Leary (hence the 'Pat Line') he was captured, imprisoned in Mauthausen, and survived the war. For helping evaders he was awarded the George Cross.

North Sea

EIRE
neutral

GREAT BRITAIN

THE NETHERLANDS

Tempsford
Beaconsfield
Cockfosters
Highgate
Tangmere
Poole

Falmouth

English Channel

The Hague
Arnhem
Venlo

GREATER GERMANY

Brussels
Lille
Mons
BELGIUM
Amiens

Mauthausen

Plouha
Rennes

Rouen
Reims

Atlantic Ocean

Paris

Orléans
Dijon
SWITZERLAND
neutral

Nevers

Bay of Biscay

Montluçon
Vichy
Lyon

Ruffec
Limoges
Clermont Ferrand

Périgueux

VICHY FRANCE

San Sebastian

Toulouse
Béziers
Arles
Avignon
Marseille

Bilbao
Bayonne
Gulf of Lions
Perpignan

Pyrenees

Barcelona

Mediterranean Sea

Madrid

SPAIN
neutral

PORTUGAL
neutral

Lisbon

GIBRALTAR
British

ITALY

FRANCE

0 kilometres 300

0 miles 200

© Martin Gilbert 2008

■ MI9 headquarters
♦ Escapee training school (Highgate)
▲ Debriefing centre (Cockfosters)
┄┄ Border of Vichy France, 1940–1942
◉ Collecting centres for evaders
▣ Delivery centres
┄◀┄ Escape line using Royal Navy gunboats; 307 men used this route successfully
◀— The 'Pat Line', initiated up in April 1941 by a Belgian, Albert-Marie Guérisse
◀— The 'Comet' escape line, established in August 1941

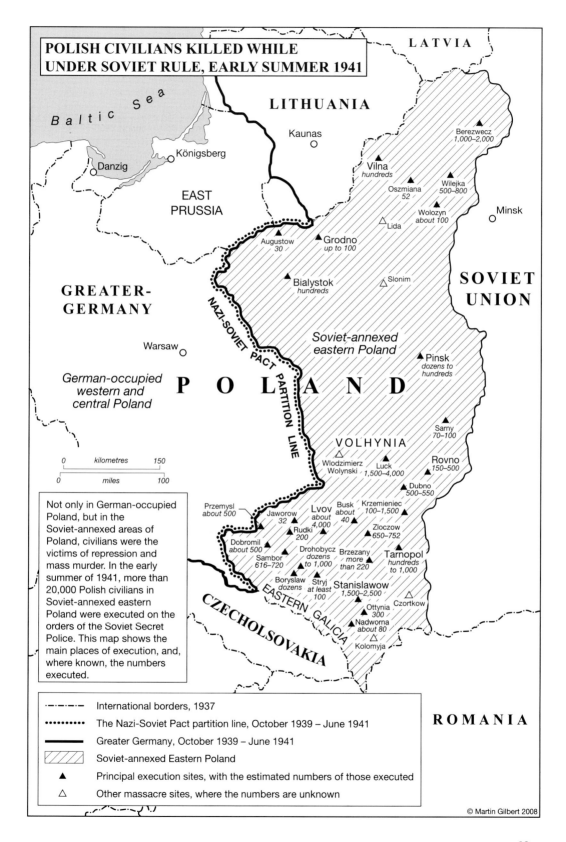

POLISH CIVILIANS KILLED WHILE
UNDER SOVIET RULE, EARLY SUMMER 1941

L A T V I A

Baltic Sea

LITHUANIA

Kaunas ○

Danzig ○

○ Königsberg

EAST
PRUSSIA

Berezwecz
1,000–2,000

Vilna
hundreds

Oszmiana
52

Wilejka
500–800

Wolozyn
about 100

Minsk ○

△ Lida

Augustow
30

Grodno
up to 100

GREATER-
GERMANY

Bialystok
hundreds

△ Slonim

SOVIET
UNION

Warsaw ○

Soviet-annexed
eastern Poland

Pinsk
*dozens to
hundreds*

*German-occupied
western and
central Poland*

P O L A N D

Sarny
70–100

VOLHYNIA

Rovno
150–500

△
Wlodzimierz
Wolynski

Luck
1,500–4,000

Dubno
500–550

0 kilometres 150
0 miles 100

Przemysl
about 500

Jaworow
32

Lvov
*about
4,000*

Busk
*about
40*

Krzemieniec
100–1,500

Zloczow
650–752

Rudki
200

Not only in German-occupied
Poland, but in the
Soviet-annexed areas of
Poland, civilians were the
victims of repression and
mass murder. In the early
summer of 1941, more than
20,000 Polish civilians in
Soviet-annexed eastern
Poland were executed on the
orders of the Soviet Secret
Police. This map shows the
main places of execution, and,
where known, the numbers
executed.

Dobromil
about 500

Sambor
616–720

Drohobycz
*dozens
to 1,000*

Brzezany
*more
than 220*

Tarnopol
*hundreds
to 1,000*

Boryslaw
dozens

Stryj
*at least
100*

Stanislawow
1,500–2,500

△ Czortkow

Ottynia
300

Nadworna
about 80

EASTERN GALICIA

△
Kolomyja

CZECHOLSOVAKIA

International borders, 1937

The Nazi-Soviet Pact partition line, October 1939 – June 1941

Greater Germany, October 1939 – June 1941

Soviet-annexed Eastern Poland

▲ Principal execution sites, with the estimated numbers of those executed

△ Other massacre sites, where the numbers are unknown

R O M A N I A

© Martin Gilbert 2008

40

Section 3

THE SOVIET UNION BECOMES AN ALLIED POWER

Russski, Russski – obernis-ka
yedet Nemets,
gost ne'izvanny

> Russian, Russian – wake yourself up
> the German is coming,
> the uninvited guest

A Russian Exhortation from the Fourteenth Century

Our war for the freedom of our motherland will merge with the struggle of the peoples of Europe and America for their independence, for democratic liberties. It will be a united front of the peoples who stand for freedom and against enslavement and threats of enslavement by Hitler's fascist armies.

JOSEPH STALIN
First Radio Address after the German invasion of the Soviet Union
3 July 1941

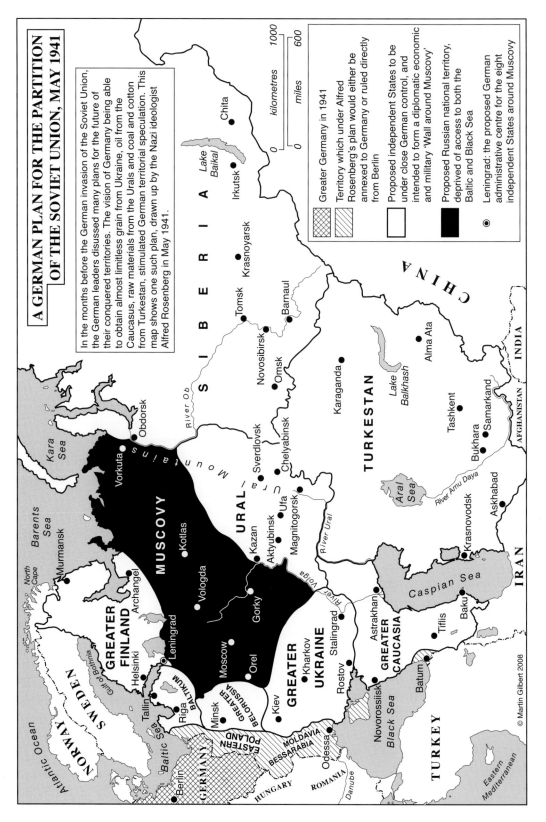

A GERMAN PLAN FOR THE PARTITION OF THE SOVIET UNION, MAY 1941

In the months before the German invasion of the Soviet Union, the German leaders disussed many plans for the future of their conquered territories. The vision of Germany being able to obtain almost limitless grain from Ukraine, oil from the Caucasus, raw materials from the Urals and coal and cotton from Turkestan, stimulated German territorial speculation. This map shows one such plan, drawn up by the Nazi ideologist Alfred Rosenberg in May 1941.

Greater Germany in 1941

Territory which under Alfred Rosenberg's plan would either be annexed to Germany or ruled directly from Berlin

Proposed independent States to be under close German control, and intended to form a diplomatic economic and military 'Wall around Muscovy'

Proposed Russian national territory, deprived of access to both the Baltic and Black Sea

Leningrad: the proposed German administrative centre for the eight independent States around Muscovy

© Martin Gilbert 2008

41

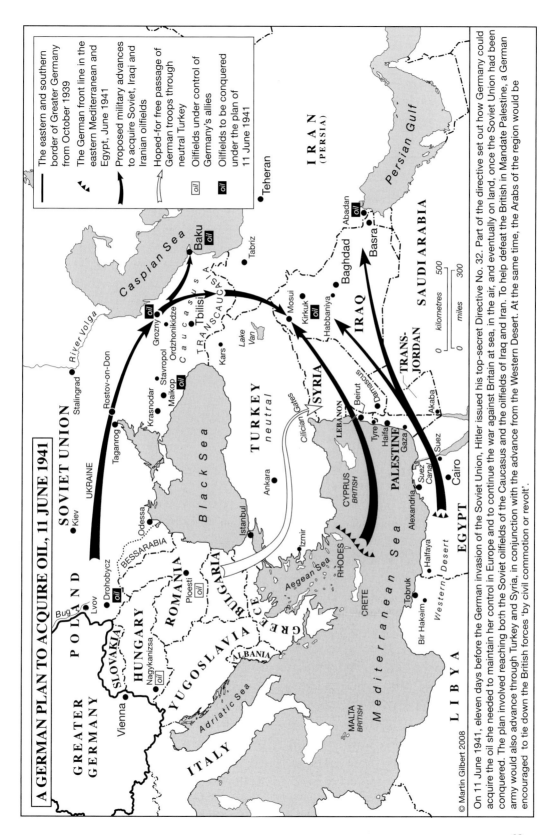

A GERMAN PLAN TO ACQUIRE OIL, 11 JUNE 1941

Legend:
- The eastern and southern border of Greater Germany from October 1939
- The German front line in the eastern Mediterranean and Egypt, June 1941
- Proposed military advances to acquire Soviet, Iraqi and Iranian oilfields
- Hoped-for free passage of German troops through neutral Turkey
- ⬜ *oil* Oilfields under control of Germany's allies
- ⬛ *oil* Oilfields to be conquered under the plan of 11 June 1941

GREATER GERMANY · Vienna · POLAND · Lvov · Bug · Drohobycz ⬜*oil* · SLOVAKIA · HUNGARY · Nagykanizsa ⬜*oil* · ROMANIA · Ploesti ⬜*oil* · BESSARABIA · Odessa · YUGOSLAVIA · ALBANIA · ITALY · Adriatic Sea · GREECE · BULGARIA · CRETE · MALTA BRITISH

SOVIET UNION · Kiev · UKRAINE · River Volga · Stalingrad · Rostov-on-Don · Taganrog · Krasnodar · Stavropol · Maikop ⬜*oil* · Grozny ⬜*oil* · Ordzhonikidze · Tbilisi · TRANSCAUCASIA · CAUCASUS · Kars · Lake Van · Caspian Sea · Baku ⬛*oil* · Tabriz · Teheran

Black Sea · Istanbul · TURKEY *neutral* · Ankara · Cilician Gates · Izmir · Aegean Sea · RHODES · Mediterranean Sea

IRAN (PERSIA) · Persian Gulf · Abadan ⬛*oil* · Baghdad · Basra · IRAQ · Mosul ⬛*oil* · Kirkuk ⬛*oil* · Habbaniya · SYRIA · LEBANON · Beirut · Damascus · TRANS-JORDAN · Akaba · SAUDI ARABIA

CYPRUS BRITISH · Tyre · Haifa · Gaza · PALESTINE · Suez · Suez Canal · Cairo · EGYPT · Alexandria · Western Desert · Tobruk · Bir Hakeim · Halfaya · Bir Hakeim · LIBYA

0 kilometres 500
0 miles 300

© Martin Gilbert 2008

On 11 June 1941, eleven days before the German invasion of the Soviet Union, Hitler issued his top-secret Directive No. 32. Part of the directive set out how Germany could acquire the oil she needed to maintain her control in Europe and to continue the war against Britain at sea, in the air, and eventually on land, once the Soviet Union had been conquered. The plan involved reaching both the Soviet oilfields of the Caucasus and the oilfields of Iraq and Iran. To help defeat the British in Mandate Palestine, a German army would also advance through Turkey and Syria, in conjunction with the advance from the Western Desert. At the same time, the Arabs of the region would be encouraged to tie down the British forces 'by civil commotion or revolt'.

THE GERMAN INVASION OF THE SOVIET UNION, 22 JUNE 1941

■ Under German rule or influence by June 1941

→ General direction of the German advance

▨ Occupied by German forces between June and December 1941

⊙ Cities besieged by the Germans, late 1941

On 22 June 1941, German forces invaded the Soviet Union; Operation Barbarossa. Within six months they had besieged Leningrad and Sebastopol, and reached to within twelve miles of the Soviet capital, Moscow.

The German Army was supported by Italian, Romanian, Hungarian and Finnish troops. A Spanish Legion also fought for Germany on the Eastern Front.

© Martin Gilbert 2008

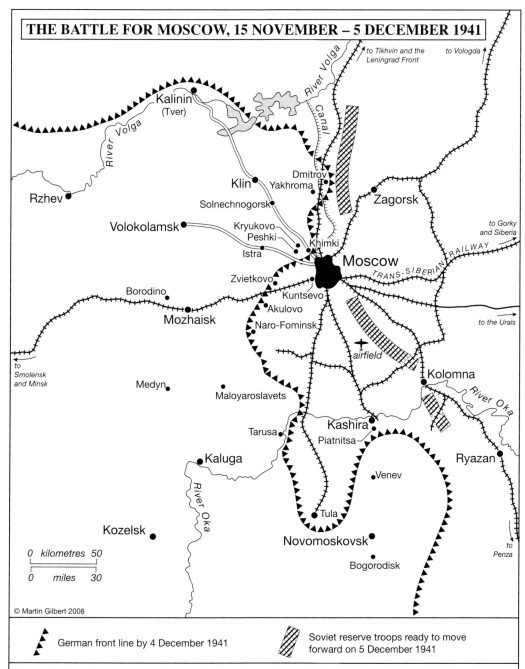

THE BATTLE FOR MOSCOW, 15 NOVEMBER – 5 DECEMBER 1941

to Tikhvin and the
Leningrad Front

to Vologda

River Volga

Canal

Kalinin
(Tver)

River Volga

Rzhev

Klin

Yakhroma

Dmitrov

Zagorsk

Solnechnogorsk

Volokolamsk

Kryukovo

Peshki

Khimki

Istra

Moscow

to Gorky
and Siberia

RAILWAY

TRANS-SIBERIAN

Zvietkovo

Borodino

Kuntsevo

Akulovo

Mozhaisk

Naro-Fominsk

to the Urals

to
Smolensk
and Minsk

airfield

Medyn

Kolomna

Maloyaroslavets

River Oka

Tarusa

Kashira

Ryazan

Piatnitsa

Kaluga

Venev

Kozelsk

River Oka

Tula

to
Penza

Novomoskovsk

Bogorodisk

0 kilometres 50

0 miles 30

© Martin Gilbert 2008

▲▲ German front line by 4 December 1941

▨ Soviet reserve troops ready to move forward on 5 December 1941

Even as Leningrad was besieged, German forces advanced towards Moscow, seeking but failing to encircle it, and being halted by Soviet reserve troops, many having been brought by train along the Trans-Siberian railway from the Soviet Far East. On 1 December 1941, German attacks on Zvietkovo and towards Kolomna were beaten back. Reaching Khimki on 2 December, the German forces were only twelve miles from the Kremlin. They were forced to a halt, during a blinding snowstorm, by hastily armed Soviet factory workers. That day, German troops entered Akulovo, from which the tall spires of the Kremlin could be seen; two days later they were driven out. The final German push began on 4 December. Two days later the Soviets launched a counter-offensive forcing the Germans to withdraw and take up defensive positions. German troops were never to come so close to Moscow again. On the Moscow Front, 85,000 German soldiers had been killed between 16 November and 4 December 1941.

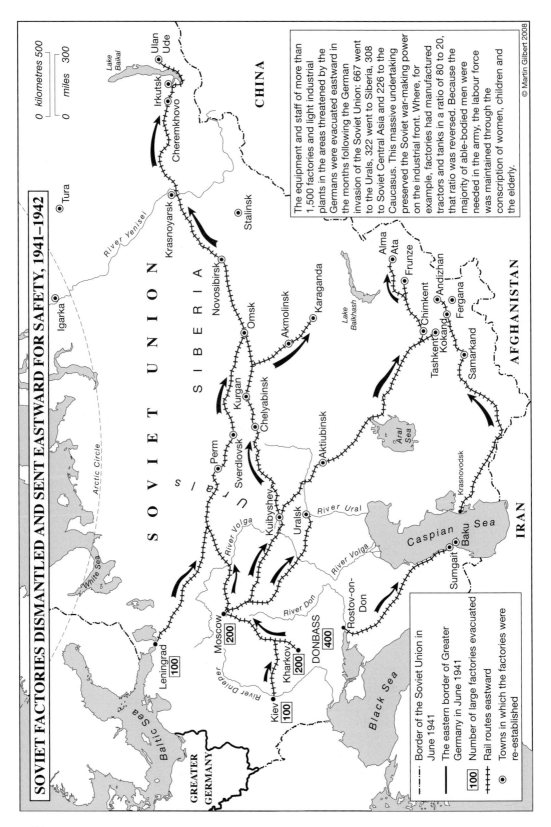

SOVIET FACTORIES DISMANTLED AND SENT EASTWARD FOR SAFETY, 1941–1942

The equipment and staff of more than 1,500 factories and light industrial plants in the areas threatened by the Germans were evacuated eastward in the months following the German invasion of the Soviet Union: 667 went to the Urals, 322 went to Siberia, 308 to Soviet Central Asia and 226 to the Caucasus. This massive undertaking preserved the Soviet war-making power on the industrial front. Where, for example, factories had manufactured tractors and tanks in a ratio of 80 to 20, that ratio was reversed. Because the majority of able-bodied men were needed in the army, the labour force was maintained through the conscription of women, children and the elderly.

© Martin Gilbert 2008

Legend:

- –··– Border of the Soviet Union in June 1941
- —— The eastern border of Greater Germany in June 1941
- [100] Number of large factories evacuated
- +++++ Rail routes eastward
- ◉ Towns in which the factories were re-established

45

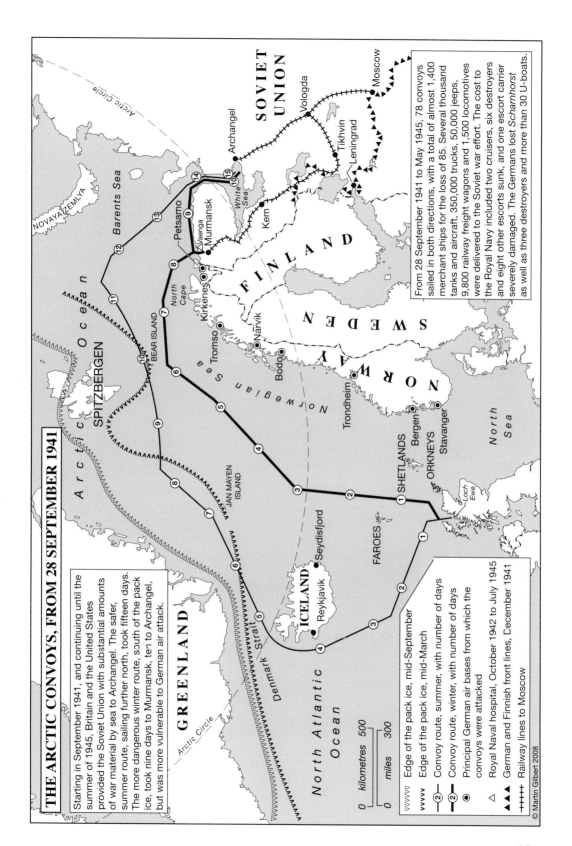

THE ARCTIC CONVOYS, FROM 28 SEPTEMBER 1941

Starting in September 1941, and continuing until the summer of 1945, Britain and the United States provided the Soviet Union with substantial amounts of war material by sea to Archangel. The safer, summer route, sailing further north, took fifteen days. The more dangerous winter route, south of the pack ice, took nine days to Murmansk, ten to Archangel, but was more vulnerable to German air attack.

From 28 September 1941 to May 1945, 78 convoys sailed in both directions, with a total of almost 1,400 merchant ships for the loss of 85. Several thousand tanks and aircraft, 350,000 trucks, 50,000 jeeps, 9,800 railway freight wagons and 1,500 locomotives were delivered to the Soviet war effort. The cost to the Royal Navy included two cruisers, six destroyers and eight other escorts sunk, and one escort carrier severely damaged. The Germans lost *Scharnhorst* as well as three destroyers and more than 30 U-boats.

SOVIET UNION

Moscow
Vologda
Archangel
Tikhvin
Leningrad

Barents Sea
NOVAYA ZEMLYA
White Sea
Kem
Petsamo
Vaenga
Murmansk
North Cape
Kirkenes
FINLAND

Arctic Ocean
SPITZBERGEN
BEAR ISLAND
Narvik
Tromso
Bodo
SWEDEN
NORWAY
Trondheim
Bergen
Stavanger

JAN MAYEN ISLAND
Norwegian Sea
SHETLANDS
ORKNEYS
Loch Ewe
North Sea

GREENLAND
Denmark Strait
Arctic Circle
ICELAND
Reykjavik
Seydisfjord
FAROES

North Atlantic Ocean

wwwww Edge of the pack ice, mid-September
vvvvv Edge of the pack ice, mid-March
—②— Convoy route, summer, with number of days
—②— Convoy route, winter, with number of days
◉ Principal German air bases from which the convoys were attacked
△ Royal Naval hospital, October 1942 to July 1945
▲▲▲ German and Finnish front lines, December 1941
++++ Railway lines to Moscow

0 kilometres 500
0 miles 300

© Martin Gilbert 2008

46

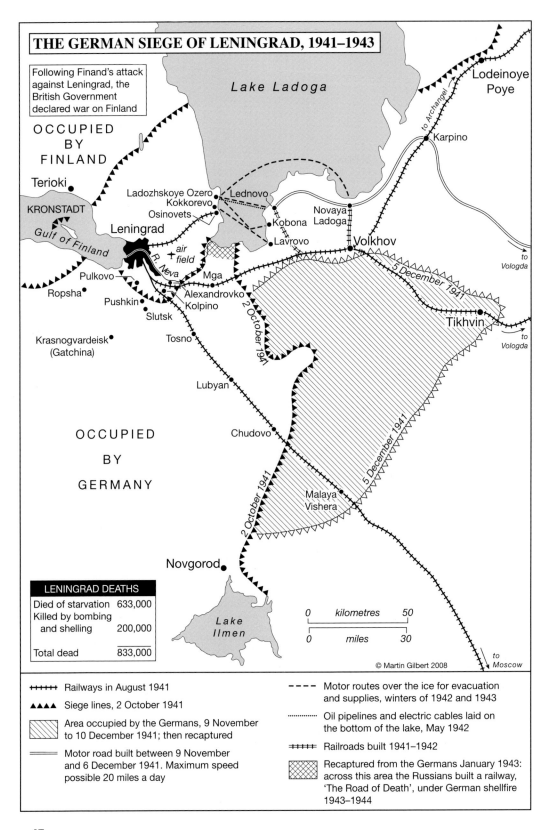

THE GERMAN SIEGE OF LENINGRAD, 1941–1943

Following Finand's attack against Leningrad, the British Government declared war on Finland

Lake Ladoga

OCCUPIED BY FINLAND

Lodeinoye Poye

to Archangel

Karpino

Terioki

KRONSTADT

Ladozhskoye Ozero
Kokkorevo
Lednovo

Osinovets

Novaya Ladoga

Gulf of Finland

Leningrad

Kobona

air field

Lavrovo

Volkhov

to Vologda

R. Neva

5 December 1941

Pulkovo

Mga

Ropsha

Alexandrovko
Kolpino

Pushkin

Slutsk

2 October 1941

Tikhvin

to Vologda

Krasnogvardeisk
(Gatchina)

Tosno

Lubyan

Chudovo

5 December 1941

OCCUPIED

BY

GERMANY

2 October 1941

Malaya Vishera

Novgorod

0	kilometres	50
0	miles	30

Lake Ilmen

to Moscow

© Martin Gilbert 2008

LENINGRAD DEATHS

Died of starvation	633,000
Killed by bombing and shelling	200,000
Total dead	833,000

+++++ Railways in August 1941

▲▲▲▲ Siege lines, 2 October 1941

Area occupied by the Germans, 9 November to 10 December 1941; then recaptured

Motor road built between 9 November and 6 December 1941. Maximum speed possible 20 miles a day

– – – Motor routes over the ice for evacuation and supplies, winters of 1942 and 1943

·········· Oil pipelines and electric cables laid on the bottom of the lake, May 1942

+++++ Railroads built 1941–1942

Recaptured from the Germans January 1943: across this area the Russians built a railway, 'The Road of Death', under German shellfire 1943–1944

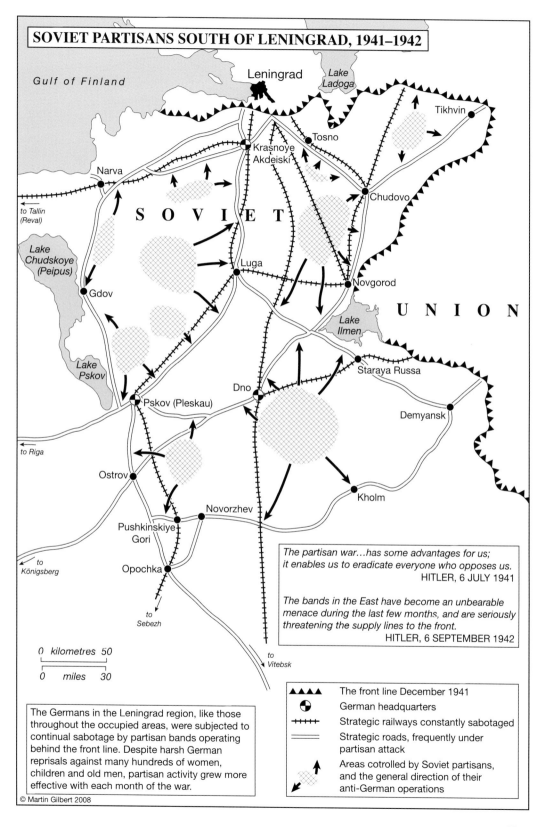

SOVIET PARTISANS SOUTH OF LENINGRAD, 1941–1942

Gulf of Finland

Leningrad

Lake Ladoga

Tikhvin

Tosno

Krasnoye Akdeiski

Narva

to Tallin (Reval)

Chudovo

S O V I E T

Lake Chudskoye (Peipus)

Luga

Novgorod

U N I O N

Gdov

Lake Pskov

Lake Ilmen

Dno

Staraya Russa

Demyansk

to Riga

Pskov (Pleskau)

Ostrov

Kholm

Novorzhev

Pushkinskiye Gori

to Königsberg

Opochka

> The partisan war...has some advantages for us;
> it enables us to eradicate everyone who opposes us.
> HITLER, 6 JULY 1941

> The bands in the East have become an unbearable
> menace during the last few months, and are seriously
> threatening the supply lines to the front.
> HITLER, 6 SEPTEMBER 1942

to Sebezh

0   kilometres 50

0   miles   30

to Vitebsk

The Germans in the Leningrad region, like those
throughout the occupied areas, were subjected to
continual sabotage by partisan bands operating
behind the front line. Despite harsh German
reprisals against many hundreds of women,
children and old men, partisan activity grew more
effective with each month of the war.

© Martin Gilbert 2008

▲▲▲▲ The front line December 1941

◑ German headquarters

╫╫╫╫╫ Strategic railways constantly sabotaged

═══ Strategic roads, frequently under
partisan attack

Areas cotrolled by Soviet partisans,
and the general direction of their
anti-German operations

48

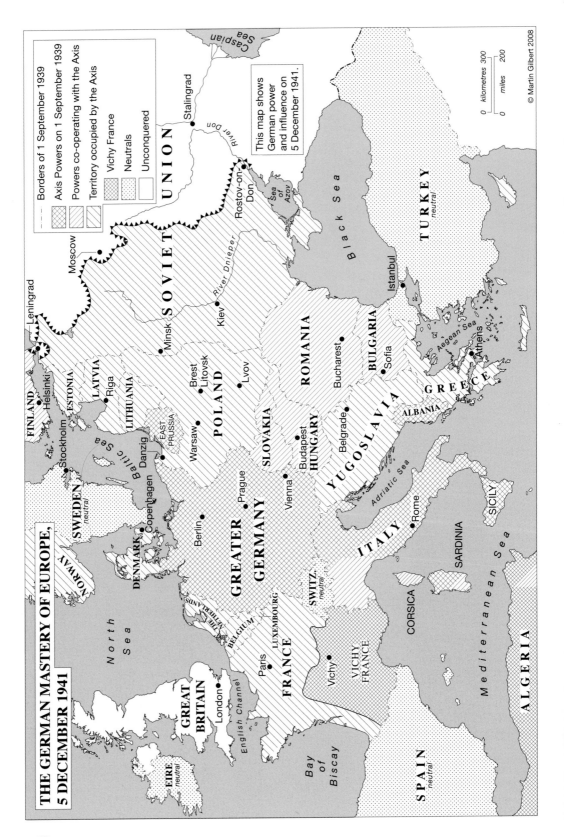

THE GERMAN MASTERY OF EUROPE, 5 DECEMBER 1941

Legend:
- Borders of 1 September 1939
- Axis Powers on 1 September 1939
- Powers co-operating with the Axis
- Territory occupied by the Axis
- Vichy France
- Neutrals
- Unconquered

This map shows German power and influence on 5 December 1941.

© Martin Gilbert 2008

SOVIET UNION

Stalingrad

River Don

Rostov-on-Don

Sea of Azov

Black Sea

TURKEY *neutral*

Moscow

Leningrad

FINLAND

Helsinki

ESTONIA

LATVIA

Riga

LITHUANIA

Minsk

Brest Litovsk

Kiev

Lvov

ROMANIA

Bucharest

BULGARIA

Sofia

Istanbul

Aegean Sea

GREECE

Athens

SWEDEN *neutral*

Stockholm

Baltic Sea

Danzig

EAST PRUSSIA

Warsaw

POLAND

SLOVAKIA

Budapest

HUNGARY

Belgrade

YUGOSLAVIA

ALBANIA

Adriatic Sea

NORWAY

DENMARK

Copenhagen

Berlin

Prague

GREATER GERMANY

Vienna

SWITZ. *neutral*

ITALY

Rome

SICILY

SARDINIA

CORSICA

North Sea

THE NETHERLANDS

BELGIUM

LUXEMBOURG

Paris

FRANCE

Vichy

VICHY FRANCE

GREAT BRITAIN

London

English Channel

EIRE *neutral*

Bay of Biscay

SPAIN *neutral*

ALGERIA

Mediterranean Sea

River Dnieper

Caspian Sea

0 kilometres 300
0 miles 200

49

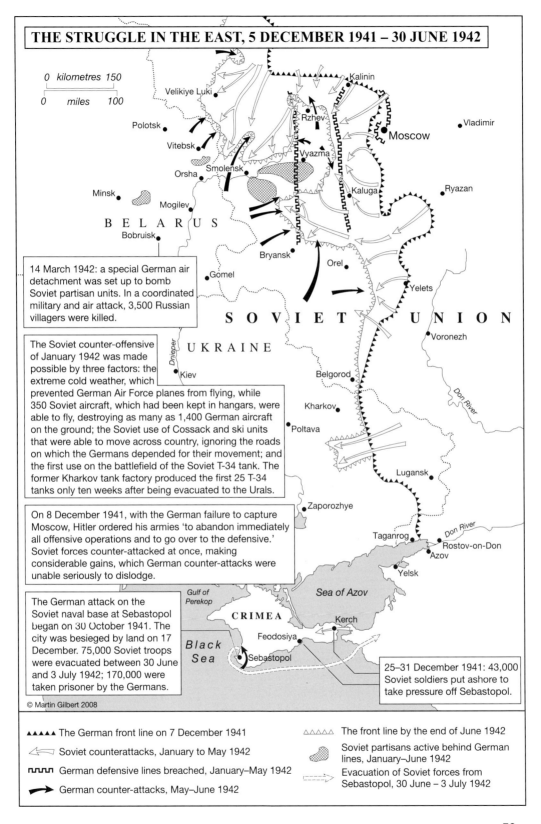

THE STRUGGLE IN THE EAST, 5 DECEMBER 1941 – 30 JUNE 1942

0 kilometres 150
0 miles 100

Velikiye Luki
Kalinin
Vladimir
Polotsk
Rzhev
Vitebsk
Moscow
Orsha
Smolensk
Vyazma
Minsk
Mogilev
Kaluga
Ryazan
B E L A R U S
Bobruisk
Bryansk
Orel
Gomel
Yelets
S O V I E T   U N I O N
U K R A I N E
Voronezh
Dnieper
Kiev
Belgorod
Kharkov
Poltava
Don River
Lugansk
Zaporozhye
Taganrog
Don River
Rostov-on-Don
Azov
Yelsk
Sea of Azov
Gulf of Perekop
C R I M E A
Kerch
Feodosiya
Black Sea
Sebastopol

14 March 1942: a special German air detachment was set up to bomb Soviet partisan units. In a coordinated military and air attack, 3,500 Russian villagers were killed.

The Soviet counter-offensive of January 1942 was made possible by three factors: the extreme cold weather, which prevented German Air Force planes from flying, while 350 Soviet aircraft, which had been kept in hangars, were able to fly, destroying as many as 1,400 German aircraft on the ground; the Soviet use of Cossack and ski units that were able to move across country, ignoring the roads on which the Germans depended for their movement; and the first use on the battlefield of the Soviet T-34 tank. The former Kharkov tank factory produced the first 25 T-34 tanks only ten weeks after being evacuated to the Urals.

On 8 December 1941, with the German failure to capture Moscow, Hitler ordered his armies 'to abandon immediately all offensive operations and to go over to the defensive.' Soviet forces counter-attacked at once, making considerable gains, which German counter-attacks were unable seriously to dislodge.

The German attack on the Soviet naval base at Sebastopol began on 30 October 1941. The city was besieged by land on 17 December. 75,000 Soviet troops were evacuated between 30 June and 3 July 1942; 170,000 were taken prisoner by the Germans.

25–31 December 1941: 43,000 Soviet soldiers put ashore to take pressure off Sebastopol.

© Martin Gilbert 2008

▲▲▲▲▲ The German front line on 7 December 1941

◁— Soviet counterattacks, January to May 1942

ⴖⴖⴖⴖ German defensive lines breached, January–May 1942

➤ German counter-attacks, May–June 1942

△△△△△ The front line by the end of June 1942

Soviet partisans active behind German lines, January–June 1942

Evacuation of Soviet forces from Sebastopol, 30 June – 3 July 1942

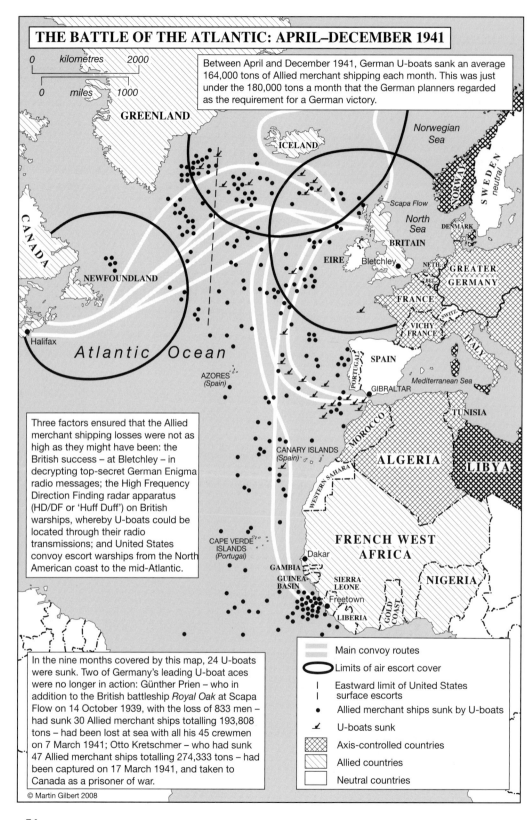

THE BATTLE OF THE ATLANTIC: APRIL–DECEMBER 1941

0 kilometres 2000
0 miles 1000

Between April and December 1941, German U-boats sank an average 164,000 tons of Allied merchant shipping each month. This was just under the 180,000 tons a month that the German planners regarded as the requirement for a German victory.

GREENLAND

Norwegian Sea

ICELAND

CANADA

NEWFOUNDLAND

Scapa Flow

North Sea

DENMARK

BRITAIN

EIRE   Bletchley

Halifax

Atlantic Ocean

AZORES (Spain)

SPAIN

PORTUGAL

GIBRALTAR

Mediterranean Sea

GREATER GERMANY

FRANCE

VICHY FRANCE

SWITZ.

ITALY

NETH.
BEL.

S W E D E N neutral

N O R W A Y

Three factors ensured that the Allied merchant shipping losses were not as high as they might have been: the British success – at Bletchley – in decrypting top-secret German Enigma radio messages; the High Frequency Direction Finding radar apparatus (HD/DF or 'Huff Duff') on British warships, whereby U-boats could be located through their radio transmissions; and United States convoy escort warships from the North American coast to the mid-Atlantic.

CANARY ISLANDS (Spain)

MOROCCO

ALGERIA

LIBYA

TUNISIA

WESTERN SAHARA

CAPE VERDE ISLANDS (Portugal)

FRENCH WEST AFRICA

Dakar

GAMBIA

GUINEA BASIN

SIERRA LEONE

Freetown

LIBERIA

GOLD COAST

NIGERIA

In the nine months covered by this map, 24 U-boats were sunk. Two of Germany's leading U-boat aces were no longer in action: Günther Prien – who in addition to the British battleship *Royal Oak* at Scapa Flow on 14 October 1939, with the loss of 833 men – had sunk 30 Allied merchant ships totalling 193,808 tons – had been lost at sea with all his 45 crewmen on 7 March 1941; Otto Kretschmer – who had sunk 47 Allied merchant ships totalling 274,333 tons – had been captured on 17 March 1941, and taken to Canada as a prisoner of war.

© Martin Gilbert 2008

Main convoy routes

Limits of air escort cover

Eastward limit of United States surface escorts

• Allied merchant ships sunk by U-boats

U-boats sunk

Axis-controlled countries

Allied countries

Neutral countries

THE BATTLE OF THE ATLANTIC: CONVOY HG76, 14-30 DECEMBER 1941

The tide of battle in the Atlantic seemed to turn with convoy HG76, which left Gibraltar on 14 December 1941. The escort commander, Commander F.J. Walker, Royal Navy, was determined to attack the U-boats rather than wait for them to attack, an idea hitherto resisted by the Admiralty. Commander Walker, whose signature tune was 'A hunting we will go', was present at the sinking of 25 U-boats before his death from natural causes in July 1944. He was awarded the Distinguished Service Order (DSO) four times.

The first convoy success came on 17 December, when four of the escorts sank *U-131*. *U-434* was sunk on 18 December; *U-574* on 19 December; *U-567* on 23 December. German Focke-Wulf aircraft attacked the convoy from their base at Bordeaux: two of them were shot down. On 21 December the U-boats were reinforced from the Bay of Biscay submarine base at Lorient, sinking the British Escort Carrier, *HMS Audacity,* that day. The convoy reached Liverpool on 30 December 1941. Britain's loss of the ability to decrypt German naval Enigma messages in 1942 brought renewed heavy losses.

Convoy HG76 consisted of 32 merchant ships – British, Norwegian and Swedish – and 14 escort vessels. Two of the escorts and two merchant ships were sunk. The two merchant ships sunk were *SS Ruckinge*, ex-Dundee (2 crewmen killed) and the Norwegian *SS Annavore* (34 crewmen killed, only 4 survived). The Escort Carrier *HMS Audacity*, with four Martlet aircraft, was a converted German merchant ship prize, *MV Hannover*. She was sunk on 21 December. The escort destroyer *HMS Stanley*, formerly the *USS McCalla*, was one of the American First World War destroyers transferred to the Royal Navy at the end of 1940.

⟢	U-boats sighted
⟤	U-boats attacked
⟍	U-boats sunk
✗	German Focke-Wulf 200 'Condor' long-range anti-shipping bombers driven off
⟍	Merchant ships torpedoed
⟍	Escorts sunk

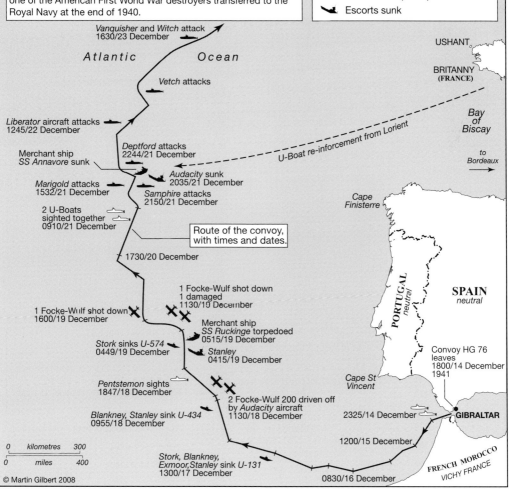

Vanquisher and *Witch* attack
1630/23 December

Atlantic   Ocean

USHANT

BRITANNY
(FRANCE)

Vetch attacks

Liberator aircraft attacks
1245/22 December

Bay
of
Biscay

Deptford attacks
2244/21 December

U-Boat re-inforcement from Lorient

to
Bordeaux

Merchant ship
SS Annavore sunk

Audacity sunk
2035/21 December

Marigold attacks
1532/21 December

Samphire attacks
2150/21 December

Cape
Finisterre

2 U-Boats
sighted together
0910/21 December

Route of the convoy,
with times and dates.

1730/20 December

1 Focke-Wulf shot down
1 damaged
1130/10 December

PORTUGAL
neutral

SPAIN
neutral

1 Focke-Wulf shot down
1600/19 December

Merchant ship
SS Ruckinge torpedoed
0515/19 December

Stork sinks *U-574*
0449/19 December

Stanley
0415/19 December

Convoy HG 76
leaves
1800/14 December
1941

Pentstemon sights
1847/18 December

Cape St
Vincent

Blankney, Stanley sink *U-434*
0955/18 December

2 Focke-Wulf 200 driven off
by *Audacity* aircraft
1130/18 December

2325/14 December

GIBRALTAR

1200/15 December

0   kilometres   300

0   miles   400

© Martin Gilbert 2008

*Stork, Blankney,
Exmoor,Stanley* sink *U-131*
1300/17 December

0830/16 December

FRENCH MOROCCO
VICHY FRANCE

Section 4

JAPAN AND THE UNITED STATES ENTER THE WAR

Yesterday, December 7, 1941 – a date which will live in infamy – the United States of America was suddenly and deliberately attacked by naval and air forces of the Empire of Japan. . . .

Yesterday the Japanese government also launched an attack against Malaya. Last night Japanese forces attacked Hong Kong. Last night Japanese forces attacked Guam. Last night Japanese forces attacked the Philippine Islands. Last night Japanese forces attacked Wake Island. And this morning the Japanese attacked Midway Island.

Japan has, therefore, undertaken a surprise offensive extending throughout the Pacific area.

The facts of yesterday and today speak for themselves. The people of the United States have already formed their opinions and well understand the implications to the very life and safety of our nation.

As Commander-in-Chief of the Army and Navy I have directed that all measures be taken for our defense. But always will our whole nation remember the character of the onslaught against us.

President Franklin D. Roosevelt
White House Radio Broadcast
8 December 1941

Now it is impossible for us to lose the war. We now have an ally who has never been vanquished in three thousand years.

Adolf Hitler
8 December 1941
Three days before declaring war on the United States

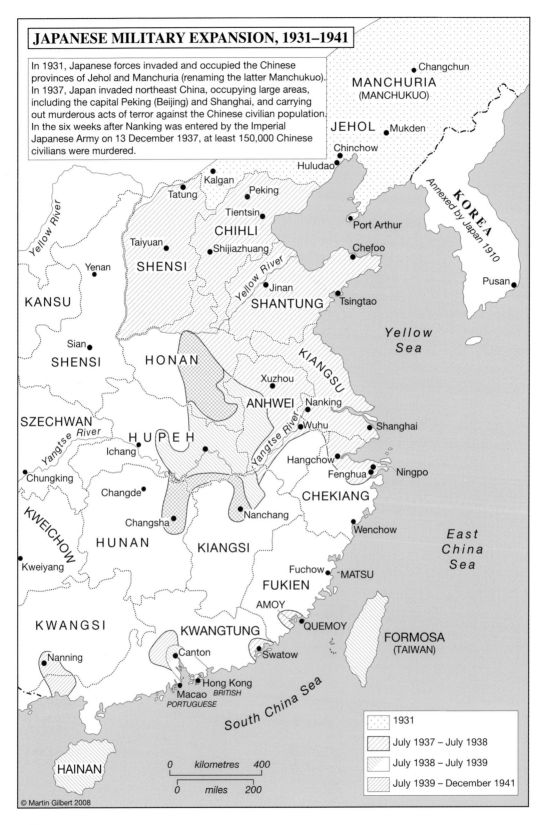

JAPANESE MILITARY EXPANSION, 1931–1941

In 1931, Japanese forces invaded and occupied the Chinese provinces of Jehol and Manchuria (renaming the latter Manchukuo). In 1937, Japan invaded northeast China, occupying large areas, including the capital Peking (Beijing) and Shanghai, and carrying out murderous acts of terror against the Chinese civilian population. In the six weeks after Nanking was entered by the Imperial Japanese Army on 13 December 1937, at least 150,000 Chinese civilians were murdered.

MANCHURIA
(MANCHUKUO)

Changchun

JEHOL · Mukden

Chinchow

Huludao

KOREA
Annexed by Japan 1910

Kalgan

Tatung

Peking

Tientsin

Port Arthur

CHIHLI

Taiyuan

Shijiazhuang

Chefoo

Pusan

Yellow River

SHENSI

Yenan

Jinan

SHANTUNG

Tsingtao

KANSU

Yellow River

Yellow
Sea

Sian

HONAN

KIANGSU

SHENSI

Xuzhou

Nanking

ANHWEI

Shanghai

SZECHWAN

Yangtse River

HUPEH

Wuhu

Yangtse River

Ichang

Hangchow

Chungking

Fenghua

Ningpo

Changde

Nanchang

CHEKIANG

Changsha

Wenchow

East
China
Sea

KWEICHOW

HUNAN

KIANGSI

Kweiyang

Fuchow · MATSU

FUKIEN

AMOY

KWANGSI

QUEMOY

FORMOSA
(TAIWAN)

KWANGTUNG

Nanning

Canton

Swatow

Hong Kong
Macao BRITISH
PORTUGUESE

South China Sea

HAINAN

0   kilometres   400

0   miles   200

1931

July 1937 – July 1938

July 1938 – July 1939

July 1939 – December 1941

© Martin Gilbert 2008

53

THE JAPANESE EMPIRE ON 6 DECEMBER 1941

On 27 September 1940, Japan signed a Tripartite Pact with Germany and Italy. This ten-year agreement, signed in Berlin, provided mutual aid if one of the parties were attacked by a country not yet involved in the European war, that is, by the United States. Within a month, Britain and the United States – still neutral but helping Britain massively in the war against Germany and Italy – responded jointly with an oil boycott of Japan. The oil shortages that resulted, and the failure to solve the dispute diplomatically, led the Japanese Government to resolve to take the oilfields in the Dutch East Indies and British rubber and raw materials in Malaya.

Kolyma

SOVIET UNION

KOMANDORSKI ISLANDS
USSR

KAMCHATKA
USSR

ALEUTIAN ISLANDS
USA

Lake Baikal

SAKHALIN

OUTER MONGOLIA

Harbin

Vladivostok

KURILE ISLANDS
JAPANESE

JAPANESE OCCUPATION
MANCHUKUO

Peking

Sea of Japan

JAPAN

Tientsin

KOREA

Tokyo
Yokohama

Pacific Ocean

Yellow Sea

Hiroshima
Kobe

TIBET

Chengdu

Nagasaki
Shanghai

British military aid to China

Chungking

RYUKYU ISLANDS
JAPANESE

IWO JIMA
JAPANESE

MIDWAY
USA

INDIA
BRITISH

Burma Road

Kunming

OKINAWA
JAPANESE

MARCUS ISLAND
USA

Lashio

FORMOSA
JAPANESE

Calcutta

BURMA
BRITISH

Hong Kong
BRITISH

WAKE
USA

HAINAN

Rangoon

THAILAND

INDO-CHINA
FRENCH

Manila

MARIANAS ISLANDS
JAPANESE

SAIPAN
TINIAN

PHILIPPINES

GUAM
USA

ENIWETOK

MARSHALL ISLANDS
JAPANESE

Bangkok

Saigon

CAROLINE ISLANDS
JAPANESE

KWAJALEIN

MALAYA
BRITISH

PELELIU
ANGAUR

TRUK

The Japanese Empire on 6 December 1941

SUMATRA

Singapore

THE NETHERLANDS EAST INDIES

BORNEO

BIAK

ADMIRALTY ISLANDS
Bismarck Sea
Rabaul
NEW BRITAIN

BAKER ISLAND

MAKIN

TARAWA

Bandung

JAVA

AMBOINA

NEW GUINEA

BOUGAINVILLE

SOLOMON ISLANDS

CHRISTMAS ISLAND
BRITISH

TIMOR

Port Moresby

RUSSELL

TULAGI
GUADALCANAL

SANTA CRUZ ISLANDS

Darwin

Coral Sea

▲▲▲ The Japanese Empire on 6 December 1941

In 1940, the The Netherlands East Indies produced 95% of the world's quinine, 50% of its tobacco, 20% of its tin, 10% of its petroleum, 50% of its coconut oil, 70% of its pepper, 60–70% of its sisal, and was rich in rice, tea, coffee, iron, silver, gold, teakwood, ebony and sandalwood. Malaya produced substantial quantities of rubber and palm oil.

| 0 | kilometres | 1500 |
| 0 | miles | 1000 |

AUSTRALIA

Sydney

Canberra
Melbourne

Following the Anglo-American oil boycott, Japan announced that it would try to organize a 'Greater East Asian Co-Prosperity Sphere', a bloc that would extend from India to New Zealand, supplying raw materials to Japan and receiving exports in return. The bloc would be controlled by the Japanese military. Japan also propagated the idea that the Asian colonies of the European powers should be free from Western control.

© Martin Gilbert 2008

NEW ZEALAND

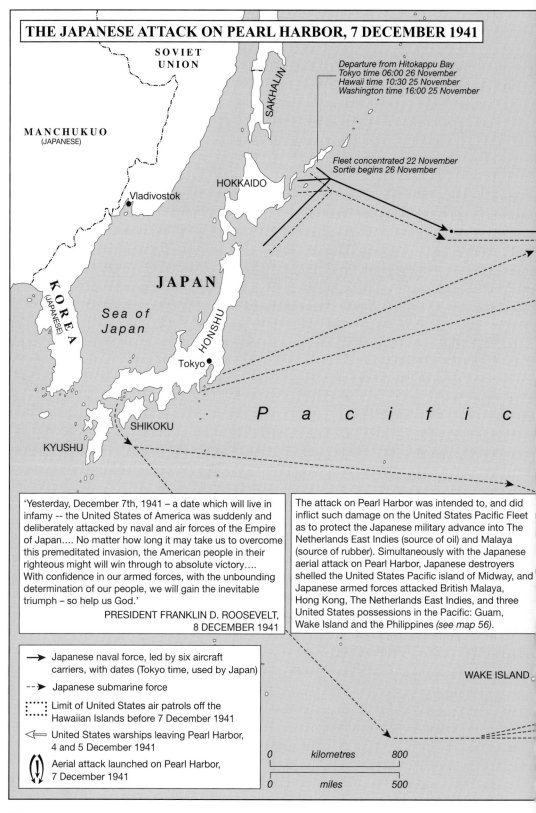

THE JAPANESE ATTACK ON PEARL HARBOR, 7 DECEMBER 1941

SOVIET UNION

SAKHALIN

Departure from Hitokappu Bay
Tokyo time 06:00 26 November
Hawaii time 10:30 25 November
Washington time 16:00 25 November

MANCHUKUO
(JAPANESE)

Fleet concentrated 22 November
Sortie begins 26 November

HOKKAIDO

Vladivostok

K O R E A
(JAPANESE)

JAPAN

Sea of Japan

HONSHU

Tokyo

P   a   c   i   f   i   c

SHIKOKU

KYUSHU

'Yesterday, December 7th, 1941 – a date which will live in infamy -- the United States of America was suddenly and deliberately attacked by naval and air forces of the Empire of Japan.... No matter how long it may take us to overcome this premeditated invasion, the American people in their righteous might will win through to absolute victory.... With confidence in our armed forces, with the unbounding determination of our people, we will gain the inevitable triumph – so help us God.'

PRESIDENT FRANKLIN D. ROOSEVELT,
8 DECEMBER 1941

The attack on Pearl Harbor was intended to, and did inflict such damage on the United States Pacific Fleet as to protect the Japanese military advance into The Netherlands East Indies (source of oil) and Malaya (source of rubber). Simultaneously with the Japanese aerial attack on Pearl Harbor, Japanese destroyers shelled the United States Pacific island of Midway, and Japanese armed forces attacked British Malaya, Hong Kong, The Netherlands East Indies, and three United States possessions in the Pacific: Guam, Wake Island and the Philippines *(see map 56)*.

WAKE ISLAND

→ Japanese naval force, led by six aircraft carriers, with dates (Tokyo time, used by Japan)

--► Japanese submarine force

⋯⋯ Limit of United States air patrols off the Hawaiian Islands before 7 December 1941

⇐ United States warships leaving Pearl Harbor, 4 and 5 December 1941

⇕ Aerial attack launched on Pearl Harbor, 7 December 1941

| 0 | kilometres | 800 |
| 0 | miles | 500 |

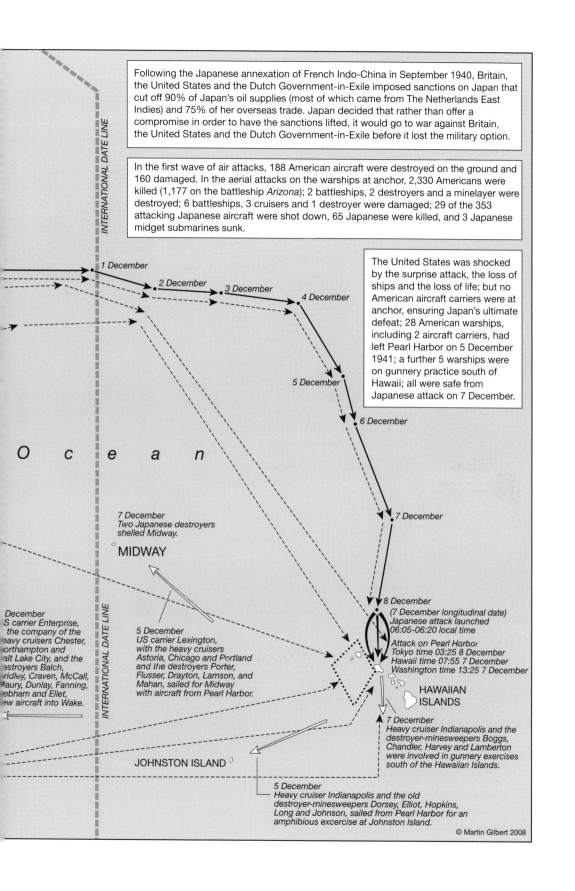

Following the Japanese annexation of French Indo-China in September 1940, Britain, the United States and the Dutch Government-in-Exile imposed sanctions on Japan that cut off 90% of Japan's oil supplies (most of which came from The Netherlands East Indies) and 75% of her overseas trade. Japan decided that rather than offer a compromise in order to have the sanctions lifted, it would go to war against Britain, the United States and the Dutch Government-in-Exile before it lost the military option.

In the first wave of air attacks, 188 American aircraft were destroyed on the ground and 160 damaged. In the aerial attacks on the warships at anchor, 2,330 Americans were killed (1,177 on the battleship *Arizona*); 2 battleships, 2 destroyers and a minelayer were destroyed; 6 battleships, 3 cruisers and 1 destroyer were damaged; 29 of the 353 attacking Japanese aircraft were shot down, 65 Japanese were killed, and 3 Japanese midget submarines sunk.

The United States was shocked by the surprise attack, the loss of ships and the loss of life; but no American aircraft carriers were at anchor, ensuring Japan's ultimate defeat; 28 American warships, including 2 aircraft carriers, had left Pearl Harbor on 5 December 1941; a further 5 warships were on gunnery practice south of Hawaii; all were safe from Japanese attack on 7 December.

INTERNATIONAL DATE LINE

1 December

2 December

3 December

4 December

5 December

6 December

7 December

8 December
(7 December longitudinal date)
Japanese attack launched
06:05–06:20 local time

Attack on Pearl Harbor
Tokyo time 03:25 8 December
Hawaii time 07:55 7 December
Washington time 13:25 7 December

O c e a n

7 December
Two Japanese destroyers
shelled Midway.

○ MIDWAY

INTERNATIONAL DATE LINE

December
S carrier Enterprise,
the company of the
eavy cruisers Chester,
orthampton and
alt Lake City, and the
estroyers Balch,
ridley, Craven, McCall,
aury, Dunlay, Fanning,
ebham and Ellet,
w aircraft into Wake.

5 December
US carrier Lexington,
with the heavy cruisers
Astoria, Chicago and Portland
and the destroyers Porter,
Flusser, Drayton, Lamson, and
Mahan, sailed for Midway
with aircraft from Pearl Harbor.

HAWAIIAN
ISLANDS

7 December
Heavy cruiser Indianapolis and the
destroyer-minesweepers Boggs,
Chandler, Harvey and Lamberton
were involved in gunnery exercises
south of the Hawaiian Islands.

JOHNSTON ISLAND ○

5 December
Heavy cruiser Indianapolis and the old
destroyer-minesweepers Dorsey, Elliot, Hopkins,
Long and Johnson, sailed from Pearl Harbor for an
amphibious excercise at Johnston Island.

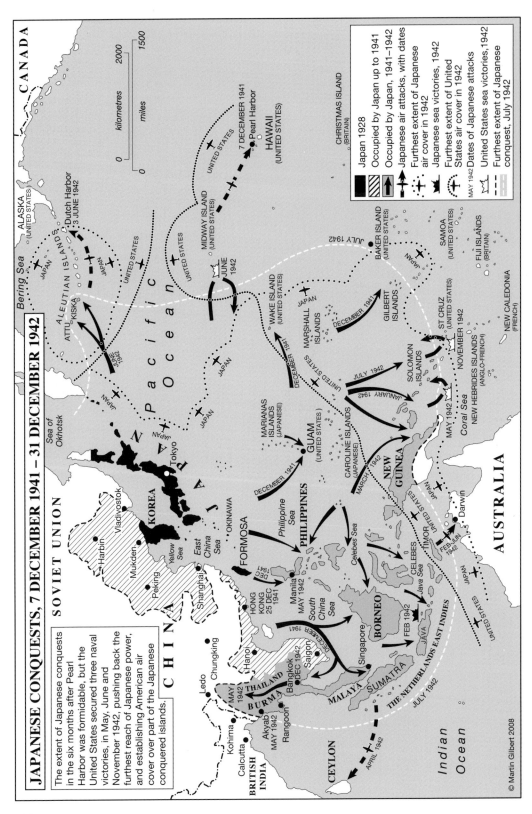

JAPANESE CONQUESTS, 7 DECEMBER 1941 – 31 DECEMBER 1942

The extent of Japanese conquests in the six months after Pearl Harbor was formidable, but the United States secured three naval victories, in May, June and November 1942, pushing back the furthest reach of Japanese power, and establishing American air cover over part of the Japanese conquered islands.

Legend

Japan 1928

Occupied by Japan up to 1941

Occupied by Japan, 1941–1942

Japanese air attacks, with dates

Furthest extent of Japanese air cover in 1942

Japanese sea victories, 1942

Furthest extent of United States air cover in 1942

MAY 1942 Dates of Japanese attacks

United States sea victories, 1942

Furthest extent of Japanese conquest, July 1942

Map labels

CANADA

ALASKA (UNITED STATES)

Bering Sea

Sea of Okhotsk

SOVIET UNION

CHINA

Vladivostok
Harbin
Mukden
Peking
Shanghai
Chungking
Hanoi
Ledo
Kohima
Calcutta
BRITISH INDIA
Akyab MAY 1942
Rangoon
BURMA
Bangkok DEC 1942
THAILAND
MAY 1942
Saigon
Singapore
MALAYA
SUMATRA
THE NETHERLANDS EAST INDIES
JULY 1942
CEYLON
APRIL 1942
Indian Ocean
BORNEO
JAVA
FEB 1942
Java Sea
CELEBES
Celebes Sea
TIMOR
FEB-JUN 1942
Darwin
AUSTRALIA
NEW GUINEA
MAY 1942
Coral Sea
NEW HEBRIDES ISLANDS (ANGLO-FRENCH)
NEW CALEDONIA (FRENCH)
NOVEMBER 1942
ST CRUZ (UNITED STATES)
SOLOMON ISLANDS
JULY 1942
JANUARY 1942
MARCH 1942
SAMOA (UNITED STATES)
FIJI ISLANDS (BRITAIN)
BAKER ISLAND (UNITED STATES)
JULY 1942
GILBERT ISLANDS
DECEMBER 1941
MARSHALL ISLANDS
WAKE ISLAND (UNITED STATES)
CAROLINE ISLANDS (JAPANESE)
GUAM (UNITED STATES)
DECEMBER 1941
MARIANAS ISLANDS (JAPANESE)
PHILIPPINES
Manila MAY 1942
Philippine Sea
South China Sea
HONG KONG 25 DEC 1941
DEC 1941
FORMOSA
OKINAWA
East China Sea
Yellow Sea
KOREA
Tokyo
JAPAN
MIDWAY ISLAND (UNITED STATES)
UNITED STATES
JUNE 1942
Pacific Ocean
JAPAN
JAPAN
JAPAN
JAPAN
ALEUTIAN ISLANDS
ATTU
KISKA
JUNE 1942
Dutch Harbor 3 JUNE 1942
UNITED STATES
UNITED STATES
7 DECEMBER 1941
Pearl Harbor
HAWAII (UNITED STATES)
CHRISTMAS ISLAND (BRITAIN)

1500
2000
kilometres
miles
0

© Martin Gilbert 2008

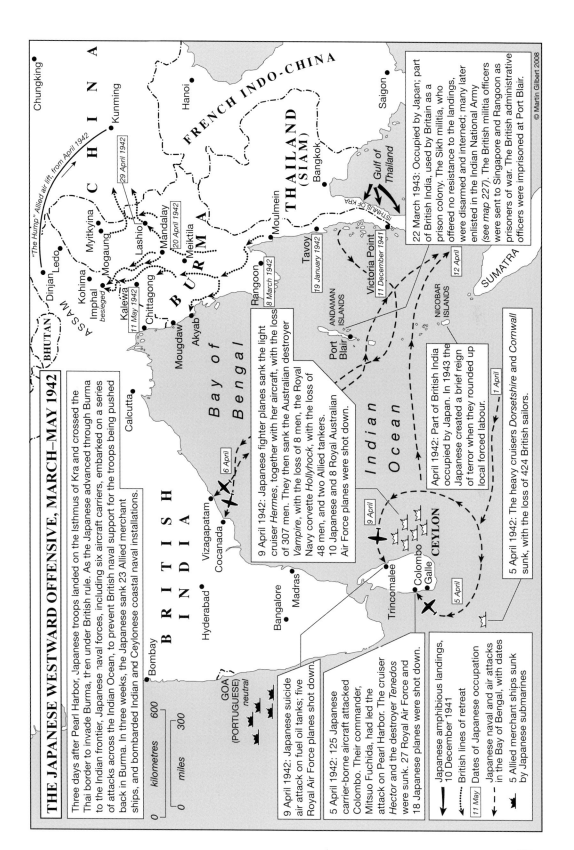

THE JAPANESE WESTWARD OFFENSIVE, MARCH–MAY 1942

Three days after Pearl Harbor, Japanese troops landed on the Isthmus of Kra and crossed the Thai border to invade Burma, then under British rule. As the Japanese advanced through Burma to the Indian frontier, Japanese naval forces, including six aircraft carriers, embarked on a series of attacks across the Indian Ocean, to prevent British naval support for the troops being pushed back in Burma. In three weeks, the Japanese sank 23 Allied merchant ships, and bombarded Indian and Ceylonese coastal naval installations.

9 April 1942: Japanese fighter planes sank the light cruiser *Hermes*, together with her aircraft, with the loss of 307 men. They then sank the Australian destroyer *Vampire*, with the loss of 8 men, the Royal Navy corvette *Hollyhock*, with the loss of 48 men, and two Allied tankers.
10 Japanese and 8 Royal Australian Air Force planes were shot down.

9 April 1942: Japanese suicide air attack on fuel oil tanks; five Royal Air Force planes shot down.

5 April 1942: 125 Japanese carrier-borne aircraft attacked Colombo. Their commander, Mitsuo Fuchida, had led the attack on Pearl Harbor. The cruiser *Hector* and the destroyer *Tenedos* were sunk. 27 Royal Air Force and 18 Japanese planes were shot down.

22 March 1943: Occupied by Japan; part of British India, used by Britain as a prison colony. The Sikh militia, who offered no resistance to the landings, were disarmed and interned; many later enlisted in the Indian National Army *(see map 227)*. The British militia officers were sent to Singapore and Rangoon as prisoners of war. The British administrative officers were imprisoned at Port Blair.

April 1942: Part of British India occupied by Japan. In 1943 the Japanese created a brief reign of terror when they rounded up local forced labour.

5 April 1942: The heavy cruisers *Dorsetshire* and *Cornwall* sunk, with the loss of 424 British sailors.

Japanese amphibious landings, 10 December 1941

⋯⋯⋯⋯ British lines of retreat

11 May · Dates of Japanese occupation and air attacks in the Bay of Bengal, with dates

5 Allied merchant ships sunk by Japanese submarines

© Martin Gilbert 2008

0   300   miles
0   600   kilometres

Chungking
Kunming
Hanoi
CHINA
"The Hump" Allied air lift, from April 1942
29 April 1942
FRENCH INDO-CHINA
BHUTAN
ASSAM
Dinjan
Ledo
Myitkyina
Mogaung
Kohima
Imphal besieged
11 May 1942
Kalewa
Lashio
Mandalay
Meiktila
20 April 1942
BURMA
Chittagong
Akyab
Mougdaw
Moulmein
Rangoon
8 March 1942
THAILAND (SIAM)
Bangkok
Saigon
Gulf of Thailand
ISTHMUS OF KRA
12 April
Tavoy
19 January 1942
Victoria Point
11 December 1941
ANDAMAN ISLANDS
Port Blair
NICOBAR ISLANDS
1 April
SUMATRA

Calcutta
BRITISH INDIA
Bombay
GOA (PORTUGUESE) neutral
Hyderabad
Bangalore
Madras
Vizagapatam
Cocanada
6 April
Bay of Bengal
Indian Ocean
9 April
CEYLON
Colombo
Galle
Trincomalee
5 April

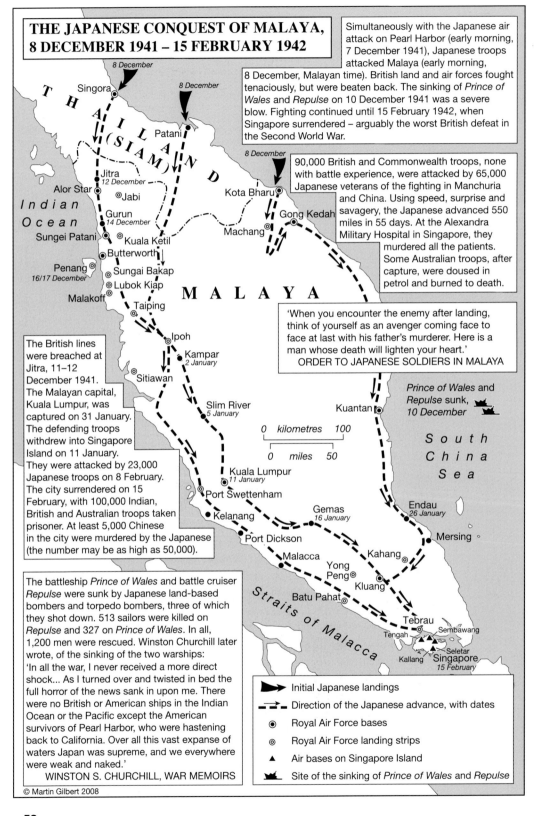

THE JAPANESE CONQUEST OF MALAYA, 8 DECEMBER 1941 – 15 FEBRUARY 1942

Simultaneously with the Japanese air attack on Pearl Harbor (early morning, 7 December 1941), Japanese troops attacked Malaya (early morning, 8 December, Malayan time). British land and air forces fought tenaciously, but were beaten back. The sinking of *Prince of Wales* and *Repulse* on 10 December 1941 was a severe blow. Fighting continued until 15 February 1942, when Singapore surrendered – arguably the worst British defeat in the Second World War.

90,000 British and Commonwealth troops, none with battle experience, were attacked by 65,000 Japanese veterans of the fighting in Manchuria and China. Using speed, surprise and savagery, the Japanese advanced 550 miles in 55 days. At the Alexandra Military Hospital in Singapore, they murdered all the patients. Some Australian troops, after capture, were doused in petrol and burned to death.

'When you encounter the enemy after landing, think of yourself as an avenger coming face to face at last with his father's murderer. Here is a man whose death will lighten your heart.'
ORDER TO JAPANESE SOLDIERS IN MALAYA

The British lines were breached at Jitra, 11–12 December 1941. The Malayan capital, Kuala Lumpur, was captured on 31 January. The defending troops withdrew into Singapore Island on 11 January. They were attacked by 23,000 Japanese troops on 8 February. The city surrendered on 15 February, with 100,000 Indian, British and Australian troops taken prisoner. At least 5,000 Chinese in the city were murdered by the Japanese (the number may be as high as 50,000).

The battleship *Prince of Wales* and battle cruiser *Repulse* were sunk by Japanese land-based bombers and torpedo bombers, three of which they shot down. 513 sailors were killed on *Repulse* and 327 on *Prince of Wales*. In all, 1,200 men were rescued. Winston Churchill later wrote, of the sinking of the two warships:
'In all the war, I never received a more direct shock... As I turned over and twisted in bed the full horror of the news sank in upon me. There were no British or American ships in the Indian Ocean or the Pacific except the American survivors of Pearl Harbor, who were hastening back to California. Over all this vast expanse of waters Japan was supreme, and we everywhere were weak and naked.'
WINSTON S. CHURCHILL, WAR MEMOIRS

© Martin Gilbert 2008

Map labels: 8 December · Singora · 8 December · Patani · 8 December · T H A I L A N D (S I A M) · Jitra 12 December · Alor Star · Jabi · Indian Ocean · Gurun 14 December · Kuala Ketil · Sungei Patani · Butterworth · Penang 16/17 December · Sungai Bakap · Lubok Kiap · Malakoff · Taiping · Kota Bharu · Gong Kedah · Machang · M A L A Y A · Ipoh · Kampar 2 January · Sitiawan · Slim River 5 January · Kuantan · *Prince of Wales* and *Repulse* sunk, 10 December · South China Sea · Kuala Lumpur 11 January · Port Swettenham · Kelanang · Gemas 16 January · Endau 26 January · Mersing · Port Dickson · Malacca · Yong Peng · Kahang · Kluang · Batu Pahat · Straits of Malacca · Tebrau · Tengah · Sembawang · Kallang · Seletar · Singapore 15 February

Scale: 0 kilometres 100 · 0 miles 50

Legend:
▶ Initial Japanese landings
⇢ Direction of the Japanese advance, with dates
◉ Royal Air Force bases
◎ Royal Air Force landing strips
▲ Air bases on Singapore Island
🐦 Site of the sinking of *Prince of Wales* and *Repulse*

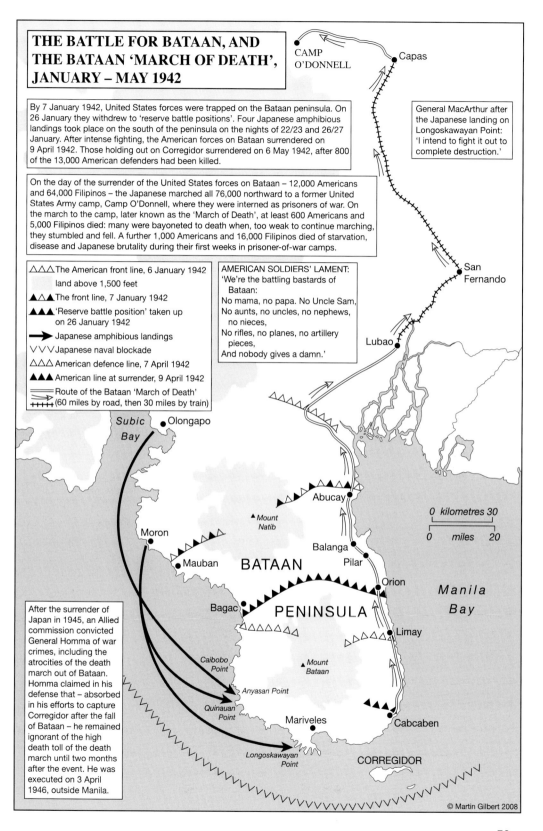

THE BATTLE FOR BATAAN, AND THE BATAAN 'MARCH OF DEATH', JANUARY – MAY 1942

CAMP O'DONNELL

Capas

By 7 January 1942, United States forces were trapped on the Bataan peninsula. On 26 January they withdrew to 'reserve battle positions'. Four Japanese amphibious landings took place on the south of the peninsula on the nights of 22/23 and 26/27 January. After intense fighting, the American forces on Bataan surrendered on 9 April 1942. Those holding out on Corregidor surrendered on 6 May 1942, after 800 of the 13,000 American defenders had been killed.

General MacArthur after the Japanese landing on Longoskawayan Point: 'I intend to fight it out to complete destruction.'

On the day of the surrender of the United States forces on Bataan – 12,000 Americans and 64,000 Filipinos – the Japanese marched all 76,000 northward to a former United States Army camp, Camp O'Donnell, where they were interned as prisoners of war. On the march to the camp, later known as the 'March of Death', at least 600 Americans and 5,000 Filipinos died: many were bayoneted to death when, too weak to continue marching, they stumbled and fell. A further 1,000 Americans and 16,000 Filipinos died of starvation, disease and Japanese brutality during their first weeks in prisoner-of-war camps.

△△△ The American front line, 6 January 1942
　land above 1,500 feet
▲△▲ The front line, 7 January 1942
▲▲▲ 'Reserve battle position' taken up on 26 January 1942
➡ Japanese amphibious landings
∨∨∨ Japanese naval blockade
△△△ American defence line, 7 April 1942
▲▲▲ American line at surrender, 9 April 1942
═══ Route of the Bataan 'March of Death' (60 miles by road, then 30 miles by train)

AMERICAN SOLDIERS' LAMENT:
'We're the battling bastards of Bataan:
No mama, no papa. No Uncle Sam,
No aunts, no uncles, no nephews, no nieces,
No rifles, no planes, no artillery pieces,
And nobody gives a damn.'

San Fernando

Lubao

Subic Bay

Olongapo

Abucay

▲ Mount Natib

Moron

Balanga

Pilar

Mauban

BATAAN

Orion

0 kilometres 30
0 miles 20

Manila Bay

After the surrender of Japan in 1945, an Allied commission convicted General Homma of war crimes, including the atrocities of the death march out of Bataan. Homma claimed in his defense that – absorbed in his efforts to capture Corregidor after the fall of Bataan – he remained ignorant of the high death toll of the death march until two months after the event. He was executed on 3 April 1946, outside Manila.

Bagac

PENINSULA

Limay

Caibobo Point

▲ Mount Bataan

Anyasan Point

Quinauan Point

Mariveles

Cabcaben

Longoskawayan Point

CORREGIDOR

© Martin Gilbert 2008

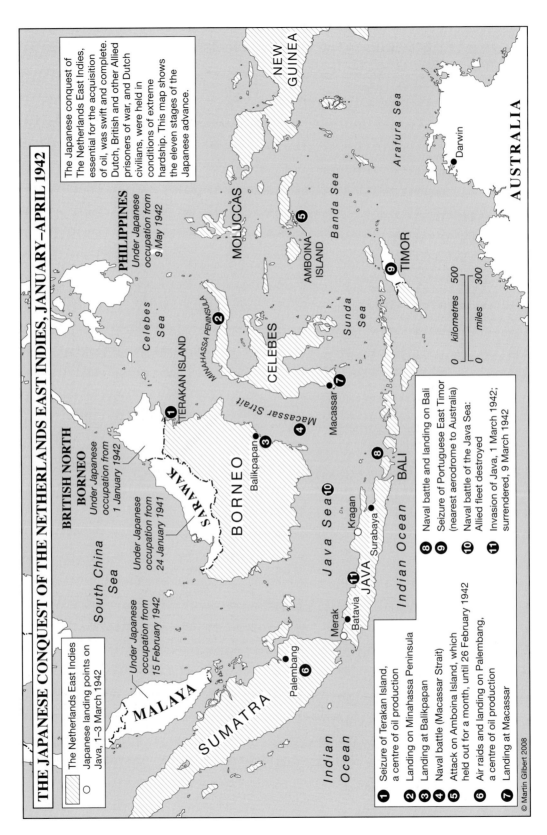

THE JAPANESE CONQUEST OF THE NETHERLANDS EAST INDIES, JANUARY–APRIL 1942

The Japanese conquest of The Netherlands East Indies, essential for the acquisition of oil, was swift and complete. Dutch, British and other Allied prisoners of war, and Dutch civilians, were held in conditions of extreme hardship. This map shows the eleven stages of the Japanese advance.

The Netherlands East Indies

○ Japanese landing points on Java, 1–3 March 1942

BRITISH NORTH BORNEO
Under Japanese occupation from 1 January 1942

Under Japanese occupation from 24 January 1941

Under Japanese occupation from 15 February 1942

PHILIPPINES
Under Japanese occupation from 9 May 1942

South China Sea

Celebes Sea

TERAKAN ISLAND

MINAHASSA PENINSULA

SARAWAK

BORNEO

Balikpapan

Macassar Strait

MOLUCCAS

CELEBES

Macassar

AMBOINA ISLAND

Banda Sea

Sunda Sea

TIMOR

NEW GUINEA

Arafura Sea

Darwin

AUSTRALIA

MALAYA

SUMATRA

Palembang

Indian Ocean

Merak
Batavia
Kragan
JAVA
Surabaya
BALI

Java Sea

Indian Ocean

0 kilometres 500
0 miles 300

1 Seizure of Terakan Island, a centre of oil production

2 Landing on Minahassa Peninsula

3 Landing at Balikpapan

4 Naval battle (Macassar Strait)

5 Attack on Amboina Island, which held out for a month, until 26 February 1942

6 Air raids and landing on Palembang, a centre of oil production

7 Landing at Macassar

8 Naval battle and landing on Bali

9 Seizure of Portuguese East Timor (nearest aerodrome to Australia)

10 Naval battle of the Java Sea: Allied fleet destroyed

11 Invasion of Java, 1 March 1942; surrendered, 9 March 1942

© Martin Gilbert 2008

60

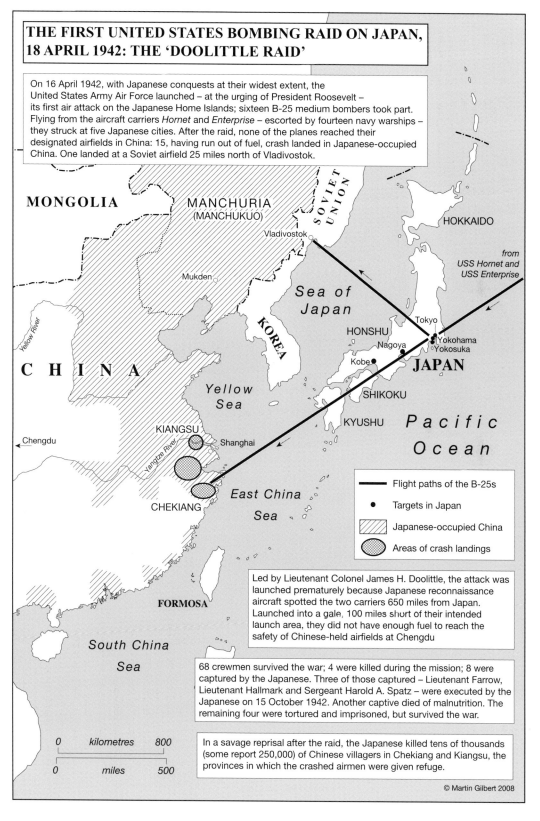

THE FIRST UNITED STATES BOMBING RAID ON JAPAN, 18 APRIL 1942: THE 'DOOLITTLE RAID'

On 16 April 1942, with Japanese conquests at their widest extent, the United States Army Air Force launched – at the urging of President Roosevelt – its first air attack on the Japanese Home Islands; sixteen B-25 medium bombers took part. Flying from the aircraft carriers *Hornet* and *Enterprise* – escorted by fourteen navy warships – they struck at five Japanese cities. After the raid, none of the planes reached their designated airfields in China: 15, having run out of fuel, crash landed in Japanese-occupied China. One landed at a Soviet airfield 25 miles north of Vladivostok.

MONGOLIA

MANCHURIA
(MANCHUKUO)

SOVIET UNION

HOKKAIDO

Vladivostok

from USS Hornet and USS Enterprise

Mukden

Sea of Japan

CHINA

KOREA

Tokyo

HONSHU

Nagoya

Yokohama
Yokosuka

Kobe

JAPAN

Yellow River

Yellow Sea

SHIKOKU

Chengdu

KYUSHU

Pacific Ocean

KIANGSU

Shanghai

Yangtze River

CHEKIANG

East China Sea

FORMOSA

Flight paths of the B-25s
● Targets in Japan
Japanese-occupied China
Areas of crash landings

South China Sea

Led by Lieutenant Colonel James H. Doolittle, the attack was launched prematurely because Japanese reconnaissance aircraft spotted the two carriers 650 miles from Japan. Launched into a gale, 100 miles short of their intended launch area, they did not have enough fuel to reach the safety of Chinese-held airfields at Chengdu

68 crewmen survived the war; 4 were killed during the mission; 8 were captured by the Japanese. Three of those captured – Lieutenant Farrow, Lieutenant Hallmark and Sergeant Harold A. Spatz – were executed by the Japanese on 15 October 1942. Another captive died of malnutrition. The remaining four were tortured and imprisoned, but survived the war.

| 0 | kilometres | 800 |

| 0 | miles | 500 |

In a savage reprisal after the raid, the Japanese killed tens of thousands (some report 250,000) of Chinese villagers in Chekiang and Kiangsu, the provinces in which the crashed airmen were given refuge.

© Martin Gilbert 2008

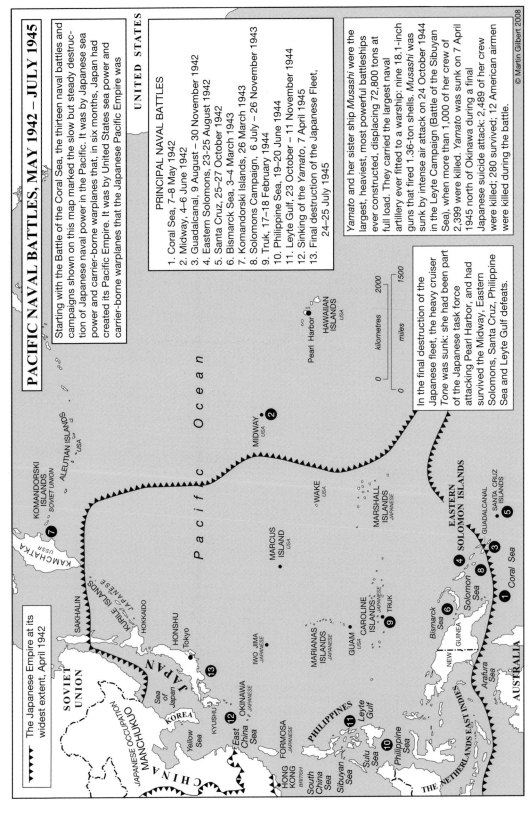

PACIFIC NAVAL BATTLES, MAY 1942 – JULY 1945

Starting with the Battle of the Coral Sea, the thirteen naval battles and campaigns shown on this map marked the slow but steady destruction of Japanese naval power in the Pacific. It was by Japanese sea power and carrier-borne warplanes that, in six months, Japan had created its Pacific Empire. It was by United States sea power and carrier-borne warplanes that the Japanese Pacific Empire was

PRINCIPAL NAVAL BATTLES

1. Coral Sea, 7–8 May 1942
2. Midway, 4–6 June 1942
3. Guadalcanal, 9 August – 30 November 1942
4. Eastern Solomons, 23–25 August 1942
5. Santa Cruz, 25–27 October 1942
6. Bismarck Sea, 3–4 March 1943
7. Komandorski Islands, 26 March 1943
8. Solomons Campaign, 6 July – 26 November 1943
9. Truk, 17–18 February 1944
10. Philippine Sea, 19–20 June 1944
11. Leyte Gulf, 23 October – 11 November 1944
12. Sinking of the *Yamato*, 7 April 1945
13. Final destruction of the Japanese Fleet,
    24–25 July 1945

Yamato and her sister ship *Musashi* were the largest, heaviest, most powerful battleships ever constructed, displacing 72,800 tons at full load. They carried the largest naval artillery ever fitted to a warship: nine 18.1-inch guns that fired 1.36-ton shells. *Musashi* was sunk by intense air attack on 24 October 1944 in the Leyte Campaign (Battle of the Sibuyan Sea), when more than 1,000 of her crew of 2,399 were killed. *Yamato* was sunk on 7 April 1945 north of Okinawa during a final Japanese suicide attack: 2,489 of her crew were killed; 280 survived; 12 American airmen were killed during the battle.

In the final destruction of the Japanese fleet, the heavy cruiser *Tone* was sunk: she had been part of the Japanese task force attacking Pearl Harbor, and had survived the Midway, Eastern Solomons, Santa Cruz, Philippine Sea and Leyte Gulf defeats.

The Japanese Empire at its widest extent, April 1942

© Martin Gilbert 2008

UNITED STATES

Pacific Ocean

Pearl Harbor
HAWAIIAN ISLANDS
USA

MIDWAY *USA* ②

WAKE *USA*

MARCUS ISLAND *USA*

MARSHALL ISLANDS *JAPANESE*

KOMANDORSKI ISLANDS *SOVIET UNION* ⑦

ALEUTIAN ISLANDS *USA*

KAMCHATKA *USSR*

SAKHALIN

KURILE ISLANDS *JAPANESE*

HOKKAIDO

HONSHU
Tokyo

Sea of Japan

JAPAN ⑬

KYUSHU

OKINAWA ⑫ *JAPANESE*

East China Sea

FORMOSA *JAPANESE*

KOREA

Yellow Sea

MANCHUKUO

JAPANESE OCCUPATION

SOVIET UNION

CHINA

HONG KONG *BRITISH*

South China Sea

IWO JIMA *JAPANESE*

MARIANAS ISLANDS *JAPANESE*

GUAM *USA*

CAROLINE ISLANDS *JAPANESE*

TRUK ⑨

PHILIPPINES

Leyte Gulf ⑪

Sibuyan Sea

Sulu Sea

Philippine Sea ⑩

THE NETHERLANDS EAST INDIES

NEW GUINEA

Arafura Sea

AUSTRALIA

Bismarck Sea ⑥

Solomon Sea

GUADALCANAL ③

EASTERN SOLOMON ISLANDS ④

⑧

SANTA CRUZ ISLANDS ⑤

Coral Sea ①

0 — 1500 kilometres
0 — 2000 miles

SOLOMON ISLANDS

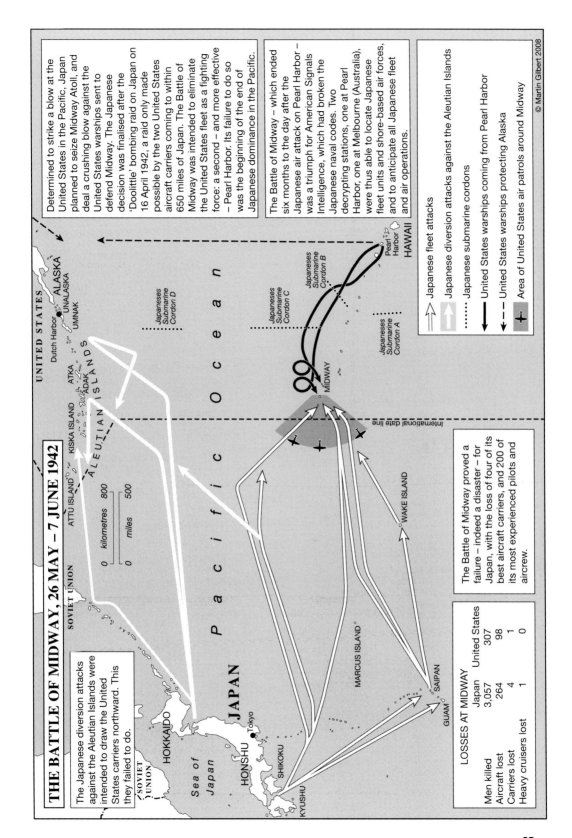

THE BATTLE OF MIDWAY, 26 MAY – 7 JUNE 1942

The Japanese diversion attacks against the Aleutian Islands were intended to draw the United States carriers northward. This they failed to do.

Determined to strike a blow at the United States in the Pacific, Japan planned to seize Midway Atoll, and deal a crushing blow against the United States warships sent to defend Midway. The Japanese decision was finalised after the 'Doolittle' bombing raid on Japan on 16 April 1942, a raid only made possible by the two United States aircraft carriers coming to within 650 miles of Japan. The Battle of Midway was intended to eliminate the United States fleet as a fighting force: a second – and more effective – Pearl Harbor. Its failure to do so was the beginning of the end of Japanese dominance in the Pacific.

The Battle of Midway – which ended six months to the day after the Japanese air attack on Pearl Harbor – was a triumph for American Signals Intelligence, which had broken the Japanese naval codes. Two decrypting stations, one at Pearl Harbor, one at Melbourne (Australia), were thus able to locate Japanese fleet units and shore-based air forces, and to anticipate all Japanese fleet and air operations.

© Martin Gilbert 2008

The Battle of Midway proved a failure – indeed a disaster – for Japan, with the loss of four of its best aircraft carriers, and 200 of its most experienced pilots and aircrew.

LOSSES AT MIDWAY

	Japan	United States
Men killed	3,057	307
Aircraft lost	264	98
Carriers lost	4	1
Heavy cruisers lost	1	0

Legend:

⇗ Japanese fleet attacks

⬜➡ Japanese diversion attacks against the Aleutian Islands

······· Japanese submarine cordons

➡ United States warships coming from Pearl Harbor

- - -➡ United States warships protecting Alaska

✈ Area of United States air patrols around Midway

UNITED STATES
ALASKA
UNALASKA
UMNAK
Dutch Harbor

SOVIET UNION

ALEUTIAN ISLANDS
ATTU ISLAND
KISKA ISLAND
ATKA
ADAK

Japaneses Submarine Cordon D

Japaneses Submarine Cordon C

Japaneses Submarine Cordon B

Japaneses Submarine Cordon A

Pearl Harbor
HAWAII

MIDWAY

International date line

Pacific Ocean

WAKE ISLAND

MARCUS ISLAND

SAIPAN
GUAM

JAPAN
Tokyo
HOKKAIDO
HONSHU
SHIKOKU
KYUSHU

Sea of Japan

SOVIET UNION

0 kilometres 800
0 miles 500

JAPANESE-AMERICANS INTERNED IN THE UNITED STATES, FROM 19 FEBRUARY 1942

0 kilometres 500

0 miles 300

CANADA

Pacific Ocean

McNeil Island
WASHINGTON

MONTANA
Fort Missoula

NORTH DAKOTA
Fort Lincoln

Kooskia

IDAHO

Minidoka
9,397▲

▲ Heart Mountain
10,767

WYOMING

WISCONSIN
Camp McCoy

Lake Superior

Lake Michigan

▲ Tule Lake
18,789

Marysville

Sacramento△

Tanforan△ △Stockton
△Turlock

Salinas△ Merced
Pinedale△ ▲Manzanar
Fresno△ △ **10,046**
Tulore △ Owens
Valley

CALIFORNIA

△△Pomona

Santa Anita

Parker Dam△

Great Salt Lake

▲Topaz
8,130

UTAH

COLORADO

Granada
7,318 ▲

KANSAS

Leavenworth

Mississippi River

ARIZONA

OKLAHOMA
Fort Sill Stringtown

ARKANSAS

Jerome
8,497 ▲

▲Rohwer
8,475

Santa Fe

▲Poston
17,814

NEW MEXICO

Gila River▲ Camp Florence
13,348 Fort Stanton
Catalina Lordsburg

Seagoville

TEXAS

Fort Sam Houston

Kennedy

Crystal City

LOUISIANA

Camp Livingstone

Gulf of Mexico

MEXICO

△ Civilian Assembly Centres, under the Western Civilian Control Administration (WCCA)

▲ War Relocation Centres, under the War Relocations Authority (WRA), with the numbers held there from 1942 to 1945

◉ Internment Camps for 'enemy sympathisers', under the United States Department of Justice

© Martin Gilbert 2008

Following President Franklin D. Roosevelt's Executive Order 9066, signed by the President on 19 February 1942 – based on fear of Japanese espionage – local military commanders could establish 'military exclusion zones' from which all people of Japanese descent on the Pacific Coast could be removed and interned: 62% of all Japanese in the United States at that time were American citizens.

110,000 Japanese-American men, women and children were sent to War Relocation Centres in remote parts of the interior. A further 7,000 Japanese-Americans, and 2,210 people of Japanese ancestry living in twelve Latin American countries (1,800 in Peru) – brought to the United States against their will – were held in the Department of Justice camps.

6% of military-age Japanese-American internees volunteered to serve in the United States armed forces. They were formed into the 442nd Regimental Combat Team, which fought in Italy in 1944, and was the most highly decorated unit in the United States Army for its size and length of service.

In December 1944, while the war against Japan was still being fought, the United States Supreme Court ruled that the detainment of 'loyal citizens' was unconstitutional, and on 2 January 1945 the exclusion zone order was rescinded. In 1988 President Ronald Reagan signed legislation apologising for the internment on behalf of the United States Government, describing the internment as based on 'race prejudice, war hysteria, and a failure of political leadership.' In 1990 the United States Government began paying reparations to the surviving internees.

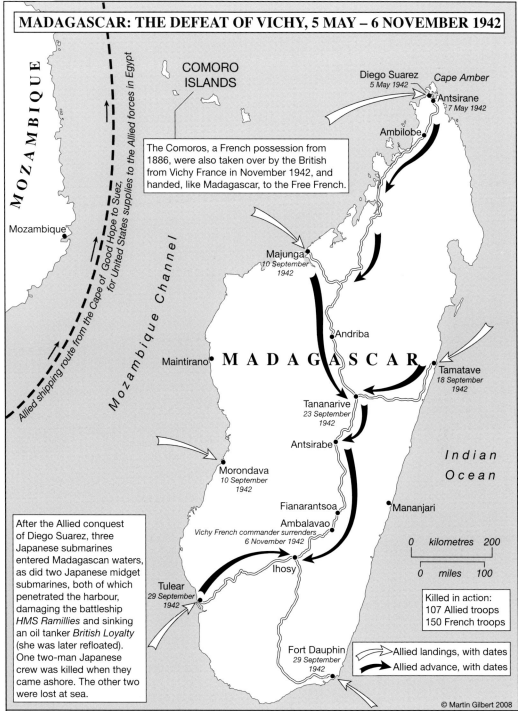

MADAGASCAR: THE DEFEAT OF VICHY, 5 MAY – 6 NOVEMBER 1942

MOZAMBIQUE

COMORO ISLANDS

Diego Suarez
5 May 1942

Cape Amber

Antsirane
7 May 1942

Ambilobe

Allied shipping route from the Cape of Good Hope to Suez,
for United States supplies to the Allied forces in Egypt

The Comoros, a French possession from 1886, were also taken over by the British from Vichy France in November 1942, and handed, like Madagascar, to the Free French.

Mozambique

Mozambique Channel

Majunga
10 September 1942

Andriba

Maintirano

M A D A G A S C A R

Tamatave
18 September 1942

Tananarive
23 September 1942

Antsirabe

Indian Ocean

Morondava
10 September 1942

Fianarantsoa

Mananjari

Ambalavao
Vichy French commander surrenders
6 November 1942

After the Allied conquest of Diego Suarez, three Japanese submarines entered Madagascan waters, as did two Japanese midget submarines, both of which penetrated the harbour, damaging the battleship *HMS Ramillies* and sinking an oil tanker *British Loyalty* (she was later refloated). One two-man Japanese crew was killed when they came ashore. The other two were lost at sea.

Ihosy

Tulear
29 September 1942

0   kilometres   200

0   miles   100

Killed in action:
107 Allied troops
150 French troops

Fort Dauphin
29 September 1942

Allied landings, with dates
Allied advance, with dates

© Martin Gilbert 2008

Madagascar, a French possession since 1883, was under Vichy French rule from June 1940. With Japanese submarines in the Indian Ocean from January 1942, there were fears that Japan would establish submarine bases on the island from which to attack Allied merchant shipping, and the supply route to British and Commonwealth forces in Egypt. Starting on 5 May 1942, more than 10,000 British, South African, East African and Rhodesian troops landed in Madagascar. After six months of fighting against 2,000 French and 6,000 Madagascan and Senegalese troops, Madagascar passed into Free French and Allied control.

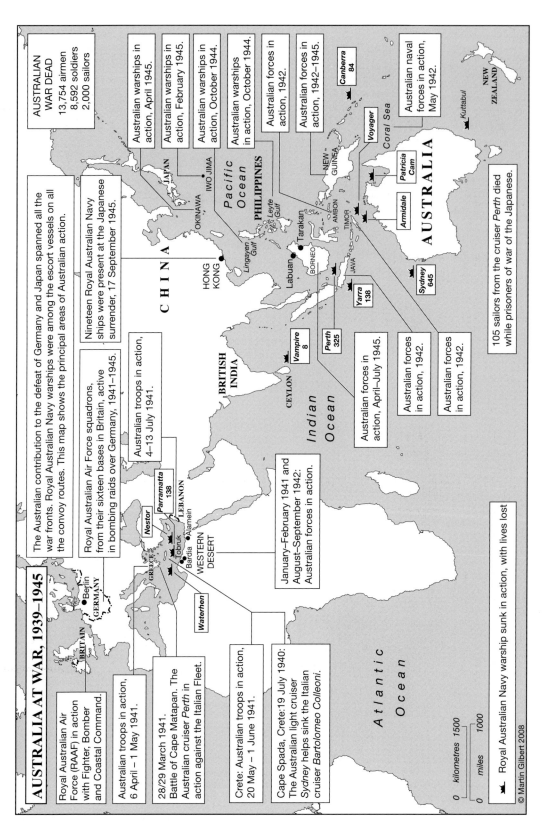

AUSTRALIA AT WAR, 1939–1945

The Australian contribution to the defeat of Germany and Japan spanned all the war fronts. Royal Australian Navy warships were among the escort vessels on all the convoy routes. This map shows the principal areas of Australian action.

Royal Australian Air Force squadrons, from their sixteen bases in Britain, active in bombing raids over Germany, 1941–1945.

Nineteen Royal Australian Navy ships were present at the Japanese surrender, 17 September 1945.

AUSTRALIAN WAR DEAD
13,754 airmen
8,592 soldiers
2,000 sailors

Australian warships in action, April 1945.

Australian warships in action, February 1945.

Australian warships in action, October 1944.

Australian warships in action, October 1944.

Australian forces in action, 1942.

Australian forces in action, 1942–1945.

Australian naval forces in action, May 1942.

Royal Australian Air Force (RAAF) in action with Fighter, Bomber and Coastal Command.

Australian troops in action, 6 April – 1 May 1941.

28/29 March 1941. Battle of Cape Matapan. The Australian cruiser *Perth* in action against the Italian Fleet.

Australian troops in action, 4–13 July 1941.

Australian troops in action, 20 May – 1 June 1941.

January–February 1941 and August–September 1942: Australian forces in action.

Cape Spada, Crete:19 July 1940: The Australian light cruiser *Sydney* helps sink the Italian cruiser *Bartolomeo Colleoni*.

Australian forces in action, April–July 1945.

Australian forces in action, 1942.

Australian forces in action, 1942.

105 sailors from the cruiser *Perth* died while prisoners of war of the Japanese.

GERMANY
Berlin
BRITAIN
GREECE
Tobruk
Bardia
Alamein
WESTERN DESERT
LEBANON
Nestor
Parramatta 138
Waterhen
CEYLON
Vampire 8
Perth 325
BRITISH INDIA
CHINA
HONG KONG
JAPAN
OKINAWA
IWO JIMA
Pacific Ocean
PHILIPPINES
Leyte Gulf
Lingayen Gulf
Tarakan
Labuan
BORNEO
JAVA
TIMOR
AMBON
NEW GUINEA
Yarra 138
Sydney 645
Voyager
Coral Sea
Patricia Cam
Armidale
Canberra 84
AUSTRALIA
Kuttabul
NEW ZEALAND
Indian Ocean
Atlantic Ocean

0   kilometres   1500
0   miles   1000

✦ Royal Australian Navy warship sunk in action, with lives lost

© Martin Gilbert 2008

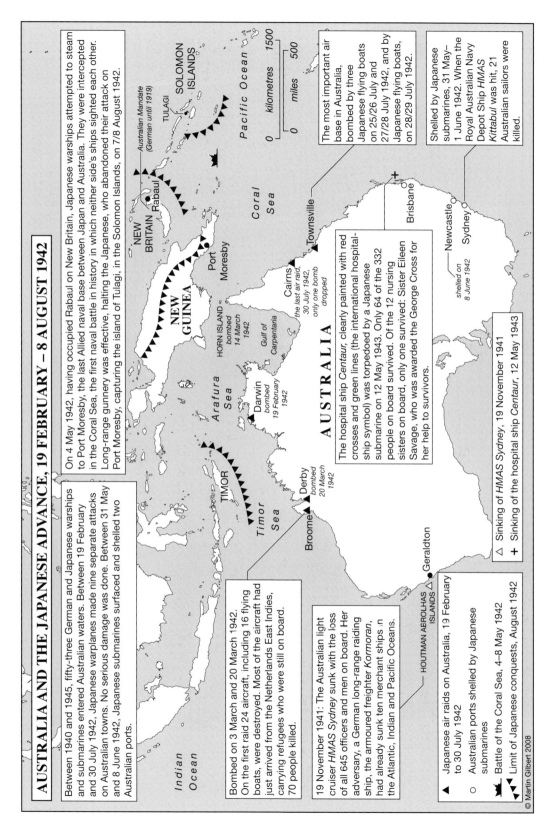

AUSTRALIA AND THE JAPANESE ADVANCE, 19 FEBRUARY – 8 AUGUST 1942

On 4 May 1942, having occupied Rabaul on New Britain, Japanese warships attempted to steam to Port Moresby, the last Allied naval base between Japan and Australia. They were intercepted in the Coral Sea, the first naval battle in history in which neither side's ships sighted each other. Long-range gunnery was effective, halting the Japanese, who abandoned their attack on Port Moresby, capturing the island of Tulagi, in the Solomon Islands, on 7/8 August 1942.

Between 1940 and 1945, fifty-three German and Japanese warships and submarines entered Australian waters. Between 19 February and 30 July 1942, Japanese warplanes made nine separate attacks on Australian towns. No serious damage was done. Between 31 May and 8 June 1942, Japanese submarines surfaced and shelled two Australian ports.

The most important air base in Australia, bombed by three Japanese flying boats on 25/26 July and 27/28 July 1942, and by Japanese flying boats, on 28/29 July 1942.

Shelled by Japanese submarines, 31 May–1 June 1942. When the Royal Australian Navy Depot Ship *HMAS Kittabul* was hit, 21 Australian sailors were killed.

Australian Mandate (German until 1919)

SOLOMON ISLANDS

TULAGI

Pacific Ocean

0   kilometres   1500

0   miles   500

NEW BRITAIN   Rabaul

NEW GUINEA

Port Moresby

Coral Sea

Townsville

Brisbane

Newcastle

Sydney

shelled on 8 June 1942

Cairns
the last air raid, 30 July 1942, only one bomb dropped

HORN ISLAND *bombed 14 March 1942*

Gulf of Carpentaria

Arafura Sea

Darwin
bombed 19 February 1942

AUSTRALIA

The hospital ship *Centaur*, clearly painted with red crosses and green lines (the international hospital-ship symbol) was torpedoed by a Japanese submarine on 12 May 1943. Only 64 of the 332 people on board survived. Of the 12 nursing sisters on board, only one survived: Sister Eileen Savage, who was awarded the George Cross for her help to survivors.

TIMOR

Timor Sea

Derby *bombed 20 March 1942*

Broome

Bombed on 3 March and 20 March 1942. On the first raid 24 aircraft, including 16 flying boats, were destroyed. Most of the aircraft had just arrived from the Netherlands East Indies, carrying refugees who were still on board. 70 people killed.

19 November 1941: The Australian light cruiser *HMAS Sydney* sunk with the loss of all 645 officers and men on board. Her adversary, a German long-range raiding ship, the armoured freighter *Kormoran*, had already sunk ten merchant ships in the Atlantic, Indian and Pacific Oceans.

Indian Ocean

HOUTMAN ABROLHAS ISLANDS

Geraldton

▲ Japanese air raids on Australia, 19 February to 30 July 1942

○ Australian ports shelled by Japanese submarines

◣ Battle of the Coral Sea, 4–8 May 1942

▼ Limit of Japanese conquests, August 1942

△ Sinking of *HMAS Sydney*, 19 November 1941

+ Sinking of the hospital ship *Centaur*, 12 May 1943

© Martin Gilbert 2008

67

JAPANESE-CANADIANS INTERNED IN BRITISH COLUMBIA, FROM 4 MARCH 1942

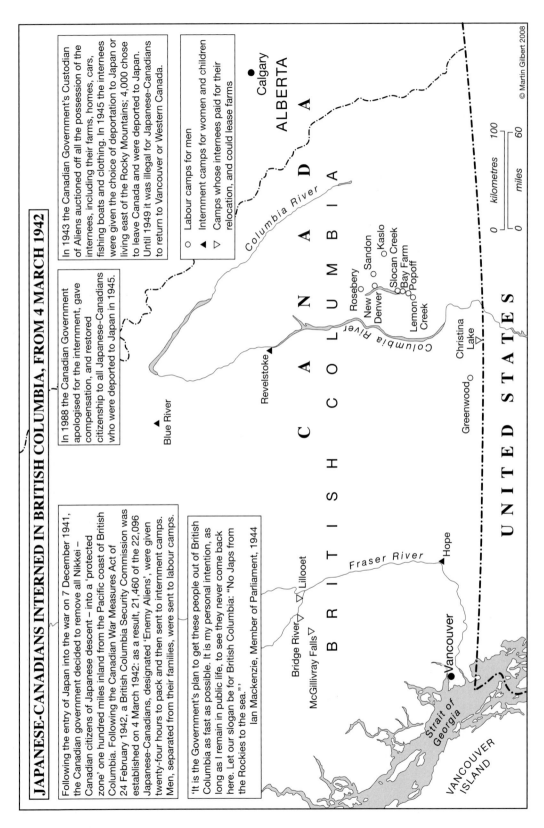

Following the entry of Japan into the war on 7 December 1941, the Canadian government decided to remove all Nikkei – Canadian citizens of Japanese descent – into a 'protected zone' one hundred miles inland from the Pacific coast of British Columbia. Following the Canadian War Measures Act of 24 February 1942, a British Columbia Security Commission was established on 4 March 1942: as a result, 21,460 of the 22,096 Japanese-Canadians, designated 'Enemy Aliens', were given twenty-four hours to pack and then sent to internment camps. Men, separated from their families, were sent to labour camps.

'It is the Government's plan to get these people out of British Columbia as fast as possible. It is my personal intention, as long as I remain in public life, to see they never come back here. Let our slogan be for British Columbia: "No Japs from the Rockies to the sea."'

Ian Mackenzie, Member of Parliament, 1944

In 1988 the Canadian Government apologised for the internment, gave compensation, and restored citizenship to all Japanese-Canadians who were deported to Japan in 1945.

In 1943 the Canadian Government's Custodian of Aliens auctioned off all the possession of the internees, including their farms, homes, cars, fishing boats and clothing. In 1945 the internees were given the choice of deportation to Japan or living east of the Rocky Mountains; 4,000 chose to leave Canada and were deported to Japan. Until 1949 it was illegal for Japanese-Canadians to return to Vancouver or Western Canada.

○ Labour camps for men

▲ Internment camps for women and children

▽ Camps whose internees paid for their relocation, and could lease farms

© Martin Gilbert 2008

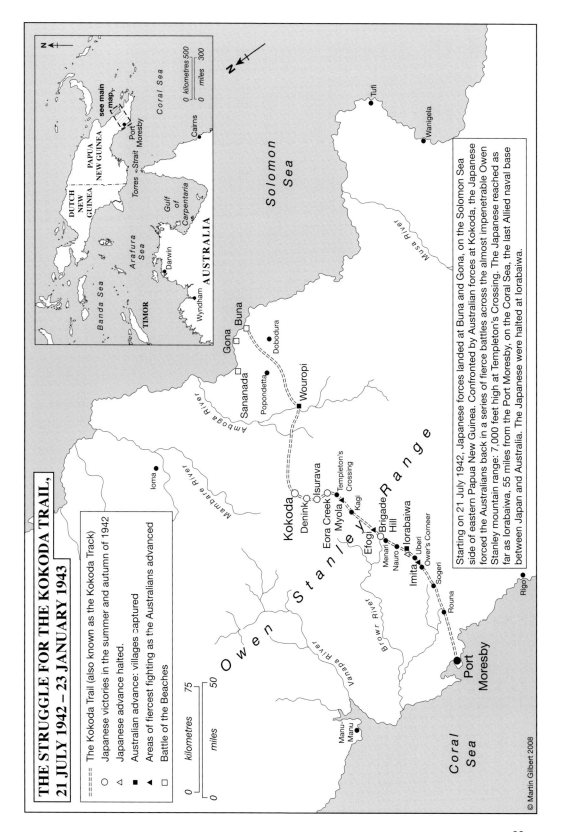

THE STRUGGLE FOR THE KOKODA TRAIL, 21 JULY 1942 – 23 JANUARY 1943

===== The Kokoda Trail (also known as the Kokoda Track)

○ Japanese victories in the summer and autumn of 1942

△ Japanese advance halted.

■ Australian advance: villages captured

▲ Areas of fiercest fighting as the Australians advanced

□ Battle of the Beaches

Starting on 21 July 1942, Japanese forces landed at Buna and Gona, on the Solomon Sea side of eastern Papua New Guinea. Confronted by Australian forces at Kokoda, the Japanese forced the Australians back in a series of fierce battles across the almost impenetrable Owen Stanley mountain range: 7,000 feet high at Templeton's Crossing. The Japanese reached as far as Iorabaiwa, 55 miles from the Port Moresby, on the Coral Sea, the last Allied naval base between Japan and Australia. The Japanese were halted at Iorabaiwa.

© Martin Gilbert 2008

Section 5

THE UNRELENTING STRUGGLE, 1942 AND BEYOND

Lili Marlene

Somewhere after midnight, in a land not mine,
Somewhere near our mud-strewn battle line,
Sleep would not lull my soul tonight,
And so awake I long to write,
To you Lili Marlen, to you Lili Marlen.

In this battered shelter lashed by icy rain,
Thoughts of you are sunshine that banish grief and pain,
Soft burns my candle, soft yet bright,
My love for you is like that light,
So true Lili Marlen, so true Lili Marlen.

My beloved darling, I can't forget that day,
The last we were together before I went away,
Rain fell like tears from sorrowing skies,
But tears not rain were in your eyes,
I knew Lili Marlen, I knew Lili Marlen.

Is your hair still golden, are your eyes as blue?
Would your voice enchant me as it used to do?
I'd trade the world to see your smile,
And hold you close just for awhile
Just you Lili Marlen, just you Lili Marlen.

Lower flames the candle, grey the eastern sky,
One more day of battle, another day to die.
God, how I hate this warring hell
But I endure each screaming shell
For you Lili Marlen, for you Lili Marlen.

Wait for me my darling till I return to thee,
When the guns are silent in hush of victory,
Even the flaming gates of hell
Against we two cannot prevail,
Adieu Lili Marlen, adieu Lili Marlen.

*Canadian version of the popular wartime soldiers' song,
found in the field notecase of Trooper S. A. Burke*

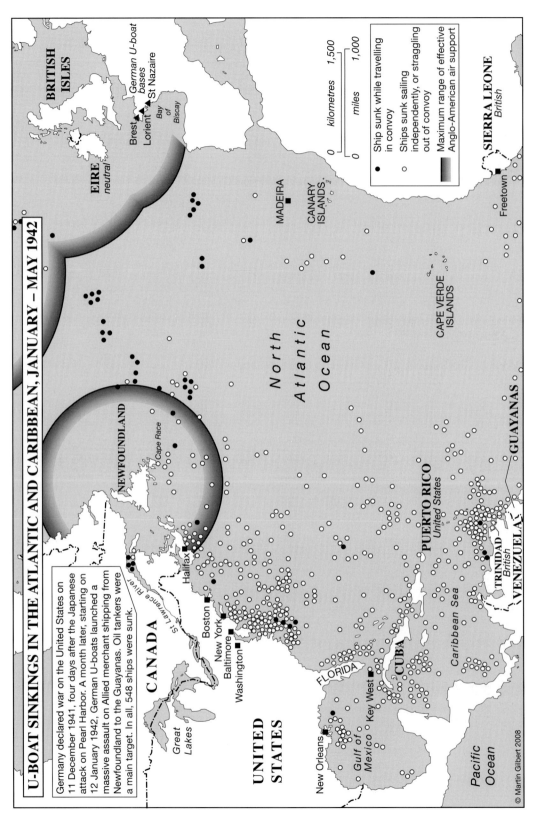

U-BOAT SINKINGS IN THE ATLANTIC AND CARIBBEAN, JANUARY – MAY 1942

Germany declared war on the United States on 11 December 1941, four days after the Japanese attack on Pearl Harbor. A month later, starting on 12 January 1942, German U-boats launched a massive assault on Allied merchant shipping from Newfoundland to the Guayanas. Oil tankers were a main target. In all, 548 ships were sunk.

Scale:
- kilometres: 0 — 1,000 — 1,500
- miles: 0 — 1,000

Legend:
- ● Ship sunk while travelling in convoy
- ○ Ships sunk sailing independently, or straggling out of convoy
- ▨ Maximum range of effective Anglo-American air support

BRITISH ISLES

German U-boat bases
Brest ▲ Lorient ▲ St Nazaire ▲
Bay of Biscay

EIRE *neutral*

SIERRA LEONE *British*
Freetown ■

MADEIRA ■
CANARY ISLANDS

CAPE VERDE ISLANDS

North Atlantic Ocean

NEWFOUNDLAND
Cape Race

CANADA
St Lawrence River
Great Lakes

Halifax ■
Boston ■
New York ■
Baltimore ■
Washington ■

UNITED STATES

New Orleans ■
Gulf of Mexico
Key West ○
FLORIDA ■
CUBA

PUERTO RICO *United States*
TRINIDAD *British*
VENEZUELA
GUAYANAS

Caribbean Sea

Pacific Ocean

© Martin Gilbert 2008

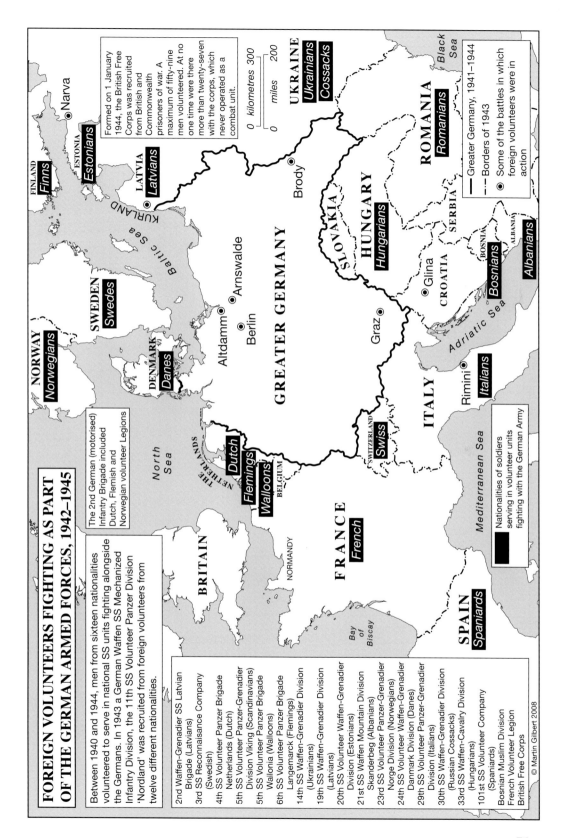

FOREIGN VOLUNTEERS FIGHTING AS PART OF THE GERMAN ARMED FORCES, 1942–1945

Between 1940 and 1944, men from sixteen nationalities volunteered to serve in national SS units fighting alongside the Germans. In 1943 a German Waffen SS Mechanized Infantry Division, the 11th SS Volunteer Panzer Division 'Nordland' was recruited from foreign volunteers from twelve different nationalities.

The 2nd German (motorised) Infantry Brigade included Dutch, Flemish and Norwegian volunteer Legions

Formed on 1 January 1944, the British Free Corps was recruited from British and Commonwealth prisoners of war. A maximum of fifty-nine men volunteered. At no one time were there more than twenty-seven with the corps, which never operated as a combat unit.

0   kilometres   300
0   miles   200

— Greater Germany, 1941–1944
–·– Borders of 1943
◉ Some of the battles in which foreign volunteers were in action

◼ Nationalities of soldiers serving in volunteer units fighting with the German Army

2nd Waffen-Grenadier SS Latvian Brigade (Latvians)
3rd SS Reconnaisance Company (Swedish)
4th SS Volunteer Panzer Brigade Netherlands (Dutch)
5th SS Volunteer Panzer-Grenadier Division Viking (Scandinavians)
5th SS Volunteer Panzer Brigade Wallonia (Walloons)
6th SS Volunteer Panzer Brigade Langemarck (Flemings)
14th SS Waffen-Grenadier Division (Ukrainians)
19th SS Waffen-Grenadier Division (Latvians)
20th SS Volunteer Waffen-Grenadier Division (Estonians)
21st SS Waffen Mountain Division Skanderbeg (Albanians)
23rd SS Volunteer Panzer-Grenadier Norge Division (Norwegians)
24th SS Volunteer Waffen-Grenadier Danmark Division (Danes)
29th SS Volunteer Panzer-Grenadier Division (Italians)
30th SS Waffen-Grenadier Division (Russian Cossacks)
33rd SS Waffen-Cavalry Division (Hungarians)
101st SS Volunteer Company (Spaniards)
Bosnian Muslim Division
French Volunteer Legion
British Free Corps

NORWAY *Norwegians*
SWEDEN *Swedes*
FINLAND *Finns*
ESTONIA *Estonians*
●Narva
LATVIA *Latvians*
KURLAND
Baltic Sea
North Sea
THE NETHERLANDS *Dutch*
Flemings
Walloons
BELGIUM
DENMARK *Danes*
Altdamm●
●Arnswalde
●Berlin
GREATER GERMANY
Brody◉
SLOVAKIA
HUNGARY *Hungarians*
Graz●
SWITZERLAND *Swiss*
UKRAINE *Ukrainians*
Cossacks
Black Sea
ROMANIA *Romanians*
SERBIA
CROATIA
BOSNIA *Bosnians*
ALBANIA *Albanians*
Glina●
Adriatic Sea
ITALY
Rimini● *Italians*
Mediterranean Sea
FRANCE *French*
NORMANDY
Bay of Biscay
BRITAIN
SPAIN *Spaniards*

© Martin Gilbert 2008

71

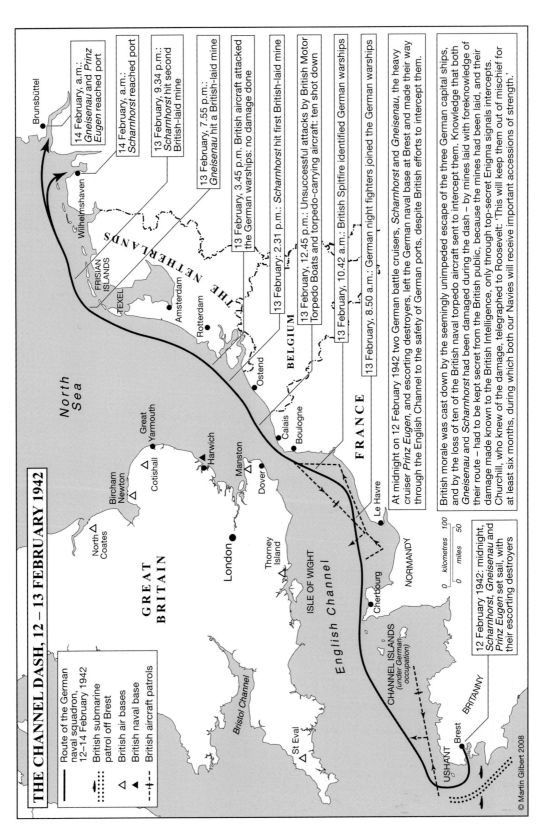

THE CHANNEL DASH, 12 – 13 FEBRUARY 1942

Route of the German
naval squadron,
12–14 February 1942

British submarine
patrol off Brest

△ British air bases

▲ British naval base

British aircraft patrols

14 February, a.m.: *Gneisenau* and *Prinz Eugen* reached port

14 February, a.m.: *Scharnhorst* reached port

13 February, 9.34 p.m.: *Scharnhorst* hit second British-laid mine

13 February, 7.55 p.m.: *Gneisenau* hit a British-laid mine

13 February, 3.45 p.m. British aircraft attacked the German warships: no damage done

13 February: *Scharnhorst* hit first British-laid mine

13 February, 2.31 p.m.: *Scharnhorst* hit first British-laid mine

13 February, 12.45 p.m.: Unsuccessful attacks by British Motor Torpedo Boats and torpedo-carrying aircraft: ten shot down

13 February, 10.42 a.m.: British Spitfire identified German warships

13 February, 8.50 a.m.: German night fighters joined the German warships

At midnight on 12 February 1942 two German battle cruisers, *Scharnhorst* and *Gneisenau*, the heavy cruiser *Prinz Eugen*, and escorting destroyers, left the German naval base at Brest and made their way through the English Channel to the safety of German ports, despite British efforts to intercept them.

British morale was cast down by the seemingly unimpeded escape of the three German capital ships, and by the loss of ten of the British naval torpedo aircraft sent to intercept them. Knowledge that both *Gneisenau* and *Scharnhorst* had been damaged during the dash – by mines laid with foreknowledge of their route – had to be kept secret from the British public, because the mines had been laid, and their damage made known to the British Intelligence, only through top-secret Enigma signals intercepts. Churchill, who knew of the damage, telegraphed to Roosevelt: 'This will keep them out of mischief for at least six months, during which both our Navies will receive important accessions of strength.'

12 February 1942: midnight, *Scharnhorst*, *Gneisenau* and *Prinz Eugen* set sail, with their escorting destroyers

Brunsbüttel

Wilhelmshaven

FRISIAN ISLANDS

TEXEL

THE NETHERLANDS

Amsterdam

Rotterdam

North Sea

Ostend

BELGIUM

Calais

Boulogne

FRANCE

Le Havre

NORMANDY

Cherbourg

CHANNEL ISLANDS
(under German occupation)

USHANT

Brest

BRITTANY

English Channel

ISLE OF WIGHT

Thorney Island

St Eval

Bristol Channel

London

GREAT BRITAIN

North Coates

Bircham Newton

Cotishall

Great Yarmouth

Harwich

Manston

Dover

0   kilometres   100
0   miles   50

© Martin Gilbert 2008

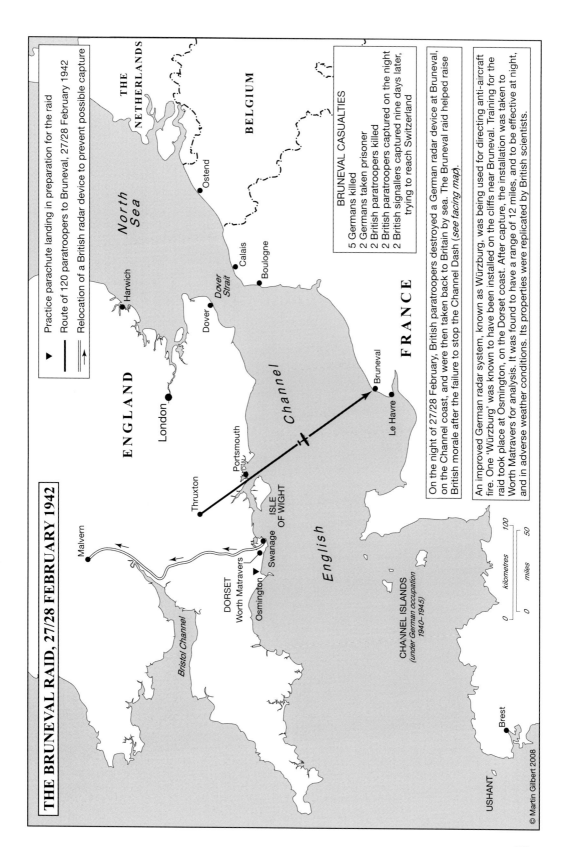

THE BRUNEVAL RAID, 27/28 FEBRUARY 1942

▼ Practice parachute landing in preparation for the raid

→ Route of 120 paratroopers to Bruneval, 27/28 February 1942

⇒ Relocation of a British radar device to prevent possible capture

ENGLAND

Malvern

London

Thruxton

Portsmouth

DORSET
Worth Matravers
Osmington
Swanage

ISLE
OF WIGHT

Bristol Channel

English

North Sea

Harwich

Dover
Dover Strait
Calais
Boulogne

Ostend

THE NETHERLANDS

BELGIUM

Channel

Bruneval
Le Havre

FRANCE

CHANNEL ISLANDS
(under German occupation 1940–1945)

USHANT

Brest

0   50   100   kilometres
0   50   miles

BRUNEVAL CASUALTIES

5 Germans killed
2 Germans taken prisoner
2 British paratroopers killed
2 British paratroopers captured on the night
2 British signallers captured nine days later,
trying to reach Switzerland

On the night of 27/28 February, British paratroopers destroyed a German radar device at Bruneval, on the Channel coast, and were then taken back to Britain by sea. The Bruneval raid helped raise British morale after the failure to stop the Channel Dash (*see facing map*).

An improved German radar system, known as Würzburg, was being used for directing anti-aircraft fire. One 'Würzburg' was known to have been installed on the cliffs near Bruneval. Training for the raid took place at Osmington, on the Dorset coast. After capture, the installation was taken to Worth Matravers for analysis. It was found to have a range of 12 miles, and to be effective at night, and in adverse weather conditions. Its properties were replicated by British scientists.

© Martin Gilbert 2008

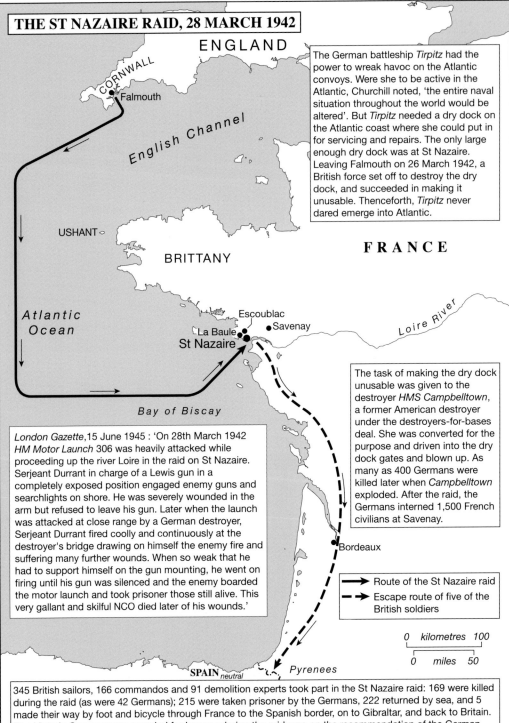

THE ST NAZAIRE RAID, 28 MARCH 1942

ENGLAND

CORNWALL
Falmouth

English Channel

USHANT

BRITTANY

FRANCE

Atlantic
Ocean

Escoublac
Savenay
La Baule
St Nazaire

Loire River

Bay of Biscay

Bordeaux

SPAIN neutral
Pyrenees

The German battleship *Tirpitz* had the power to wreak havoc on the Atlantic convoys. Were she to be active in the Atlantic, Churchill noted, 'the entire naval situation throughout the world would be altered'. But *Tirpitz* needed a dry dock on the Atlantic coast where she could put in for servicing and repairs. The only large enough dry dock was at St Nazaire. Leaving Falmouth on 26 March 1942, a British force set off to destroy the dry dock, and succeeded in making it unusable. Thenceforth, *Tirpitz* never dared emerge into Atlantic.

The task of making the dry dock unusable was given to the destroyer *HMS Campbelltown*, a former American destroyer under the destroyers-for-bases deal. She was converted for the purpose and driven into the dry dock gates and blown up. As many as 400 Germans were killed later when *Campbelltown* exploded. After the raid, the Germans interned 1,500 French civilians at Savenay.

London Gazette,15 June 1945 : 'On 28th March 1942 *HM Motor Launch* 306 was heavily attacked while proceeding up the river Loire in the raid on St Nazaire. Serjeant Durrant in charge of a Lewis gun in a completely exposed position engaged enemy guns and searchlights on shore. He was severely wounded in the arm but refused to leave his gun. Later when the launch was attacked at close range by a German destroyer, Serjeant Durrant fired coolly and continuously at the destroyer's bridge drawing on himself the enemy fire and suffering many further wounds. When so weak that he had to support himself on the gun mounting, he went on firing until his gun was silenced and the enemy boarded the motor launch and took prisoner those still alive. This very gallant and skilful NCO died later of his wounds.'

→ Route of the St Nazaire raid
⇢ Escape route of five of the British soldiers

0 kilometres 100
0 miles 50

345 British sailors, 166 commandos and 91 demolition experts took part in the St Nazaire raid: 169 were killed during the raid (as were 42 Germans); 215 were taken prisoner by the Germans, 222 returned by sea, and 5 made their way by foot and bicycle through France to the Spanish border, on to Gibraltar, and back to Britain. Five Victoria Crosses were awarded for bravery during the raid: one on the recommendation of the German naval captain who had witnessed the bravery of Sergeant Thomas Frank Durrant in action at close range against the German captain's destroyer. Together with others killed on the raid, Durrant is buried in the Commonwealth War Graves Commission cemetery at Escoublac-La Baule. Of the 16 Motor launches that took part in the raid, only one returned.

© Martin Gilbert 2008

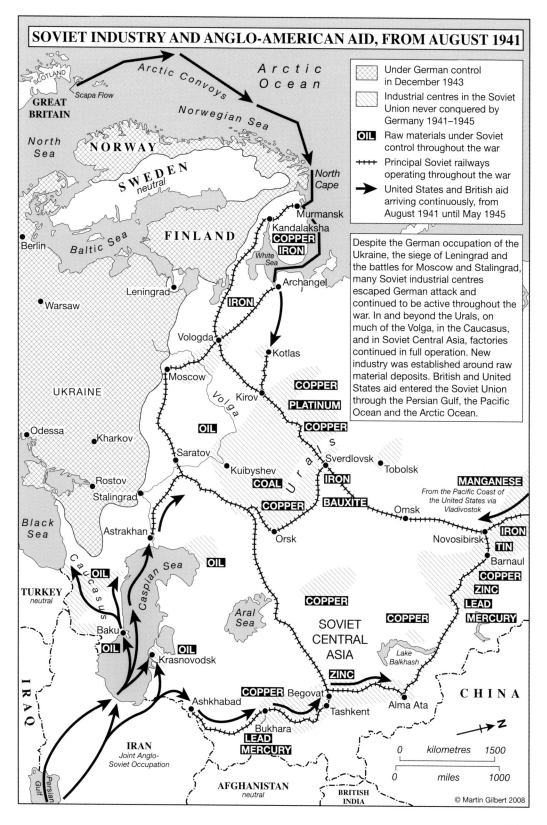

SOVIET INDUSTRY AND ANGLO-AMERICAN AID, FROM AUGUST 1941

Legend:

- Under German control in December 1943
- Industrial centres in the Soviet Union never conquered by Germany 1941–1945
- **OIL** Raw materials under Soviet control throughout the war
- ++++ Principal Soviet railways operating throughout the war
- → United States and British aid arriving continuously, from August 1941 until May 1945

Despite the German occupation of the Ukraine, the siege of Leningrad and the battles for Moscow and Stalingrad, many Soviet industrial centres escaped German attack and continued to be active throughout the war. In and beyond the Urals, on much of the Volga, in the Caucasus, and in Soviet Central Asia, factories continued in full operation. New industry was established around raw material deposits. British and United States aid entered the Soviet Union through the Persian Gulf, the Pacific Ocean and the Arctic Ocean.

Arctic Convoys
Arctic Ocean
Norwegian Sea
SCOTLAND
Scapa Flow
GREAT BRITAIN
North Sea
NORWAY
SWEDEN neutral
North Cape
Murmansk
Kandalaksha **COPPER** **IRON**
White Sea
Archangel
Berlin
Baltic Sea
FINLAND
Leningrad
Warsaw
IRON
Vologda
Kotlas
Moscow
Volga
Kirov **COPPER** **PLATINUM** **COPPER**
UKRAINE
Odessa
Kharkov
Saratov **OIL**
Kuibyshev
Sverdlovsk
Tobolsk
MANGANESE *From the Pacific Coast of the United States via Vladivostok*
Rostov
Stalingrad **COAL** **IRON**
COPPER **BAUXITE**
Omsk
IRON
TIN
Black Sea
Astrakhan
Orsk
Novosibirsk
Barnaul
COPPER
ZINC
LEAD
MERCURY
Caucasus
OIL
Caspian Sea **OIL**
TURKEY neutral
Aral Sea
SOVIET CENTRAL ASIA
COPPER
COPPER
Baku
OIL
Krasnovodsk **OIL**
Lake Balkhash
IRAQ
ZINC
Ashkhabad
COPPER Begovat
Tashkent
Alma Ata
CHINA
Bukhara
LEAD
MERCURY
IRAN *Joint Anglo-Soviet Occupation*
Persian Gulf
AFGHANISTAN neutral
BRITISH INDIA

0 kilometres 1500
0 miles 1000
N

© Martin Gilbert 2008

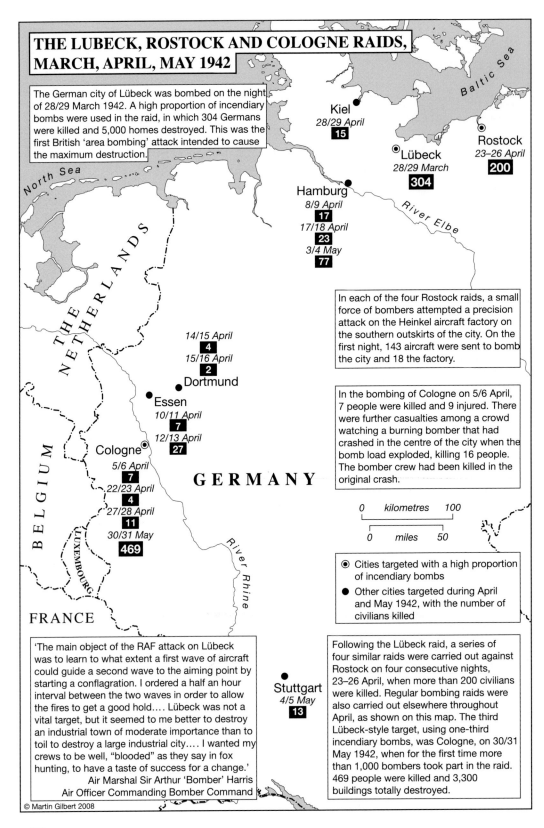

THE LUBECK, ROSTOCK AND COLOGNE RAIDS, MARCH, APRIL, MAY 1942

The German city of Lübeck was bombed on the night of 28/29 March 1942. A high proportion of incendiary bombs were used in the raid, in which 304 Germans were killed and 5,000 homes destroyed. This was the first British 'area bombing' attack intended to cause the maximum destruction.

Baltic Sea

Kiel
28/29 April
15

Rostock
23–26 April
200

Lübeck
28/29 March
304

North Sea

River Elbe

Hamburg
8/9 April
17
17/18 April
23
3/4 May
77

THE NETHERLANDS

In each of the four Rostock raids, a small force of bombers attempted a precision attack on the Heinkel aircraft factory on the southern outskirts of the city. On the first night, 143 aircraft were sent to bomb the city and 18 the factory.

14/15 April
4
15/16 April
2
Dortmund

Essen
10/11 April
7
12/13 April
27

Cologne
5/6 April
7
22/23 April
4
27/28 April
11
30/31 May
469

GERMANY

In the bombing of Cologne on 5/6 April, 7 people were killed and 9 injured. There were further casualties among a crowd watching a burning bomber that had crashed in the centre of the city when the bomb load exploded, killing 16 people. The bomber crew had been killed in the original crash.

BELGIUM

LUXEMBOURG

River Rhine

| 0 | kilometres | 100 |
| 0 | miles | 50 |

- ◉ Cities targeted with a high proportion of incendiary bombs
- ● Other cities targeted during April and May 1942, with the number of civilians killed

FRANCE

'The main object of the RAF attack on Lübeck was to learn to what extent a first wave of aircraft could guide a second wave to the aiming point by starting a conflagration. I ordered a half an hour interval between the two waves in order to allow the fires to get a good hold…. Lübeck was not a vital target, but it seemed to me better to destroy an industrial town of moderate importance than to toil to destroy a large industrial city…. I wanted my crews to be well, "blooded" as they say in fox hunting, to have a taste of success for a change.'
Air Marshal Sir Arthur 'Bomber' Harris
Air Officer Commanding Bomber Command

Stuttgart
4/5 May
13

Following the Lübeck raid, a series of four similar raids were carried out against Rostock on four consecutive nights, 23–26 April, when more than 200 civilians were killed. Regular bombing raids were also carried out elsewhere throughout April, as shown on this map. The third Lübeck-style target, using one-third incendiary bombs, was Cologne, on 30/31 May 1942, when for the first time more than 1,000 bombers took part in the raid. 469 people were killed and 3,300 buildings totally destroyed.

© Martin Gilbert 2008

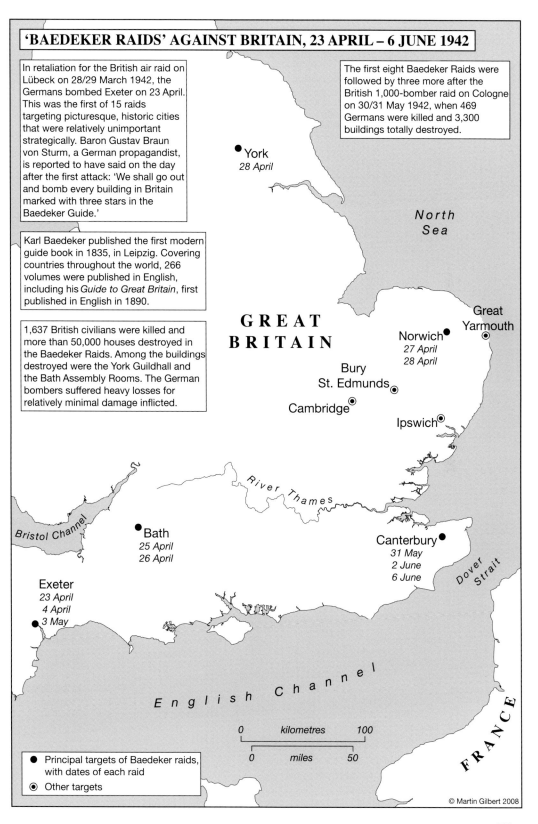

'BAEDEKER RAIDS' AGAINST BRITAIN, 23 APRIL – 6 JUNE 1942

In retaliation for the British air raid on Lübeck on 28/29 March 1942, the Germans bombed Exeter on 23 April. This was the first of 15 raids targeting picturesque, historic cities that were relatively unimportant strategically. Baron Gustav Braun von Sturm, a German propagandist, is reported to have said on the day after the first attack: 'We shall go out and bomb every building in Britain marked with three stars in the Baedeker Guide.'

Karl Baedeker published the first modern guide book in 1835, in Leipzig. Covering countries throughout the world, 266 volumes were published in English, including his *Guide to Great Britain*, first published in English in 1890.

1,637 British civilians were killed and more than 50,000 houses destroyed in the Baedeker Raids. Among the buildings destroyed were the York Guildhall and the Bath Assembly Rooms. The German bombers suffered heavy losses for relatively minimal damage inflicted.

The first eight Baedeker Raids were followed by three more after the British 1,000-bomber raid on Cologne on 30/31 May 1942, when 469 Germans were killed and 3,300 buildings totally destroyed.

North Sea

York
28 April

GREAT BRITAIN

Great Yarmouth

Norwich
27 April
28 April

Bury St. Edmunds

Cambridge

Ipswich

River Thames

Bristol Channel

Bath
25 April
26 April

Canterbury
31 May
2 June
6 June

Dover Strait

Exeter
23 April
4 April
3 May

English Channel

FRANCE

| 0 | kilometres | 100 |
| 0 | miles | 50 |

● Principal targets of Baedeker raids, with dates of each raid

⊙ Other targets

© Martin Gilbert 2008

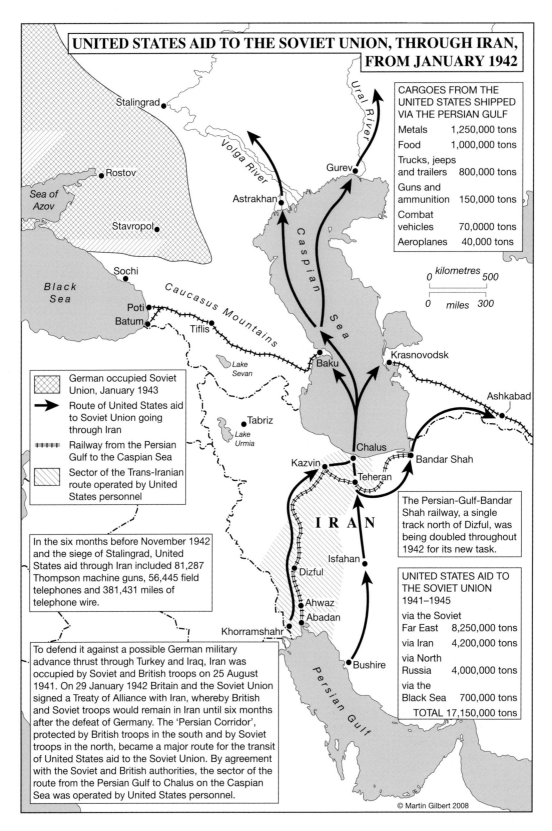

UNITED STATES AID TO THE SOVIET UNION, THROUGH IRAN, FROM JANUARY 1942

Stalingrad

Ural River

Rostov

Sea of Azov

Stavropol

Volga River

Astrakhan

Gurev

CARGOES FROM THE UNITED STATES SHIPPED VIA THE PERSIAN GULF

Metals	1,250,000 tons
Food	1,000,000 tons
Trucks, jeeps and trailers	800,000 tons
Guns and ammunition	150,000 tons
Combat vehicles	70,0000 tons
Aeroplanes	40,000 tons

Sochi

Black Sea

Caucasus Mountains

Poti
Batum

Tiflis

Lake Sevan

Caspian Sea

Baku

Krasnovodsk

Ashkabad

German occupied Soviet Union, January 1943

Route of United States aid to Soviet Union going through Iran

Railway from the Persian Gulf to the Caspian Sea

Sector of the Trans-Iranian route operated by United States personnel

Tabriz
Lake Urmia

Chalus

Kazvin

Bandar Shah

Teheran

I R A N

In the six months before November 1942 and the siege of Stalingrad, United States aid through Iran included 81,287 Thompson machine guns, 56,445 field telephones and 381,431 miles of telephone wire.

Isfahan

Dizful

The Persian-Gulf-Bandar Shah railway, a single track north of Dizful, was being doubled throughout 1942 for its new task.

Ahwaz
Abadan

Khorramshahr

UNITED STATES AID TO THE SOVIET UNION 1941–1945

via the Soviet Far East	8,250,000 tons
via Iran	4,200,000 tons
via North Russia	4,000,000 tons
via the Black Sea	700,000 tons
TOTAL	17,150,000 tons

To defend it against a possible German military advance thrust through Turkey and Iraq, Iran was occupied by Soviet and British troops on 25 August 1941. On 29 January 1942 Britain and the Soviet Union signed a Treaty of Alliance with Iran, whereby British and Soviet troops would remain in Iran until six months after the defeat of Germany. The 'Persian Corridor', protected by British troops in the south and by Soviet troops in the north, became a major route for the transit of United States aid to the Soviet Union. By agreement with the Soviet and British authorities, the sector of the route from the Persian Gulf to Chalus on the Caspian Sea was operated by United States personnel.

Bushire

Persian Gulf

© Martin Gilbert 2008

kilometres
0   500

0   *miles*   300

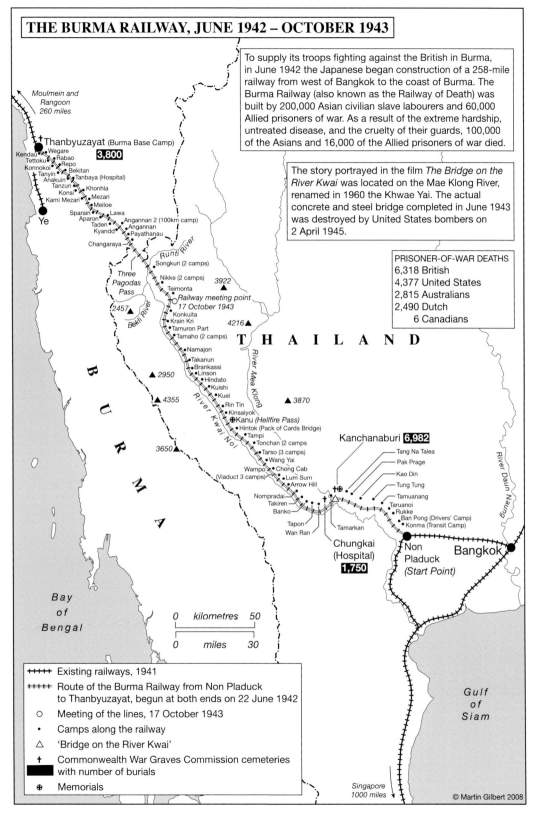

THE BURMA RAILWAY, JUNE 1942 – OCTOBER 1943

To supply its troops fighting against the British in Burma, in June 1942 the Japanese began construction of a 258-mile railway from west of Bangkok to the coast of Burma. The Burma Railway (also known as the Railway of Death) was built by 200,000 Asian civilian slave labourers and 60,000 Allied prisoners of war. As a result of the extreme hardship, untreated disease, and the cruelty of their guards, 100,000 of the Asians and 16,000 of the Allied prisoners of war died.

The story portrayed in the film *The Bridge on the River Kwai* was located on the Mae Klong River, renamed in 1960 the Khwae Yai. The actual concrete and steel bridge completed in June 1943 was destroyed by United States bombers on 2 April 1945.

PRISONER-OF-WAR DEATHS
6,318 British
4,377 United States
2,815 Australians
2,490 Dutch
6 Canadians

Moulmein and Rangoon 260 miles

† Thanbyuzayat (Burma Base Camp) **3,800**
Kendau
Tettoku · Wegare
Konnokoi · Rabao
Tanyin · Repo
Anakuin · Bekitan
Tanzun · Tanbaya (Hospital)
Konsi · Khonhla
Kami Mezari · Mezari
· Meiloe
Ye
Sparain · Lawa
Aparon
Taden · Angannan 2 (100km camp)
Kyandd · Angannan
· Payathanau
Changaraya

Runti River

Three Pagodas Pass
Songkuri (2 camps)
Nikke (2 camps) 3922 ▲
Teimonta
○ Railway meeting point 17 October 1943
2457 ▲ *Bekli River*
Konkuita
Krain Kri
Tamuron Part 4216 ▲
Tamaho (2 camps)

T H A I L A N D

Namajon
Takanun
Brankassi
▲ 2950 Linson
Hindato
Kuishi
▲ 4355 Kuei
Rin Tin ▲ 3870
Kinsaiyok
⊕ Kanu (*Hellfire Pass*)
Hintok (Pack of Cards Bridge)
3650 ▲ Tampi
Tonchan (2 camps)
Tarso (3 camps)
Wang Yai
Wampo · Chong Cab
(Viaduct 3 camps) Lum Sum
· Arrow Hill

Kanchanaburi **6,982**
Tang Na Talea
Pak Prage
Kao Din
Tung Tung
Tamuanang
Nompradai Taruanoi
Takiren Rukke
Banko Ban Pong (Drivers' Camp)
Konma (Transit Camp)
Tapon Tamarkan
Wan Ran
Chungkai (Hospital) Non Pladuck (Start Point) Bangkok
1,750

River Mea Klong

River Kwai Noi

River Daun Naung

Bay of Bengal

B U R M A

0 kilometres 50

0 miles 30

Gulf of Siam

+++++ Existing railways, 1941
+++++ Route of the Burma Railway from Non Pladuck to Thanbyuzayat, begun at both ends on 22 June 1942
○ Meeting of the lines, 17 October 1943
· Camps along the railway
△ 'Bridge on the River Kwai'
† Commonwealth War Graves Commission cemeteries with number of burials
⊕ Memorials

Singapore 1000 miles

© Martin Gilbert 2008

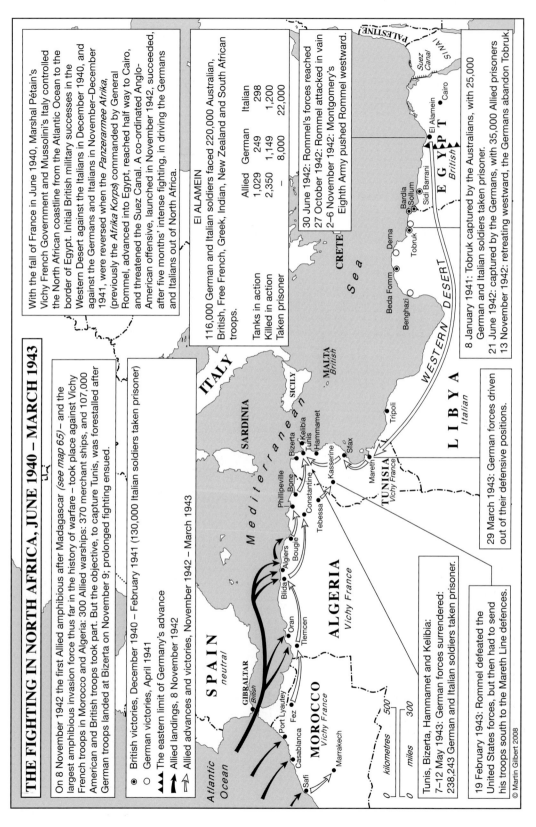

THE FIGHTING IN NORTH AFRICA, JUNE 1940 – MARCH 1943

On 8 November 1942 the first Allied amphibious after Madagascar *(see map 65)* – and the largest amphibious invasion force thus far in the history of warfare – took place against Vichy French troops in Morocco and Algeria: 300 Allied warships: 370 merchant ships, and 107,000 American and British troops took part. But the objective, to capture Tunis, was forestalled after German troops landed at Bizerta on November 9; prolonged fighting ensued.

- ◉ British victories, December 1940 – February 1941 (130,000 Italian soldiers taken prisoner)
- ○ German victories, April 1941
- ▲▲▲ The eastern limit of Germany's advance
- ➤ Allied landings, 8 November 1942
- ⇨ Allied advances and victories, November 1942 – March 1943

With the fall of France in June 1940, Marshal Pétain's Vichy French Government and Mussolini's Italy controlled the North African coastline from the Atlantic Ocean to the border of Egypt. Initial British military successes in the Western Desert against the Italians in December 1940, and against the Germans and Italians in November–December 1941, were reversed when the *Panzerarmee Afrika*, (previously the *Afrika Korps*) commanded by General Rommel, advanced into Egypt, reached half way to Cairo, and threatened the Suez Canal. A co-ordinated Anglo-American offensive, launched in November 1942, succeeded, after five months' intense fighting, in driving the Germans and Italians out of North Africa.

EL ALAMEIN

116,000 German and Italian soldiers faced 220,000 Australian, British, Free French, Greek, Indian, New Zealand and South African troops.

	Allied	German	Italian
Tanks in action	1,029	249	298
Killed in action	2,350	1,149	1,200
Taken prisoner	–	8,000	22,000

30 June 1942: Rommel's forces reached
27 October 1942: Rommel attacked in vain
2–6 November 1942: Montgomery's Eighth Army pushed Rommel westward.

8 January 1941: Tobruk captured by the Australians, with 25,000 German and Italian soldiers taken prisoner.
21 June 1942: captured by the Germans, with 35,000 Allied prisoners
13 November 1942: retreating westward, the Germans abandon Tobruk.

29 March 1943: German forces driven out of their defensive positions.

19 February 1943: Rommel defeated the United States forces, but then had to send his troops south to the Mareth Line defences.

Tunis, Bizerta, Hammamet and Kelibia: 7–12 May 1943: German forces surrendered: 238,243 German and Italian soldiers taken prisoner.

© Martin Gilbert 2008

SPAIN *neutral*
GIBRALTAR *British*
Atlantic Ocean
MOROCCO *Vichy France*
Port Lyautey
Casablanca
Safi
Marrakech
Fez
ALGERIA *Vichy France*
Tlemcen
Oran
Blida
Algiers
Bougie
Phillipeville
Bone
Constantine
Tebessa
Kasserine
Mareth
TUNISIA *Vichy France*
Sfax
Tunis
Bizerta
Kelibia
Hammamet
SARDINIA
ITALY
SICILY
MALTA *British*
Tripoli
LIBYA *Italian*
Mediterranean Sea
Benghazi
Beda Fomm
Derna
Tobruk
Bardia
Sollum
Sidi Barrani
WESTERN DESERT
El Alamein
EGYPT *British*
Cairo
Suez Canal
SINAI
PALESTINE
CRETE

kilometres 0 300 500
miles 0 300

80

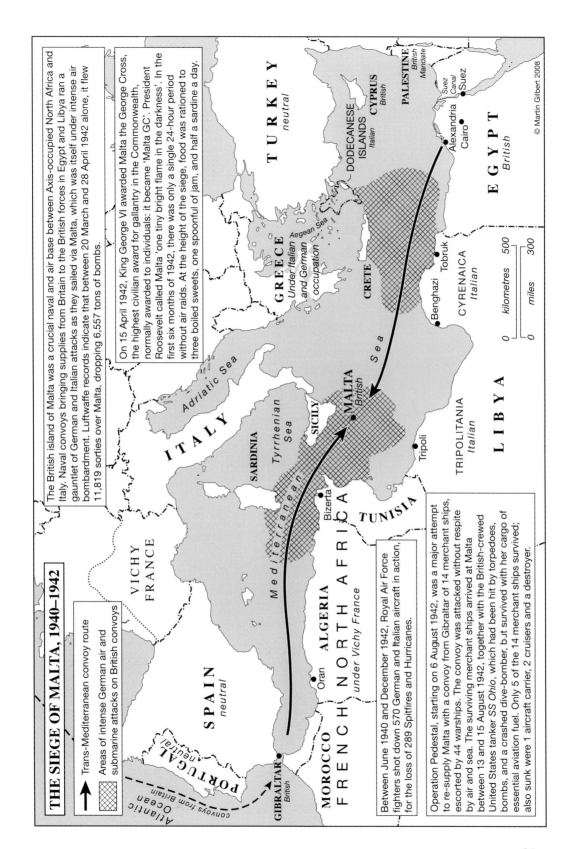

THE SIEGE OF MALTA, 1940–1942

Trans-Mediterranean convoy route

Areas of intense German air and submarine attacks on British convoys

The British island of Malta was a crucial naval and air base between Axis-occupied North Africa and Italy. Naval convoys bringing supplies from Britain to the British forces in Egypt and Libya ran a gauntlet of German and Italian attacks as they sailed via Malta, which was itself under intense air bombardment. Luftwaffe records indicate that between 20 March and 28 April 1942 alone, it flew 11,819 sorties over Malta, dropping 6,557 tons of bombs.

On 15 April 1942, King George VI awarded Malta the George Cross, the highest civilian award for gallantry in the Commonwealth, normally awarded to individuals: it became 'Malta GC'. President Roosevelt called Malta 'one tiny bright flame in the darkness'. In the first six months of 1942, there was only a single 24-hour period without air raids. At the height of the siege, food was rationed to three boiled sweets, one spoonful of jam, and half a sardine a day.

Between June 1940 and December 1942, Royal Air Force fighters shot down 570 German and Italian aircraft in action, for the loss of 289 Spitfires and Hurricanes.

Operation Pedestal, starting on 6 August 1942, was a major attempt to re-supply Malta with a convoy from Gibraltar of 14 merchant ships, escorted by 44 warships. The convoy was attacked without respite by air and sea. The surviving merchant ships arrived at Malta between 13 and 15 August 1942, together with the British-crewed United States tanker SS *Ohio*, which had been hit by torpedoes, bombs, and a crashed dive-bomber, but survived with her cargo of essential aviation fuel. Only 5 of the 14 merchant ships survived; also sunk were 1 aircraft carrier, 2 cruisers and a destroyer.

© Martin Gilbert 2008

81

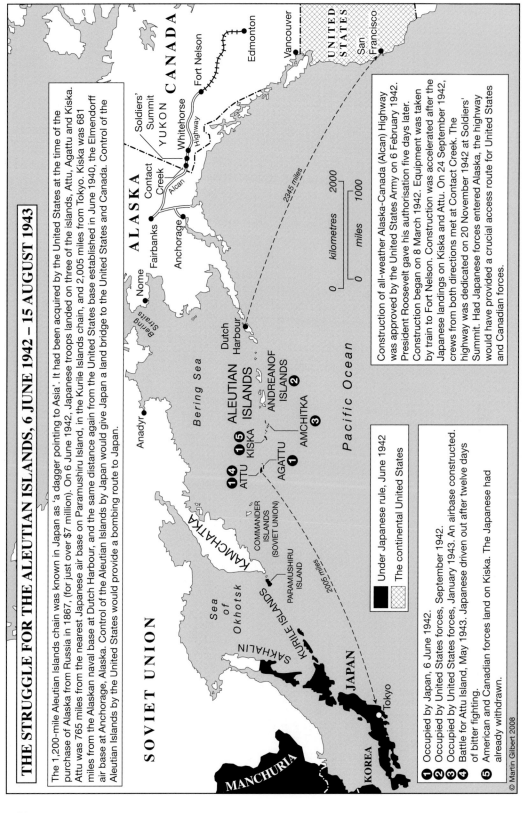

THE STRUGGLE FOR THE ALEUTIAN ISLANDS, 6 JUNE 1942 – 15 AUGUST 1943

The 1,200-mile Aleutian Islands chain was known in Japan as 'a dagger pointing to Asia'. It had been acquired by the United States at the time of the purchase of Alaska from Russia in 1867, (for just over $7 million). On 6 June 1942, Japanese troops landed on three of the islands, Attu, Agattu and Kiska. Attu was 765 miles from the nearest Japanese air base on Paramushiru Island, in the Kurile Islands chain, and 2,005 miles from Tokyo. Kiska was 681 miles from the Alaskan naval base at Dutch Harbour, and the same distance again from the United States base established in June 1940, the Elmendorf air base at Anchorage, Alaska. Control of the Aleutian Islands by Japan would give Japan a land bridge to the United States and Canada. Control of the Aleutian Islands by the United States would provide a bombing route to Japan.

Construction of all-weather Alaska-Canada (Alcan) Highway was approved by the United States Army on 6 February 1942. President Roosevelt gave his authorisation five days later. Construction began on 8 March 1942. Equipment was taken by train to Fort Nelson. Construction was accelerated after the Japanese landings on Kiska and Attu. On 24 September 1942, crews from both directions met at Contact Creek. The highway was dedicated on 20 November 1942 at Soldiers' Summit. Had Japanese forces entered Alaska, the highway would have provided a crucial access route for United States and Canadian forces.

Under Japanese rule, June 1942

The continental United States

❶ Occupied by Japan, 6 June 1942.
❷ Occupied by United States forces, September 1942.
❸ Occupied by United States forces, January 1943. An airbase constructed.
❹ Battle for Attu Island, May 1943. Japanese driven out after twelve days of bitter fighting.
❺ American and Canadian forces land on Kiska. The Japanese had already withdrawn.

© Martin Gilbert 2008

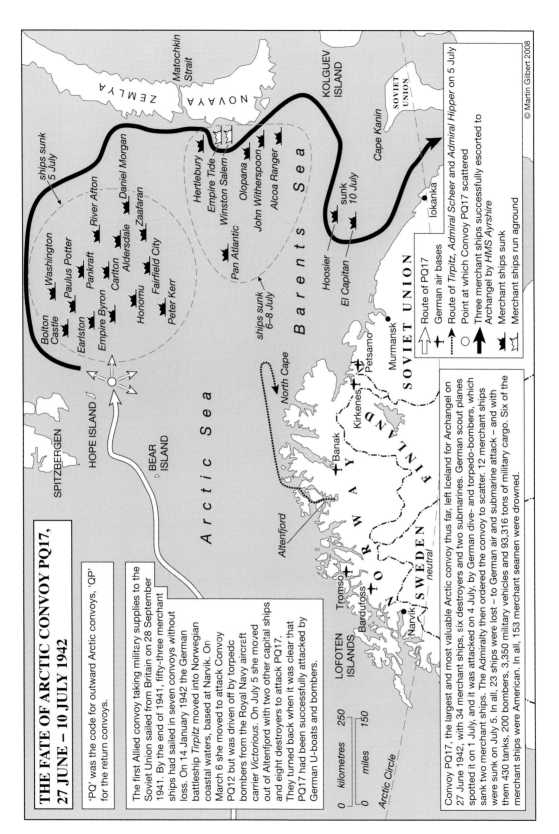

THE FATE OF ARCTIC CONVOY PQ17,
27 JUNE – 10 JULY 1942

'PQ' was the code for outward Arctic convoys, 'QP' for the return convoys.

The first Allied convoy taking military supplies to the Soviet Union sailed from Britain on 28 September 1941. By the end of 1941, fifty-three merchant ships had sailed in seven convoys without loss. On 14 January 1942 the German battleship *Tirpitz* moved into Norwegian coastal waters, based at Narvik. On March 6 she moved to attack Convoy PQ12 but was driven off by torpedo bombers from the Royal Navy aircraft carrier *Victorious*. On July 5 she moved out of Altenfjord with two other capital ships and eight destroyers to attack PQ17. They turned back when it was clear that PQ17 had been successfully attacked by German U-boats and bombers.

Convoy PQ17, the largest and most valuable Arctic convoy thus far, left Iceland for Archangel on 27 June 1942, with 34 merchant ships, six destroyers and two submarines. German scout planes spotted it on 1 July, and it was attacked on 4 July, by German dive- and torpedo-bombers, which sank two merchant ships. The Admiralty then ordered the convoy to scatter. 12 merchant ships were sunk on July 5. In all, 23 ships were lost – to German air and submarine attack – and with them 430 tanks, 200 bombers, 3,350 military vehicles and 93,316 tons of military cargo. Six of the merchant ships were American. In all, 153 merchant seamen were drowned.

Route of PQ17

German air bases

Route of *Tirpitz*, *Admiral Scheer* and *Admiral Hipper* on 5 July

Point at which Convoy PQ17 scattered

Three merchant ships successfully escorted to Archangel by HMS *Ayrshire*

Merchant ships sunk

Merchant ships run aground

© Martin Gilbert 2008

83

ESTONIAN BATTALIONS IN THE GERMAN-OCCUPIED EAST, 1942–1943

The German Army made use of the Estonian volunteer battalions to secure the rear areas and its long supply routes from Soviet partisan attacks. These attacks intensified from the early months of 1942, throwing a heavy burden on the Estonian battalions, as well as on their Lithuanian, Latvian and Ukrainian fellow-volunteers. Four battalions of Estonian soldiers served in the German Army.

Helsinki

Lake Ladoga

Gulf of Finland

Tallin

ESTONIA

Lake Peipus

Lake Ilmen

Lake Pskov

Riga

LATVIA

SEE FACING MAP 85

Moscow

River Volga

▲ Towns and areas in which Estonian volunteer battalions were serving during the German occupation of Lithuania, Poland and Ukraine.

▲▲▲ The furthest German advance into the Soviet Union, December 1942

Panevezys

Utena

LITHUANIA

Glebokiye

Ukmerge

Wilejka

Vilnius

Lida

Minsk

Grodno

Baranowicze

POLAND

Gomel

UKRAINE

Kiev

River Dnieper

Kharkov

Surovikino

Poltava

Izyum

River Don

Cherkassy

Khanzhenkovo

Lvov

River Dniester

Stalino

River Don

Kishinev

Odessa

Sea of Azov

0   kilometres   300

0   miles   200

Black Sea

© Martin Gilbert 2008

84

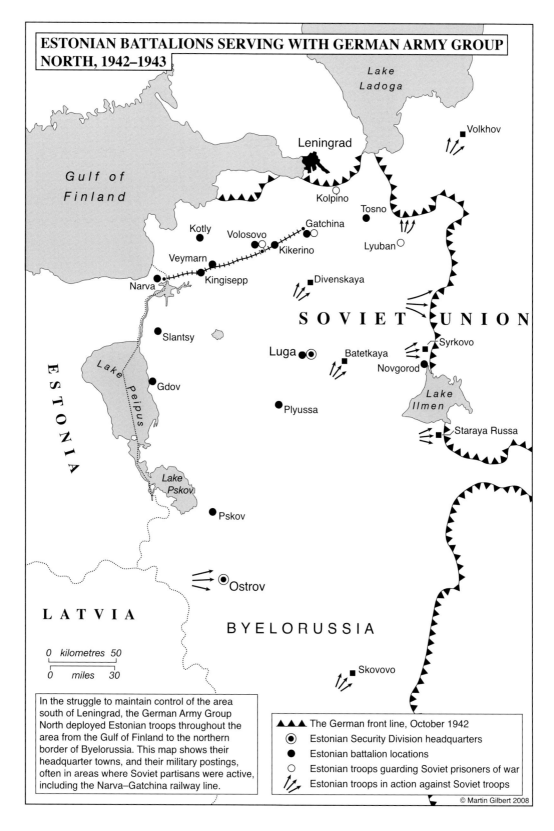

ESTONIAN BATTALIONS SERVING WITH GERMAN ARMY GROUP NORTH, 1942–1943

Lake Ladoga

■ Volkhov

Leningrad

Gulf of Finland

○ Kolpino

Tosno ●

Lyuban ○

Kotly ●

Volosovo ○ ● Gatchina ○

Veymarn ● ● Kikerino

Narva ● ● Kingisepp

■ Divenskaya

S O V I E T   U N I O N

● Slantsy

Luga ● ◉

Batetkaya ■

■ Syrkovo

Novgorod ■

● Gdov

Lake Peipus

● Plyussa

Lake Ilmen

■ Staraya Russa

Lake Pskov

● Pskov

E S T O N I A

◉ Ostrov

L A T V I A

B Y E L O R U S S I A

0 kilometres 50

0 miles 30

In the struggle to maintain control of the area south of Leningrad, the German Army Group North deployed Estonian troops throughout the area from the Gulf of Finland to the northern border of Byelorussia. This map shows their headquarter towns, and their military postings, often in areas where Soviet partisans were active, including the Narva–Gatchina railway line.

■ Skovovo

▲▲▲ The German front line, October 1942
◉ Estonian Security Division headquarters
● Estonian battalion locations
○ Estonian troops guarding Soviet prisoners of war
↗↑↗ Estonian troops in action against Soviet troops

© Martin Gilbert 2008

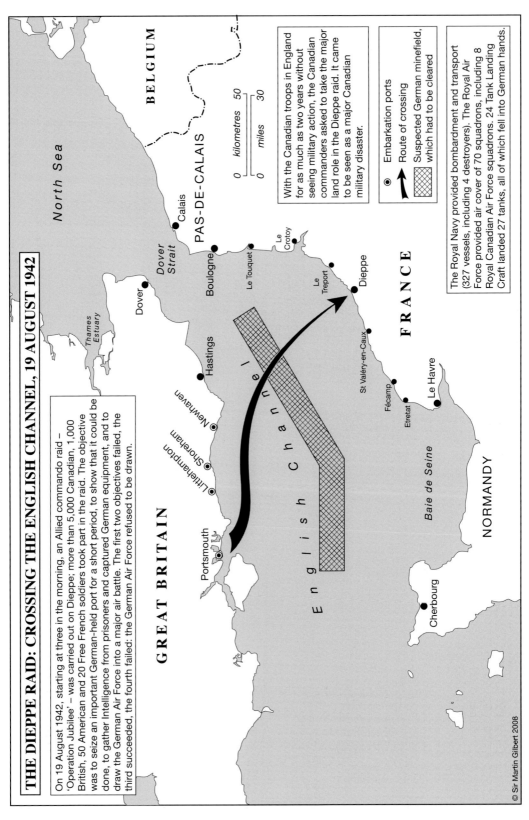

THE DIEPPE RAID: CROSSING THE ENGLISH CHANNEL, 19 AUGUST 1942

On 19 August 1942, starting at three in the morning, an Allied commando raid – 'Operation Jubilee' – was carried out on Dieppe; more than 5,000 Canadian, 1,000 British, 50 American and 20 Free French soldiers took part in the raid. The objective was to seize an important German-held port for a short period, to show that it could be done, to gather Intelligence from prisoners and captured German equipment, and to draw the German Air Force into a major air battle. The first two objectives failed, the third succeeded, the fourth failed: the German Air Force refused to be drawn.

With the Canadian troops in England for as much as two years without seeing military action, the Canadian commanders asked to take the major land role in the Dieppe raid. It came to be seen as a major Canadian military disaster.

- ⊙ Embarkation ports
- ➤ Route of crossing
- ▨ Suspected German minefield, which had to be cleared

The Royal Navy provided bombardment and transport (327 vessels, including 4 destroyers). The Royal Air Force provided air cover of 70 squadrons, including 8 Royal Canadian Air Force squadrons. 24 Tank Landing Craft landed 27 tanks, all of which fell into German hands.

North Sea

BELGIUM

PAS-DE-CALAIS

Calais

Dover Strait

Boulogne

Le Touquet

Le Crotoy

Dover

Thames Estuary

Hastings

Newhaven

Shoreham

Littlehampton

GREAT BRITAIN

Portsmouth

English Channel

Dieppe

Le Tréport

St Valéry-en-Caux

Fécamp

Etretat

Le Havre

FRANCE

Baie de Seine

Cherbourg

NORMANDY

0 kilometres 50
0 miles 30

© Sir Martin Gilbert 2008

THE DIEPPE RAID: THE BATTLE, 19 AUGUST 1942

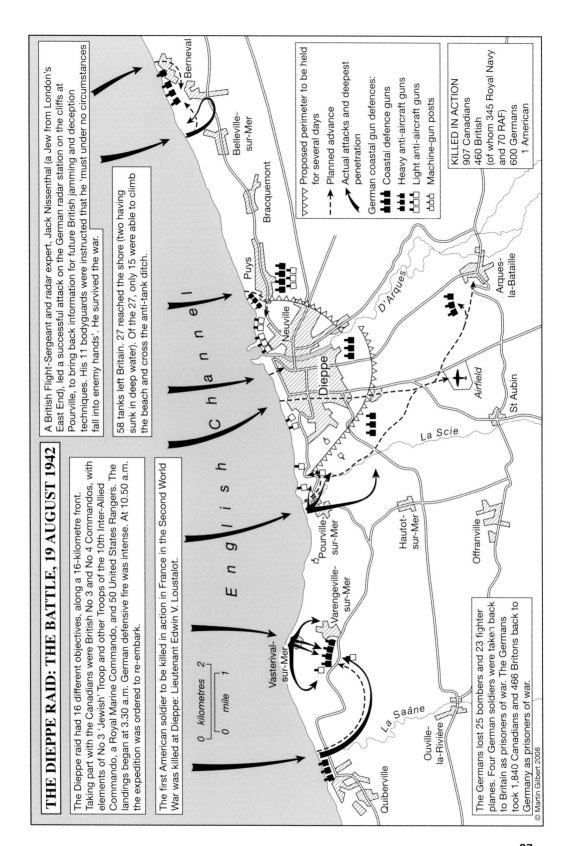

The Dieppe raid had 16 different objectives, along a 16-kilometre front. Taking part with the Canadians were British No 3 and No 4 Commandos, with elements of No 3 'Jewish' Troop and other Troops of the 10th Inter-Allied Commando, a Royal Marine Commando, and 50 United States Rangers. The landings began at 3.30 a.m. German defensive fire was intense. At 10.50 a.m. the expedition was ordered to re-embark.

The first American soldier to be killed in action in France in the Second World War was killed at Dieppe: Lieutenant Edwin V. Loustalot.

A British Flight-Sergeant and radar expert, Jack Nissenthal (a Jew from London's East End), led a successful attack on the German radar station on the cliffs at Pourville, to bring back information for future British jamming and deception techniques. His 11 bodyguards were instructed that he 'must under no circumstances fall into enemy hands'. He survived the war.

58 tanks left Britain. 27 reached the shore (two having sunk in deep water). Of the 27, only 15 were able to climb the beach and cross the anti-tank ditch.

The Germans lost 25 bombers and 23 fighter planes. Four German soldiers were taken back to Britain as prisoners of war. The Germans took 1,840 Canadians and 466 Britons back to Germany as prisoners of war.

English Channel

KILLED IN ACTION
907 Canadians
460 British
(of whom 345 Royal Navy
and 70 RAF)
600 Germans
1 American

Berneval
Belleville-sur-Mer
Bracquemont
Puys
Neuville
Dieppe
D'Arques
Arques-la-Bataille
Airfield
St Aubin
La Scie
Hautot-sur-Mer
Pourville-sur-Mer
Varengeville-sur-Mer
Vasterival-sur-Mer
Offranville
La Saâne
Ouville-la-Rivière
Quiberville

▽▽▽▽ Proposed perimeter to be held for several days
- - - ➔ Planned advance
➔ Actual attacks and deepest penetration

German coastal gun defences:
Coastal defence guns
Heavy anti-aircraft guns
Light anti-aircraft guns
Machine-gun posts

0 kilometres 2
0 mile 1

© Martin Gilbert 2008

Section 6

THE UNARMED AND THE CIVILIANS

I push wagons, I work with a shovel, I turn rotten in the rain, I shiver in the wind; already my own body is no longer mine: my belly is swollen, my limbs emaciated, my face is thick in the morning, hollow in the evening; some of us have yellow skin, others grey. When we do not meet for a few days we hardly recognize each other.

PRIMO LEVI
recalling the first two weeks in Buna-Monowitz
Survival in Auschwitz, The Nazi Assault on Humanity
1961

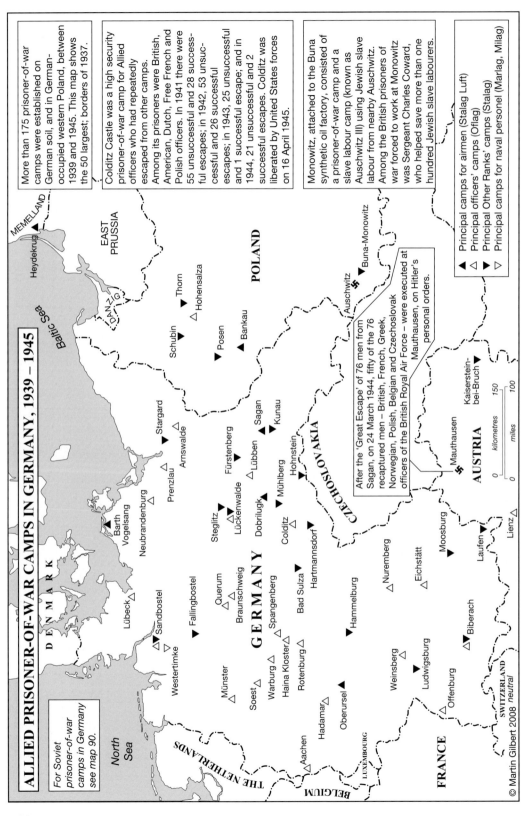

ALLIED PRISONER-OF-WAR CAMPS IN GERMANY, 1939 – 1945

For Soviet prisoner-of-war camps in Germany see map 90.

More than 175 prisoner-of-war camps were established on German soil, and in German-occupied western Poland, between 1939 and 1945. This map shows the 50 largest; borders of 1937.

Colditz Castle was a high security prisoner-of-war camp for Allied officers who had repeatedly escaped from other camps. Among its prisoners were British, American, Dutch, Free French and Polish officers. In 1941 there were 55 unsuccessful and 28 successful escapes; in 1942, 53 unsuccessful and 26 successful escapes; in 1943, 25 unsuccessful and 1 successful escape; and in 1944, 21 unsuccessful and 2 successful escapes. Colditz was liberated by United States forces on 16 April 1945.

Monowitz, attached to the Buna synthetic oil factory, consisted of a prisoner-of-war camp and a slave labour camp (known as Auschwitz III) using Jewish slave labour from nearby Auschwitz. Among the British prisoners of war forced to work at Monowitz was Sergeant Charles Coward, who helped save more than one hundred Jewish slave labourers.

▲ Principal camps for airmen (Stalag Luft)
△ Principal officers' camps (Oflag)
▼ Principal Other Ranks' camps (Stalag)
▽ Principal camps for naval personel (Marlag, Milag)

After the 'Great Escape' of 76 men from Sagan, on 24 March 1944, fifty of the 76 recaptured men – British, French, Greek, Norwegian, Polish, Belgian and Czechoslovak officers of the British Royal Air Force – were executed at Mauthausen, on Hitler's personal orders.

MEMELLAND
Heydekrug ▲
EAST PRUSSIA
Baltic Sea
DANZIG
POLAND

Thorn ▼
Hohensalza △
Posen ▼
Bankau ▲
Auschwitz 卐
Buna-Monowitz ▲

North Sea
DENMARK

Stargard ▼
Arnswalde △
Prenzlau △
Neubrandenburg △
Barth ▲
Vogelsang
Lübeck △
Sandbostel △▽
Westertimke ▽
Fallingpostel ▼
Münster △
Querum △
Braunschweig △
Soest △
Warburg △
Haina Kloster △
Rotenburg △
Hadamar △
Oberursel ▼
Aachen △

Steglitz ▼
Lückenwalde △
Fürstenberg ▼
Lübben △
Sagan ▲
Kunau ▲
Dobrilugk ▼
Mühlberg △
Hohnstein △
Colditz △
Hartmannsdorf ▼
Bad Sulza ▼
Spangenberg △
Hammelburg ▼
Nuremberg △
Eichstätt △
Weinsberg △
Ludwigsburg
Offenburg △
Biberach △▽
Moosburg ▼

GERMANY
CZECHOSLOVAKIA

Mauthausen 卐
Kaiserstein-bei-Bruch ▼
Laufen ▼
Lienz △
AUSTRIA

THE NETHERLANDS
BELGIUM
LUXEMBOURG
FRANCE
SWITZERLAND *neutral*

0 _____ 150 kilometres
0 _____ 100 miles

© Martin Gilbert 2008

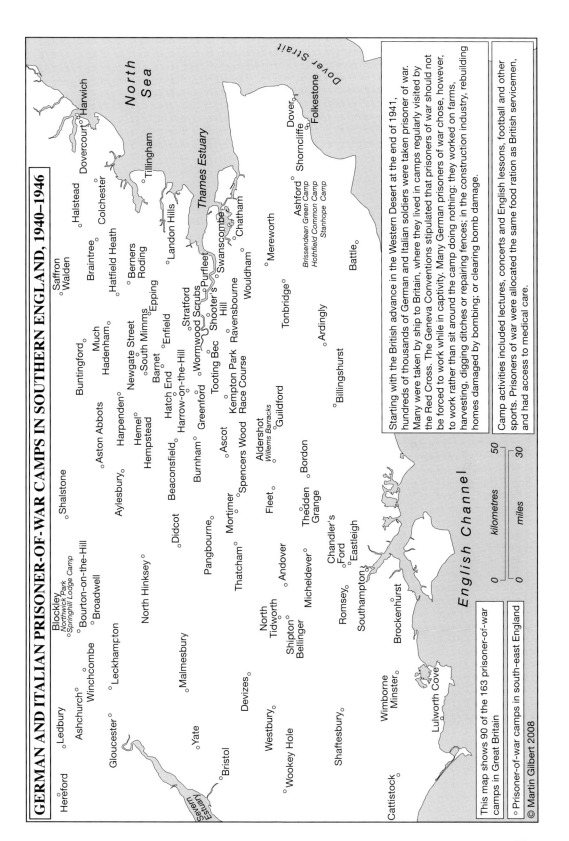

GERMAN AND ITALIAN PRISONER-OF-WAR CAMPS IN SOUTHERN ENGLAND, 1940–1946

Starting with the British advance in the Western Desert at the end of 1941, hundreds of thousands of German and Italian soldiers were taken prisoner of war. Many were taken by ship to Britain, where they lived in camps regularly visited by the Red Cross. The Geneva Conventions stipulated that prisoners of war should not be forced to work while in captivity. Many German prisoners of war chose, however, to work rather than sit around the camp doing nothing: they worked on farms, harvesting, digging ditches or repairing fences; in the construction industry, rebuilding homes damaged by bombing; or clearing bomb damage.

Camp activities included lectures, concerts and English lessons, football and other sports. Prisoners of war were allocated the same food ration as British servicemen, and had access to medical care.

This map shows 90 of the 163 prisoner-of-war camps in Great Britain

○ Prisoner-of-war camps in south-east England

© Martin Gilbert 2008

89

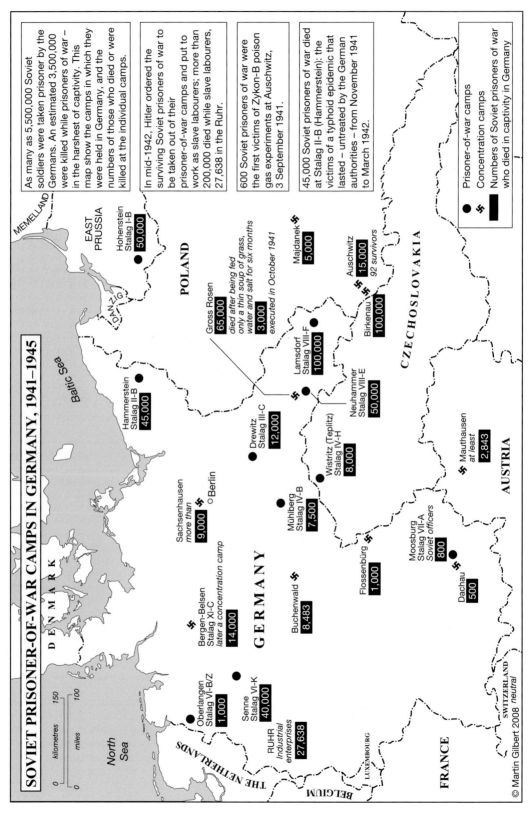

SOVIET PRISONER-OF-WAR CAMPS IN GERMANY, 1941–1945

As many as 5,500,000 Soviet soldiers were taken prisoner by the Germans. An estimated 3,500,000 were killed while prisoners of war – in the harshest of captivity. This map show the camps in which they were held in Germany, and the numbers of those who died or were killed at the individual camps.

In mid-1942, Hitler ordered the surviving Soviet prisoners of war to be taken out of their prisoner-of-war camps and put to work as slave labourers; more than 200,000 died while slave labourers, 27,638 in the Ruhr.

600 Soviet prisoners of war were the first victims of Zykon-B poison gas experiments at Auschwitz, 3 September 1941.

45,000 Soviet prisoners of war died at Stalag II-B (Hammerstein): the victims of a typhoid epidemic that lasted – untreated by the German authorities – from November 1941 to March 1942.

● Prisoner-of-war camps

卐 Concentration camps

▬ Numbers of Soviet prisoners of war who died in captivity in Germany

Baltic Sea

North Sea

MEMELLAND

DANZIG

EAST PRUSSIA

Hohenstein Stalag I-B
50,000 ●

POLAND

Hammerstein Stalag II-B
45,000 ●

Gross Rosen
65,000
died after being fed only a thin soup of grass, water and salt for six months
3,000
executed in October 1941

Majdanek 卐
5,000

Auschwitz 卐 卐 15,000
92 survivors

Birkenau
100,000

CZECHOSLOVAKIA

Lamsdorf Stalag VIII-F
100,000

Neuhammer Stalag VIII-E
50,000

Drewitz Stalag III-C
12,000

Wistritz (Teplitz) Stalag IV-H
8,000

DENMARK

Sachsenhausen
more than
9,000 卐

○ Berlin

Mühlberg Stalag IV-B
7,500

Mauthausen
at least
2,843 卐

AUSTRIA

GERMANY

Bergen-Belsen Stalag XI-C
later a concentration camp
14,000 卐

Buchenwald 卐
8,483

Flossenbürg 卐
1,000

Moosburg Stalag VII-A
Soviet officers
800 ●

Dachau 卐
500

Oberlangen Stalag VI-B/Z
1,000 ●

Senne Stalag VI-K
40,000 ●

RUHR
Industrial enterprises
27,638

THE NETHERLANDS

BELGIUM

LUXEMBOURG

FRANCE

SWITZERLAND *neutral*

kilometres 0   150
miles   0   100

© Martin Gilbert 2008

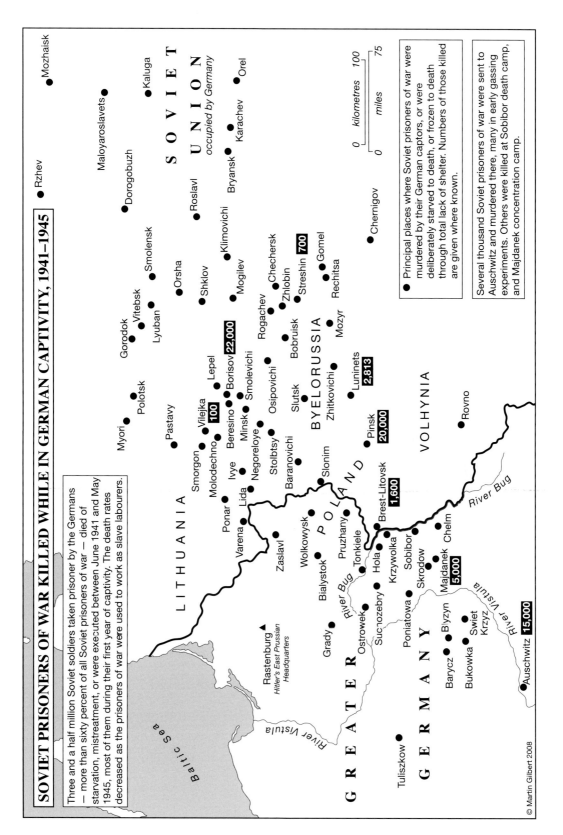

SOVIET PRISONERS OF WAR KILLED WHILE IN GERMAN CAPTIVITY, 1941–1945

Three and a half million Soviet soldiers taken prisoner by the Germans — more than sixty percent of all Soviet prisoners of war — died of starvation, mistreatment, or were executed between June 1941 and May 1945, most of them during their first year of captivity. The death rates decreased as the prisoners of war were used to work as slave labourers.

● Principal places where Soviet prisoners of war were murdered by their German captors, or were deliberately starved to death, or frozen to death through total lack of shelter. Numbers of those killed are given where known.

Several thousand Soviet prisoners of war were sent to Auschwitz and murdered there, many in early gassing experiments. Others were killed at Sobibor death camp, and Majdanek concentration camp.

0   kilometres   100
0   miles   75

S O V I E T

U N I O N
occupied by Germany

Mozhaisk

Maloyaroslavets

Kaluga

Rzhev

Orel

Karachev

Bryansk

Dorogobuzh

Roslavl

Klimovichi

Smolensk

Orsha

Shklov

Mogilev

Chechersk

Zhlobin

Streshin **700**

Gomel

Rechitsa

Chernigov

Mozyr

B Y E L O R U S S I A

Rogachev

Bobruisk

Zhitkovichi

Luninets **2,813**

Pinsk **20,000**

V O L H Y N I A

Rovno

Vitebsk

Gorodok

Lyuban

Polotsk

Myori

Pastavy

Vilejka **100**

Lepel

Borisov **22,000**

Smolevichi

Beresino

Osipovichi

Slutsk

Minsk

Negoreloye

Stolbtsy

Molodechno

Smorgon

Ivye

Baranovichi

Slonim

L I T H U A N I A

Lida

Ponar

Varena

Zaslavl

Wolkowysk

Brest-Litovsk **1,600**

P O L A N D

Pruzhany

Tonkiele

Hola

Krzywolka

Sobibor

Chelm

Skrodow

Majdanek **5,000**

Bialystok

Ostrowek

Suchozebry

Poniatowa

Grady

River Bug

River Bug

Barycz

Blyzyn

Bukowka

Swiet Krzyz

Auschwitz **15,000**

G R E A T E R

G E R M A N Y

Tuliszkow

River Vistula

River Vistula

Baltic Sea

Rastenburg ▲
Hitler's East Prussian Headquarters

© Martin Gilbert 2008

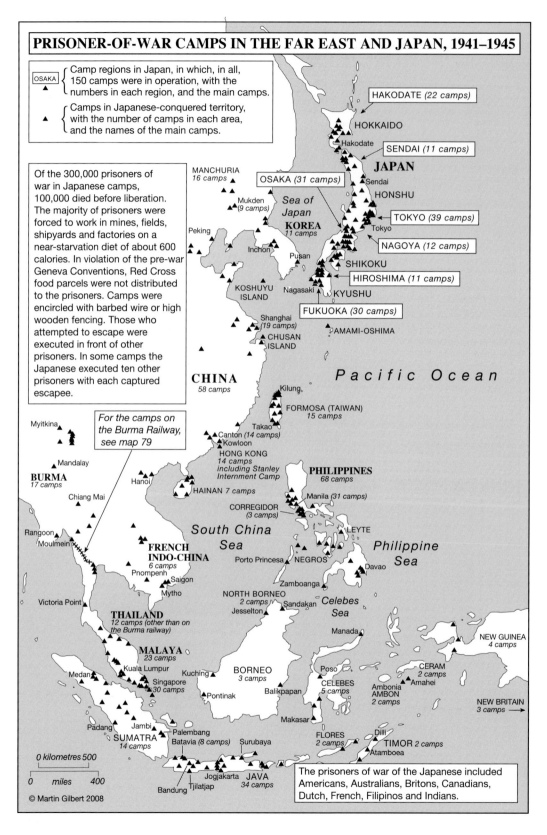

PRISONER-OF-WAR CAMPS IN THE FAR EAST AND JAPAN, 1941–1945

OSAKA ▲ { Camp regions in Japan, in which, in all, 150 camps were in operation, with the numbers in each region, and the main camps.

▲ { Camps in Japanese-conquered territory, with the number of camps in each area, and the names of the main camps.

Of the 300,000 prisoners of war in Japanese camps, 100,000 died before liberation. The majority of prisoners were forced to work in mines, fields, shipyards and factories on a near-starvation diet of about 600 calories. In violation of the pre-war Geneva Conventions, Red Cross food parcels were not distributed to the prisoners. Camps were encircled with barbed wire or high wooden fencing. Those who attempted to escape were executed in front of other prisoners. In some camps the Japanese executed ten other prisoners with each captured escapee.

For the camps on the Burma Railway, see map 79

HAKODATE *(22 camps)*

HOKKAIDO

Hakodate

SENDAI *(11 camps)*

JAPAN

OSAKA *(31 camps)*

Sendai

HONSHU

TOKYO *(39 camps)*

Tokyo

NAGOYA *(12 camps)*

SHIKOKU

HIROSHIMA *(11 camps)*

KYUSHU

FUKUOKA *(30 camps)*

AMAMI-OSHIMA

MANCHURIA
16 camps ▲

Mukden
(9 camps)

Sea of Japan

KOREA
11 camps

Peking

Inchon

Pusan

KOSHUYU
ISLAND

Nagasaki

Shanghai
(19 camps)

CHUSAN
ISLAND

CHINA
58 camps

Kilung

FORMOSA (TAIWAN)
15 camps

Takao

Canton (14 camps)

Kowloon

HONG KONG
14 camps
including Stanley
Internment Camp

HAINAN 7 camps

PHILIPPINES
68 camps

Manila (31 camps)

CORREGIDOR
(3 camps)

LEYTE

Pacific Ocean

Philippine Sea

Myitkina

Mandalay

BURMA
17 camps

Chiang Mai

Rangoon

Moulmein

Hanoi

FRENCH
INDO-CHINA
6 camps

Pnompenh

Saigon

Mytho

South China Sea

Porto Princesa

NEGROS

Davao

Zamboanga

NORTH BORNEO
2 camps

Jesselton

Sandakan

Celebes Sea

Victoria Point

THAILAND
12 camps (other than on the Burma railway)

MALAYA
23 camps

Kuala Lumpur

Kuching

BORNEO
3 camps

Poso

Manada

NEW GUINEA
4 camps

Medan

Singapore
30 camps

Pontinak

Balikpapan

CELEBES
5 camps

Ambonia
AMBON
2 camps

CERAM
2 camps

Amahei

NEW BRITAIN
3 camps →

Padang

Jambi

Palembang

SUMATRA
14 camps

Batavia (8 camps)

Surubaya

Makasar

FLORES
2 camps

Dilli

TIMOR 2 camps

Atamboea

0 kilometres 500

0 miles 400

Bandung

Tjilatjap

Jogjakarta

JAVA
34 camps

The prisoners of war of the Japanese included Americans, Australians, Britons, Canadians, Dutch, French, Filipinos and Indians.

© Martin Gilbert 2008

92

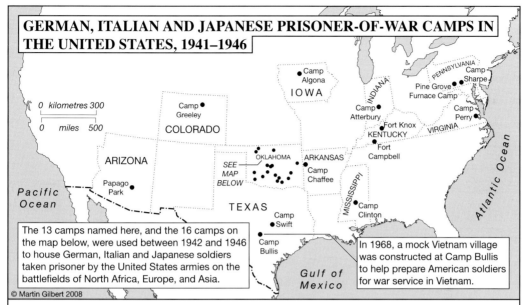

GERMAN, ITALIAN AND JAPANESE PRISONER-OF-WAR CAMPS IN THE UNITED STATES, 1941–1946

0 kilometres 300
0 miles 500

Camp Algona — IOWA

Camp Greeley — COLORADO

ARIZONA

Papago Park

Pacific Ocean

SEE MAP BELOW — OKLAHOMA — ARKANSAS

Camp Chaffee

TEXAS

Camp Swift

Camp Bullis

Gulf of Mexico

Camp Atterbury — INDIANA — PENNSYLVANIA — Camp Sharpe

Pine Grove Furnace Camp

Fort Knox — KENTUCKY — VIRGINIA — Camp Perry

Fort Campbell

MISSISSIPPI

Camp Clinton

Atlantic Ocean

The 13 camps named here, and the 16 camps on the map below, were used between 1942 and 1946 to house German, Italian and Japanese soldiers taken prisoner by the United States armies on the battlefields of North Africa, Europe, and Asia.

In 1968, a mock Vietnam village was constructed at Camp Bullis to help prepare American soldiers for war service in Vietnam.

© Martin Gilbert 2008

Pine Grove Furnace POW Camp was originally intended to house German Naval Officers. It was enlarged to include prisoners from Rommel's Afrika Korps. Later Japanese Officers were imprisoned here. The camp housed 1,500 prisoners and 150 American personnel and guards. When questioned by outsiders, guards were instructed to say they were stationed at Carlisle Barracks, thirty minutes away by car, to maintain the secrecy of the POW camp. In all, 15 prisoners escaped. The camp was declared 'surplus' on 29 November 1945. It later became Camp Michaux, operated by the Dickinson United Presbyterian Church as a youth church camp.

GERMAN, ITALIAN AND JAPANESE PRISONER-OF-WAR CAMPS IN OKLAHOMA, 1941–1946

KANSAS

North Canadian River

Alva — Tonkawa

Waynoka

Cimarron River

Canadian River

OKLAHOMA

Fort Reno

Oklahoma City Camp — Oklahoma City

Camp Gruber

TEXAS

Hobart — Chickasha

Fort Sill — Pauls Valley

Tipton

Horseshoe Ranch

Gene Autry

Tishomingo

McAlester POW Camp

Stringtown POW Camp

● Prisoner-of-war camps in Oklahoma

The 16 camps shown here, and the 13 camps on the above map, were used between 1942 and 1946 to house German, Italian and Japanese soldiers taken prisoner by the United States armies on the battlefields of North Africa, Europe, and Asia.

0 kilometres 100
0 miles 50

TEXAS

Red River

© Martin Gilbert 2008

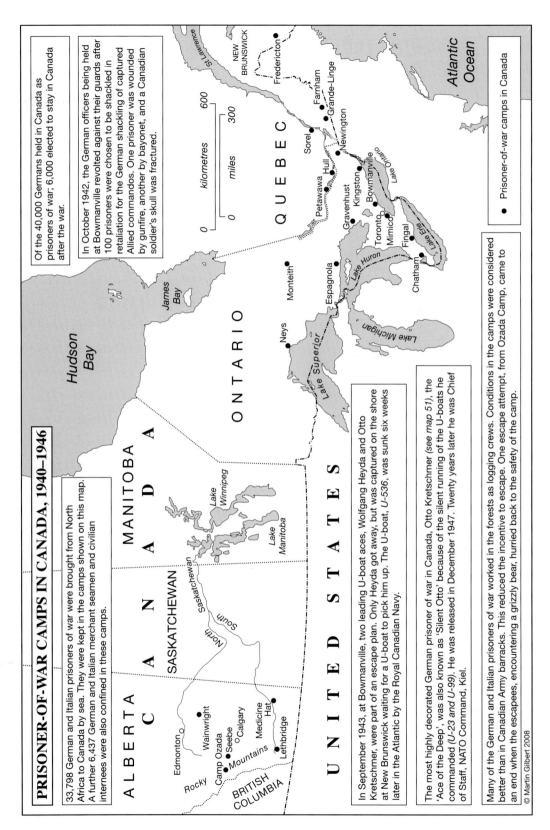

PRISONER-OF-WAR CAMPS IN CANADA, 1940–1946

33,798 German and Italian prisoners of war were brought from North Africa to Canada by sea. They were kept in the camps shown on this map. A further 6,437 German and Italian merchant seamen and civilian internees were also confined in these camps.

Of the 40,000 Germans held in Canada as prisoners of war; 6,000 elected to stay in Canada after the war.

In October 1942, the German officers being held at Bowmanville revolted against their guards after 100 prisoners were chosen to be shackled in retaliation for the German shackling of captured Allied commandos. One prisoner was wounded by gunfire, another by bayonet, and a Canadian soldier's skull was fractured.

In September 1943, at Bowmanville, two leading U-boat aces, Wolfgang Heyda and Otto Kretschmer, were part of an escape plan. Only Heyda got away, but was captured on the shore at New Brunswick waiting for a U-boat to pick him up. The U-boat, *U-536*, was sunk six weeks later in the Atlantic by the Royal Canadian Navy.

The most highly decorated German prisoner of war in Canada, Otto Kretschmer (*see map 51*), the 'Ace of the Deep', was also known as 'Silent Otto' because of the silent running of the U-boats he commanded (*U-23 and U-99*). He was released in December 1947. Twenty years later he was Chief of Staff, NATO Command, Kiel.

Many of the German and Italian prisoners of war worked in the forests as logging crews. Conditions in the camps were considered better than in Canadian Army barracks. This reduced the incentive to escape. One escape attempt, from Ozada Camp, came to an end when the escapees, encountering a grizzly bear, hurried back to the safety of the camp.

● Prisoner-of-war camps in Canada

© Martin Gilbert 2008

NEW BRUNSWICK — Fredericton

QUEBEC — Grande-Linge, Farnham, Newington, Sorel, Hull, Petawawa, Gravenhurst, Kingston, Bowmanville, Toronto, Mimico, Fingal, Chatham

ONTARIO — Espagnola, Monteith, Neys

MANITOBA — Lake Winnipeg, Lake Manitoba

SASKATCHEWAN — North Saskatchewan, South Saskatchewan

ALBERTA — Edmonton, Wainwright, Camp Ozada, Seebe, Calgary, Medicine Hat, Lethbridge

BRITISH COLUMBIA

CANADA

UNITED STATES

Hudson Bay

James Bay

St Lawrence

Lake Ontario, Lake Erie, Lake Huron, Lake Superior, Lake Michigan

Rocky Mountains

Atlantic Ocean

kilometres 0 300 600
miles

95

GERMAN-AMERICANS INTERNED IN THE UNITED STATES, 1942–1945

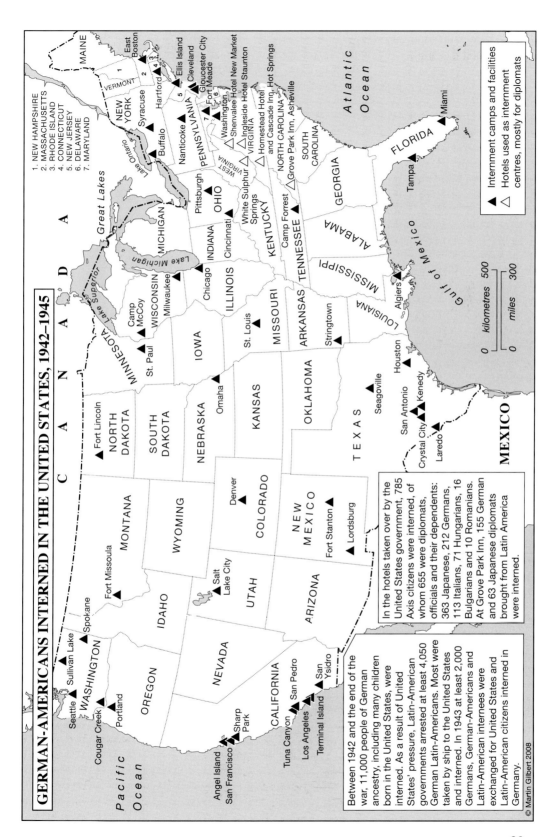

Key:
1. NEW HAMPSHIRE
2. MASSACHUSETTS
3. RHODE ISLAND
4. CONNECTICUT
5. NEW JERSEY
6. DELAWARE
7. MARYLAND

▲ Internment camps and facilities

△ Hotels used as internment centres, mostly for diplomats

In the hotels taken over by the United States government, 785 Axis citizens were interned, of whom 655 were diplomats, officials and their dependents: 363 Japanese, 212 Germans, 113 Italians, 71 Hungarians, 16 Bulgarians and 10 Romanians. At Grove Park Inn, 155 German and 63 Japanese diplomats brought from Latin America were interned.

Between 1942 and the end of the war, 11,000 people of German ancestry, including many children born in the United States, were interned. As a result of United States' pressure, Latin-American governments arrested at least 4,050 German Latin-Americans. Most were taken by ship to the United States and interned. In 1943 at least 2,000 Germans, German-Americans and Latin-American internees were exchanged for United States and Latin-American citizens interned in Germany.

© Martin Gilbert 2008

96

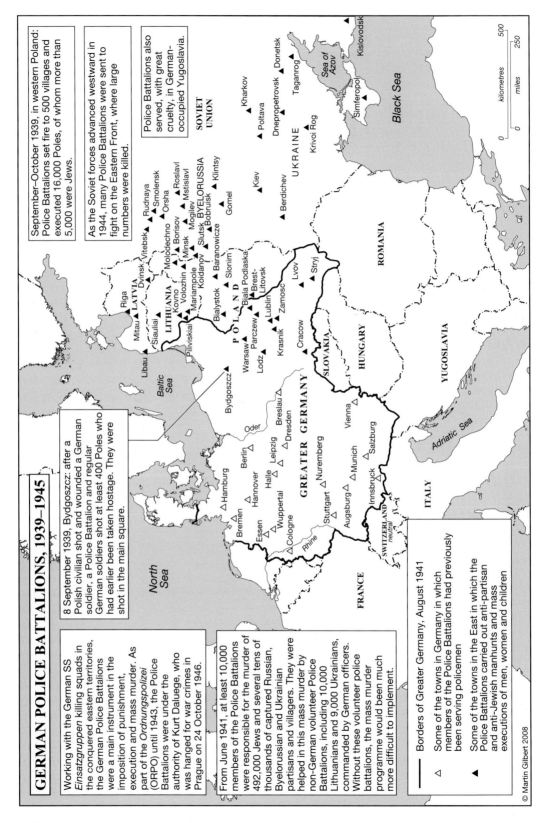

GERMAN POLICE BATTALIONS, 1939–1945

Working with the German SS *Einsatzgruppen* killing squads in the conquered eastern territories, the German Police Battalions were a main instrument in the imposition of punishment, execution and mass murder. As part of the *Ordnungspolizei* (ORPO) until 1943, the Police Battalions were under the authority of Kurt Daluege, who was hanged for war crimes in Prague on 24 October 1946.

From June 1941, at least 10,000 members of the Police Battalions were responsible for the murder of 492,000 Jews and several tens of thousands of captured Russian, Byelorussian and Ukrainian partisans and villagers. They were helped in this mass murder by non-German volunteer Police Battalions, including 10,000 Lithuanians and 9,000 Ukrainians, commanded by German officers. Without these volunteer police battalions, the mass murder programme would been much more difficult to implement.

8 September 1939, Bydgoszcz: after a Polish civilian shot and wounded a German soldier, a Police Battalion and regular German soldiers shot at least 400 Poles who had earlier been taken hostage. They were shot in the main square.

September–October 1939, in western Poland: Police Battalions set fire to 500 villages and executed 16,000 Poles, of whom more than 5,000 were Jews.

As the Soviet forces advanced westward in 1944, many Police Battalions were sent to fight on the Eastern Front, where large numbers were killed.

Police Battalions also served, with great cruelty, in German-occupied Yugoslavia.

Borders of Greater Germany, August 1941

△ Some of the towns in Germany in which members of the Police Battalions had previously been serving policemen

▲ Some of the towns in the East in which the Police Battalions carried out anti-partisan and anti-Jewish manhunts and mass executions of men, women and children

© Martin Gilbert 2008

SOVIET UNION

UKRAINE

ROMANIA

HUNGARY

SLOVAKIA

POLAND

LITHUANIA

LATVIA

BYELORUSSIA

GREATER GERMANY

FRANCE

ITALY

YUGOSLAVIA

SWITZERLAND neutral

North Sea

Baltic Sea

Black Sea

Sea of Azov

Adriatic Sea

Rhine

Oder

Kislovodsk
Simferopol
Taganrog
Donetsk
Dnepropetrovsk
Kharkov
Poltava
Krivoi Rog
Kiev
Berdichev
Lvov
Stryi
Klintsy
Gomel
Roslavl
Mstislavl
Mogilev
Slutsk
Bobruisk
Smolensk
Orsha
Rudnaya
Borisov
Minsk
Volozhin
Koidanov
Mariampole
Baranowicze
Slonim
Molodechno
Vitebsk
Dvinsk
Riga
Mitau
Siauliai
Libau
Pilliviskiai
Kovno
Bialystok
Biala Podlaska
Brest-Litovsk
Parczew
Lublin
Zamosc
Krasnik
Cracow
Warsaw
Lodz
Bydgoszcz
Breslau
Dresden
Leipzig
Halle
Berlin
Hannover
Bremen
Hamburg
Essen
Wuppertal
Cologne
Stuttgart
Augsburg
Munich
Nuremberg
Vienna
Salzburg
Innsbruck

0   250   500 miles
0   500 kilometres

97

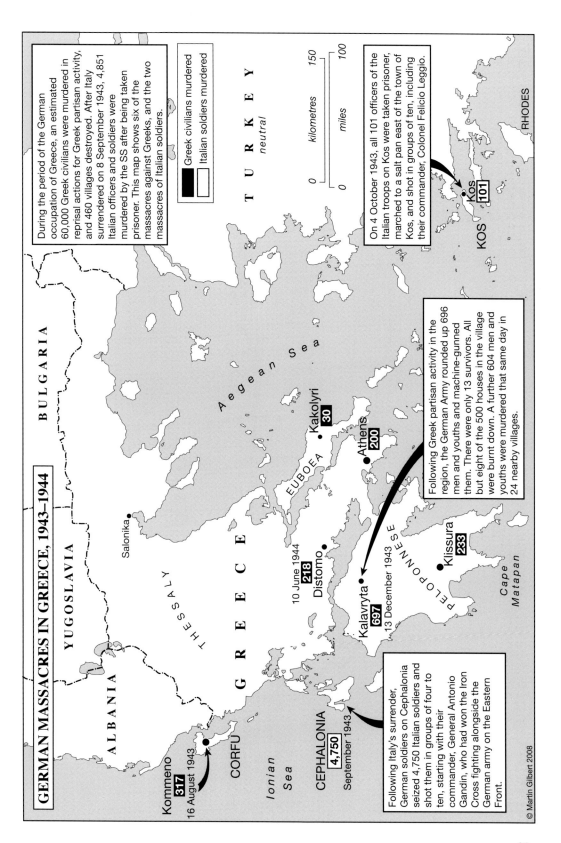

GERMAN MASSACRES IN GREECE, 1943–1944

During the period of the German occupation of Greece, an estimated 60,000 Greek civilians were murdered in reprisal actions for Greek partisan activity, and 460 villages destroyed. After Italy surrendered on 8 September 1943, 4,851 Italian officers and soldiers were murdered by the SS after being taken prisoner. This map shows six of the massacres against Greeks, and the two massacres of Italian soldiers.

Greek civilians murdered
Italian soldiers murdered

0   kilometres   150
0   miles   100

On 4 October 1943, all 101 officers of the Italian troops on Kos were taken prisoner, marched to a salt pan east of the town of Kos, and shot in groups of ten, including their commander, Colonel Felicio Leggio.

T U R K E Y
neutral

KOS
Kos **101**

RHODES

B U L G A R I A

YUGOSLAVIA

A L B A N I A

THESSALY

G R E E C E

Salonika•

Aegean Sea

EUBOEA

Kakolyri **30**

Athens **200**

Distomo• **218**
10 June 1944

Kalavryta• **697**
13 December 1943

PELOPONNESE

Klissura **233**

Cape Matapan

Following Greek partisan activity in the region, the German Army rounded up 696 men and youths and machine-gunned them. There were only 13 survivors. All but eight of the 500 houses in the village were burnt down. A further 604 men and youths were murdered that same day in 24 nearby villages.

Kommeno **317**
16 August 1943

CORFU

Ionian Sea

CEPHALONIA
4,750
September 1943

Following Italy's surrender, German soldiers on Cephalonia seized 4,750 Italian soldiers and shot them in groups of four to ten, starting with their commander, General Antonio Gandin, who had won the Iron Cross fighting alongside the German army on the Eastern Front.

© Martin Gilbert 2008

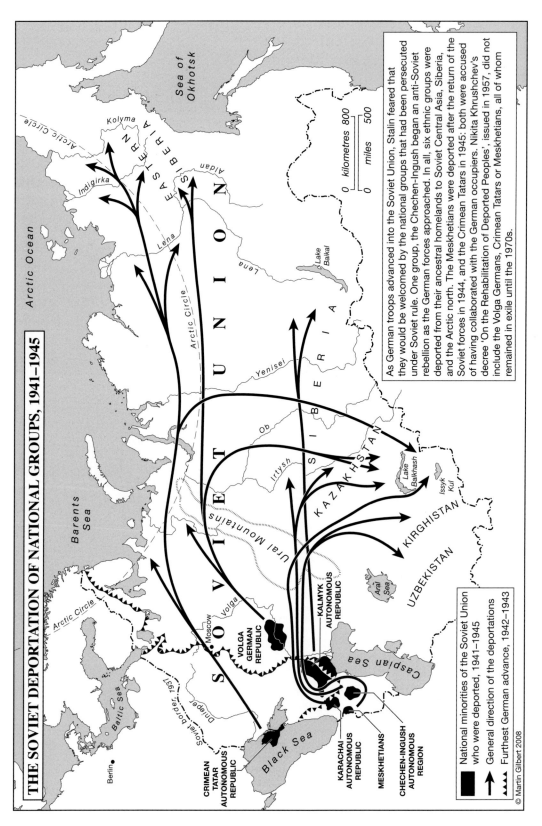

THE SOVIET DEPORTATION OF NATIONAL GROUPS, 1941–1945

As German troops advanced into the Soviet Union, Stalin feared that they would be welcomed by the national groups that had been persecuted under Soviet rule. One group, the Chechen-Ingush began an anti-Soviet rebellion as the German forces approached. In all, six ethnic groups were deported from their ancestral homelands to Soviet Central Asia, Siberia, and the Arctic north. The Meskhetians were deported after the return of the Soviet forces in 1944, and the Crimean Tatars in 1945: both were accused of having collaborated with the German occupiers. Nikita Khrushchev's decree 'On the Rehabilitation of Deported Peoples', issued in 1957, did not include the Volga Germans, Crimean Tatars or Meskhetians, all of whom remained in exile until the 1970s.

National minorities of the Soviet Union who were deported, 1941–1945

General direction of the deportations

Furthest German advance, 1942–1943

Sea of Okhotsk

Arctic Ocean

Barents Sea

EASTERN SIBERIA

SIBERIA

SOVIET UNION

KAZAKHSTAN

KIRGHISTAN

UZBEKISTAN

Black Sea

Caspian Sea

Baltic Sea

Aral Sea

Lake Baikal

Lake Balkhash

Issyk Kul

Kolyma

Indigirka

Lena

Aldan

Arctic Circle

Yenisei

Ob

Irtysh

Ural Mountains

Volga

Dnieper

Moscow

Berlin

VOLGA GERMAN REPUBLIC

KALMYK AUTONOMOUS REPUBLIC

CRIMEAN TATAR AUTONOMOUS REPUBLIC

MESKHETIANS

KARACHAI AUTONOMOUS REPUBLIC

CHECHEN-INGUSH AUTONOMOUS REGION

Soviet border, 1937

0 kilometres 800

0 miles 500

© Martin Gilbert 2008

99

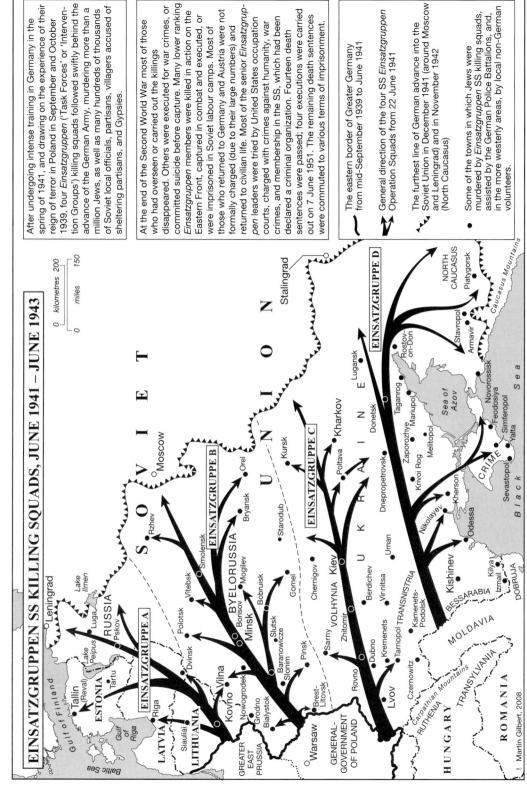

EINSATZGRUPPEN SS KILLING SQUADS, JUNE 1941 – JUNE 1943

After undergoing intense training in Germany in the spring of 1941, and drawing on the experience of their reign of terror in Poland in September and October 1939, four *Einsatzgruppen* ('Task Forces' or 'Intervention Groups') killing squads followed swiftly behind the advance of the German Army, murdering more than a million Jews, as well as many hundreds of thousands of Soviet local officials, partisans, villagers accused of sheltering partisans, and Gypsies.

At the end of the Second World War most of those who had overseen or carried out the killings disappeared. Others were executed for war crimes, or committed suicide before capture. Many lower ranking *Einsatzgruppen* members were killed in action on the Eastern Front, captured in combat and executed, or were imprisoned in Soviet labour camps. Most of those who returned to Germany and Austria were not formally charged (due to their large numbers) and returned to civilian life. Most of the senior *Einsatzgruppen* leaders were tried by United States occupation courts, charged with crimes against humanity, war crimes, and membership in the SS, which had been declared a criminal organization. Fourteen death sentences were passed; four executions were carried out on 7 June 1951. The remaining death sentences were commuted to various terms of imprisonment.

⌐⌐⌐ The eastern border of Greater Germany from mid-September 1939 and October 1941

The general direction of the four SS *Einsatzgruppen* Operation Squads from 22 June 1941

The furthest line of German advance into the Soviet Union in December 1941 (around Moscow and Leningrad) and in November 1942 (North Caucasus)

• Some of the towns in which Jews were murdered by *Einsatzgruppen* SS killing squads, assisted by the German Police Battalions, and, in the more westerly areas, by local non-German volunteers.

! Martin Gilbert, 2008

100

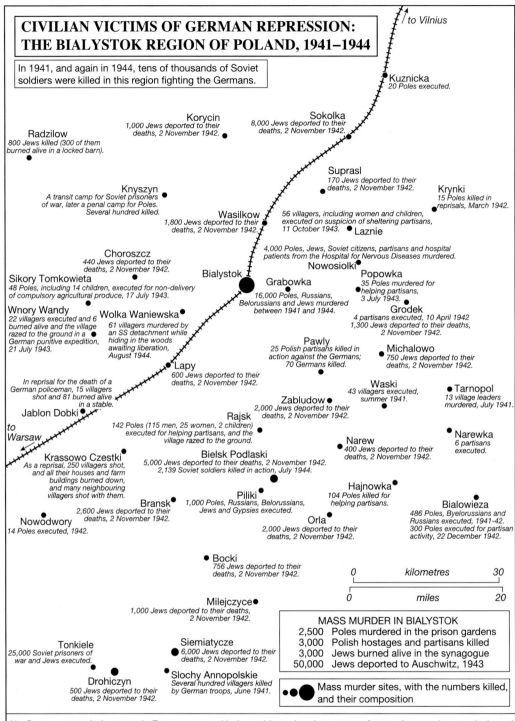

CIVILIAN VICTIMS OF GERMAN REPRESSION:
THE BIALYSTOK REGION OF POLAND, 1941–1944

to Vilnius

In 1941, and again in 1944, tens of thousands of Soviet soldiers were killed in this region fighting the Germans.

Kuznicka
20 Poles executed.

Korycin
1,000 Jews deported to their deaths, 2 November 1942.

Sokolka
8,000 Jews deported to their deaths, 2 November 1942.

Radzilow
800 Jews killed (300 of them burned alive in a locked barn).

Suprasl
170 Jews deported to their deaths, 2 November 1942.

Krynki
15 Poles killed in reprisals, March 1942.

Knyszyn
A transit camp for Soviet prisoners of war, later a penal camp for Poles. Several hundred killed.

Wasilkow
1,800 Jews deported to their deaths, 2 November 1942.

56 villagers, including women and children, executed on suspicion of sheltering partisans, 11 October 1943. **Laznie**

Choroszcz
440 Jews deported to their deaths, 2 November 1942.

4,000 Poles, Jews, Soviet citizens, partisans and hospital patients from the Hospital for Nervous Diseases murdered.
Nowosiolki

Bialystok

Sikory Tomkowieta
48 Poles, including 14 children, executed for non-delivery of compulsory agricultural produce, 17 July 1943.

Grabowka
16,000 Poles, Russians, Belorussians and Jews murdered between 1941 and 1944.

Popowka
35 Poles murdered for helping partisans, 3 July 1943.

Wnory Wandy
22 villagers executed and 6 burned alive and the village razed to the ground in a German punitive expedition, 21 July 1943.

Wolka Waniewska
61 villagers murdered by an SS detachment while hiding in the woods awaiting liberation, August 1944.

Grodek
*4 partisans executed, 10 April 1942
1,300 Jews deported to their deaths, 2 November 1942.*

Pawly
25 Polish partisans killed in action against the Germans; 70 Germans killed.

Michalowo
750 Jews deported to their deaths, 2 November 1942.

Lapy
600 Jews deported to their deaths, 2 November 1942.

Waski
43 villagers executed, summer 1941.

Tarnopol
13 village leaders murdered, July 1941.

In reprisal for the death of a German policeman, 15 villagers shot and 81 burned alive in a stable.

Zabludow
2,000 Jews deported to their deaths, 2 November 1942.

Jablon Dobki

Rajsk
142 Poles (115 men, 25 women, 2 children) executed for helping partisans, and the village razed to the ground.

Narew
400 Jews deported to their deaths, 2 November 1942.

Narewka
6 partisans executed.

to Warsaw

Krassowo Czestki
As a reprisal, 250 villagers shot, and all their houses and farm buildings burned down, and many neighbouring villagers shot with them.

Bielsk Podlaski
*5,000 Jews deported to their deaths, 2 November 1942.
2,139 Soviet soldiers killed in action, July 1944.*

Hajnowka
104 Poles killed for helping partisans.

Piliki
1,000 Poles, Russians, Belorussians, Jews and Gypsies executed.

Bransk
2,600 Jews deported to their deaths, 2 November 1942.

Orla
2,000 Jews deported to their deaths, 2 November 1942.

Bialowieza
486 Jews, Byelorussians and Russians executed, 1941-42. 300 Poles executed for partisan activity, 22 December 1942.

Nowodwory
14 Poles executed, 1942.

Bocki
756 Jews deported to their deaths, 2 November 1942.

| 0 | kilometres | 30 |

| 0 | miles | 20 |

Milejczyce
1,000 Jews deported to their deaths, 2 November 1942.

MASS MURDER IN BIALYSTOK

2,500	Poles murdered in the prison gardens
3,000	Polish hostages and partisans killed
3,000	Jews burned alive in the synagogue
50,000	Jews deported to Auschwitz, 1943

Tonkiele
25,000 Soviet prisoners of war and Jews executed.

Siemiatycze
6,000 Jews deported to their deaths, 2 November 1942.

Drohiczyn
500 Jews deported to their deaths, 2 November 1942.

Slochy Annopolskie
Several hundred villagers killed by German troops, June 1941.

● ● **●** Mass murder sites, with the numbers killed, and their composition

No German-occupied country in Europe escaped being subjected to the severest forms of repression, reprisals and mass executions. Greece, Yugoslavia, western Russia and Poland were the most harshly treated; the reprisals intensified as partisan groups challenged the occupation forces. This map takes a small region in Poland - in and around the city of Bialystok - to give a picture in microcosm of the nature and scale of the terror in 42 towns and villages in a mainly agricultural area: killings directed against local Poles, Belorussians, Jews, Gypsies, and Soviet prisoners of war.

© Martin Gilbert 2008

GREEK VILLAGES DESTROYED IN GERMAN REPRISALS, JUNE – DECEMBER 1943: THE TRIKALA REGION OF GREECE

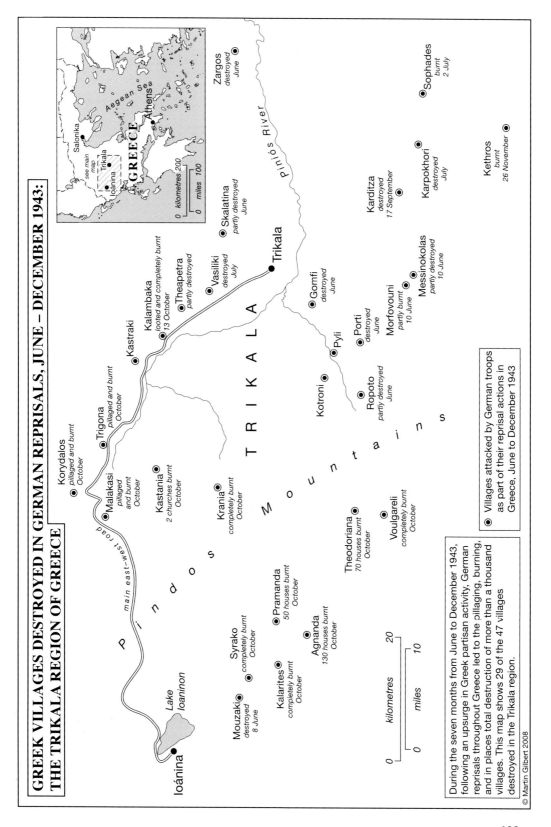

Zargos
destroyed June

Sophades
burnt 2 July

Aegean Sea

Salonika

Athens

GREECE

Trikala

Ioánina

see main map

Piniós River

Kethros
burnt 26 November

Karpokhori
destroyed July

Karditza
destroyed 17 September

Skalatina
partly destroyed June

Messinokolas
partly destroyed July

Kalambaka
looted and completely burnt 13 October

Theapetra
partly destroyed

Vasiliki
destroyed July

Trikala

Gomfi
destroyed June

Morfovouni
partly burnt 10 June

Kastraki

Korydalos
pillaged and burnt October

Trigona
pillaged and burnt October

Malakasi
pillaged and burnt October

Kastania
2 churches burnt October

Krania
completely burnt October

Porti
destroyed June

Pyli

Kotroni

Ropoto
partly destroyed June

T R I K A L A

P i n d o s   M o u n t a i n s

Theodoriana
70 houses burnt October

Voulgareli
completely burnt October

main east-west road

Lake Ioaninon

Mouzaki
destroyed 8 June

Syrako
completely burnt October

Kalarites
completely burnt October

Pramanda
50 houses burnt October

Agnanda
130 houses burnt October

Ioánina

0   10   20 kilometres

0   10 miles

⦿ Villages attacked by German troops as part of their reprisal actions in Greece, June to December 1943

During the seven months from June to December 1943, following an upsurge in Greek partisan activity, German reprisals throughout Greece led to the pillaging, burning, and in places total destruction of more than a thousand villages. This map shows 29 of the 47 villages destroyed in the Trikala region.

0   kilometres   200
0   miles   100

© Martin Gilbert 2008

102

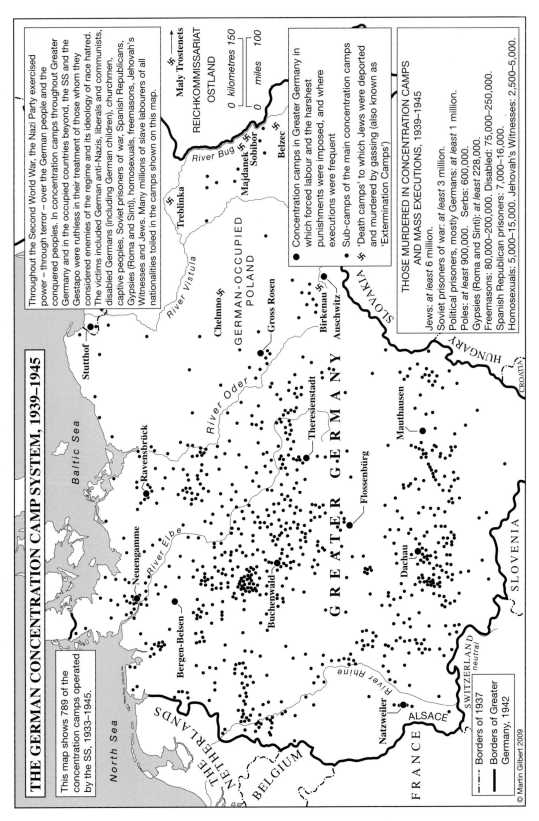

THE GERMAN CONCENTRATION CAMP SYSTEM, 1939–1945

This map shows 789 of the concentration camps operated by the SS, 1933–1945.

Throughout the Second World War, the Nazi Party exercised power – through terror – over the German people and the conquered peoples. In concentration camps throughout Greater Germany and in the occupied countries beyond, the SS and the Gestapo were ruthless in their treatment of those whom they considered enemies of the regime and its ideology of race hatred. The victims included German anti-Nazis, liberals and communists, disabled Germans (including German children), churchmen, captive peoples, Soviet prisoners of war, Spanish Republicans, Gypsies (Roma and Sinti), homosexuals, freemasons, Jehovah's Witnesses and Jews. Many millions of slave labourers of all nationalities toiled in the camps shown on this map.

● Concentration camps in Greater Germany in which forced labour and the harshest punishments were imposed, and where executions were frequent

· Sub-camps of the main concentration camps

卍 'Death camps' to which Jews were deported and murdered by gassing (also known as 'Extermination Camps')

0 kilometres 150
0 miles 100

THOSE MURDERED IN CONCENTRATION CAMPS AND MASS EXECUTIONS, 1939–1945

Jews: *at least* 6 million.
Soviet prisoners of war: *at least* 3 million.
Political prisoners, mostly Germans: *at least* 1 million.
Poles: *at least* 900,000.   Serbs: 600,000.
Gypsies (Roma and Sinti): *at least* 228,000.
Freemasons: 80,000–200,000. Disabled: 75,000–250,000.
Spanish Republican prisoners: 7,000–16,000.
Homosexuals: 5,000–15,000. Jehovah's Witnesses: 2,500–5,000.

REICHKOMMISSARIAT OSTLAND

Maly Trostenets

Treblinka

Majdanek Sobibor

Belzec

River Bug

River Vistula

Chelmno

GERMAN-OCCUPIED POLAND

Gross Rosen

Birkenau
Auschwitz

SLOVAKIA

HUNGARY

CROATIA

Stutthof

Baltic Sea

Ravensbrück

River Oder

Theresienstadt

Mauthausen

GREATER GERMANY

Neuengamme

River Elbe

Flossenbürg

Dachau

Bergen-Belsen

Buchenwald

North Sea

SLOVENIA

THE NETHERLANDS

BELGIUM

River Rhine

SWITZERLAND *neutral*

Natzweiler ALSACE

FRANCE

-·-·- Borders of 1937

—— Borders of Greater Germany, 1942

© Martin Gilbert 2009

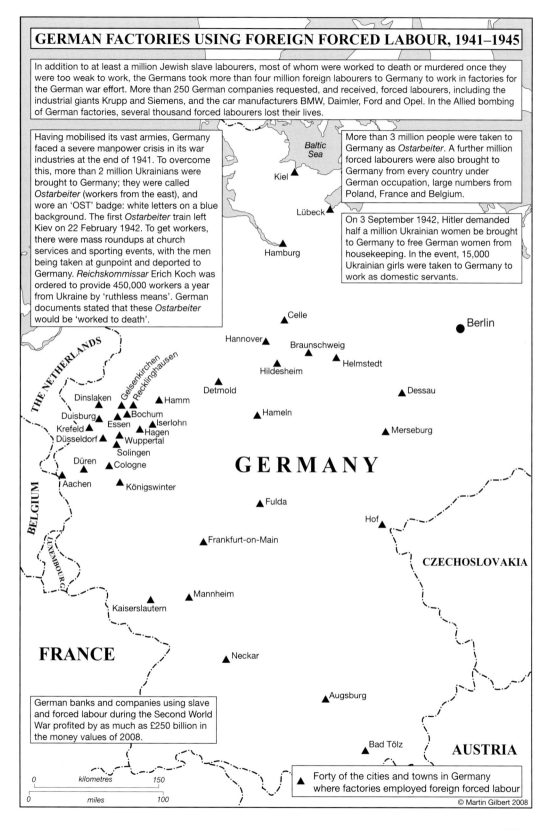

GERMAN FACTORIES USING FOREIGN FORCED LABOUR, 1941–1945

In addition to at least a million Jewish slave labourers, most of whom were worked to death or murdered once they were too weak to work, the Germans took more than four million foreign labourers to Germany to work in factories for the German war effort. More than 250 German companies requested, and received, forced labourers, including the industrial giants Krupp and Siemens, and the car manufacturers BMW, Daimler, Ford and Opel. In the Allied bombing of German factories, several thousand forced labourers lost their lives.

Having mobilised its vast armies, Germany faced a severe manpower crisis in its war industries at the end of 1941. To overcome this, more than 2 million Ukrainians were brought to Germany; they were called *Ostarbeiter* (workers from the east), and wore an 'OST' badge: white letters on a blue background. The first *Ostarbeiter* train left Kiev on 22 February 1942. To get workers, there were mass roundups at church services and sporting events, with the men being taken at gunpoint and deported to Germany. *Reichskommissar* Erich Koch was ordered to provide 450,000 workers a year from Ukraine by 'ruthless means'. German documents stated that these *Ostarbeiter* would be 'worked to death'.

More than 3 million people were taken to Germany as *Ostarbeiter*. A further million forced labourers were also brought to Germany from every country under German occupation, large numbers from Poland, France and Belgium.

On 3 September 1942, Hitler demanded half a million Ukrainian women be brought to Germany to free German women from housekeeping. In the event, 15,000 Ukrainian girls were taken to Germany to work as domestic servants.

Baltic Sea

Kiel
Lübeck
Hamburg

THE NETHERLANDS

Celle
Hannover
Braunschweig
Helmstedt
Hildesheim
Detmold
Dessau
Dinslaken
Gelsenkirchen
Recklinghausen
Hamm
Duisburg
Bochum
Essen
Iserlohn
Krefeld
Hagen
Düsseldorf
Wuppertal
Solingen
Düren
Cologne
Aachen
Königswinter

Berlin

Hameln
Merseburg

GERMANY

Fulda
Hof

Frankfurt-on-Main

CZECHOSLOVAKIA

BELGIUM
LUXEMBOURG

Mannheim
Kaiserslautern

FRANCE

Neckar

Augsburg

German banks and companies using slave and forced labour during the Second World War profited by as much as £250 billion in the money values of 2008.

Bad Tölz
AUSTRIA

▲ Forty of the cities and towns in Germany where factories employed foreign forced labour

0   kilometres   150
0   miles   100

© Martin Gilbert 2008

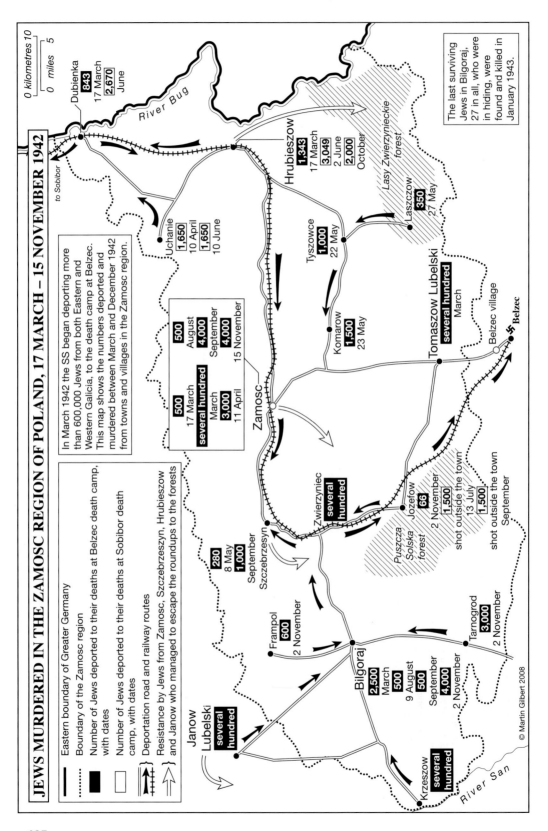

JEWS MURDERED IN THE ZAMOSC REGION OF POLAND, 17 MARCH – 15 NOVEMBER 1942

In March 1942 the SS began deporting more than 600,000 Jews from both Eastern and Western Galicia, to the death camp at Belzec. This map shows the numbers deported and murdered between March and December 1942 from towns and villages in the Zamosc region.

Eastern boundary of Greater Germany

Boundary of the Zamosc region

Number of Jews deported to their deaths at Belzec death camp, with dates

Number of Jews deported to their deaths at Sobibor death camp, with dates

Deportation road and railway routes

Resistance by Jews from Zamosc, Szczebrzeszyn, Hrubieszow and Janow who managed to escape the roundups to the forests

The last surviving Jews in Bilgoraj, 27 in all, who were in hiding, were found and killed in January 1943.

Dubienka
843 17 March
2,670 June

River Bug

to Sobibor

Uchanie
1,650 10 April
1,650 10 June

Hrubieszow
1,343 17 March
3,049 2 June
2,000 October

Lasy Zwierzynieckie forest

Laszczow
350 27 May

Tyszowce
1,000 22 May

Komarow
1,500 23 May

Zamosc
500 17 March
several hundred March
3,000 11 April
500 August
4,000 September
4,000 15 November

Tomaszow Lubelski
several hundred March

Belzec village

Belzec

Szczebrzeszyn
280 8 May
1,000 September

Zwierzyniec
several hundred

Jozefow
66 2 November
1,500 shot outside the town 13 July
1,500 shot outside the town September

Puszcza Solska forest

Frampol
600 2 November

Bilgoraj
2,500 March
500 9 August
500 September
4,000 2 November

Tarnogrod
3,000 2 November

Janow Lubelski
several hundred

Krzeszow
several hundred

River San

© Martin Gilbert 2008

0 kilometres 10
0 miles 5

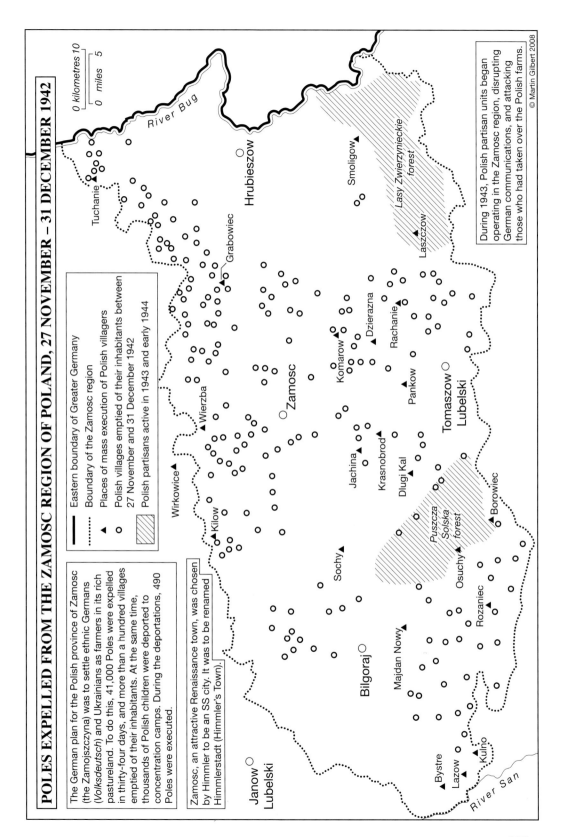

POLES EXPELLED FROM THE ZAMOSC REGION OF POLAND, 27 NOVEMBER – 31 DECEMBER 1942

The German plan for the Polish province of Zamosc (the Zamojszczyna) was to settle ethnic Germans (*Volksdeutsch*) and Ukrainians as farmers in its rich pastureland. To do this, 41,000 Poles were expelled in thirty-four days, and more than a hundred villages emptied of their inhabitants. At the same time, thousands of Polish children were deported to concentration camps. During the deportations, 490 Poles were executed.

Zamosc, an attractive Renaissance town, was chosen by Himmler to be an SS city. It was to be renamed Himmlerstadt (Himmler's Town).

	Eastern boundary of Greater Germany
	Boundary of the Zamosc region
▲	Places of mass execution of Polish villagers
○	Polish villages emptied of their inhabitants between 27 November and 31 December 1942
▨	Polish partisans active in 1943 and early 1944

During 1943, Polish partisan units began operating in the Zamosc region, disrupting German communications, and attacking those who had taken over the Polish farms.

0 kilometres 10
0 miles 5

River Bug

Tuchanie ▲

Hrubieszow ○

Smoligow ▲

Lasy Zwierzynieckie forest

Laszczow ▲

Grabowiec ▲

Komarow ▲

Dzierazna ▲

Rachanie ▲

Pankow

Wierzba ▲

○ Zamosc

Tomaszow ○ Lubelski

Wirkowice ▲

Jachina ▲

Krasnobrod ▲

Dlugi Kal ▲

Kilow ▲

Borowiec

Puszcza Solska forest

Osuchy ▲

Rozaniec ▲

Sochy ▲

Janow ○ Lubelski

Bilgoraj ○

Majdan Nowy ▲

Bystre ▲

Lazow ▲

Kulno ▲

River San

© Martin Gilbert 2008

106

RAILWAY DEPORTATION ROUTES OF JEWS TO AUSCHWITZ, 1942–1944

Between the summer of 1942 and late 1944 more than one million Jews were deported by train to Auschwitz and murdered there. This map shows the main railway deportation routes and some of the cities and towns from which Jews were deported to their deaths.

A German refugee from Frankfurt-on-Main, Anne Frank, was hidden in Amsterdam until she and those hidden with her were betrayed. Deported to Auschwitz in August 1944, she died in Belsen in March 1945, a month before Belsen was liberated.

Atlantic Ocean

NORWAY

SWEDEN neutral

FINLAND

Helsinki

Bergen

Oslo

Narva

line of furthest German advance 1942

Lake Peipus

North Sea

Baltic Sea

Kovno

Vilna

Grodno

Wolkowysk

Bialystok

Pruzana

BRITAIN

Hamburg

Sachsenhausen

Plonsk

Westerbork

Berlin

Amsterdam

Belsen

Lodz

Radom

Lublin

Vught

Leipzig

Breslau

English Channel

Malines

Lille

Brussels

Buchenwald

Theresienstadt

Cracow

Auschwitz

Luxembourg

Rouen

Frankfurt-on-Main

Vienna

Munkacs

Kosice

Beregszasz

Caen

Nancy

Eger

Debrecen

Marmarossziget

Angers

Paris

Orléans

Munich

Salzburg

Budapest

Mako

Szeged

Beszterce

Szaszregen

Cluj

Sepiszentgyorgy

Nantes

Tours

Dijon

SWITZERLAND neutral

Brenner Pass

Merano

Padua

Trieste

Zagreb

Bonyhad

Pecs

Black Sea

Lyon

Milan

Turin

Fossoli

Bordeaux

Genoa

Florence

Adriatic Sea

TURKEY neutral

Toulouse

Avignon

Pisa

Gurs

Rivesaltes

Marseille

Veles

Pyrenees

Florina

Salonika

SPAIN neutral

Rome

Kastoria

Larissa

Aegean Sea

CORFU

Arta

Athens

KOS

Patras

RHODES

Ionian Sea

Mediterranean Sea

0   kilometres   400

0   miles   250

© Martin Gilbert 2008

107

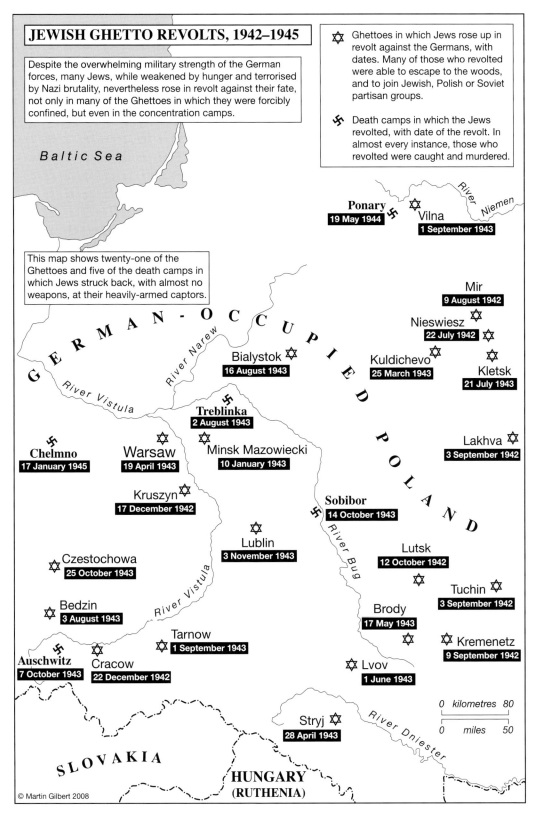

JEWISH GHETTO REVOLTS, 1942–1945

Despite the overwhelming military strength of the German forces, many Jews, while weakened by hunger and terrorised by Nazi brutality, nevertheless rose in revolt against their fate, not only in many of the Ghettoes in which they were forcibly confined, but even in the concentration camps.

✡ Ghettoes in which Jews rose up in revolt against the Germans, with dates. Many of those who revolted were able to escape to the woods, and to join Jewish, Polish or Soviet partisan groups.

卐 Death camps in which the Jews revolted, with date of the revolt. In almost every instance, those who revolted were caught and murdered.

Baltic Sea

This map shows twenty-one of the Ghettoes and five of the death camps in which Jews struck back, with almost no weapons, at their heavily-armed captors.

Ponary 卐
19 May 1944

Vilna ✡
1 September 1943

River Niemen

G E R M A N - O C C U P I E D   P O L A N D

River Narew

River Vistula

Mir ✡
9 August 1942

Nieswiesz ✡
22 July 1942

Bialystok ✡
16 August 1943

Kuldichevo ✡
25 March 1943

Kletsk ✡
21 July 1943

Treblinka 卐
2 August 1943

Chelmno 卐
17 January 1945

Warsaw ✡
19 April 1943

Minsk Mazowiecki ✡
10 January 1943

Lakhva ✡
3 September 1942

Kruszyn ✡
17 December 1942

Sobibor 卐
14 October 1943

River Bug

Lublin ✡
3 November 1943

Lutsk ✡
12 October 1942

Czestochowa ✡
25 October 1943

River Vistula

Tuchin ✡
3 September 1942

Bedzin ✡
3 August 1943

Brody ✡
17 May 1943

Tarnow ✡
1 September 1943

Kremenetz ✡
9 September 1942

Auschwitz 卐
7 October 1943

Cracow ✡
22 December 1942

Lvov ✡
1 June 1943

0 kilometres 80

0 miles 50

Stryj ✡
28 April 1943

River Dniester

S L O V A K I A

HUNGARY
(RUTHENIA)

© Martin Gilbert 2008

THE MUFTI OF JERUSALEM AND THE GERMAN WAR EFFORT, 1941–1945

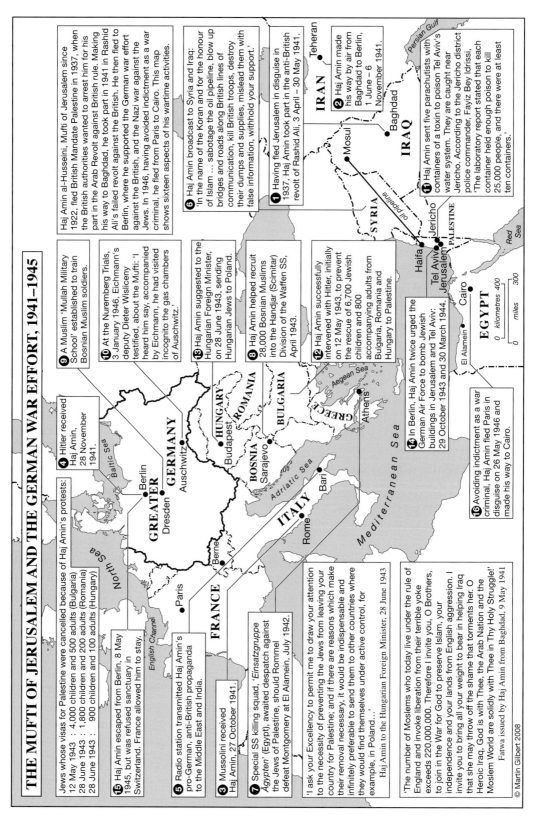

Jews whose visas for Palestine were cancelled because of Haj Amin's protests:
12 May 1943 : 4,000 children and 500 adults (Bulgaria)
28 June 1943 : 1,800 children and 200 adults (Romania)
28 June 1943 : 900 children and 100 adults (Hungary)

9 A Muslim 'Mullah Military School' established to train Bosnian Muslim soldiers.

Haj Amin al-Husseini, Mufti of Jerusalem since 1922, fled British Mandate Palestine in 1937, when the British authorities wanted to arrest him for his part in the Arab Revolt against British rule. Making his way to Baghdad, he took part in 1941 in Rashid Ali's failed revolt against the British. He then fled to Berlin, where he supported the German war effort against the British, and the Nazi war against the Jews. In 1946, having avoided indictment as a war criminal, he fled from Paris to Cairo. This map shows sixteen aspects of his wartime activities.

6 Haj Amin broadcast to Syria and Iraq: 'In the name of the Koran and for the honour of Islam ... sabotage the oil pipeline, blow up bridges and roads along British lines of communication, kill British troops, destroy their dumps and supplies, mislead them with false information, withhold your support.'

1 Having fled Jerusalem in disguise in 1937, Haj Amin took part in the anti-British revolt of Rashid Ali, 3 April – 30 May 1941.

2 Haj Amin made his way by air from Baghdad to Berlin, 1 June – November 1941.

11 Haj Amin sent five parachutists with containers of a toxin to poison Tel Aviv's water system. They are caught near Jericho. According to the Jericho district police commander, Fayiz Bey Idrissi, 'The laboratory report stated that each container held enough poison to kill 25,000 people, and there were at least ten containers.'

4 Hitler received Haj Amin, 28 November 1941.

10 At the Nuremberg Trials, 3 January 1946, Eichmann's deputy Dieter Wisliceny testified, about the Mufti: 'I heard him say, accompanied by Eichmann, he had visited incognito the gas chambers of Auschwitz.'

13 Haj Amin suggested to the Hungarian Foreign Minister, on 28 June 1943, sending Hungarian Jews to Poland.

8 Haj Amin helped recruit 28,000 Bosnian Muslims into the Handjar (Scimitar) Division of the Waffen SS, April 1943.

12 Haj Amin successfully intervened with Hitler, initially on 12 May 1943, to prevent the rescue of 6,700 Jewish children and 800 accompanying adults from Bulgaria, Romania and Hungary to Palestine.

15 Haj Amin escaped from Berlin, 8 May 1945, but was refused sanctuary in Switzerland. France allowed him to stay.

5 Radio station transmitted Haj Amin's pro-German, anti-British propaganda to the Middle East and India.

3 Mussolini received Haj Amin, 27 October 1941.

7 Special SS killing squad, '*Einsatzgruppe Ägypten*' (Egypt), awaited despatch against the Jews of Palestine, should Rommel defeat Montgomery at El Alamein, July 1942.

14 In Berlin, Haj Amin twice urged the German Air Force to bomb Jewish buildings in Jerusalem and Tel Aviv: 29 October 1943 and 30 March 1944.

16 Avoiding indictment as a war criminal, Haj Amin fled Paris in disguise on 26 May 1946 and made his way to Cairo.

'I ask your Excellency to permit me to draw your attention to the necessity of preventing the Jews from leaving your country for Palestine; and if there are reasons which make their removal necessary, it would be indispensable and infinitely preferable to send them to other countries where they would find themselves under active control, for example, in Poland....'

Haj Amin to the Hungarian Foreign Minister, 28 June 1943

'The number of Moslems who today live under the rule of England and invoke liberation from their terrible yoke exceeds 220,000,000. Therefore I invite you, O Brothers, to join in the War for God to preserve Islam, your independence and your lands from English aggression. I invite you to bring all your weight to bear in helping Iraq that she may throw off the shame that torments her. O Heroic Iraq, God is with Thee, the Arab Nation and the Moslem World are solidly with Thee in Thy Holy Struggle!'

Fatwa issued by Haj Amin from Baghdad, 9 May 1941

IRAN • Teheran

IRAQ • Baghdad • Mosul

oil pipeline

SYRIA

Jericho • PALESTINE

Haifa • Tel Aviv • Jerusalem

Red Sea

Persian Gulf

Cairo • EGYPT • El Alamein

0 kilometres 400
0 miles 300

North Sea

Baltic Sea

Berlin • GREATER GERMANY • Dresden • Auschwitz

HUNGARY • Budapest

ROMANIA

BOSNIA • Sarajevo

BULGARIA

GREECE • Athens

Aegean Sea

English Channel

Paris • FRANCE

Berne • ITALY • Rome • Bari

Adriatic Sea

Mediterranean Sea

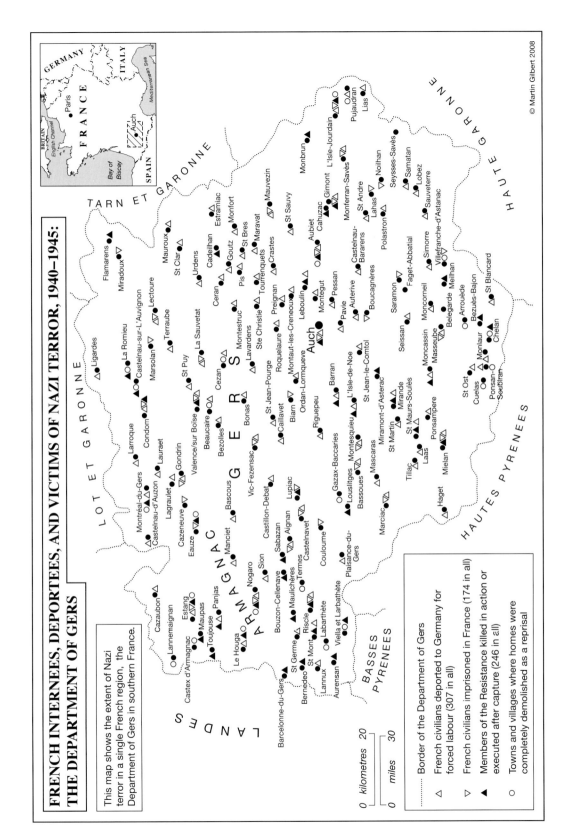

FRENCH INTERNEES, DEPORTEES, AND VICTIMS OF NAZI TERROR, 1940–1945: THE DEPARTMENT OF GERS

This map shows the extent of Nazi terror in a single French region, the Department of Gers in southern France.

© Martin Gilbert 2008

GERMANY
ITALY
FRANCE
Paris
Auch
SPAIN
BRITAIN
English Channel
Bay of Biscay
Mediterranean Sea

TARN ET GARONNE
LOT ET GARONNE
HAUTE GARONNE
HAUTES PYRENEES
BASSES PYRENEES
LANDES

G E R S
A R M A G N A C

Auch

0 kilometres 20
0 miles 30

.... Border of the Department of Gers

△ French civilians deported to Germany for forced labour (307 in all)

▽ French civilians imprisoned in France (174 in all)

▲ Members of the Resistance killed in action or executed after capture (246 in all)

○ Towns and villages where homes were completely demolished as a reprisal

110

Section 7

TOTAL WAR

The total war effort has become a matter of the entire German people. No one has any excuse for ignoring its demands.

A storm of applause greeted my call on 30 January for total war. I can therefore assure you that the leadership's measures are in full agreement with the desires of the German people at home and at the front.

The people are willing to bear any burden, even the heaviest, to make any sacrifice, if it leads to the great goal of victory.

DR JOSEF GOEBBELS
Speech in Berlin
18 February 1943

Over a year and a half ago I said this to the Congress: The militarists in Berlin, and Rome and Tokyo started this war, but the massed angered forces of common humanity will finish it.

Today that prophecy is in the process of being fulfilled. The massed, angered forces of common humanity are on the march. They are going forward – on the Russian front, in the vast Pacific area, and into Europe – converging upon their ultimate objectives: Berlin and Tokyo.

I think the first crack in the Axis has come. The criminal, corrupt Fascist regime in Italy is going to pieces. The pirate philosophy of the Fascists and the Nazis cannot stand adversity. The military superiority of the United Nations – on sea and land, and in the air – has been applied in the right place and at the right time.

PRESIDENT FRANKLIN D. ROOSEVELT
White House Radio Broadcast
28 July 1943

THE GERMAN PLAN TO DEFEAT THE SOVIET UNION IN 1942

Despite fierce German efforts, Moscow was not captured in 1941. Hitler planned a more southerly attack for 1942, hoping to capture Stalingrad, drive north along the Volga, and cut off Moscow from the east. This plan failed, as did the plan to capture the oil fields of the Caucasus.

Volga

Gorky

Moscow

Vladimir

Kazan

Smolensk

Ryazan

Tula

Kuibyshev

Bryansk

Orel

S O V I E T   U N I O N

Kursk

Voronezh

Saratov

UKRAINE

Kiev

Kharkov

Don

Volga

Stalingrad

Stalino

Rostov-on-Don

Astrakhan

Taganrog

Sea of Azov

CRIMEA

Sebastopol

Anapa

Armavir

Maikop
oilfields

Caspian Sea

Black Sea

0   kilometres   300
0   miles   200

Sukhumi

Grozny
oilfields

Derbent

Under German control by June 1942

The objectives of the German General Staff

Hitler's First Plan

Hitler's Second Plan

Soviet territory conquered by Germany between June and December 1942. This included the Maikop oilfields, but not the larger oilfields of Baku or Grozny

Batum

Tiflis

T U R K E Y
neutral

Caucasus Mountains

Baku
oilfields

I R A N
under Anglo-Soviet control

© Martin Gilbert 2008

111

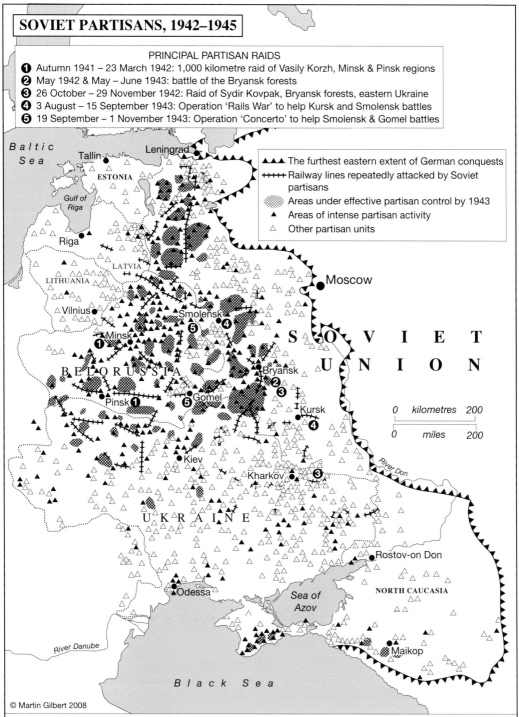

SOVIET PARTISANS, 1942–1945

PRINCIPAL PARTISAN RAIDS
❶ Autumn 1941 – 23 March 1942: 1,000 kilometre raid of Vasily Korzh, Minsk & Pinsk regions
❷ May 1942 & May – June 1943: battle of the Bryansk forests
❸ 26 October – 29 November 1942: Raid of Sydir Kovpak, Bryansk forests, eastern Ukraine
❹ 3 August – 15 September 1943: Operation 'Rails War' to help Kursk and Smolensk battles
❺ 19 September – 1 November 1943: Operation 'Concerto' to help Smolensk & Gomel battles

▲▲▲ The furthest eastern extent of German conquests
╫╫╫╫ Railway lines repeatedly attacked by Soviet partisans
▨ Areas under effective partisan control by 1943
▲ Areas of intense partisan activity
△ Other partisan units

Baltic Sea
Tallin
Leningrad
ESTONIA
Gulf of Riga
Riga
LATVIA
LITHUANIA
Vilnius
Minsk ❶
BELORUSSIA
Pinsk ❶
Smolensk ❹
❺
❺ Gomel
Bryansk ❷❸
Kursk ❹
Kiev
Kharkov ❸
UKRAINE
Odessa
Sea of Azov
Rostov-on Don
NORTH CAUCASIA
Maikop
River Don
River Danube
Black Sea

S O V I E T
U N I O N

Moscow

0   kilometres   200
0   miles   200

© Martin Gilbert 2008

Within a few days of the German attack on the Soviet Union on 22 June 1941, Soviet partisan units were being established behind German lines: 220,000 partisans were active in 1942; 550,000 in 1943, reinforced from Soviet-held territory by parachute drops of men and weapons. Partisan units attacked German road and rail communications, supply dumps, air strips, barracks and army patrols, making many areas impassable and impenetrable to German troops. German reprisals were savage: in Belorusssia 2,200,000 people were murdered, 209 towns (out of 270) largely destroyed, and 9,000 villages raised to the ground.

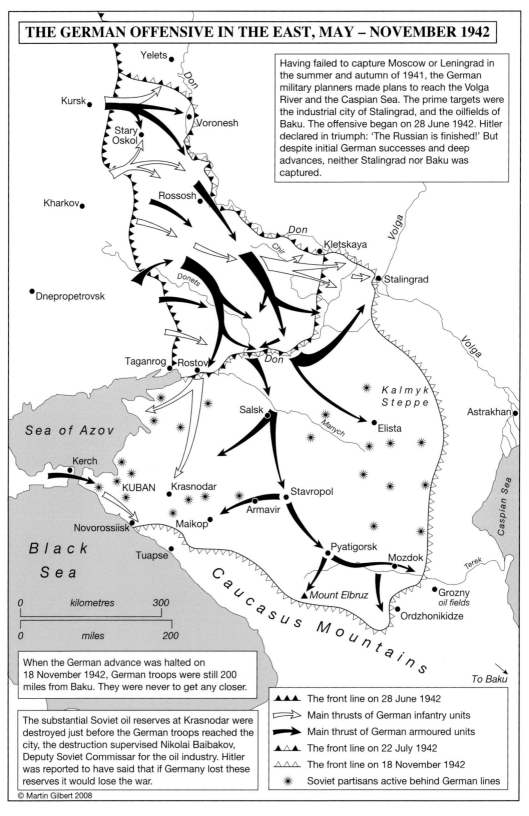

THE GERMAN OFFENSIVE IN THE EAST, MAY – NOVEMBER 1942

Having failed to capture Moscow or Leningrad in the summer and autumn of 1941, the German military planners made plans to reach the Volga River and the Caspian Sea. The prime targets were the industrial city of Stalingrad, and the oilfields of Baku. The offensive began on 28 June 1942. Hitler declared in triumph: 'The Russian is finished!' But despite initial German successes and deep advances, neither Stalingrad nor Baku was captured.

Yelets

Kursk

Voronesh

Stary Oskol

Don

Rossosh

Kharkov

Don

Chir

Kletskaya

Volga

Dnepropetrovsk

Donets

Stalingrad

Taganrog   Rostov

Don

Volga

Kalmyk Steppe

Astrakhan

Salsk

Manych

Elista

Sea of Azov

Kerch

KUBAN   Krasnodar

Stavropol

Armavir

Caspian Sea

Novorossiisk   Maikop

Pyatigorsk

Mozdok

Terek

Black Sea

Tuapse

Caucasus Mountains

| 0 | kilometres | 300 |

| 0 | miles | 200 |

Mount Elbruz

Grozny oil fields

Ordzhonikidze

To Baku

When the German advance was halted on 18 November 1942, German troops were still 200 miles from Baku. They were never to get any closer.

The substantial Soviet oil reserves at Krasnodar were destroyed just before the German troops reached the city, the destruction supervised Nikolai Baibakov, Deputy Soviet Commissar for the oil industry. Hitler was reported to have said that if Germany lost these reserves it would lose the war.

▲▲▲ The front line on 28 June 1942
⇒   Main thrusts of German infantry units
➤   Main thrust of German armoured units
▲▲▲ The front line on 22 July 1942
△△△ The front line on 18 November 1942
✳   Soviet partisans active behind German lines

© Martin Gilbert 2008

113

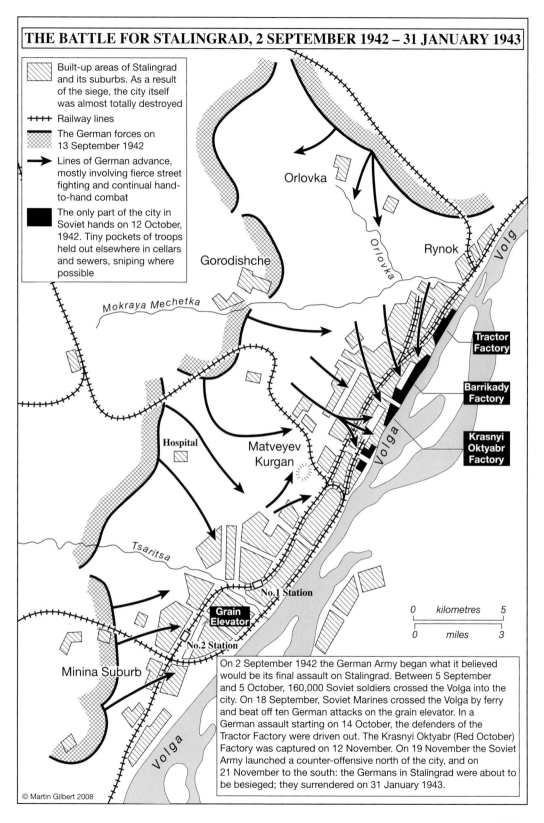

THE BATTLE FOR STALINGRAD, 2 SEPTEMBER 1942 – 31 JANUARY 1943

Built-up areas of Stalingrad and its suburbs. As a result of the siege, the city itself was almost totally destroyed

++++ Railway lines

The German forces on 13 September 1942

Lines of German advance, mostly involving fierce street fighting and continual hand-to-hand combat

The only part of the city in Soviet hands on 12 October, 1942. Tiny pockets of troops held out elsewhere in cellars and sewers, sniping where possible

Orlovka

Orlovka

Rynok

Volga

Gorodishche

Mokraya Mechetka

Tractor Factory

Barrikady Factory

Krasnyi Oktyabr Factory

Hospital

Matveyev Kurgan

Volga

Tsaritsa

No.1 Station

0 kilometres 5

0 miles 3

Grain Elevator

No.2 Station

Minina Suburb

Volga

© Martin Gilbert 2008

On 2 September 1942 the German Army began what it believed would be its final assault on Stalingrad. Between 5 September and 5 October, 160,000 Soviet soldiers crossed the Volga into the city. On 18 September, Soviet Marines crossed the Volga by ferry and beat off ten German attacks on the grain elevator. In a German assault starting on 14 October, the defenders of the Tractor Factory were driven out. The Krasnyi Oktyabr (Red October) Factory was captured on 12 November. On 19 November the Soviet Army launched a counter-offensive north of the city, and on 21 November to the south: the Germans in Stalingrad were about to be besieged; they surrendered on 31 January 1943.

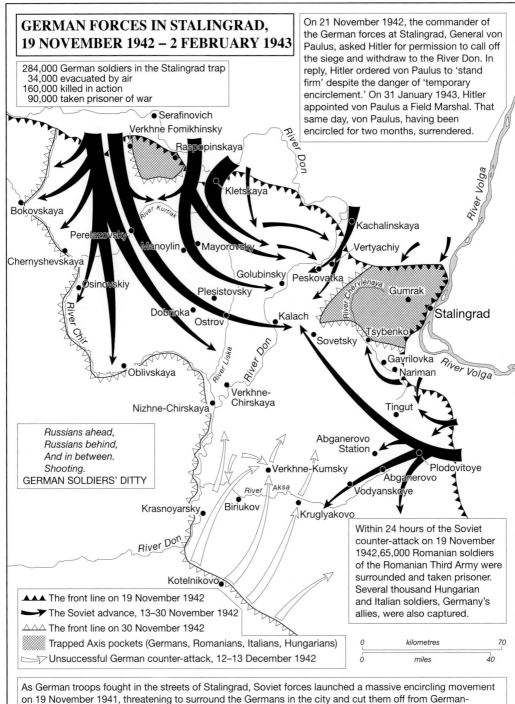

GERMAN FORCES IN STALINGRAD, 19 NOVEMBER 1942 – 2 FEBRUARY 1943

284,000 German soldiers in the Stalingrad trap
34,000 evacuated by air
160,000 killed in action
90,000 taken prisoner of war

On 21 November 1942, the commander of the German forces at Stalingrad, General von Paulus, asked Hitler for permission to call off the siege and withdraw to the River Don. In reply, Hitler ordered von Paulus to 'stand firm' despite the danger of 'temporary encirclement.' On 31 January 1943, Hitler appointed von Paulus a Field Marshal. That same day, von Paulus, having been encircled for two months, surrendered.

Serafinovich
Verkhne Fomikhinsky
Raspopinskaya
River Don
River Volga
Kletskaya
Bokovskaya
River Kurtlak
Kachalinskaya
Perelazovsky
Manoylin   Mayorovsky
Vertyachiy
Chernyshevskaya
Golubinsky Peskovatka
River Chervlenaya
Gumrak
Osinovskiy
Plesistovsky
River Chir
Dobrinka
Ostrov
Kalach
Stalingrad
Tsybenko
Sovetsky
River Don
River Volga
Gavrilovka
Nariman
River Liska
Oblivskaya
Tingut
Verkhne-Chirskaya
Nizhne-Chirskaya

Russians ahead,
Russians behind,
And in between.
Shooting.
GERMAN SOLDIERS' DITTY

Abganerovo
Station
Verkhne-Kumsky
Plodovitoye
River Aksa
Abganerovo
Vodyanskoye
Krasnoyarsky   Biriukov
Kruglyakovo

Within 24 hours of the Soviet counter-attack on 19 November 1942, 65,000 Romanian soldiers of the Romanian Third Army were surrounded and taken prisoner. Several thousand Hungarian and Italian soldiers, Germany's allies, were also captured.

River Don

Kotelnikovo

▲▲▲ The front line on 19 November 1942
➤ The Soviet advance, 13–30 November 1942
△△△ The front line on 30 November 1942
▨ Trapped Axis pockets (Germans, Romanians, Italians, Hungarians)
⇨ Unsuccessful German counter-attack, 12–13 December 1942

0   kilometres   70
0   miles   40

As German troops fought in the streets of Stalingrad, Soviet forces launched a massive encircling movement on 19 November 1941, threatening to surround the Germans in the city and cut them off from German-occupied Soviet Union. Hitler at once called a halt to the advance in the Caucasus and ordered priority to the Stalingrad front, but in vain. By 23 November the encircling Soviet armies linked up. By 30 November the German forces in Stalingrad were besieged. A German attempt to break through to the defenders was halted on 13 December, when the Italian Eighth Army, and part of the Romanian Fourth Army, were destroyed. The German forces in Stalingrad surrendered on 31 January 1943; final pockets of German resistance surrendered on 2 February 1943.

© Martin Gilbert 2008

ITALY AT WAR, 1940–1943

Legend:
- —— Under Italian rule, November 1942
- French territory annexed by Italy, June 1940
- Greek territory occupied by Italy, April 1941
- Dalmatian and Montenegran coast annexed by Italy, May 1941
- French territory occupied by Italy, November 1942
- Under joint Italian-German military control (Tunisia)
- Royal Air Force (RAF) and, after March 1942, United States Army Air Force (USAAF) air raids on Italian naval and military facilities, June 1940–August 1943

GREATER GERMANY

SWITZERLAND
neutral

Lyon

Cislago
Milan
Turin
San Giovanni
Genoa
Savona
Bologna
La Spezia
Leghorn (Livorno)

FRANCE

River Rhône

Ligurian Sea

CORSICA

SARDINIA
Cagliari

Tyrrhenian Sea

ITALY

Rome

Venice

Adriatic Sea

CROATIA
DALMATIA

GERMAN-OCCUPIED SERBIA

MONTENEGRO

ALBANIA

GREECE

Naples

Taranto
Brindisi

Palermo

SICILY

'On this tenth day of June 1940, the hand that held the dagger has struck it into the back of its neighbor.'
PRESIDENT ROOSEVELT ON LEARNING OF THE ITALIAN ATTACK ON FRANCE

Mediterranean Sea

Tunis

MALTA
British

United States bombers made six bombing raids on the Italian naval facilities at Genoa between 22 October and 15 November 1942, and bombed military targets in Turin on 18 and 20 November 1942.

On 11 November 1940 Britain launched the first aircraft carrier based attack of the war, on the Italian naval base at Taranto: 3 Italian battleships were put out of action by torpedo bombers. The Japanese carefully studied this technique, emulating it at Pearl Harbor. From 1940 to 1942, Italian warships in the Mediterranean sank 28 Allied merchant ships (111,527 tons) and two British battleships, *Queen Elizabeth* and *Valiant*.

Tripoli

TRIPOLITANIA (LIBYA)

Benghazi
under Allied control from 20 November 1942

CYRENAICA (LIBYA)

TUNISIA

| 0 | kilometres | 300 |
| 0 | miles | 200 |

© Martin Gilbert 2008

Between Italy's attack on France on 10 June 1940 – when 1,247 Italian soldiers were killed – and the Allied landings on Sicily on 10 July 1943, Italian forces were in action in North Africa, Ethiopia and Greece. Italy also sent 200,000 Italian soldiers to fight against the Soviet Union alongside the German Army: 20,000 Italians were killed in the Soviet Union and 64,000 made prisoner of war.

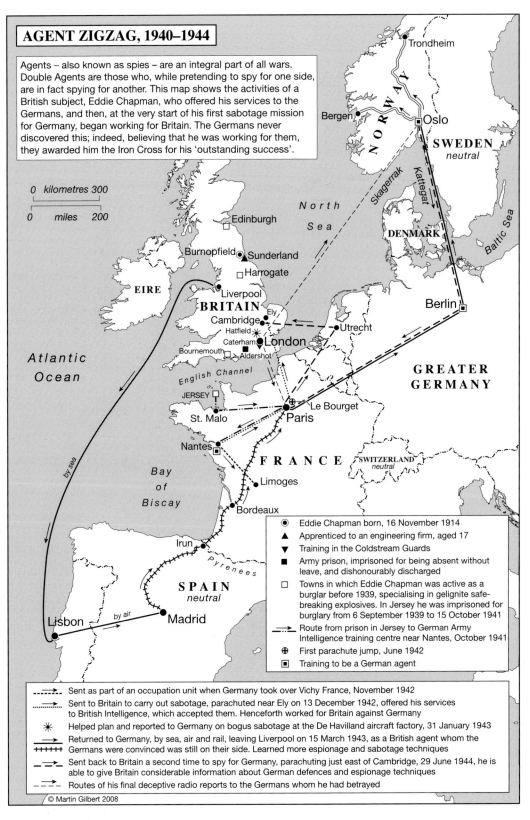

AGENT ZIGZAG, 1940–1944

Agents – also known as spies – are an integral part of all wars. Double Agents are those who, while pretending to spy for one side, are in fact spying for another. This map shows the activities of a British subject, Eddie Chapman, who offered his services to the Germans, and then, at the very start of his first sabotage mission for Germany, began working for Britain. The Germans never discovered this; indeed, believing that he was working for them, they awarded him the Iron Cross for his 'outstanding success'.

Trondheim

NORWAY

Bergen

Oslo

SWEDEN
neutral

Skagerrak

Kattegat

Baltic Sea

North Sea

DENMARK

0 kilometres 300

0 miles 200

Edinburgh

Burnopfield Sunderland

Harrogate

EIRE

Liverpool

BRITAIN Ely

Cambridge

Hatfield

Caterham London

Bournemouth Aldershot

Utrecht

Berlin

Atlantic Ocean

English Channel

JERSEY

St. Malo

Le Bourget

Paris

GREATER GERMANY

Nantes

FRANCE SWITZERLAND
neutral

by sea

Bay of Biscay

Limoges

Bordeaux

Irun

Pyrenees

SPAIN
neutral

Lisbon by air Madrid

⊙	Eddie Chapman born, 16 November 1914
▲	Apprenticed to an engineering firm, aged 17
▼	Training in the Coldstream Guards
■	Army prison, imprisoned for being absent without leave, and dishonourably discharged
☐	Towns in which Eddie Chapman was active as a burglar before 1939, specialising in gelignite safe-breaking explosives. In Jersey he was imprisoned for burglary from 6 September 1939 to 15 October 1941
⟶	Route from prison in Jersey to German Army Intelligence training centre near Nantes, October 1941
⊕	First parachute jump, June 1942
▣	Training to be a German agent

⟶	Sent as part of an occupation unit when Germany took over Vichy France, November 1942
⟶	Sent to Britain to carry out sabotage, parachuted near Ely on 13 December 1942, offered his services to British Intelligence, which accepted them. Henceforth worked for Britain against Germany
✳	Helped plan and reported to Germany on bogus sabotage at the De Havilland aircraft factory, 31 January 1943
⟶	Returned to Germany, by sea, air and rail, leaving Liverpool on 15 March 1943, as a British agent whom the Germans were convinced was still on their side. Learned more espionage and sabotage techniques
⟶	Sent back to Britain a second time to spy for Germany, parachuting just east of Cambridge, 29 June 1944, he is able to give Britain considerable information about German defences and espionage techniques
⟶	Routes of his final deceptive radio reports to the Germans whom he had betrayed

© Martin Gilbert 2008

117

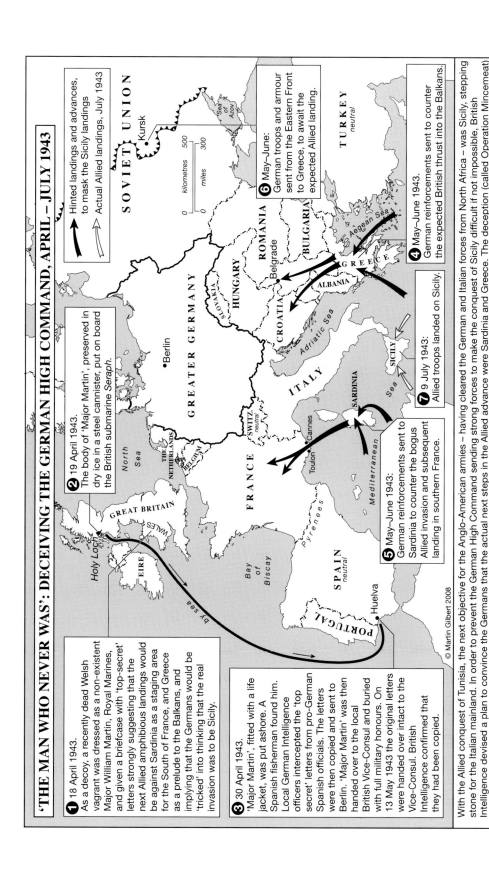

'THE MAN WHO NEVER WAS': DECEIVING THE GERMAN HIGH COMMAND, APRIL – JULY 1943

➤ Hinted landings and advances, to mask the Sicily landings

⇢ Actual Allied landings, July 1943

❶ 18 April 1943.
As a decoy, a recently dead Welsh vagrant was dressed as a non-existent Major William Martin, Royal Marines, and given a briefcase with 'top-secret' letters strongly suggesting that the next Allied amphibious landings would be against Sardinia as a staging area for the South of France, and Greece as a prelude to the Balkans, and implying that the Germans would be 'tricked' into thinking that the real invasion was to be Sicily.

❷ 19 April 1943.
The body of 'Major Martin', preserved in dry ice in a steel cannister, put on board the British submarine *Seraph*.

❸ 30 April 1943.
'Major Martin', fitted with a life jacket, was put ashore. A Spanish fisherman found him. Local German Intelligence officers intercepted the 'top secret' letters from pro-German Spanish officials. The letters were then copied and sent to Berlin. 'Major Martin' was then handed over to the local British Vice-Consul and buried with full military honours. On 13 May 1943 the original letters were handed over intact to the Vice-Consul. British Intelligence confirmed that they had been copied.

❹ May–June 1943.
German reinforcements sent to counter the expected British thrust into the Balkans.

❺ May–June 1943:
German reinforcements sent to Sardinia to counter the bogus Allied invasion and subsequent landing in southern France.

❻ May–June:
German troops and armour sent from the Eastern Front to Greece, to await the expected Allied landing.

❼ 9 July 1943:
Allied troops landed on Sicily.

© Martin Gilbert 2008

With the Allied conquest of Tunisia, the next objective for the Anglo-American armies – having cleared the German and Italian forces from North Africa – was Sicily, stepping stone for the Italian mainland. In order to prevent the German High Command sending strong forces to make the conquest of Sicily difficult if not impossible, British Intelligence devised a plan to convince the Germans that the actual next steps in the Allied advance were Sardinia and Greece. The deception (called Operation Mincemeat) succeeded, with Hitler personally ordering reinforcements to Sardinia and Greece. Because Greece had been made to seem the most likely point of attack, Hitler sent Field Marshal Erwin Rommel there to command an Army Group, and diverted two Panzer Divisions to Greece from the Eastern Front, where they were most needed. German minelayers and minesweepers that were off Sicily were diverted to Greek waters. On 14 May 1943, Churchill, then in Washington, received a telegram from his Defence Staff: 'Mincemeat swallowed rod, line and sinker by right people and from best information they look like acting on it.' The Germans had been successfully deceived.

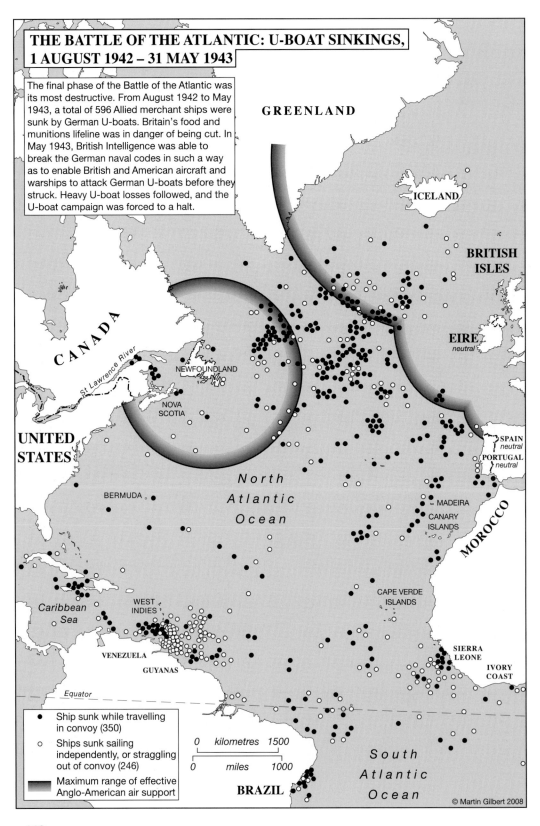

THE BATTLE OF THE ATLANTIC: U-BOAT SINKINGS, 1 AUGUST 1942 – 31 MAY 1943

The final phase of the Battle of the Atlantic was its most destructive. From August 1942 to May 1943, a total of 596 Allied merchant ships were sunk by German U-boats. Britain's food and munitions lifeline was in danger of being cut. In May 1943, British Intelligence was able to break the German naval codes in such a way as to enable British and American aircraft and warships to attack German U-boats before they struck. Heavy U-boat losses followed, and the U-boat campaign was forced to a halt.

GREENLAND

ICELAND

BRITISH ISLES

CANADA

St Lawrence River

NEWFOUNDLAND

NOVA SCOTIA

EIRE
neutral

UNITED STATES

SPAIN
neutral

PORTUGAL
neutral

BERMUDA

North Atlantic Ocean

MADEIRA

CANARY ISLANDS

MOROCCO

Caribbean Sea

WEST INDIES

CAPE VERDE ISLANDS

VENEZUELA

GUYANAS

SIERRA LEONE

IVORY COAST

Equator

- Ship sunk while travelling in convoy (350)
○ Ships sunk sailing independently, or straggling out of convoy (246)

Maximum range of effective Anglo-American air support

0   kilometres   1500

0   miles   1000

South Atlantic Ocean

BRAZIL

© Martin Gilbert 2008

THE BATTLE OF THE ATLANTIC: FOUR CONVOYS, 7–22 MARCH 1943

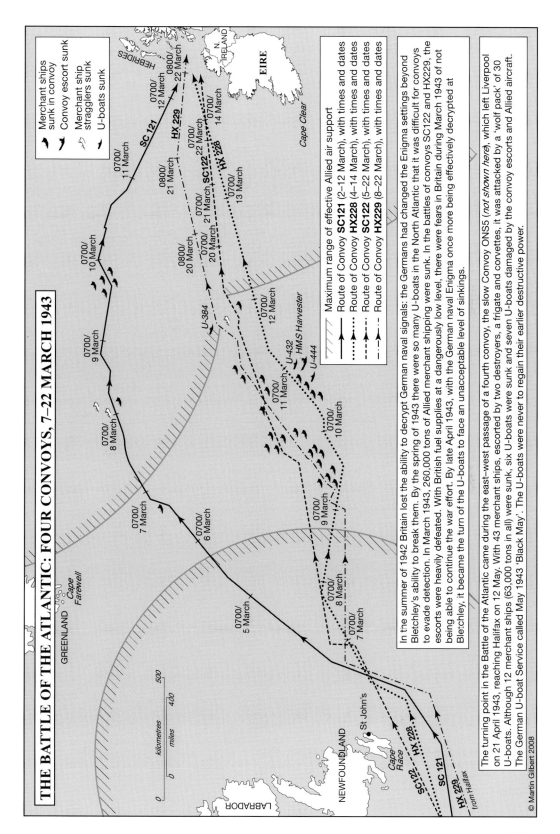

Legend:

↘ Merchant ships sunk in convoy
↙ Convoy escort sunk
↗ Merchant ship stragglers sunk
↑ U-boats sunk

///// Maximum range of effective Allied air support

——— Route of Convoy **SC121** (2–12 March), with times and dates
········ Route of Convoy **HX228** (4–14 March), with times and dates
–·–·– Route of Convoy **SC122** (5–22 March), with times and dates
– · – · – Route of Convoy **HX229** (8–22 March), with times and dates

GREENLAND
Cape Farewell
LABRADOR
NEWFOUNDLAND
St John's
Cape Race
N. IRELAND
EIRE
HEBRIDES
Cape Clear

U-384
U-432
HMS Harvester
U-444

SC122 · HX228 · SC121 · HX229 from Halifax

kilometres 0 400 500
miles 0

In the summer of 1942 Britain lost the ability to decrypt German naval signals: the Germans had changed the Enigma settings beyond Bletchley's ability to break them. By the spring of 1943 there were so many U-boats in the North Atlantic that it was difficult for convoys to evade detection. In March 1943, 260,000 tons of Allied merchant shipping were sunk. In the battles of convoys SC122 and HX229, the escorts were heavily defeated. With British fuel supplies at a dangerously low level, there were fears in Britain during March 1943 of not being able to continue the war effort. By late April 1943, with the German naval Enigma once more being effectively decrypted at Bletchley, it became the turn of the U-boats to face an unacceptable level of sinkings.

The turning point in the Battle of the Atlantic came during the east–west passage of a fourth convoy, the slow Convoy ONS5 (*not shown here*), which left Liverpool on 21 April 1943, reaching Halifax on 12 May. With 43 merchant ships, escorted by two destroyers, a frigate and corvettes, it was attacked by a 'wolf pack' of 30 U-boats. Although 12 merchant ships (63,000 tons in all) were sunk, six U-boats were sunk and seven U-boats damaged by the convoy escorts and Allied aircraft. The German U-boat Service called May 1943 'Black May'. The U-boats were never to regain their earlier destructive power.

© Martin Gilbert 2008

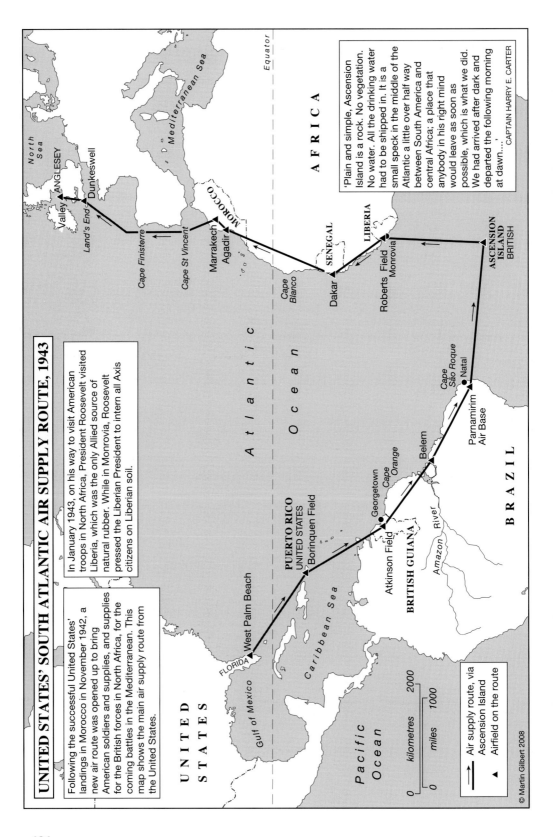

UNITED STATES' SOUTH ATLANTIC AIR SUPPLY ROUTE, 1943

Following the successful United States' landings in Morocco in November 1942, a new air route was opened up to bring American soldiers and supplies, and supplies for the British forces in North Africa, for the coming battles in the Mediterranean. This map shows the main air supply route from the United States.

In January 1943, on his way to visit American troops in North Africa, President Roosevelt visited Liberia, which was the only Allied source of natural rubber. While in Monrovia, Roosevelt pressed the Liberian President to intern all Axis citizens on Liberian soil.

'Plain and simple, Ascension Island is a rock. No vegetation. No water. All the drinking water had to be shipped in. It is a small speck in the middle of the Atlantic a little over half way between South America and central Africa; a place that anybody in his right mind would leave as soon as possible, which is what we did. We had arrived after dark and departed the following morning at dawn....'

CAPTAIN HARRY E. CARTER

North Sea

Mediterranean Sea

Equator

A F R I C A

Valley
ANGLESEY
Land's End
Dunkeswell

Cape Finisterre

Cape St Vincent

Marrakech
MOROCCO
Agadir

SENEGAL

LIBERIA

Cape
Blanco

Dakar

Roberts Field
Monrovia

ASCENSION
ISLAND
BRITISH

A t l a n t i c

O c e a n

Cape
São Roque
Natal

Parnamirim
Air Base

B R A Z I L

West Palm Beach

FLORIDA

Gulf of Mexico

PUERTO RICO
UNITED STATES
Borinquen Field

Caribbean Sea

Pacific
Ocean

Atkinson Field

BRITISH GUIANA

Georgetown
Cape
Orange

Belem

Amazon River

U N I T E D
S T A T E S

| 0 | kilometres | 2000 |
| 0 | miles | 1000 |

Air supply route, via
Ascension Island

Airfield on the route

© Martin Gilbert 2008

121

LANDING CRAFT BUILDING YARDS IN THE UNITED STATES, 1942–1945

CANADA

The Allies were dependent for all their amphibious landings on an adequate supply of landing craft: including throughout the Pacific and the Far East, and in Madagascar (5 May 1942), North Africa (8 November 1942), Sicily (10 July 1943), Straits of Messina (3 September 1943), Salerno (9 September 1943), Anzio (22 January 1944), Normandy (6 June 1944), and the South of France (15 August 1944) This map shows the principal building yards in the United States in which more than a thousand landing craft were built.

St Lawrence River

Lake Huron

Lake Ontario

Lake Erie

Lake Michigan

Boston
NAVY YARD

New York
NAVY YARD

Baltimore
BETHLEHEM
FAIRFIELD
COMPANY

Philadelphia
NAVY YARD

Quincy
BETHLEHEM
STEEL

Ambridge
AMERICAN
BRIDGE
COMPANY

Pittsburgh
DRAVO
CORPORATION

Seneca
CHICAGO
BRIDGE
AND IRON
COMPANY

Ohio River

Illinois River

Jeffersonville
BOAT AND
MACHINE
COMPANY

Evansville
MISSOURI
VALLEY BRIDGE
AND
IRON COMPANY

Newport News
SHIP BUILDING AND
DRY DOCK COMPANY

Norfolk
NAVY YARD

Mississippi River

UNITED
STATES

Atlantic
Ocean

Charleston
NAVY YARD

Mississippi River

New Orleans
HIGGINS
BOATS

'Andrew Higgins ... is the man who won the war for us. ... If Higgins had not designed and built those LCVPs, we never could have landed over an open beach. The whole strategy of the war would have been different.'

GENERAL DWIGHT D. EISENHOWER

Gulf of
Mexico

| 0 | kilometres | 500 |
| 0 | miles | 300 |

© Martin Gilbert 2008

TYPES OF LANDING CRAFT

LCA: Landing Craft Assault (36 fully armed men)
LCI: Landing Craft Infantry (200 men)
LCVP: Landing Craft, Vehicle, Personnel. Also known as the Higgins Boat (36 men)
LCM: Landing Craft Mechanised (one small tank or 100 men); it could be slung under the davits of ships
LST: Landing Ship, Tanks (up to four tanks)

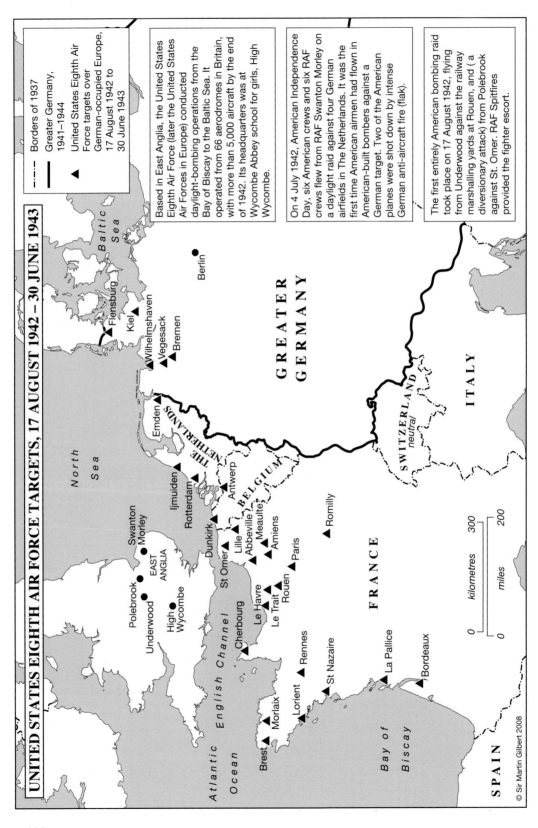

UNITED STATES EIGHTH AIR FORCE TARGETS, 17 AUGUST 1942 – 30 JUNE 1943

Borders of 1937

Greater Germany, 1941–1944

▲ United States Eighth Air Force targets over German-occupied Europe, 17 August 1942 to 30 June 1943

Based in East Anglia, the United States Eighth Air Force (later the United States Air Forces in Europe) conducted daylight-bombing operations from the Bay of Biscay to the Baltic Sea. It operated from 66 aerodromes in Britain, with more than 5,000 aircraft by the end of 1942. Its headquarters was at Wycombe Abbey school for girls, High Wycombe.

On 4 July 1942, American Independence Day, six American crews and six RAF crews flew from RAF Swanton Morley on a daylight raid against four German airfields in The Netherlands. It was the first time American airmen had flown in American-built bombers against a German target. Two of the American planes were shot down by intense German anti-aircraft fire (flak).

The first entirely American bombing raid took place on 17 August 1942, flying from Underwood against the railway marshalling yards at Rouen, and (a diversionary attack) from Polebrook against St. Omer. RAF Spitfires provided the fighter escort.

Baltic Sea

North Sea

Atlantic Ocean

English Channel

Flensburg

Kiel

Wilhelmshaven
Vegesack
Bremen

Berlin

Emden

GREATER GERMANY

THE NETHERLANDS

Ijmuiden

Rotterdam

Antwerp

BELGIUM

Dunkirk

St Omer

Lille
Abbeville
Meaulte
Amiens

Romilly

FRANCE

Paris

Rouen

Le Trait

Le Havre

Cherbourg

Swanton Morley

Polebrook
Underwood
EAST ANGLIA
High Wycombe

Morlaix

Brest

Lorient
Rennes

St Nazaire

La Pallice

Bordeaux

Bay of Biscay

SWITZERLAND
neutral

ITALY

SPAIN

0   kilometres   300

0   miles   200

© Sir Martin Gilbert 2008

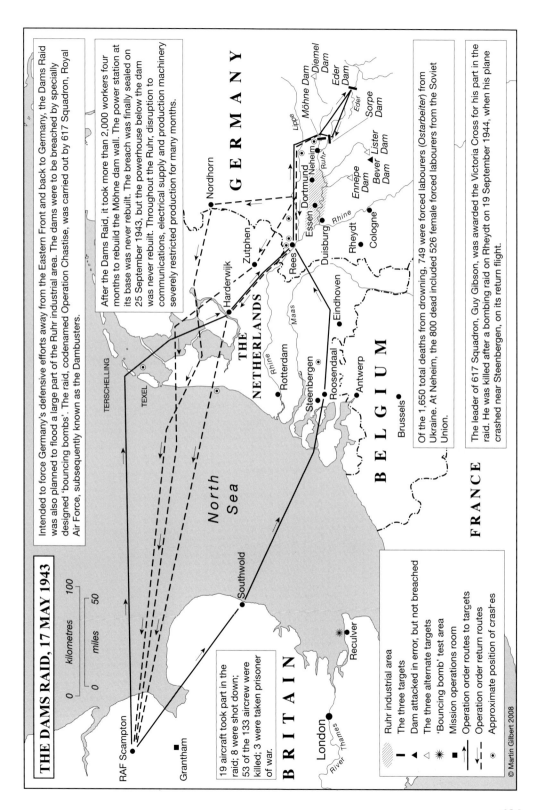

THE DAMS RAID, 17 MAY 1943

0   kilometres   100

0   miles   50

Intended to force Germany's defensive efforts away from the Eastern Front and back to Germany, the Dams Raid was also planned to flood a large part of the Ruhr industrial area. The dams were to be breached by specially designed 'bouncing bombs'. The raid, codenamed Operation Chastise, was carried out by 617 Squadron, Royal Air Force, subsequently known as the Dambusters.

After the Dams Raid, it took more than 2,000 workers four months to rebuild the Möhne dam wall. The power station at its base was never rebuilt. The breach was finally sealed on 25 September 1943, but the powerhouse below the dam was never rebuilt. Throughout the Ruhr, disruption to communications, electrical supply and production machinery severely restricted production for many months.

Of the 1,650 total deaths from drowning, 749 were forced labourers (*Ostarbeiter*) from Ukraine. At Neheim, the 800 dead included 526 female forced labourers from the Soviet Union.

The leader of 617 Squadron, Guy Gibson, was awarded the Victoria Cross for his part in the raid. He was killed after a bombing raid on Rheydt on 19 September 1944, when his plane crashed near Steenbergen, on its return flight.

19 aircraft took part in the raid; 8 were shot down; 53 of the 133 aircrew were killed; 3 were taken prisoner of war.

Ruhr industrial area

The three targets

Dam attacked in error, but not breached

The three alternate targets

'Bouncing bomb' test area

Mission operations room

Operation order routes to targets

Operation order return routes

Approximate position of crashes

GERMANY

THE NETHERLANDS

BELGIUM

FRANCE

BRITAIN

North Sea

Möhne Dam
Diemel Dam
Eder Dam
Sorpe Dam
Lister Dam
Bever Dam
Ennepe Dam
Neheim
Dortmund
Essen
Duisburg
Rees
Rheydt
Cologne
Nordhorn
Zutphen
Harderwijk
Eindhoven
Antwerp
Roosendaal
Steenbergen
Rotterdam
Brussels
TEXEL
TERSCHELLING
Southwold
RAF Scampton
Grantham
London
Reculver

River Thames
Rhine
Maas
Lippe
Ruhr
Eder

© Martin Gilbert 2008

124

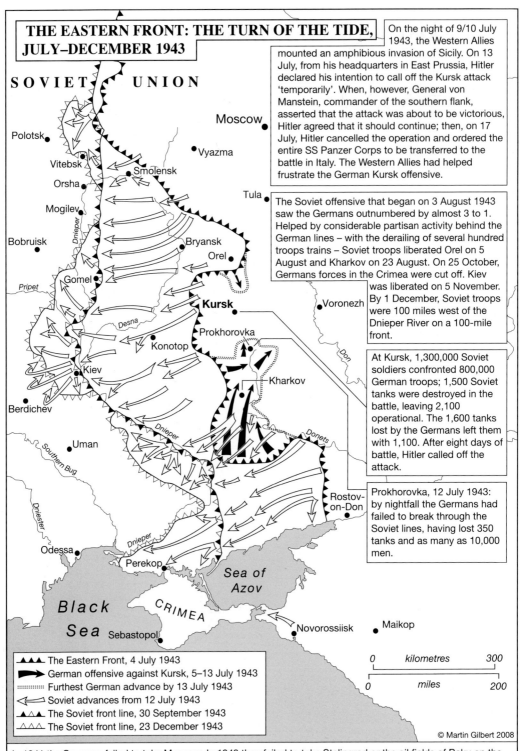

THE EASTERN FRONT: THE TURN OF THE TIDE, JULY–DECEMBER 1943

On the night of 9/10 July 1943, the Western Allies mounted an amphibious invasion of Sicily. On 13 July, from his headquarters in East Prussia, Hitler declared his intention to call off the Kursk attack 'temporarily'. When, however, General von Manstein, commander of the southern flank, asserted that the attack was about to be victorious, Hitler agreed that it should continue; then, on 17 July, Hitler cancelled the operation and ordered the entire SS Panzer Corps to be transferred to the battle in Italy. The Western Allies had helped frustrate the German Kursk offensive.

The Soviet offensive that began on 3 August 1943 saw the Germans outnumbered by almost 3 to 1. Helped by considerable partisan activity behind the German lines – with the derailing of several hundred troops trains – Soviet troops liberated Orel on 5 August and Kharkov on 23 August. On 25 October, Germans forces in the Crimea were cut off. Kiev was liberated on 5 November. By 1 December, Soviet troops were 100 miles west of the Dnieper River on a 100-mile front.

At Kursk, 1,300,000 Soviet soldiers confronted 800,000 German troops; 1,500 Soviet tanks were destroyed in the battle, leaving 2,100 operational. The 1,600 tanks lost by the Germans left them with 1,100. After eight days of battle, Hitler called off the attack.

Prokhorovka, 12 July 1943: by nightfall the Germans had failed to break through the Soviet lines, having lost 350 tanks and as many as 10,000 men.

SOVIET UNION

Polotsk
Moscow
Vyazma
Vitebsk
Smolensk
Orsha
Mogilev
Tula
Bobruisk
Bryansk
Orel
Dnieper
Pripet
Gomel
Kursk
Voronezh
Desna
Prokhorovka
Konotop
Kiev
Kharkov
Berdichev
Dnieper
Donets
Uman
Southern Bug
Don
Dniester
Dnieper
Rostov-on-Don
Odessa
Perekop
Sea of Azov
Black Sea
CRIMEA
Sebastopol
Novorossiisk
Maikop

The Eastern Front, 4 July 1943
German offensive against Kursk, 5–13 July 1943
Furthest German advance by 13 July 1943
Soviet advances from 12 July 1943
The Soviet front line, 30 September 1943
The Soviet front line, 23 December 1943

0   kilometres   300
0   miles   200

© Martin Gilbert 2008

In 1941 the Germans failed to take Moscow. In 1942 they failed to take Stalingrad or the oil fields of Baku on the Caspian Sea. In 1943 they made a third attempt to defeat the Soviet Union, by a major breakthrough in the Kursk region. When this failed, and with German loss of air superiority for the first time over the Soviet Union, the tide of war in the east began to turn emphatically against Germany.

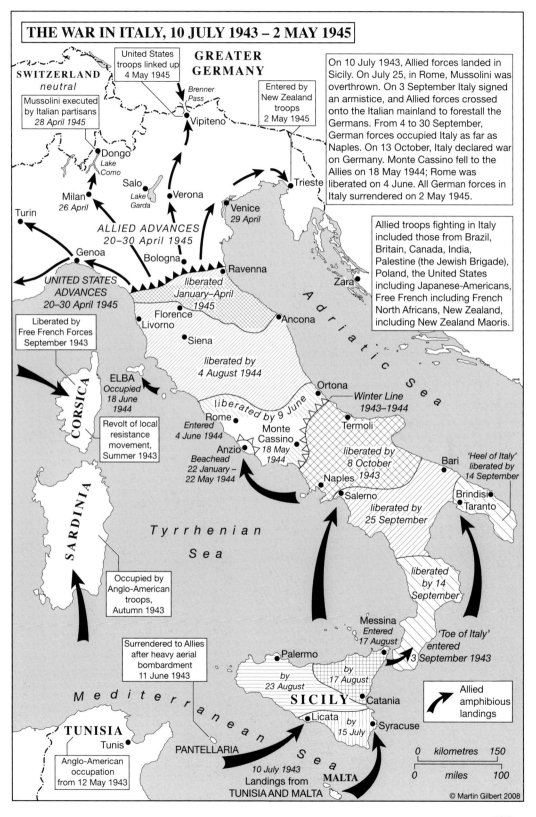

THE WAR IN ITALY, 10 JULY 1943 – 2 MAY 1945

GREATER GERMANY

SWITZERLAND *neutral*

United States troops linked up 4 May 1945

Brenner Pass

Vipiteno

Entered by New Zealand troops 2 May 1945

Mussolini executed by Italian partisans 28 April 1945

Dongo
Lake Como

Salo
Lake Garda

Milan
26 April

Verona

Trieste

Venice
29 April

Turin

Genoa

Bologna

Ravenna

Zara

ALLIED ADVANCES 20–30 April 1945

liberated January–April 1945

UNITED STATES ADVANCES 20–30 April 1945

Florence
Livorno

Siena

Ancona

Liberated by Free French Forces September 1943

ELBA *Occupied 18 June 1944*

liberated by 4 August 1944

liberated by 9 June

Ortona

Winter Line 1943–1944

CORSICA

Revolt of local resistance movement, Summer 1943

Rome
Entered 4 June 1944

Monte Cassino
18 May 1944

Termoli

liberated by 8 October 1943

Bari

'Heel of Italy' liberated by 14 September

Anzio
Beachhead 22 January – 22 May 1944

Naples

Brindisi
Taranto

SARDINIA

T y r r h e n i a n   S e a

Salerno

liberated by 25 September

Occupied by Anglo-American troops, Autumn 1943

liberated by 14 September

'Toe of Italy' entered 3 September 1943

Messina
Entered 17 August

Surrendered to Allies after heavy aerial bombardment 11 June 1943

Palermo

by 23 August

by 17 August

SICILY
Catania

Allied amphibious landings

Licata
by 15 July

Syracuse

TUNISIA
Tunis

Anglo-American occupation from 12 May 1943

PANTELLARIA

M e d i t e r r a n e a n   S e a

10 July 1943 Landings from TUNISIA AND MALTA

MALTA

On 10 July 1943, Allied forces landed in Sicily. On July 25, in Rome, Mussolini was overthrown. On 3 September Italy signed an armistice, and Allied forces crossed onto the Italian mainland to forestall the Germans. From 4 to 30 September, German forces occupied Italy as far as Naples. On 13 October, Italy declared war on Germany. Monte Cassino fell to the Allies on 18 May 1944; Rome was liberated on 4 June. All German forces in Italy surrendered on 2 May 1945.

Allied troops fighting in Italy included those from Brazil, Britain, Canada, India, Palestine (the Jewish Brigade), Poland, the United States including Japanese-Americans, Free French including French North Africans, New Zealand, including New Zealand Maoris.

A d r i a t i c   S e a

| 0 | kilometres | 150 |
| 0 | miles | 100 |

© Martin Gilbert 2008

126

UNITED STATES EIGHTH AIR FORCE BASES IN EASTERN ENGLAND AND EAST ANGLIA, AUGUST 1942 – MAY 1945

North Sea

Balderton
Fulbeck
Bottesford
Barkston Heath
The Wash
Langar
Sculthorpe
River Bure
Saltby
Folkingham
Oulton
North Witham
Horsham
St. Faith
Cottesmore
Wendling
Attlebridge
Rackheath
River Welland
North Pickenham
Shipdham
River Yare
Great Ouse
Deopham Green
Watton
Spanhoe
Wittering
Bodney
Hethel
Seething
King's Cliffe
East Wretham
Old Buckingham
Hardwick
Deenethorpe
Snetterton Heath
Tibenham
Bungay
Polebrook
Glatton
Knettishall
Fersfield
Thorpe Abbotts
Halesworth
Harrington
Grafton
Molesworth
Alconbury
Honington
Great Ashfield
Eye
Metfield
Underwood
Horham
Brampton Grange
Snailwell
Chelveston
Bury
St Edmunds
Mendlesham
Thurleigh
Little
Framlingham
Leiston
Podington
Staughton
Bottisham
Lavenham
Rattlesden
Wattisham
Debach
Bassingbourn
Fowlmere
Ridgewell
Sudbury
Martlesham Heath
Steeple Morden
Duxford
Little Walden
Wethersfield
Wormingford
Raydon
Nuthampstead
Debden
Gosfield
Boxted
Andrew's Field
Earls Colne
Birch
Stansted
Great Dunmow
Rivenhall
Cheddington
Matching Green
Boreham
Bovingdon
Chipping Ongar
0 kilometres 30
0 miles 20
Heston
River Thames
Thames Estuary

⊙ United States Eighth Air Force bases in eastern England and East Anglia, 1942–1945

© Martin Gilbert 2008

Between August 1942 and May 1945, more than 26,000 United States Eighth Air Force aircrew were killed in action.

The bases of the United States Eighth Air Force in Britain were a formidable factor in the daylight bombing of Germany. They were the bases for the 'Big Week' attack on German aircraft manufacturing factories *(see map 136)*, for strikes against German ground forces during the Battle of the Bulge *(see map 168)*, and for the daylight phase of the Anglo-American raid on Dresden *(see map 175)*. This map shows the 89 bases in eastern England and East Anglia.

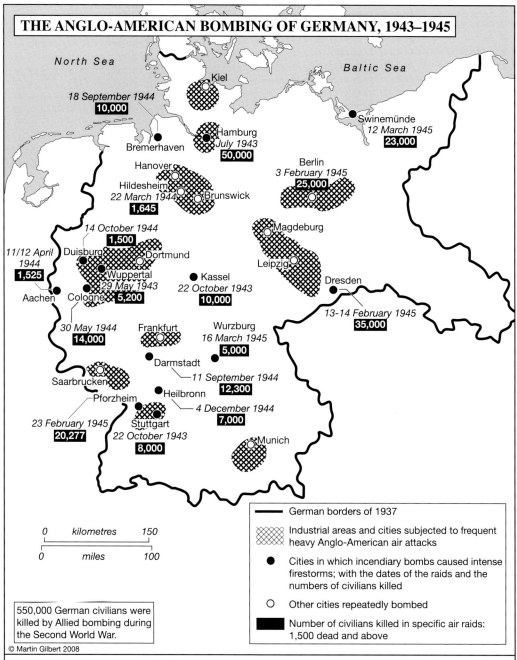

THE ANGLO-AMERICAN BOMBING OF GERMANY, 1943–1945

North Sea

Baltic Sea

Kiel
18 September 1944
10,000

Swinemünde
12 March 1945
23,000

Hamburg
July 1943
50,000

Bremerhaven

Hanover

Berlin
3 February 1945
25,000

Hildesheim
22 March 1944
1,645
Brunswick

Magdeburg

14 October 1944
1,500

Leipzig

11/12 April
1944
1,525
Duisburg
Dortmund

Dresden
13-14 February 1945
35,000

Wuppertal
29 May 1943
5,200

Kassel
22 October 1943
10,000

Aachen
Cologne

30 May 1944
14,000
Frankfurt

Wurzburg
16 March 1945
5,000

Darmstadt
11 September 1944
12,300

Saarbrucken

Pforzheim
Heilbronn
4 December 1944
7,000

23 February 1945
20,277
Stuttgart
22 October 1943
8,000

Munich

——— German borders of 1937

▨▨▨ Industrial areas and cities subjected to frequent heavy Anglo-American air attacks

● Cities in which incendiary bombs caused intense firestorms; with the dates of the raids and the numbers of civilians killed

○ Other cities repeatedly bombed

■ Number of civilians killed in specific air raids: 1,500 dead and above

0   kilometres   150
0   miles   100

550,000 German civilians were killed by Allied bombing during the Second World War.

© Martin Gilbert 2008

Royal Air Force Bomber Command deaths included 38,462 Britons, 9,980 Canadians (58% of the Canadians who flew with Bomber Command were killed), 4,050 Australians, 1,703 New Zealanders, 977 Poles, 480 Czechoslovaks, 218 Free French, 188 Rhodesians, 68 Americans attached to Bomber Command from the United States Army Air Force, 34 Norwegians, 12 South Africans, three Indians, and 1,479 ground crew. Ninety-one members of the Women's Auxiliary Air Force (WAAF) also died while on duty with Bomber Command. 10,999 members of Bomber Command were taken prisoner of war, and 8,403 were wounded in action. As many as a thousand evaded capture after being shot down, most of them making their way back to Britain, to fly again (see map 39). More than 26,000 aircrew of the United States Army Air Force were killed on operations over Germany.

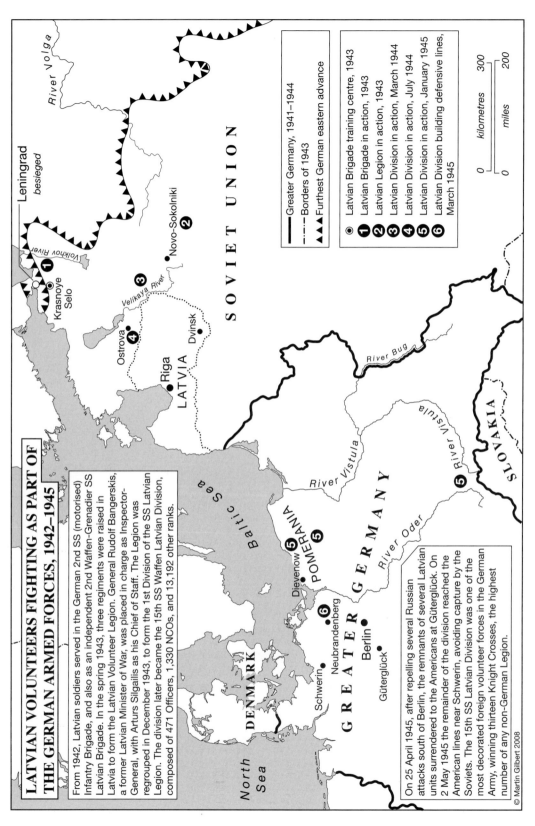

LATVIAN VOLUNTEERS FIGHTING AS PART OF THE GERMAN ARMED FORCES, 1942–1945

From 1942, Latvian soldiers served in the German 2nd SS (motorised) Infantry Brigade, and also as an independent 2nd Waffen-Grenadier SS Latvian Brigade. In the spring 1943, three regiments were raised in Latvia to form the Latvian Volunteer Legion. General Rudolf Bangerskis, a former Latvian Minister of War, was placed in charge as Inspector-General, with Arturs Silgailis as his Chief of Staff. The Legion was regrouped in December 1943, to form the 1st Division of the SS Latvian Legion. The division later became the 15th SS Waffen Latvian Division, composed of 471 Officers, 1,330 NCOs, and 13,192 other ranks.

On 25 April 1945, after repelling several Russian attacks south of Berlin, the remnants of several Latvian units surrendered to the Americans at Güterglück. On 2 May 1945 the remainder of the division reached the American lines near Schwerin, avoiding capture by the Soviets. The 15th SS Latvian Division was one of the most decorated foreign volunteer forces in the German Army, winning thirteen Knight Crosses, the highest number of any non-German Legion.

— Greater Germany, 1941–1944
---- Borders of 1943
▲▲▲ Furthest German eastern advance

◉ Latvian Brigade training centre, 1943
❶ Latvian Brigade in action, 1943
❷ Latvian Legion in action, 1943
❸ Latvian Division in action, March 1944
❹ Latvian Division in action, July 1944
❺ Latvian Division in action, January 1945
❻ Latvian Division building defensive lines, March 1945

0   kilometres   300
0   miles   200

River Volga
Leningrad besieged
Volkhov River
Krasnoye Selo
Novo-Sokolniki
Velikaya River
Ostrova
Dvinsk
Riga
LATVIA
SOVIET UNION
River Bug
River Vistula
River Oder
SLOVAKIA
Baltic Sea
Dievenow
POMERANIA
Neubrandenberg
Berlin
Schwerin
Güterglück
GREATER GERMANY
DENMARK
North Sea

© Martin Gilbert 2008

ANGLO-AMERICAN BOMBING RAIDS ON HAMBURG, 24 JULY – 3 AUGUST 1943

Between 24 July and 3 August 1943, the Royal Air Force Bomber Command and the United States Eighth Air Force made six major and three smaller raids on the German port city of Hamburg. This map shows the route of the first of these raids, on the night of 24/25 July: 1,500 civilians were killed that night. The final civilian death toll for all nine raids was 45,000, some 40,000 of whom died in the firestorm on the night of 27/28 July.

The bombing raid that took place on the night of 24/25 July 1943 on Hamburg was the 98th Allied bombing raid on the city. Bombs had also been dropped on 39 other occasions by bombers mistaking Hamburg for another target, or bombing Hamburg when they could not reach their target city. Between 1940 and 1945, 55,000 civilians were killed in Hamburg by bombing.

The airmen taking part in the raids on Hamburg included Australians, Americans, Britons, Canadians, New Zealanders, Poles and South Africans. The track distance for the flights varied between 980 and 1,020 miles from base and back.

The principal targets for the American day raids were the Blohm and Voss U-Boat Yards and the Kloehner Aero-Engine Factory. Both were massively damaged.

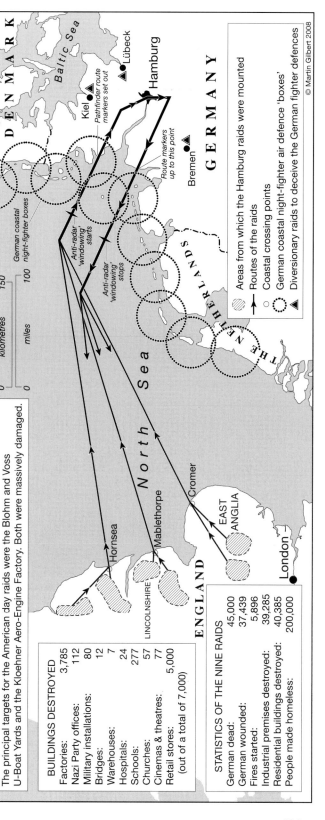

BUILDINGS DESTROYED

Factories:	3,785
Nazi Party offices:	112
Military installations:	80
Bridges:	12
Warehouses:	7
Hospitals:	24
Schools:	277
Churches:	57
Cinemas & theatres:	77
Retail stores:	5,000
(out of a total of 7,000)	

STATISTICS OF THE NINE RAIDS

German dead:	45,000
German wounded:	37,439
Fires started:	5,896
Industrial premises destroyed:	39,285
Residential buildings destroyed:	40,385
People made homeless:	200,000

© Martin Gilbert 2008

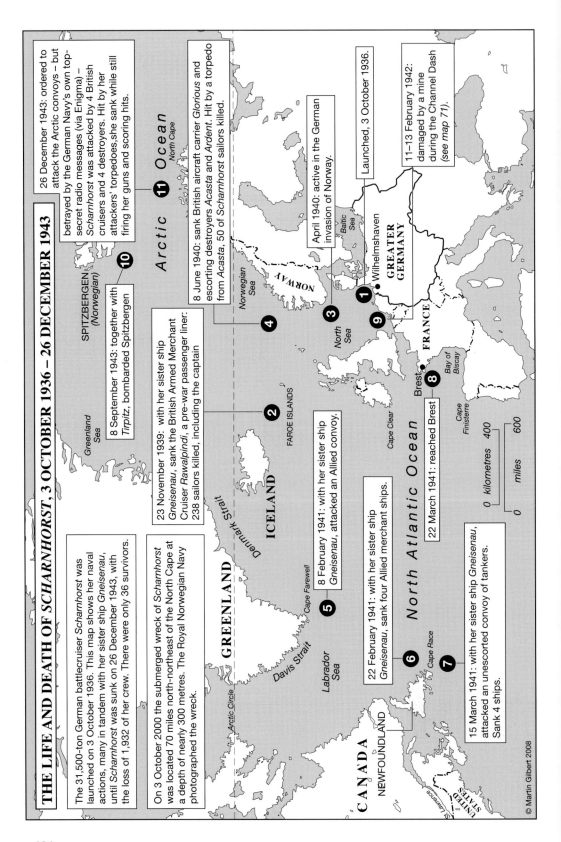

THE LIFE AND DEATH OF SCHARNHORST, 3 OCTOBER 1936 – 26 DECEMBER 1943

The 31,500-ton German battlecruiser *Scharnhorst* was launched on 3 October 1936. This map shows her naval actions, many in tandem with her sister ship *Gneisenau*, until *Scharnhorst* was sunk on 26 December 1943, with the loss of 1,932 of her crew. There were only 36 survivors.

On 3 October 2000 the submerged wreck of *Scharnhorst* was located 70 miles north-northeast of the North Cape at a depth of nearly 300 metres. The Royal Norwegian Navy photographed the wreck.

26 December 1943: ordered to attack the Arctic convoys – but betrayed by the German Navy's own top-secret radio messages (via Enigma) – *Scharnhorst* was attacked by 4 British cruisers and 4 destroyers. Hit by her attackers' torpedoes, she sank while still firing her guns and scoring hits.

8 September 1943: together with *Tirpitz*, bombarded Spitzbergen

Launched, 3 October 1936.

11–13 February 1942: damaged by a mine during the Channel Dash (*see map 71*).

April 1940: active in the German invasion of Norway.

8 June 1940: sank British aircraft carrier *Glorious* and escorting destroyers *Acasta* and *Ardent*. Hit by a torpedo from *Acasta*, 50 of *Scharnhorst* sailors killed.

23 November 1939: with her sister ship *Gneisenau*, sank the British Armed Merchant Cruiser *Rawalpindi*, a pre-war passenger liner: 238 sailors killed, including the captain

8 February 1941: with her sister ship *Gneisenau*, attacked an Allied convoy.

22 February 1941: with her sister ship *Gneisenau*, sank four Allied merchant ships.

22 March 1941: reached Brest

15 March 1941: with her sister ship *Gneisenau*, attacked an unescorted convoy of tankers. Sank 4 ships.

SPITZBERGEN (Norwegian)

Greenland Sea

Arctic Ocean
North Cape

Norwegian Sea

NORWAY

Baltic Sea

GREATER GERMANY

Wilhelmshaven

North Sea

FRANCE

Bay of Biscay

Brest

Cape Finisterre

Cape Clear

FAROE ISLANDS

ICELAND

Denmark Strait

Cape Farewell

GREENLAND

Davis Strait

Labrador Sea

Arctic Circle

North Atlantic Ocean

Cape Race

CANADA

NEWFOUNDLAND

UNITED STATES

St Lawrence

0   kilometres   400   600
0   miles

© Martin Gilbert 2008

131

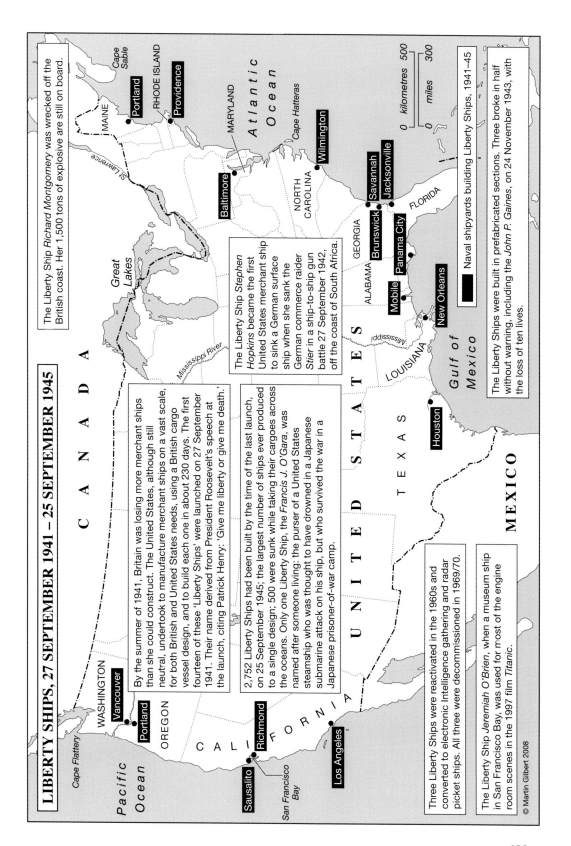

LIBERTY SHIPS, 27 SEPTEMBER 1941 – 25 SEPTEMBER 1945

The Liberty Ship *Richard Montgomery* was wrecked off the British coast. Her 1,500 tons of explosive are still on board.

By the summer of 1941, Britain was losing more merchant ships than she could construct. The United States, although still neutral, undertook to manufacture merchant ships on a vast scale, for both British and United States needs, using a British cargo vessel design, and to build each one in about 230 days. The first fourteen of these 'Liberty Ships' were launched on 27 September 1941. Their name derived from President Roosevelt's speech at the launch, citing Patrick Henry: 'Give me liberty or give me death.'

2,752 Liberty Ships had been built by the time of the last launch, on 25 September 1945; the largest number of ships ever produced to a single design; 500 were sunk while taking their cargoes across the oceans. Only one Liberty Ship, the *Francis J. O'Gara*, was named after someone living: the purser of a United States steamship who was thought to have drowned in a Japanese submarine attack on his ship, but who survived the war in a Japanese prisoner-of-war camp.

The Liberty Ship *Stephen Hopkins* became the first United States merchant ship to sink a German surface ship when she sank the German commerce raider *Stier* in a ship-to-ship gun battle 27 September 1942, off the coast of South Africa.

Three Liberty Ships were reactivated in the 1960s and converted to electronic intelligence gathering and radar picket ships. All three were decommissioned in 1969/70.

The Liberty Ship *Jeremiah O'Brien*, when a museum ship in San Francisco Bay, was used for most of the engine room scenes in the 1997 film *Titanic*.

The Liberty Ships were built in prefabricated sections. Three broke in half without warning, including the *John P. Gaines*, on 24 November 1943, with the loss of ten lives.

■ Naval shipyards building Liberty Ships, 1941–45

0 kilometres 500
0 miles 300

Pacific Ocean

Atlantic Ocean

Gulf of Mexico

C A N A D A

U N I T E D   S T A T E S

MEXICO

Cape Flattery
WASHINGTON
Vancouver
Portland
OREGON
CALIFORNIA
Sausalito
Richmond
San Francisco Bay
Los Angeles
T E X A S
Houston
LOUISIANA
Mississippi
New Orleans
Mobile
ALABAMA
Panama City
Brunswick
GEORGIA
FLORIDA
Jacksonville
Savannah
Wilmington
NORTH CAROLINA
Cape Hatteras
Baltimore
MARYLAND
Great Lakes
Mississippi River
St Lawrence
MAINE
Portland
RHODE ISLAND
Providence
Cape Sable

© Martin Gilbert 2008

132

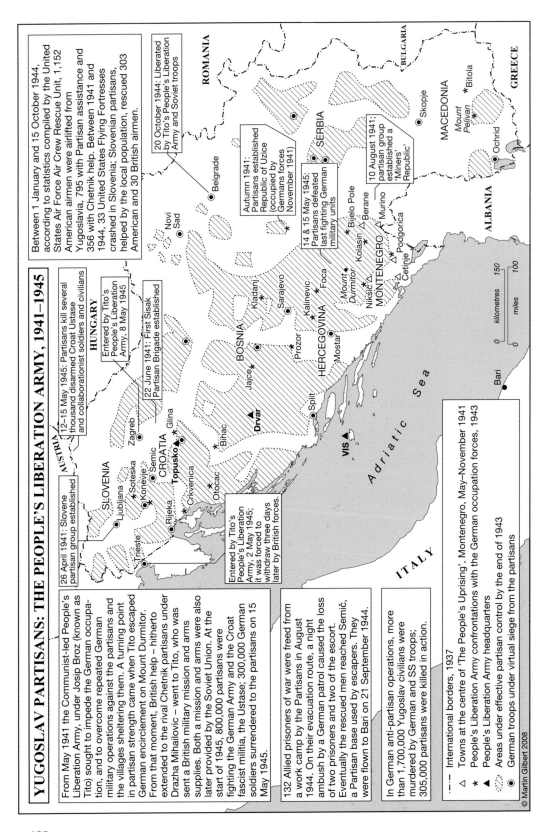

YUGOSLAV PARTISANS: THE PEOPLE'S LIBERATION ARMY, 1941–1945

From May 1941 the Communist-led People's Liberation Army, under Josip Broz (known as Tito) sought to impede the German occupation, and to overcome repeated German military operations against the partisans and the villages sheltering them. A turning point in partisan strength came when Tito escaped German encirclement on Mount Durmitor. From that moment, British help – hitherto extended to the rival Chetnik partisans under Drazha Mihailovic – went to Tito, who was sent a British military mission and arms supplies. Both a mission and arms were also later provided by the Soviet Union. At the start of 1945, 800,000 partisans were fighting the German Army and the Croat fascist militia, the Ustase; 300,000 German soldiers surrendered to the partisans on 15 May 1945.

132 Allied prisoners of war were freed from a work camp by the Partisans in August 1944. On their evacuation route, a night ambush by a German patrol caused the loss of two prisoners and two of the escort. Eventually the rescued men reached Semič, a Partisan base used by escapers. They were flown to Bari on 21 September 1944.

In German anti-partisan operations, more than 1,700,000 Yugoslav civilians were murdered by German and SS troops; 305,000 partisans were killed in action.

Between 1 January and 15 October 1944, according to statistics compiled by the United States Air Force Air Crew Rescue Unit, 1,152 American airmen were airlifted from Yugoslavia, 795 with Partisan assistance and 356 with Chetnik help. Between 1941 and 1944, 33 United States Flying Fortresses crashed in Slovenia; Slovenian partisans, helped by the local population, rescued 303 American and 30 British airmen.

20 October 1944: Liberated by Tito's People's Liberation Army and Soviet troops

Autumn 1941: Partisans established Republic of Uzice (occupied by Germans forces November 1941)

14 & 15 May 1945: Partisans defeated last fighting German military units

10 August 1941: partisan group established a 'Miners' Republic'

12–15 May 1945: Partisans kill several thousand disarmed Croat Ustase and collaborationist soldiers and civilians

Entered by Tito's People's Liberation Army, 8 May 1945

22 June 1941: First Sisak Partisan Brigade established

26 April 1941: Slovene partisan group established

Entered by Tito's People's Liberation Army, 2 May 1945; it was forced to withdraw three days later by British forces.

--- International borders, 1937

△ Towns at the centre of 'The People's Uprising', Montenegro, May–November 1941

✶ People's Liberation Army confrontations with the German occupation forces, 1943

▲ People's Liberation Army headquarters

Areas under effective partisan control by the end of 1943

German troops under virtual siege from the partisans

© Martin Gilbert 2008

ROMANIA

HUNGARY

AUSTRIA

SLOVENIA

CROATIA

BOSNIA

HERCEGOVINA

MONTENEGRO

SERBIA

MACEDONIA

BULGARIA

GREECE

ALBANIA

ITALY

Adriatic Sea

Belgrade
Novi Sad
Zagreb
Rijeka
Trieste
Ljubljana
Soteska
Konevje
Semič
Crkvenica
Otocac
Bihac
Glina
Topusko
Drvar
VIS
Split
Mostar
Prozor
Jajce
Kladani
Kalinevic
Foca
Sarajevo
Mount Durmitor
Niksić
Bijelo Pole
Berane
Kolasin
Podgorica
Cetinje
Murino
Mount Peljivan
Skopje
Ochrid
Bitola
Bari

0   kilometres   150
0   miles   100

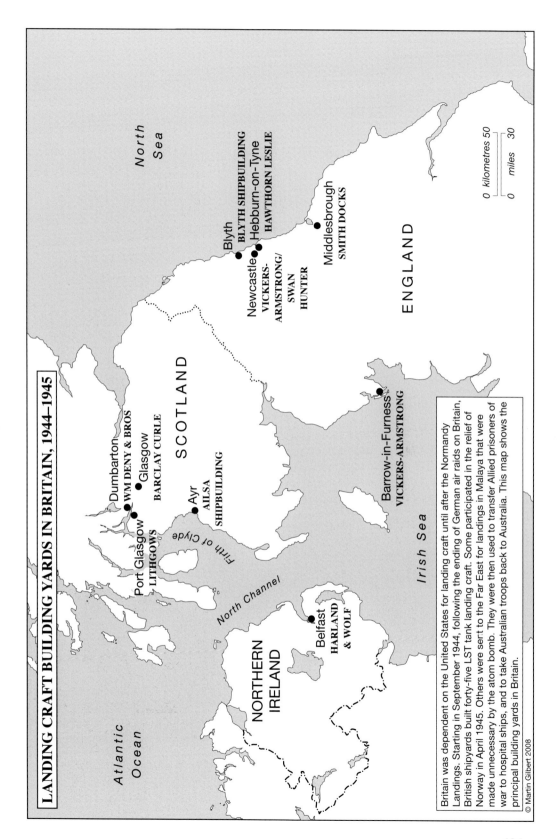

LANDING CRAFT BUILDING YARDS IN BRITAIN, 1944–1945

North Sea

Blyth
BLYTH SHIPBUILDING
Hebburn-on-Tyne **HAWTHORN LESLIE**

Newcastle
VICKERS-ARMSTRONG/ SWAN HUNTER

Middlesbrough **SMITH DOCKS**

ENGLAND

Atlantic Ocean

Dumbarton **WM DENY & BROS**
Glasgow **BARCLAY CURLE**

SCOTLAND

Ayr **AILSA SHIPBUILDING**

Port Glasgow **LITHGOWS**

Firth of Clyde

Barrow-in-Furness **VICKERS-ARMSTRONG**

Irish Sea

North Channel

Belfast **HARLAND & WOLF**

NORTHERN IRELAND

0 kilometres 50
0 miles 30

Britain was dependent on the United States for landing craft until after the Normandy Landings. Starting in September 1944, following the ending of German air raids on Britain, British shipyards built forty-five LST tank landing craft. Some participated in the relief of Norway in April 1945. Others were sent to the Far East for landings in Malaya that were made unnecessary by the atom bomb. They were then used to transfer Allied prisoners of war to hospital ships, and to take Australian troops back to Australia. This map shows the principal building yards in Britain.

© Martin Gilbert 2008

Section 8

YEAR OF DECISION: 1944

Much of Warsaw is ours again!

In many areas, the red and white flag of Poland is flying over the scarred but proud city for the first time in almost five years, and the hated Swastikas have been torn down and burned.

JULIAN KULSKI
A participant in the Warsaw Uprising
Diary entry
4 August 1944

If your new weapons, in which such burning faith is placed, do not bring success, then, my Führer, take the decision to end the war.

The German people have suffered such unspeakable ills, that the time has come to put an end to these horrors.

FIELD MARSHAL GÜNTHER VON KLUGE
Letter to Hitler
17 August 1944

THE YUGOSLAV PARTISAN AIR FORCE, MAY 1942 – MAY 1945

Gorica
captured by partisans
from September 1943,
many Italian aircraft
seized

Meduvodje
captured by
partisans
May-June 1942

Lacarac
used by partisans,
December 1944 -
May 1945

Ruma
partisan air bases,
December 1944

Zaluzani
captured by
partisans,
September 1944

Zemun
used by partisans for
training aircrew
October 1944

Prijedor
captured by
partisans
May 1942

Pancevo
used for training
Yugoslav aircrew and
by Soviet Air Force,
from October 1944

Lusca Palanka
captured by partisans,
July 1942, used for
bombing raids by
single aircraft

Livno
used by
partisans from
14 October 1943

Skrabrnje
captured by
partisans,
May 1943

Divulje
captured by
partisans from
September 1943

VIS
liberated by
partisans,
August 1944

Mostar
captured by
partisans
April 1945

Glamocko Polje
captured by partisans from
November 1943. Partisan
leader Ivo Lola Ribar killed
by a German bomber on
27 November 1943 while
about to take off for Allied
Headquarters in Italy

Niksic
German aircraft
captured by
partisans, August–
September 1944

Ljubljana · Zagreb · Fiume · Ljubija · C R O A T I A · Banja Luka · Belgrade · ROMANIA · Zadar · DALMATIA · Split · BOSNIA · Sarajevo · S E R B I A · HERZEGOVINA · Nish · MONTENEGRO · Sofia · BULGARIA · Dubrovnik · Kotor · Skopje · Adriatic Sea · MACEDONIA · ALBANIA · Durazzo · Tirana · Ochrid · Bitola · Brindisi · Valona · Klisura · G R E E C E · Salonika · Aegean Sea

```
0    kilometres    150
0      miles       100
```

Legend:
- ▨ German-occupied Yugoslavia
- ═ Borders of independent Croatia
- ▬ ▬ Borders of the Italian Zone of Occupation
- ▲ Partisan airstrips

As the Yugoslav partisans established
their control over larger and larger areas
of German-occupied Serbia, Slovenia,
the territory of the pro-German Croatian
government, and – after the surrender of
Italy in September 1943 – the Italian
Zone of Occupation, they were able to
use small air strips to attack German
lines of communications, military units
and supply dumps, and to receive
support flown in from Allied air bases in
southern Italy.

Two Croatian Air Force pilots, Franjo Kluz and Rudi Cajavec
with his mechanic Milos Jazbec, escaped to the partisans on 23
May 1942, with their two planes, flying from Banja Luka to the
partisan-held town of Prijedor. Their defection marked the start
of Yugoslav partisan aviation. From the airfield near Prijedor
and another airfield near Medjuvodje, the two pilots flew their
first sortie on 4 June 1942 against the German occupation
forces. The pipe bombs they dropped by hand had been
produced by the partisans at the Ljubija mine, the largest
iron-ore mine in Yugoslavia. Cajavec was killed during the first
mission; wounded and forced to land near a Croat-held village,
he shot himself to avoid capture. His mechanic, Milos Jazbec,
was captured and later executed in Zagreb. Kluz completed
three more missions, attacking German transport columns and
garrisons with his machine gun and pipe bombs. On 6 July
1942 his plane was destroyed on the ground by a German
fighter at the airfield near Lusca Palanka.

© Martin Gilbert 2008

135

THE UNITED STATES 'BIG WEEK' BOMBING OFFENSIVE, 19–25 FEBRUARY 1944

GREAT BRITAIN

North Sea

DENMARK

Baltic Sea

EAST ANGLIA
United States Strategic Air Force bases →

London

Rostock ●
AIR PARK

Tutow ●
AIR ASSEMBLY PLANT

Bremen ●
AIRCRAFT FACTORY

Braunschweig ●
AIRCRAFT FACTORY

●Berlin

Halberstadt ●
AIRCRAFT FACTORY

Bernberg ● *AIR PARK*

Aschersleben ● *AIRCRAFT FACTORY*

Kassel ●
AIRCRAFT FACTORY

Gotha
●*AIRCRAFT FACTORY*

Brussels ●
AIRCRAFT FACTORY

English Channel

●Caen

NORMANDY

● Paris

FRANCE

Rhine

GREATER GERMANY

Schweinfurt ●
BALL BEARING FACTORY

Fürth ●
AIRCRAFT FACTORY

Stuttgart ●
BALL BEARING FACTORY

Regensburg ●
AIRCRAFT FACTORY

Danube

Vienna ●

Augsburg ●
AIRCRAFT FACTORY

Steyr ●
BALL BEARING FACTORY

Neustadt ●
AIR PARK

Zell-am-See ●
RAILWAY LINES

SWITZERLAND
neutral

Graz ●
AIRFIELD

Pola ● *WAREHOUSES*

Fiume ●
PORT INSTALLATIONS

Adriatic Sea

Zara ●
PORT INSTALLATIONS

Mediterranean

0   kilometres   200
0   miles   100

ITALY

Sea

Rome ●

Allied front line during 'Big Week'

Foggia ●
Allied air base

Bari ●
Allied air base

—— Greater Germany
● Principal 'Big Week' targets

© Martin Gilbert 2008

To prevent German aircraft interfering with the planned Allied landings in Normandy, the United States Strategic Air Force launched 3,000 sorties from Britain and 500 from southern Italy against German aircraft industry, including airframe manufacturing and aircraft assembly plants. During the 'Big Week' offensive, the United States Eighth Air Force lost 226 heavy bombers and 2,600 crewmen. A total of 8,000 tons of bombs were dropped. The German Air Force, with more than 500 fighter aircraft destroyed, lost the ability to control the air above German soil.

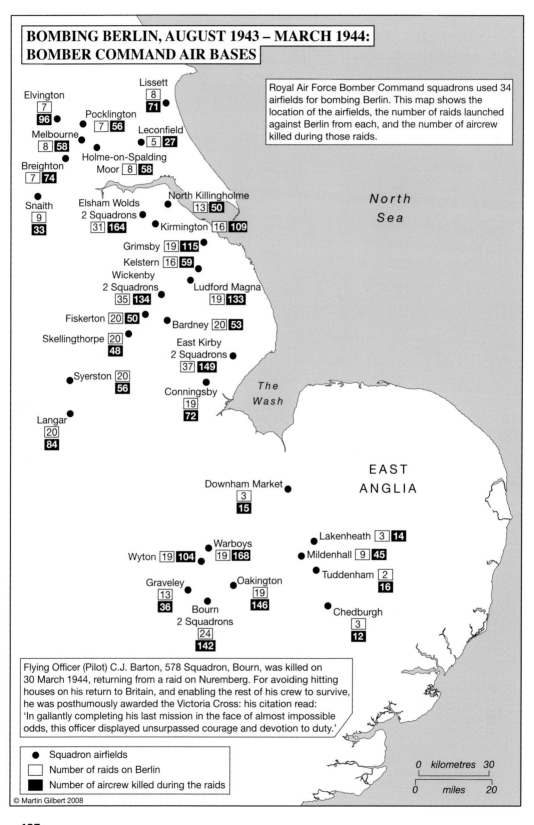

BOMBING BERLIN, AUGUST 1943 – MARCH 1944: BOMBER COMMAND AIR BASES

Royal Air Force Bomber Command squadrons used 34 airfields for bombing Berlin. This map shows the location of the airfields, the number of raids launched against Berlin from each, and the number of aircrew killed during those raids.

Lissett 8 71

Elvington 7 96

Pocklington 7 56

Melbourne 8 58

Leconfield 5 27

Breighton 7 74

Holme-on-Spalding Moor 8 58

Snaith 9 33

Elsham Wolds 2 Squadrons 31 164

North Killingholme 13 50

Kirmington 16 109

Grimsby 19 115

Kelstern 16 59

Wickenby 2 Squadrons 35 134

Ludford Magna 19 133

Fiskerton 20 50

Bardney 20 53

Skellingthorpe 20 48

East Kirby 2 Squadrons 37 149

Syerston 20 56

Conningsby 19 72

Langar 20 84

North Sea

The Wash

EAST ANGLIA

Downham Market 3 15

Lakenheath 3 14

Mildenhall 9 45

Warboys 19 168

Wyton 19 104

Tuddenham 2 16

Graveley 13 36

Oakington 19 146

Bourn 2 Squadrons 24 142

Chedburgh 3 12

Flying Officer (Pilot) C.J. Barton, 578 Squadron, Bourn, was killed on 30 March 1944, returning from a raid on Nuremberg. For avoiding hitting houses on his return to Britain, and enabling the rest of his crew to survive, he was posthumously awarded the Victoria Cross: his citation read: 'In gallantly completing his last mission in the face of almost impossible odds, this officer displayed unsurpassed courage and devotion to duty.'

● Squadron airfields
☐ Number of raids on Berlin
■ Number of aircrew killed during the raids

0 kilometres 30
0 miles 20

© Martin Gilbert 2008

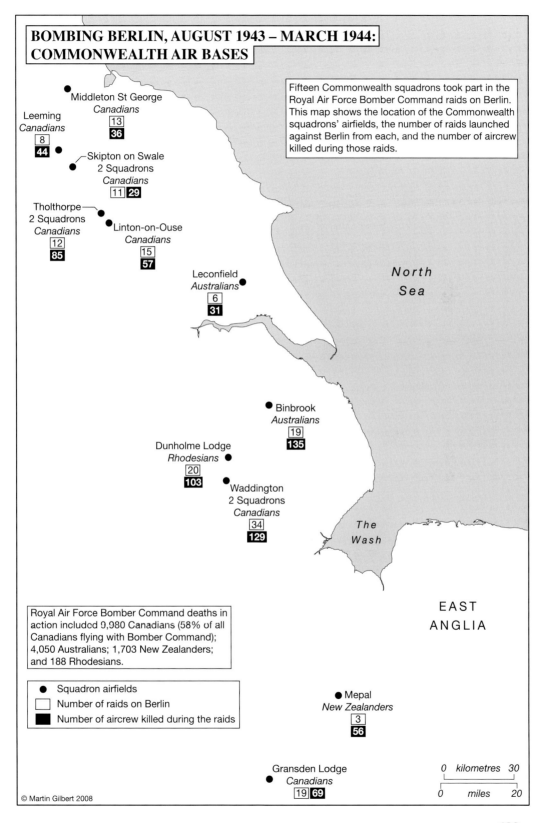

BOMBING BERLIN, AUGUST 1943 – MARCH 1944: COMMONWEALTH AIR BASES

Fifteen Commonwealth squadrons took part in the Royal Air Force Bomber Command raids on Berlin. This map shows the location of the Commonwealth squadrons' airfields, the number of raids launched against Berlin from each, and the number of aircrew killed during those raids.

Middleton St George
Canadians
13
36

Leeming
Canadians
8
44

Skipton on Swale
2 Squadrons
Canadians
11 29

Tholthorpe
2 Squadrons
Canadians
12
85

Linton-on-Ouse
Canadians
15
57

Leconfield
Australians
6
31

North Sea

Binbrook
Australians
19
135

Dunholme Lodge
Rhodesians
20
103

Waddington
2 Squadrons
Canadians
34
129

The Wash

EAST ANGLIA

Royal Air Force Bomber Command deaths in action included 9,980 Canadians (58% of all Canadians flying with Bomber Command); 4,050 Australians; 1,703 New Zealanders; and 188 Rhodesians.

● Squadron airfields
☐ Number of raids on Berlin
■ Number of aircrew killed during the raids

Mepal
New Zealanders
3
56

Gransden Lodge
Canadians
19 69

0 kilometres 30
0 miles 20

© Martin Gilbert 2008

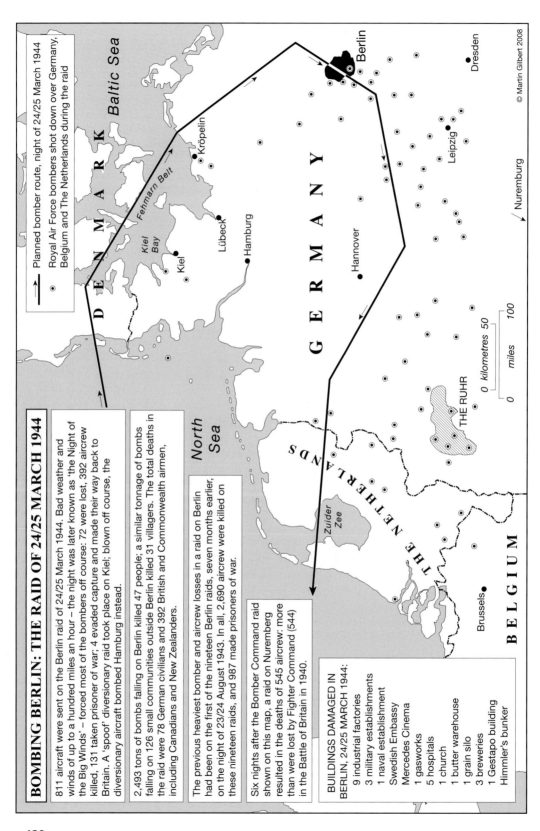

BOMBING BERLIN: THE RAID OF 24/25 MARCH 1944

811 aircraft were sent on the Berlin raid of 24/25 March 1944. Bad weather and winds of up to a hundred miles an hour – the night was later known as 'the Night of the Big Winds' – forced most of the bombers off course: 72 were lost, 392 aircrew killed, 131 taken prisoner of war; 4 evaded capture and made their way back to Britain. A 'spoof' diversionary raid took place on Kiel; blown off course, the diversionary aircraft bombed Hamburg instead.

2,493 tons of bombs falling on Berlin killed 47 people; a similar tonnage of bombs falling on 126 small communities outside Berlin killed 31 villagers. The total deaths in the raid were 78 German civilians and 392 British and Commonwealth airmen, including Canadians and New Zealanders.

The previous heaviest bomber and aircrew losses in a raid on Berlin had been on the first of the nineteen Berlin raids, seven months earlier, on the night of 23/24 August 1943. In all, 2,690 aircrew were killed on these nineteen raids, and 987 made prisoners of war.

Six nights after the Bomber Command raid shown on this map, a raid on Nuremberg resulted in the deaths of 545 aircrew: more than were lost by Fighter Command (544) in the Battle of Britain in 1940.

BUILDINGS DAMAGED IN
BERLIN, 24/25 MARCH 1944:
9 industrial factories
3 military establishments
1 naval establishment
Swedish Embassy
Mercedes Cinema
1 gasworks
5 hospitals
1 church
1 butter warehouse
1 grain silo
3 breweries
1 Gestapo building
Himmler's bunker

→ Planned bomber route, night of 24/25 March 1944

⊙ Royal Air Force bombers shot down over Germany, Belgium and The Netherlands during the raid

© Martin Gilbert 2008

Baltic Sea

Berlin

Dresden

Kröpelin

Fehmarn Belt

Kiel Bay

Lübeck

Hamburg

Kiel

Leipzig

D E N M A R K

G E R M A N Y

Hannover

North Sea

T H E   N E T H E R L A N D S

Zuider Zee

THE RUHR

0 kilometres 50   100

0   miles

↓ Nuremburg

Brussels

B E L G I U M

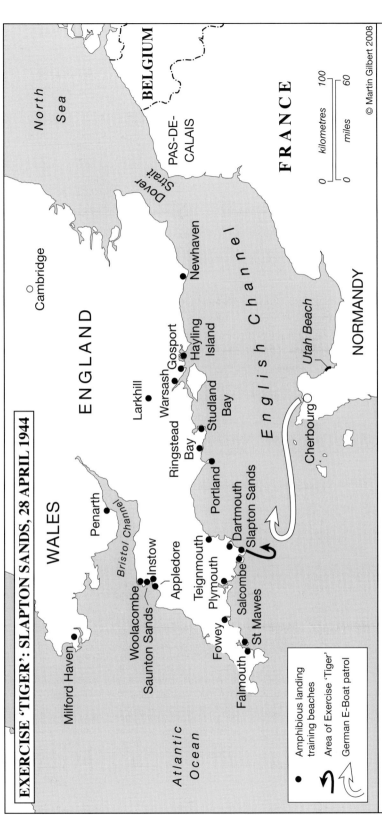

EXERCISE 'TIGER': SLAPTON SANDS, 28 APRIL 1944

In preparation for the cross-Channel landings, exercises were held in which troops were put ashore on British beaches. Exercise Tiger was a practice landing on Slapton Sands, carried out by the 4th United States Infantry Division, as part of its preparation for the Utah Beach landing. In the early hours of 28 April 1944, a German E-boat force, sailing from Cherbourg, came across the exercise, and – mistaking the American landing craft for destroyers – torpedoed two of the eight landing craft: *LST 507*, on which 127 men were drowned, and *LST 531*, on which 424 men were drowned.

Many more men were killed in the Exercise Tiger practice landing (551 soldiers and 198 sailors) than were killed thirty-eight days later in the actual Utah Beach landing (197). The names of the Exercise Tiger dead are engraved in the American Battle Monuments Commission cemetery just outside Cambridge, England.

Ten of the American officers on Exercise Tiger knew the location of the landing beaches in Normandy. An intense search was made to find their bodies; had a single one of them been captured by the Germans, the secret destination might have been revealed. Fortunately for the allies, although more than one hundred bodies were not recovered, after more than a week of searches, all ten bodies of those who knew the secret were recovered. The D-Day secret was safe.

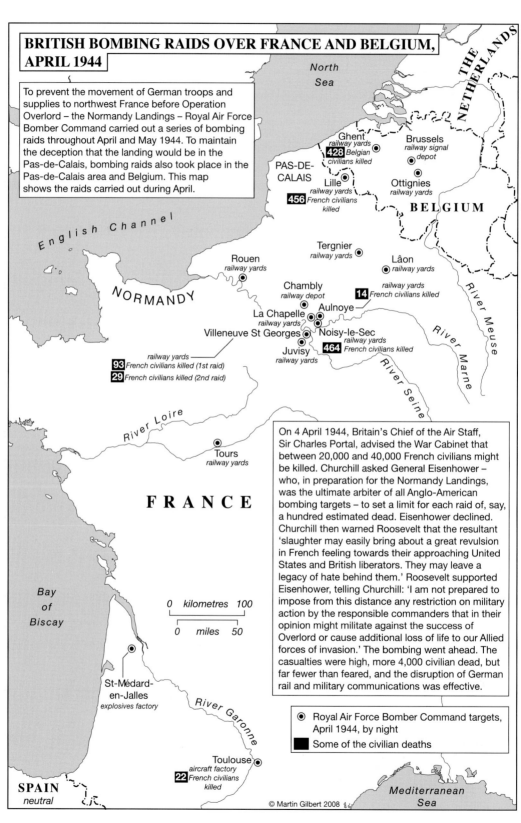

BRITISH BOMBING RAIDS OVER FRANCE AND BELGIUM, APRIL 1944

To prevent the movement of German troops and supplies to northwest France before Operation Overlord – the Normandy Landings – Royal Air Force Bomber Command carried out a series of bombing raids throughout April and May 1944. To maintain the deception that the landing would be in the Pas-de-Calais, bombing raids also took place in the Pas-de-Calais area and Belgium. This map shows the raids carried out during April.

North Sea

THE NETHERLANDS

Ghent
railway yards
428 *Belgian civilians killed*

Brussels
railway signal
depot

PAS-DE-CALAIS

Ottignies
railway yards

Lille
railway yards
456 *French civilians killed*

BELGIUM

English Channel

NORMANDY

Tergnier
railway yards

Lâon
railway yards

Rouen
railway yards

Chambly
railway depot

Aulnoye
railway yards
14 *French civilians killed*

La Chapelle
railway yards

Noisy-le-Sec
railway yards
464 *French civilians killed*

Villeneuve St Georges

Juvisy
railway yards

railway yards
93 *French civilians killed (1st raid)*
29 *French civilians killed (2nd raid)*

River Meuse

River Marne

River Seine

River Loire

Tours
railway yards

FRANCE

On 4 April 1944, Britain's Chief of the Air Staff, Sir Charles Portal, advised the War Cabinet that between 20,000 and 40,000 French civilians might be killed. Churchill asked General Eisenhower – who, in preparation for the Normandy Landings, was the ultimate arbiter of all Anglo-American bombing targets – to set a limit for each raid of, say, a hundred estimated dead. Eisenhower declined. Churchill then warned Roosevelt that the resultant 'slaughter may easily bring about a great revulsion in French feeling towards their approaching United States and British liberators. They may leave a legacy of hate behind them.' Roosevelt supported Eisenhower, telling Churchill: 'I am not prepared to impose from this distance any restriction on military action by the responsible commanders that in their opinion might militate against the success of Overlord or cause additional loss of life to our Allied forces of invasion.' The bombing went ahead. The casualties were high, more 4,000 civilian dead, but far fewer than feared, and the disruption of German rail and military communications was effective.

Bay of Biscay

0   kilometres   100

0   miles   50

St-Médard-en-Jalles
explosives factory

River Garonne

⊙   Royal Air Force Bomber Command targets, April 1944, by night

■   Some of the civilian deaths

SPAIN
neutral

Toulouse
aircraft factory
22 *French civilians killed*

© Martin Gilbert 2008

Mediterranean Sea

ANGLO-AMERICAN BOMBING ATTACKS ON GERMANY, 1 MAY – 5 JUNE 1944

In the six weeks before the Normandy Landings, Anglo-American bomber forces based in Britain struck, often repeatedly, at twenty military and industrial targets in Germany.

North Sea

Baltic Sea

Kiel
mine laying in the Kiel Canal

Kiel Canal

Pölitz
synthetic oil factory

Tutow
aircraft assembly

Hamburg
port area

River

Oldenburg
airfield

Osnabrück

Hannover

Berlin
diesel engine works

THE NETHERLANDS

22/23 May
335 Germans and **26** Allied POWs killed 6 industrial buildings and 852 houses destroyed

Brunswick
marshalling yards

River Elbe

Xanten
ammunition dump

Dortmund

Duisburg

Wuppertal

Düsseldorf

21/22 May
factories
350 buildings destroyed
124 people killed

Leverkusen

Cologne

Aachen

Zeitz
synthetic oil factory

Bombed in error for Düsseldorf
20/21 May
71 people killed

BELGIUM

24/25 May
railway marshalling yards
259 people killed
27/28 May
railway marshalling yards
167 people killed
(this raid, by 162 bombers, lasted only twelve minutes)

GERMANY

River Rhine

River Main

CZECHOSLOVAKIA

LUXEMBOURG

Saarbrücken
marshalling yards

● Main targets inside Germany, 1 May – 5 June 1944, of the United States Army Air Force bomber forces based in Britain

◉ Main targets of the Royal Air Force, Bomber Command, 1 May – 5 June 1944

■ German civilians killed (total 956)

□ Allied prisoners of war killed (total 26)

FRANCE

0 kilometres 100

0 miles 50

Ludwigshaven

Meersburg
synthetic oil factory

SWITZERLAND
neutral

Lake Constance

© Martin Gilbert 2008

142

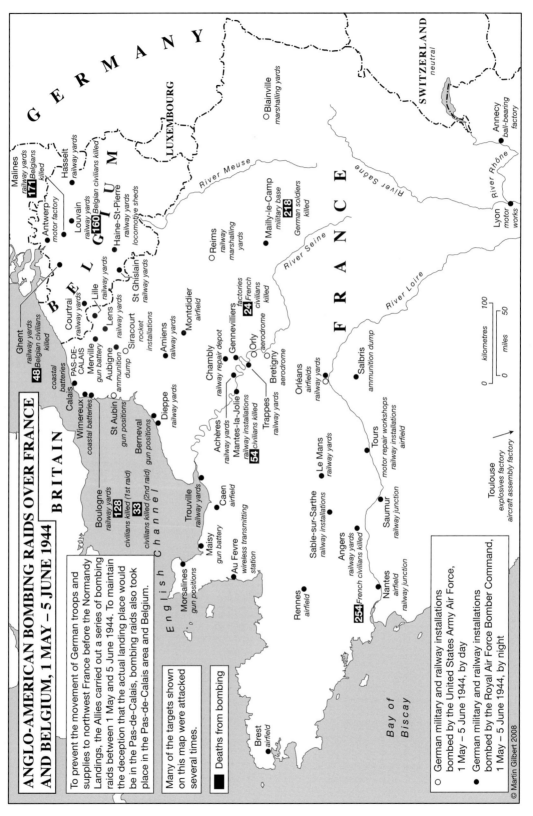

ANGLO-AMERICAN BOMBING RAIDS OVER FRANCE AND BELGIUM, 1 MAY – 5 JUNE 1944

BRITAIN

To prevent the movement of German troops and supplies to northwest France before the Normandy Landings, the Allies carried out a series of bombing raids between 1 May and 5 June 1944. To maintain the deception that the actual landing place would be in the Pas-de-Calais, bombing raids also took place in the Pas-de-Calais area and Belgium.

Many of the targets shown on this map were attacked several times.

■ Deaths from bombing

○ German military and railway installations bombed by the United States Army Air Force, 1 May – 5 June 1944, by day

● German military and railway installations bombed by the Royal Air Force Bomber Command, 1 May – 5 June 1944, by night

GERMANY

LUXEMBOURG

BELGIUM

FRANCE

SWITZERLAND
neutral

Malines
railway yards
171 *Belgians killed*

Hasselt
railway yards

Antwerp
motor factory

Louvain
railway yards

Ghent
railway yards
48 *Belgian civilians killed*

G 160 *Belgian civilians killed*

Haine-St-Pierre
railway yards
locomotive sheds

St Ghislain
railway yards

Courtrai
railway yards

Lille
railway yards

Lens
railway yards

Merville
gun battery

PAS-DE-CALAIS
coastal batteries

Calais
coastal batteries

Wimereux
coastal batteries

Aubigne
ammunition dump

Siracourt
rocket installations

Amiens
railway yards

Montdidier
airfield

Reims
railway marshalling yards

Blainville
marshalling yards

Mailly-le-Camp
military base
218 *German soldiers killed*

Genneviliers
factories

Orly
aerodrome
24 *French civilians killed*

Bretigny
aerodrome

Chambly
railway repair depot

Achères
railway yards

Mantes-la-Jolie
railway installations
54 *civilians killed*

Trappes
railway yards

St Aubin
gun positions

Berneval
gun positions

Dieppe
railway yards

Boulogne
railway yards
128 *civilians killed (1st raid)*
33 *civilians killed (2nd raid)*

Trouville
railway yards

Caen
airfield

Orléans
railway yards

Salbris
ammunition dump

Tours
motor repair workshops
railway installations
airfield

Maisy
gun battery

Au Fevre
wireless transmitting station

Morsalines
gun positions

Sable-sur-Sarthe
railway installations

Le Mans
railway yards

Angers
railway yards

Saumur
railway junction

Nantes
airfield
railway junction
254 *French civilians killed*

Rennes
airfield

Brest
airfield

Toulouse
explosives factory
aircraft assembly factory

Lyon
motor works

Annecy
ball-bearing factory

River Meuse

River Seine

River Loire

River Saône

River Rhône

English Channel

Bay of Biscay

0   50   100
kilometres
0   50
miles

© Martin Gilbert 2008

143

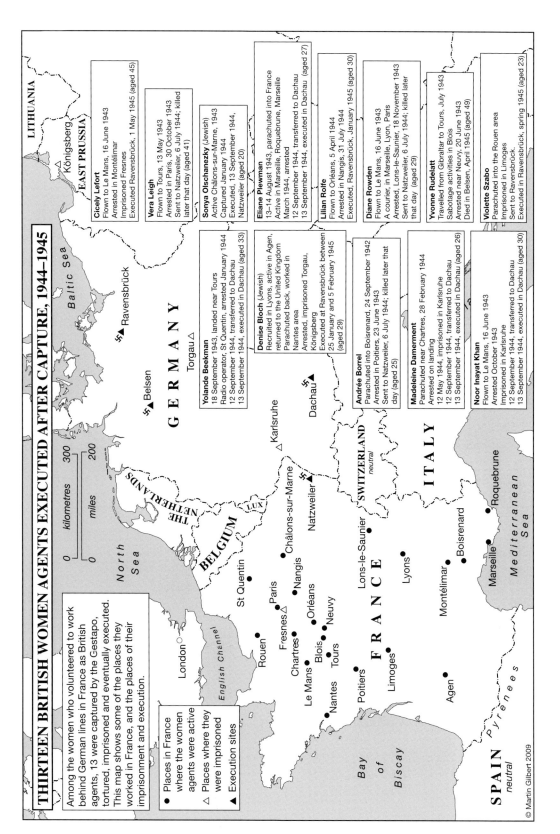

THIRTEEN BRITISH WOMEN AGENTS EXECUTED AFTER CAPTURE, 1944–1945

Among the women who volunteered to work behind German lines in France as British agents, 13 were captured by the Gestapo, tortured, imprisoned and eventually executed. This map shows some of the places they worked in France, and the places of their imprisonment and execution.

- ● Places in France where the women agents were active
- △ Places where they were imprisoned
- ▲ Execution sites

Cicely Lefort
Flown to Le Mans, 16 June 1943
Arrested in Montélimar
Imprisoned Fresnes
Executed Ravensbrück, 1 May 1945 (aged 45)

Vera Leigh
Flown to Tours, 13 May 1943
Arrested in Paris, 30 October 1943
Sent to Natzweiler, 6 July 1944; killed later that day (aged 41)

Sonya Olschanezky (Jewish)
Active Châlons-sur-Marne, 1943
Captured January 1944
Executed, 13 September 1944, Natzweiler (aged 20)

Eliane Plewman
13–14 August 1943, parachuted into France
Active in Marseille, Roquebrune, Marseille
March 1944, arrested
12 September 1944, transferred to Dachau
13 September 1944, executed in Dachau (aged 27)

Lilian Rolfe
Flown to Orléans, 5 April 1944
Arrested in Nangis, 31 July 1944
Executed, Ravensbrück, January 1945 (aged 30)

Diane Rowden
Flown to Le Mans, 16 June 1943
A courier, in Marseille, Lyon, Paris
Arrested, Lons-le-Saunier, 18 November 1943
Sent to Natzweiler, 6 July 1944; killed later that day (aged 29)

Yvonne Rudelatt
Travelled from Gibraltar to Tours, July 1943
Sabotage activities in Blois
Arrested near Neuvy, 20 June 1943
Died in Belsen, April 1945 (aged 49)

Violette Szabo
Parachuted into the Rouen area
Imprisoned in Limoges
Sent to Ravensbrück.
Executed in Ravensbrück, spring 1945 (aged 23)

Yolande Beekman
18 September 1943, landed near Tours
Radio operator, St Quentin, arrested January 1944
12 September 1944, transferred to Dachau
13 September 1944, executed in Dachau (aged 33)

Denise Bloch (Jewish)
Recruited in Lyons, active in Agen,
returned to the United Kingdom
Parachuted back, worked in
Nantes area
Arrested, imprisoned Torgau,
Königsberg
Executed at Ravensbrück between
25 January and 5 February 1945
(aged 29)

Andrée Borrel
Parachuted into Boisrenard, 24 September 1942
Arrested in Poitiers, 23 June 1943
Sent to Natzweiler, 6 July 1944; killed later that day (aged 25)

Madeleine Damerment
Parachuted near Chartres, 28 February 1944
Arrested on landing
12 May 1944, imprisoned in Karlsruhe
12 September 1944, transferred to Dachau
13 September 1944, executed in Dachau (aged 26)

Noor Inayat Khan
Flown to Le Mans, 16 June 1943
Arrested October 1943
Imprisoned in Karlsruhe
12 September 1944, transferred to Dachau
13 September 1944, executed in Dachau (aged 30)

LITHUANIA

EAST PRUSSIA

Königsberg △

Baltic Sea

Ravensbrück ▲

Torgau △

GERMANY

Belsen ▲

Dachau ▲

Karlsruhe △

Natzweiler ▲

THE NETHERLANDS

BELGIUM

LUX

North Sea

English Channel

0 kilometres 300
0 miles 200

London ○

Rouen ●
Fresnes △
Paris ●
Chartres ●
Le Mans ●
Blois ●
Tours ●
Nantes ●
Poitiers ●
Orléans ●
Neuvy ●
Nangis ●
Châlons-sur-Marne ●
Lons-le-Saunier ●
Lyons ●
Boisrenard ●
Montélimar ●
Limoges ●
Agen ●
Marseille ●
Roquebrune ●

St Quentin ●

FRANCE

SWITZERLAND
neutral

ITALY

Mediterranean Sea

Bay of Biscay

SPAIN
neutral

Pyrenees

© Martin Gilbert 2009

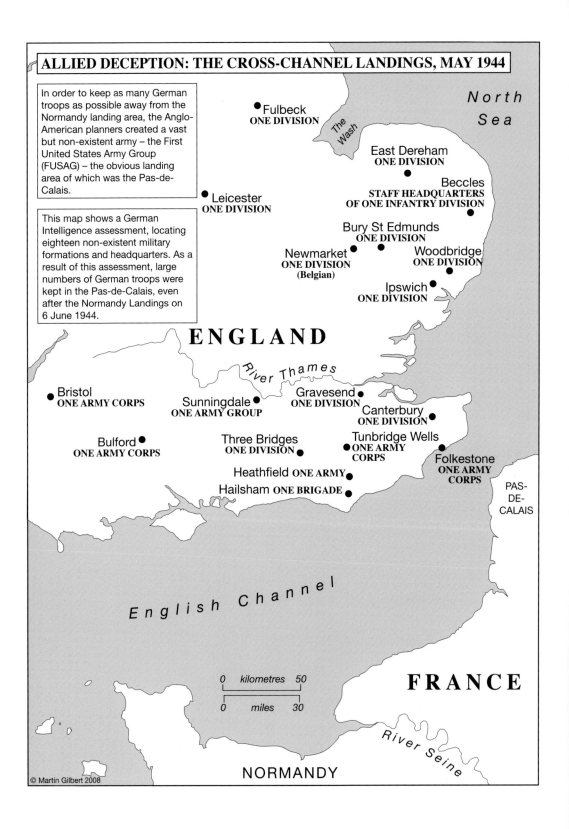

ALLIED DECEPTION: THE CROSS-CHANNEL LANDINGS, MAY 1944

In order to keep as many German troops as possible away from the Normandy landing area, the Anglo-American planners created a vast but non-existent army – the First United States Army Group (FUSAG) – the obvious landing area of which was the Pas-de-Calais.

This map shows a German Intelligence assessment, locating eighteen non-existent military formations and headquarters. As a result of this assessment, large numbers of German troops were kept in the Pas-de-Calais, even after the Normandy Landings on 6 June 1944.

North Sea

Fulbeck
ONE DIVISION

The Wash

East Dereham
ONE DIVISION

Beccles
STAFF HEADQUARTERS
OF ONE INFANTRY DIVISION

Leicester
ONE DIVISION

Bury St Edmunds
ONE DIVISION

Woodbridge
ONE DIVISION

Newmarket
ONE DIVISION
(Belgian)

Ipswich
ONE DIVISION

ENGLAND

River Thames

Bristol
ONE ARMY CORPS

Sunningdale
ONE ARMY GROUP

Gravesend
ONE DIVISION

Canterbury
ONE DIVISION

Bulford
ONE ARMY CORPS

Three Bridges
ONE DIVISION

Tunbridge Wells
ONE ARMY CORPS

Folkestone
ONE ARMY CORPS

Heathfield ONE ARMY

Hailsham ONE BRIGADE

PAS-DE-CALAIS

English Channel

| 0 | kilometres | 50 |
| 0 | miles | 30 |

FRANCE

River Seine

© Martin Gilbert 2008

NORMANDY

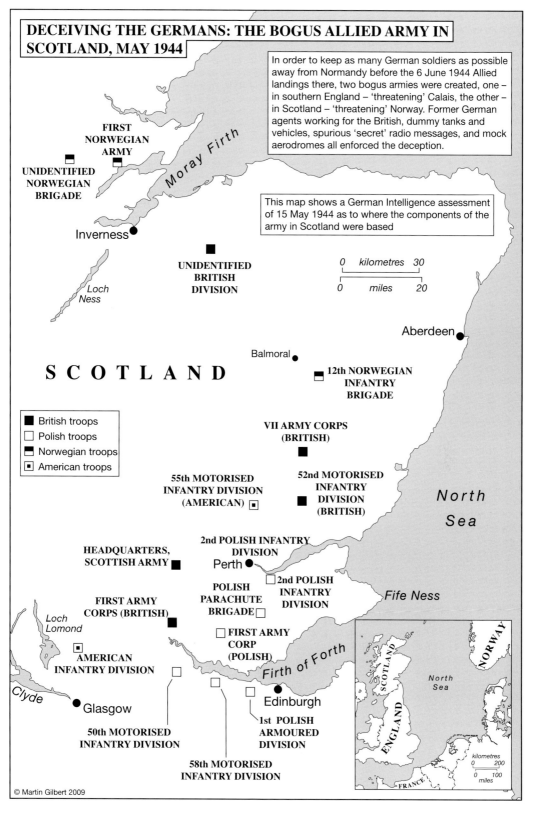

DECEIVING THE GERMANS: THE BOGUS ALLIED ARMY IN SCOTLAND, MAY 1944

In order to keep as many German soldiers as possible away from Normandy before the 6 June 1944 Allied landings there, two bogus armies were created, one – in southern England – 'threatening' Calais, the other – in Scotland – 'threatening' Norway. Former German agents working for the British, dummy tanks and vehicles, spurious 'secret' radio messages, and mock aerodromes all enforced the deception.

This map shows a German Intelligence assessment of 15 May 1944 as to where the components of the army in Scotland were based

FIRST NORWEGIAN ARMY

UNIDENTIFIED NORWEGIAN BRIGADE

Moray Firth

Inverness

Loch Ness

UNIDENTIFIED BRITISH DIVISION

| 0 | kilometres | 30 |
| 0 | miles | 20 |

Aberdeen

Balmoral

12th NORWEGIAN INFANTRY BRIGADE

S C O T L A N D

VII ARMY CORPS (BRITISH)

55th MOTORISED INFANTRY DIVISION (AMERICAN)

52nd MOTORISED INFANTRY DIVISION (BRITISH)

North Sea

- ■ British troops
- □ Polish troops
- ◫ Norwegian troops
- ▣ American troops

2nd POLISH INFANTRY DIVISION

HEADQUARTERS, SCOTTISH ARMY

Perth

2nd POLISH INFANTRY DIVISION

POLISH PARACHUTE BRIGADE

Fife Ness

FIRST ARMY CORPS (BRITISH)

Loch Lomond

FIRST ARMY CORP (POLISH)

AMERICAN INFANTRY DIVISION

Firth of Forth

Clyde

Glasgow

Edinburgh

50th MOTORISED INFANTRY DIVISION

1st POLISH ARMOURED DIVISION

58th MOTORISED INFANTRY DIVISION

NORWAY

SCOTLAND

North Sea

ENGLAND

kilometres		
0		200
0		100
miles		

FRANCE

© Martin Gilbert 2009

146

SPECIAL OPERATIONS EXECUTIVE (SOE): SABOTAGE MISSIONS IN FRANCE, JANUARY–JUNE 1944

North Sea

WALES

ENGLAND

THE NETHERLANDS

Amsterdam

London

English Channel

Brussels

GERMANY

BELGIUM

LUXEMBOURG

▲ Lieven *petrol*

Somme

Asnières *ball bearings*

▲ Choissy-au-Bac *tyres*

Levallois-Perret *artillery pieces*

▲ Aubervillers *ball bearings*

Courbevoie *aircraft parts*

Paris

Boulogne-sur-Seine *tank parts*

Ivry-sur-Seine *ball bearings*

River Seine

River Rhine

▲ Sochaux - Montbéliard *tank factory*

Dijon

Blois *wireless equipment* ▲

River Loire

Tours

Nantes

SWITZERLAND *neutral*

F R A N C E

Montluçon ▲ *tyres*

▲ Ancizes *steel*

Bar *hydro-electricity* ▲

Lyon *aircraft engine parts*

Ugine ▲ *hydro-electricity*

Bay of Biscay

Tulle ▲ *artillery pieces*

St Marcel ▲ *rolling stock*

L'Eau Rousses *hydro-electricity*

ITALY

▲ Brive-la-Gaillarde *wireless valves*

Bordeaux

Figéac *aircraft propellers*

▲ Decazaville *coal mines*

River Rhône

Toulouse

Marseille

Tarbes ▲ *aero engines, guns*

Lannemezan *hydrogen, aluminium*

Bagnères de Bigorre ▲ *self-propelled guns*

Lavelanet ▲ *hydro-electricity*

Perpignan

P y r e n e e s

SPAIN

Mediterranean Sea

| 0 | kilometres | 200 |
| 0 | miles | 150 |

Special Operations Executive (SOE) carried out thirty-seven acts of sabotage in France in 1943, and a further ninety-five in 1944. More than 3,000 pounds of explosive, mostly plastic, was needed to carry out these actions.

▲ Important sabotage actions carried out by SOE operatives, January–June 1944

© Martin Gilbert 2008

GERMAN-DOMINATED EUROPE ON 6 JUNE 1944: THE DAY OF THE NORMANDY LANDINGS

German-dominated Europe on 6 June 1944
Borders of European countries, 1941–1944
Allied forces on 6 June 1944
The Normandy landings, 6 June 1944

Arctic Ocean

Atlantic Ocean

Soviet forces

White Sea

NORWAY

SWEDEN *neutral*

FINLAND

Gulf of Bothnia

ESTONIA

Soviet forces

Moscow

North Sea

Skagerrak

Kattegat

DENMARK

Baltic Sea

LATVIA

LITHUANIA

Dublin

GREAT BRITAIN

EIRE *neutral*

London

THE NETHERLANDS

BELGIUM

Berlin

POLAND

SOVIET UNION

Soviet forces

Paris

LUXEMBOURG

GREATER GERMANY

Bay of Biscay

FRANCE

SWITZERLAND *neutral*

AUSTRIA

SLOVAKIA

HUNGARY

Soviet forces

ROMANIA

ITALY

CROATIA

SERBIA

Black Sea

SPAIN *neutral*

Adriatic Sea

BULGARIA

Rome
Allied forces
liberated, 4 June 1944

ALBANIA

GREECE

TURKEY *neutral*

Aegean Sea

Mediterranean Sea

ALGERIA

| 0 | kilometres | 500 |
| 0 | miles | 300 |

TUNISIA

RHODES

CRETE

© Martin Gilbert 2008

148

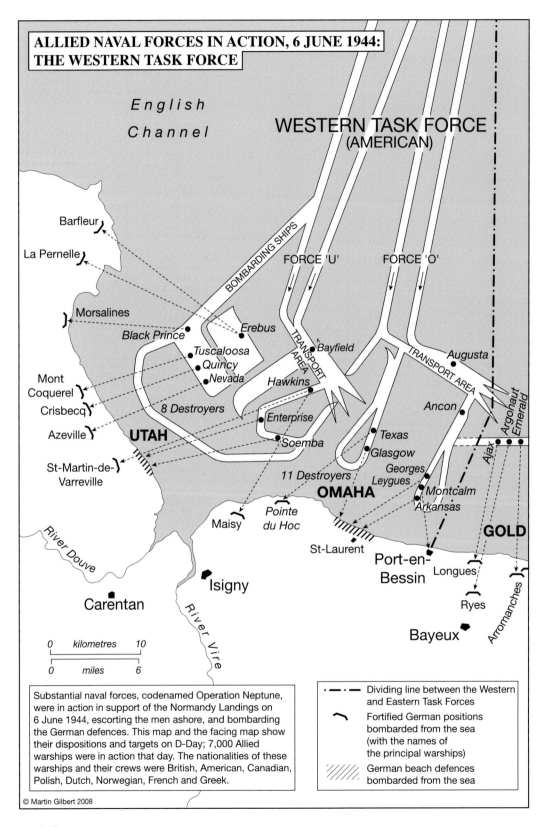

ALLIED NAVAL FORCES IN ACTION, 6 JUNE 1944: THE WESTERN TASK FORCE

English Channel

WESTERN TASK FORCE (AMERICAN)

Barfleur

La Pernelle

BOMBARDING SHIPS

FORCE 'U'   FORCE 'O'

Morsalines

Erebus

Black Prince

TRANSPORT AREA

Bayfield

Tuscaloosa

Quincy

Nevada

Hawkins

Mont Coquerel

Crisbecq

8 Destroyers

Azeville

UTAH

Enterprise

Soemba

St-Martin-de-Varreville

11 Destroyers

Maisy

Pointe du Hoc

OMAHA

St-Laurent

Augusta

TRANSPORT AREA

Argohaut
Emerald

Ancon

Texas

Glasgow

Georges Leygues

Montcalm

Arkansas

Ajax

GOLD

Port-en-Bessin

Longues

Ryes

Arromanches

River Douve

Isigny

Carentan

River Vire

Bayeux

| 0 | kilometres | 10 |
| 0 | miles | 6 |

Substantial naval forces, codenamed Operation Neptune, were in action in support of the Normandy Landings on 6 June 1944, escorting the men ashore, and bombarding the German defences. This map and the facing map show their dispositions and targets on D-Day; 7,000 Allied warships were in action that day. The nationalities of these warships and their crews were British, American, Canadian, Polish, Dutch, Norwegian, French and Greek.

– · – · – Dividing line between the Western and Eastern Task Forces

⌒ Fortified German positions bombarded from the sea (with the names of the principal warships)

//// German beach defences bombarded from the sea

© Martin Gilbert 2008

149

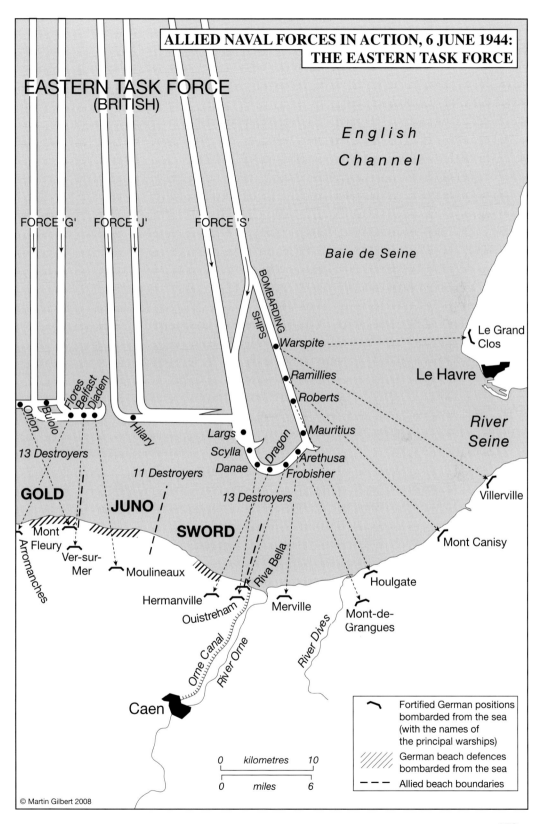

ALLIED NAVAL FORCES IN ACTION, 6 JUNE 1944: THE EASTERN TASK FORCE

EASTERN TASK FORCE
(BRITISH)

English Channel

FORCE 'G'   FORCE 'J'   FORCE 'S'

Baie de Seine

BOMBARDING SHIPS

Warspite

Ramillies

Roberts

Mauritius

Largs

Scylla   Dragon

Danae   Arethusa

Frobisher

Orion   Bulolo   Flores   Belfast   Diadem

Hilary

13 Destroyers

11 Destroyers

13 Destroyers

Le Grand Clos

Le Havre

River Seine

Villerville

Mont Canisy

GOLD

JUNO

SWORD

Mont Fleury

Ver-sur-Mer

Moulineaux

Arromanches

Hermanville

Ouistreham

Orne Canal

River Orne

Riva Bella

Merville

River Dives

Houlgate

Mont-de-Grangues

Caen

0 kilometres 10	
0 miles 6	

⌐	Fortified German positions bombarded from the sea (with the names of the principal warships)
//////	German beach defences bombarded from the sea
– – –	Allied beach boundaries

© Martin Gilbert 2008

150

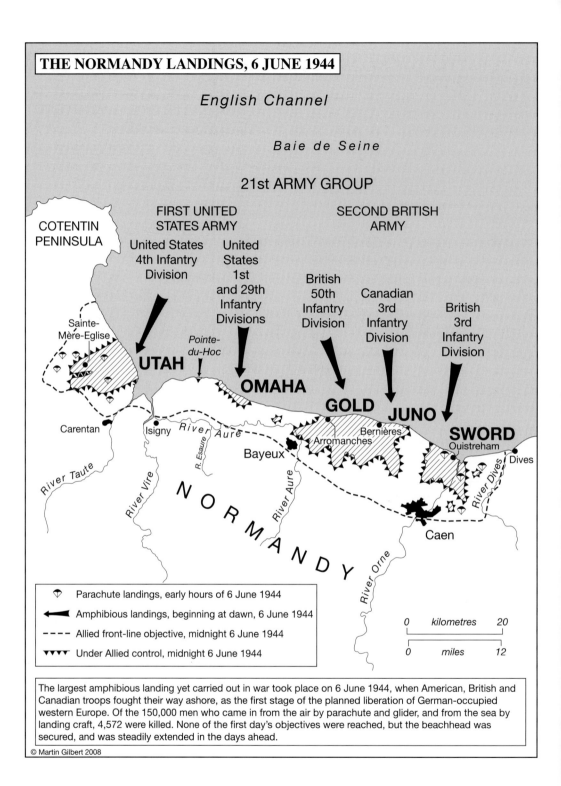

THE NORMANDY LANDINGS, 6 JUNE 1944

English Channel

Baie de Seine

21st ARMY GROUP

FIRST UNITED
STATES ARMY

SECOND BRITISH
ARMY

COTENTIN
PENINSULA

United States
4th Infantry
Division

United
States
1st
and 29th
Infantry
Divisions

British
50th
Infantry
Division

Canadian
3rd
Infantry
Division

British
3rd
Infantry
Division

Sainte-
Mère-Eglise

*Pointe-
du-Hoc*

UTAH

OMAHA

GOLD

JUNO

SWORD

Carentan

Isigny

River Aure

Bernières

Arromanches

Ouistreham

Dives

R. Esaure

Bayeux

River Taute

River Vire

River Aure

River Dives

N O R M A N D Y

Caen

River Orne

⬦	Parachute landings, early hours of 6 June 1944
◄	Amphibious landings, beginning at dawn, 6 June 1944
- - - -	Allied front-line objective, midnight 6 June 1944
▼▼▼▼	Under Allied control, midnight 6 June 1944

| 0 | kilometres | 20 |
| 0 | miles | 12 |

The largest amphibious landing yet carried out in war took place on 6 June 1944, when American, British and
Canadian troops fought their way ashore, as the first stage of the planned liberation of German-occupied
western Europe. Of the 150,000 men who came in from the air by parachute and glider, and from the sea by
landing craft, 4,572 were killed. None of the first day's objectives were reached, but the beachhead was
secured, and was steadily extended in the days ahead.

© Martin Gilbert 2008

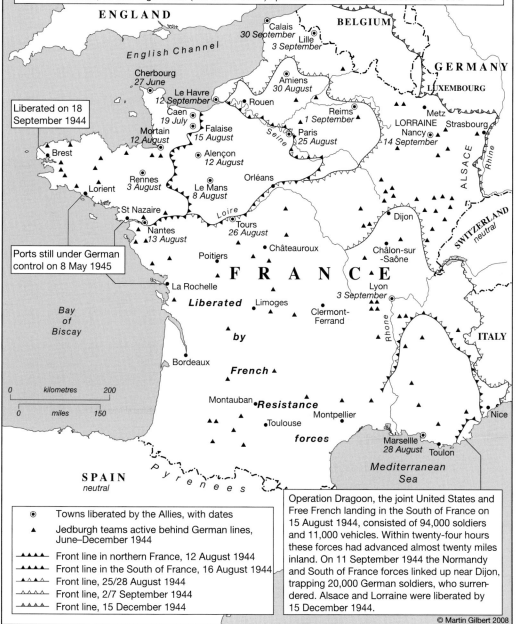

THE BATTLE FOR FRANCE, 6 JUNE – 15 SEPTEMBER 1944

Following the Normandy Landings on 6 June 1944, American, British and Canadian forces, later joined by Polish, Czechoslovak, Belgian, Dutch, Luxembourg and Free French forces, fought for more than three months to liberate France, overcoming particularly tenacious German resistance at Caen and Falaise.

As the Allied forces advanced from Normandy (from 6 June 1944) and the South of France (from 15 August 1944), special teams of British and American commandos – three-man 'Jedburgh Teams' organised by the British Special Operations Executive (SOE), the United States Office of Strategic Services (OSS) and the Free French Intelligence and Operations Bureau – were parachuted behind German lines, causing considerable disruption to the movement of German troops and supplies. Jedburgh was the Scottish town near where the teams had trained; 91 Jedburgh teams (known as 'Jeds') operated in France June to December 1944.

ENGLAND

English Channel

BELGIUM

GERMANY

LUXEMBOURG

Calais
30 September
Lille
3 September

Cherbourg
27 June

Amiens
30 August

Metz

Le Havre
12 September

Rouen

Reims
1 September

LORRAINE
Nancy
14 September

Strasbourg

Liberated on 18
September 1944

Caen
19 July

Falaise
15 August

Mortain
12 August

Paris
25 August

Seine

ALSACE

Rhine

Brest

Alençon
12 August

Rennes
3 August

Le Mans
8 August

Orléans

Lorient

St Nazaire

Loire

Dijon

SWITZERLAND
neutral

Ports still under German
control on 8 May 1945

Nantes
13 August

Tours
26 August

Châteauroux

Châlon-sur
-Saône

Poitiers

F R A N C E

La Rochelle

Lyon
3 September

Bay
of
Biscay

Liberated

Limoges

Clermont-
Ferrand

Rhone

ITALY

by

0   kilometres   200
0   miles   150

Bordeaux

French

Montauban

Resistance

Toulouse

Montpellier

Nice

forces

Marseille
28 August

Toulon

SPAIN
neutral

Pyrenees

Mediterranean
Sea

Operation Dragoon, the joint United States and Free French landing in the South of France on 15 August 1944, consisted of 94,000 soldiers and 11,000 vehicles. Within twenty-four hours these forces had advanced almost twenty miles inland. On 11 September 1944 the Normandy and South of France forces linked up near Dijon, trapping 20,000 German soldiers, who surrendered. Alsace and Lorraine were liberated by 15 December 1944.

⊙ Towns liberated by the Allies, with dates

▲ Jedburgh teams active behind German lines,
   June–December 1944

▲▲▲▲ Front line in northern France, 12 August 1944
▲▲▲▲ Front line in the South of France, 16 August 1944
▲▲▲▲ Front line, 25/28 August 1944
▲▲▲▲ Front line, 2/7 September 1944
▲▲▲▲ Front line, 15 December 1944

© Martin Gilbert 2008

THE THREE-FRONT ADVANCE TOWARDS GERMANY, 6 JUNE – 31 DECEMBER 1944

On 23 June 1944, two weeks after the Normandy Landings, the Soviet Army – by prior agreement with the Western Allies – launched its summer offensive. It had delayed this since May at the Allied request so that the Germans would be forced to take troops back from the Normandy Front. The Allied armies then advanced simultaneously towards the borders of Greater Germany.

On the Eastern Front, between 23 June and 29 August 1944, more than 375,000 German soldiers were killed and 158,000 taken prisoner. The Soviet forces captured 2,000 German tanks and 10,000 artillery pieces. In two months, the Soviet forces had advanced 450 miles, outstripping their own supply lines.

On the Western Front, the Allied forces struggled against strong German opposition to break out of the Normandy beachhead. With the breakthrough came rapid advances; Paris was liberated on 25 August, and on 12 September, at Le Havre, 12,000 German soldiers surrendered. On the central Italian Front, the German defence line was broken by 20 September.

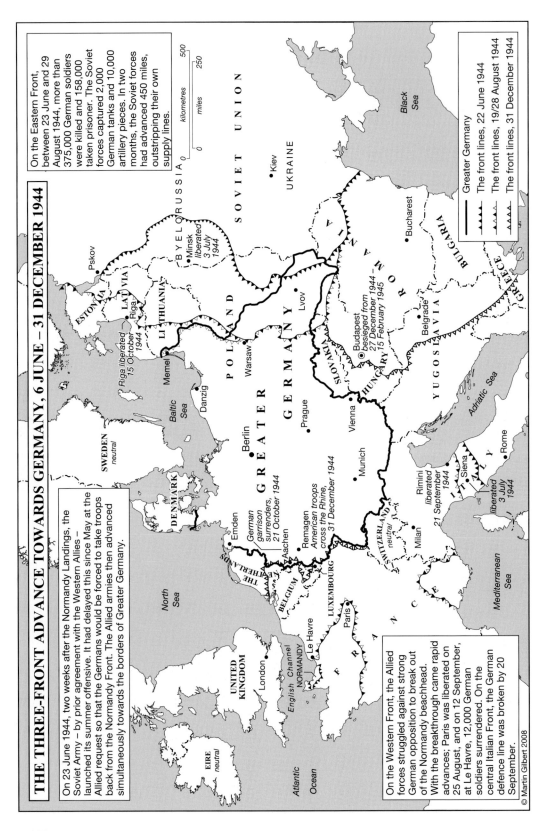

— Greater Germany
— The front lines, 22 June 1944
— The front lines, 19/28 August 1944
— The front lines, 31 December 1944

SOVIET UNION

Kiev

UKRAINE

BYELORUSSIA

Minsk
liberated
3 July
1944

Pskov

ESTONIA

LATVIA

Riga

Riga liberated
15 October
1944

LITHUANIA

Memel

Baltic
Sea

Danzig

POLAND

Warsaw

Lvov

ROMANIA

Bucharest

Budapest
besieged from
27 December 1944 –
15 February 1945

HUNGARY

SLOVAKIA

Belgrade

YUGOSLAVIA

BULGARIA

GREECE

Adriatic Sea

GREATER
GERMANY

Berlin

Prague

Vienna

Munich

Rome

ITALY

Siena
liberated
3 July
1944

Rimini
liberated
21 September
1944

Milan

SWITZERLAND
neutral

Mediterranean
Sea

SWEDEN
neutral

DENMARK

Emden

German
garrison
surrenders,
21 October 1944

Aachen

Remagen
American troops
cross the Rhine,
31 December 1944

THE NETHERLANDS

BELGIUM

LUXEMBOURG

Paris

Le Havre

FRANCE

NORMANDY

English Channel

London

UNITED
KINGDOM

North
Sea

EIRE
neutral

Atlantic
Ocean

Black
Sea

kilometres
0   250   500
miles
0   250

© Martin Gilbert 2008

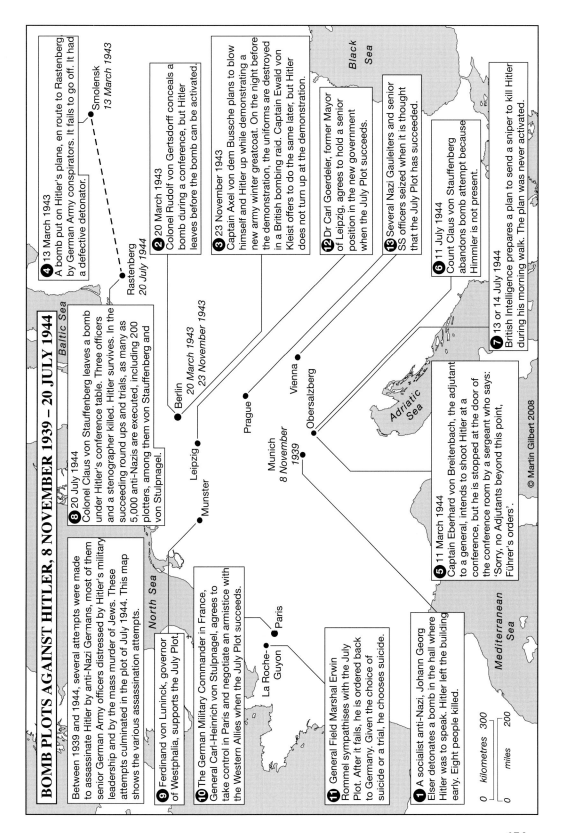

BOMB PLOTS AGAINST HITLER, 8 NOVEMBER 1939 – 20 JULY 1944

Between 1939 and 1944, several attempts were made to assassinate Hitler by anti-Nazi Germans, most of them senior German Army officers distressed by Hitler's military leadership and by the mass murder of Jews. These attempts culminated in the plot of July 1944. This map shows the various assassination attempts.

4 13 March 1943
A bomb put on Hitler's plane, en route to Rastenberg, by German Army conspirators. It fails to go off. It had a defective detonator.

2 20 March 1943
Colonel Rudolf von Gertsdorff conceals a bomb during a conference, but Hitler leaves before the bomb can be activated.

3 23 November 1943
Captain Axel von dem Bussche plans to blow himself and Hitler up while demonstrating a new army winter greatcoat. On the night before the demonstration, the uniforms are destroyed in a British bombing raid. Captain Ewald von Kleist offers to do the same later, but Hitler does not turn up at the demonstration.

12 Dr Carl Goerdeler, former Mayor of Leipzig, agrees to hold a senior position in the new government when the July Plot succeeds.

13 Several Nazi Gauleiters and senior SS officers seized when it is thought that the July Plot has succeeded.

6 11 July 1944
Count Claus von Stauffenberg abandons bomb attempt because Himmler is not present.

7 13 or 14 July 1944
British Intelligence prepares a plan to send a sniper to kill Hitler during his morning walk. The plan was never activated.

8 20 July 1944
Colonel Claus von Stauffenberg leaves a bomb under Hitler's conference table. Three officers and a stenographer killed. Hitler survives. In the succeeding round ups and trials, as many as 5,000 anti-Nazis are executed, including 200 plotters, among them von Stauffenberg and von Stulpnagel.

9 Ferdinand von Luninck, governor of Westphalia, supports the July Plot.

10 The German Military Commander in France, General Carl-Heinrich von Stulpnagel, agrees to take control in Paris and negotiate an armistice with the Western Allies when the July Plot succeeds.

11 General Field Marshal Erwin Rommel sympathises with the July Plot. After it fails, he is ordered back to Germany. Given the choice of suicide or a trial, he chooses suicide.

5 11 March 1944
Captain Eberhard von Breitenbach, the adjutant to a general, intends to shoot Hitler at a conference, but he is stopped at the door of the conference room by a sergeant who says: 'Sorry, no Adjutants beyond this point, Führer's orders'.

1 A socialist anti-Nazi, Johann Georg Elser detonates a bomb in the hall where Hitler was to speak. Hitler left the building early. Eight people killed.

Smolensk
13 March 1943

Rastenberg
20 July 1944

Baltic Sea

Black Sea

Berlin
20 March 1943
23 November 1943

Leipzig

Munster

Prague

Vienna

Obersalzberg

Munich
8 November 1939

North Sea

La Roche-
Guyon ● Paris

Adriatic Sea

Mediterranean Sea

0   kilometres   300
0   miles   200

© Martin Gilbert 2008

154

SPECIAL OPERATIONS EXECUTIVE (SOE) RESISTANCE CIRCUITS ACTIVE IN FRANCE, JUNE – NOVEMBER 1944

BRITAIN

North Sea

THE NETHERLANDS

BELGIUM

GERMANY

River Rhine

English Channel

Calais
FARMER

MUSICIAN

LUXEMBOURG

Le Havre • SALESMAN

River Seine

Reims

Nancy

NORMANDY
HELMSMAN
HEADMASTER

Paris
PROFESSOR
SCIENTIST
(fragment)

River Marne

St Mâlo

RACKETEER
BRITTANY

SCIENTIST

TINKER

River Seine

STOCKBROKER
Belfort

HILLBILLY

River Loire

Tours

DONKEYMAN

CHANCELLOR

Nevers

SWITZERLAND
neutral

F R A N C E

Mâcon

MARKSMAN

Bay of Biscay

W R E S T L E R

Limoges

SHIPWRIGHT

Lyon
ACOLYTE

ITALY

Bordeaux

A C T O R

part of
WHEELWRIGHT

Cahors

part of
PIMENTO

River Rhône

J O C K E Y

Gap

Bayonne

River Garonne

part of
WHEELWRIGHT

part of
PIMENTO

Toulouse

Avignon

GARDENER

Pau

STATIONER (detachment)

Marseille

Toulon

SPAIN
neutral

Pyrenees

Mediterranean Sea

© Martin Gilbert 2008

Special Operations Executive (SOE), established by Churchill in June 1940 to 'Set Europe ablaze', established circuits throughout France, organising, arming and maintaining resistance groups. This map shows those circuits disrupting German troop and munitions movements after the Normandy and South of France landings (June and August 1944).

Of the 470 British agents sent in to France between 1941 and 1944 (39 of them women), 117 were killed.

0   kilometres   100

0   miles   50

—·—·— International borders, 1937

☐ Code names of SOE resistance circuits active in 1944

155

THE SS MASSACRE AT ORADOUR-SUR-GLANE, 10 JUNE 1944

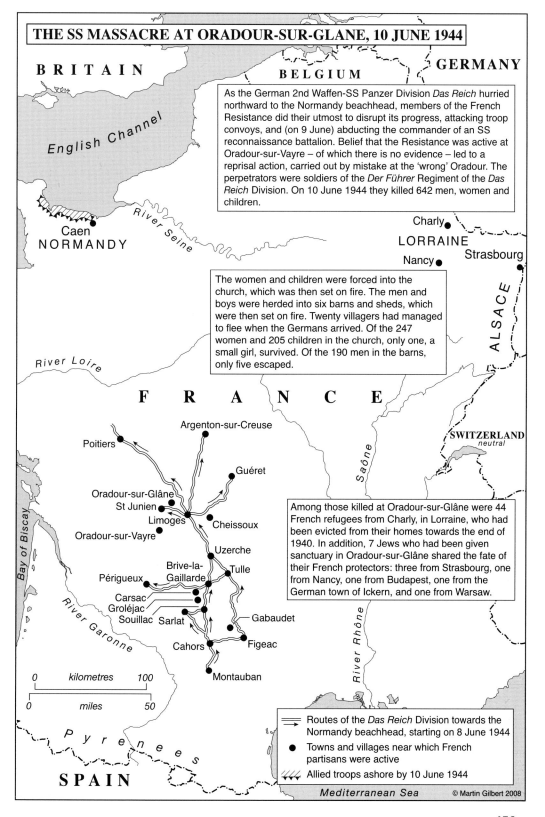

BRITAIN

English Channel

River Seine

Caen
NORMANDY

BELGIUM

GERMANY

As the German 2nd Waffen-SS Panzer Division *Das Reich* hurried northward to the Normandy beachhead, members of the French Resistance did their utmost to disrupt its progress, attacking troop convoys, and (on 9 June) abducting the commander of an SS reconnaissance battalion. Belief that the Resistance was active at Oradour-sur-Vayre – of which there is no evidence – led to a reprisal action, carried out by mistake at the 'wrong' Oradour. The perpetrators were soldiers of the *Der Führer* Regiment of the *Das Reich* Division. On 10 June 1944 they killed 642 men, women and children.

Charly
LORRAINE
Nancy
Strasbourg

ALSACE

F R A N C E

River Loire

The women and children were forced into the church, which was then set on fire. The men and boys were herded into six barns and sheds, which were then set on fire. Twenty villagers had managed to flee when the Germans arrived. Of the 247 women and 205 children in the church, only one, a small girl, survived. Of the 190 men in the barns, only five escaped.

Argenton-sur-Creuse

Poitiers

Guéret

Saône

SWITZERLAND
neutral

Oradour-sur-Glâne
St Junien
Limoges
Cheissoux
Oradour-sur-Vayre

Uzerche

Brive-la-Gaillarde
Tulle
Périgueux

Carsac
Groléjac
Souillac Sarlat
Gabaudet

Cahors
Figeac

Montauban

Among those killed at Oradour-sur-Glâne were 44 French refugees from Charly, in Lorraine, who had been evicted from their homes towards the end of 1940. In addition, 7 Jews who had been given sanctuary in Oradour-sur-Glâne shared the fate of their French protectors: three from Strasbourg, one from Nancy, one from Budapest, one from the German town of Ickern, and one from Warsaw.

River Rhône

Bay of Biscay

River Garonne

| 0 | kilometres | 100 |
| 0 | miles | 50 |

P y r e n e e s

SPAIN

⇒ Routes of the *Das Reich* Division towards the Normandy beachhead, starting on 8 June 1944

● Towns and villages near which French partisans were active

//// Allied troops ashore by 10 June 1944

Mediterranean Sea   © Martin Gilbert 2008

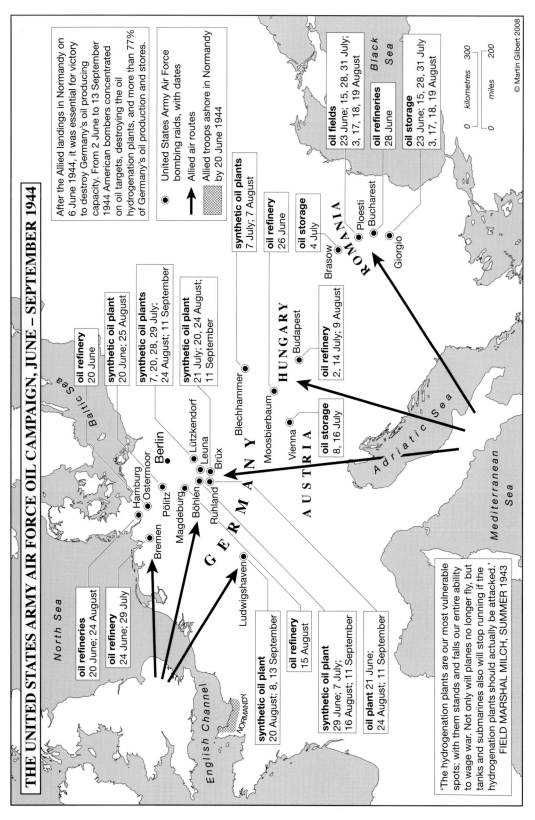

THE UNITED STATES ARMY AIR FORCE OIL CAMPAIGN, JUNE – SEPTEMBER 1944

After the Allied landings in Normandy on 6 June 1944, it was essential for victory to destroy Germany's oil producing capacity. From 2 June to 13 September 1944 American bombers concentrated on oil targets, destroying the oil hydrogenation plants, and more than 77% of Germany's oil production and stores.

- ● United States Army Air Force bombing raids, with dates
- → Allied air routes
- ▨ Allied troops ashore in Normandy by 20 June 1944

© Martin Gilbert 2008

oil fields
23 June; 15, 28, 31 July; 3, 17, 18, 19 August

oil refineries
28 June

oil storage
23 June; 15, 28, 31 July; 3, 17, 18, 19 August

0 — 300 kilometres
0 — 200 miles

synthetic oil plants
7 July; 7 August

oil refinery
26 June

oil storage
4 July

Ploesti
Bucharest
Giorgio

ROMANIA

Brasov

oil refinery
2, 14 July; 9 August

Budapest

HUNGARY

oil storage
8, 16 July

Vienna

AUSTRIA

Moosbierbaum

Blechhammer

Black Sea

Adriatic Sea

Mediterranean Sea

oil refinery
20 June

synthetic oil plant
20 June; 25 August

synthetic oil plants
7, 20, 28, 29 July; 24 August; 11 September

synthetic oil plant
21 July; 20, 24 August; 11 September

Baltic Sea

North Sea

Hamburg
Ostermoor
Berlin
Pölitz
Magdeburg
Böhlen
Lützkendorf
Leuna
Ruhland
Brüx
Bremen

G E R M A N Y

Ludwigshaven

synthetic oil plant
20 August; 8, 13 September

oil refinery
15 August

synthetic oil plant
29 June; 7 July; 16 August; 11 September

oil plant 21 June; 24 August; 11 September

NORMANDY

English Channel

'The hydrogenation plants are our most vulnerable spots; with them stands and falls our entire ability to wage war. Not only will planes no longer fly, but tanks and submarines also will stop running if the hydrogenation plants should actually be attacked.'
FIELD MARSHAL MILCH, SUMMER 1943

157

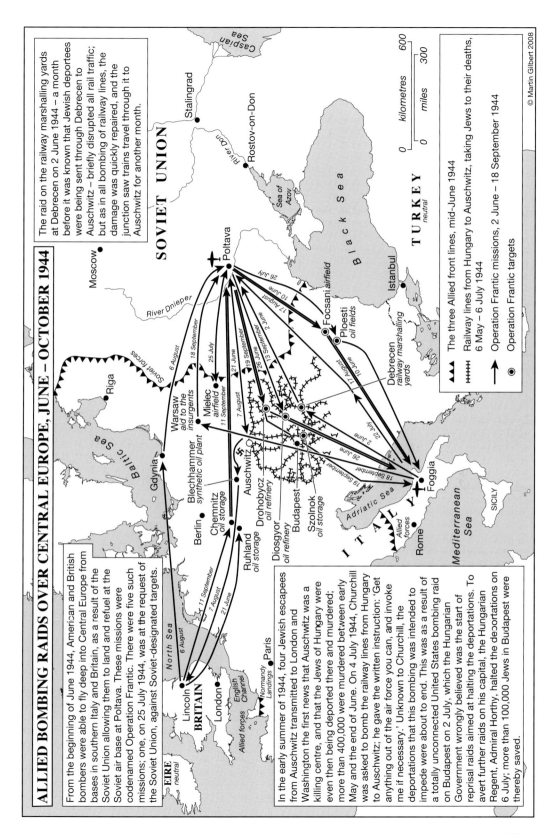

ALLIED BOMBING RAIDS OVER CENTRAL EUROPE, JUNE – OCTOBER 1944

From the beginning of June 1944, American and British bombers were able to fly deep into Central Europe from bases in southern Italy and Britain, as a result of the Soviet Union allowing them to land and refuel at the Soviet air base at Poltava. These missions were codenamed Operation Frantic. There were five such missions; one, on 25 July 1944, was at the request of the Soviet Union, against Soviet-designated targets.

The raid on the railway marshalling yards at Debrecen on 2 June 1944 – a month before it was known that Jewish deportees were being sent through Debrecen to Auschwitz – briefly disrupted all rail traffic; but as in all bombing of railway lines, the damage was quickly repaired, and the junction saw trains travel through it to Auschwitz for another month.

In the early summer of 1944, four Jewish escapees from Auschwitz transmitted to London and Washington the first news that Auschwitz was a killing centre, and that the Jews of Hungary were even then being deported there and murdered; more than 400,000 were murdered between early May and the end of June. On 4 July 1944, Churchill was asked to bomb the railway lines from Hungary to Auschwitz; he gave the written instruction: 'Get anything out of the air force you can, and invoke me if necessary.' Unknown to Churchill, the deportations that this bombing was intended to impede were about to end. This was as a result of a totally unconnected United States bombing raid on Budapest on 2 July, which the Hungarian Government wrongly believed was the start of reprisal raids aimed at halting the deportations. To avert further raids on his capital, the Hungarian Regent, Admiral Horthy, halted the deportations on 6 July; more than 100,000 Jews in Budapest were thereby saved.

SOVIET UNION

Stalingrad

Rostov-on-Don

River Don

Caspian Sea

Sea of Azov

Black Sea

Istanbul

TURKEY
neutral

Moscow

River Dnieper

Poltava

Focsani airfield

Ploesti oil fields

Debrecen railway marshalling yards

Foggia

Allied forces

Rome

I T A L Y

Adriatic Sea

Mediterranean Sea

SICILY

Riga

Baltic Sea

Soviet forces

Warsaw aid to the insurgents

Mielec airfield

Blechhammer synthetic oil plant

Auschwitz

Drohobycz oil refinery

Budapest

Szolnok oil storage

Diosgyor oil refinery

Chemnitz oil storage

Berlin

Ruhland oil storage

North Sea

Gdynia

Lincoln

BRITAIN

London

English Channel

Allied forces

Normandy Landings

Paris

EIRE
neutral

6 August

18 September

25 July

21 June

11 September

26 June

13 September

19 September

7 August

22 July

2 June

10 June

17 August

26 July

10 June

11 September

7 August

21 June

17 September

The three Allied front lines, mid-June 1944

Railway lines from Hungary to Auschwitz, taking Jews to their deaths, 6 May – 6 July 1944

Operation Frantic missions, 2 June – 18 September 1944

Operation Frantic targets

0   kilometres   600
0   miles   300

© Martin Gilbert 2008

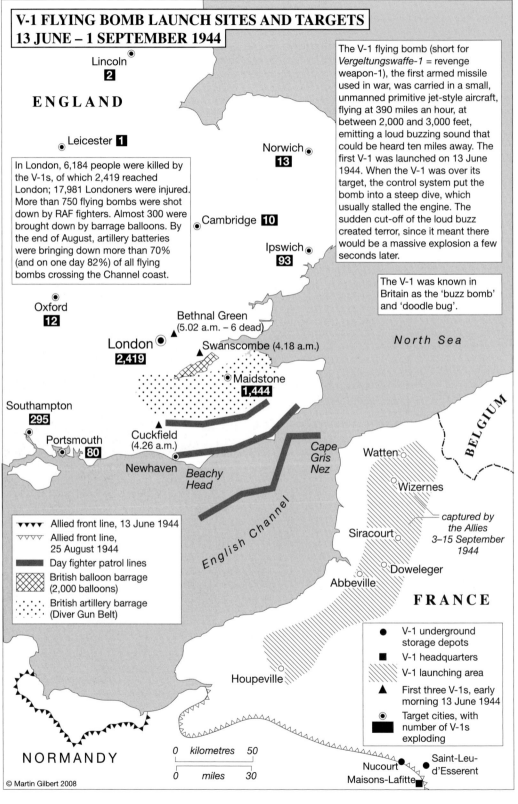

V-1 FLYING BOMB LAUNCH SITES AND TARGETS
13 JUNE – 1 SEPTEMBER 1944

Lincoln
2

ENGLAND

Leicester **1**

The V-1 flying bomb (short for *Vergeltungswaffe-1* = revenge weapon-1), the first armed missile used in war, was carried in a small, unmanned primitive jet-style aircraft, flying at 390 miles an hour, at between 2,000 and 3,000 feet, emitting a loud buzzing sound that could be heard ten miles away. The first V-1 was launched on 13 June 1944. When the V-1 was over its target, the control system put the bomb into a steep dive, which usually stalled the engine. The sudden cut-off of the loud buzz created terror, since it meant there would be a massive explosion a few seconds later.

Norwich
13

In London, 6,184 people were killed by the V-1s, of which 2,419 reached London; 17,981 Londoners were injured. More than 750 flying bombs were shot down by RAF fighters. Almost 300 were brought down by barrage balloons. By the end of August, artillery batteries were bringing down more than 70% (and on one day 82%) of all flying bombs crossing the Channel coast.

Cambridge **10**

Ipswich
93

The V-1 was known in Britain as the 'buzz bomb' and 'doodle bug'.

Oxford
12

Bethnal Green
(5.02 a.m. – 6 dead)

North Sea

London ◉
2,419

Swanscombe (4.18 a.m.)

Maidstone
1,444

Southampton
295

Portsmouth
80

Cuckfield
(4.26 a.m.)

Newhaven

Beachy Head

Cape Gris Nez

Watten

Wizernes

captured by the Allies 3–15 September 1944

BELGIUM

Siracourt

▼▼▼▼ Allied front line, 13 June 1944
▽▽▽▽ Allied front line, 25 August 1944
▬▬▬ Day fighter patrol lines
▨▨▨ British balloon barrage (2,000 balloons)
∴∴∴ British artillery barrage (Diver Gun Belt)

English Channel

Doweleger

Abbeville

FRANCE

● V-1 underground storage depots
■ V-1 headquarters
▨ V-1 launching area
▲ First three V-1s, early morning 13 June 1944
◉ Target cities, with number of V-1s exploding

Houpeville

NORMANDY

0   kilometres   50

0   miles   30

© Martin Gilbert 2008

Nucourt

Saint-Leu-d'Esserent

Maisons-Lafitte

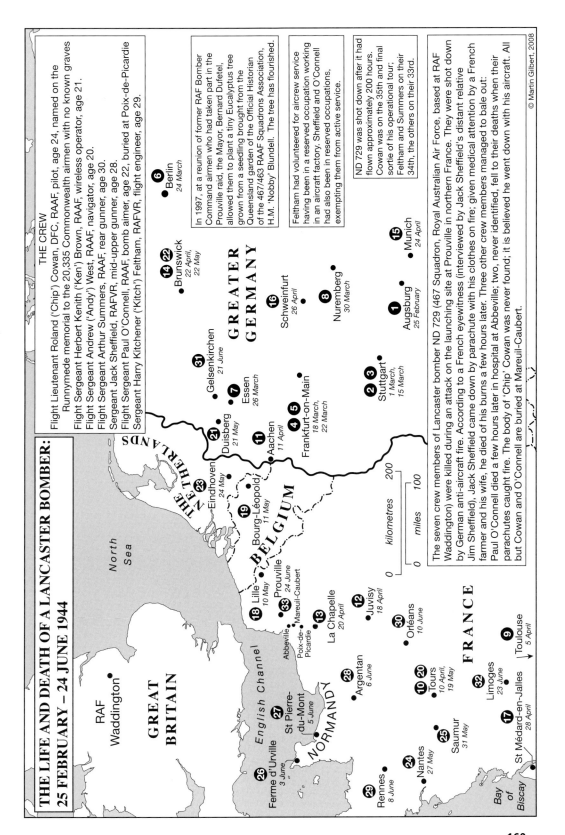

ALLIED AIRBORNE AID TO THE WARSAW UPRISING, 4 AUGUST – 20 SEPTEMBER 1944

▲▲▲ Soviet forces on 15 September 1944

═══ Air flight paths across German-occupied Europe, to the dropping zones

▨ Limits of the dropping zones

○ Soviet air bases

Grodno

Baranowicze

Slonim

Dropping zone limit

Warsaw

Kalisz

Lodz

Dropping zone limit

S O V I E T

Dropping zone

Radom

F O R C E S

Dropping zone

Czestochowa

Kielce

G R E A T E R

Dropping zone

Cracow

Zywiec

Przemysl

G E R M A N Y

EASTERN GALICIA

Kosice

S L O V A K I A

Vienna

Diosgyor

RUTHENIA

A U S T R I A

Budapest

H U N G A R Y

U N D E R   G E R M A N   C O N T R O L

Szeged

S O V I E T

Zagreb

F O R C E S

C R O A T I A

Belgrade

0   kilometres   150

0   miles   100

S E R B I A

ISTRIA

Split

Ancona

Adriatic Sea

The flights on 4, 8, 9 August 1944, and each day between 12 and 17 August, were carried out by Royal Air Force and South African Air Force squadrons. Australian and Canadian crews also took part. A total of ninety-three aircraft took part in these nine missions; seventeen were lost. As a result of these high losses, almost all subsequent flights were carried out by Polish volunteer pilots and crews. In all, 223 sorties were flown; 34 aircraft were lost. Much of the 104 tons of supplies fell into areas under German control.

I T A L Y
under Allied control

THE LAST TWO MISSIONS
On 18 September the American Army Air Force Eighth Bomber Group (in the first and only American air mission to Warsaw) dropped 1,284 containers of arms and supplies. Nearly a thousand fell into German hands. Fewer than a hundred reached the Polish insurgents. On 20 September, twenty aircraft with Polish volunteer crews flew the final mission. Five aircraft were shot down. Since the start of the mission, 200 aircrew had been killed.

Foggia

© Martin Gilbert 2008

Within four days of the outbreak of the Warsaw Uprising on 1 August 1944, Allied air crews based at Foggia in Italy volunteered to fly to Warsaw and drop supplies by parachute to the insurgents. The return journey was at the limit of their fuel carrying capacity; on some missions one in six of the aircraft failed to return. Despite a personal appeal from Churchill to Stalin on 12 August 1944, and a joint appeal to Stalin by Churchill and Roosevelt on 20 August, the Soviet Union refused to allow the planes to land and refuel at Soviet air bases within 100 miles (160 kilometres) of Warsaw, or to use those bases from which to drop their supplies.

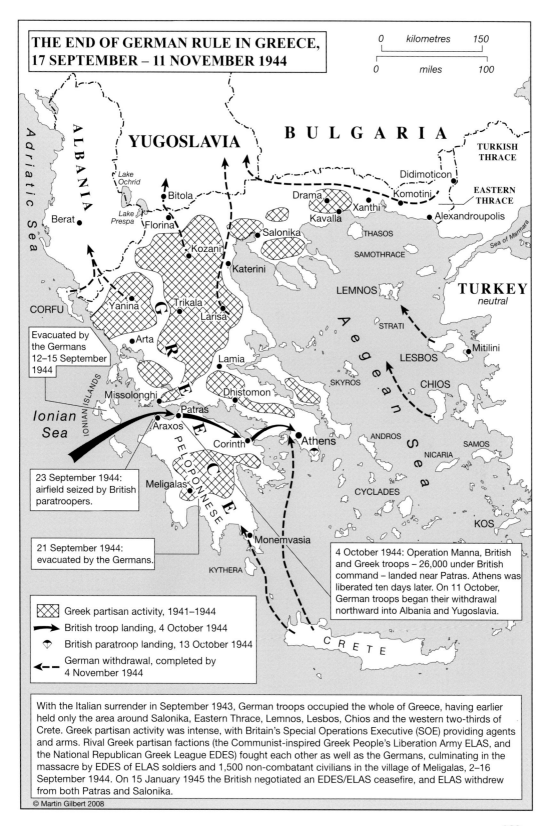

THE END OF GERMAN RULE IN GREECE, 17 SEPTEMBER – 11 NOVEMBER 1944

0   kilometres   150

0   miles   100

Adriatic Sea

ALBANIA

YUGOSLAVIA

BULGARIA

TURKISH THRACE

EASTERN THRACE

Lake Ochrid

Bitola

Berat

Lake Prespa

Florina

Drama

Komotini

Didimoticon

Xanthi

Kavalla

Alexandroupolis

Sea of Marmara

Kozani

Salonika

THASOS

Katerini

SAMOTHRACE

LEMNOS

TURKEY
neutral

CORFU

Yanini

Trikala

Larisa

STRATI

Aegean Sea

Mitilini

Evacuated by the Germans 12–15 September 1944

Arta

Lamia

LESBOS

CHIOS

Missolonghi

Dhistomon

SKYROS

Ionian Sea

IONIAN ISLANDS

Patras

Araxos

Corinth

Athens

ANDROS

SAMOS

NICARIA

23 September 1944: airfield seized by British paratroopers.

Meligalas

PELOPONNESE

CYCLADES

KOS

21 September 1944: evacuated by the Germans.

KYTHERA

Monemvasia

4 October 1944: Operation Manna, British and Greek troops – 26,000 under British command – landed near Patras. Athens was liberated ten days later. On 11 October, German troops began their withdrawal northward into Albania and Yugoslavia.

CRETE

Greek partisan activity, 1941–1944

British troop landing, 4 October 1944

British paratroop landing, 13 October 1944

German withdrawal, completed by 4 November 1944

With the Italian surrender in September 1943, German troops occupied the whole of Greece, having earlier held only the area around Salonika, Eastern Thrace, Lemnos, Lesbos, Chios and the western two-thirds of Crete. Greek partisan activity was intense, with Britain's Special Operations Executive (SOE) providing agents and arms. Rival Greek partisan factions (the Communist-inspired Greek People's Liberation Army ELAS, and the National Republican Greek League EDES) fought each other as well as the Germans, culminating in the massacre by EDES of ELAS soldiers and 1,500 non-combatant civilians in the village of Meligalas, 2–16 September 1944. On 15 January 1945 the British negotiated an EDES/ELAS ceasefire, and ELAS withdrew from both Patras and Salonika.

© Martin Gilbert 2008

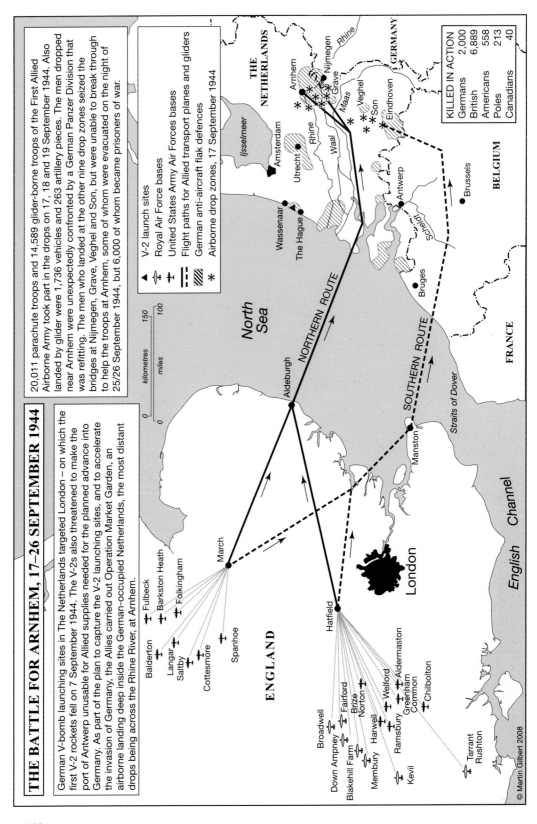

THE BATTLE FOR ARNHEM, 17–26 SEPTEMBER 1944

German V-bomb launching sites in The Netherlands targeted London – on which the first V-2 rockets fell on 7 September 1944. The V-2s also threatened to make the port of Antwerp unusable for Allied supplies needed for the planned advance into Germany. As part of the plan to capture the V-2 launching sites, and to accelerate the invasion of Germany, the Allies carried out Operation Market Garden, an airborne landing deep inside the German-occupied Netherlands, the most distant drops being across the Rhine River, at Arnhem.

20,011 parachute troops and 14,589 glider-borne troops of the First Allied Airborne Army took part in the drops on 17, 18 and 19 September 1944. Also landed by glider were 1,736 vehicles and 263 artillery pieces. The men dropped near Arnhem were unexpectedly confronted by a German Panzer Division that was refitting. The men who landed at the other nine drop zones seized the bridges at Nijmegen, Grave, Veghel and Son, but were unable to break through to help the troops at Arnhem, some of whom were evacuated on the night of 25/26 September 1944, but 6,000 of whom became prisoners of war.

KILLED IN ACTION	
Germans	2,000
British	6,889
Americans	558
Poles	213
Canadians	40

Legend:
- ◀ V-2 launch sites
- ✈ Royal Air Force bases
- ✈ United States Army Air Forces bases
- ╫ Flight paths for Allied transport planes and gliders
- ▨ German anti-aircraft flak defences
- ✳ Airborne drop zones, 17 September 1944

© Martin Gilbert 2008

163

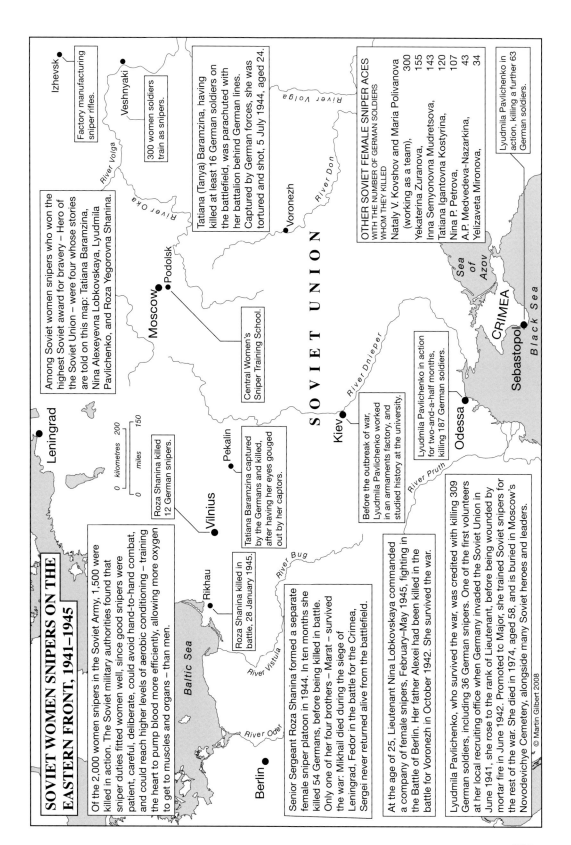

SOVIET WOMEN SNIPERS ON THE EASTERN FRONT, 1941–1945

Of the 2,000 women snipers in the Soviet Army, 1,500 were killed in action. The Soviet military authorities found that sniper duties fitted women well, since good snipers were patient, careful, deliberate, could avoid hand-to-hand combat, and could reach higher levels of aerobic conditioning – training the heart to pump blood more efficiently, allowing more oxygen to get to muscles and organs – than men.

Factory manufacturing sniper rifles.

300 women soldiers train as snipers.

Among Soviet women snipers who won the highest Soviet award for bravery – Hero of the Soviet Union – were four whose stories are told on this map: Tatiana Baramzina, Nina Alexeyevna Lobkovskaya, Lyudmila Pavlichenko, and Roza Yegorovna Shanina.

Tatiana (Tanya) Baramzina, having killed at least 16 German soldiers on the battlefield, was parachuted with her battalion behind German lines. Captured by German forces, she was tortured and shot, 5 July 1944, aged 24.

OTHER SOVIET FEMALE SNIPER ACES
WITH THE NUMBER OF GERMAN SOLDIERS WHOM THEY KILLED

Nataly V. Kovshov and Maria Polivanova (working as a team),	300
Yekaterina Zuranova,	155
Inna Semyonovna Mudretsova,	143
Tatiana Igantovna Kostyrina,	120
Nina P. Petrova,	107
A.P. Medvedeva-Nazarkina,	43
Yelizaveta Mironova,	34

Lyudmila Pavlichenko in action, killing a further 63 German soldiers.

Central Women's Sniper Training School.

Roza Shanina killed 12 German snipers.

Tatiana Baramzina captured by the Germans and killed, after having her eyes gouged out by her captors.

Roza Shanina killed in battle, 28 January 1945.

Before the outbreak of war, Lyudmila Pavlichenko worked in an armaments factory, and studied history at the university.

Lyudmila Pavlichenko in action for two-and-a-half months, killing 187 German soldiers.

Senior Sergeant Roza Shanina formed a separate female sniper platoon in 1944. In ten months she killed 54 Germans, before being killed in battle. Only one of her four brothers – Marat – survived the war: Mikhail died during the siege of Leningrad, Fedor in the battle for the Crimea, Sergei never returned alive from the battlefield.

At the age of 25, Lieutenant Nina Lobkovskaya commanded a company of female snipers, February–May 1945, fighting in the Battle of Berlin. Her father Alexei had been killed in the battle for Voronezh in October 1942. She survived the war.

Lyudmila Pavlichenko, who survived the war, was credited with killing 309 German soldiers, including 36 German snipers. One of the first volunteers at her local recruiting office when Germany invaded the Soviet Union in June 1941, she rose to the rank of Lieutenant, before being wounded by mortar fire in June 1942. Promoted to Major, she trained Soviet snipers for the rest of the war. She died in 1974, aged 58, and is buried in Moscow's Novodevichye Cemetery, alongside many Soviet heroes and leaders.

Izhevsk

Veshnyaki

Leningrad

Moscow

Podolsk

Voronezh

River Volga

River Oka

River Don

River Volga

S O V I E T   U N I O N

Sea of Azov

Black Sea

CRIMEA

Sebastopol

Kiev

Odessa

River Dnieper

River Pruth

Vilnius

Pekalin

Rikhau

Baltic Sea

River Bug

River Vistula

River Oder

Berlin

0   kilometres   200
0   miles   150

© Martin Gilbert 2008

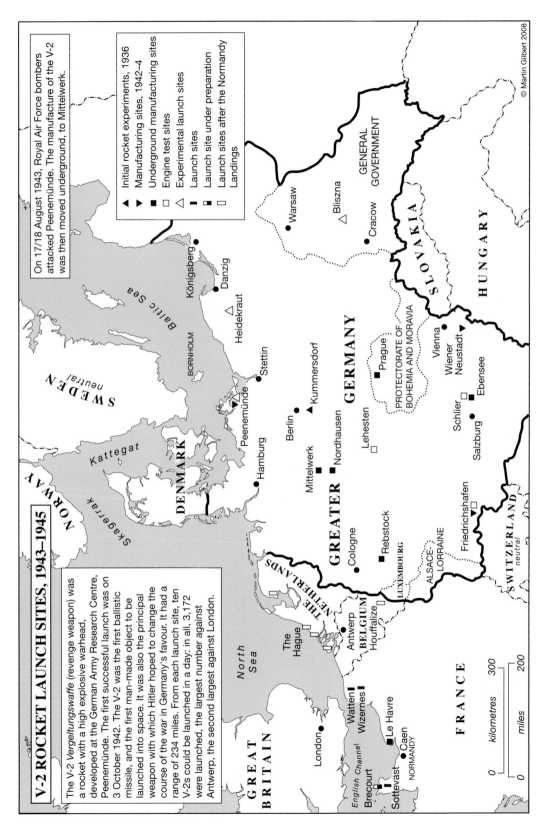

V-2 ROCKET LAUNCH SITES, 1943–1945

The V-2 *Vergeltungswaffe* (revenge weapon) was a rocket with a high explosive warhead, developed at the German Army Research Centre, Peenemünde. The first successful launch was on 3 October 1942. The V-2 was the first ballistic missile, and the first man-made object to be launched into space. It was also the principal weapon with which Hitler hoped to change the course of the war in Germany's favour. It had a range of 234 miles. From each launch site, ten V-2s could be launched in a day: in all, 3,172 were launched, the largest number against Antwerp, the second largest against London.

On 17/18 August 1943, Royal Air Force bombers attacked Peenemünde. The manufacture of the V-2 was then moved underground, to Mittelwerk.

Initial rocket experiments, 1936 ◀
Manufacturing sites, 1942–4 ▶
Underground manufacturing sites ■
Engine test sites □
Experimental launch sites △
Launch sites ▬
Launch site under preparation ▭
Launch sites after the Normandy Landings ▭

© Martin Gilbert 2008

165

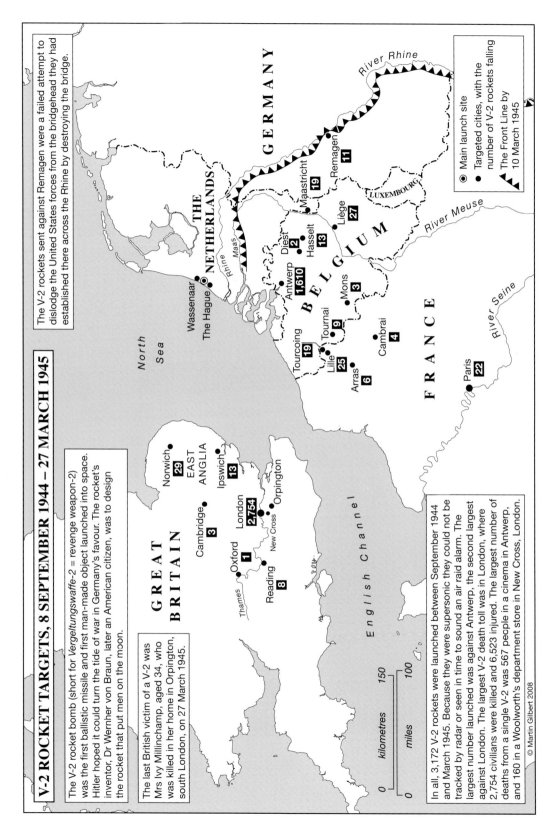

V-2 ROCKET TARGETS, 8 SEPTEMBER 1944 – 27 MARCH 1945

The V-2 rocket bomb (short for *Vergeltungswaffe-2* = revenge weapon-2) was the first ballistic missile and first man-made object launched into space. Hitler hoped it could turn the tide of war in Germany's favour. The rocket's inventor, Dr Wernher von Braun, later an American citizen, was to design the rocket that put men on the moon.

The last British victim of a V-2 was Mrs Ivy Millinchamp, aged 34, who was killed in her home in Orpington, south London, on 27 March 1945.

The V-2 rockets sent against Remagen were a failed attempt to dislodge the United States forces from the bridgehead they had established there across the Rhine by destroying the bridge.

In all, 3,172 V-2 rockets were launched between September 1944 and March 1945. Because they were supersonic they could not be tracked by radar or seen in time to sound an air raid alarm. The largest number launched was against Antwerp, the second largest against London. The largest V-2 death toll was in London, where 2,754 civilians were killed and 6,523 injured. The largest number of deaths from a single V-2 was 567 people in a cinema in Antwerp, and 160 in a Woolworth's department store in New Cross, London.

Main launch site

Targeted cities, with the number of V-2 rockets falling

The Front Line by 10 March 1945

GERMANY

THE NETHERLANDS

BELGIUM

LUXEMBOURG

FRANCE

GREAT BRITAIN

River Rhine

River Meuse

River Seine

North Sea

English Channel

Thames

Maas

Rhine

Wassenaar
The Hague

Remagen **11**
Maastricht **19**
Liège **27**
Diest **2**
Hasselt **13**
Antwerp **1,610**
Mons **3**
Tournai **9**
Tourcoing **19**
Lille **25**
Cambrai **4**
Arras **6**
Paris **22**

Norwich **29**
EAST ANGLIA
Ipswich **13**
Cambridge **3**
London **2,754**
Orpington
New Cross
Oxford **1**
Reading **8**

kilometres 0   100   150
miles 0   100

© Martin Gilbert 2008

166

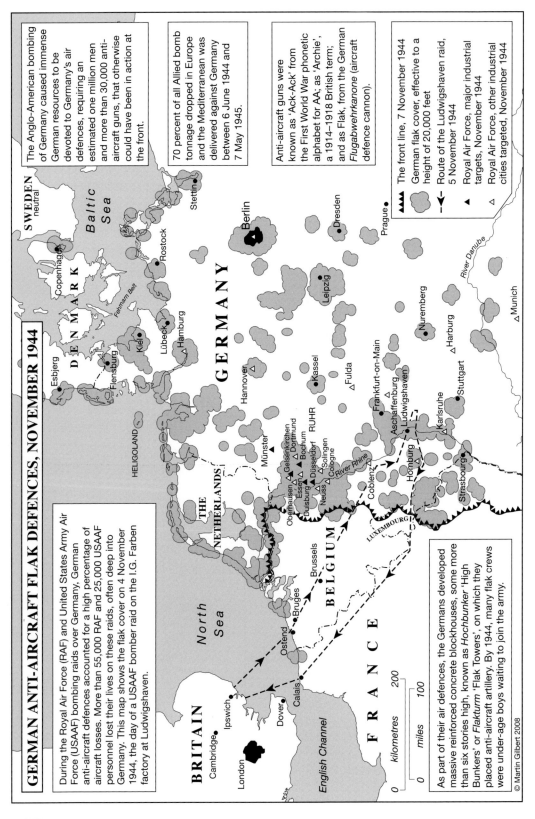

GERMAN ANTI-AIRCRAFT FLAK DEFENCES, NOVEMBER 1944

During the Royal Air Force (RAF) and United States Army Air Force (USAAF) bombing raids over Germany, German anti-aircraft defences accounted for a high percentage of aircraft losses. More than 55,000 RAF and 25,000 USAAF personnel lost their lives on these raids, often deep into Germany. This map shows the flak cover on 4 November 1944, the day of a USAAF bomber raid on the I.G. Farben factory at Ludwigshaven.

The Anglo-American bombing of Germany caused immense German resources to be devoted to Germany's air defences, requiring an estimated one million men and more than 30,000 anti-aircraft guns, that otherwise could have been in action at the front.

70 percent of all Allied bomb tonnage dropped in Europe and the Mediterranean was delivered against Germany between 6 June 1944 and 7 May 1945.

Anti-aircraft guns were known as 'Ack-Ack' from the First World War phonetic alphabet for AA; as 'Archie', a 1914–1918 British term; and as Flak, from the German *Flugabwehrkanone* (aircraft defence cannon).

- ▲▲▲▲ The front line, 7 November 1944
- German flak cover, effective to a height of 20,000 feet
- – – ◄ Route of the Ludwigshaven raid, 5 November 1944
- ▲ Royal Air Force, major industrial targets, November 1944
- △ Royal Air Force, other industrial cities targeted, November 1944

As part of their air defences, the Germans developed massive reinforced concrete blockhouses, some more than six stories high, known as *Hochbunker* 'High Bunkers' or *Flakturm* 'Flak Towers', on which they placed anti-aircraft artillery. By 1944, many flak crews were under-age boys waiting to join the army.

SWEDEN neutral

Baltic Sea

Copenhagen●

DENMARK

Esbjerg●   Flensburg●
Kiel●   Lübeck●
△Hamburg

Rostock●

Stettin●

Berlin●

Dresden●

Prague●

River Danube

GERMANY

Leipzig●

Nuremberg●

△Harburg

Hannover●
△

HELIGOLAND

THE NETHERLANDS

Münster▲
Gelsenkirchen△ △Dortmund
Oberhausen△ ▲Bochum
Essen△ Düsseldorf△ RUHR
Duisburg△ Solingen△
Neuss△ Cologne△

River Rhine

Coblenz△

Kassel●

△Fulda

Frankfurt-on-Main●
Aschaffenburg△
Ludwigshaven△
Homburg△
Karlsruhe△
Stuttgart●
Strasbourg●

△Munich

BELGIUM

Brussels●

Bruges●
Ostend●

LUXEMBOURG

FRANCE

North Sea

English Channel

BRITAIN

London●
Cambridge●   Ipswich●
Dover●
Calais●

0   100   200 kilometres
0   100 miles

© Martin Gilbert 2008

THE GERMAN COUNTER-OFFENSIVE IN THE ARDENNES, 16 DECEMBER 1944 – 7 FEBRUARY 1945

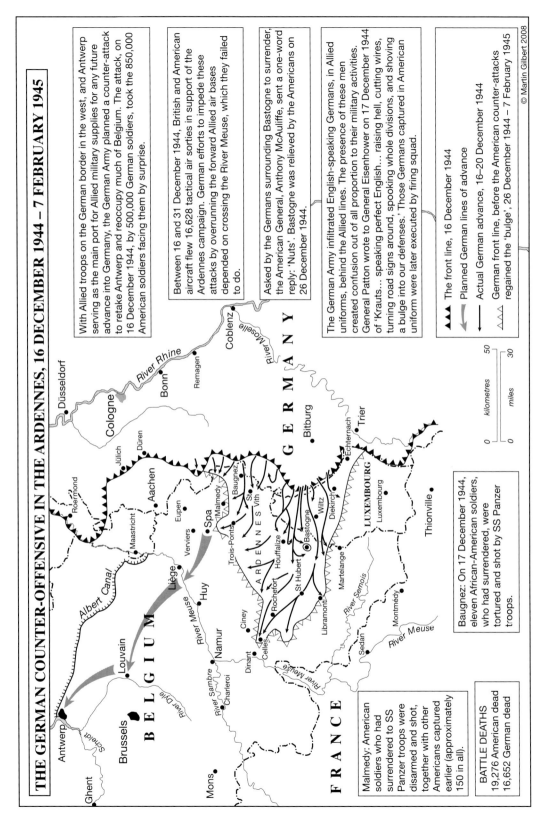

With Allied troops on the German border in the west, and Antwerp serving as the main port for Allied military supplies for any future advance into Germany, the German Army planned a counter-attack to retake Antwerp and reoccupy much of Belgium. The attack, on 16 December 1944, by 500,000 German soldiers, took the 850,000 American soldiers facing them by surprise.

Between 16 and 31 December 1944, British and American aircraft flew 16,628 tactical air sorties in support of the Ardennes campaign. German efforts to impede these attacks by overrunning the forward Allied air bases depended on crossing the River Meuse, which they failed to do.

Asked by the Germans surrounding Bastogne to surrender, the American General, Anthony McAuliffe, sent a one-word reply: 'Nuts'. Bastogne was relieved by the Americans on 26 December 1944.

The German Army infiltrated English-speaking Germans, in Allied uniforms, behind the Allied lines. The presence of these men created confusion out of all proportion to their military activities. General Patton wrote to General Eisenhower on 17 December 1944 of 'Krauts... speaking perfect English... raising hell, cutting wires, turning road signs around, spooking whole divisions, and shoving a bulge into our defenses.' Those Germans captured in American uniform were later executed by firing squad.

▲▲▲ The front line, 16 December 1944

Planned German lines of advance

Actual German advance, 16–20 December 1944

△△△ German front line, before the American counter-attacks regained the 'bulge', 26 December 1944 – 7 February 1945

© Martin Gilbert 2008

Baugnez: On 17 December 1944, eleven African-American soldiers, who had surrendered, were tortured and shot by SS Panzer troops.

Malmedy: American soldiers who had surrendered to SS Panzer troops were disarmed and shot, together with other Americans captured earlier (approximately 150 in all).

BATTLE DEATHS
19,276 American dead
16,652 German dead

GERMANY

Düsseldorf

River Rhine

Cologne

Bonn

Remagen

Moselle

River

Coblenz

Bitburg

Trier

Echternach

Roermond

Jülich

Düren

Aachen

Eupen

Verviers

Spa

Malmedy

Baugnez

St Vith

A R D E N N E S

Houffalize

St Hubert

Martelange

Wiltz

Diekirch

LUXEMBOURG

Luxembourg

Thionville

Maastricht

Liège

Huy

River Meuse

Namur

Ciney

Rochefort

Libramont

River Semois

Montmédy

River Meuse

Sedan

Trois-Ponts

Celles

Dinant

River Sambre

River Meuse

Charleroi

River Dyle

Albert Canal

Louvain

Brussels

BELGIUM

Antwerp

Scheldt

Ghent

Mons

FRANCE

0   kilometres   50

0   miles   30

THE LIFE AND DEATH OF *TIRPITZ*, 1 APRIL 1939 – 14 NOVEMBER 1944

The German battleship *Tirpitz*, launched at Wilhelmshaven on 1 April 1939 in Hitler's presence, and completed in February 1941, was, by 1944, the last heavy warship left to the German Navy. Shaken by the sinking of *Bismarck*, her sister ship, on 27 May 1941, Hitler did not want *Tirpitz* risked in battle. On 15 January 1942 she was ordered to the relative safety of Norwegian waters, where she remained for 34 months; for the British, her presence there was a grave potential threat to Allied convoys to Murmansk, and she had to be sunk.

7 11–12 September 1943: Six British midget submarines attack *Tirpitz*. Two VCs won. Badly damaged, *Tirpitz* never reached her full speed (more than 30 knots) again.

6 8 September 1943: *Tirpitz* attacked Spitzbergen weather station. The only time she put her full eight 18-inch gun armament to use.

8 2–3 April 1944: attacked by carrier-borne aircraft from Scapa Flow. 14 hits; 122 of her crew killed. Only 4 of the 121 attacking aircraft lost. *Tirpitz* disabled for 3 months.

3 6 March 1942: *Tirpitz* sailed to Bear Island, to attack Convoy PQ12 but driven off by torpedo bombers from the British aircraft carrier *Victorious*.

9 Air attacks on 28 April, 15 May, 28 May, 17 July and 22 August 1944; all failed.

4 5 July 1942: *Tirpitz* moved out of Altenfjord with two other capital ships and eight destroyers to attack the Arctic Convoy PQ17. Turned back when it was clear that PQ17 had been successfully attacked by German U-boats and bombers.

10 24 August 1944: two hits during an air attack. One bomb penetrated the main armoured deck, but failed to explode.

11 29 August 1944: further failed air attack.

13 15 September 1944: British bombing raid via Yagodnik Soviet air base, badly damaged the upper deck, which peeled back 'like a sardine tin'. Damage so severe that *Tirpitz* could henceforth only make 8 knots (as opposed to her possible 30+ knots).

5 26 October 1942: A team of 2-man steerable torpedoes ('Chariots') driven off by a storm only five miles from *Tirpitz*.

12 11 September 1944: after the first successful British air attack, *Tirpitz* sent south to Haakoy Island to serve as a floating fortress to help ward off any Allied invasion of Norway.

2 31 March 1942: 33 bombers attack, but *Tirpitz* protected by a smokescreen.

16 The German fighters that could have intercepted the final British bomber attack on *Tirpitz* thought that the bombers were aiming at their airfield, Bardufoss, and turned back from Haakoy to protect Bardufoss.

1 28/29 January 1942: first unsuccessful British attempt to bomb *Tirpitz*.

14 29 October 1944: bomber raid from Lossiemouth; bad visibility.

15 12 November 1944: *Tirpitz* attacked by bombers from Lossiemouth, using 12,000-pound bombs. *Tirpitz* sunk; 1,000 of her crew of 1,700 drowned.

SPITZBERGEN

Arctic Ocean

BEAR ISLAND

North Cape

Barents Sea

HAAKOY ISLAND — Altenfjord
Tromsö — Murmansk
Bardufoss
Narvik

White Sea
Yagodnik

Norwegian Sea

Trondheim

Gulf of Bothnia

NORWAY

Scapa Flow
Lossiemouth

North Sea

Baltic Sea

London

Wilhelmshaven
Berlin

English Channel

Tirpitz was known to the Norwegians as 'The Lone Queen of the North'.

0   kilometres   600
0   miles   400

Movements of *Tirpitz*, 1942–1945
⊙ British attempts to sink *Tirpitz*

© Martin Gilbert 2008

THE GERMAN AIR OFFENSIVE, 1 JANUARY 1945

North Sea

Rotterdam
River Rhine
Arnhem

THE

River Waal
Heesch
Volkel

River Lippe

RUHR

NETHERLANDS

Woensdrecht
Gilze Rijen
Eindhoven

Limburg
Düsseldorf

River Ruhr

GERMANY

Maldegem
Ursel
Antwerp
Scheldt

Ophoven

St Trond
Asch

River Rhine

Cologne

Ghent

Grimbergen
Melsbroeke
Evere
Brussels

BELGIUM

Liège

Namur
River Meuse

Coblenz

Malmedy
St Vith

Le Culot

LUXEMBOURG

River Moselle

Luxembourg

Kaiserslautern

F R A N C E

River Meuse

Metz

LORRAINE

Nancy

River Moselle

River Rhine

A L S A C E

0   *kilometres*   100

0   *miles*   50

▲▲▲ The Western Front, 15 December 1944
△△△ Front line in the Ardennes, 1 January 1945
◉ Allied airfields attacked on 1 January 1945
◄—·— Route of German air attack on St Trond

The Ardennes battle was followed on 1 January 1945 by an air attack by 1,035 German fighter bombers on Allied air bases. While destroying 120 British and 36 American aircraft, and seriously damaging a further 268, the attackers failed to obtain the German air dominance essential if the Allied advance into Germany was to be prevented. During the attack, 300 German planes were shot down, 85 by their own anti-aircraft guns.

St Trond had been the German night-fighter base of Heinz-Wolfgang Schnaufer, known to the British night bomber crews as 'The Ghost of St Trond'. Schnaufer shot down in total 121 Allied bombers. In a single night, 21 February 1945, from a base in Germany, he shot down nine British bombers, seven of them in just 19 minutes. He was killed in a car crash in France in 1950, aged 28.

© Martin Gilbert 2008

Section 9

THE DEFEAT OF GERMANY

Once we were crossing the Rhine and progressing through Germany, we came across lots of Germans fleeing. Once, we passed a convoy of horses and carts, and a young girl was sitting on top of one cart with all her possessions on the cart behind her. She stared at me with a look of cold hatred. I knew a bit of German so I called at her, '*Denken sie an. . .*' to tell her to remember Poland and France and Russia and the terrible things the Germans had done. She carried on staring at me, full of hate.

CORPORAL ERIC LORD
British Army
Quoted in Max Arthur, *Forgotten Voices of World War II*
2004

Now it was their turn to carry their babies and drag their children behind them. The bewildered women, hair covered by turban-like kerchiefs, were pushing their carts. In many carts sat ill and elderly relatives wrapped in blankets. They had been sending our people straight to the gas chambers, I thought as I watched a woman bend lovingly over an old man to rearrange a blanket as she pushed the cart. Your turn has come, I thought with immense sorrow.

ERIKA KOUNIO AMARIGLIO
From Thessaloniki to Auschwitz and Back
2000

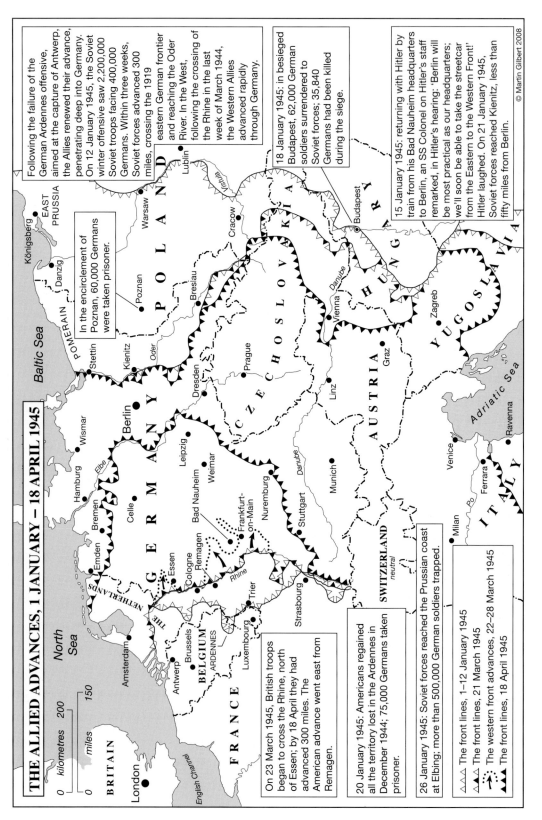

THE ALLIED ADVANCES, 1 JANUARY – 18 APRIL 1945

Following the failure of the German Ardennes offensive, aimed at the capture of Antwerp, the Allies renewed their advance, penetrating deep into Germany. On 12 January 1945, the Soviet winter offensive saw 2,200,000 Soviet troops facing 400,000 Germans. Within three weeks, Soviet forces advanced 300 miles, crossing the 1919 eastern German frontier and reaching the Oder River. In the West, following the crossing of the Rhine in the last week of March 1944, the Western Allies advanced rapidly through Germany.

In the encirclement of Poznan, 60,000 Germans were taken prisoner.

18 January 1945: in besieged Budapest, 62,000 German soldiers surrendered to Soviet forces; 35,840 Germans had been killed during the siege.

15 January 1945: returning with Hitler by train from his Bad Nauheim headquarters to Berlin, an SS Colonel on Hitler's staff remarked, in Hitler's hearing: 'Berlin will be most practical as our headquarters; we'll soon be able to take the streetcar from the Eastern to the Western Front!' Hitler laughed. On 21 January 1945, Soviet forces reached Kienitz, less than fifty miles from Berlin.

On 23 March 1945, British troops began to cross the Rhine, north of Essen; by 18 April they had advanced 300 miles. The American advance went east from Remagen.

20 January 1945: Americans regained all the territory lost in the Ardennes in December 1944; 75,000 Germans taken prisoner.

26 January 1945: Soviet forces reached the Prussian coast at Elbing; more than 500,000 German soldiers trapped.

△△△ The front lines, 1–12 January 1945
▲▲▲ The front lines, 21 March 1945
 ⌒⌒ The western front advances, 22–28 March 1945
▲▲▲ The front lines, 18 April 1945

© Martin Gilbert 2008

North Sea
Baltic Sea
Adriatic Sea
English Channel

BRITAIN
London

EAST PRUSSIA
Königsberg
Danzig
POMERAIN
Stettin
Kienitz
Poznan
POLAND
Warsaw
Lublin
Cracow
Breslau
Vistula
Oder

Amsterdam
THE NETHERLANDS
Emden
Bremen
Hamburg
Wismar
Berlin
Celle
Leipzig
Weimar
Bad Nauheim
Dresden
Elbe
GERMANY
Essen
Cologne
Remagen
Frankfurt-on-Main
Nuremburg
Trier
Strasbourg
Stuttgart
Rhine
Danube
Prague
CZECHOSLOVAKIA
Vienna
Linz
Danube
Munich
AUSTRIA
Graz
SWITZERLAND
neutral

Antwerp
Brussels
BELGIUM
ARDENNES
Luxembourg
FRANCE

Zagreb
HUNGARY
Budapest
YUGOSLAVIA

Milan
Po
Ferrara
Ravenna
Venice
ITALY

0 kilometres 200
0 miles 150

171

CIVILIANS, CAPTIVES AND PRISONERS OF WAR EVACUATED WESTWARD, JANUARY – MAY 1945

The Soviet offensive that began on 12 January 1945 drove through East Prussia and penetrated deep into Germany. On 23 January, as the Soviet advance gained pace, the Commander of the German Navy, Admiral Dönitz, radioed to Gotenhafen (Gdynia) to evacuate as many people as possible away from the Soviets. The operation, codenamed 'Hannibal', was one of the largest emergency sea evacuations in history. In 15 weeks, as many as 1,000 merchant ships and numerous naval craft, including Germany's largest remaining naval units, transported 264,887 refugees and soldiers across the Baltic Sea to Germany: as many as 17,000 of those being evacuated were drowned in three sinkings.

▲▲▲ The Soviet front line, 12 January 1945
△△△ The Soviet front line, 24 February 1945
→ Main German evacuation routes

© Martin Gilbert 2008

30 January 1945: while evacuating German soldiers, U-boat personnel, and German refugees trapped by the Red Army in East Prussia, the ocean liner *Wilhelm Gustloff* – on route from Gdynia (Gotenhafen) to Kiel – was hit by three torpedoes from a Soviet submarine: 4,974 refugees and 1,626 military personnel – 6,600 people in all – were drowned, probably the largest loss of life in a single sinking in maritime history; 1,252 were saved.

20 January 1945: 700 Jewish concentration camp prisoners were killed during a forced march from Königsberg; 3,000 were machine gunned to death at the shore; only 60 escaped.

Starting in October 1944, several million East Prussians fled westward, to the River Oder and beyond. As many as half a million perished, many from Soviet shelling and bombing of roads crowded with German troops and armour moving eastward.

The further west Soviet forces advanced, the more chaotic the land evacuations became, and the higher the death toll of the evacuees. Tens of thousands of Jews were also being taken under SS supervision to slave labour camps inside Germany.

On the former German ocean liner *General von Steuben*, 4,267 Germans being evacuated from East Prussia were drowned when the ship was torpedoed by a Soviet submarine off Kolberg. The dead included 2,800 wounded German soldiers. There were only 300 survivors.

Of the 29,000 Jews on a forced march to Sachsenhausen (men) and Ravensbrück (women), 26,000 perished on the journey.

In April 1945 the German Navy and merchant marine safely evacuated 264,887 German refugees from East Prussia to Lübeck, Kiel and Warnemünde.

16 April 1945: the German ocean liner *Goya*, with German refugees on board, was torpedoed by a Soviet submarine as it left Danzig for Copenhagen. More than 6,000 were drowned; only 183 were saved.

LITHUANIA

Tilsit

EAST PRUSSIA

Memel

Palmnicken

Pillau

Königsberg

Rastenburg
Hitler's headquarters

Hel

Stutthof

Gdynia

Danzig

Grossendorf

POLAND

Warsaw

River Vistula

River Vistula

SWEDEN
neutral

Baltic Sea

BORNHOLM
(Denmark)

Kolberg

P O M E R A N I A

Stettin

River Oder

Swinemünde

Warnemünde

Berlin

DENMARK
(under German occupation)

Copenhagen

Lübeck

Kiel

Ravensbrück
Sachsenhausen

0   kilometres   200

0   miles   150

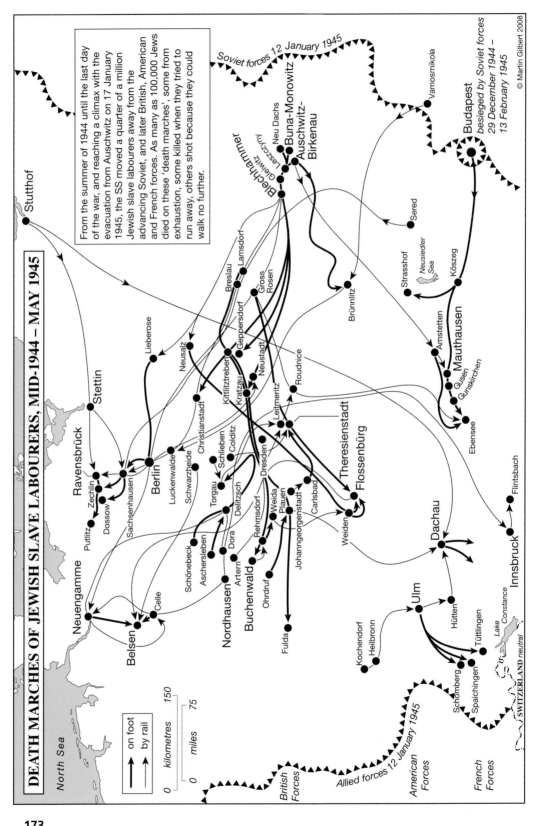

DEATH MARCHES OF JEWISH SLAVE LABOURERS, MID-1944 – MAY 1945

North Sea

From the summer of 1944 until the last day of the war, and reaching a climax with the evacuation from Auschwitz on 17 January 1945, the SS moved a quarter of a million Jewish slave labourers away from the advancing Soviet, and later British, American and French forces. As many as 100,000 Jews died on these 'death marches', some from exhaustion, some killed when they tried to run away, others shot because they could walk no further.

© Martin Gilbert 2008

on foot
by rail

kilometres 0 ... 150
miles 0 ... 75

Soviet forces 12 January 1945

Budapest *besieged by Soviet forces 29 December 1944 – 13 February 1945*

Vámosmikola

Stutthof

Neu Dachs
Buna-Monowitz
Auschwitz-Birkenau
Leszczyny
Gleiwitz
Blechhammer

Sered

Strasshof
Neusiedler Sea
Kőszeg
Amstetten
Mauthausen
Gusen
Gunskirchen
Ebensee

Breslau
Lamsdorf
Gross Rosen
Geppersdorf
Neustadt
Brünnlitz

Lieberose
Neusalz
Kittlitztreben
Kratzau
Roudnice
Leitmeritz

Stettin
Ravensbrück
Zechlin
Putlitz
Dossow
Berlin
Sachsenhausen
Luckenwalde
Schwarzheide
Christianstadt
Schlieben
Colditz
Torgau
Delitzsch
Dresden
Carlsbad

Theresienstadt
Flossenbürg
Weiden

Flintsbach

Neuengamme
Belsen
Celle
Schönebeck
Aschersleben
Dora
Artern
Rehmsdorf
Weida
Plauen
Johanngeorgenstadt
Dachau
Innsbruck

Nordhausen
Buchenwald
Ohrdruf
Fulda

Ulm
Hütten
Kochendorf
Heilbronn
Schömberg
Spaichingen
Tüttlingen
Lake Constance
SWITZERLAND *neutral*

Allied forces 12 January 1945

American Forces
British Forces
French Forces

173

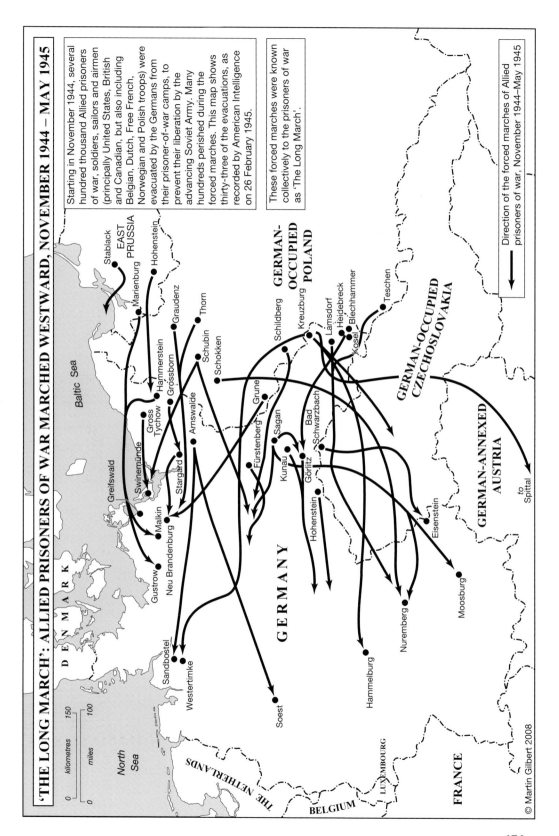

'THE LONG MARCH': ALLIED PRISONERS OF WAR MARCHED WESTWARD, NOVEMBER 1944 – MAY 1945

Starting in November 1944, several hundred thousand Allied prisoners of war, soldiers, sailors and airmen (principally United States, British and Canadian, but also including Belgian, Dutch, Free French, Norwegian and Polish troops) were evacuated by the Germans from their prisoner-of-war camps, to prevent their liberation by the advancing Soviet Army. Many hundreds perished during the forced marches. This map shows thirty-three of the evacuations, as recorded by American Intelligence on 26 February 1945.

These forced marches were known collectively to the prisoners of war as 'The Long March'.

→ Direction of the forced marches of Allied prisoners of war, November 1944–May 1945

North Sea

Baltic Sea

DENMARK

EAST PRUSSIA

Stablack
Hohenstein
Marienburg
Graudenz
Thorn
Hammerstein
Grössborn
Schubin
Schokken

GERMAN-OCCUPIED POLAND

Schildberg
Kreuzburg
Lamsdorf
Heidebreck
Blechhammer
Kosel
Teschen

GERMAN-OCCUPIED CZECHOSLOVAKIA

Greifswald
Swinemünde
Gross Tychow
Stargard
Arnswalde
Grune
Fürstenberg
Sagan
Kunau
Görlitz
Bad Schwarzbach

Gustrow
Malkin
Neu Brandenburg

Hohenstein
Eisenstein

GERMAN-ANNEXED AUSTRIA

to Spittal

GERMANY

Sandbostel
Westertimke

Soest

Hammelburg

Nuremberg

Moosburg

THE NETHERLANDS

BELGIUM

LUXEMBOURG

FRANCE

kilometres 0 100 150
miles 0 100

© Martin Gilbert 2008

174

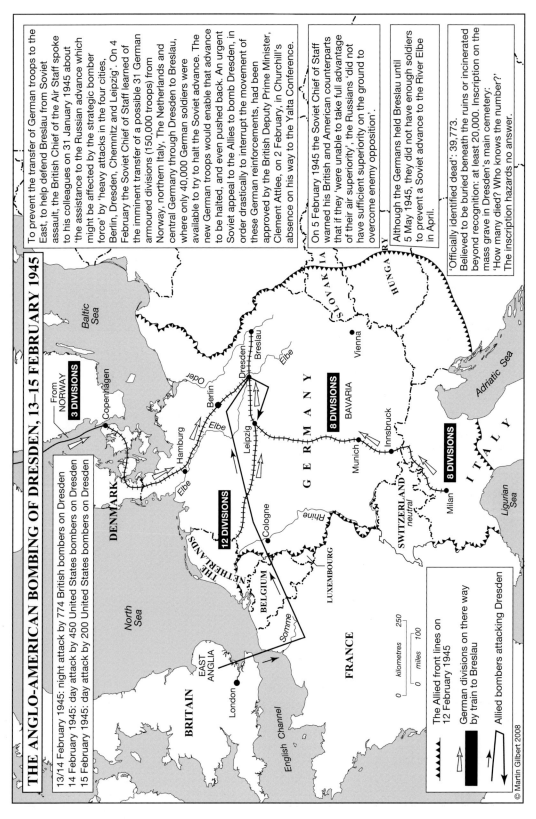

THE ANGLO-AMERICAN BOMBING OF DRESDEN, 13–15 FEBRUARY 1945

13/14 February 1945: night attack by 774 British bombers on Dresden
14 February 1945: day attack by 450 United States bombers on Dresden
15 February 1945: day attack by 200 United States bombers on Dresden

To prevent the transfer of German troops to the East, to help defend Breslau from Soviet assault, the British Chief of the Air Staff spoke to his colleagues on 31 January 1945 about 'the assistance to the Russian advance which might be affected by the strategic bomber force' by 'heavy attacks in the four cities, Berlin, Dresden, Chemnitz and Leipzig'. On 4 February the Soviet Chief of Staff learned of the imminent transfer of a possible 31 German armoured divisions (150,000 troops) from Norway, northern Italy, The Netherlands and central Germany through Dresden to Breslau, where only 40,000 German soldiers were available to try to halt the Soviet advance. The new German troops would enable that advance to be halted, and even pushed back. An urgent Soviet appeal to the Allies to bomb Dresden, in order drastically to interrupt the movement of these German reinforcements, had been approved by the British Deputy Prime Minister, Clement Attlee, on 2 February, in Churchill's absence on his way to the Yalta Conference.

On 5 February 1945 the Soviet Chief of Staff warned his British and American counterparts that if they 'were unable to take full advantage of their air superiority', the Russians 'did not have sufficient superiority on the ground to overcome enemy opposition'.

Although the Germans held Breslau until 5 May 1945, they did not have enough soldiers to prevent a Soviet advance to the River Elbe in April.

'Officially identified dead': 39,773.
Believed to be buried beneath the ruins or incinerated beyond recognition: at least 20,000. Inscription on the mass grave in Dresden's main cemetery:
'How many died? Who knows the number?'
The inscription hazards no answer.

Baltic Sea

From NORWAY
3 DIVISIONS

Copenhagen

DENMARK

Hamburg

Elbe

Elbe

Berlin

Oder

Leipzig

Dresden

Breslau

Elbe

12 DIVISIONS

Cologne

Rhine

NETHERLANDS

BELGIUM

LUXEMBOURG

Somme

GERMANY

SLOVAKIA

HUNGARY

Vienna

8 DIVISIONS

BAVARIA

Munich

Innsbruck

SWITZERLAND
neutral

Milan

8 DIVISIONS

ITALY

Adriatic Sea

Ligurian Sea

North Sea

BRITAIN

EAST ANGLIA

London

English Channel

FRANCE

0   kilometres   250
0   miles   100

⌃⌃⌃⌃   The Allied front lines on 12 February 1945

▮   German divisions on there way by train to Breslau

⇧   Allied bombers attacking Dresden

© Martin Gilbert 2008

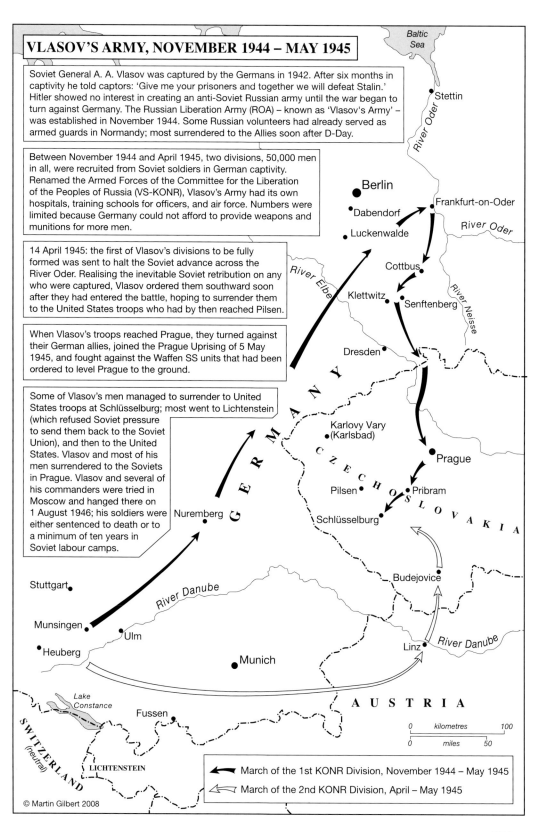

VLASOV'S ARMY, NOVEMBER 1944 – MAY 1945

Soviet General A. A. Vlasov was captured by the Germans in 1942. After six months in captivity he told captors: 'Give me your prisoners and together we will defeat Stalin.' Hitler showed no interest in creating an anti-Soviet Russian army until the war began to turn against Germany. The Russian Liberation Army (ROA) – known as 'Vlasov's Army' – was established in November 1944. Some Russian volunteers had already served as armed guards in Normandy; most surrendered to the Allies soon after D-Day.

Between November 1944 and April 1945, two divisions, 50,000 men in all, were recruited from Soviet soldiers in German captivity. Renamed the Armed Forces of the Committee for the Liberation of the Peoples of Russia (VS-KONR), Vlasov's Army had its own hospitals, training schools for officers, and air force. Numbers were limited because Germany could not afford to provide weapons and munitions for more men.

14 April 1945: the first of Vlasov's divisions to be fully formed was sent to halt the Soviet advance across the River Oder. Realising the inevitable Soviet retribution on any who were captured, Vlasov ordered them southward soon after they had entered the battle, hoping to surrender them to the United States troops who had by then reached Pilsen.

When Vlasov's troops reached Prague, they turned against their German allies, joined the Prague Uprising of 5 May 1945, and fought against the Waffen SS units that had been ordered to level Prague to the ground.

Some of Vlasov's men managed to surrender to United States troops at Schlüsselburg; most went to Lichtenstein (which refused Soviet pressure to send them back to the Soviet Union), and then to the United States. Vlasov and most of his men surrendered to the Soviets in Prague. Vlasov and several of his commanders were tried in Moscow and hanged there on 1 August 1946; his soldiers were either sentenced to death or to a minimum of ten years in Soviet labour camps.

Baltic Sea

Stettin

River Oder

Berlin

Dabendorf

Luckenwalde

Frankfurt-on-Oder

River Oder

River Elbe

Cottbus

Klettwitz

Senftenberg

River Neisse

Dresden

Karlovy Vary (Karlsbad)

Prague

C Z E C H O S L O V A K I A

Pilsen

Pribram

Schlüsselburg

Budejovice

G E R M A N Y

Nuremberg

Stuttgart

River Danube

Munsingen

Ulm

Heuberg

Munich

Linz

River Danube

Lake Constance

Fussen

A U S T R I A

| 0 | kilometres | 100 |
| 0 | miles | 50 |

S W I T Z E R L A N D (neutral)

LICHTENSTEIN

⬅ March of the 1st KONR Division, November 1944 – May 1945

⇐ March of the 2nd KONR Division, April – May 1945

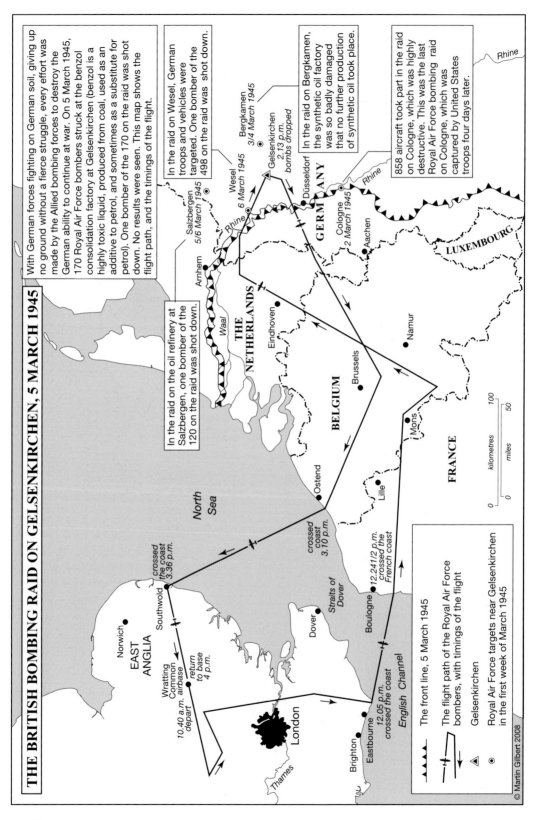

THE BRITISH BOMBING RAID ON GELSENKIRCHEN, 5 MARCH 1945

With German forces fighting on German soil, giving up no ground without a fierce struggle, every effort was made by the Allied bombing forces to destroy the German ability to continue at war. On 5 March 1945, 170 Royal Air Force bombers struck at the benzol consolidation factory at Gelsenkirchen (benzol is a highly toxic liquid, produced from coal, used as an additive to petrol, and sometimes as a substitute for petrol). One bomber of the 170 on the raid was shot down. No results were seen. This map shows the flight path, and the timings of the flight.

In the raid on Wesel, German troops and vehicles were targeted. One bomber of the 498 on the raid was shot down.

In the raid on Bergkamen, the synthetic oil factory was so badly damaged that no further production of synthetic oil took place.

858 aircraft took part in the raid on Cologne, which was highly destructive. This was the last Royal Air Force bombing raid on Cologne, which was captured by United States troops four days later.

In the raid on the oil refinery at Salzbergen, one bomber of the 120 on the raid was shot down.

Salzbergen 5/6 March 1945

Bergkamen 3/4 March 1945

Gelsenkirchen 2.13 p.m. bombs dropped

Wesel 6 March 1945

Düsseldorf

Cologne 2 March 1945

Aachen

Rhine

Arnhem

Rhine

Waal

THE NETHERLANDS

GERMANY

LUXEMBOURG

Eindhoven

Brussels

BELGIUM

Namur

Mons

Lille

FRANCE

Ostend

crossed coast 3.10 p.m.

North Sea

Boulogne

12.24/2 p.m. crossed the French coast

Straits of Dover

Dover

English Channel

London

Thames

Eastbourne

12.05 p.m. crossed the coast

Brighton

Gelsenkirchen

Southwold

crossed the coast 3.36 p.m.

Norwich

EAST ANGLIA

Wratting Common airbase

10.40 a.m. depart

return to base 4 p.m.

The front line, 5 March 1945

The flight path of the Royal Air Force bombers, with timings of the flight

Gelsenkirchen

Royal Air Force targets near Gelsenkirchen in the first week of March 1945

kilometres 100
miles 50
0

© Martin Gilbert 2008

177

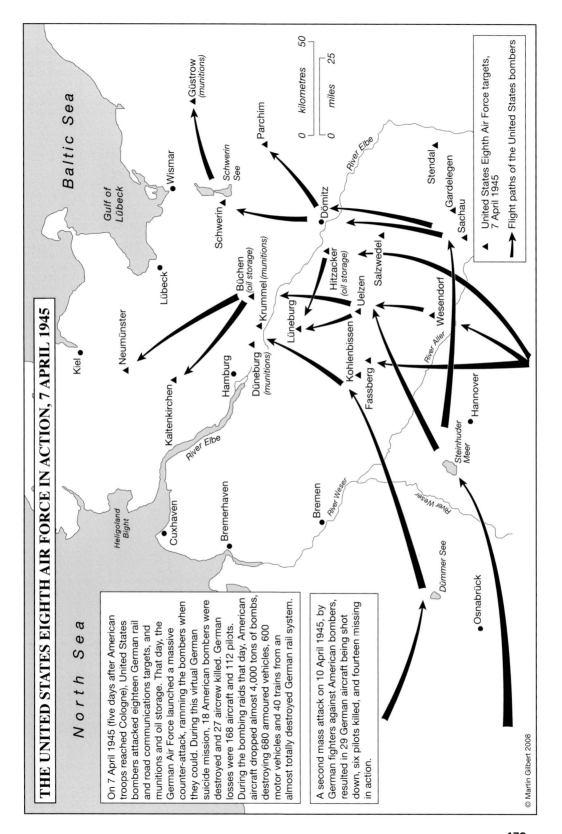

THE UNITED STATES EIGHTH AIR FORCE IN ACTION, 7 APRIL 1945

North Sea

Baltic Sea

Heligoland Bight

Gulf of Lübeck

Kiel

Neumünster

Kaltenkirchen

Cuxhaven

Bremerhaven

Bremen

Hamburg

Lübeck

Wismar

Schwerin
Schwerin See

Parchim

▲Güstrow *(munitions)*

Büchen *(oil storage)*

Krummel *(munitions)*

Düneburg *(munitions)*

Lüneburg

Hitzacker *(oil storage)*

Uelzen

Dömitz

Salzwedel

Stendal

Gardelegen

Sachau

Wesendorf

Kohlenbissen

Fassberg

Hannover

Steinhuder Meer

Dümmer See

Osnabrück

River Elbe

River Elbe

River Weser

River Weser

River Aller

kilometres 0 — 50
miles 0 — 25

▲ United States Eighth Air Force targets, 7 April 1945

→ Flight paths of the United States bombers

On 7 April 1945 (five days after American troops reached Cologne), United States bombers attacked eighteen German rail and road communications targets, and munitions and oil storage. That day, the German Air Force launched a massive counter-attack, ramming the bombers when they could. During this virtual German suicide mission, 18 American bombers were destroyed and 27 aircrew killed. German losses were 168 aircraft and 112 pilots. During the bombing raids that day, American aircraft dropped almost 4,000 tons of bombs, destroying 680 armoured vehicles, 600 motor vehicles and 40 trains from an almost totally destroyed German rail system.

A second mass attack on 10 April 1945, by German fighters against American bombers, resulted in 29 German aircraft being shot down, six pilots killed, and fourteen missing in action.

© Martin Gilbert 2008

178

THE ALLIED ADVANCE FROM WEST AND EAST BY 19 APRIL 1945

As Soviet forces moved westward from the Oder, British and American forces reached and crossed the Elbe.

On 10 April 1945, American aircraft shot down 14 German jet aircraft above Oranienburg, in what became known as the Great Jet Massacre.

DENMARK
under German occupation

Copenhagen

North Sea

Baltic Sea

Kiel

Rostock

Kolberg

POMERANIA

Lübeck

Stettin

Hamburg

Wilhelmshaven

Bremen

Elbe

Wittenberge

Ravensbrück

River Oder

19 April 1945

Osnabrück

Hannover

Braunschweig

Oranienburg

Berlin

Küstrin

Poznan

Paderborn

Harz Mountains

Magdeburg

Potsdam

Frankfurt-on-Oder

RUHR

Göttingen

Halle

Elbe

Western Neisse

Düsseldorf

Eschwege

Leipzig

Breslau

River Oder

Remagen

Erfurt

THURINGIA

Dresden

19 April 1945

Fulda

19 April 1945

River Elbe

River Rhine

Frankfurt-on-Main

SUDETENLAND

Bayreuth

Flossenbürg

Prague

Olomouc

Pilsen

BOHEMIA

0 kilometres 100

Nuremberg

SUDETENLAND

Brno

MORAVIA

0 miles 50

19 April 1945

BAVARIA

SLOVAKIA

Stuttgart

Bratislava

River Danube

River Inn

Linz

Danube

Vienna

Munich

Salzburg

AUSTRIA

STYRIA

HUNGARY

Berchtesgaden

Innsbruck

Graz

SWITZERLAND
neutral

CARINTHIA

River Adige

NORTHERN ITALY
under German occupation

YUGOSLAVIA

Trieste

ISTRIA

© Martin Gilbert 2008

—·—·— Borders of 1937

▲▲▲▲ Allied front lines on 19 April 1945

LIBERATING THE CONCENTRATION CAMPS, 4 APRIL – 7 MAY 1945

As the Allied armies advanced into Germany from the west, they came across signs of horrific brutality: SS-run concentration camps in which the dead and the living were intermingled, and where many of the victims were too weak to survive liberation. The majority of the inmates of these camps were Jews. There were also political prisoners from all the formerly German-occupied nations, as well as Gypsies (Roma and Sinti), homosexuals, and other 'enemies' of Hitler's Third Reich. Most of the concentration camps that were liberated were in the United States Army's areas of operation. Bergen-Belsen was liberated by British troops on 15 April 1945.

North Sea

Baltic Sea

The first concentration camp to be liberated in the west was Ohrdruf, in which 4,000 inmates had died of disease and starvation, or been murdered, in the previous three months. Hundreds had been shot on the eve of the arrival of the United States forces on 4 April 1945. The inmates – Jews, and Polish and Soviet prisoners of war – were being forced to build a huge underground radio and telephone centre for the German Army in the event of the evacuation of Berlin.

'You were our liberators, but we, the diseased, emaciated, barely human survivors were your teachers. We taught you to understand the Kingdom of Night'.
ELIE WIESEL, LIBERATED AT BUCHENWALD (AUTHOR OF *NIGHT*)

Hamburg

Lüneberg

Wöbbelin
8th Infantry Division

Berlin

Bergen-Belsen

Salzwedel
84th Infantry Division

THE NETHERLANDS

Ahlem
84th Infantry Division

Gardelegen
102nd Infantry Division

G E R M A N Y

Dinslaken
29th Infantry Division

Halberstadt
8th Armoured Division

Werl
95th Infantry Division

Mittelbau-Dora
104th Infantry Division

Thekla
69th Infantry Division

Schönefeld
2nd Infantry Division

Cologne

Attendorn
86th Infantry Division

Leipzig

Immediately after the war, Nazi officials were imprisoned at Werl. In 2008, Werl was one of the largest prisons in Germany.

Ohrdruf
89th Infantry Division and 4th Armoured Division

Buchenwald
80th Infantry Division 6th Armoured Division

Frankfurt-on-Main

Falkenau-on-the-Eger
1st Infantry Division and 9th Armoured Division

S U D E T E N L A N D

Every year, a ceremony is held under the Rotunda in the Capitol Building, Washington DC, when the flags of the liberating divisions are paraded before American dignatories, veterans, and Holocaust survivors.

Flossenbürg
65th and 90th Infantry Divisions

B O H E M I A

S U D E T E N L A N D

FRANCE

Stuttgart

26th Infantry Division

Dachau
42nd and 45th Infantry Divisions

Gusen

Mauthausen

Kaufering
36th and 63rd and 103rd Infantry Divisions

Munich

Gunskirchen
71st Infantry Division

Langenstein
83rd Infantry Division

| 0 | kilometres | 150 |
| 0 | miles | 100 |

Ebensee
80th Infantry Division

AUSTRIA

▲▲▲▲▲▲ The Front Lines on 19 April 1945

卐 Twenty-two of the concentration camps liberated by United States troops, with the names of the liberating divisions

© Martin Gilbert 2008

THE BATTLE FOR BERLIN, FROM ENCIRCLEMENT TO CONQUEST, 19 APRIL – 2 MAY 1945

Pankow

Jungfern Heath

Wedding

26 April 1945

26 April 1945

River Spree

Moabit

1 May

Charlottenburg

Moabit Prison

■ Reichstag
■ Brandenburg Gate
■ Chancellery
(Hitler's Bunker)

Lichtenberg

1 May

1 May 1945

Tiergarten

River Spree

1 May

Potsdam Station

Grünwald

1 May

BERLIN DEFENCE PERIMETER

Wilmersdorf

Berlin

Schöneberg

Landwehr Canal

Neukölln

Spandau Forest

Templehof
Airport ✈

Friedenau

Dahlem

Steglitz

Britz

26 April 1945

Legend:

ˇˇˇˇ Berlin Defence Perimeter, 19 April 1945
➤ Direction of Soviet advance
▲▲▲▲ Soviet front line, 26 April 1945
△△△△ Front line on 1 May 1945

| 0 | kilometres | 3 |
| 0 | miles | 2 |

© Martin Gilbert 2008

By 25 April 1945 the Berlin Defence Perimeter had been breached in the north and south by Soviet troops, with Tempelhof airfield under Soviet control. By the end of 27 April, three-quarters of Berlin was under Soviet control.

On 27 April, during the fighting in Berlin, Reginald Cornford, a British volunteer in the British Free Corps, knocked out a Soviet tank with his anti-tank gun: then defended himself for half an hour before being killed. On 28 April, Eugene Vaulot, a French SS volunteer, destroyed six Soviet tanks.

With the entry of Soviet troops, commanded by Colonel Zinchenko, into the Moabit Prison on 28 April, more than 7,000 prisoners, including many Allied prisoners of war, were liberated.

With the Soviet capture of Berlin's Potsdam Railway Station on 29 April, the German defenders had no more anti-tank guns with which to defend Hitler's Chancellery. On 30 April the German Ninth Army, which Hitler had ordered to come to the defence of Berlin, was surrounded thirty miles away. On 30 April, Soviet troops were fighting inside the Reichstag. That day, Hitler committed suicide. At ten minutes to eleven that night the Soviet Red banner flew on the roof of the Reichstag; the whole building was not secured until 1 p.m. on 2 May, two hours before the German surrender in Berlin.

In the battle for the Reichstag building, 2,500 German and 2,200 Soviet soldiers were killed.

THE LAST THREE WEEKS OF THE WAR IN EUROPE, 25 APRIL – 7 MAY 1945

On 26 April 1945, British Intelligence decrypted a top-secret Enigma message sent by the SS to Himmler, warning that food for the German-controlled civilian population would not last beyond 10 May 1945.

Significant German surrenders began on 25 April 1945 and continued until the signing of the Unconditional Surrender on 7 May 1945, at Reims, when all but a few groups of German soldiers laid down their arms.

On 3 May 1945, during a British bombing raid on what were thought to be German troopships in Lübeck harbour, 2,750 Jewish concentration camp evacuees who were on board *Thielbeck*, and 3,500 on board *Cap Arcona*, (which had been used in a German pre-war film as a stand-in for *Titanic*) as well a several hundred Soviet prisoners of war, were drowned; 150 of the 500 Jews who managed to swim to the shore were killed by German Marines and Hitler Youth. There were 350 survivors.

With Soviet troops only 400 yards away above ground, Adolf Hitler committed suicide in his underground bunker on 30 April 1945, ten days after his 56th birthday.

0 kilometres 200
0 miles 100

North Atlantic Ocean

Trondheim

Bergen

NORWAY

Oslo

2 May
The first wartime defection of a German bomber, flying from Norway, with a crew of five
Fraserburgh

SCOTLAND

ISLE OF MAY
7 May
German submarine U-2336 sank a Norwegian and a British merchant ship. Seven Norwegian and two British merchant seamen killed

Ventspils

LATVIA

Kiel
5 May
All German submarines ordered back to German ports

2 May
President Eamon de Valera expressed condolences on the death of Hitler

EIRE
Dublin

3 May
Hamburg's mayor negotiated the city's surrender

DENMARK

BORNHOLM

Baltic Sea

Danzig

2 May, 3 p.m.
German-Soviet ceasefire came into effect

On 29 April 1945, British bombers carried out Operation Manna, dropping more than 6,000 tons of supplies behind German lines, to help feed the starving Dutch.

THE NETHERLANDS

Lübeck
Hamburg

Lüneberg Heath
4 May, 6.25 p.m.
German Army emissaries sign unconditional surrender of all German forces to General Montgomery

Wageningen
5 May
Surrender of all German forces in The Netherlands

Berlin

Torgau

6 May
Surrender of German forces besieged for more than three months
Breslau

25 April
United States and Soviet troops linked up

Lorient

St Nazaire

FRANCE

Reims
7 May, 2.41 a.m.
Germany signed the Unconditional Surrender of all its forces

GERMANY

30 April
Entered by United States troops
Munich

Brno
26 April
Liberated by Soviet troops

Bay of Biscay

Oberammergau
2 May
Wernher von Braun and two other German scientists surrendered to the Americans. They were taken to Paris, en route to the United States (Operation Paperclip)

SWITZERLAND
neutral

Dongo

Venice

Ebensee
6 May
Revolt of Jewish concentration camp prisoners

Milan

25 April
Liberated by Italian partisans

NORTHERN ITALY
2 May
All German forces in Italy surrendered

29 April
Liberated by Allied forces

Baldham
5 May
Surrender of all German forces in southern Germany

SPAIN
neutral

28 April
Mussolini shot dead by Italian partisans

ITALY

Adriatic Sea

© Martin Gilbert 2008

▲ German forces surrendering, and other events, 25 April – 6 May 1945

■ Areas under German military control on 7 May 1945

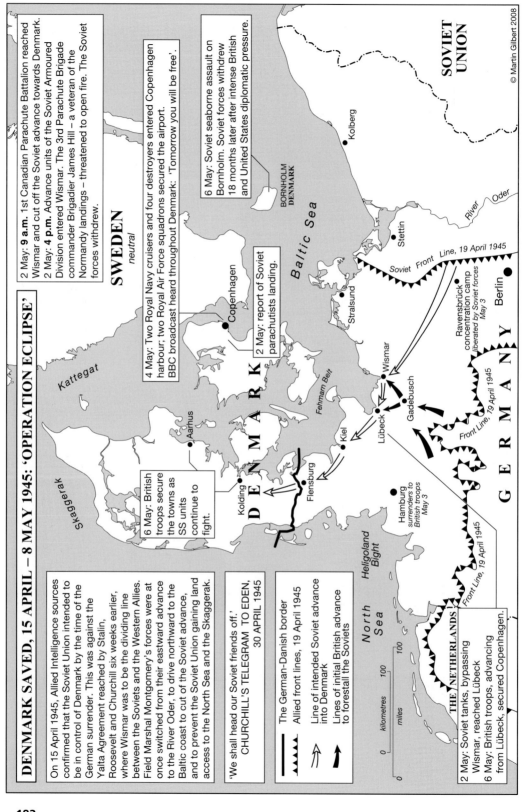

DENMARK SAVED, 15 APRIL – 8 MAY 1945: 'OPERATION ECLIPSE'

On 15 April 1945, Allied Intelligence sources confirmed that the Soviet Union intended to be in control of Denmark by the time of the German surrender. This was against the Yalta Agreement reached by Stalin, Roosevelt and Churchill six weeks earlier, where Wismar was to be the dividing line between the Soviets and the Western Allies. Field Marshal Montgomery's forces were at once switched from their eastward advance to the River Oder, to drive northward to the Baltic coast to cut off the Soviet advance, and to prevent the Soviet Union gaining land access to the North Sea and the Skaggerak.

'We shall head our Soviet friends off.'
CHURCHILL'S TELEGRAM TO EDEN, 30 APRIL 1945

2 May: **9 a.m.** 1st Canadian Parachute Battalion reached Wismar and cut off the Soviet advance towards Denmark.
2 May: **4 p.m.** Advance units of the Soviet Armoured Division entered Wismar. The 3rd Parachute Brigade commander Brigadier James Hill – a veteran of the Normandy landings – threatened to open fire. The Soviet forces withdrew.

SWEDEN
neutral

4 May: Two Royal Navy cruisers and four destroyers entered Copenhagen harbour; two Royal Air Force squadrons secured the airport. BBC broadcast heard throughout Denmark: 'Tomorrow you will be free'.

2 May: report of Soviet parachutists landing.

6 May: Soviet seaborne assault on Bornholm. Soviet forces withdrew 18 months later after intense British and United States diplomatic pressure.

BORNHOLM
DENMARK

Baltic Sea

Kattegat

Copenhagen

Skaggerak

Aarhus

Kolding

D E N M A R K

6 May: British troops secure the towns as SS units continue to fight.

Flensburg

Kiel

Fehmarn Belt

Lübeck

Gadebusch

Wismar

Stralsund

Stettin

Kolberg

River Oder

Soviet Front Line, 19 April 1945

Ravensbrück concentration camp liberated by Soviet forces May 5

Berlin

G E R M A N Y

Front Line, 19 April 1945

Hamburg surrenders to British troops May 3

Heligoland Bight

North Sea

THE NETHERLANDS

Front Line, 19 April 1945

The German-Danish border
Allied front lines, 19 April 1945
Line of intended Soviet advance into Denmark
Lines of initial British advance to forestall the Soviets

0   100 kilometres
0   100 miles

2 May: Soviet tanks, bypassing Wismar, reached Lübeck
6 May: British troops, advancing from Lübeck, secured Copenhagen.

SOVIET UNION

© Martin Gilbert 2008

183

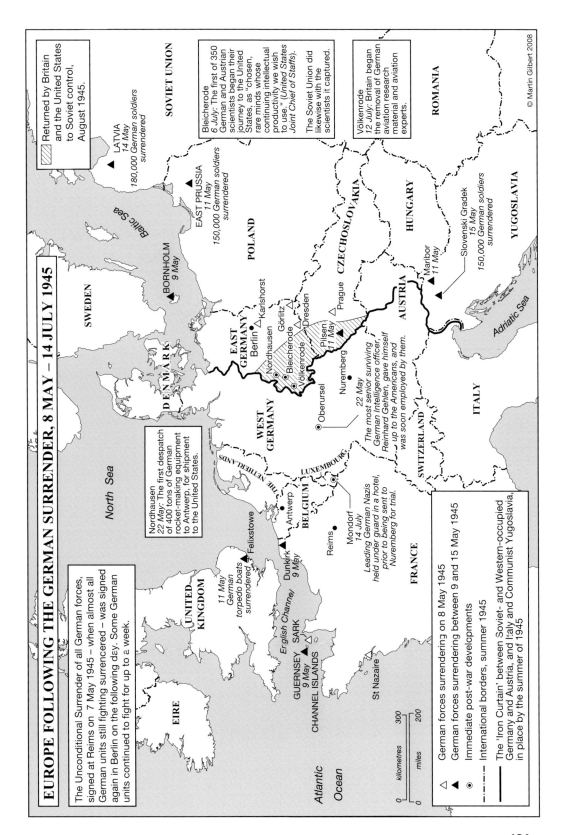

EUROPE FOLLOWING THE GERMAN SURRENDER, 8 MAY – 14 JULY 1945

The Unconditional Surrender of all German forces, signed at Reims on 7 May 1945 – when almost all German units still fighting surrendered – was signed again in Berlin on the following day. Some German units continued to fight for up to a week.

Returned by Britain and the United States to Soviet control, August 1945.

SOVIET UNION

LATVIA
14 May
180,000 German soldiers surrendered

Bleicherode
6 July: The first of 350 German and Austrian scientists began their journey to the United States, as "chosen, rare minds whose continuing intellectual productivity we wish to use." (United States Joint Chief of Staffs).

The Soviet Union did likewise with the scientists it captured.

EAST PRUSSIA
11 May
150,000 German soldiers surrendered

Völkenrode
12 July: Britain began the removal of German aviation research material and aviation experts.

ROMANIA

Baltic Sea

BORNHOLM
9 May

SWEDEN

POLAND

CZECHOSLOVAKIA

HUNGARY

Slovenski Gradek
15 May
150,000 German soldiers surrendered

Karlshorst

Görlitz
Dresden

Maribor
11 May

YUGOSLAVIA

DENMARK

EAST GERMANY
Berlin
Nordhausen
Bleicherode
Völkenrode

Prague

Pilsen
11 May

AUSTRIA

Adriatic Sea

North Sea

Nuremberg

22 May
The most senior surviving German Intelligence officer, Reinhard Gehlen, gave himself up to the Americans, and was soon employed by them.

Oberursel

Nordhausen
22 May: The first despatch of 400 tons of German rocket-making equipment to Antwerp, for shipment to the United States.

WEST GERMANY

THE NETHERLANDS

LUXEMBOURG

SWITZERLAND

ITALY

Antwerp

BELGIUM

Mondorf
14 July
Leading German Nazis held under guard in a hotel, prior to being sent to Nuremberg for trial.

Reims

11 May
German torpedo boats surrendered

Felixstowe

UNITED KINGDOM

Dunkirk
9 May

FRANCE

English Channel

GUERNSEY
9 May
SARK
9 May
CHANNEL ISLANDS

St Nazaire

EIRE

Atlantic Ocean

0   300
kilometres
0   200
miles

△   German forces surrendering on 8 May 1945

▲   German forces surrendering between 9 and 15 May 1945

⊙   Immediate post-war developments

–··–··   International borders, summer 1945

——   The 'Iron Curtain' between Soviet- and Western-occupied Germany and Austria, and Italy and Communist Yugoslavia, in place by the summer of 1945

© Martin Gilbert 2008

184

Section 10

THE DEFEAT OF JAPAN

'My God, look at that son-of-a-bitch go!'

Paul Tibbets
Commander of the Enola Gay, watching the first atomic bomb explode
6 August 1945

It is far too early to say that the war is lost. That we will inflict severe losses on the enemy when he invades Japan is certain, and it is by no means impossible that we may be able to reverse the situation in our favour, pulling victory out of defeat.

General Korechika Anami
Japanese Minister of War
9 August 1945

To our good and loyal subjects: After pondering deeply the general trends of the world and the actual conditions obtaining in our empire today, we have decided to effect a settlement of the present situation by resorting to an extraordinary measure. We have ordered our Government to communicate to the Governments of the United States, Great Britain, China and the Soviet Union that our empire accepts the provisions of their joint declaration. . . .

Despite the best that has been done by everyone . . . the war situation has developed not necessarily to Japan's advantage, while the general trends of the world have all turned against her interest. Moreover, the enemy has begun to employ a new and most cruel bomb, the power of which to do damage is, indeed, incalculable, taking the toll of many innocent lives. Should we continue to fight, it would not only result in an ultimate collapse and obliteration of the Japanese nation, but also it would lead to the total extinction of human civilization.

Emperor Hirohito
Radio Broadcast
14 August 1945

– Japs licked –

A street banner in Chicago
15 August 1945

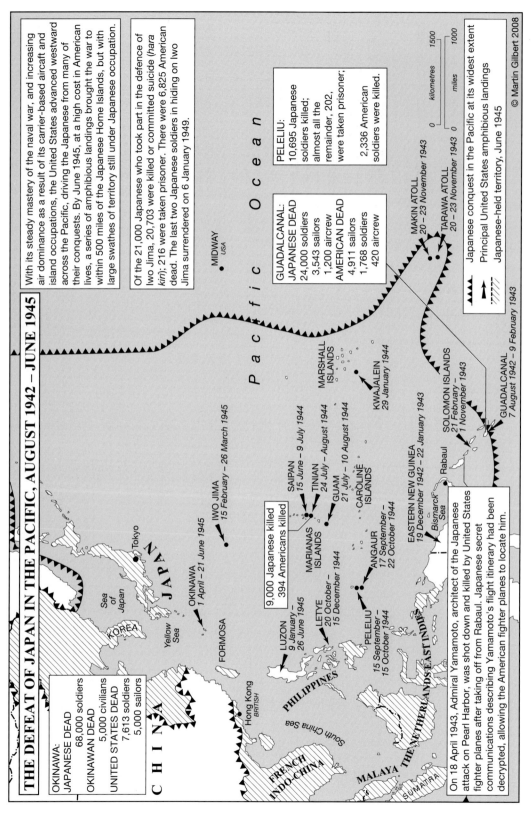

THE DEFEAT OF JAPAN IN THE PACIFIC, AUGUST 1942 – JUNE 1945

With its steady mastery of the naval war, and increasing air dominance as a result of its carrier-based aircaft and island occupations, the United States advanced westward across the Pacific, driving the Japanese from many of their conquests. By June 1945, at a high cost in American lives, a series of amphibious landings brought the war to within 500 miles of the Japanese Home Islands, but with large swathes of territory still under Japanese occupation.

Of the 21,000 Japanese who took part in the defence of Iwo Jima, 20,703 were killed or committed suicide (*hara kiri*); 216 were taken prisoner. There were 6,825 American dead. The last two Japanese soldiers in hiding on Iwo Jima surrendered on 6 January 1949.

PELELIU:
10,695 Japanese
soldiers killed;
almost all the
remainder, 202,
were taken prisoner;

2,336 American
soldiers were killed.

GUADALCANAL:
JAPANESE DEAD
24,000 soldiers
3,543 sailors
1,200 aircrew
AMERICAN DEAD
4,911 sailors
1,768 soldiers
420 aircrew

OKINAWA:
JAPANESE DEAD
68,000 soldiers
OKINAWAN DEAD
5,000 civilians
UNITED STATES DEAD
7,613 soldiers
5,000 sailors

On 18 April 1943, Admiral Yamamoto, architect of the Japanese attack on Pearl Harbor, was shot down and killed by United States fighter planes after taking off from Rabaul. Japanese secret communications describing Yamamoto's flight itinerary had been decrypted, allowing the American fighter planes to locate him.

MAKIN ATOLL
20 – 23 November 1943

TARAWA ATOLL
20 – 23 November 1943

SOLOMON ISLANDS
21 February –
1 November 1943

GUADALCANAL
7 August 1942 – 9 February 1943

EASTERN NEW GUINEA
19 December 1942 – 22 January 1943

Rabaul

Bismarck Sea

KWAJALEIN
29 January 1944

MARSHALL
ISLANDS

MIDWAY
USA

SAIPAN
15 June – 9 July 1944

TINIAN
24 July – August 1944

GUAM
21 July – 10 August 1944

CAROLINE
ISLANDS

MARIANAS
ISLANDS

9,000 Japanese killed
394 Americans killed

ANGAUR
17 September –
22 October 1944

PELELIU
15 September –
15 October 1944

LETYE
20 October –
15 December 1944

PHILIPPINES

LUZON
9 January –
26 June 1945

IWO JIMA
15 February – 26 March 1945

OKINAWA
1 April – 21 June 1945

FORMOSA

Tokyo

JAPAN

Sea
of
Japan

KOREA

Yellow
Sea

Hong Kong
BRITISH

South China Sea

CHINA

FRENCH
INDO-CHINA

MALAYA

THE NETHERLANDS EAST INDIES

SUMATRA

P a c i f i c   O c e a n

Japanese conquest in the Pacific at its widest extent

Principal United States amphibious landings

Japanese-held territory, June 1945

0   kilometres   1500
0   miles   1000

© Martin Gilbert 2008

185

THE GERMAN U-BOAT WAR IN THE INDIAN OCEAN AND PACIFIC, 1942–1945

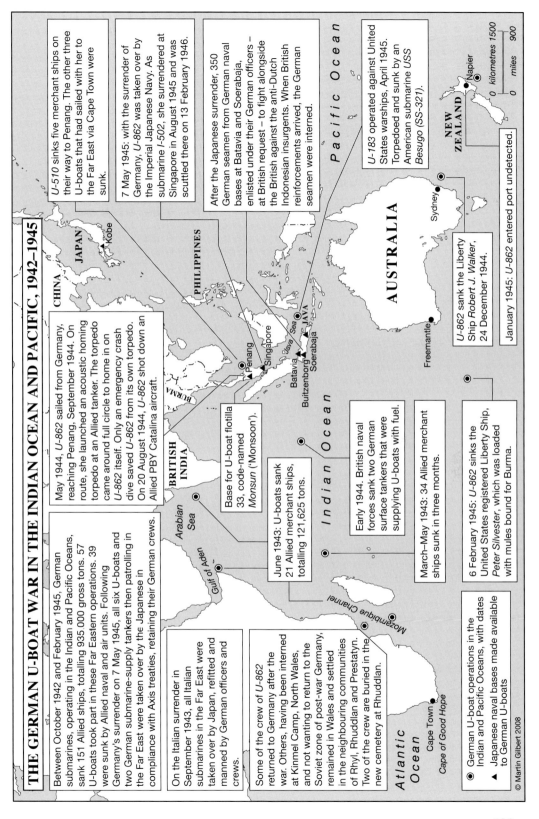

Between October 1942 and February 1945, German submarines, operating in the Indian and Pacific Oceans, sank 151 Allied ships, totalling 935 000 gross tons. 57 U-boats took part in these Far Eastern operations. 39 were sunk by Allied naval and air units. Following Germany's surrender on 7 May 1945, all six U-boats and two German submarine-supply tankers then patrolling in the Far East were taken over by the Japanese in compliance with Axis treaties, retaining their German crews.

On the Italian surrender in September 1943, all Italian submarines in the Far East were taken over by Japan, refitted and manned by German officers and crews.

Some of the crew of U-862 returned to Germany after the war. Others, having been interned at Kinmel Camp, North Wales, and not wanting to return to the Soviet zone of post-war Germany, remained in Wales and settled in the neighbouring communities of Rhyl, Rhuddlan and Prestatyn. Two of the crew are buried in the new cemetery at Rhuddlan.

May 1944, U-862 sailed from Germany, reaching Penang, September 1944. On route, she launched an acoustic homing torpedo at an Allied tanker. The torpedo came around full circle to home in on U-862 itself. Only an emergency crash dive saved U-862 from its own torpedo. On 20 August 1944, U-862 shot down an Allied PBY Catalina aircraft.

7 May 1945: with the surrender of Germany, U-862 was taken over by the Imperial Japanese Navy. As submarine I-502, she surrendered at Singapore in August 1945 and was scuttled there on 13 February 1946.

U-510 sinks five merchant ships on their way to Penang. The other three U-boats that had sailed with her to the Far East via Cape Town were sunk.

After the Japanese surrender, 350 German seamen from German naval bases at Batavia and Soerabaja, enlisted under their German officers – at British request – to fight alongside the anti-Dutch Indonesian insurgents. When British reinforcements arrived, the German seamen were interned.

U-183 operated against United States warships, April 1945. Torpedoed and sunk by an American submarine USS Besugo (SS-321).

Base for U-boat flotilla 33, code-named Monsun ('Monsoon').

June 1943: U-boats sank 21 Allied merchant ships, totalling 121,625 tons.

Early 1944. British naval forces sank two German surface tankers that were supplying U-boats with fuel.

March–May 1943: 34 Allied merchant ships sunk in three months.

6 February 1945: U-862 sinks the United States registered Liberty Ship, Peter Silvester, which was loaded with mules bound for Burma.

U-862 sank the Liberty Ship Robert J. Walker, 24 December 1944.

January 1945: U-862 entered port undetected.

⊙ German U-boat operations in the Indian and Pacific Oceans, with dates
▲ Japanese naval bases made available to German U-boats

Atlantic Ocean

Indian Ocean

Pacific Ocean

CHINA

JAPAN

Kobe

PHILIPPINES

BURMA

BRITISH INDIA

Arabian Sea

Gulf of Aden

Mozambique Channel

Cape Town
Cape of Good Hope

Penang

Singapore

Java Sea

Batavia
Buitzenborg
Soerabaja

JAVA

AUSTRALIA

Freemantle

Sydney

NEW ZEALAND

Napier

0 kilometres 1500
0 miles 900

© Martin Gilbert 2008

CHINDIT EXPEDITIONS BEHIND JAPANESE LINES IN BURMA, FEBRUARY 1943 AND MARCH 1944

Wingate chose the name Chindit from the Chinthe, a mythical creature that stands guard outside Burmese pagodas.

The Chindits were the largest of the Allied Special Forces of the Second World War. They were formed and led by a British officer, Major-General Orde Wingate. The Chindits operated deep behind Japanese lines in northern Burma, relying on airdrops for their supplies. There were two Chindit expeditions: the first in February 1943, Operation Longcloth, when 3,000 men marched more than 1,000 miles; the second, Operation Thursday, in March 1944.

Operation Thursday, launched on 6 March 1944; 20,000 British and Commonwealth soldiers, with Chinese troop support, and air support provided by the United States Army Air Force; the second largest airborne invasion of the Second World War (the Normandy landings three months later were the largest). Wingate was killed on 24 March 1944 when his aeroplane, returning from Imphal to rejoin his men, crashed in a thunderstorm. When the expedition ended in mid-August 1944, in all, 1,392 men had been killed.

Mogaung:
Captured by the Chindits, 6–27 June 1944. They held it until relieved by advancing British troops, 17 August 1944.

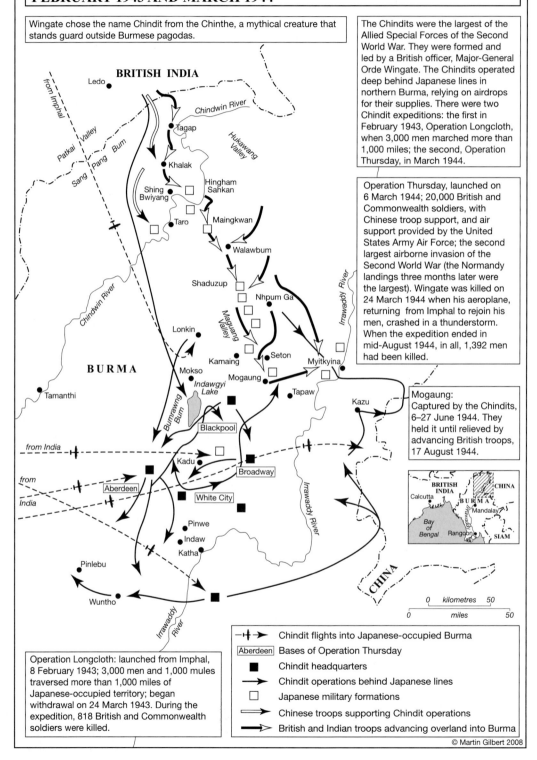

Operation Longcloth: launched from Imphal, 8 February 1943; 3,000 men and 1,000 mules traversed more than 1,000 miles of Japanese-occupied territory; began withdrawal on 24 March 1943. During the expedition, 818 British and Commonwealth soldiers were killed.

-++-> Chindit flights into Japanese-occupied Burma
[Aberdeen] Bases of Operation Thursday
■ Chindit headquarters
→ Chindit operations behind Japanese lines
□ Japanese military formations
⇒ Chinese troops supporting Chindit operations
➤ British and Indian troops advancing overland into Burma

© Martin Gilbert 2008

187

THE BATTLE FOR KOHIMA AND IMPHAL, 4 APRIL – 22 JUNE 1944

The memorial at the Commonwealth War Graves Commission cemetery at Kohima bears the words of John Maxwell Edmonds, a British classicist: 'When You Go Home, Tell Them Of Us And Say: For Their Tomorrow, We Gave Our Today.'

On 15 March 1944, Japanese troops crossed the Chindwin river and marched to the Indian border, from where they advanced more than 100 miles into British India. Reaching Kohima on 16 April, they laid siege to the town and its garrison. Kohima, defended with tenacity, became known as the 'Stalingrad of the East'. Japanese troops also besieged Imphal, and advanced towards the main British army base at Dimapur. It was not until 22 June that the British troops in Kohima were able to break the siege and link up with those in Imphal. The Japanese, their supply lines bombed and harrassed, were forced to retreat back into Burma.

The Royal Air Force flew 19,000 tons of supplies and 12,000 men into Kohima and Imphal. They flew out 13,000 wounded soldiers and 43,000 civilians.

In the Commonwealth War Graves Commission cemetery at Kohima are 1,400 British, and 917 Hindu and Sikh dead. At Imphal, there are 1,600 British graves.

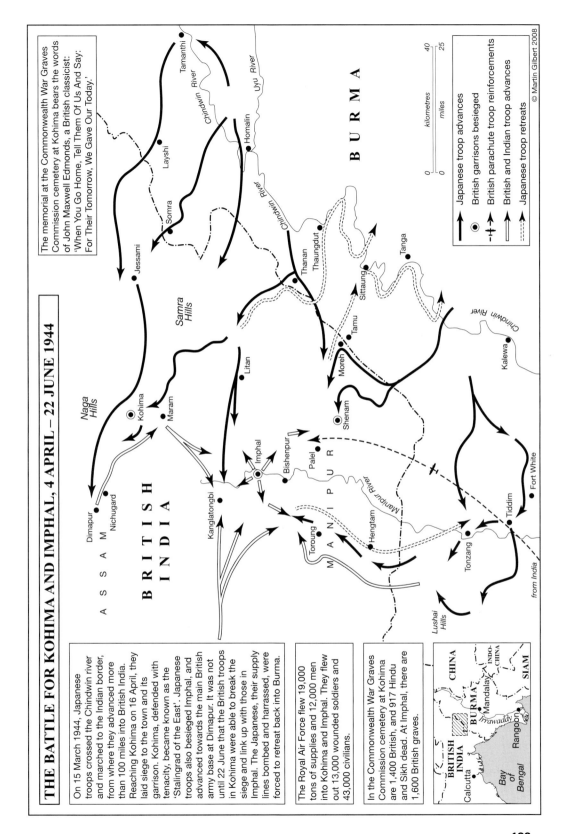

© Martin Gilbert 2008

Japanese troop advances
British garrisons besieged
British parachute troop reinforcements
British and Indian troop advances
Japanese troop retreats

kilometres 40
miles 25
0

BURMA

Tamanthi
Chindwin River
Uyu River
Homalin
Layshi
Somra
Jessami
Chindwin River
Thanan
Thaungdut
Tanga
Sittaung
Naga Hills
Samra Hills
Litan
Tamu
Moreh
Kohima
Maram
Shenam
Chindwin River
Imphal
Bishenpur
Palel
M A N I P U R
Kalewa
Kanglatongbi
Toroung
Hengtam
Manipur River
Tonzang
Tiddim
Fort White
Dimapur
Nichugard
A S S A M
B R I T I S H   I N D I A
Lushai Hills
from India

CHINA
BRITISH INDIA
Calcutta
Bay of Bengal
BURMA
Mandalay
Irrawaddy
Rangoon
INDO-CHINA
SIAM

JAPANESE 'HELLSHIP' VOYAGES, 1942–1945

Between 1 January 1942 and 26 July 1945, more than 170 Japanese merchant ships – known as 'Hellships' – carrying prisoners of war and civilian internees on board in the cruellest of confinement in their cargo holds, crossed the Japanese-controlled seas. Seemingly regular merchant ships, they were the frequent target of United States bombers.

● ▶ Main departure ports of the 'Hellships'
▷ ● Main destination ports of the 'Hellships'

The 'Hellship' *Tottori Maru* and its sister ship *Tokushima Maru*, were built in Glasgow in 1913–14.

Tamahoko Maru left Takao, Formosa, on 18 June 1944, with 267 Australian, 266 Dutch, 190 British and 18 American prisoners of war. Torpedoed by *USS Tang* on 24 June 1944, near Nagasaki, 650 of the 722 prisoners of war were drowned.

On 11 October 1944, *Arisan Maru* left Manila with 1,800 prisoners of war in its cargo holds. Torpedoed 200 miles northwest of Luzon by *USS Shark* on 24 October 1944, all but 9 of the prisoners of war died, the largest loss in history of American lives in a single maritime disaster.

When United States aircraft attacked *Enoura Maru* on 2 January 1945, while she was in harbour at Takao, 350 prisoners of war in the forward hold were killed.

When *Brazil Maru* reached Moji from the Phillipines on 14 January 1945, only 425 prisoners of war out of the 1,619 who began the journey a month earlier were still alive.

On 20 August 1944, at Lasang, Mindanao, 750 American prisoners of war were loaded into the cargo holds of the *Shinyo Maru*, a small, 2,600-ton freighter built in Glasgow in 1894. Torpedoed by *USS Paddle* near Zamboanga, many of the prisoners who tried to leave the ship or waited in the sea to be rescued were killed by the Japanese guards; in all, 668 were drowned on the ship or killed by the guards; 82 reached the shore and were sheltered by local Filipinos.

© Martin Gilbert 2008

189

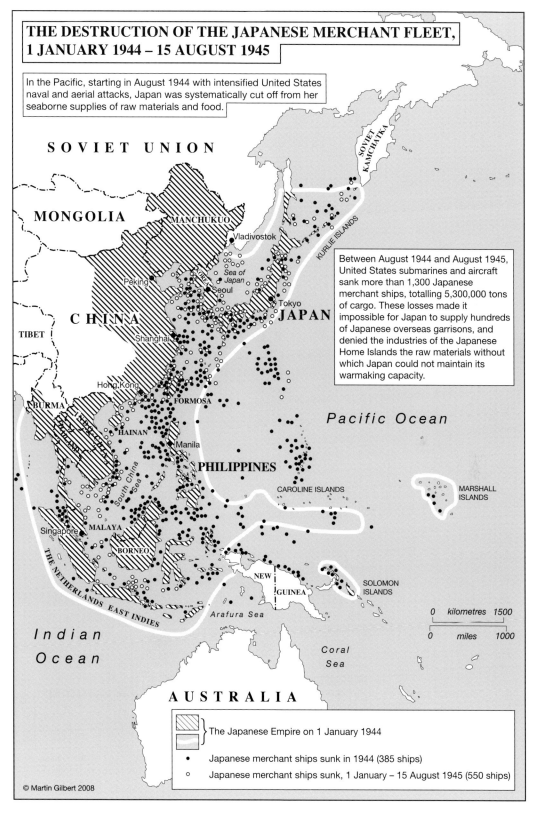

THE DESTRUCTION OF THE JAPANESE MERCHANT FLEET, 1 JANUARY 1944 – 15 AUGUST 1945

In the Pacific, starting in August 1944 with intensified United States naval and aerial attacks, Japan was systematically cut off from her seaborne supplies of raw materials and food.

Between August 1944 and August 1945, United States submarines and aircraft sank more than 1,300 Japanese merchant ships, totalling 5,300,000 tons of cargo. These losses made it impossible for Japan to supply hundreds of Japanese overseas garrisons, and denied the industries of the Japanese Home Islands the raw materials without which Japan could not maintain its warmaking capacity.

SOVIET UNION

MONGOLIA

MANCHUKUO

Vladivostok

SOVIET KAMCHATKA

KURILE ISLANDS

Peking

Sea of Japan

Seoul

Tokyo

CHINA

JAPAN

TIBET

Shanghai

Pacific Ocean

Hong Kong

FORMOSA

BURMA

HAINAN

Manila

South China Sea

PHILIPPINES

CAROLINE ISLANDS

MARSHALL ISLANDS

Singapore

MALAYA

BORNEO

THE NETHERLANDS EAST INDIES

NEW GUINEA

SOLOMON ISLANDS

Arafura Sea

Indian Ocean

Coral Sea

| 0 | kilometres | 1500 |
| 0 | miles | 1000 |

AUSTRALIA

The Japanese Empire on 1 January 1944

• Japanese merchant ships sunk in 1944 (385 ships)

○ Japanese merchant ships sunk, 1 January – 15 August 1945 (550 ships)

© Martin Gilbert 2008

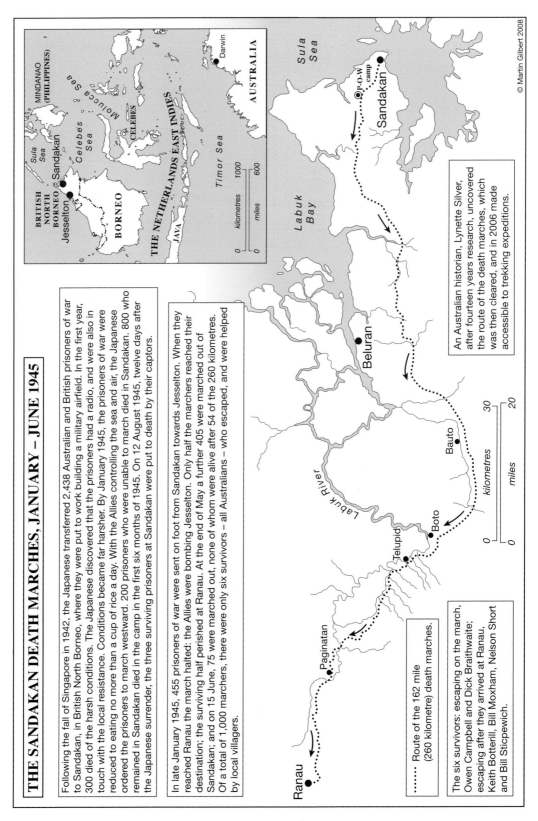

THE SANDAKAN DEATH MARCHES, JANUARY – JUNE 1945

Following the fall of Singapore in 1942, the Japanese transferred 2,438 Australian and British prisoners of war to Sandakan, in British North Borneo, where they were put to work building a military airfield. In the first year, 300 died of the harsh conditions. The Japanese discovered that the prisoners had a radio, and were also in touch with the local resistance. Conditions became far harsher. By January 1945, the prisoners of war were reduced to eating no more than a cup of rice a day. With the Allies controlling the sea and air, the Japanese ordered the prisoners to march westward. 200 prisoners who were unable to march died in Sandakan. 800 who remained in Sandakan died in the camp in the first six months of 1945. On 12 August 1945, twelve days after the Japanese surrender, the three surviving prisoners at Sandakan were put to death by their captors.

In late January 1945, 455 prisoners of war were sent on foot from Sandakan towards Jesselton. When they reached Ranau the march halted: the Allies were bombing Jesselton. Only half the marchers reached their destination; the surviving half perished at Ranau. At the end of May a further 405 were marched out of Sandakan; and on 15 June, 75 were marched out, none of whom were alive after 54 of the 260 kilometres. Of a total of 1,000 marchers, there were only six survivors – all Australians – who escaped, and were helped by local villagers.

An Australian historian, Lynette Silver, after fourteen years research, uncovered the route of the death marches, which was then cleared, and in 2006 made accessible to trekking expeditions.

∙∙∙∙∙∙ Route of the 162 mile (260 kilometre) death marches.

The six survivors: escaping on the march, Owen Campbell and Dick Braithwaite; escaping after they arrived at Ranau, Keith Botterill, Bill Moxham, Nelson Short and Bill Sticpewich.

MINDANAO (PHILIPPINES)

BRITISH NORTH BORNEO
Jesselton
Sandakan

BORNEO

Sula Sea

Celebes Sea

Molucca Sea

CELEBES

THE NETHERLANDS EAST INDIES

JAVA

Timor Sea

AUSTRALIA

Darwin

kilometres 1000
miles 600

Sula Sea

P·O·W camp
Sandakan

Labuk Bay

Beluran

Labuk River

Bauto

Boto

Telupid

Paginatan

Ranau

kilometres 0 30
miles 0 20

© Martin Gilbert 2008

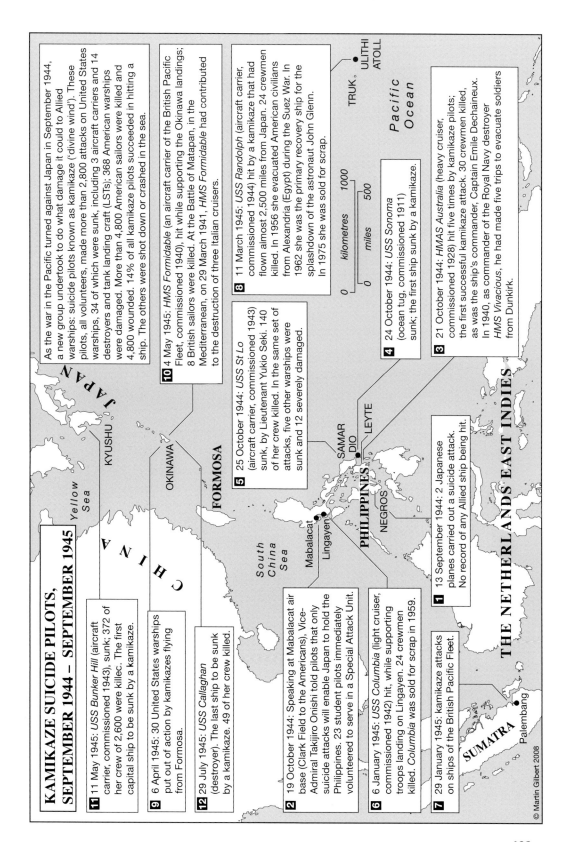

KAMIKAZE SUICIDE PILOTS, SEPTEMBER 1944 – SEPTEMBER 1945

As the war in the Pacific turned against Japan in September 1944, a new group undertook to do what damage it could to Allied warships: suicide pilots known as kamikaze ('divine wind'). These pilots, all volunteers, made more than 2,800 attacks on United States warships, 34 of which were sunk, including 3 aircraft carriers and 14 destroyers and tank landing craft (LSTs); 368 American warships were damaged. More than 4,800 American sailors were killed and 4,800 wounded. 14% of all kamikaze pilots succeeded in hitting a ship. The others were shot down or crashed in the sea.

11 11 May 1945: *USS Bunker Hill* (aircraft carrier, commissioned 1943), sunk; 372 of her crew of 2,600 were killed. The first capital ship to be sunk by a kamikaze.

9 6 April 1945: 30 United States warships put out of action by kamikazes flying from Formosa.

12 29 July 1945: *USS Callaghan* (destroyer). The last ship to be sunk by a kamikaze. 49 of her crew killed.

10 4 May 1945: *HMS Formidable* (an aircraft carrier of the British Pacific Fleet, commissioned 1940), hit while supporting the Okinawa landings; 8 British sailors were killed. At the Battle of Matapan, in the Mediterranean, on 29 March 1941, *HMS Formidable* had contributed to the destruction of three Italian cruisers.

8 11 March 1945: *USS Randolph* (aircraft carrier, commissioned 1944) hit by a kamikaze that had flown almost 2,500 miles from Japan. 24 crewmen killed. In 1956 she evacuated American civilians from Alexandria (Egypt) during the Suez War. In 1962 she was the primary recovery ship for the splashdown of the astronaut John Glenn. In 1975 she was sold for scrap.

4 24 October 1944: *USS Sonoma* (ocean tug, commissioned 1911) sunk; the first ship sunk by a kamikaze.

5 25 October 1944: *USS St Lo* (aircraft carrier, commissioned 1943) sunk, by Lieutenant Yukio Seki. 140 of her crew killed. In the same set of attacks, five other warships were sunk and 12 severely damaged.

3 21 October 1944: *HMAS Australia* (heavy cruiser, commissioned 1928) hit five times by kamikaze pilots; the first successful kamikaze attack. 30 crewmen killed, as was the ship's commander, Captain Emile Dechaineux. In 1940, as commander of the Royal Navy destroyer *HMS Vivacious*, he had made five trips to evacuate soldiers from Dunkirk.

2 19 October 1944: Speaking at Mabalacat air base (Clark Field to the Americans), Vice-Admiral Takijiro Onishi told pilots that only suicide attacks will enable Japan to hold the Philippines. 23 student pilots immediately volunteered to serve in a Special Attack Unit.

6 6 January 1945: *USS Columbia* (light cruiser, commissioned 1942) hit, while supporting troops landing on Lingayen. 24 crewmen killed. *Columbia* was sold for scrap in 1959.

1 13 September 1944: 2 Japanese planes carried out a suicide attack. No record of any Allied ship being hit.

7 29 January 1945: kamikaze attacks on ships of the British Pacific Fleet.

JAPAN

KYUSHU

OKINAWA

FORMOSA

CHINA

Yellow Sea

Pacific Ocean

TRUK

ULITHI ATOLL

South China Sea

PHILIPPINES

LEYTE

SAMAR

DIO

NEGROS

Mabalacat

Lingayen

THE NETHERLANDS EAST INDIES

SUMATRA

Palembang

kilometres 1000 500

0 miles

0

© Martin Gilbert 2008

ANTI-JAPANESE PARTISAN MOVEMENTS, 1941–1945

SOVIET UNION

In offering a 'Greater East Asia Co-Prosperity Sphere' to its conquered nations, Japan posed as the liberator from colonial rule. But harsh Japanese occupation policies created anti-Japanese partisan movements, which were supported by the British Special Operations Executive (SOE) and the United States Organization of Strategic Services (OSS).

Chinese anti-Japanese guerrilla forces supported by agents from OSS. United States naval weather technicians, who had set up radio-linked weather stations in Japanese-occupied China, cooperated with local Chinese guerrillas, and formed the Sino-American Cooperative Organization (SACO), sabotaging Japanese lines of communications.

MANCHURIA (MANCHUKUO)
• Harbin

Chinese Communists under Mao Tse-Tung active in anti-Japanese resistance.

C H I N A

• Peking

KOREA

JAPAN

SOE active in helping local population during the Japanese occupation.

Agents from SOE's Force 136 and OSS's Force 101 supported the Kachin people in their resistance.

Agents from SOE's Force 136 supported the Karen people in their resistance. Karen guerrillas killed 12,500 Japanese soldiers in May and June 1945.

Yellow Sea

Meerut
◉
△
New Delhi

Chungking
▲

Communist-led Hukbalahap (the 'Huks': the People's Army Against The Japanese); and guerrilla groups led by United States officers, one of whom, Captain Walter Cushing, published a clandestine news sheet, *The Echo of the Free North*.

From the start of the war, Filipinos fought alongside United States troops. After the Japanese conquest, Filipinos were active in anti-Japanese activities. To deter resistance, the Japanese placed the severed heads of reprisal victims on stakes around Philippine villages. In May 1943, two United States lieutenant colonels, Martin Moses and Arthur K. Noble – the most senior American leaders of Filipino resistance – were captured by the Japanese and executed.

ASSAM

BRITISH INDIA
Calcutta
●

OSS helped Communist anti-Japanese guerrillas, headed by Vo Nguyen Giap.

BURMA

VIETNAM

1943: General Aung San (father of Aung San Suu Kyi) led anti-Japanese resistance – the Burma National Army – supported by SOE. On 12 March 1945 he assembled 10,000 soldiers outside Rangoon and attacked Japanese lines of communication throughout southern Burma.

9 January 1945: American landing supported by guerrilla fighting in the interior.

Lingayen •
LUZON

THAILAND
FRENCH INDO-CHINA
Bangkok

A Free Thai underground movement, led by the Regent (Pridi Phanamyong, codename 'Ruth'), supported by OSS, provided Intelligence information to the United States, and helped rescue shot-down Allied airmen and escaped prisoners of war.

OSS officers worked with Thai insurgents from January 1945.

OSS helped Communist anti-Japanese guerrillas, headed by Ho Chi Minh.

PHILIPPINES
CEBU

Kandy △ CEYLON

SABAH
Api ●

A United States officer, Lieutenant Colonel James Cushing, captured a Japanese admiral and sent his secret documents to Australia. In retaliation, the Japanese began a massacre of the civilian population. To halt the massacre, Cushing released the admiral.

British SOE agents trained the Malayan People's Anti-Japanese Army.

MALAYA
PERAK

SARAWAK

JOHORE
Singapore

Overseas Chinese, including Communists, released from Changi prison in Singapore, trained to resist the invaders, forming the Malayan People's Anti-Japanese Army. By 1945 they numbered more than 3,000 soldiers, supported by tens of thousands of local sympathisers. From 1948 to 1960, the Malayan People's Anti-Japanese Army fought against British rule.

Anti-Japanese activity supported by SOE, led to a national uprising on 10 October 1943, led by the local guerrillas: 200 Chinese and 100 natives. The rebellion was crushed by the Japanese forces, after the rebel leader, Albert Kwok, was captured (December 1943) and executed (January 1944). Several thousand locals were executed by the Japanese.

SOE sent Tom Harrisson (later one of the founders of Mass Observation) to work with local guerrillas.

JAVA

PORTUGUESE TIMOR

Communist guerrillas led by Sutan Sjahrir, launch an anti-Japanese insurgency.

SOE sent in several officers and arms to the local guerrillas.

△ Special Operations Executive (SOE) headquarters for the Far East

◉ SOE branch offices in India

▲ SOE staging post

△ Organization of Strategic Services (OSS) headquarters for planning activity behind Japanese lines in South-East Asia

AUSTRALIA

October 1942: General MacArthur's message to Filipino guerrillas: 'Strike wherever possible'.

0   kilometres   1000

0   miles   500

© Martin Gilbert 2008

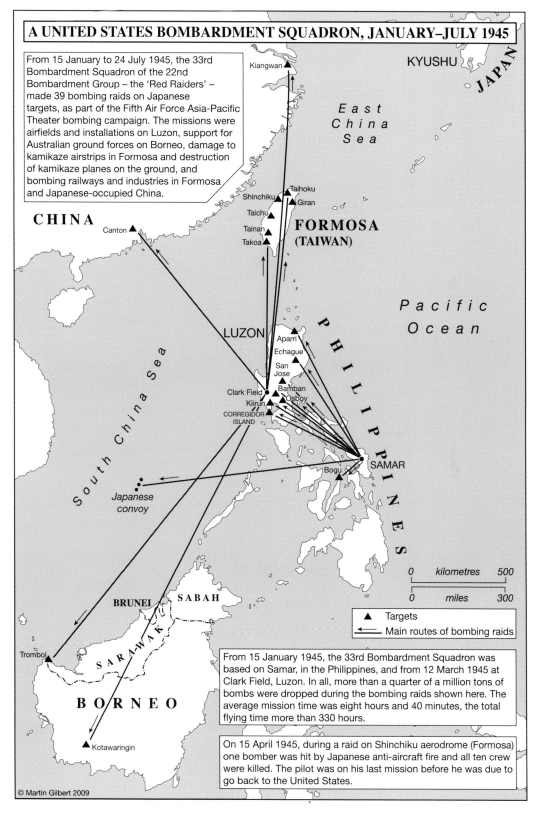

A UNITED STATES BOMBARDMENT SQUADRON, JANUARY–JULY 1945

From 15 January to 24 July 1945, the 33rd Bombardment Squadron of the 22nd Bombardment Group – the 'Red Raiders' – made 39 bombing raids on Japanese targets, as part of the Fifth Air Force Asia-Pacific Theater bombing campaign. The missions were airfields and installations on Luzon, support for Australian ground forces on Borneo, damage to kamikaze airstrips in Formosa and destruction of kamikaze planes on the ground, and bombing railways and industries in Formosa and Japanese-occupied China.

KYUSHU

JAPAN

Kiangwan

East China Sea

CHINA

Canton

Taihoku
Shinchiku
Giran
Taichu
Tainan
Takoa

FORMOSA (TAIWAN)

Pacific Ocean

LUZON

Aparri
Echague
San Jose
Bamban
Clark Field
Kiirun
Osboy
CORREGIDOR ISLAND

South China Sea

PHILIPPINES

Bogu
SAMAR

Japanese convoy

BRUNEI   SABAH

SARAWAK

Trombol

BORNEO

Kotawaringin

| 0 | kilometres | 500 |
| 0 | miles | 300 |

▲ Targets
← Main routes of bombing raids

From 15 January 1945, the 33rd Bombardment Squadron was based on Samar, in the Philippines, and from 12 March 1945 at Clark Field, Luzon. In all, more than a quarter of a million tons of bombs were dropped during the bombing raids shown here. The average mission time was eight hours and 40 minutes, the total flying time more than 330 hours.

On 15 April 1945, during a raid on Shinchiku aerodrome (Formosa) one bomber was hit by Japanese anti-aircraft fire and all ten crew were killed. The pilot was on his last mission before he was due to go back to the United States.

© Martin Gilbert 2009

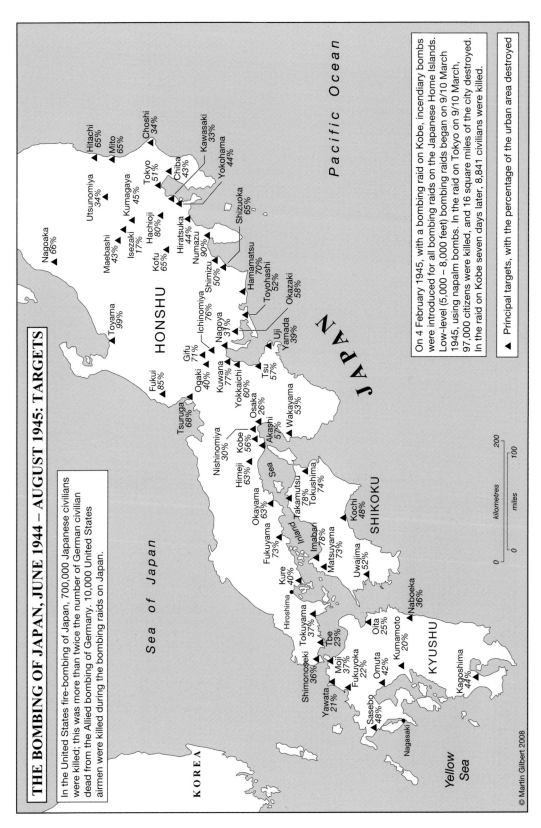

THE BOMBING OF JAPAN, JUNE 1944 – AUGUST 1945: TARGETS

In the United States fire-bombing of Japan, 700,000 Japanese civilians were killed; this was more than twice the number of German civilian dead from the Allied bombing of Germany. 10,000 United States airmen were killed during the bombing raids on Japan.

On 4 February 1945, with a bombing raid on Kobe, incendiary bombs were introduced for all bombing raids on the Japanese Home Islands. Low-level (5,000 – 8,000 feet) bombing raids began on 9/10 March 1945, using napalm bombs. In the raid on Tokyo on 9/10 March, 97,000 citizens were killed, and 16 square miles of the city destroyed. In the raid on Kobe seven days later, 8,841 civilians were killed.

▲ Principal targets, with the percentage of the urban area destroyed

Pacific Ocean

HONSHU

Sea of Japan

KOREA

Yellow Sea

JAPAN

SHIKOKU

KYUSHU

Inland Sea

Hitachi 65%
Mito 65%
Choshi 34%
Kawasaki 33%
Yokohama 44%
Chiba 43%
Tokyo 51%
Utsunomiya 34%
Kumagaya 45%
Hachioji 80%
Hiratsuka 44%
Numazu 90%
Shizuoka 65%
Isezaki 17%
Kofu 65%
Shimizu 50%
Hamamatsu 70%
Toyohashi 52%
Okazaki 58%
Maebashi 43%
Nagaoka 66%
Toyama 99%
Fukui 85%
Gifu 71%
Ogaki 40%
Ichinomiya 76%
Nagoya 31%
Uji Yamada 39%
Tsu 57%
Tsuruga 68%
Kuwana 77%
Yokkaichi 60%
Osaka 26%
Wakayama 53%
Nishinomiya 30%
Kobe 56%
Akashi 57%
Himeji 63%
Okayama 63%
Takamutsu 78%
Tokushima 74%
Fukuyama 73%
Imabari 78%
Matsuyama 73%
Kochi 48%
Uwajima 52%
Hiroshima
Kure 40%
Tokuyama 37%
Ube 23%
Shimonoseki 36%
Moji 37%
Fukuyoka 22%
Omuta 42%
Kumamoto 20%
Oita 25%
Naboeka 36%
Yawata 21%
Sasebo 48%
Kagoshima 44%
Nagasaki

kilometres   200
miles   100
0

© Martin Gilbert 2008

195

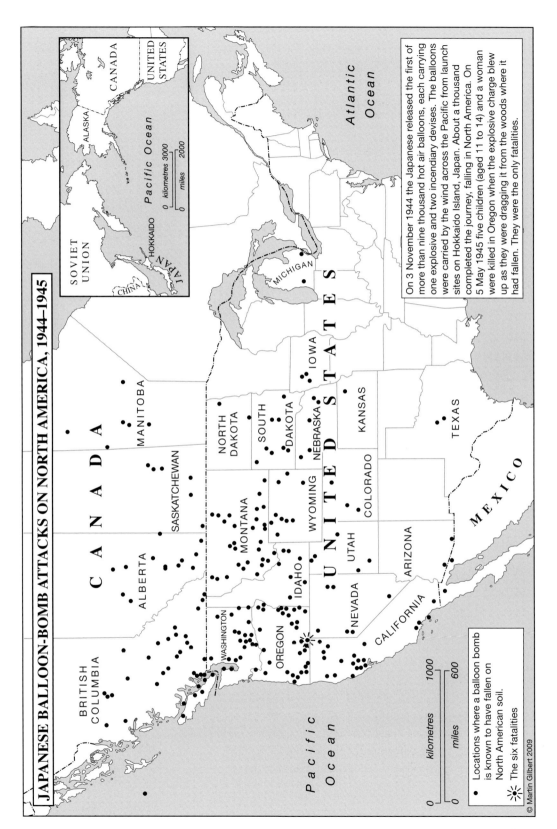

JAPANESE BALLOON-BOMB ATTACKS ON NORTH AMERICA, 1944–1945

SOVIET UNION

CHINA

JAPAN

HOKKAIDO

Pacific Ocean

0 kilometres 3000
0 miles 2000

ALASKA

CANADA

UNITED STATES

Atlantic Ocean

On 3 November 1944 the Japanese released the first of more than nine thousand hot air balloons, each carrying one explosive and two incendiary devises. The balloons were carried by the wind across the Pacific from launch sites on Hokkaido Island, Japan. About a thousand completed the journey, falling in North America. On 5 May 1945 five children (aged 11 to 14) and a woman were killed in Oregon when the explosive charge blew up as they were dragging it from the woods where it had fallen. They were the only fatalities.

C A N A D A

BRITISH COLUMBIA

ALBERTA

SASKATCHEWAN

MANITOBA

MICHIGAN

U N I T E D   S T A T E S

WASHINGTON

OREGON

IDAHO

MONTANA

WYOMING

NORTH DAKOTA

SOUTH DAKOTA

NEBRASKA

IOWA

NEVADA

UTAH

COLORADO

KANSAS

CALIFORNIA

ARIZONA

TEXAS

M E X I C O

Pacific Ocean

0 kilometres 1000
0 miles 600

• Locations where a balloon bomb is known to have fallen on North American soil.

☀ The six fatalities

© Martin Gilbert 2009

196

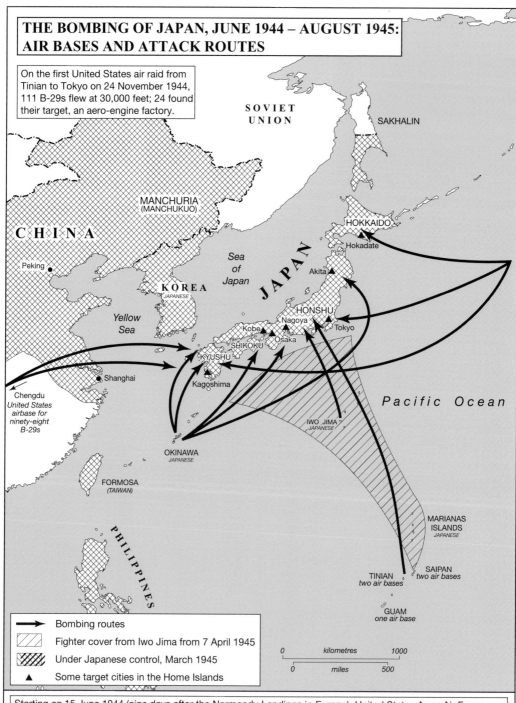

THE BOMBING OF JAPAN, JUNE 1944 – AUGUST 1945: AIR BASES AND ATTACK ROUTES

On the first United States air raid from Tinian to Tokyo on 24 November 1944, 111 B-29s flew at 30,000 feet; 24 found their target, an aero-engine factory.

SOVIET UNION

SAKHALIN

MANCHURIA (MANCHUKUO)

C·H·I·N·A

HOKKAIDO

Hokadate

Peking

Sea of Japan

Akita

KOREA
JAPANESE

JAPAN

HONSHU

Yellow Sea

Nagoya

Kobe

Tokyo

SHIKOKU

Osaka

KYUSHU

Shanghai

Kagoshima

Chengdu
United States airbase for ninety-eight B-29s

Pacific Ocean

IWO JIMA
JAPANESE

OKINAWA
JAPANESE

FORMOSA
(TAIWAN)

MARIANAS ISLANDS
JAPANESE

P H I L I P P I N E S

TINIAN
two air bases

SAIPAN
two air bases

GUAM
one air base

→ Bombing routes

▨ Fighter cover from Iwo Jima from 7 April 1945

▨ Under Japanese control, March 1945

▲ Some target cities in the Home Islands

| 0 | kilometres | 1000 |
| 0 | miles | 500 |

Starting on 15 June 1944 (nine days after the Normandy Landings in Europe), United States Army Air Force bombers were able to attack the Japanese Home Islands from their air base at Chengdu, in China, a distance of 1,500 miles to Kyushu, using the new B-29 Superfortress long-range bomber with a heavy bomb load. Attacks from Tinian, 1,500 miles from Tokyo, began on 24 November 1944. Each of the five Pacific Ocean bases – on Tinian, Saipan and Guam – could accommodate 180 B-29s. Following the capture of Iwo Jima, from 7 April 1945 bombing raids on Japan could be launched, for the first time with fighter support, from a distance of 900 miles. From 1 July 1945, the capture of Okinawa brought the bombers to within 300 miles of Kyushu.

© Martin Gilbert 2008

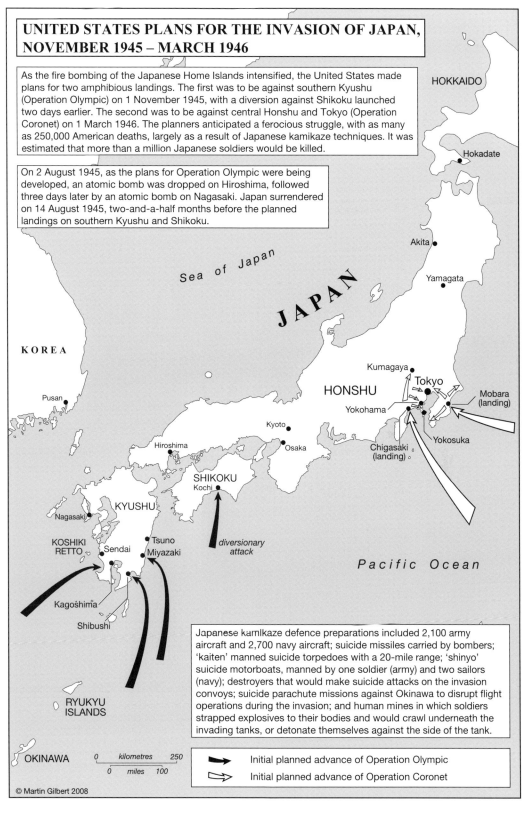

UNITED STATES PLANS FOR THE INVASION OF JAPAN, NOVEMBER 1945 – MARCH 1946

As the fire bombing of the Japanese Home Islands intensified, the United States made plans for two amphibious landings. The first was to be against southern Kyushu (Operation Olympic) on 1 November 1945, with a diversion against Shikoku launched two days earlier. The second was to be against central Honshu and Tokyo (Operation Coronet) on 1 March 1946. The planners anticipated a ferocious struggle, with as many as 250,000 American deaths, largely as a result of Japanese kamikaze techniques. It was estimated that more than a million Japanese soldiers would be killed.

On 2 August 1945, as the plans for Operation Olympic were being developed, an atomic bomb was dropped on Hiroshima, followed three days later by an atomic bomb on Nagasaki. Japan surrendered on 14 August 1945, two-and-a-half months before the planned landings on southern Kyushu and Shikoku.

HOKKAIDO

Hokadate

Akita

Yamagata

Sea of Japan

JAPAN

KOREA

Pusan

Kumagaya

Tokyo

HONSHU

Yokohama

Mobara (landing)

Kyoto

Osaka

Yokosuka

Chigasaki (landing)

Hiroshima

SHIKOKU
Kochi

KYUSHU

Nagasaki

KOSHIKI RETTO
Sendai

Tsuno
Miyazaki

diversionary attack

Pacific Ocean

Kagoshima

Shibushi

Japanese kamikaze defence preparations included 2,100 army aircraft and 2,700 navy aircraft; suicide missiles carried by bombers; 'kaiten' manned suicide torpedoes with a 20-mile range; 'shinyo' suicide motorboats, manned by one soldier (army) and two sailors (navy); destroyers that would make suicide attacks on the invasion convoys; suicide parachute missions against Okinawa to disrupt flight operations during the invasion; and human mines in which soldiers strapped explosives to their bodies and would crawl underneath the invading tanks, or detonate themselves against the side of the tank.

RYUKYU ISLANDS

OKINAWA

| 0 | kilometres | 250 |
| 0 | miles | 100 |

➤ Initial planned advance of Operation Olympic
▷ Initial planned advance of Operation Coronet

© Martin Gilbert 2008

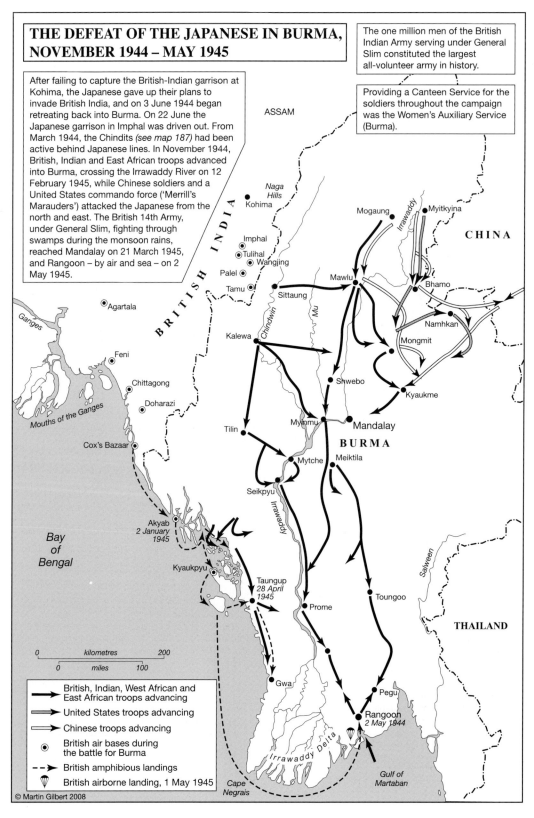

THE DEFEAT OF THE JAPANESE IN BURMA, NOVEMBER 1944 – MAY 1945

The one million men of the British Indian Army serving under General Slim constituted the largest all-volunteer army in history.

After failing to capture the British-Indian garrison at Kohima, the Japanese gave up their plans to invade British India, and on 3 June 1944 began retreating back into Burma. On 22 June the Japanese garrison in Imphal was driven out. From March 1944, the Chindits *(see map 187)* had been active behind Japanese lines. In November 1944, British, Indian and East African troops advanced into Burma, crossing the Irrawaddy River on 12 February 1945, while Chinese soldiers and a United States commando force ('Merrill's Marauders') attacked the Japanese from the north and east. The British 14th Army, under General Slim, fighting through swamps during the monsoon rains, reached Mandalay on 21 March 1945, and Rangoon – by air and sea – on 2 May 1945.

Providing a Canteen Service for the soldiers throughout the campaign was the Women's Auxiliary Service (Burma).

ASSAM

Naga Hills

Kohima

BRITISH INDIA

Imphal
Tulihal
Wangjing
Palel
Tamu

Mogaung
Myitkyina

Irrawaddy

CHINA

Mawlu
Bhamo
Namhkan
Mongmit

Sittaung

Mu

Chindwin

Agartala

Ganges

Feni

Chittagong

Doharazi

Kalewa

Shwebo

Kyaukme

Mouths of the Ganges

Cox's Bazaar

Tilin

Myinmu
Mandalay

BURMA

Meiktila

Mytche

Seikpyu

Irrawaddy

Bay
of
Bengal

Akyab
2 January
1945

Kyaukpyu

Taungup
28 April
1945

Prome

Toungoo

THAILAND

Salween

Gwa

Pegu

Rangoon
2 May 1944

Irrawaddy Delta

Cape
Negrais

Gulf of
Martaban

scale	
0 kilometres 200	
0 miles 100	

British, Indian, West African and East African troops advancing

United States troops advancing

Chinese troops advancing

British air bases during the battle for Burma

British amphibious landings

British airborne landing, 1 May 1945

© Martin Gilbert 2008

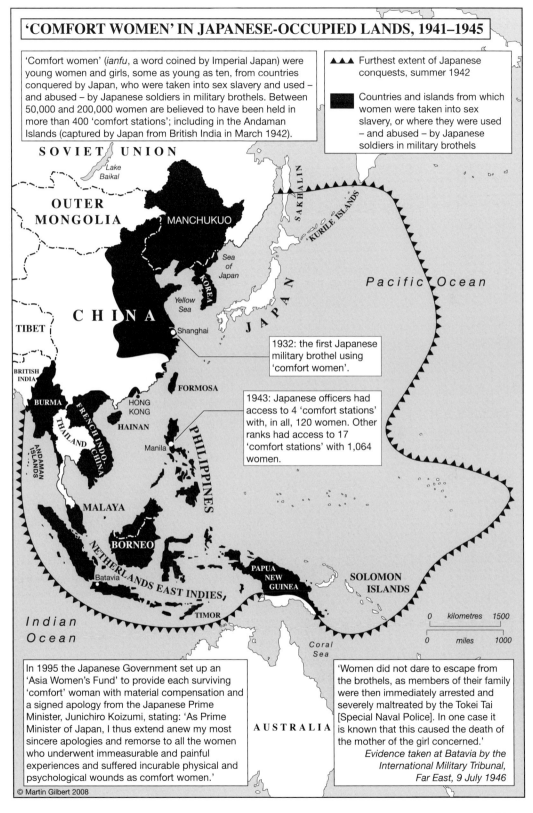

'COMFORT WOMEN' IN JAPANESE-OCCUPIED LANDS, 1941–1945

'Comfort women' (*ianfu*, a word coined by Imperial Japan) were young women and girls, some as young as ten, from countries conquered by Japan, who were taken into sex slavery and used – and abused – by Japanese soldiers in military brothels. Between 50,000 and 200,000 women are believed to have been held in more than 400 'comfort stations'; including in the Andaman Islands (captured by Japan from British India in March 1942).

▲▲▲ Furthest extent of Japanese conquests, summer 1942

■ Countries and islands from which women were taken into sex slavery, or where they were used – and abused – by Japanese soldiers in military brothels

SOVIET UNION

Lake Baikal

OUTER MONGOLIA

MANCHUKUO

SAKHALIN

KURILE ISLANDS

Sea of Japan

KOREA

Pacific Ocean

CHINA

Yellow Sea

TIBET

JAPAN

Shanghai

1932: the first Japanese military brothel using 'comfort women'.

BRITISH INDIA

FORMOSA

1943: Japanese officers had access to 4 'comfort stations' with, in all, 120 women. Other ranks had access to 17 'comfort stations' with 1,064 women.

BURMA

HONG KONG

HAINAN

FRENCH INDO-CHINA

THAILAND

ANDAMAN ISLANDS

Manila

PHILIPPINES

MALAYA

BORNEO

NETHERLANDS EAST INDIES

Batavia

PAPUA NEW GUINEA

SOLOMON ISLANDS

TIMOR

Indian Ocean

0 kilometres 1500

0 miles 1000

Coral Sea

In 1995 the Japanese Government set up an 'Asia Women's Fund' to provide each surviving 'comfort' woman with material compensation and a signed apology from the Japanese Prime Minister, Junichiro Koizumi, stating: 'As Prime Minister of Japan, I thus extend anew my most sincere apologies and remorse to all the women who underwent immeasurable and painful experiences and suffered incurable physical and psychological wounds as comfort women.'

AUSTRALIA

'Women did not dare to escape from the brothels, as members of their family were then immediately arrested and severely maltreated by the Tokei Tai [Special Naval Police]. In one case it is known that this caused the death of the mother of the girl concerned.'
Evidence taken at Batavia by the International Military Tribunal, Far East, 9 July 1946

© Martin Gilbert 2008

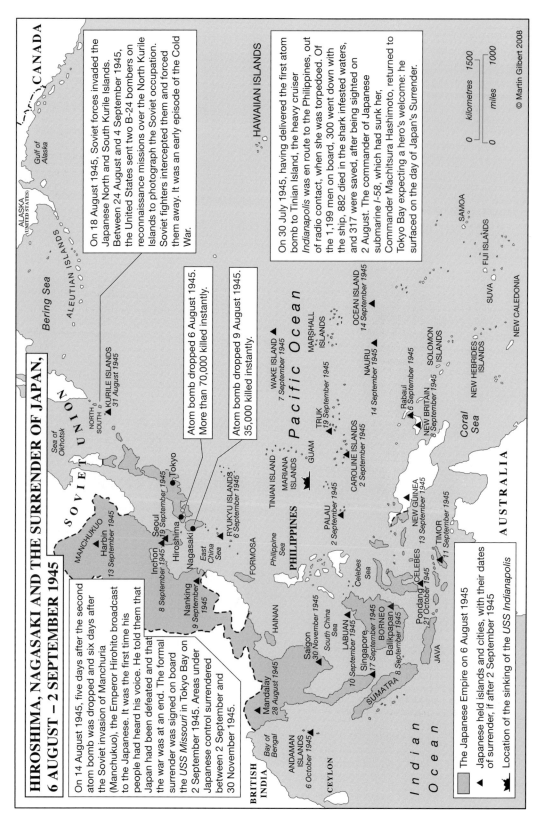

HIROSHIMA, NAGASAKI AND THE SURRENDER OF JAPAN, 6 AUGUST – 2 SEPTEMBER 1945

On 14 August 1945, five days after the second atom bomb was dropped and six days after the Soviet invasion of Manchuria (Manchukuo), the Emperor Hirohito broadcast to the Japanese. It was the first time his people had heard his voice. He told them that Japan had been defeated and that the war was at an end. The formal surrender was signed on board the *USS Missouri* in Tokyo Bay on 2 September 1945. Areas under Japanese control surrendered between 2 September and 30 November 1945.

On 18 August 1945, Soviet forces invaded the Japanese North and South Kurile Islands. Between 24 August and 4 September 1945, the United States sent two B-24 bombers on reconnaissance missions over the North Kurile Islands to photograph the Soviet occupation. Soviet fighters intercepted them and forced them away. It was an early episode of the Cold War.

On 30 July 1945, having delivered the first atom bomb to Tinian Island, the heavy cruiser *Indianapolis* was en route to the Philippines, out of radio contact, when she was torpedoed. Of the 1,199 men on board, 300 went down with the ship, 882 died in the shark infested waters, and 317 were saved, after being sighted on 2 August. The commander of Japanese submarine *I-58*, which had sunk her, Commander Machitsura Hashimoto, returned to Tokyo Bay expecting a hero's welcome: he surfaced on the day of Japan's Surrender.

Atom bomb dropped 6 August 1945. More than 70,000 killed instantly.

Atom bomb dropped 9 August 1945. 35,000 killed instantly.

The Japanese Empire on 6 August 1945

▲ Japanese held islands and cities, with their dates of surrender, if after 2 September 1945

⚓ Location of the sinking of the *USS Indianapolis*

© Martin Gilbert 2008

CANADA
ALASKA (UNITED STATES)
Gulf of Alaska
Bering Sea
ALEUTIAN ISLANDS
Sea of Okhotsk
SOVIET UNION
KURILE ISLANDS 31 August 1945
NORTH SOUTH
Seoul 19 September 1945
Inchon 8 September 1945
Tokyo
Hiroshima
Nagasaki 9 September 1945
MANCHUKUO
Harbin 13 September 1945
Nanking 1945
East China Sea
FORMOSA
RYUKYU ISLANDS 6 September 1945
HAWAIIAN ISLANDS
Pacific Ocean
WAKE ISLAND 7 September 1945
MARSHALL ISLANDS
OCEAN ISLAND 14 September 1945
TRUK 19 September 1945
TINIAN ISLAND
MARIANA ISLANDS
GUAM
CAROLINE ISLANDS 2 September 1945
NAURU 14 September 1945
Rabaul 6 September 1945
NEW BRITAIN 8 September 1945
SOLOMON ISLANDS
SAMOA
FIJI ISLANDS
SUVA
NEW HEBRIDES ISLANDS
NEW CALEDONIA
Philippine Sea
PHILIPPINES
PALAU 2 September 1945
NEW GUINEA 13 September 1945
TIMOR 11 September 1945
Coral Sea
AUSTRALIA
HAINAN
Saigon 30 November 1945
South China Sea
Celebes Sea
CELEBES
Pondang 21 October 1945
LABUAN 10 September 1945
Singapore 17 September 1945
BORNEO
Balikpapan 8 September 1945
SUMATRA
JAVA
Mandalay 28 August 1945
Bay of Bengal
ANDAMAN ISLANDS 6 October 1945
BRITISH INDIA
CEYLON
Indian Ocean

0 kilometres 1500
0 miles 1000

THE SOVIET INVASION OF MANCHURIA, 8 AUGUST – 13 SEPTEMBER 1945

At the Yalta Conference in February 1945, Stalin promised Roosevelt and Churchill that the Soviet Union would enter the war against Japan within three months of the defeat of Germany. Germany surrendered on 7 May 1945. On 8 August 1945 (three months and a day after the German surrender) the Soviet Union declared war on Japan, and attacked Manchuria (Manchukuo); this was two days after the first atom bomb had been dropped on Hiroshima. Had the Japanese not surrendered on 2 September 1945, the Soviet Union had intended to invade Hokkaido, from Sakhalin, well before the United States plan to invade Kyushu.

BALANCE OF FORCES IN MANCHURIA		
	Soviet	Japanese
Troops:	1,577,225	1,040,000
Artillery:	26,137	6,700
Aircraft:	5,368	1,800
Tanks:	3,704	1,000

KILLED IN ACTION
21,000 Japanese soldiers
8,219 Soviet soldiers

The Soviet border
Soviet troop advances, 8 August – 1 September 1945
Soviet amphibious landings
The front line on 1 September 1945

Between May and August 1945, Stalin transferred one million Soviet troops to the Manchurian border. The Soviet troops were better equipped and more experienced; the best Japanese military units had long since been transferred to the Pacific islands.

Soviet amphibious landings in northern Korea were intended to help the Soviet troops when they approached the Korean border from the north. The Soviet units in northern Korea were forestalled in moving south by a United States landing at Inchon on 8 September 1945.

Before leaving Manchuria in 1946, Soviet forces dismantled the considerable industry there and transferred it to the Soviet Union.

© Martin Gilbert 2008

Section 11

GLOBAL WAR

In former days, when wars arose from individual causes, from the policy of a Minister or the passion of a King, when they were fought by small regular armies of professional soldiers, and when their course was retarded by the difficulties of communication and supply, and often suspended by the winter season, it was possible to limit the liabilities of the combatants.

But now, when mighty populations are impelled on each other, each individual severally embittered and inflamed – when the resources of science and civilisation sweep away everything that might mitigate their fury, a European war can only end in the ruin of the vanquished and the scarcely less fatal commercial dislocation and exhaustion of the conquerors.

Democracy is more vindictive than Cabinets. The wars of peoples will be more terrible than those of kings.

WINSTON CHURCHILL
House of Commons
13 May 1901

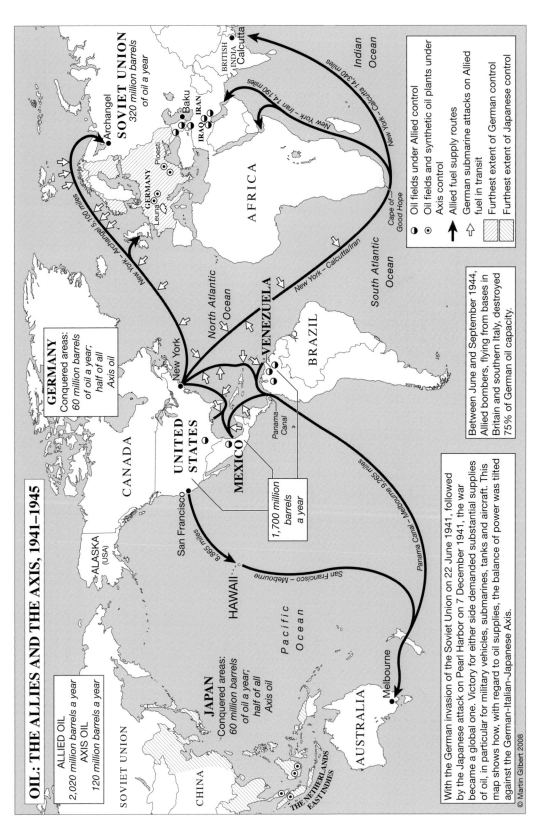

OIL: THE ALLIES AND THE AXIS, 1941–1945

ALLIED OIL
2,020 million barrels a year
AXIS OIL
120 million barrels a year

GERMANY
Conquered areas:
60 million barrels
of oil a year;
half of all
Axis oil

JAPAN
Conquered areas:
60 million barrels
of oil a year;
half of all
Axis oil

SOVIET UNION
320 million barrels
of oil a year

1,700 million
barrels
a year

Archangel

Baku
IRAN
IRAQ

Ploesti

GERMANY
Leuna

AFRICA

BRITISH
INDIA
Calcutta

Indian
Ocean

Cape of
Good Hope

New York – Calcutta 14,340 miles

New York – Iran 14,190 miles

New York – Archangel 5,100 miles

New York – Calcutta/Iran

North Atlantic
Ocean

South Atlantic
Ocean

CANADA

ALASKA
(USA)

UNITED
STATES

New York

San Francisco

MEXICO

VENEZUELA

BRAZIL

Panama
Canal

Panama Canal – Melbourne 9,265 miles

San Francisco – Melbourne

San Francisco – Melbourne 8,865 miles

HAWAII

Pacific
Ocean

SOVIET UNION

CHINA

THE NETHERLANDS
EAST INDIES

AUSTRALIA

Melbourne

Legend:
◑ Oil fields under Allied control
◉ Oil fields and synthetic oil plants under Axis control
→ Allied fuel supply routes
⇨ German submarine attacks on Allied fuel in transit
▨ Furthest extent of German control
▨ Furthest extent of Japanese control

Between June and September 1944, Allied bombers, flying from bases in Britain and southern Italy, destroyed 75% of German oil capacity.

With the German invasion of the Soviet Union on 22 June 1941, followed by the Japanese attack on Pearl Harbor on 7 December 1941, the war became a global one. Victory for either side demanded substantial supplies of oil, in particular for military vehicles, submarines, tanks and aircraft. This map shows how, with regard to oil supplies, the balance of power was tilted against the German-Italian-Japanese Axis.

© Martin Gilbert 2008

203

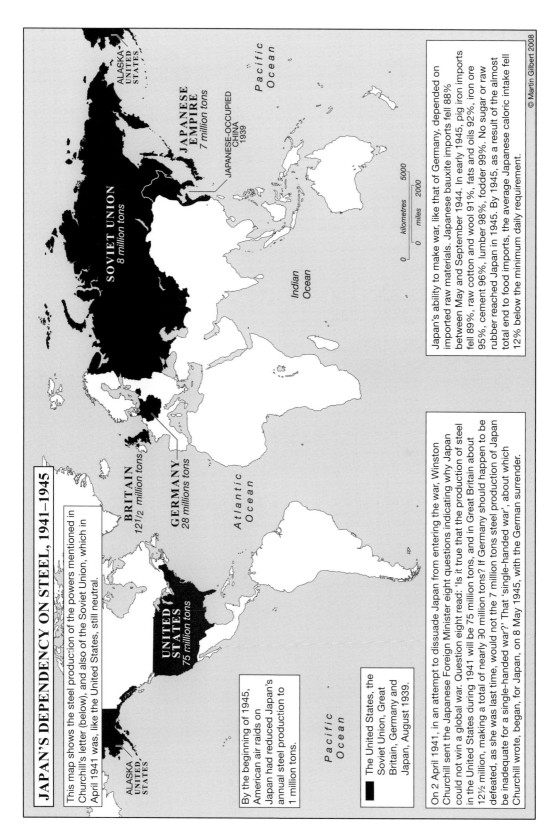

JAPAN'S DEPENDENCY ON STEEL, 1941–1945

This map shows the steel production of the powers mentioned in Churchill's letter (below), and also of the Soviet Union, which in April 1941 was, like the United States, still neutral.

ALASKA
UNITED
STATES

**JAPANESE
EMPIRE**
7 million tons

JAPANESE-OCCUPIED
CHINA
1939

*Pacific
Ocean*

SOVIET UNION
8 million tons

BRITAIN
12½ million tons

GERMANY
28 millions tons

*Indian
Ocean*

*Atlantic
Ocean*

**UNITED
STATES**
75 million tons

ALASKA
UNITED
STATES

*Pacific
Ocean*

By the beginning of 1945, American air raids on Japan had reduced Japan's annual steel production to 1 million tons.

■ The United States, the Soviet Union, Great Britain, Germany and Japan, August 1939.

Japan's ability to make war, like that of Germany, depended on imported raw materials. Japanese bauxite imports fell 88% between May and September 1944. In early 1945, pig iron imports fell 89%, raw cotton and wool 91%, fats and oils 92%, iron ore 95%, cement 96%, lumber 98%, fodder 99%. No sugar or raw rubber reached Japan in 1945. By 1945, as a result of the almost total end to food imports, the average Japanese caloric intake fell 12% below the minimum daily requirement.

On 2 April 1941, in an attempt to dissuade Japan from entering the war, Winston Churchill sent the Japanese Foreign Minister eight questions indicating why Japan could not win a global war. Question eight read: 'Is it true that the production of steel in the United States during 1941 will be 75 million tons, and in Great Britain about 12½ million, making a total of nearly 90 million tons? If Germany should happen to be defeated, as she was last time, would not the 7 million tons steel production of Japan be inadequate for a single-handed war', about which Churchill wrote, began, for Japan, on 8 May 1945, with the German surrender.

0   2000   5000
kilometres
0   miles

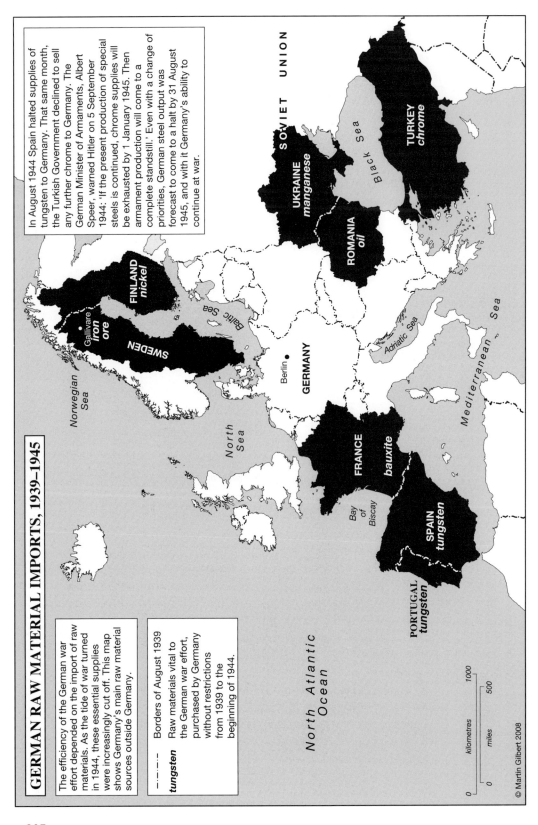

GERMAN RAW MATERIAL IMPORTS, 1939–1945

The efficiency of the German war effort depended on the import of raw materials. As the tide of war turned in 1944, these essential supplies were increasingly cut off. This map shows Germany's main raw material sources outside Germany.

—·—·— Borders of August 1939

tungsten Raw materials vital to the German war effort, purchased by Germany without restrictions from 1939 to the beginning of 1944.

In August 1944 Spain halted supplies of tungsten to Germany. That same month, the Turkish Government declined to sell any further chrome to Germany. The German Minister of Armaments, Albert Speer, warned Hitler on 5 September 1944: 'If the present production of special steels is continued, chrome supplies will be exhausted by 1 January 1945. Then armament production will come to a complete standstill'. Even with a change of priorities, German steel output was forecast to come to a halt by 31 August 1945, and with it Germany's ability to continue at war.

SOVIET UNION

UKRAINE *manganese*

ROMANIA *oil*

TURKEY *chrome*

Black Sea

FINLAND *nickel*

SWEDEN

Gällivare *iron ore*

Baltic Sea

Norwegian Sea

North Sea

GERMANY

Berlin ●

Adriatic Sea

Mediterranean Sea

FRANCE *bauxite*

Bay of Biscay

SPAIN *tungsten*

PORTUGAL *tungsten*

North Atlantic Ocean

0   500   1000 kilometres

0   500   miles

© Martin Gilbert 2008

205

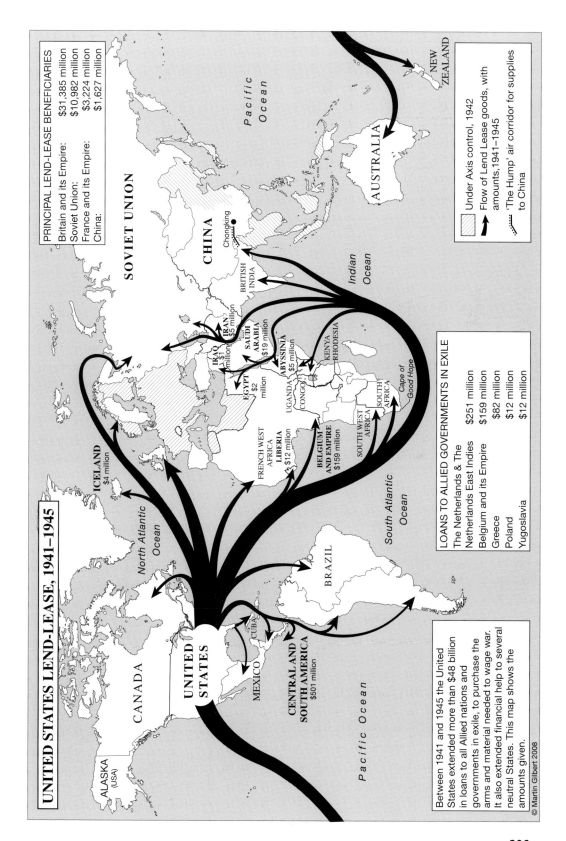

UNITED STATES LEND-LEASE, 1941–1945

PRINCIPAL LEND-LEASE BENEFICIARIES

Britain and its Empire:	$31,385 million
Soviet Union:	$10,982 million
France and its Empire:	$3,224 million
China:	$1,627 million

LOANS TO ALLIED GOVERNMENTS IN EXILE

The Netherlands & The Netherlands East Indies	$251 million
Belgium and its Empire	$159 million
Greece	$82 million
Poland	$12 million
Yugoslavia	$12 million

Between 1941 and 1945 the United States extended more than $48 billion in loans to all Allied nations and governments in exile, to purchase the arms and material needed to wage war. It also extended financial help to several neutral States. This map shows the amounts given.

ALASKA (USA)

CANADA

UNITED STATES

North Atlantic Ocean

Pacific Ocean

MEXICO

CUBA

CENTRAL AND SOUTH AMERICA
$501 million

BRAZIL

South Atlantic Ocean

ICELAND
$4 million

SOVIET UNION

FRENCH WEST AFRICA

LIBERIA
$12 million

BELGIUM AND EMPIRE
$159 million

EGYPT
$2 million

IRAQ
$1 million

IRAN
$5 million

SAUDI ARABIA
$19 million

ABYSSINIA
$5 million

UGANDA

CONGO

KENYA

RHODESIA

SOUTH WEST AFRICA

SOUTH AFRICA

Cape of Good Hope

CHINA

Chongking

BRITISH INDIA

Indian Ocean

Pacific Ocean

AUSTRALIA

NEW ZEALAND

Under Axis control, 1942

Flow of Lend Lease goods, with amounts, 1941–1945

'The Hump' air corridor for supplies to China

© Martin Gilbert 2008

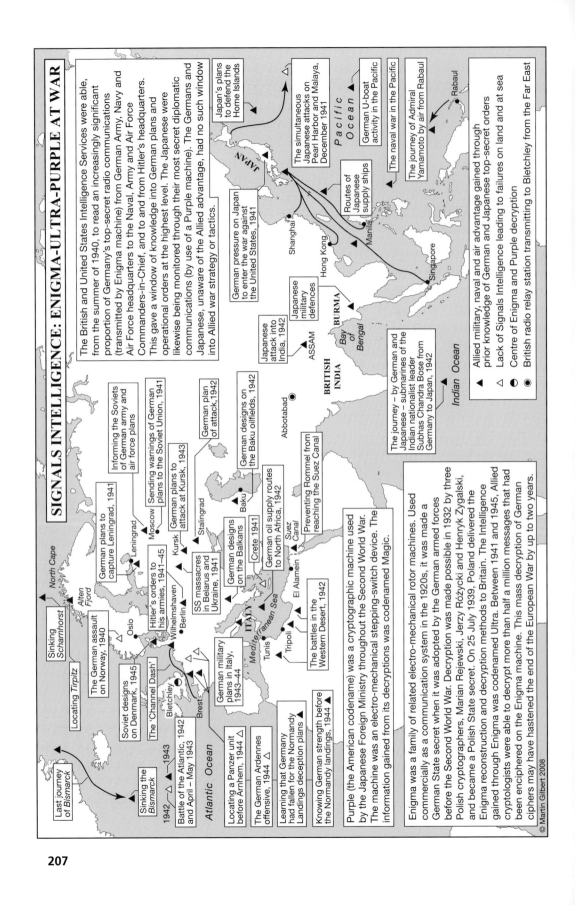

SIGNALS INTELLIGENCE: ENIGMA-ULTRA-PURPLE AT WAR

The British and United States Intelligence Services were able, from the summer of 1940, to read an increasingly significant proportion of Germany's top-secret radio communications (transmitted by Enigma machine) from German Army, Navy and Air Force headquarters to the Naval, Army and Air Force Commanders-in-Chief, and to and from Hitler's headquarters. This gave a window of knowledge into German plans and operational orders at the highest level. The Japanese were likewise being monitored through their most secret diplomatic communications (by use of a Purple machine). The Germans and Japanese, unaware of the Allied advantage, had no such window into Allied war strategy or tactics.

Japan's plans to defend the Home Islands

The simultaneous Japanese attacks on Pearl Harbor and Malaya, December 1941

German U-boat activity in the Pacific

The naval war in the Pacific

The journey of Admiral Yamamoto by air from Rabaul

Pacific Ocean

Rabaul

German pressure on Japan to enter the war against the United States, 1941

JAPAN

Routes of Japanese supply ships

Shanghai

Hong Kong

Manila

Singapore

Japanese attack into India, 1942

Japanese military defences

BURMA

ASSAM

Bay of Bengal

BRITISH INDIA

Indian Ocean

The journey – by German and Japanese – submarines of the Indian nationalist leader Subhas Chandra Bose from Germany to Japan, 1942

Abbotabad

Informing the Soviets of German army and air force plans

German plans to capture Leningrad, 1941

Leningrad

Moscow

Sending warnings of German plans to the Soviet Union, 1941

German plans to attack at Kursk, 1943

Kursk

Stalingrad

Baku

German designs on the Baku oilfields, 1942

German plan of attack,1942

German designs on the Balkans

Crete 1941

German oil supply routes to North Africa, 1942

Suez Canal

Preventing Rommel from reaching the Suez Canal

El Alamein

The battles in the Western Desert, 1942

Tripoli

Tunis

ITALY

Mediterranean Sea

SS massacres in Belarus and Ukraine, 1941

Hitler's orders to his armies, 1941–45

Wilhelmshaven

Berlin

Brest

Oslo

Bletchley

Soviet designs on Denmark, 1945

The 'Channel Dash'

Alten Fjord

North Cape

Locating *Tirpitz*

Sinking *Scharnhorst*

The German assault on Norway, 1940

Last journey of *Bismarck*

Sinking the *Bismarck*

1942 △ —— 1943

Battle of the Atlantic, 1942 and April – May 1943

Atlantic Ocean

Locating a Panzer unit before Arnhem, 1944

The German Ardennes offensive, 1944

Learning that Germany had fallen for the Normandy Landings deception plans

Knowing German strength before the Normandy landings, 1944

German military plans in Italy, 1943–44

Purple (the American codename) was a cryptographic machine used commercially as a communication system in the 1920s. Used by the Japanese Foreign Ministry throughout the Second World War. The machine was an electro-mechanical stepping-switch device. The information gained from its decryptions was codenamed Magic.

Enigma was a family of related electro-mechanical rotor machines. Used commercially as a communication system in the 1920s, it was made a German State secret when it was adopted by the German armed forces before the Second World War. Decryption was made possible in 1932 by three Polish cryptographers, Marian Rejewski, Jerzy Różycki and Henryk Zygalski, and became a Polish State secret. On 25 July 1939, Poland delivered the Enigma reconstruction and decryption methods to Britain. The Intelligence gained through Enigma was codenamed Ultra. Between 1941 and 1945, Allied cryptologists were able to decrypt more than half a million messages that had been enciphered on the Enigma machine. This mass decryption of German ciphers may have hastened the end of the European War by up to two years.

▲ Allied military, naval and air advantage gained through prior knowledge of German and Japanese top-secret orders

△ Lack of Signals Intelligence leading to failures on land and at sea

◑ Centre of Enigma and Purple decryption

● British radio relay station transmitting to Bletchley from the Far East

© Martin Gilbert 2008

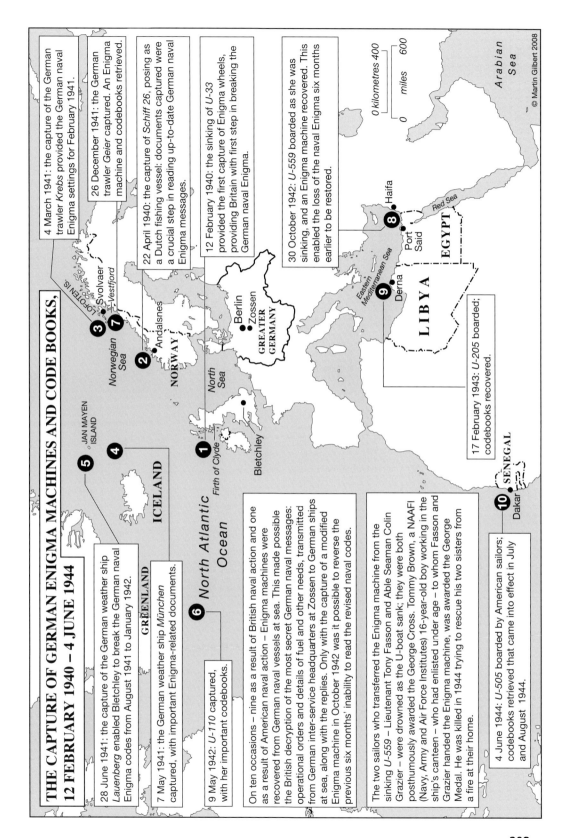

THE CAPTURE OF GERMAN ENIGMA MACHINES AND CODE BOOKS, 12 FEBRUARY 1940 – 4 JUNE 1944

4 March 1941: the capture of the German trawler *Krebs* provided the German naval Enigma settings for February 1941.

26 December 1941: the German trawler *Geier* captured. An Enigma machine and codebooks retrieved.

22 April 1940: the capture of *Schiff 26*, posing as a Dutch fishing vessel: documents captured were a crucial step in reading up-to-date German naval Enigma messages.

12 February 1940: the sinking of *U-33* provided the first capture of Enigma wheels, providing Britain with first step in breaking the German naval Enigma.

30 October 1942: *U-559* boarded as she was sinking, and an Enigma machine recovered. This enabled the loss of the naval Enigma six months earlier to be restored.

28 June 1941: the capture of the German weather ship *Lauenberg* enabled Bletchley to break the German naval Enigma codes from August 1941 to January 1942.

7 May 1941: the German weather ship *München* captured, with important Enigma-related documents.

9 May 1942: *U-110* captured, with her important codebooks.

On ten occasions – nine as a result of British naval action and one as a result of American naval action – Enigma machines were recovered from German naval vessels at sea. This made possible the British decryption of the most secret German naval messages: operational orders and details of fuel and other needs, transmitted from German inter-service headquarters at Zossen to German ships at sea, along with the replies. Only with the capture of a modified Enigma machine in October 1942 was it possible to reverse the previous six months' inability to read the revised naval codes.

The two sailors who transferred the Enigma machine from the sinking *U-559* – Lieutenant Tony Fasson and Able Seaman Colin Grazier – were drowned as the U-boat sank; they were both posthumously awarded the George Cross. Tommy Brown, a NAAFI (Navy, Army and Air Force Institutes) 16-year-old boy working in the ship's canteen – who had enlisted under age – to whom Fasson and Grazier handed the Enigma machine, was awarded the George Medal. He was killed in 1944 trying to rescue his two sisters from a fire at their home.

17 February 1943: *U-205* boarded; codebooks recovered.

4 June 1944: *U-505* boarded by American sailors; codebooks retrieved that came into effect in July and August 1944.

© Martin Gilbert 2008

0 kilometres 400

0 miles 600

GREENLAND

ICELAND

JAN MAYEN ISLAND

North Atlantic Ocean

Firth of Clyde

Bletchley

Norwegian Sea

LOFOTEN IS.
Svolvaer
Vestfjord

Andalsnes
NORWAY

North Sea

Berlin
Zossen
GREATER GERMANY

Eastern Mediterranean Sea

Haifa
Port Said
Red Sea
EGYPT

Derna
LIBYA

Arabian Sea

SENEGAL
Dakar

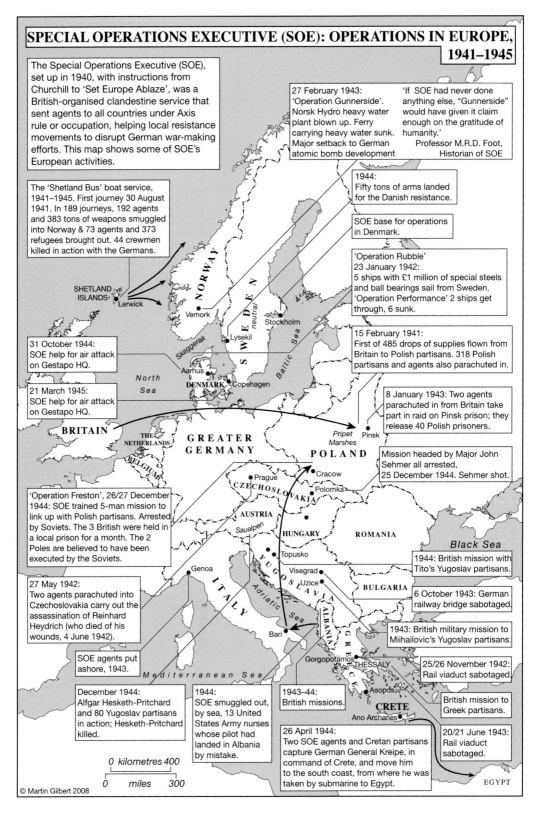

SPECIAL OPERATIONS EXECUTIVE (SOE): OPERATIONS IN EUROPE, 1941–1945

The Special Operations Executive (SOE), set up in 1940, with instructions from Churchill to 'Set Europe Ablaze', was a British-organised clandestine service that sent agents to all countries under Axis rule or occupation, helping local resistance movements to disrupt German war-making efforts. This map shows some of SOE's European activities.

27 February 1943: 'Operation Gunnerside'. Norsk Hydro heavy water plant blown up. Ferry carrying heavy water sunk. Major setback to German atomic bomb development

'If SOE had never done anything else, "Gunnerside" would have given it claim enough on the gratitude of humanity.'
Professor M.R.D. Foot, Historian of SOE

The 'Shetland Bus' boat service, 1941–1945. First journey 30 August 1941. In 189 journeys, 192 agents and 383 tons of weapons smuggled into Norway & 73 agents and 373 refugees brought out. 44 crewmen killed in action with the Germans.

1944: Fifty tons of arms landed for the Danish resistance.

SOE base for operations in Denmark.

'Operation Rubble' 23 January 1942: 5 ships with £1 million of special steels and ball bearings sail from Sweden. 'Operation Performance' 2 ships get through, 6 sunk.

15 February 1941: First of 485 drops of supplies flown from Britain to Polish partisans. 318 Polish partisans and agents also parachuted in.

31 October 1944: SOE help for air attack on Gestapo HQ.

21 March 1945: SOE help for air attack on Gestapo HQ.

8 January 1943: Two agents parachuted in from Britain take part in raid on Pinsk prison; they release 40 Polish prisoners.

Mission headed by Major John Sehmer all arrested, 25 December 1944. Sehmer shot.

'Operation Freston', 26/27 December 1944: SOE trained 5-man mission to link up with Polish partisans. Arrested by Soviets. The 3 British were held in a local prison for a month. The 2 Poles are believed to have been executed by the Soviets.

27 May 1942: Two agents parachuted into Czechoslovakia carry out the assassination of Reinhard Heydrich (who died of his wounds, 4 June 1942).

1944: British mission with Tito's Yugoslav partisans.

6 October 1943: German railway bridge sabotaged.

1943: British military mission to Miihailovic's Yugoslav partisans.

25/26 November 1942: Rail viaduct sabotaged.

SOE agents put ashore, 1943.

December 1944: Alfgar Hesketh-Pritchard and 80 Yugoslav partisans in action; Hesketh-Pritchard killed.

1944: SOE smuggled out, by sea, 13 United States Army nurses whose pilot had landed in Albania by mistake.

1943–44: British missions.

British mission to Greek partisans.

20/21 June 1943: Rail viaduct sabotaged.

26 April 1944: Two SOE agents and Cretan partisans capture German General Kreipe, in command of Crete, and move him to the south coast, from where he was taken by submarine to Egypt.

SHETLAND ISLANDS · Lerwick
NORWAY
Vemork
SWEDEN neutral
Stockholm
Skaggerak Lysekil
Baltic Sea
North Sea
Aarhus
DENMARK · Copenhagen
BRITAIN
THE NETHERLANDS
BELGIUM
GREATER GERMANY
POLAND
Pripet Marshes · Pinsk
Prague · Cracow
CZECHOSLOVAKIA Polomka
AUSTRIA
Saualpen
HUNGARY
ROMANIA
Black Sea
Topusko
Genoa
YUGOSLAVIA
Visegrad · Uzice
BULGARIA
ITALY
Adriatic Sea
ALBANIA
GREECE
Bari
Gorgopotamos THESSALY
Mediterranean Sea
Asopos
CRETE
Ano Archanes
EGYPT

0 kilometres 400
0 miles 300

© Martin Gilbert 2008

209

GERMAN REFUGEES WHO FOUGHT IN BRITAIN'S ARMED FORCES, 1940–1945

'I decided that we had to win the war, and we had to get rid of Hitler and the Nazis.'
KEN ADAM, THE ONLY KNOWN GERMAN FIGHTER PILOT IN THE ROYAL AIR FORCE

Klaus Hugo Adam (Keith Howard Adam, later known as 'Ken'), born Berlin 1921; a fighter pilot, he took part in an RAF/USAAF bombing raid against the radar station at Bruneval, 11 May 1944, and against Gestapo headquarters at Dunkirk, 11 November 1944.

Otto Hess, born Mainz, 1921; served with Special Intelligence Services (SIS) as Peter Giles; captured behind German lines in Yugoslavia, interrogated, tortured and killed, 1 October 1944.

Friederich Berliner; parachuted, late 1944, as Michael O'Hara, behind German lines; captured, tortured and killed, April 1945.

Rudi Friedlaender, born Munich,1908; served in the Special Air Service (SAS) as Robert Lodge; killed on 18 August 1944 after being parachuted behind German lines; buried at Moussey-dans-le-Vosges.

Bletchley
Signals Intelligence

Hamburg
capture

Osnabrück ▲ Belsen
liberation of

▲ Berlin
Victory Parade

Arnhem ▲
parachute drop

Rotterdam ▲
WALCHEREN ▲
Nijmegen ▲

ENGLAND

Goch ▲ ▲ Echt
Wesel

GREATER
GERMANY

Dunkirk ▲ Antwerp ▲ ▲
Arras ▲ Brussels
liberation

● Mainz

CHANNEL
ISLANDS

HERM ▲
commando raid

Bruneval ▲

Caen ▲ NORMANDY

● Brest
naval intelligence

Villers Bocage ● Paris

RHINELAND
parachuted behind German lines

FRANCE

Moussey-dans-le-Vosges ▲
fighting behind German lines

● Munich

Loeben ▲
Graz ▲
sabotage behind German lines

SWITZERLAND
neutral

Tramonti ▲
*parachuted behind
German lines*

▲ Lekenik
*fighting behind
German lines*

YUGOSLAVIA

Bay of
Biscay

0   kilometres   300

0   miles   200

Valli di Comacchio ▲

Adriatic

BRAC ▲ ▲
HVAR ▲
commando raids

Sea

SPAIN
neutral

CORSICA

Anzio ▲

ITALY

● Cassino ▲

Salerno ▲

CORFU
commando raid

SARDINIA

Mediterranean   Sea

SICILY

▲ Thirty-three of the battles in which German refugees to Britain fought against Germany, and other locations where members of 'The King's Most Loyal Enemy Aliens' were in action, 1940-1945

Bone ▲

TUNISIA

ALGERIA

LAMPEDUSA ▲

MALTA ▲
naval escort duties

10,000 Germans and Austrians – mostly Jewish refugees from Nazism – fought in the British Army in the Second World War. Most had been interned in 1939 and 1940 by the British Government as enemy aliens. All volunteered to serve in the British armed forces. Known affectionately as 'The King's Most Loyal Enemy Aliens', they constituted one in seven of all refugees who had come to Britain between 1933 and 1939. At least 300 were killed in action.

© Martin Gilbert 2008

JAPANESE-AMERICAN – *NISEI* – SOLDIERS IN ACTION, 1943–1945

Scouts from the 522nd Field Artillery (Japanese-American) Battalion were among the first Allied troops to enter Dachau concentration camp.

Among the Japanese-American soldiers in action was the future Senator Daniel Inoye (Democrat, Hawaii, from 1962), Senator Spark Matsunaga (Democrat, Hawaii, 1977–1990), and Susumu Ito, Professor of Cell Biology and Anatomy, Harvard Medical School.

Battle zones in which first Japanese-American – *Nisei* – soldiers were in action.

❶ NAPLES-FOGGIA CAMPAIGN
   9 September 1943 – 21 January 1944

❷ ROME-ARNO CAMPAIGN
   22 January – 9 September 1944

❸ SOUTHERN FRANCE CAMPAIGN
   15 August – 14 September 1944

❹ NORTHERN APENNINES
   10 September 1944 – 4 April 1945

❺ ALSACE-RHINELAND
   15 September 1944 – 21 March 1945

❻ CENTRAL EUROPE
   22 March – 11 May 1945

❼ PO VALLEY CAMPAIGN
   5 April – 8 May 1945

© Martin Gilbert 2009

Between December 1941 and July 1945, more than 33,000 Japanese-Americans – *Nisei* – served in the United States Army, most of them in the 442nd Regimental Combat team (later the 442nd Infantry Regiment). The unit, many members of which were Japanese-Americans from Hawaii, fought in Italy, France, Germany, Austria and Czechoslovakia. They were the most highly decorated military unit in the history of the United States Armed Forces, including one Medal of Honor. Because so many in the 100th Battalion had been wounded and awarded the Purple Heart, they were known as the 'Purple Heart Battalion'. More than 700 were killed in action.

The first Japanese-Americans to be killed in action were 29 soldiers on a military transport vessel torpedoed by a Japanese submarine off Hawaii on 28 January 1942, less than two months after Pearl Harbor. The first rifle-carrying Japanese-American to fall in combat was Joe Takata, killed on 29 September 1943 at Monte Milleto near Salerno, in Italy.

The one Japanese-American Medal of Honor recipient was Private First Class Sadao Munemori, killed in action at Serevezza in Italy on 5 April 1945. In June 2000, 19 Distinguished Service Crosses – of 52 awarded during the war to Japanese-American soldiers – and one Bronze Star (of 4,000) were upgraded to Medals of Honor.

AFRICAN-AMERICAN SOLDIERS IN ACTION, 1944–1945

Baltic Sea

More than 12,000 African-American soldiers saw action with the United States forces in the Second World War. More than 550 were killed. Because these soldiers were black, they were not considered suitable for the highest bravery award, the Medal of Honor. On 13 January 1997, more than 50 years after the end of the war, President Clinton presented seven Medals of Honor – six of them posthumously – to African-American soldiers judged to have merited the award. The research needed to make the awards was carried out at the request of the Army at Shaw University, Raleigh, North Carolina.

● Berlin

The 92nd Infantry 'Buffalo' Division was the last segregated (all-black) United States Army Division, and the only black division to fight in Europe in the Second World War. It arrived in Europe on 22 September 1944 and returned to the United States on 26 November 1945. It was disbanded two days later.

Lippoldsberg
7 April 1945
● Private First Class Willy F. James Jr

卐 **Buchenwald**

The 332nd Fighter Group (the 'Tuskegee Airmen') were an all-black unit of the United States Army Air Force. They shot down more than a hundred German warplanes over Europe.

CZECHOSLOVAKIA

BELGIUM

LUX

Ardennes

GERMANY

Speyer
● *23 March 1945*
Staff Sergeant Edward A. Carter Jr

Guebling
15–19 November 1944 ●
Staff Sergeant
Ruben Rivers

Climbach
14 December 1944
Captain Charles L. Thomas

FRANCE

卐 **Gunskirchen**

● Places in Europe where six of the seven African-American Medals of Honor were won. The seventh was won in the Pacific. *(see below)*

卐 Concentration camps reached by advancing African-American troops

AUSTRIA

YUGOSLAVIA

African-American soldiers were among the United States troops who liberated the concentration camps in Germany in April and early May 1945. They were members of the 761st Tank Battalion and the 183rd Combat Engineers, who had distinguished themselves in the Ardennes at the Battle of the Bulge at the end of 1944. Thirty-three years later the 761st was awarded a Presidential Unit Citation for heroism.

ITALY

On 8 March 1943, Private George Watson was on board a ship off Papua New Guinea that was attacked by Japanese bombers. When the ship was abandoned, Private Watson refused to be rescued until he could help several soldiers – who could not swim – to reach the safety of the raft. His Medal of Honor citation reads: 'Weakened by his exertions, he was dragged down by the suction of the sinking ship and was drowned. Private Watson's extraordinary valorous actions, daring leadership, and self-sacrificing devotion to his fellow-man exemplify the finest traditions of military service.'

Sommocolonia
26 December 1944
First Lieutenant John R. Fox
●

● **Viareggio**
5 and 6 April 1945
First Lieutenant Vernon J. Baker

Adriatic Sea

0   kilometres   200
0   miles   100

© Martin Gilbert 2009

212

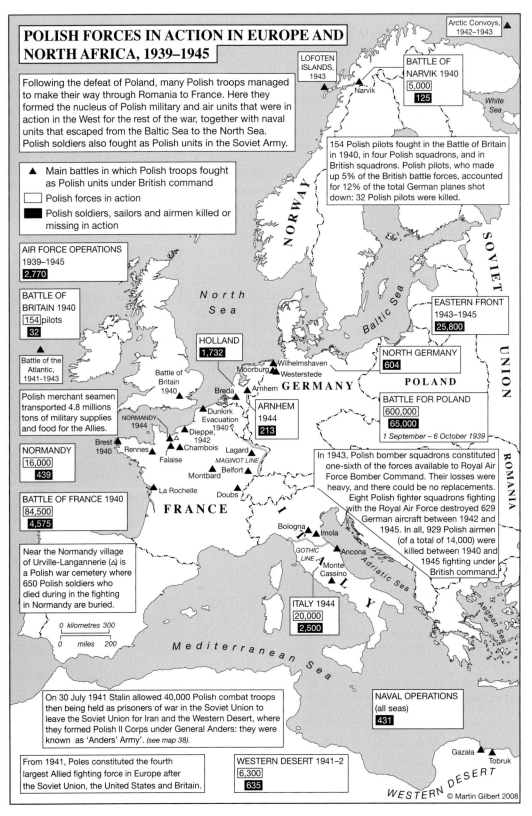

POLISH FORCES IN ACTION IN EUROPE AND NORTH AFRICA, 1939–1945

Following the defeat of Poland, many Polish troops managed to make their way through Romania to France. Here they formed the nucleus of Polish military and air units that were in action in the West for the rest of the war, together with naval units that escaped from the Baltic Sea to the North Sea. Polish soldiers also fought as Polish units in the Soviet Army.

▲ Main battles in which Polish troops fought as Polish units under British command

☐ Polish forces in action

■ Polish soldiers, sailors and airmen killed or missing in action

AIR FORCE OPERATIONS
1939–1945
2,770

BATTLE OF BRITAIN 1940
154 pilots
32

Battle of the Atlantic, 1941-1943

Polish merchant seamen transported 4.8 millions tons of military supplies and food for the Allies.

NORMANDY 1940
16,000
439

BATTLE OF FRANCE 1940
84,500
4,575

Near the Normandy village of Urville-Langannerie (△) is a Polish war cemetery where 650 Polish soldiers who died during in the fighting in Normandy are buried.

Arctic Convoys, 1942–1943 ▲

LOFOTEN ISLANDS, 1943 ▲

BATTLE OF NARVIK 1940
5,000
125
Narvik ▲

White Sea

154 Polish pilots fought in the Battle of Britain in 1940, in four Polish squadrons, and in British squadrons. Polish pilots, who made up 5% of the British battle forces, accounted for 12% of the total German planes shot down: 32 Polish pilots were killed.

North Sea

NORWAY

Baltic Sea

EASTERN FRONT 1943–1945
25,800

NORTH GERMANY
604

SOVIET UNION

HOLLAND
1,732

Wilhelmshaven
Moorburg ▲ Westerstede
Battle of Britain 1940
Breda ▲ Arnhem **GERMANY**
Dunkirk
Evacuation 1940 **ARNHEM** 1944
213
NORMANDY 1944
Dieppe, 1942
Brest 1940 ▲△ Chambois
Rennes ▲ Falaise
Lagard
MAGINOT LINE
Belfort ▲
Montbard
La Rochelle ▲ Doubs

POLAND

BATTLE FOR POLAND
600,000
65,000
1 September – 6 October 1939

In 1943, Polish bomber squadrons constituted one-sixth of the forces available to Royal Air Force Bomber Command. Their losses were heavy, and there could be no replacements. Eight Polish fighter squadrons fighting with the Royal Air Force destroyed 629 German aircraft between 1942 and 1945. In all, 929 Polish airmen (of a total of 14,000) were killed between 1940 and 1945 fighting under British command.

FRANCE

Bologna ▲ Imola
GOTHIC LINE ▲ Ancona
Monte Cassino ▲
ROMANIA
Adriatic Sea
Aegean Sea

ITALY 1944
20,000
2,500

Mediterranean Sea

NAVAL OPERATIONS
(all seas)
431

0 kilometres 300
0 miles 200

On 30 July 1941 Stalin allowed 40,000 Polish combat troops then being held as prisoners of war in the Soviet Union to leave the Soviet Union for Iran and the Western Desert, where they formed Polish II Corps under General Anders: they were known as 'Anders' Army'. *(see map 38).*

From 1941, Poles constituted the fourth largest Allied fighting force in Europe after the Soviet Union, the United States and Britain.

WESTERN DESERT 1941–2
6,300
635

Gazala ▲ ▲ Tobruk
WESTERN DESERT

© Martin Gilbert 2008

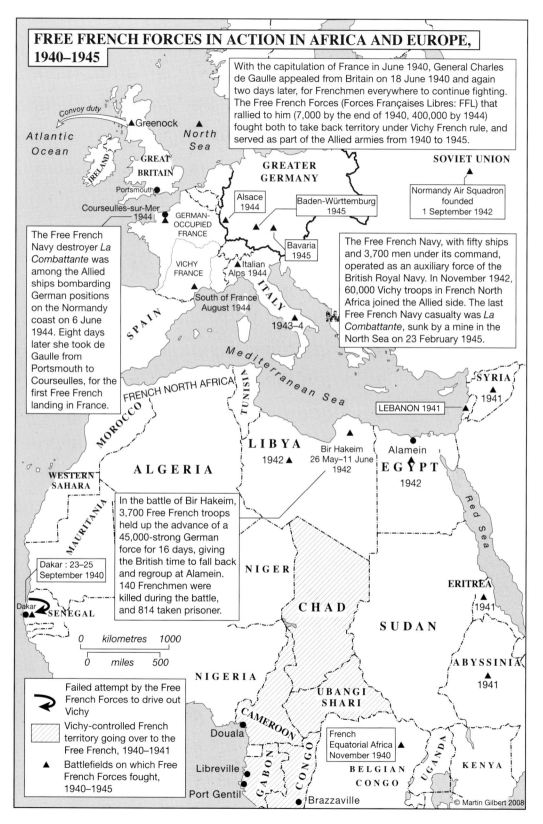

FREE FRENCH FORCES IN ACTION IN AFRICA AND EUROPE, 1940–1945

With the capitulation of France in June 1940, General Charles de Gaulle appealed from Britain on 18 June 1940 and again two days later, for Frenchmen everywhere to continue fighting. The Free French Forces (Forces Françaises Libres: FFL) that rallied to him (7,000 by the end of 1940, 400,000 by 1944) fought both to take back territory under Vichy French rule, and served as part of the Allied armies from 1940 to 1945.

Convoy duty

Atlantic Ocean

Greenock ▲

▲ *North Sea*

GREAT BRITAIN

IRELAND

Portsmouth ●

Courseulles-sur-Mer 1944

GERMAN-OCCUPIED FRANCE

GREATER GERMANY

Alsace 1944

Baden-Württemburg 1945

SOVIET UNION ▲

Normandy Air Squadron founded 1 September 1942

VICHY FRANCE

Bavaria 1945

▲ Italian Alps 1944

▲ South of France August 1944

SPAIN

ITALY

1943–4 ▲

The Free French Navy destroyer *La Combattante* was among the Allied ships bombarding German positions on the Normandy coast on 6 June 1944. Eight days later she took de Gaulle from Portsmouth to Courseulles, for the first Free French landing in France.

The Free French Navy, with fifty ships and 3,700 men under its command, operated as an auxiliary force of the British Royal Navy. In November 1942, 60,000 Vichy troops in French North Africa joined the Allied side. The last Free French Navy casualty was *La Combattante*, sunk by a mine in the North Sea on 23 February 1945.

Mediterranean Sea

SYRIA ▲ 1941

FRENCH NORTH AFRICA

TUNISIA

LEBANON 1941

MOROCCO

LIBYA 1942 ▲

Bir Hakeim 26 May–11 June 1942

Alamein ▲

EGYPT 1942

WESTERN SAHARA

ALGERIA

Red Sea

In the battle of Bir Hakeim, 3,700 Free French troops held up the advance of a 45,000-strong German force for 16 days, giving the British time to fall back and regroup at Alamein. 140 Frenchmen were killed during the battle, and 814 taken prisoner.

MAURITANIA

Dakar : 23–25 September 1940

NIGER

CHAD

SUDAN

ERITREA ▲ 1941

Dakar ● ▲▲ SENEGAL

0   kilometres   1000
0   miles   500

ABYSSINIA ▲ 1941

NIGERIA

UBANGI SHARI

Failed attempt by the Free French Forces to drive out Vichy

Vichy-controlled French territory going over to the Free French, 1940–1941

▲ Battlefields on which Free French Forces fought, 1940–1945

CAMEROON

Douala

French Equatorial Africa November 1940 ▲

UGANDA

KENYA

Libreville

GABON

CONGO

BELGIAN CONGO

Port Gentil

● Brazzaville

© Martin Gilbert 2008

214

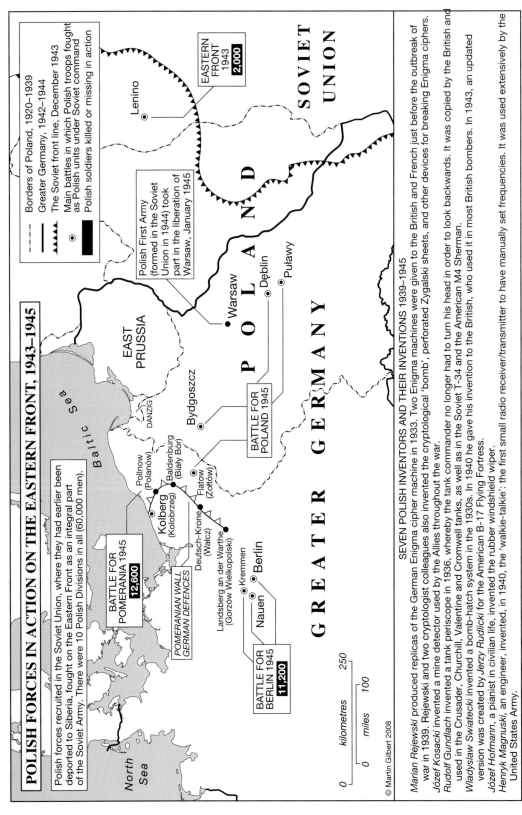

POLISH FORCES IN ACTION ON THE EASTERN FRONT, 1943–1945

Polish forces recruited in the Soviet Union, where they had earlier been deported to Siberia, fought on the Eastern Front as an integral part of the Soviet Army. There were 10 Polish Divisions in all (60,000 men).

Borders of Poland, 1920–1939
Greater Germany, 1942–1944
The Soviet front line, December 1943
Main battles in which Polish troops fought as Polish units under Soviet command
Polish soldiers killed or missing in action

EASTERN FRONT 1943 **2,000**

Polish First Army (formed in the Soviet Union in 1944) took part in the liberation of Warsaw, January 1945

BATTLE FOR POLAND 1945

BATTLE FOR POMERANIA 1945 **12,600**

POMERANIAN WALL GERMAN DEFENCES

BATTLE FOR BERLIN 1945 **11,200**

SOVIET UNION

Lenino

POLAND

Warsaw
Dęblin
Puławy

EAST PRUSSIA

Bydgoszcz

DANZIG

Pollnow (Polanów)
Baldenburg (Biały Bór)
Kolberg (Kołobrzeg)
Flatow (Złotów)
Deutsch-Krone (Wałcz)
Landsberg an der Warthe (Gorzów Wielkopolski)
Kremmen
Nauen
Berlin

GREATER GERMANY

Baltic Sea

North Sea

0   kilometres   250
0   miles   100

© Martin Gilbert 2008

SEVEN POLISH INVENTORS AND THEIR INVENTIONS 1939–1945

Marian Rejewski produced replicas of the German Enigma cipher machine in 1933. Two Enigma machines were given to the British and French just before the outbreak of war in 1939. Rejewski and two cryptologist colleagues also invented the cryptological 'bomb', perforated Zygalski sheets, and other devices for breaking Enigma ciphers.

Józef Kosacki invented a mine detector used by the Allies throughout the war.

Rudolf Gundlach invented a tank periscope in 1936, whereby the tank commander no longer had to turn his head in order to look backwards. It was copied by the British and used in the Crusader, Churchill, Valentine and Cromwell tanks, as well as in the Soviet T-34 and the American M4 Sherman.

Władysław Świątecki invented a bomb-hatch system in the 1930s. In 1940 he gave his invention to the British, who used it in most British bombers. In 1943, an updated version was created by *Jerzy Rudlicki* for the American B-17 Flying Fortress.

Józef Hofmann, a pianist in civilian life, invented the rubber windshield wiper.

Henryk Magnuski, an engineer, invented, in 1940, the 'walkie-talkie': the first small radio receiver/transmitter to have manually set frequencies. It was used extensively by the United States Army.

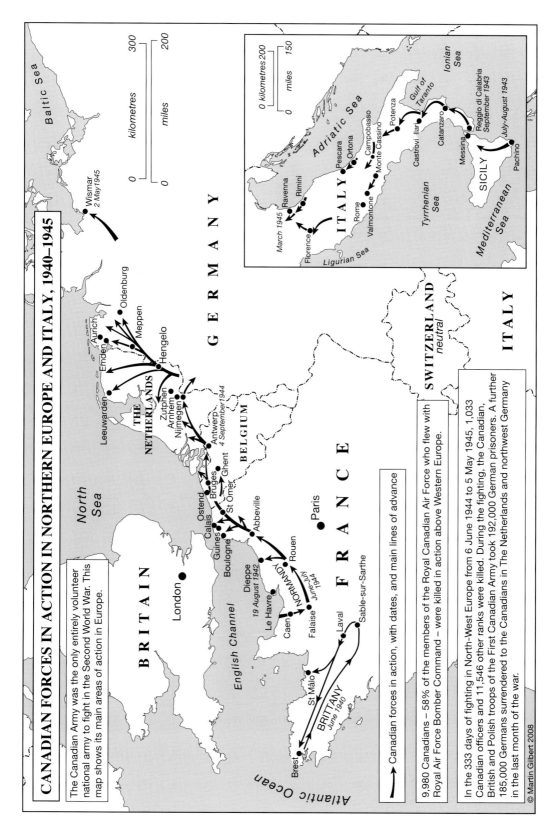

CANADIAN FORCES IN ACTION IN NORTHERN EUROPE AND ITALY, 1940–1945

The Canadian Army was the only entirely volunteer national army to fight in the Second World War. This map shows its main areas of action in Europe.

→ Canadian forces in action, with dates, and main lines of advance

9,980 Canadians – 58% of the members of the Royal Canadian Air Force who flew with Royal Air Force Bomber Command – were killed in action above Western Europe.

In the 333 days of fighting in North-West Europe from 6 June 1944 to 5 May 1945, 1,033 Canadian officers and 11,546 other ranks were killed. During the fighting, the Canadian, British and Polish troops of the First Canadian Army took 192,000 German prisoners. A further 185,000 Germans surrendered to the Canadians in The Netherlands and northwest Germany in the last month of the war.

© Martin Gilbert 2008

Baltic Sea

North Sea

BRITAIN

London

English Channel

Atlantic Ocean

Brest

BRITTANY
June 1940

St Mâlo

Laval

Sable-sur-Sarthe

Falaise

Caen

NORMANDY
June–July 1944

Le Havre

Dieppe
19 August 1942

Rouen

Paris

FRANCE

Abbeville

Boulogne

Guînes

Calais

Ostend

Bruges

Ghent

St Omer

BELGIUM

Antwerp
4 September 1944

Nijmegen

Arnhem

Zutphen

THE NETHERLANDS

Leeuwarden

Hengelo

Emden

Aurich

Meppen

Oldenburg

GERMANY

Wismar
2 May 1945

SWITZERLAND
neutral

ITALY

kilometres 0   200   300
miles   0   200

Italy inset

0 kilometres 200
0 miles 150

Adriatic Sea

Ionian Sea

Ravenna

Rimini

March 1945

Florence

Ligurian Sea

Rome

Valmontone

Tyrrhenian Sea

Pescara

Ortona

Campobasso

Monte Cassino

Potenza

Gulf of Taranto

Castrovi Ilari

Catanzaro

Reggio di Calabria
September 1943

Messina

SICILY

Pachino

July–August 1943

ITALY

Mediterranean Sea

216

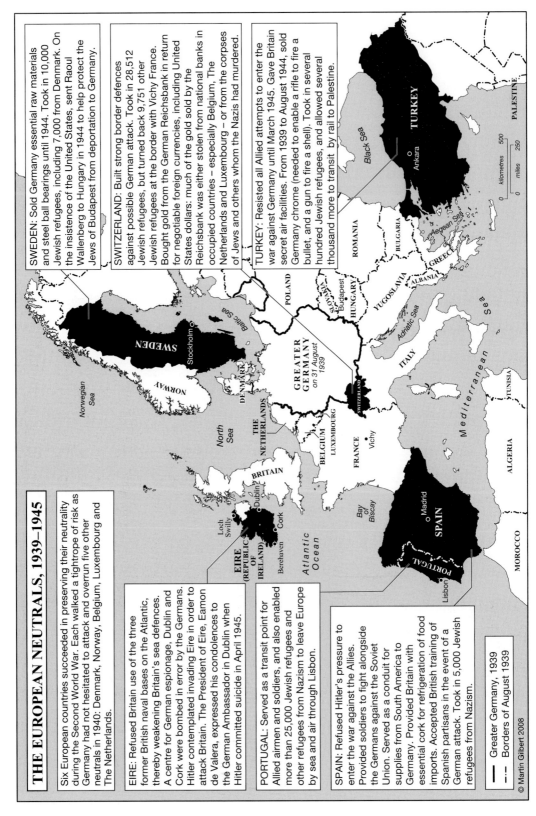

THE EUROPEAN NEUTRALS, 1939–1945

Six European countries succeeded in preserving their neutrality during the Second World War. Each walked a tightrope of risk as Germany had not hesitated to attack and overrun five other neutrals in 1940: Denmark, Norway, Belgium, Luxembourg and The Netherlands.

SWEDEN: Sold Germany essential raw materials and steel ball bearings until 1944. Took in 10,000 Jewish refugees, including 7,000 from Denmark. On the insistence of the United States, sent Raoul Wallenberg to Hungary in 1944 to help protect the Jews of Budapest from deportation to Germany.

SWITZERLAND: Built strong border defences against possible German attack. Took in 28,512 Jewish refugees, but turned back 9,751 other Jewish refugees at the border with Vichy France. Bought gold from the German Reichsbank in return for negotiable foreign currencies, including United States dollars: much of the gold sold by the Reichsbank was either stolen from national banks in occupied countries – especially Belgium, The Netherlands and Luxembourg – or from the corpses of Jews and others whom the Nazis had murdered.

TURKEY: Resisted all Allied attempts to enter the war against Germany until March 1945. Gave Britain secret air facilities. From 1939 to August 1944, sold Germany chrome (needed to enable a rifle to fire a bullet, and a gun to fire a shell). Took in several hundred Jewish refugees, and allowed several thousand more to transit by rail to Palestine.

EIRE: Refused Britain use of the three former British naval bases on the Atlantic, thereby weakening Britain's sea defences. A centre for German espionage, Dublin and Cork were bombed in error by the Germans. Hitler contemplated invading Eire in order to attack Britain. The President of Eire, Eamon de Valera, expressed his condolences to the German Ambassador in Dublin when Hitler committed suicide in April 1945.

PORTUGAL: Served as a transit point for Allied airmen and soldiers, and also enabled more than 25,000 Jewish refugees and other refugees from Nazism to leave Europe by sea and air through Lisbon.

SPAIN: Refused Hitler's pressure to enter the war against the Allies. Provided soldiers to fight alongside the Germans against the Soviet Union. Served as a conduit for supplies from South America to Germany. Provided Britain with essential cork for refrigeration of food imports. Accepted British training of Spanish partisans in the event of a German attack. Took in 5,000 Jewish refugees from Nazism.

Greater Germany, 1939
Borders of August 1939

© Martin Gilbert 2008

217

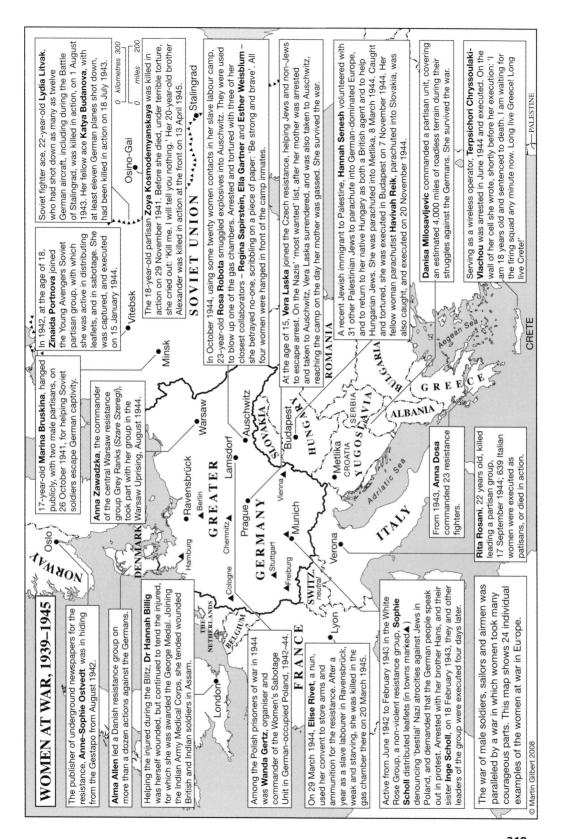

WOMEN AT WAR, 1939–1945

The publisher of underground newspapers for the resistance, **Anne-Sophie Ostvedt** was in hiding from the Gestapo from August 1942.

Alma Allen led a Danish resistance group on more than a dozen actions against the Germans.

17-year-old **Marina Bruskina**, hanged publicly, with two male partisans, on 26 October 1941, for helping Soviet soldiers escape German captivity.

In 1942, at the age of 18, **Zinaida Portnova** joined the Young Avengers Soviet partisan group, with which she was active in distributing leaflets, and in sabotage. She was captured, and executed on 15 January 1944.

Soviet fighter ace, 22-year-old **Lydia Litvak**, who had shot down as many as twelve German aircraft, including during the Battle of Stalingrad, was killed in action, on 1 August 1943. Her fellow ace **Katya Budanova**, with at least eleven German planes shot down, had been killed in action on 18 July 1943.

The 18-year-old partisan **Zoya Kosmodemyanskaya** was killed in action on 29 November 1941. Before she died, under terrible torture, she cried out: 'Kill me. I will tell you nothing.' Her 20-year-old brother Alexander was killed in action at the front on 13 April 1945.

Helping the injured during the Blitz, **Dr Hannah Billig** was herself wounded, but continued to tend the injured, for which she was awarded the George Medal. Joining the Indian Army Medical Corps, she tended wounded British and Indian soldiers in Assam.

Anna Zawadzka, the commander of the central Warsaw resistance group Grey Ranks (*Szare Szeregi*), took part with her group in the Warsaw Uprising, August 1944.

In October 1944, using some twenty women contacts in her slave labour camp, 23-year-old **Rosa Robota** smuggled explosives into Auschwitz. They were used to blow up one of the gas chambers. Arrested and tortured with three of her closest collaborators – **Regina Sapirstein**, **Ella Gartner** and **Esther Weisblum** – she betrayed no-one, scribbling on a piece of paper: 'Be strong and brave'. All four women were hanged in front of the camp inmates.

At the age of 15, **Vera Laska** joined the Czech resistance, helping Jews and non-Jews to escape arrest. On the Nazis' 'most wanted' list, after her mother was arrested and taken to Auschwitz, Vera Laska surrendered, and was also taken to Auschwitz, reaching the camp on the day her mother was gassed. She survived the war.

A recent Jewish immigrant to Palestine, **Hannah Senesh** volunteered with 31 other Palestinian Jews to parachute into German-dominated Europe, and to return to her native Hungary as both a British agent and to help Hungarian Jews. She was parachuted into Metlika, 8 March 1944. Caught and tortured, she was executed in Budapest on 7 November 1944. Her fellow woman parachutist **Havivah Reik**, parachuted into Slovakia, was also caught, and executed on 20 November 1944.

Danisa Milosavljevic commanded a partisan unit, covering an estimated 4,000 miles of roadless terrain during their struggles against the Germans. She survived the war.

Serving as a wireless operator, **Terpsichori Chryssoulaki-Vlachou** was arrested in June 1944 and executed. On the wall of her cell she wrote, shortly before her execution: 'I am 18 years old and sentenced to death. I am waiting for the firing squad any minute now. Long live Greece! Long live Crete!'

Among the Polish prisoners of war in 1944 was **Wanda Gertz**, organiser and commander of the Women's Sabotage Unit in German-occupied Poland, 1942–44.

On 29 March 1944, **Elise Rivet**, a nun, used her convent to store arms and ammunition for the resistance. After a year as a slave labourer in Ravensbrück, weak and starving, she was killed in the gas chamber there on 20 March 1945.

Active from June 1942 to February 1943 in the White Rose Group, a non-violent resistance group, **Sophie Scholl** distributed leaflets (in towns marked▲) denouncing 'bestial' Nazi atrocities against Jews in Poland, and demanded that the German people speak out in protest. Arrested with her brother Hans, and their sister **Inge Scholl**, on 18 February 1943, they and other leaders of the group were executed four days later.

From 1943, **Anna Dosa** commanded 23 resistance fighters.

Rita Rosani, 22 years old, killed leading a partisan group, 17 September 1944; 639 Italian women were executed as partisans, or died in action.

The war of male soldiers, sailors and airmen was paralleled by a war in which women took many courageous parts. This map shows 24 individual examples of the women at war in Europe.

0 kilometres 300
0 miles 200

SOVIET UNION
Stalingrad
Osino-Gai
Vitebsk
Minsk

GREATER GERMANY
Berlin
Ravensbrück
Warsaw
Auschwitz
Lamsdorf
Chemnitz
Prague
Vienna
Budapest
SLOVAKIA
HUNGARY
ROMANIA
Munich
Stuttgart
Freiburg
Verona
Metlika
CROATIA
SERBIA
YUGOSLAVIA
ALBANIA
GREECE
BULGARIA
ITALY
Aegean Sea
Adriatic Sea
CRETE
PALESTINE

NORWAY
Oslo
DENMARK
Hamburg
Cologne
THE NETHERLANDS
BELGIUM
London
FRANCE
Lyon
SWITZ. neutral

© Martin Gilbert 2008

218

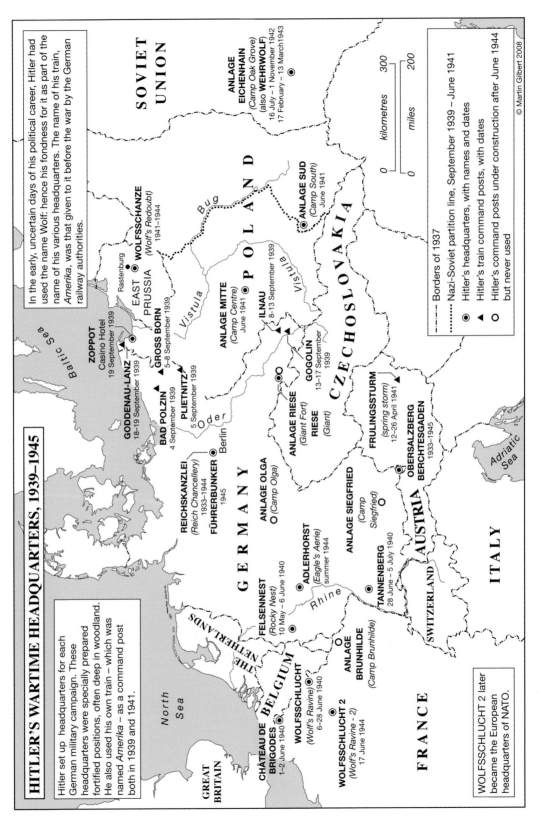

HITLER'S WARTIME HEADQUARTERS, 1939–1945

Hitler set up headquarters for each German military campaign. These headquarters were specially prepared fortified positions, often deep in woodland. He also used his own train – which was named *Amerika* – as a command post both in 1939 and 1941.

In the early, uncertain days of his political career, Hitler had used the name Wolf: hence his fondness for it as part of the name of his various headquarters. The name of his train, *Amerika*, was that given to it before the war by the German railway authorities.

SOVIET UNION

ANLAGE EICHENHAIN
(Camp Oak Grove)
(also **WEHRWOLF**)
16 July – 1 November 1942
17 February – 13 March 1943 ◉

Rastenburg
EAST ● **WOLFSSCHANZE**
PRUSSIA *(Wolf's Redoubt)*
1941–1944

Bug

ANLAGE SUD
(Camp South)
June 1941 ◉

Vistula

ZOPPOT
Casino Hotel
19 September 1939
GODDENAU-LANZ ◉
18–19 September 1939
GROSS BORN ▲
5–8 September 1939
BAD POLZIN ▲
4 September 1939
PLIETNITZ ▲
5 September 1939

Baltic Sea

ANLAGE MITTE
(Camp Centre)
June 1941 ◉

P O L A N D

ILNAU ◉
8–13 September 1939

GOGOLIN
13–17 September
1939

Oder

Vistula

C Z E C H O S L O V A K I A

ANLAGE SUD

Berlin

REICHSKANZLEI
(Reich Chancellery)
1933–1944
FÜHRERBUNKER ◉
1945

ANLAGE OLGA
O *(Camp Olga)*

ANLAGE RIESE
(Giant Fort)
RIESE ▲
(Giant)

FRULINGSSTURM
(spring storm)
12–26 April 1941 ▲

OBERSALZBERG
BERCHTESGADEN ◉
1933–1945

G E R M A N Y

FELSENNEST
(Rocky Nest)
10 May – 6 June 1940 ◉

ADLERHORST
(Eagle's Aerie)
summer 1944 ◉

Rhine

TANNENBERG
28 June – 5 July 1940 ◉

ANLAGE SIEGFRIED
(Camp Siegfried) O

A U S T R I A

I T A L Y

Adriatic Sea

North Sea

T H E   N E T H E R L A N D S

B E L G I U M

WOLFSSCHLUCHT
(Wolf's Ravine) ◉
6–28 June 1940

WOLFSSCHLUCHT 2
(Wolf's Ravine - 2)

ANLAGE BRUNHILDE
O *(Camp Brunhilde)*

CHÂTEAU DE BRIGODES ◉
1–2 June 1940

WOLFSSCHLUCHT 2
(Wolf's Ravine - 2)
17 June 1944

GREAT BRITAIN

F R A N C E

SWITZERLAND

WOLFSSCHLUCHT 2 later became the European headquarters of NATO.

Borders of 1937
- - - - - Nazi-Soviet partition line, September 1939 – June 1941
◉ Hitler's headquarters, with names and dates
▲ Hitler's train command posts, with dates
O Hitler's command posts under construction after June 1944 but never used

0 ___ 200 miles
0 ___ 300 kilometres

© Martin Gilbert 2008

219

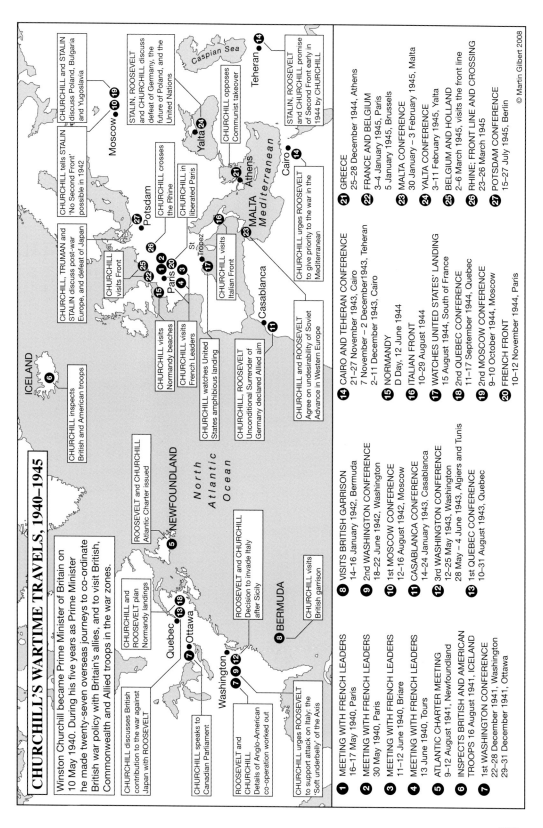

CHURCHILL'S WARTIME TRAVELS, 1940–1945

Winston Churchill became Prime Minister of Britain on 10 May 1940. During his five years as Prime Minister he made twenty-seven overseas journeys to co-ordinate British war policy with Britain's allies, and to visit British, Commonwealth and Allied troops in the war zones.

CHURCHILL inspects British and American troops

CHURCHILL tells STALIN 'No Second Front' possible in 1942

CHURCHILL and STALIN discuss Poland, Bulgaria and Yugoslavia

STALIN, ROOSEVELT and CHURCHILL discuss defeat of Germany, the future of Poland, and the United Nations

CHURCHILL opposes Communist takeover

CHURCHILL, TRUMAN and STALIN discuss post-war Europe, and defeat of Japan

STALIN, ROOSEVELT and CHURCHILL promise of Second Front early in 1944 by CHURCHILL

CHURCHILL crosses the Rhine

CHURCHILL in liberated Paris

CHURCHILL discusses British contribution to the war against Japan with ROOSEVELT

CHURCHILL and ROOSEVELT plan Normandy landings

ROOSEVELT and CHURCHILL Atlantic Charter issued

CHURCHILL visits Front

CHURCHILL visits Normandy beaches

CHURCHILL visits French Leaders

CHURCHILL visits Italian Front

CHURCHILL urges ROOSEVELT to give priority to the war in the Mediterranean

CHURCHILL speaks to Canadian Parliament

ROOSEVELT and CHURCHILL Details of Anglo-American co-operation worked out

CHURCHILL watches United States amphibious landing

CHURCHILL, ROOSEVELT Unconditional Surrender of Germany declared Allied aim

CHURCHILL and ROOSEVELT Agree on undesirability of Soviet Advance in Western Europe

ROOSEVELT and CHURCHILL Decision to invade Italy: the 'Soft underbelly' of the Axis

CHURCHILL visits British garrison

CHURCHILL urges ROOSEVELT to support attack on Italy: the 'Soft underbelly' of the Axis

Caspian Sea

Mediterranean

North Atlantic Ocean

ICELAND
NEWFOUNDLAND
BERMUDA
Quebec
Ottawa
Washington
Moscow
Teheran
Yalta
Potsdam
Paris
St Tropez
Athens
MALTA
Cairo
Casablanca

© Martin Gilbert 2008

1 MEETING WITH FRENCH LEADERS
16–17 May 1940, Paris

2 MEETING WITH FRENCH LEADERS
30 May 1940, Paris

3 MEETING WITH FRENCH LEADERS
11–12 June 1940, Briare

4 MEETING WITH FRENCH LEADERS
13 June 1940, Tours

5 ATLANTIC CHARTER MEETING
9–12 August 1941, Newfoundland

6 INSPECTS BRITISH AND AMERICAN TROOPS 16 August 1941, ICELAND

7 1st WASHINGTON CONFERENCE
22–28 December 1941, Washington
29–31 December 1941, Ottawa

8 VISITS BRITISH GARRISON
14–16 January 1942, Bermuda

9 2nd WASHINGTON CONFERENCE
18–22 June 1942, Washington

10 1st MOSCOW CONFERENCE
12–16 August 1942, Moscow

11 CASABLANCA CONFERENCE
14–24 January 1943, Casablanca

12 3rd WASHINGTON CONFERENCE
12–25 May 1943, Washington
28 May – 4 June 1943, Algiers and Tunis

13 1st QUEBEC CONFERENCE
10–31 August 1943, Quebec

14 CAIRO AND TEHERAN CONFERENCE
21–27 November 1943, Cairo
7 November – 2 December1943, Teheran
2–11 December 1943, Cairo

15 NORMANDY
D Day, 12 June 1944

16 ITALIAN FRONT
10–29 August 1944

17 WATCHES UNITED STATES' LANDING
15 August 1944, South of France

18 2nd QUEBEC CONFERENCE
11–17 September 1944, Quebec

19 2nd MOSCOW CONFERENCE
9–10 October 1944, Moscow

20 FRENCH FRONT
10–12 November 1944, Paris

21 GREECE
25–28 December 1944, Athens

22 FRANCE AND BELGIUM
3–4 January 1945, Paris
5 January 1945, Brussels

23 MALTA CONFERENCE
30 January – 3 February 1945, Malta

24 YALTA CONFERENCE
3–11 February 1945, Yalta

25 BELGIUM AND HOLLAND
2–6 March 1945, visits the front line

26 RHINE: FRONT LINE AND CROSSING
23–26 March 1945

27 POTSDAM CONFERENCE
15–27 July 1945, Berlin

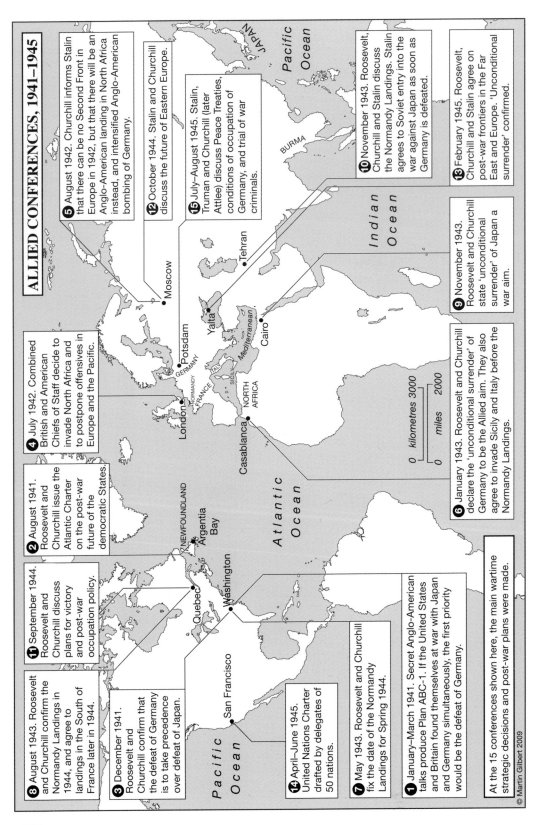

ALLIED CONFERENCES, 1941–1945

1 January–March 1941. Secret Anglo-American talks produce Plan ABC-1. If the United States and Britain found themselves at war with Japan and Germany simultaneously, the first priority would be the defeat of Germany.

2 August 1941. Roosevelt and Churchill issue the Atlantic Charter on the post-war future of the democratic States.

3 December 1941. Roosevelt and Churchill confirm that the defeat of Germany is to take precedence over defeat of Japan.

4 July 1942. Combined British and American Chiefs of Staff decide to invade North Africa and to postpone offensives in Europe and the Pacific.

5 August 1942. Churchill informs Stalin that there can be no Second Front in Europe in 1942, but that there will be an Anglo-American landing in North Africa instead, and intensified Anglo-American bombing of Germany.

6 January 1943. Roosevelt and Churchill declare the 'unconditional surrender' of Germany to be the Allied aim. They also agree to invade Sicily and Italy before the Normandy Landings.

7 May 1943. Roosevelt and Churchill fix the date of the Normandy Landings for Spring 1944.

8 August 1943. Roosevelt and Churchill confirm the Normandy Landings in 1944, and agree to landings in the South of France later in 1944.

9 November 1943. Roosevelt and Churchill state 'unconditional surrender' of Japan a war aim.

10 November 1943. Roosevelt, Churchill and Stalin discuss the Normandy Landings. Stalin agrees to Soviet entry into the war against Japan as soon as Germany is defeated.

11 September 1944. Roosevelt and Churchill discuss plans for victory and post-war occupation policy.

12 October 1944. Stalin and Churchill discuss the future of Eastern Europe.

13 February 1945. Roosevelt, Churchill and Stalin agree on post-war frontiers in the Far East and Europe. 'Unconditional surrender' confirmed.

14 April–June 1945. United Nations Charter drafted by delegates of 50 nations.

15 July–August 1945. Stalin, Truman and Churchill (later Attlee) discuss Peace Treaties, conditions of occupation of Germany, and trial of war criminals.

At the 15 conferences shown here, the main wartime strategic decisions and post-war plans were made.

JAPAN

Pacific Ocean

BURMA

Indian Ocean

Moscow

Potsdam

GERMANY

Tehran

Yalta

Mediterranean

Cairo

ITALY

SICILY

NORTH AFRICA

FRANCE

NORMANDY

London

Casablanca

Atlantic Ocean

NEWFOUNDLAND

Argentia Bay

Quebec

Washington

San Francisco

Pacific Ocean

0 kilometres 3000

0 miles 2000

© Martin Gilbert 2009

BELGIUM AT WAR, 1939–1945

Atlantic Ocean

BATTLE OF THE ATLANTIC
(350 Belgian sailors served)

A Belgian Wing Commander, Michael Donnet, led the British air raid on Gestapo headquarters in Copenhagen, 22 March 1945.

NORWAY

North Sea

SWEDEN
neutral

Baltic Sea

DENMARK

Copenhagen

Belgian soldiers also saw active service in East Africa *(see inset map)*. A Belgian Casualty Clearing Station helped wounded Allied soldiers in Burma

BATTLE OF BRITAIN
(29 Belgian pilots flew, 7 were killed)

BRITAIN

NETHERLANDS

THE AIR WAR
1,200 Belgians served in the Royal Air Force
128 Belgian airmen killed in action

GERMANY

WALCHEREN

Nijmegen

Dunkirk

BELGIUM

Remagen

Arromanches

Rhine

CZECHOSLOVAKIA

Pilsen

Bay of Biscay

FRANCE

SWITZERLAND
neutral

AUSTRIA

HUNGARY

YUGOSLAVIA

Adriatic Sea

ITALY

SPAIN
neutral

ALBANIA

GREECE

| 0 | kilometres | 300 |
| 0 | miles | 200 |

Mediterranean Sea

☐ Belgian forces in action, 1940–1945

■ Belgian commandos in action behind German lines

raw materials for the Allied war effort:
copper
gold
rubber
cotton
uranium (for the atom bomb)

ABYSSINIA
Belgian Expeditionary Forces in action

BELGIAN CONGO

Atlantic Ocean

Indian Ocean

| 0 | kilometres | 1000 |
| 0 | miles | 500 |

AFRICA

After fighting bravely against an overwhelmingly strong German attack in May 1940, Belgian troops were in action on many Allied war fronts. On 25 May 1940, 163 Belgian soldiers rescued from Dunkirk formed the basis of the 1st Belgian Infantry Brigade. On 8 August 1944, Belgian soldiers landed in Normandy. Belgium also provided the Allies with essential raw materials from the Belgian Congo.

Inside Belgium, the Belgian resistance harassed the German occupation authorities, and were active in enabling Allied airmen who had been shot down to avoid capture, and to escape to neutral Spain.

© Martin Gilbert 2009

222

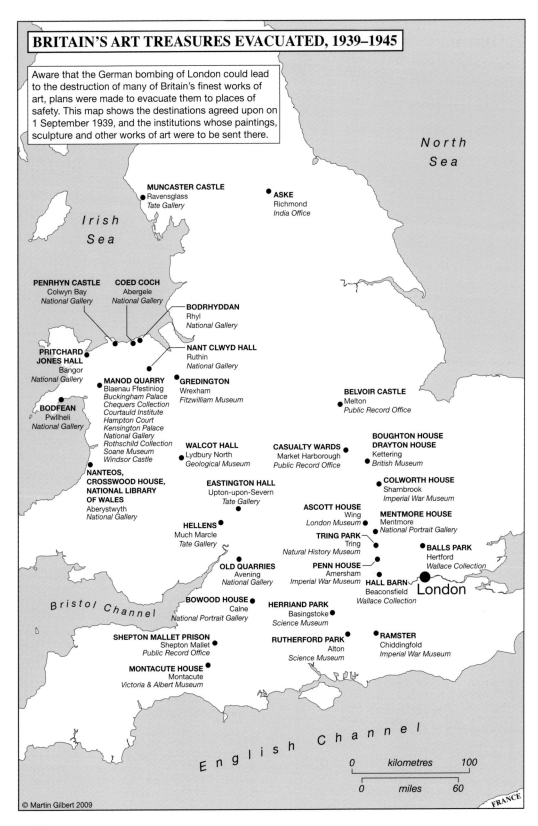

BRITAIN'S ART TREASURES EVACUATED, 1939–1945

Aware that the German bombing of London could lead to the destruction of many of Britain's finest works of art, plans were made to evacuate them to places of safety. This map shows the destinations agreed upon on 1 September 1939, and the institutions whose paintings, sculpture and other works of art were to be sent there.

North Sea

Irish Sea

MUNCASTER CASTLE
Ravensglass
Tate Gallery

ASKE
Richmond
India Office

PENRHYN CASTLE
Colwyn Bay
National Gallery

COED COCH
Abergele
National Gallery

BODRHYDDAN
Rhyl
National Gallery

PRITCHARD JONES HALL
Bangor
National Gallery

NANT CLWYD HALL
Ruthin
National Gallery

MANOD QUARRY
Blaenau Ffestiniog
Buckingham Palace
Chequers Collection
Courtauld Institute
Hampton Court
Kensington Palace
National Gallery
Rothschild Collection
Soane Museum
Windsor Castle

GREDINGTON
Wrexham
Fitzwilliam Museum

BELVOIR CASTLE
Melton
Public Record Office

BODFEAN
Pwllheli
National Gallery

WALCOT HALL
Lydbury North
Geological Museum

CASUALTY WARDS
Market Harborough
Public Record Office

BOUGHTON HOUSE DRAYTON HOUSE
Kettering
British Museum

NANTEOS, CROSSWOOD HOUSE, NATIONAL LIBRARY OF WALES
Aberystwyth
National Gallery

EASTINGTON HALL
Upton-upon-Severn
Tate Gallery

COLWORTH HOUSE
Sharnbrook
Imperial War Museum

ASCOTT HOUSE
Wing
London Museum

MENTMORE HOUSE
Mentmore
National Portrait Gallery

HELLENS
Much Marcle
Tate Gallery

TRING PARK
Tring
Natural History Museum

BALLS PARK
Hertford
Wallace Collection

OLD QUARRIES
Avening
National Gallery

PENN HOUSE
Amersham
Imperial War Museum

HALL BARN
Beaconsfield
Wallace Collection

London

Bristol Channel

BOWOOD HOUSE
Calne
National Portrait Gallery

HERRIAND PARK
Basingstoke
Science Museum

SHEPTON MALLET PRISON
Shepton Mallet
Public Record Office

RUTHERFORD PARK
Alton
Science Museum

RAMSTER
Chiddingfold
Imperial War Museum

MONTACUTE HOUSE
Montacute
Victoria & Albert Museum

English Channel

| 0 | kilometres | 100 |
| 0 | miles | 60 |

© Martin Gilbert 2009

FRANCE

223

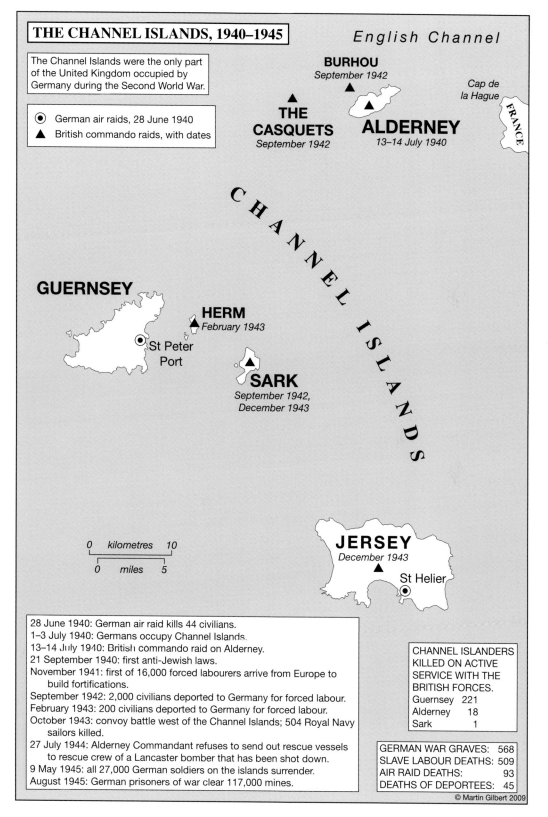

THE CHANNEL ISLANDS, 1940–1945

English Channel

The Channel Islands were the only part of the United Kingdom occupied by Germany during the Second World War.

⊙ German air raids, 28 June 1940
▲ British commando raids, with dates

BURHOU
September 1942
▲

THE CASQUETS
September 1942
▲

ALDERNEY
13–14 July 1940
▲

Cap de la Hague

FRANCE

C H A N N E L   I S L A N D S

GUERNSEY

HERM
▲ *February 1943*

⊙ St Peter Port

SARK
September 1942,
December 1943
▲

0   kilometres   10
0   miles   5

JERSEY
December 1943
▲
St Helier ⊙

28 June 1940: German air raid kills 44 civilians.
1–3 July 1940: Germans occupy Channel Islands.
13–14 July 1940: British commando raid on Alderney.
21 September 1940: first anti-Jewish laws.
November 1941: first of 16,000 forced labourers arrive from Europe to build fortifications.
September 1942: 2,000 civilians deported to Germany for forced labour.
February 1943: 200 civilians deported to Germany for forced labour.
October 1943: convoy battle west of the Channel Islands; 504 Royal Navy sailors killed.
27 July 1944: Alderney Commandant refuses to send out rescue vessels to rescue crew of a Lancaster bomber that has been shot down.
9 May 1945: all 27,000 German soldiers on the islands surrender.
August 1945: German prisoners of war clear 117,000 mines.

CHANNEL ISLANDERS KILLED ON ACTIVE SERVICE WITH THE BRITISH FORCES.
Guernsey   221
Alderney   18
Sark   1

GERMAN WAR GRAVES: 568
SLAVE LABOUR DEATHS: 509
AIR RAID DEATHS: 93
DEATHS OF DEPORTEES: 45

© Martin Gilbert 2009

224

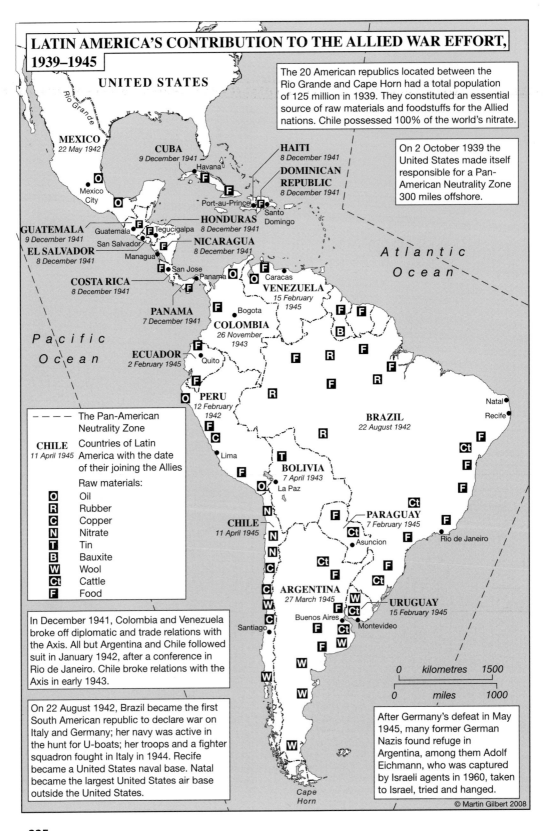

LATIN AMERICA'S CONTRIBUTION TO THE ALLIED WAR EFFORT, 1939–1945

UNITED STATES

The 20 American republics located between the Rio Grande and Cape Horn had a total population of 125 million in 1939. They constituted an essential source of raw materials and foodstuffs for the Allied nations. Chile possessed 100% of the world's nitrate.

On 2 October 1939 the United States made itself responsible for a Pan-American Neutrality Zone 300 miles offshore.

MEXICO
22 May 1942

CUBA
9 December 1941

Havana

HAITI
8 December 1941

DOMINICAN REPUBLIC
8 December 1941

Port-au-Prince

Santo Domingo

Mexico City

GUATEMALA
9 December 1941

Guatemala

HONDURAS
8 December 1941

Tegucigalpa

NICARAGUA
8 December 1941

EL SALVADOR
8 December 1941

San Salvador

Managua

COSTA RICA
8 December 1941

San Jose

Panama

Caracas

VENEZUELA
15 February 1945

PANAMA
7 December 1941

Bogota

COLOMBIA
26 November 1943

ECUADOR
2 February 1945

Quito

PERU
12 February 1942

Lima

Atlantic Ocean

Pacific Ocean

BRAZIL
22 August 1942

Natal

Recife

BOLIVIA
7 April 1943

La Paz

PARAGUAY
7 February 1945

Asuncion

Rio de Janeiro

CHILE
11 April 1945

ARGENTINA
27 March 1945

Santiago

Buenos Aires

Montevideo

URUGUAY
15 February 1945

Cape Horn

Legend

- – – – The Pan-American Neutrality Zone

CHILE
11 April 1945 — Countries of Latin America with the date of their joining the Allies

Raw materials:
- **O** Oil
- **R** Rubber
- **C** Copper
- **N** Nitrate
- **T** Tin
- **B** Bauxite
- **W** Wool
- **Ct** Cattle
- **F** Food

In December 1941, Colombia and Venezuela broke off diplomatic and trade relations with the Axis. All but Argentina and Chile followed suit in January 1942, after a conference in Rio de Janeiro. Chile broke relations with the Axis in early 1943.

On 22 August 1942, Brazil became the first South American republic to declare war on Italy and Germany; her navy was active in the hunt for U-boats; her troops and a fighter squadron fought in Italy in 1944. Recife became a United States naval base. Natal became the largest United States air base outside the United States.

After Germany's defeat in May 1945, many former German Nazis found refuge in Argentina, among them Adolf Eichmann, who was captured by Israeli agents in 1960, taken to Israel, tried and hanged.

0   kilometres   1500
0   miles   1000

© Martin Gilbert 2008

INDIA'S CONTRIBUTION TO THE DEFEAT OF ITALY, GERMANY AND JAPAN, 1939–1945

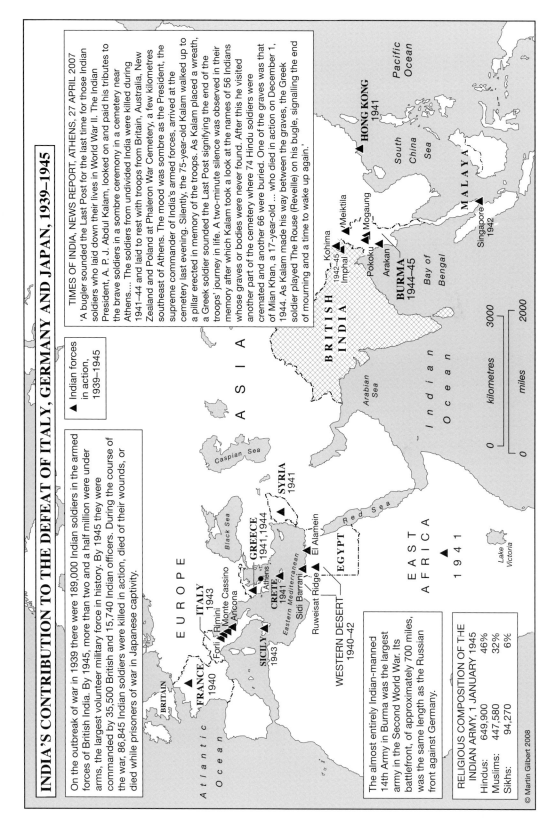

On the outbreak of war in 1939 there were 189,000 Indian soldiers in the armed forces of British India. By 1945, more than two and a half million were under arms, the largest volunteer military force in history. By 1945 they were commanded by 35,500 British and 15,740 Indian officers. During the course of the war, 86,845 Indian soldiers were killed in action, died of their wounds, or died while prisoners of war in Japanese captivity.

TIMES OF INDIA, NEWS REPORT, ATHENS, 27 APRIL 2007
'A bugler sounded the Last Post for the last time for those Indian soldiers who laid down their lives in World War II. The Indian President, A. P. J. Abdul Kalam, looked on and paid his tributes to the brave soldiers in a sombre ceremony in a cemetery near Athens.... The soldiers from undivided India were killed during 1941–44 and laid to rest with troops from Britain, Australia, New Zealand and Poland at Phaleron War Cemetery, a few kilometres southeast of Athens. The mood was sombre as the President, the supreme commander of India's armed forces, arrived at the cemetery last evening. Silently, the 75-year-old Kalam walked up to a pillar erected in memory of the troops. As Kalam placed a wreath, a Greek soldier sounded the Last Post signifying the end of the troops' journey in life. A two-minute silence was observed in their memory after which Kalam took a look at the names of 56 Indians whose graves or bodies were never found. After this he visited another part of the cemetery where 74 Hindu soldiers were cremated and another 66 were buried. One of the graves was that of Mian Khan, a 17-year-old ... who died in action on December 1, 1944. As Kalam made his way between the graves, the Greek soldier played The Rouse (Reveille) on his bugle, signalling the end of mourning and a time to wake up again.'

▲ Indian forces in action, 1939–1945

The almost entirely Indian-manned 14th Army in Burma was the largest army in the Second World War. Its battlefront, of approximately 700 miles, was the same length as the Russian front against Germany.

RELIGIOUS COMPOSITION OF THE INDIAN ARMY, 1 JANUARY 1945
Hindus:	649,900	46%
Muslims:	447,580	32%
Sikhs:	94,270	6%

WESTERN DESERT 1940–42

© Martin Gilbert 2008

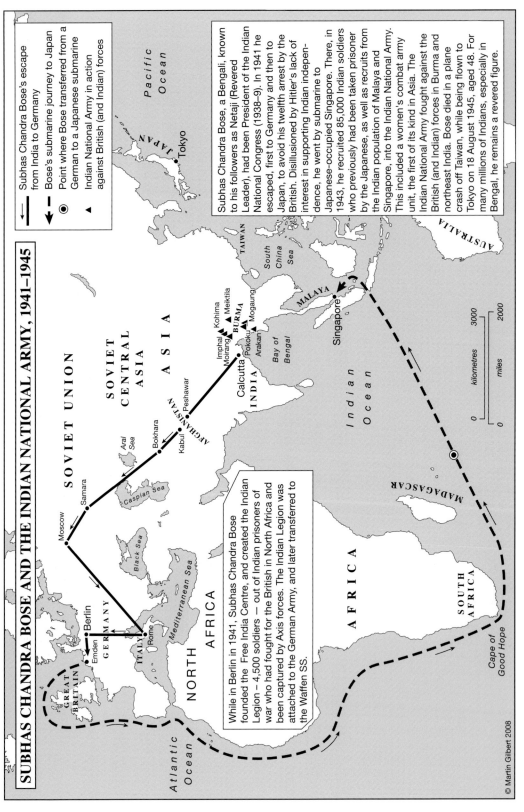

SUBHAS CHANDRA BOSE AND THE INDIAN NATIONAL ARMY, 1941–1945

→   Subhas Chandra Bose's escape from India to Germany

↠   Bose's submarine journey to Japan

◉   Point where Bose transferred from a German to a Japanese submarine

▲   Indian National Army in action against British (and Indian) forces

Subhas Chandra Bose, a Bengali, known to his followers as Netaji (Revered Leader), had been President of the Indian National Congress (1938–9). In 1941 he escaped, first to Germany and then to Japan, to avoid his twelfth arrest by the British. Disillusioned by Hitler's lack of interest in supporting Indian independence, he went by submarine to Japanese-occupied Singapore. There, in 1943, he recruited 85,000 Indian soldiers who previously had been taken prisoner by the Japanese, as well as recruits from the Indian population of Malaya and Singapore, into the Indian National Army. This included a women's combat army unit, the first of its kind in Asia. The Indian National Army fought against the British (and Indian) forces in Burma and northeast India. Bose died in a plane crash off Taiwan, while being flown to Tokyo on 18 August 1945, aged 48. For many millions of Indians, especially in Bengal, he remains a revered figure.

While in Berlin in 1941, Subhas Chandra Bose founded the Free India Centre, and created the Indian Legion – 4,500 soldiers – out of Indian prisoners of war who had fought for the British in North Africa and been captured by Axis forces. The Indian Legion was attached to the German Army, and later transferred to the Waffen SS.

© Martin Gilbert 2008

227

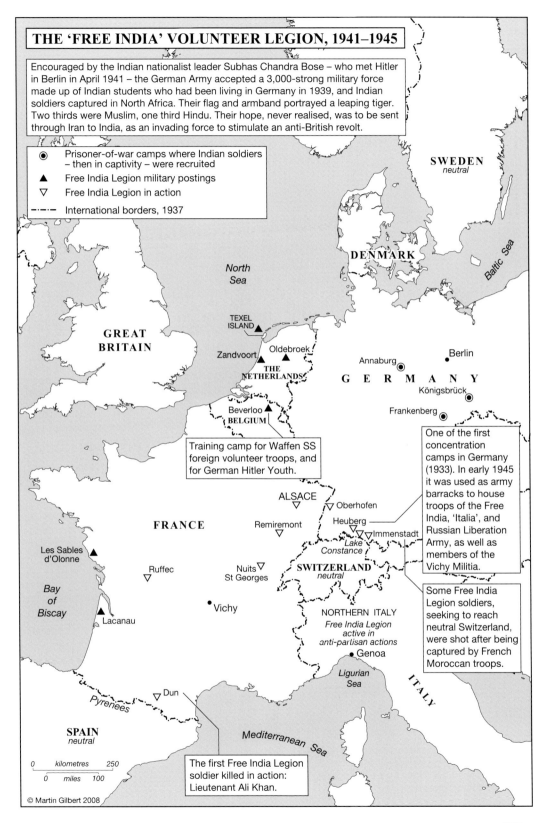

THE 'FREE INDIA' VOLUNTEER LEGION, 1941–1945

Encouraged by the Indian nationalist leader Subhas Chandra Bose – who met Hitler in Berlin in April 1941 – the German Army accepted a 3,000-strong military force made up of Indian students who had been living in Germany in 1939, and Indian soldiers captured in North Africa. Their flag and armband portrayed a leaping tiger. Two thirds were Muslim, one third Hindu. Their hope, never realised, was to be sent through Iran to India, as an invading force to stimulate an anti-British revolt.

⊙   Prisoner-of-war camps where Indian soldiers – then in captivity – were recruited

▲   Free India Legion military postings

▽   Free India Legion in action

–·–·–   International borders, 1937

SWEDEN
neutral

DENMARK

North Sea

Baltic Sea

GREAT BRITAIN

TEXEL ISLAND ▲

Zandvoort ▲   Oldebroek ▲
THE NETHERLANDS

Annaburg ⊙   • Berlin

G E R M A N Y

Königsbrück ⊙

Beverloo ▲
BELGIUM

Frankenberg ⊙

Training camp for Waffen SS foreign volunteer troops, and for German Hitler Youth.

One of the first concentration camps in Germany (1933). In early 1945 it was used as army barracks to house troops of the Free India, 'Italia', and Russian Liberation Army, as well as members of the Vichy Militia.

ALSACE

▽ Oberhofen

Heuberg

FRANCE

Remiremont ▽

▽ Immenstadt

Lake Constance

Les Sables d'Olonne ▲

Ruffec ▽

Nuits ▽ St Georges

SWITZERLAND
neutral

Some Free India Legion soldiers, seeking to reach neutral Switzerland, were shot after being captured by French Moroccan troops.

Bay of Biscay

• Vichy

Lacanau ▲

NORTHERN ITALY
Free India Legion active in anti-partisan actions

• Genoa

Ligurian Sea

▽ Dun

Pyrenees

I T A L Y

SPAIN
neutral

Mediterranean Sea

| 0 | kilometres | 250 |
| 0 | miles | 100 |

The first Free India Legion soldier killed in action: Lieutenant Ali Khan.

© Martin Gilbert 2008

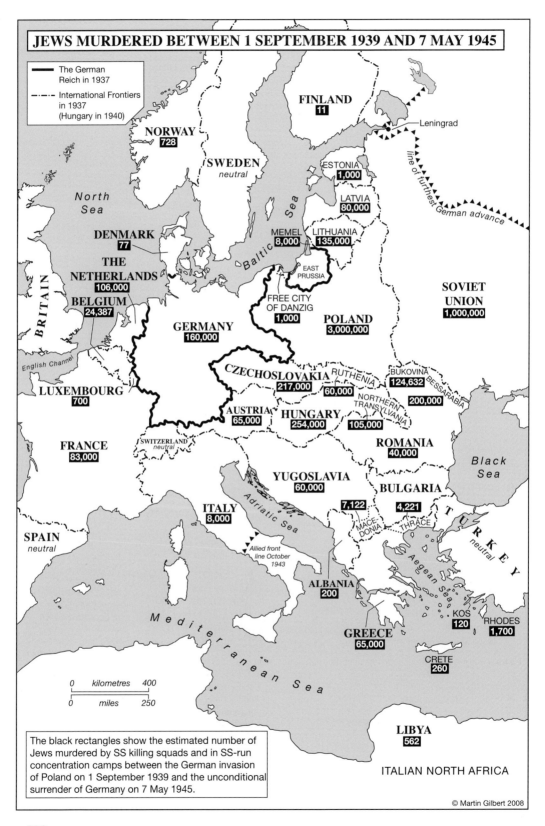

JEWS MURDERED BETWEEN 1 SEPTEMBER 1939 AND 7 MAY 1945

The German Reich in 1937

International Frontiers in 1937 (Hungary in 1940)

FINLAND
11

Leningrad

line of furthest German advance

NORWAY
728

SWEDEN
neutral

ESTONIA
1,000

LATVIA
80,000

North Sea

Baltic Sea

MEMEL
8,000

LITHUANIA
135,000

DENMARK
77

THE NETHERLANDS
106,000

EAST PRUSSIA

SOVIET UNION
1,000,000

BELGIUM
24,387

FREE CITY OF DANZIG
1,000

BRITAIN

GERMANY
160,000

POLAND
3,000,000

English Channel

LUXEMBOURG
700

CZECHOSLOVAKIA
217,000

RUTHENIA
60,000

BUKOVINA
124,632

BESSARABIA
200,000

AUSTRIA
65,000

HUNGARY
254,000

NORTHERN TRANSYLVANIA
105,000

FRANCE
83,000

SWITZERLAND
neutral

ROMANIA
40,000

Black Sea

YUGOSLAVIA
60,000

BULGARIA
4,221

TURKEY
neutral

ITALY
8,000

Adriatic Sea

7,122

MACEDONIA

THRACE

SPAIN
neutral

Allied front line October 1943

Aegean Sea

ALBANIA
200

KOS
120

RHODES
1,700

GREECE
65,000

CRETE
260

Mediterranean Sea

0 kilometres 400

0 miles 250

LIBYA
562

The black rectangles show the estimated number of Jews murdered by SS killing squads and in SS-run concentration camps between the German invasion of Poland on 1 September 1939 and the unconditional surrender of Germany on 7 May 1945.

ITALIAN NORTH AFRICA

© Martin Gilbert 2008

CHRISTIANS WHO SAVED JEWS FROM DEATH, 1939–1945

NORWAY 42

SWEDEN 10

ESTONIA 3

RUSSIA 163

North Sea

DENMARK 22

LATVIA 120

Baltic Sea

LITHUANIA 761
Kaunas

GREAT BRITAIN 14

THE NETHERLANDS 4,947

BELARUS 602

Berlin

GERMANY 460

POLAND 6,135

Kharkov

1,512

BELGIUM 1

CZECH REPUBLIC 108

UKRAINE 2,246

LUXEMBOURG

SLOVAKIA 489

Vienna

MOLDOVA 78

FRANCE 2,991

SWITZERLAND 45

AUSTRIA 85

Budapest

HUNGARY 725

Bordeaux

SLOVENIA 6

ROMANIA 56

Marseille

CROATIA 102

BOSNIA 40

SERBIA 125

SPAIN 4

ITALY 468

Adriatic Sea

YUGOSLAVIA

BULGARIA 19

Black Sea

MONTENEGRO 1

MACEDONIA 9

68

GREECE 282

TURKEY 1

ALBANIA

Aegean Sea

Mediterranean Sea

0 kilometres 300
0 miles 200

Rhodes

—·—·— International borders, 1937
·········· Post-1991 divisions of the Soviet Union
© Martin Gilbert 2008

The total number of Christians who saved Jewish lives during the Holocaust, and have been honoured by the State of Israel and the Yad Vashem Holocaust memorial in Jerusalem since 1953 reached 22,765 on 1 January 2009 (as shown on this map). They are given the title 'Righteous Among the Nations'. They are also known as 'Righteous Gentiles'. This map shows the awards given country by country, during that fifty-five-year period.

At their own request, the Norwegian and Danish resistance movements received their honours collectively.

Also recognized by Yad Vashem as Righteous are thirteen Armenians (including one in Budapest and one in Vienna), two Chinese (one in Kharkov, the other in Vienna), a Brazilian diplomat (in Berlin), a Portuguese diplomat (in Bordeaux), a Japanese diplomat (in Kaunas), and three United States citizens, one of whom Varian Fry, who, from Marseille, enabled many hundreds of Jews to leave Europe through Marseille and Spain. The one Turkish citizen indicated on the map was also a diplomat, the Turkish Consul on the island of Rhodes.

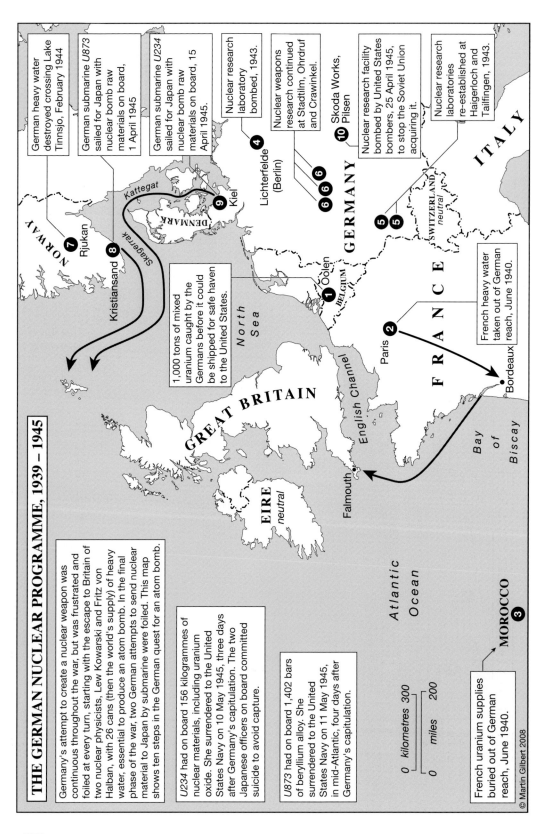

THE GERMAN NUCLEAR PROGRAMME, 1939 – 1945

German heavy water destroyed crossing Lake Tinnsjo, February 1944

German submarine *U873* sailed for Japan with nuclear bomb raw materials on board, 1 April 1945

German submarine *U234* sailed for Japan with nuclear bomb raw materials on board, 15 April 1945.

Nuclear research laboratory bombed, 1943.

Nuclear weapons research continued at Stadtilm, Ohrdruf and Crawinkel.

Nuclear research facility bombed by United States bombers, 25 April 1945, to stop the Soviet Union acquiring it.

Nuclear research laboratories re-established at Haigerloch and Tailfingen, 1943.

Skoda Works, Pilsen

ITALY

Kattegat

Skagerrak

NORWAY

Rjukan

Kristiansand

DENMARK

Kiel

Lichterfelde (Berlin)

GERMANY

SWITZERLAND neutral

Oolen

Paris

BELGIUM

FRANCE

French heavy water taken out of German reach, June 1940.

North Sea

1,000 tons of mixed uranium caught by the Germans before it could be shipped for safe haven to the United States.

Bordeaux

GREAT BRITAIN

English Channel

Bay of Biscay

Falmouth

EIRE neutral

Atlantic Ocean

MOROCCO

Germany's attempt to create a nuclear weapon was continuous throughout the war, but was frustrated and foiled at every turn, starting with the escape to Britain of two nuclear physicists, Lew Kowarski and Fritz von Halban, with 26 cans (then the world's supply) of heavy water, essential to produce an atom bomb. In the final phase of the war, two German attempts to send nuclear material to Japan by submarine were foiled. This map shows ten steps in the German quest for an atom bomb.

U234 had on board 156 kilogrammes of nuclear materials, including uranium oxide. She surrendered to the United States Navy on 10 May 1945, three days after Germany's capitulation. The two Japanese officers on board committed suicide to avoid capture.

U873 had on board 1,402 bars of beryllium alloy. She surrendered to the United States Navy on 11 May 1945, in mid-Atlantic, four days after Germany's capitulation.

0 kilometres 300
0 miles 200

French uranium supplies buried out of German reach, June 1940.

© Martin Gilbert 2008

231

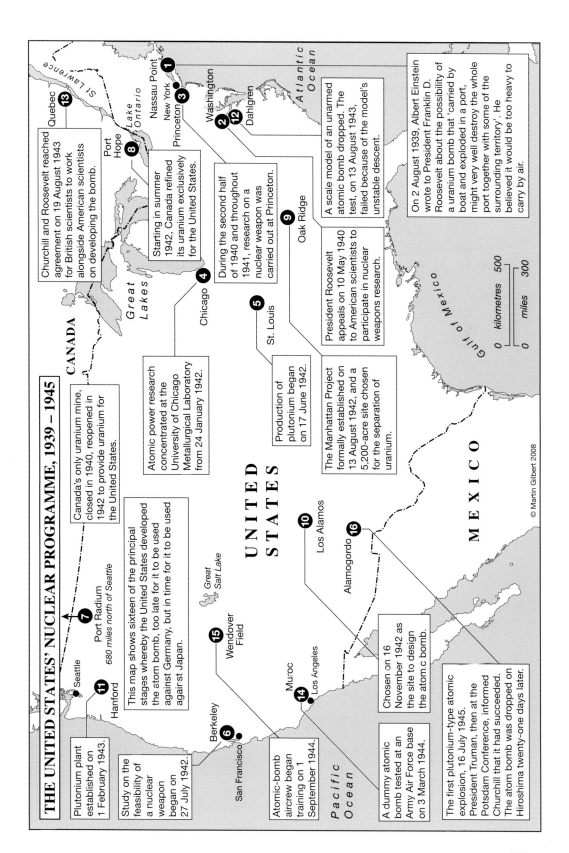

THE UNITED STATES' NUCLEAR PROGRAMME, 1939 – 1945

CANADA

Churchill and Roosevelt reached agreement on 19 August 1943 for British scientists to work alongside American scientists on developing the bomb.

Canada's only uranium mine, closed in 1940, reopened in 1942 to provide uranium for the United States.

Starting in summer 1942, Canada refined its uranium exclusively for the United States.

During the second half of 1940 and throughout 1941, research on a nuclear weapon was carried out at Princeton.

A scale model of an unarmed atomic bomb dropped. The test, on 13 August 1943, failed because of the model's unstable descent.

On 2 August 1939, Albert Einstein wrote to President Franklin D. Roosevelt about the possibility of a uranium bomb that 'carried by boat and exploded in a port, might very well destroy the whole port together with some of the surrounding territory'. He believed it would be too heavy to carry by air.

Atomic power research concentrated at the University of Chicago Metallurgical Laboratory from 24 January 1942.

President Roosevelt appeals on 10 May 1940 to American scientists to participate in nuclear weapons research.

Production of plutonium began on 17 June 1942.

The Manhattan Project formally established on 13 August 1942, and a 5,200-acre site chosen for the separation of uranium.

Plutonium plant established on 1 February 1943.

Study on the feasibility of a nuclear weapon began on 27 July 1942.

This map shows sixteen of the principal stages whereby the United States developed the atom bomb, too late for it to be used against Germany, but in time for it to be used against Japan.

Atomic-bomb aircrew began training on 1 September 1944.

Chosen on 16 November 1942 as the site to design the atomic bomb.

A dummy atomic bomb tested at an Army Air Force base on 3 March 1944.

The first plutonium-type atomic explosion, 16 July 1945. President Truman, then at the Potsdam Conference, informed Churchill that it had succeeded. The atom bomb was dropped on Hiroshima twenty-one days later.

Port Radium
680 miles north of Seattle

UNITED STATES

MEXICO

Great Lakes

Lake Ontario

Atlantic Ocean

St Lawrence

Quebec

Port Hope

Nassau Point

New York

Princeton

Washington

Dahlgren

Chicago

St. Louis

Oak Ridge

Seattle

Hanford

Berkeley

San Francisco

Great Salt Lake

Wendover Field

Muroc

Los Angeles

Los Alamos

Alamogordo

Gulf of Mexico

Pacific Ocean

© Martin Gilbert 2008

0   kilometres   500

0   miles   300

232

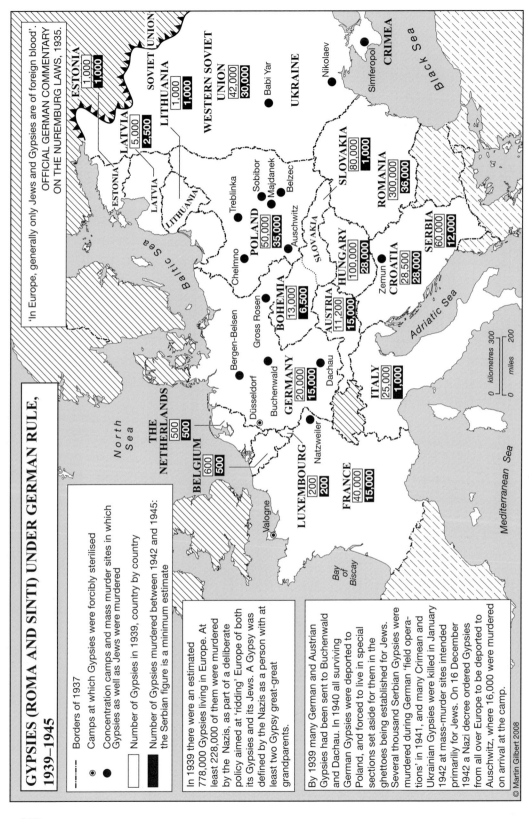

GYPSIES (ROMA AND SINTI) UNDER GERMAN RULE, 1939–1945

'In Europe, generally only Jews and Gypsies are of foreign blood'.
OFFICIAL GERMAN COMMENTARY
ON THE NUREMBURG LAWS, 1935.

Borders of 1937

⊙ Camps at which Gypsies were forcibly sterilised

● Concentration camps and mass murder sites in which Gypsies as well as Jews were murdered

☐ Number of Gypsies in 1939, country by country

■ Number of Gypsies murdered between 1942 and 1945: the Serbian figure is a minimum estimate

In 1939 there were an estimated 778,000 Gypsies living in Europe. At least 228,000 of them were murdered by the Nazis, as part of a deliberate policy aimed at 'ridding' Europe of both its Gypsies and its Jews. A Gypsy was defined by the Nazis as a person with at least two Gypsy great-great grandparents.

By 1939 many German and Austrian Gypsies had been sent to Buchenwald and Dachau. In 1940 all surviving German Gypsies were deported to Poland, and forced to live in special sections set aside for them in the ghettoes being established for Jews. Several thousand Serbian Gypsies were murdered during German 'field operations' in 1941, and many Crimean and Ukrainian Gypsies were killed in January 1942 at mass-murder sites intended primarily for Jews. On 16 December 1942 a Nazi decree ordered Gypsies from all over Europe to be deported to Auschwitz, where 16,000 were murdered on arrival at the camp.

© Martin Gilbert 2008

ESTONIA 1,000 / 1,000

SOVIET UNION

LITHUANIA 1,000 / 1,000

LATVIA 5,000 / 2,500

WESTERN SOVIET UNION 42,000 / 30,000

UKRAINE

● Babi Yar

● Nikolaev

● Simferopol

CRIMEA

Black Sea

ESTONIA
LATVIA
LITHUANIA

Baltic Sea

● Treblinka
● Sobibor
● Majdanek
● Belzec

SLOVAKIA 80,000 / 1,000

ROMANIA 300,000 / 36,000

POLAND 50,000 / 35,000

● Auschwitz

● Chelmno

SLOVAKIA

HUNGARY 100,000 / 28,000

SERBIA 60,000 / 12,000

CROATIA 28,500 / 28,000

● Zemun

BOHEMIA 13,000 / 6,500

● Gross Rosen

AUSTRIA 11,200 / 15,000

Adriatic Sea

North Sea

● Bergen-Belsen

GERMANY 20,000 / 15,000

● Buchenwald

● Düsseldorf

● Dachau

ITALY 25,000 / 1,000

THE NETHERLANDS 500 / 500

BELGIUM 600 / 500

● Natzweiler

LUXEMBOURG 200 / 200

FRANCE 40,000 / 15,000

⊙ Valogne

Bay of Biscay

Mediterranean Sea

0 kilometres 300
0 miles 200

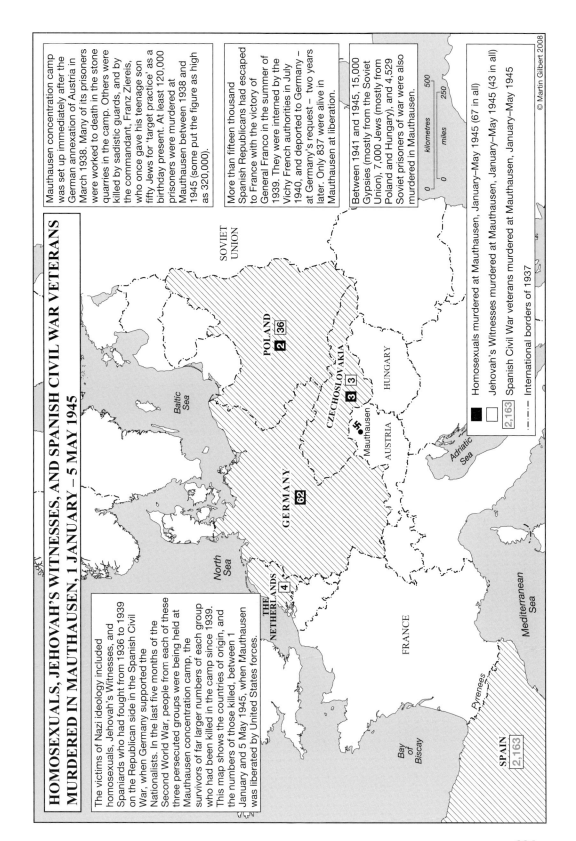

HOMOSEXUALS, JEHOVAH'S WITNESSES, AND SPANISH CIVIL WAR VETERANS MURDERED IN MAUTHAUSEN, 1 JANUARY – 5 MAY 1945

The victims of Nazi ideology included homosexuals, Jehovah's Witnesses, and Spaniards who had fought from 1936 to 1939 on the Republican side in the Spanish Civil War, when Germany supported the Nationalists. In the last five months of the Second World War, people from each of these three persecuted groups were being held at Mauthausen concentration camp, the survivors of far larger numbers of each group who had been killed in the camp since 1939. This map shows the countries of origin, and the numbers of those killed, between 1 January and 5 May 1945, when Mauthausen was liberated by United States forces.

Mauthausen concentration camp was set up immediately after the German annexation of Austria in March 1938. Many of its prisoners were worked to death in the stone quarries in the camp. Others were killed by sadistic guards, and by the commandant, Franz Ziereis, who once gave his teenage son fifty Jews for 'target practice' as a birthday present. At least 120,000 prisoners were murdered at Mauthausen between 1938 and 1945 (some put the figure as high as 320,000).

More than fifteen thousand Spanish Republicans had escaped to France with the victory of General Franco in the summer of 1939. They were interned by the Vichy French authorities in July 1940, and deported to Germany – at Germany's request – two years later. Only 837 were alive in Mauthausen at liberation.

Between 1941 and 1945, 15,000 Gypsies (mostly from the Soviet Union), 7,000 Jews (mostly from Poland and Hungary), and 4,529 Soviet prisoners of war were also murdered in Mauthausen.

SOVIET UNION

Baltic Sea

POLAND 2 36

CZECHOSLOVAKIA 3 3

3

HUNGARY

Mauthausen

AUSTRIA

GERMANY 62

North Sea

THE NETHERLANDS 4

Adriatic Sea

FRANCE

Bay of Biscay

Pyrenees

SPAIN 2,163

Mediterranean Sea

■ Homosexuals murdered at Mauthausen, January–May 1945 (67 in all)

□ Jehovah's Witnesses murdered at Mauthausen, January–May 1945 (43 in all)

2,163 Spanish Civil War veterans murdered at Mauthausen, January–May 1945

International borders of 1937

0   250   500
kilometres
0   250   miles

© Martin Gilbert 2008

234

AFTERMATH

The White Cliffs of Dover

I'll never forget the people I met
Braving those angry skies
I remember well as the shadows fell
The light of hope in their eyes

And though I'm far away
I still can hear them say
'Thumbs up. . .'
But when the dawn comes up

There'll be bluebirds over
The white cliffs of Dover
Tomorrow
Just you wait and see

There'll be love and laughter
And peace ever after
Tomorrow
When the world is free

The shepherd will tend his sheep
The valley will bloom again
And Jimmy will go to sleep
In his own little room again

There'll be bluebirds over
The white cliffs of Dover
Tomorrow
Just you wait and see

Music by Walter Kent
Lyrics by Nat Burton
Published in 1941

Made famous by Vera Lynn
The lyricist, Nat Burton, an American who had never been
to England, died on 21 March 1945, at the age of forty-four,
seven weeks before the end of the war in Europe.

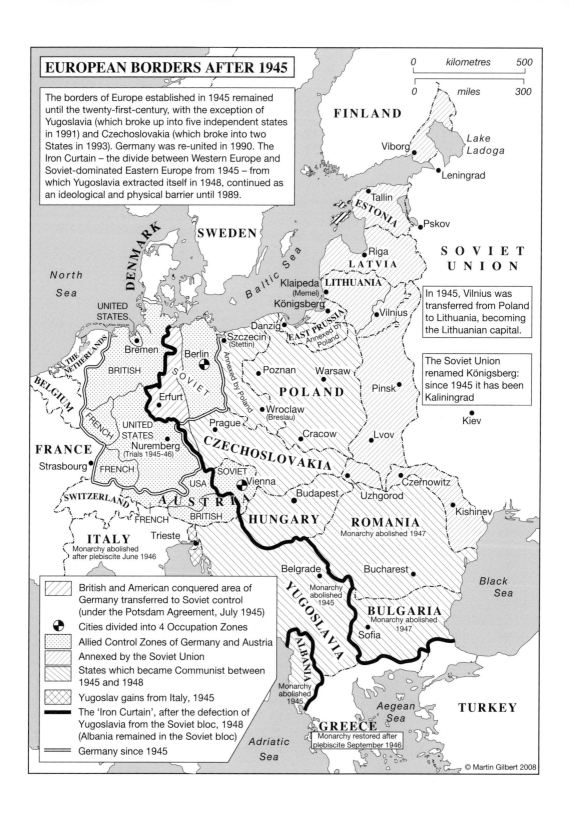

EUROPEAN BORDERS AFTER 1945

The borders of Europe established in 1945 remained until the twenty-first-century, with the exception of Yugoslavia (which broke up into five independent states in 1991) and Czechoslovakia (which broke into two States in 1993). Germany was re-united in 1990. The Iron Curtain – the divide between Western Europe and Soviet-dominated Eastern Europe from 1945 – from which Yugoslavia extracted itself in 1948, continued as an ideological and physical barrier until 1989.

0   kilometres   500

0   miles   300

FINLAND

Viborg

Lake Ladoga

Leningrad

Tallin

ESTONIA

Pskov

SWEDEN

DENMARK

Riga

LATVIA

SOVIET UNION

North Sea

Klaipeda (Memel)

LITHUANIA

Königsberg

Vilnius

In 1945, Vilnius was transferred from Poland to Lithuania, becoming the Lithuanian capital.

Baltic Sea

UNITED STATES

Danzig

EAST PRUSSIA Annexed by Poland

THE NETHERLANDS

Bremen

Szczecin (Stettin)

Berlin

Annexed by Poland

Poznan

Warsaw

Pinsk

The Soviet Union renamed Königsberg: since 1945 it has been Kaliningrad

BELGIUM

BRITISH

SOVIET

POLAND

Erfurt

Wroclaw (Breslau)

Kiev

UNITED STATES

Prague

Cracow

Lvov

FRANCE

Nuremberg (Trials 1945-46)

CZECHOSLOVAKIA

Strasbourg

FRENCH

USA

SOVIET

Vienna

Czernowitz

SWITZERLAND

AUSTRIA

Budapest

Uzhgorod

Kishinev

FRENCH

BRITISH

HUNGARY

ROMANIA

Monarchy abolished 1947

ITALY

Monarchy abolished after plebiscite June 1946

Trieste

Belgrade

Bucharest

Black Sea

Monarchy abolished 1945

YUGOSLAVIA

BULGARIA

Monarchy abolished 1947

Sofia

ALBANIA

Monarchy abolished 1945

Aegean Sea

TURKEY

Legend

- British and American conquered area of Germany transferred to Soviet control (under the Potsdam Agreement, July 1945)
- Cities divided into 4 Occupation Zones
- Allied Control Zones of Germany and Austria
- Annexed by the Soviet Union
- States which became Communist between 1945 and 1948
- Yugoslav gains from Italy, 1945
- The 'Iron Curtain', after the defection of Yugoslavia from the Soviet bloc, 1948 (Albania remained in the Soviet bloc)
- Germany since 1945

Adriatic Sea

GREECE

Monarchy restored after plebiscite September 1946

© Martin Gilbert 2008

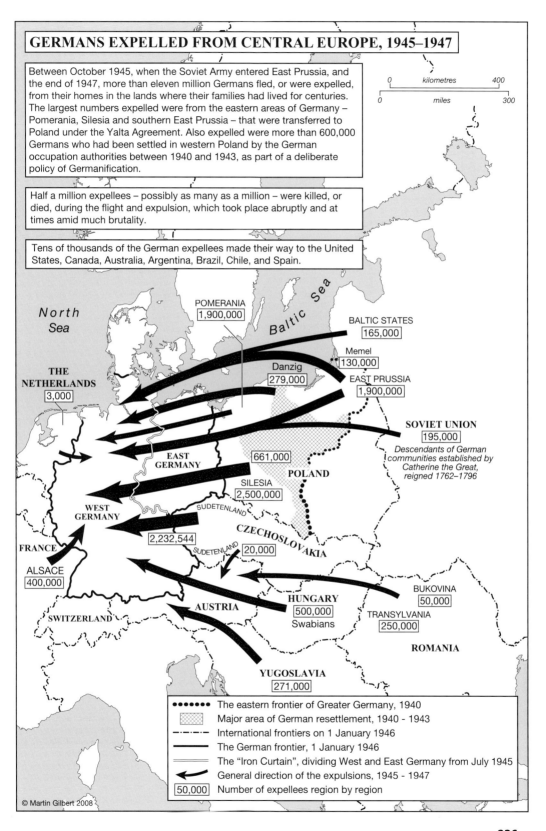

GERMANS EXPELLED FROM CENTRAL EUROPE, 1945–1947

Between October 1945, when the Soviet Army entered East Prussia, and the end of 1947, more than eleven million Germans fled, or were expelled, from their homes in the lands where their families had lived for centuries. The largest numbers expelled were from the eastern areas of Germany – Pomerania, Silesia and southern East Prussia – that were transferred to Poland under the Yalta Agreement. Also expelled were more than 600,000 Germans who had been settled in western Poland by the German occupation authorities between 1940 and 1943, as part of a deliberate policy of Germanification.

Half a million expellees – possibly as many as a million – were killed, or died, during the flight and expulsion, which took place abruptly and at times amid much brutality.

Tens of thousands of the German expellees made their way to the United States, Canada, Australia, Argentina, Brazil, Chile, and Spain.

0 | kilometres | 400
0 | miles | 300

North Sea

Baltic Sea

POMERANIA
1,900,000

BALTIC STATES
165,000

Memel
130,000

Danzig
279,000

EAST PRUSSIA
1,900,000

THE NETHERLANDS
3,000

SOVIET UNION
195,000

Descendants of German communities established by Catherine the Great, reigned 1762–1796

EAST GERMANY

661,000

POLAND

SILESIA
2,500,000

SUDETENLAND

WEST GERMANY

CZECHOSLOVAKIA

2,232,544

SUDETENLAND
20,000

FRANCE

ALSACE
400,000

BUKOVINA
50,000

AUSTRIA

HUNGARY
500,000
Swabians

TRANSYLVANIA
250,000

SWITZERLAND

ROMANIA

YUGOSLAVIA
271,000

•••••• The eastern frontier of Greater Germany, 1940
▨ Major area of German resettlement, 1940 - 1943
–·–·– International frontiers on 1 January 1946
—— The German frontier, 1 January 1946
═══ The "Iron Curtain", dividing West and East Germany from July 1945
← General direction of the expulsions, 1945 - 1947
50,000 Number of expellees region by region

© Martin Gilbert 2008

236

DISPLACED PERSONS' CAMPS (DP CAMPS) IN GERMANY AND AUSTRIA, 1945–1957

--·--·-- European borders, 1946

▲ Displace Persons' camps (DP camps)

North Sea

Baltic Sea

POLAND

BERLIN
Düppel
Mariendorf

SOVIET SECTOR

CZECHOSLOVAKIA

THE NETHERLANDS

BELGIUM

LUX

G E R M A N Y

BRITISH SECTOR

Flensburg
Eckernförde
Rendsburg Kiel
Itzehoe
Lübeck
Pinneberg
Emden
Bremen
Meppen
Lingen
Bergen-Belsen
Hannover Peine
Minden Braunschweig
Gronau
Greven Hameln Hildesheim
Detmold
Bocholt Lippstadt Goslar
Gladbeck Paderborn
Göttingen
Mülheim Bochum
Hann-Münden
Mönchengladbach Düsseldorf
Remscheid Eschwege
Zigenhain Cornberg
Aachen Trutzhain Bad Hersfeld
Wetzlar Wildflecken
Frankfurt-Zeilsheim Altenstadt
Schauenstein
Babenhausen Aschaffenburg
Bensheim Lindenfels Bayreuth
Lampertheim Bamberg
Hersbruck
Bad Mergentheim Amberg
Fürth
Heilbronn Ansbach
Dinkelsbühl
Stuttgart
Heidenheim

FRENCH SECTOR

FRENCH SECTOR

FRANCE

AMERICAN SECTOR

Deggendorf
Pocking
Leipheim
Augsburg Kloster Indersdorf
Landsberg Munich Braunau-am-Inn
Bad Gabersee Linz-Bindemichel
Wörishofen Feldafing Bad Aibling Ebensee
Ainring Salzburg
Bad Reichenhall Hallein
Mittenwald Föhrenwald Admont
Saalfelden Trofaiach
Innsbruck Kapfenberg
Bad Gastein Judenburg
Lienz-Peggetz Leibnitz
Klagenfurt

Ried im Innkris

AUSTRIA

HUNGARY

SWITZERLAND
neutral

0 kilometres 150
0 miles 100

© Martin Gilbert 2008

At least eleven million people were displaced from their homes by the Second World War. Many were not welcome back, or had no homes to which to return. Displaced Persons' camps were set up in occupied zones of Germany and Austria: some were in former German concentration camps, others in hotels, hostels, hospitals, former military barracks and private homes. On 1 October 1945 the United Nations Relief and Rehabilitation Administration (UNRRA), which had been running many of the camps, took responsibility for their administration.

Föhrenwald camp was built in 1939 to house construction workers for IG Farben. During the war it was populated by slave labourers. In June 1945 it was taken over by the United States Army administration of postwar Germany's American sector, to house DPs, at first of Jewish, Yugoslav, Hungarian and Baltic origin. On 3 October 1945, General Dwight D. Eisenhower ordered that Föhrenwald become an exclusively Jewish DP camp, after he had found living conditions at Feldafing Jewish DPcamp unacceptable. Föhrenwald, whose last inmate left on 28 February 1957, was the final DP camp to be closed.

DISPLACED PERSONS' CAMPS (DP CAMPS) IN ITALY, 1945–1950

The Rimini DP camp housed 7,100 Ukrainians – former prisoners of war of the British – members of the Ukrainian National Army who had earlier fought in the SS Galicia Division against Soviet forces, and against Yugoslav partisans.

The 1,650 Jewish DPs in Adriatica organised both a Yiddish and an Israeli-style theatre, and had a daily radio show. They also formed football, volleyball and table tennis teams, which travelled to Bari to compete with DP camp teams in southern Italy.

▲ Displaced Persons' camps (DP camps)

The DP camps at Naples and Reggio Emilia housed Yugoslav, Lithuanian, Latvian, Polish, Hungarian and Ukrainian DPs. The camp at Fermo housed Croatians.

Milan • ▲ Adriatica
Rivoli
River Po ▲ Cremona
▲ Turin
Grugliasco
Praglia ▲ • Genoa
Carbonara ▲
Reggio Emilia ▲ ▲ Modena
Bologna ▲
Imola ▲ ▲ Rimini
Forli ▲ Riccione
• Pisa Senigallia ▲ Ancona
Livorno (Leghorn)
Jesi
Fermo

Trieste
Venice
Adriatic
Sea

Ligurian Sea
Apennine Mountains
ITALY

CORSICA

Rome •
Cinecittà
▲ Bagnoli
Barletta ▲ Trani
Bari ▲
Naples ▲ Accera
Vesuvius
• Salerno

SARDINIA

Ferramonti di Tarsia ▲
Tricase ▲
Santa Maria di Leuca ▲

• Cosenza

Tyrrhenian Sea

Mediterranean Sea

SICILY

0   kilometres   150
0   miles   100
© Martin Gilbert 2008

The Displaced Persons' (DP) camps in Italy housed Jewish survivors of the Holocaust; former members of Ukrainian, Croatian, Lithuanian and Latvian military units that had fought as part of the German army; and men, women and children who had fled from Central Europe to escape the ravages of war and the arrival of Communism.

A Jewish-organised clandestine operation (Aliyah Bet: Immigration B) brought survivors of the Holocaust from Eastern Europe, and from the DP camps of Germany and Austria, to Italy, from where they were sent by ship to Palestine, without the necessary British-issued certificates. Many were intercepted by the Royal Navy as their ships approached the shore of Palestine, and were deported to internment camps on Cyprus.

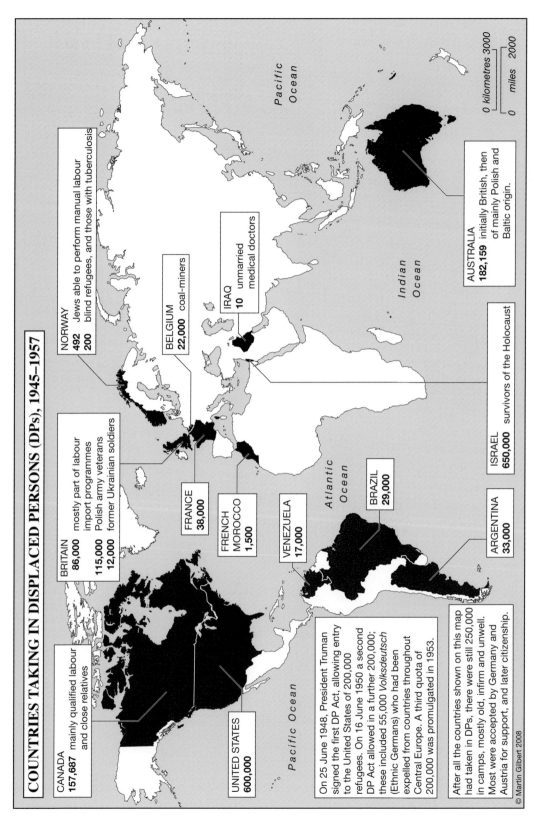

COUNTRIES TAKING IN DISPLACED PERSONS (DPs), 1945–1957

CANADA
157,687 mainly qualified labour and close relatives

NORWAY
492 Jews able to perform manual labour
200 blind refugees, and those with tuberculosis

BRITAIN
86,000 mostly part of labour import programmes
115,000 Polish army veterans
12,000 former Ukrainian soldiers

BELGIUM
22,000 coal-miners

IRAQ
10 unmarried medical doctors

AUSTRALIA **182,159** initially British, then of mainly Polish and Baltic origin.

FRANCE
38,000

FRENCH MOROCCO
1,500

VENEZUELA
17,000

BRAZIL
29,000

ISRAEL
650,000 survivors of the Holocaust

ARGENTINA
33,000

UNITED STATES
600,000

On 25 June 1948, President Truman signed the first DP Act, allowing entry to the United States of 200,000 refugees. On 16 June 1950 a second DP Act allowed in a further 200,000; these included 55,000 *Volksdeutsch* (Ethnic Germans) who had been expelled from countries throughout Central Europe. A third quota of 200,000 was promulgated in 1953.

After all the countries shown on this map had taken in DPs, there were still 250,000 in camps, mostly old, infirm and unwell. Most were accepted by Germany and Austria for support, and later citizenship.

Pacific Ocean

Pacific Ocean

Atlantic Ocean

Indian Ocean

0 kilometres 3000
0 miles 2000

© Martin Gilbert 2008

239

GERMAN SOLDIERS DEPORTED TO LABOUR CAMPS IN THE SOVIET UNION, 1942 – 1956

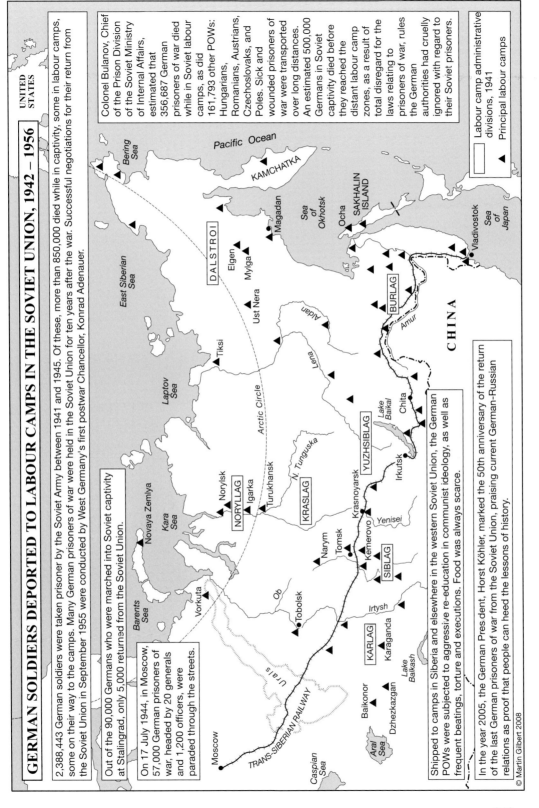

2,388,443 German soldiers were taken prisoner by the Soviet Army between 1941 and 1945. Of these, more than 850,000 died while in captivity, some in labour camps, some on their way to the camps. Many German prisoners of war were held in the Soviet Union for ten years after the war. Successful negotiations for their return from the Soviet Union in September 1955 were conducted by West Germany's first postwar Chancellor, Konrad Adenauer.

Out of the 90,000 Germans who were marched into Soviet captivity at Stalingrad, only 5,000 returned from the Soviet Union.

On 17 July 1944, in Moscow, 57,000 German prisoners of war, headed by 20 generals and 1,200 officers, were paraded through the streets.

Colonel Bulanov, Chief of the Prison Division of the Soviet Ministry of Internal Affairs, estimated that 356,687 German prisoners of war died while in Soviet labour camps, as did 161,793 other POWs: Hungarians, Romanians, Austrians, Czechoslovaks, and Poles. Sick and wounded prisoners of war were transported over long distances. An estimated 500,000 Germans in Soviet captivity died before they reached the distant labour camp zones, as a result of total disregard for the laws relating to prisoners of war, rules the German authorities had cruelly ignored with regard to their Soviet prisoners.

Shipped to camps in Siberia and elsewhere in the western Soviet Union, the German POWs were subjected to aggressive re-education in communist ideology, as well as frequent beatings, torture and executions. Food was always scarce.

In the year 2005, the German President, Horst Köhler, marked the 50th anniversary of the return of the last German prisoners of war from the Soviet Union, praising current German-Russian relations as proof that people can heed the lessons of history.

Labour camp administrative divisions, 1941

▲ Principal labour camps

UNITED STATES

Pacific Ocean

Bering Sea

KAMCHATKA

Sea of Okhotsk

SAKHALIN ISLAND

Ocha

Magadan

DALSTROI

Elgen

Mylga

Ust Nera

East Siberian Sea

Vladivostok

Sea of Japan

BURLAG

Amur

CHINA

Laptov Sea

Tiksi

Aldan

Lena

Chita

Lake Baikal

YUZHSIBLAG

Irkutsk

Arctic Circle

Kara Sea

Novaya Zemlya

Norylsk

NORYLLAG

Igarka

Turukhansk

N. Tunguska

Krasnoyarsk

KRASLAG

Yenisei

Kemerovo

SIBLAG

Narym

Tomsk

Barents Sea

Vorkuta

Tobolsk

Ob

Irtysh

Urals

Moscow

TRANS-SIBERIAN RAILWAY

Baikonor

Dzhezkazgan

KARLAG

Karaganda

Lake Balkash

Aral Sea

Caspian Sea

© Martin Gilbert 2008

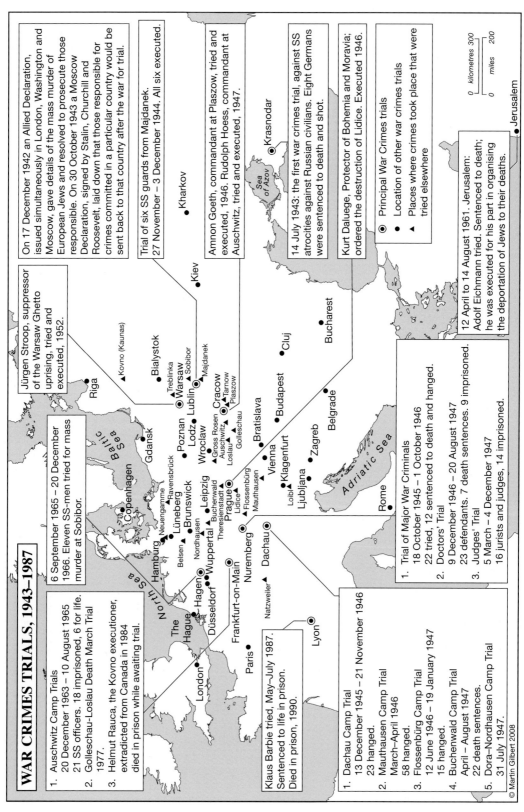

WAR CRIMES TRIALS, 1943–1987

1. Auschwitz Camp Trials
   20 December 1963 – 10 August 1965
   21 SS officers. 18 imprisoned, 6 for life.

2. Golleschau-Loslau Death March Trial
   1977.

3. Helmut Rauca, the Kovno executioner,
   extradicted from Canada in 1984
   died in prison while awaiting trial.

6 September 1965 – 20 December
1966. Eleven SS-men tried for mass
murder at Sobibor.

Jürgen Stroop, suppressor
of the Warsaw Ghetto
uprising, tried and
executed, 1952.

On 17 December 1942 an Allied Declaration,
issued simultaneously in London, Washington and
Moscow, gave details of the mass murder of
European Jews and resolved to prosecute those
responsible. On 30 October 1943 a Moscow
Declaration, signed by Stalin, Churchill and
Roosevelt, laid down that those responsible for
crimes committed in a particular country would be
sent back to that country after the war for trial.

Trial of six SS guards from Majdanek.
27 November – 3 December 1944. All six executed.

Amnon Goeth, commandant at Plaszow, tried and
executed, 1946. Rudolph Hoess, commandant at
Auschwitz, tried and executed, 1947.

14 July 1943: the first war crimes trial, against SS
atrocities against Russian civilians. Eight Germans
were sentenced to death and shot.

Kurt Daluege, Protector of Bohemia and Moravia;
ordered the destruction of Lidice. Executed 1946.

- ◉ Principal War Crimes trials
- ● Location of other war crimes trials
- ▲ Places where crimes took place that were
  tried elsewhere

0 — kilometres 300
0 — miles 200

12 April to 14 August 1961. Jerusalem:
Adolf Eichmann tried. Sentenced to death;
he was executed for his part in organising
the deportation of Jews to their deaths.

1. Trial of Major War Criminals
   18 October 1945 – 1 October 1946
   22 tried, 12 sentenced to death and hanged.

2. Doctors' Trial
   9 December 1946 – 20 August 1947
   23 defendants. 7 death sentences. 9 imprisoned.

3. Judges' Trial
   5 March – 4 December 1947
   16 jurists and judges, 14 imprisoned.

Klaus Barbie tried, May–July 1987.
Sentenced to life in prison.
Died in prison, 1990.

1. Dachau Camp Trial
   13 December 1945 – 21 November 1946
   23 hanged.

2. Mauthausen Camp Trial
   March–April 1946
   58 hanged.

3. Flossenbürg Camp Trial
   12 June 1946 – 19 January 1947
   15 hanged.

4. Buchenwald Camp Trial
   April – August 1947
   22 death sentences.

5. Dora-Nordhausen Camp Trial
   31 July 1947.

© Martin Gilbert 2008

241

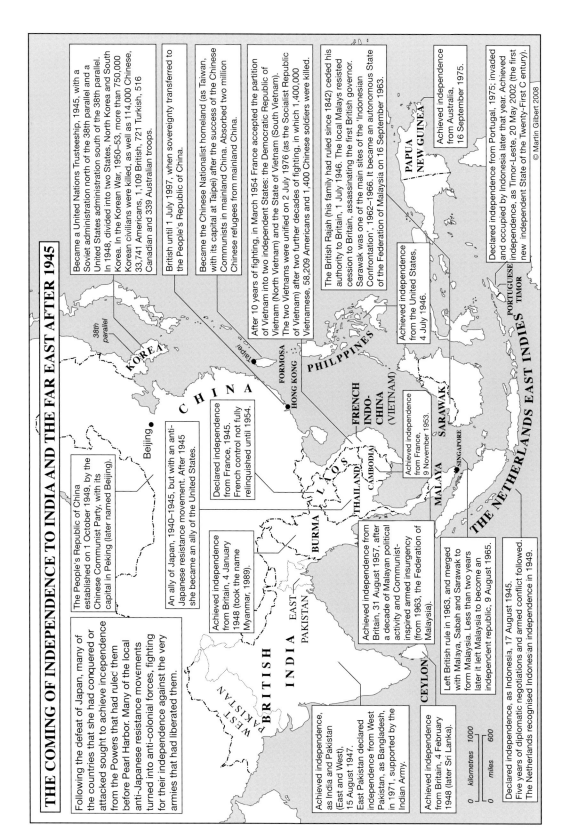

THE COMING OF INDEPENDENCE TO INDIA AND THE FAR EAST AFTER 1945

Following the defeat of Japan, many of the countries that she had conquered or attacked sought to achieve independence from the Powers that had ruled them before Pearl Harbor. Many of the local anti-Japanese resistance movements turned into anti-colonial forces, fighting for their independence against the very armies that had liberated them.

Became a United Nations Trusteeship, 1945, with a Soviet administration north of the 38th parallel and a United States administration south of the 38th parallel. In 1948, divided into two States, North Korea and South Korea. In the Korean War, 1950–53, more than 750,000 Korean civilians were killed, as well as 114,000 Chinese, 33,741 Americans, 1,109 British, 721 Turkish, 516 Canadian and 339 Australian troops.

British until 1 July 1997, when sovereignty transferred to the People's Republic of China.

Became the Chinese Nationalist homeland (as Taiwan, with its capital at Taipei) after the success of the Chinese Communists in mainland China. Absorbed two million Chinese refugees from mainland China.

After 10 years of fighting, in March 1954 France accepted the partition of Vietnam into two independent States: the Democratic Republic of Vietnam (North Vietnam) and the State of Vietnam (South Vietnam). The two Vietnams were unified on 2 July 1976 (as the Socialist Republic of Vietnam) after two further decades of fighting, in which 1,400,000 Vietnamese, 58,209 Americans and 1,400 Chinese soldiers were killed.

The British Rajah (his family had ruled since 1842) ceded his authority to Britain, 1 July 1946. The local Malays resisted cession to Britain, assassinating the first British governor. Sarawak was one of the main sites of the 'Indonesian Confrontation', 1962–1966. It became an autonomous State of the Federation of Malaysia on 16 September 1963.

Achieved independence from the United States, 4 July 1946.

Achieved independence from Australia, 16 September 1975.

Declared independence from Portugal, 1975; invaded and occupied by Indonesia later that year. Achieved independence, as Timor-Leste, 20 May 2002 (the first new independent State of the Twenty-First C century).

The People's Republic of China established on 1 October 1949, by the Chinese Communist Party, with its capital in Peking (later named Beijing).

An ally of Japan, 1940–1945, but with an anti-Japanese resistance movement. After 1945 she became an ally of the United States.

Declared independence from France, 1945. French control not fully relinquished until 1954.

Achieved independence from Britain, 4 January 1948 (took the name Myanmar, 1989).

Achieved independence from Britain, 31 August 1957, after a decade of Malayan political activity and Communist-inspired armed insurgency (from 1963, the Federation of Malaysia).

Achieved independence from France, 9 November 1953.

Achieved independence, as India and Pakistan (East and West), 15 August 1947. East Pakistan declared independence from West Pakistan, as Bangladesh, in 1971, supported by the Indian Army.

Achieved independence from Britain, 4 February 1948 (later Sri Lanka).

Left British rule in 1963, and merged with Malaya, Sabah and Sarawak to form Malaysia. Less than two years later it left Malaysia to become an independent republic, 9 August 1965.

Declared independence, as Indonesia, 17 August 1945. Five years of diplomatic negotiations and armed conflict followed. The Netherlands recognised Indonesian independence in 1949.

© Martin Gilbert 2008

242

REPAIRING THE RAVAGES OF WAR: THE MARSHALL PLAN, 1947–1951

Stalin, fearing United States' influence in Eastern Europe, where his political control was paramount, refused to allow Czechoslovakia and Poland to attend the inaugural Paris Conference. Finland opted out to avoid offending the Soviet Union.

0 kilometres 500
0 miles 300

ICELAND
$43 million

To protect against Communist aggression, President Truman announced, on 12 March 1947, the Truman Doctrine, initially on behalf of Greece and Turkey, offering both economic and military aid, 'to work out a way of life free from coercion'.

The Marshall Plan (officially the European Recovery Programme) was a joint European-American venture, in which the resources of the United States were complemented with local resources, and where the participants worked toward a common goal of freedom and prosperity.

SWEDEN
$347 million

FINLAND

NORWAY
$372 million

North Sea

UNITED KINGDOM
$3,297 million

THE NETHERLANDS
$1,128 million

REPUBLIC OF IRELAND
$133 million

DENMARK
$385 million

Baltic Sea

Atlantic Ocean

NORWAY $372 million — Countries receiving Marshall Aid, with the total sum in millions of dollars, 1948–1951

------ European borders, 1948

BELGIUM & LUXEMBOURG
$777 million

Paris

EAST GERMANY

POLAND

SOVIET UNION

WEST GERMANY

CZECHOSLOVAKIA

$1,445 million

PORTUGAL
$70 million

Bay of Biscay

FRANCE
$2,296 million

AUSTRIA
$468 million

HUNGARY

ROMANIA

ITALY
$1,204 million

YUGOSLAVIA

BULGARIA

Black Sea

SPAIN

SWITZERLAND
$250 million

Adriatic Sea

ALBANIA

TURKEY
$137 million

Aegean Sea

GREECE
$366 million

PRINCIPAL DIVISION OF MARSHALL AID
$3.4 billion: raw materials and semi-manufactured products
$3.2 billion: food, animal feed and fertilizer
$1.9 billion: machines, vehicles, equipment
$1.6 billion: fuel

© Martin Gilbert 2008

Mediterranean Sea

On 5 June 1947, speaking to the graduating class at Harvard University, Secretary of State George C. Marshall laid the foundation for United States assistance to war-ravaged Europe. Marshall called on the United States to 'do whatever it is able to do to assist in the return of normal economic health in the world, without which there can be no political stability and no assured peace.' Sixteen nations attended a conference in Paris on 12 July 1947 to participate. After the United States Congress approved the Marshall Plan, President Truman signed it into law on 3 April 1948. From then until the end of 1951, the United States sent $13 billion in economic aid and technical assistance to 16 European countries; these countries saw their gross national product rise more than 30% and industrial production by 40% over prewar levels.

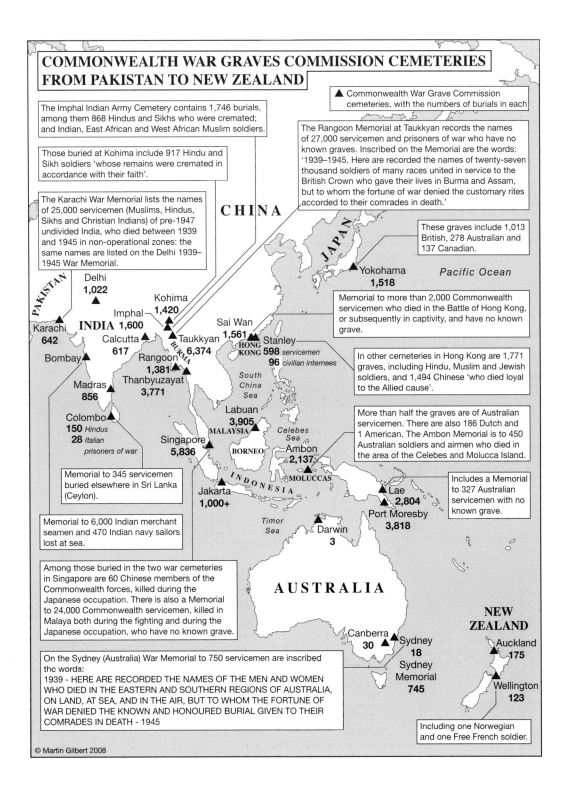

COMMONWEALTH WAR GRAVES COMMISSION CEMETERIES FROM PAKISTAN TO NEW ZEALAND

▲ Commonwealth War Grave Commission cemeteries, with the numbers of burials in each

The Imphal Indian Army Cemetery contains 1,746 burials, among them 868 Hindus and Sikhs who were cremated; and Indian, East African and West African Muslim soldiers.

The Rangoon Memorial at Taukkyan records the names of 27,000 servicemen and prisoners of war who have no known graves. Inscribed on the Memorial are the words: '1939–1945. Here are recorded the names of twenty-seven thousand soldiers of many races united in service to the British Crown who gave their lives in Burma and Assam, but to whom the fortune of war denied the customary rites accorded to their comrades in death.'

Those buried at Kohima include 917 Hindu and Sikh soldiers 'whose remains were cremated in accordance with their faith'.

The Karachi War Memorial lists the names of 25,000 servicemen (Muslims, Hindus, Sikhs and Christian Indians) of pre-1947 undivided India, who died between 1939 and 1945 in non-operational zones: the same names are listed on the Delhi 1939–1945 War Memorial.

These graves include 1,013 British, 278 Australian and 137 Canadian.

CHINA

JAPAN

Yokohama
1,518

Pacific Ocean

Memorial to more than 2,000 Commonwealth servicemen who died in the Battle of Hong Kong, or subsequently in captivity, and have no known grave.

PAKISTAN

Delhi
1,022
▲

Kohima
1,420
▲

Imphal
1,600
▲

INDIA

Sai Wan
1,561
▲

Stanley
598 *servicemen*
96 *civilian internees*

HONG KONG

Karachi
642
▲

Calcutta ▲
617

BURMA

Taukkyan
6,374

In other cemeteries in Hong Kong are 1,771 graves, including Hindu, Muslim and Jewish soldiers, and 1,494 Chinese 'who died loyal to the Allied cause'.

Bombay ▲

Rangoon
1,381

South China Sea

Thanbyuzayat
3,771

Madras ▲
856

Labuan
3,905

MALAYSIA

Celebes Sea

More than half the graves are of Australian servicemen. There are also 186 Dutch and 1 American. The Ambon Memorial is to 450 Australian soldiers and airmen who died in the area of the Celebes and Molucca Island.

Colombo ▲
150 *Hindus*
28 *Italian prisoners of war*

Singapore
5,836

BORNEO

Ambon
2,137

MOLUCCAS

Memorial to 345 servicemen buried elsewhere in Sri Lanka (Ceylon).

INDONESIA

Jakarta
1,000+

Lae
2,804

Port Moresby
3,818

Includes a Memorial to 327 Australian servicemen with no known grave.

Memorial to 6,000 Indian merchant seamen and 470 Indian navy sailors lost at sea.

Timor Sea

Darwin
3

Among those buried in the two war cemeteries in Singapore are 60 Chinese members of the Commonwealth forces, killed during the Japanese occupation. There is also a Memorial to 24,000 Commonwealth servicemen, killed in Malaya both during the fighting and during the Japanese occupation, who have no known grave.

AUSTRALIA

NEW ZEALAND

On the Sydney (Australia) War Memorial to 750 servicemen are inscribed the words:
1939 - HERE ARE RECORDED THE NAMES OF THE MEN AND WOMEN WHO DIED IN THE EASTERN AND SOUTHERN REGIONS OF AUSTRALIA, ON LAND, AT SEA, AND IN THE AIR, BUT TO WHOM THE FORTUNE OF WAR DENIED THE KNOWN AND HONOURED BURIAL GIVEN TO THEIR COMRADES IN DEATH - 1945

Canberra
30
▲

Sydney
18

Sydney Memorial
745

Auckland ▲
175

Wellington
123

Including one Norwegian and one Free French soldier.

© Martin Gilbert 2008

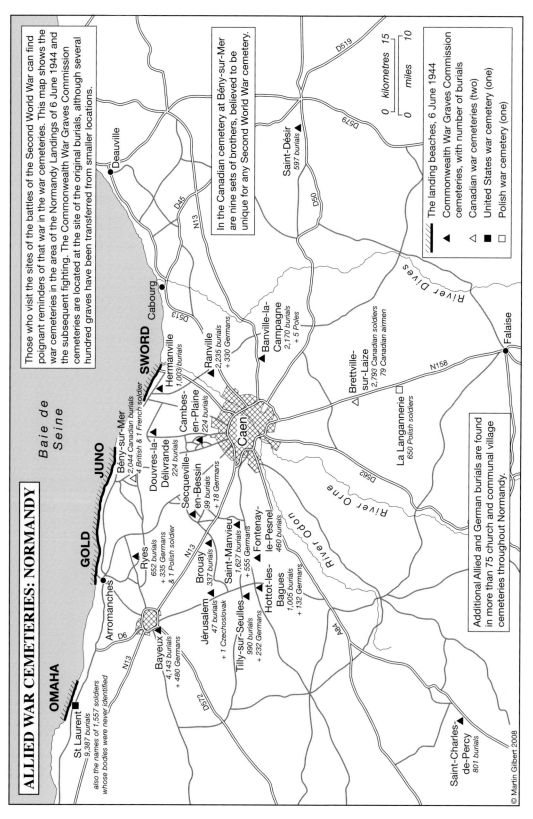

ALLIED WAR CEMETERIES: NORMANDY

Those who visit the sites of the battles of the Second World War can find poignant reminders of that war in the war cemeteries. This map shows the war cemeteries in the area of the Normandy Landings of 6 June 1944 and the subsequent fighting. The Commonwealth War Graves Commission cemeteries are located at the site of the original burials, although several hundred graves have been transferred from smaller locations.

In the Canadian cemetery at Bény-sur-Mer are nine sets of brothers, believed to be unique for any Second World War cemetery.

Additional Allied and German burials are found in more than 75 church and communal village cemeteries throughout Normandy.

///// The landing beaches, 6 June 1944

▲ Commonwealth War Graves Commission cemeteries, with number of burials

△ Canadian war cemeteries (two)

■ United States war cemetery (one)

□ Polish war cemetery (one)

0   kilometres   15

0   miles   10

Baie de Seine

OMAHA

St Laurent ■
9,387 burials
*also the names of 1,557 soldiers
whose bodies were never identified*

GOLD

JUNO

SWORD

Cabourg

Deauville

Arromanches

Bény-sur-Mer △
2,044 Canadian burials
4 British & 1 French soldier

Hermanville ▲
1,003 burials

Ranville ▲
2,235 burials
+ 330 Germans

Cambes-
en-Plaine ▲
224 burials

Douvres-la-
Délivrande ▲
224 burials

Secqueville-
en-Bessin ▲
99 burials
+ 18 Germans

Ryes ▲
652 burials
+ 335 Germans
& 1 Polish soldier

Brouay ▲
337 burials

Saint-Manvieu ▲
1,627 burials
+ 555 Germans

Fontenay-
le-Pesnel ▲
460 burials

Jérusalem ▲
47 burials
+ 1 Czechoslovak

Tilly-sur-Seulles ▲
990 burials
+ 232 Germans

Hottot-les-
Bagues ▲
1,005 burials
+ 132 Germans

Bayeux ▲
4,143 burials
+ 480 Germans

Banville-la-
Campagne ▲
2,170 burials
+ 5 Poles

Brettville-
sur-Laize △
2,793 Canadian soldiers
79 Canadian airmen

La Langannerie □
650 Polish soldiers

Saint-Désir ▲
597 burials

Caen

Falaise

Saint-Charles-
de-Percy ▲
801 burials

River Orne

River Odon

River Dives

D519

D79

D50

D45

N13

D513

N158

D562

A84

N13

D6

D572

N13

© Martin Gilbert 2008

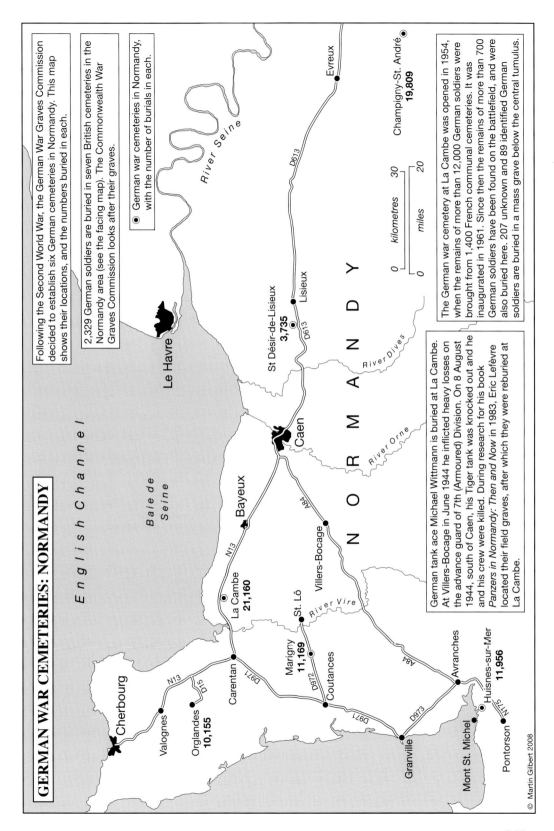

GERMAN WAR CEMETERIES: NORMANDY

Following the Second World War, the German War Graves Commission decided to establish six German cemeteries in Normandy. This map shows their locations, and the numbers buried in each.

2,329 German soldiers are buried in seven British cemeteries in the Normandy area (see the facing map). The Commonwealth War Graves Commission looks after their graves.

⊙ German war cemeteries in Normandy, with the number of burials in each.

The German war cemetery at La Cambe was opened in 1954, when the remains of more than 12,000 German soldiers were brought from 1,400 French communal cemeteries. It was inaugurated in 1961. Since then the remains of more than 700 German soldiers have been found on the battlefield, and were also buried here. 207 unknown and 89 identified German soldiers are buried in a mass grave below the central tumulus.

German tank ace Michael Wittmann is buried at La Cambe. At Villers-Bocage in June 1944 he inflicted heavy losses on the advance guard of 7th (Armoured) Division. On 8 August 1944, south of Caen, his Tiger tank was knocked out and he and his crew were killed. During research for his book *Panzers in Normandy: Then and Now* in 1983, Eric Lefèvre located their field graves, after which they were reburied at La Cambe.

English Channel

Baie de Seine

River Seine

Le Havre

Champigny-St. André
19,809

Evreux

St Désir-de-Lisieux
3,735

Lisieux

Caen

River Orne

River Dives

N O R M A N D Y

Bayeux

Villers-Bocage

La Cambe
21,160

St. Lô

River Vire

Marigny
11,169

Coutances

Carentan

Cherbourg

Valognes

Orglandes
10,155

Avranches

Granville

Mont St. Michel

Huisnes-sur-Mer
11,956

Pontorson

N13

D15

D971

D972

D973

D971

A84

A84

N175

D613

D613

0   kilometres   30
0   miles   20

© Martin Gilbert 2008

POLISH WAR GRAVES IN SCOTLAND

Several million soldiers, sailors and airmen, from many different nationalities, died hundreds and even thousands of miles from their homes. Their graves can be found in cemeteries large and small in every land. This map shows the Polish soldiers, sailors and airmen whose graves are in cemeteries in Scotland.

▲ Cemeteries in Scotland in which Polish servicemen are buried, with the number in each cemetery.

ORKNEYS

OUTER HEBRIDES

Thurso **1**
Wick **3**

Moray Firth

Evanton **9**
Fraserburgh **1**
Lossiemouth **1**
Rathen **1**
Longside **1**
Portree **1**
SKYE
Inverness **6**
Carrbridge **1**
Petty **5**
Dyce **1**
Aberdeen **2**

S C O T L A N D

North Sea

Brechin **1**
Montrose **1**
Blairgowrie **1**
Arbroath **2**
Dundee **11**
Carnoustie **2**
Perth **353**
St. Andrews **1**
Auchterarder **2**
Ceres **1**
Grangemouth **8**
Dunfermline two cemeteries **3**
Firth of Forth
Glasgow five cemeteries **8**
Larbert **1**
Falkirk **2**
Edinburgh three cemeteries **206**
Rothesay **8**
Renfrew **3**
Cambuslang **1**
Paisley **1**
Bothwell **1**
Airbles **2**
Hutton **1**
Kilmarnock **1**
Lanark **1**
Peebles **5**
Monkton **1**
Covington **1**
Mauchline **1**
Douglas **1**
Firth of Clyde
Sanquhar **9**
Harwick **3**

Auchinleck **11**

ENGLAND

Stranraer **3**

0 kilometres 50
0 miles 30

In the Westhill Cemetery in Perth are 353 Polish war graves: 339 soldiers, 4 sailors, 9 airmen and 1 nurse. The earliest war casualty is that of Officer Cadet Ulrych-Ulenski, who died on 10 November 1940.

A stone monument in the Westhill Cemetery, Perth, is inscribed, in both English and Polish:
ETERNAL GLORY
TO THE POLISH SOLDIERS
WHO DIED IN 1939-1945
FOR OUR FREEDOM AND
YOURS

Among the Polish war dead in Scotland were three Polish Jews: two are buried in the Glasgow Glenduff Hill Jewish Cemetery and one in the Glasgow Cathcart Hebrew Cemetery.

© Martin Gilbert 2008

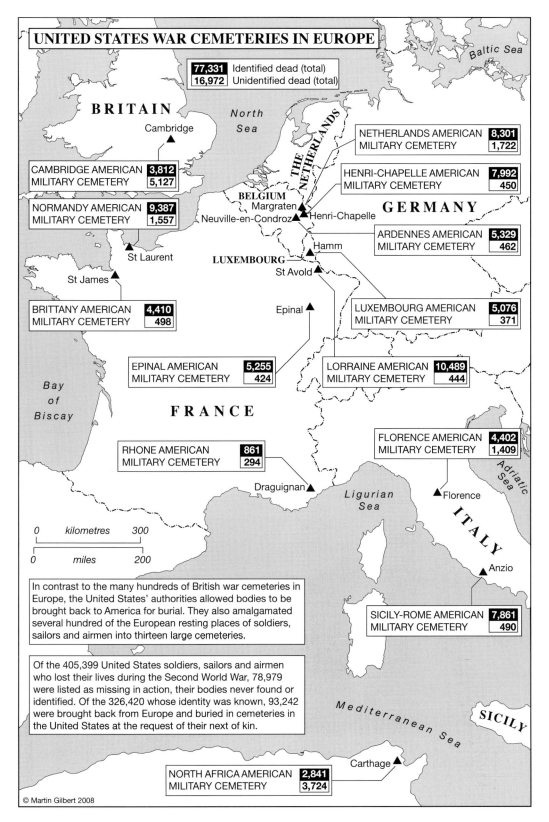

UNITED STATES WAR CEMETERIES IN EUROPE

77,331 Identified dead (total)
16,972 Unidentified dead (total)

BRITAIN

North Sea

Cambridge ▲

| CAMBRIDGE AMERICAN MILITARY CEMETERY | **3,812** **5,127** |

| NORMANDY AMERICAN MILITARY CEMETERY | **9,387** **1,557** |

St Laurent ▲

BELGIUM
Margraten ▲
Neuville-en-Condroz ▲ Henri-Chapelle

THE NETHERLANDS

| NETHERLANDS AMERICAN MILITARY CEMETERY | **8,301** **1,722** |

| HENRI-CHAPELLE AMERICAN MILITARY CEMETERY | **7,992** **450** |

GERMANY

| ARDENNES AMERICAN MILITARY CEMETERY | **5,329** **462** |

Hamm ▲
LUXEMBOURG
St Avold ▲

| LUXEMBOURG AMERICAN MILITARY CEMETERY | **5,076** **371** |

St James ▲

| BRITTANY AMERICAN MILITARY CEMETERY | **4,410** **498** |

Epinal ▲

Bay of Biscay

| EPINAL AMERICAN MILITARY CEMETERY | **5,255** **424** |

| LORRAINE AMERICAN MILITARY CEMETERY | **10,489** **444** |

FRANCE

| RHONE AMERICAN MILITARY CEMETERY | **861** **294** |

Draguignan ▲

Ligurian Sea

| FLORENCE AMERICAN MILITARY CEMETERY | **4,402** **1,409** |

▲ Florence

Adriatic Sea

ITALY

| 0 | kilometres | 300 |
| 0 | miles | 200 |

▲ Anzio

In contrast to the many hundreds of British war cemeteries in Europe, the United States' authorities allowed bodies to be brought back to America for burial. They also amalgamated several hundred of the European resting places of soldiers, sailors and airmen into thirteen large cemeteries.

| SICILY-ROME AMERICAN MILITARY CEMETERY | **7,861** **490** |

Of the 405,399 United States soldiers, sailors and airmen who lost their lives during the Second World War, 78,979 were listed as missing in action, their bodies never found or identified. Of the 326,420 whose identity was known, 93,242 were brought back from Europe and buried in cemeteries in the United States at the request of their next of kin.

Mediterranean Sea

SICILY

Carthage ▲

| NORTH AFRICA AMERICAN MILITARY CEMETERY | **2,841** **3,724** |

© Martin Gilbert 2008

Baltic Sea

248

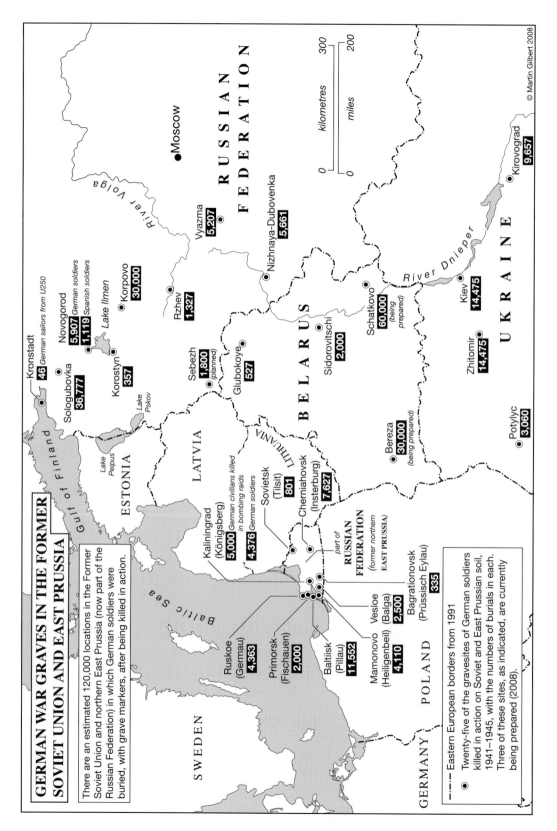

GERMAN WAR GRAVES IN THE FORMER SOVIET UNION AND EAST PRUSSIA

There are an estimated 120,000 locations in the Former Soviet Union and northern East Prussia (now part of the Russian Federation) in which German soldiers were buried, with grave markers, after being killed in action.

SWEDEN

GERMANY

POLAND

Baltic Sea

Gulf of Finland

Kronstadt
46 *German sailors from U250*

Sologubovka
36,777

Novgorod
5,907 *German soldiers*
1,119 *Spanish soldiers*

Lake Ilmen

Korpovo
30,000

Korostyn
357

Lake Pskov

Lake Peipus

ESTONIA

LATVIA

LITHUANIA

Sebezh
1,800 *(planned)*

Glubokoye
527

Rzhev
1,327

Vyazma
5,207

Nizhnaya-Dubovenka
5,661

River Volga

●Moscow

R U S S I A N
F E D E R A T I O N

Kaliningrad (Königsberg)
5,000 *German civilians killed in bombing raids*

4,376 *German soldiers*

Sovietsk (Tilsit)
801

Cherniahovsk (Insterburg)
7,627

part of
RUSSIAN FEDERATION
(former northern EAST PRUSSIA)

Ruskoe (Germau)
4,363

Primorsk (Fischhauen)
2,000

Baltiisk (Pillau)
11,552

Mamonovo (Heiligenbeil)
4,110

Vesloe (Balga)
2,500

Bagrationovsk (Prüssisch Eylau)
335

Sidorovitschi
2,000

Schatkovo
60,000 *(being prepared)*

River Dnieper

Kiev
14,475

Zhitomir
14,475

U K R A I N E

Potylyc
3,060

Kirovograd
9,657

Bereza
30,000 *(being prepared)*

B E L A R U S

0   200   300
kilometres
0   200
miles

© Martin Gilbert 2008

–––– Eastern European borders from 1991

● Twenty-five of the gravesites of German soldiers killed in action on Soviet and East Prussian soil, 1941–1945, with the numbers of burials in each. Three of these sites, as indicated, are currently being prepared (2008).

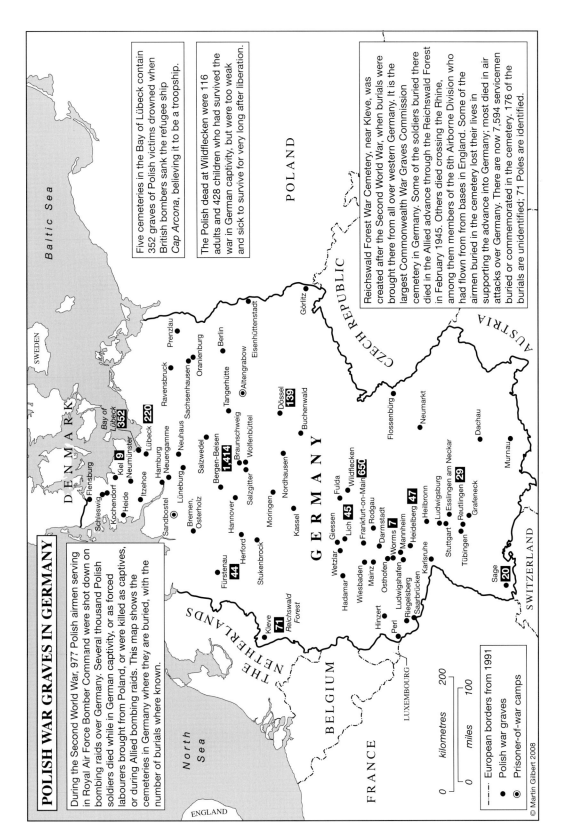

POLISH WAR GRAVES IN GERMANY

During the Second World War, 977 Polish airmen serving in Royal Air Force Bomber Command were shot down on bombing raids over Germany. Several thousand Polish soldiers died while in German captivity, or as forced labourers brought from Poland, or were killed as captives, or during Allied bombing raids. This map shows the cemeteries in Germany where they are buried, with the number of burials where known.

Five cemeteries in the Bay of Lübeck contain 352 graves of Polish victims drowned when British bombers sank the refugee ship *Cap Arcona*, believing it to be a troopship.

The Polish dead at Wildflecken were 116 adults and 428 children who had survived the war in German captivity, but were too weak and sick to survive for very long after liberation.

Reichswald Forest War Cemetery, near Kleve, was created after the Second World War, when burials were brought there from all over western Germany. It is the largest Commonwealth War Graves Commission cemetery in Germany. Some of the soldiers buried there died in the Allied advance through the Reichswald Forest in February 1945. Others died crossing the Rhine, among them members of the 6th Airborne Division who had flown from from bases in England. Some of the airmen buried in the cemetery lost their lives in supporting the advance into Germany; most died in air attacks over Germany. There are now 7,594 servicemen buried or commemorated in the cemetery. 176 of the burials are unidentified; 71 Poles are identified.

Baltic Sea

North Sea

ENGLAND

DENMARK

SWEDEN

POLAND

CZECH REPUBLIC

AUSTRIA

SWITZERLAND

FRANCE

LUXEMBOURG

BELGIUM

THE NETHERLANDS

GERMANY

Bay of Lübeck **352**

Flensburg
Schleswig
Kochendorf
Heide
Kiel **9**
Neumünster
Itzehoe
Hamburg
Neuengamme
Lüneburg
Lübeck **220**
Sandbostel
Bremen, Osterholz
Neuhaus
Salzwedel
Hannover
Ravensbrück
Sachsenhausen
Oranienburg
Berlin
Altengrabow
Eisenhüttenstadt
Görlitz
Prenzlau
Tangerhütte
Braunschweig **1,414**
Bergen-Belsen
Wolfenbüttel
Dössel **139**
Buchenwald
Salzgitter
Moringen
Nordhausen
Kassel
Fürstenau **44**
Herford
Stukenbrock
Reichswald Forest **71**
Kleve
Wetzlar
Giessen
Lich **45**
Hadamar
Fulda
Wildflecken **650**
Frankfurt-on-Main
Rodgau
Wiesbaden
Mainz
Darmstadt
Osthofen
Worms **7**
Mannheim
Heidelberg **47**
Ludwigshafen
Riegelsberg
Saarbrücken
Karlsruhe
Heilbronn
Ludwigsburg
Stuttgart
Esslingen am Neckar
Reutlingen **29**
Tübingen
Grafeneck
Sage **20**
Neumarkt
Flossenbürg
Dachau
Murnau
Hinzert
Perl

European borders from 1991
● Polish war graves
■ Prisoner-of-war camps

0   kilometres   200
0   miles   100

© Martin Gilbert 2008

250

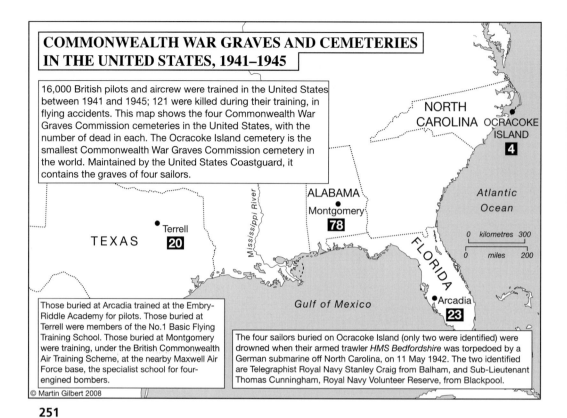

COMMONWEALTH WAR GRAVES AND CEMETERIES IN THE UNITED STATES, 1941–1945

16,000 British pilots and aircrew were trained in the United States between 1941 and 1945; 121 were killed during their training, in flying accidents. This map shows the four Commonwealth War Graves Commission cemeteries in the United States, with the number of dead in each. The Ocracoke Island cemetery is the smallest Commonwealth War Graves Commission cemetery in the world. Maintained by the United States Coastguard, it contains the graves of four sailors.

NORTH CAROLINA OCRACOKE ISLAND
4

Atlantic Ocean

ALABAMA
Montgomery
78

Terrell
TEXAS **20**

Mississippi River

FLORIDA

0 kilometres 300
0 miles 200

Gulf of Mexico

Arcadia
23

Those buried at Arcadia trained at the Embry-Riddle Academy for pilots. Those buried at Terrell were members of the No.1 Basic Flying Training School. Those buried at Montgomery were training, under the British Commonwealth Air Training Scheme, at the nearby Maxwell Air Force base, the specialist school for four-engined bombers.

The four sailors buried on Ocracoke Island (only two were identified) were drowned when their armed trawler *HMS Bedfordshire* was torpedoed by a German submarine off North Carolina, on 11 May 1942. The two identified are Telegraphist Royal Navy Stanley Craig from Balham, and Sub-Lieutenant Thomas Cunningham, Royal Navy Volunteer Reserve, from Blackpool.

© Martin Gilbert 2008

251

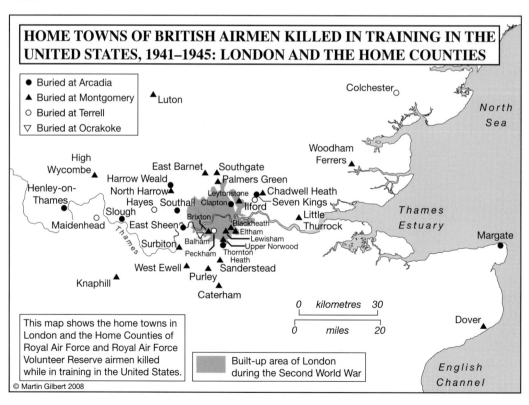

HOME TOWNS OF BRITISH AIRMEN KILLED IN TRAINING IN THE UNITED STATES, 1941–1945: LONDON AND THE HOME COUNTIES

● Buried at Arcadia
▲ Buried at Montgomery
○ Buried at Terrell
▽ Buried at Ocrakoke

Colchester○

North Sea

▲Luton

High Wycombe▲
Henley-on-Thames
Maidenhead○

East Barnet Southgate
Harrow Weald Palmers Green
North Harrow Chadwell Heath
Hayes Southall Clapton Ilford Seven Kings
Slough Brixton
East Sheen Blackheath Little Thurrock
Surbiton Balham Eltham
Peckham Lewisham
Thornton Upper Norwood
Heath
West Ewell▲ Sanderstead

Woodham Ferrers▲

Leytonstone

Thames Estuary

Margate▲

Knaphill▲

Purley
Caterham

0 kilometres 30
0 miles 20

Dover▲

This map shows the home towns in London and the Home Counties of Royal Air Force and Royal Air Force Volunteer Reserve airmen killed while in training in the United States.

Built-up area of London during the Second World War

English Channel

© Martin Gilbert 2008

252

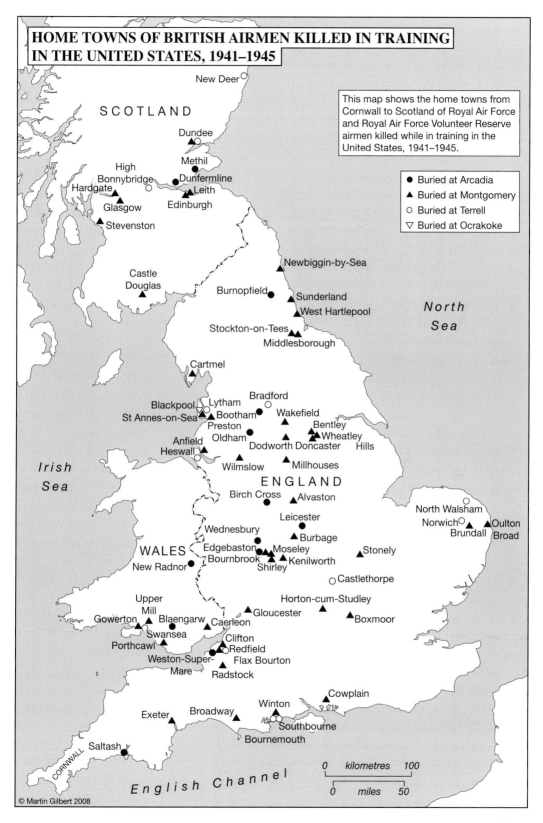

HOME TOWNS OF BRITISH AIRMEN KILLED IN TRAINING IN THE UNITED STATES, 1941–1945

New Deer

SCOTLAND

Dundee

Methil

High Bonnybridge
Hardgate
Dunfermline
Leith
Glasgow
Edinburgh
Stevenston

This map shows the home towns from Cornwall to Scotland of Royal Air Force and Royal Air Force Volunteer Reserve airmen killed while in training in the United States, 1941–1945.

● Buried at Arcadia
▲ Buried at Montgomery
○ Buried at Terrell
▽ Buried at Ocrakoke

Castle Douglas

Newbiggin-by-Sea

Burnopfield
Sunderland
West Hartlepool

North Sea

Stockton-on-Tees
Middlesborough

Cartmel

Bradford

Blackpool
St Annes-on-Sea
Lytham
Bootham
Wakefield
Preston
Bentley
Anfield
Oldham
Wheatley
Heswall
Dodworth Doncaster
Hills
Wilmslow
Millhouses

Irish Sea

ENGLAND

Birch Cross
Alvaston

North Walsham

Leicester

Norwich
Oulton Broad
Brundall

Wednesbury
Burbage

WALES
Edgebaston
Moseley
Stonely
Bournbrook
Kenilworth
New Radnor
Shirley

Castlethorpe

Horton-cum-Studley

Upper Mill
Gloucester
Gowerton
Blaengarw
Caerleon
Boxmoor
Swansea
Porthcawl
Clifton
Redfield
Weston-Super-Mare
Flax Bourton
Radstock

Cowplain

Winton
Broadway
Exeter
Southbourne
Bournemouth
Saltash

CORNWALL

English Channel

0   kilometres   100
0   miles   50

© Martin Gilbert 2008

253

GERMAN WAR GRAVES IN THE BALTIC STATES

More than 150,000 German soldiers are buried in cemeteries in the three Baltic States, This map shows the main cemeteries, and the numbers of Germans buried there.

The German names of towns are given in brackets. Daugavpils was also known, in Russian, as Dvinsk; Shauliai in Yiddish as Shavli; Vilnius as Vilna, and Kaunas as Kovno.

FINLAND

Gulf of Finland

Tallin

Pirita 251

Marjamae 2,386

Toila 2,160

Narva 9,467

Rakvere (Wesenberg) 15,568

Johvi 3,522

ESTONIA

Lake Peipus

Lavassaare 65

Pärnu (Parnau) 922

Viljandi (Fellin) 770

Tartu (Dorpat) 2,052

ÖSEL (SAAREMAA)

Kuresaari (Ahrensburg) 1,334

Baltic Sea

Gulf of Riga

Lake Pskov

Valga (Walk) 244

Cemetery includes Hungarian soldiers who fought as part of the German forces.

15,000 6,700 431

Riga (three cemeteries)

Cesis (Wenden) 376

Ergili 200

Cemetery includes Latvian soldiers who fought as part of the German forces.

Dzukste 416

Saldus (Frauenburg) 21,834

Jelgava (Mitau) 700

Olaine 100

LATVIA

Siauliai 722

A second cemetery includes 155 German soldiers killed while prisoners of war.

Daugavpils (Dunaburg) 2,580

RUSSIA

Klaipeda (Memel) 1,529

Naumiestis 281

Taurage (Tauroggen) 675

LITHUANIA

Kaunas 2,713

Kaliningrad

RUSSIA

formerly northern East Prussia

Vilnius 2,338

| 0 | kilometres | 100 |
| 0 | miles | 50 |

POLAND

▲ Towns with German soldiers' cemeteries.

—·—·— International borders since 1991.

© Martin Gilbert 2008

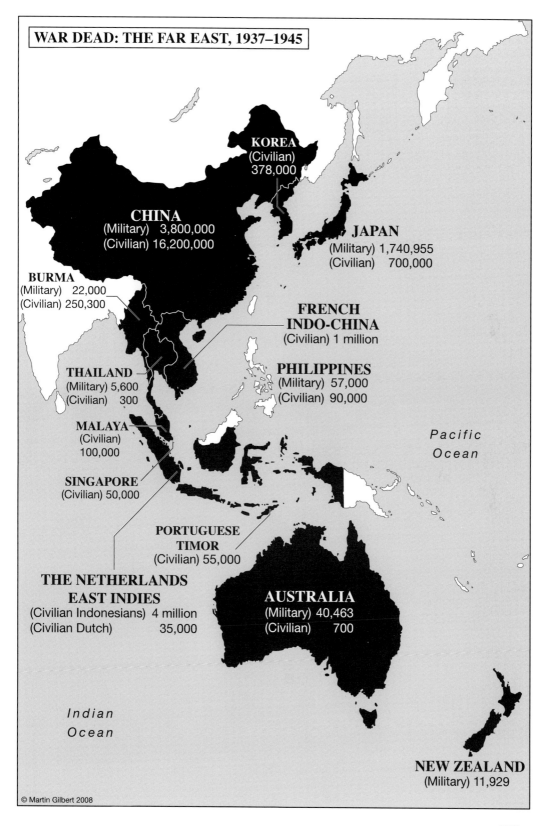

WAR DEAD: THE FAR EAST, 1937–1945

KOREA
(Civilian)
378,000

CHINA
(Military) 3,800,000
(Civilian) 16,200,000

JAPAN
(Military) 1,740,955
(Civilian) 700,000

BURMA
(Military) 22,000
(Civilian) 250,300

FRENCH
INDO-CHINA
(Civilian) 1 million

THAILAND
(Military) 5,600
(Civilian) 300

PHILIPPINES
(Military) 57,000
(Civilian) 90,000

MALAYA
(Civilian)
100,000

SINGAPORE
(Civilian) 50,000

*Pacific
Ocean*

PORTUGUESE
TIMOR
(Civilian) 55,000

THE NETHERLANDS
EAST INDIES
(Civilian Indonesians) 4 million
(Civilian Dutch)   35,000

AUSTRALIA
(Military) 40,463
(Civilian)   700

*Indian
Ocean*

NEW ZEALAND
(Military) 11,929

© Martin Gilbert 2008

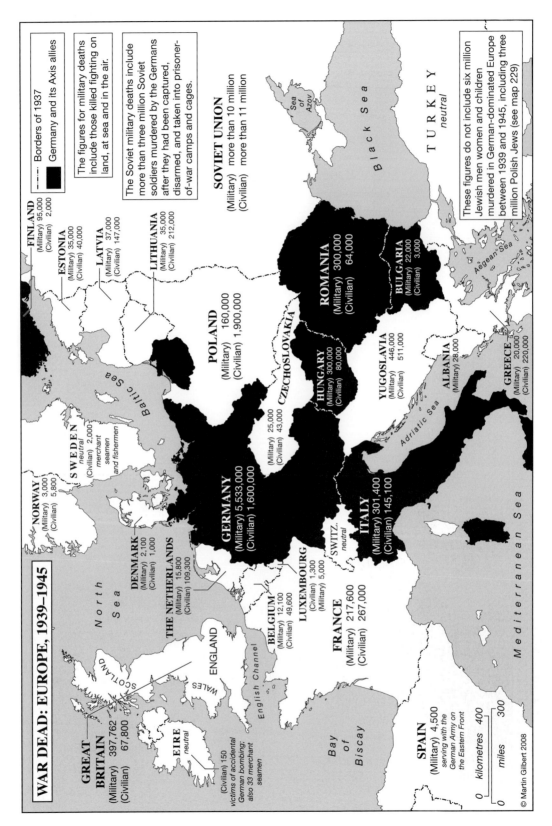

WAR DEAD: EUROPE, 1939–1945

- - - - Borders of 1937

■ Germany and its Axis allies

The figures for military deaths include those killed fighting on land, at sea and in the air.

The Soviet military deaths include more than three million Soviet soldiers murdered by the Germans after they had been captured, disarmed, and taken into prisoner-of-war camps and cages.

These figures do not include six million Jewish men women and children murdered in German-dominated Europe between 1939 and 1945, including three million Polish Jews (see map 229)

SOVIET UNION
(Military) more than 10 million
(Civilian) more than 11 million

FINLAND
(Military) 95,000
(Civilian) 2,000

ESTONIA
(Military) 35,000
(Civilian) 40,000

LATVIA
(Military) 37,000
(Civilian) 147,000

LITHUANIA
(Military) 35,000
(Civilian) 212,000

ROMANIA
(Military) 300,000
(Civilian) 64,000

BULGARIA
(Military) 22,000
(Civilian) 3,000

POLAND
(Military) 160,000
(Civilian) 1,900,000

CZECHOSLOVAKIA
(Military) 25,000
(Civilian) 43,000

HUNGARY
(Military) 300,000
(Civilian) 80,000

YUGOSLAVIA
(Military) 446,000
(Civilian) 511,000

ALBANIA
(Military) 28,000

GREECE
(Military) 20,000
(Civilian) 220,000

SWEDEN
neutral
(Civilian) 2,000 merchant seamen and fishermen

NORWAY
(Military) 3,000
(Civilian) 5,800

GERMANY
(Military) 5,533,000
(Civilian) 1,600,000

SWITZ.
neutral

ITALY
(Military) 301,400
(Civilian) 145,100

DENMARK
(Military) 2,100
(Civilian) 1,000

THE NETHERLANDS
(Military) 15,800
(Civilian) 109,300

BELGIUM
(Military) 12,100
(Civilian) 49,600

LUXEMBOURG
(Military) 1,300
(Military) 5,000

FRANCE
(Military) 217,600
(Civilian) 267,000

GREAT BRITAIN
(Military) 397,762
(Civilian) 67,800

(Civilian) 150 victims of accidental German bombing; also 33 merchant seamen

EIRE
neutral

SPAIN
(Military) 4,500 serving with the German Army on the Eastern Front

TURKEY
neutral

North Sea

Baltic Sea

Black Sea

Sea of Azov

Aegean Sea

Adriatic Sea

Mediterranean Sea

Bay of Biscay

English Channel

SCOTLAND

ENGLAND

WALES

0   300   400
kilometres
0   300
miles

© Martin Gilbert 2008

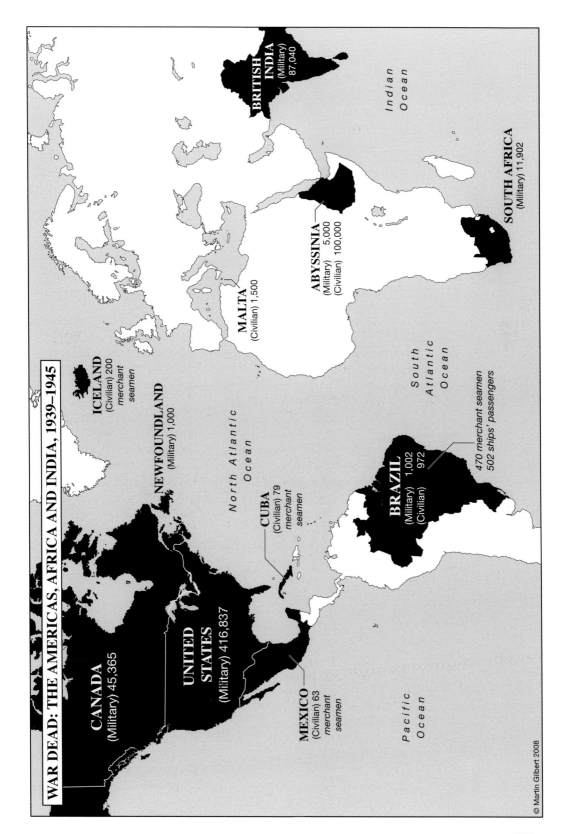

WAR DEAD: THE AMERICAS, AFRICA AND INDIA, 1939–1945

BRITISH INDIA
(Military)
87,040

SOUTH AFRICA
(Military) 11,902

ABYSSINIA
(Military)   5,000
(Civilian)   100,000

MALTA
(Civilian) 1,500

Indian Ocean

ICELAND
(Civilian) 200
merchant seamen

NEWFOUNDLAND
(Military) 1,000

North Atlantic Ocean

South Atlantic Ocean

CUBA
(Civilian) 79
merchant seamen

BRAZIL
(Military)   1,002
(Civilian)   972

*470 merchant seamen
502 ships' passengers*

CANADA
(Military) 45,365

UNITED STATES
(Military) 416,837

MEXICO
(Civilian) 63
merchant seamen

Pacific Ocean

© Martin Gilbert 2008

Epilogue

When the Second World War came to an end in 1945, large tracts of Europe and the Far East were in ruins. The territorial ambitions of pre-war Germany, Italy and Japan had been crushed. Their wartime allies, Hungary, Bulgaria and Romania, were mauled and defeated. The captive nations, most cruelly Poland and Yugoslavia, had suffered terrible repression. In every country under German rule, the Jews had been singled out for physical annihilation. Under Japanese rule, captive peoples had been denied their rights and dignity, murdered in large numbers, and, as the war ended, had taken up the struggle for independence from European colonial rule. The British and French Empires in Asia and Africa had been shaken. China, the world's most populous country, having been ravaged by almost ten years of savage conflict, was on the brink of revolution. India, the world's second most populous country, while insisting on independence from Britain, was soon to break up into two nations, one mainly Muslim, the other predominantly Hindu. Dutch rule in the Far East was under attack. United States rule in the Philippines was coming to an end.

Compounding this turmoil, the ending of the war had seen the creation of a new ideological divide. The victorious western Allies, led by the United States, found themselves face to face across an Iron Curtain with the victorious eastern Allies in the orbit of the Soviet Union. A new war, the Cold War, had come into being. The NATO and Warsaw Pact powers, headed respectively by the United States and the Soviet Union, faced each other across a continuous line of minefields, barbed wire and watchtowers stretching, as Churchill told the British parliament, 'From Stettin on the Baltic to Trieste on the Adriatic'. The atomic bomb that had brought Japan to surrender became, in even more powerful forms, the gravest threat to humanity, and, as it emerged, the guarantee that nations would hesitate before unleashing such a destructive weapon.

The Second World War had ended in victory for some and defeat for others; it had ended in the despair created by widespread destruction, and in the hopes of millions for a world in which personal and national sufferings would become a thing of the past.

The victorious nations had fought for different ideals, some for liberating those who had been defeated and subjugated, others to establish their own new order; all had also fought for self-preservation. The victors and vanquished had passed through the worst torment and pain they could inflict upon each other. As the post-war era began, they faced the task of rebuilding their lives, while often still grieving over the loss of loved ones in the conflagration that had just ended. This atlas portrays many aspects of that suffering, and also the courage and perseverance that had been shown throughout the war. These qualities were still needed after 1945, and are still needed today, if, from the rubble and the human suffering, a more civilised human society is to be achieved, with more peace, more national contentment, and a life of less fear.

Sixty-three years after the harsh guns of the Second World War fell silent and the fearful silhouettes of the bombers of all the warring nations disappeared from the skies, sixty-three years after the wounded, the prisoners of war and the surviving captives in concentration camps began to return home, much of humanity is still hoping for a world without war.

Bibliography of works consulted

SINGLE-SHEET MAPS

M. Bixel, *Internés, Déportés, Fusillés, Victimes Civiles du Gers*. No date.

Coombs Cartographic Unit, Australian National University, *Japanese Prisoner-of-War Camps During World War II, 1941–1945*. Medical Research Committee of the American Ex-Prisoners of War Organization.

Philip Cross, *The Death Railway: Map of Prisoner-of-War Camps: Bangkok–Burma Railway, June 1942 – October 1943*, August 2001.

I.G Farben Factory-Ludwigshaven, 5 November 1944 (bombing raid, German anti-aircraft defences).

Tonie and Valmai Holt, *Major and Mrs Holt's Battle of the Normandy Landing Beaches*, 1999.

Edward Kossoy, *Mitteleuropa in der ersten Hälfte des Jahres 1945*. Munich, 1968.

Jan Laskowski (ed.), *Hitlerowskie Obozy Na Ziemiach Polskich w Latach 1939–1945*. Warsaw: Main Commission for the Study of Hitlerite Crimes in Poland, 1968

Frances Worthington Lipe, *Japanese Prisoner-of-War Camps During World War II, 1941–1945: Known Locations where American, British, Dutch, Australian, Canadian, Indian and other Allied Military and Civilian Personnel Were Imprisoned by the Japanese*. Brownsville, Texas: Medical Research Committee of American Ex-Prisoners of War Inc, 1980.

Map of Lost U-boats (interactive). Updated November 2000. Nova Online. www.pbs.org/wgbh/nova/lostsub/map.html

'F/O Matthews, Gelsenkirchen, 5/3/45': The British Bombing Raid on Gelsenkirchen, 5 March 1945.

Will Newton, *The Kokoda Track: Territory of Papua New Guinea*. August 2001.

Oil Targets Attacked by Allied Strategic Air Forces April 1944 – April 1945 (with list of 101 oil and benzol plants, oilfields, oil storage and oil refineries 'classified according to contemporary Allied sources').

'Operation Chastise: planned routes': the Dams Raid of 17 May 1943.

Sandakan Death March: www.sandakan-deathmarch.com/

Soviet partisan movement activities over the 1941–1944 period. Moscow, 1975.

Sowjetische Kriegsgefangenenlager 1944 (showing prisoner-of-war camps established in 1941/2, 1943 and 1944).

Supreme Headquarters, Allied Expeditionary Force *Location of PW Camps*. 1 November 1944, amended 26 February 1945.

Lieutenant-Colonel Erwin Tschudi (historical ed.), *Les Opérations Militaires en Europe, 1939–1945*. Kümmerly & Frey, Berne. No date.

Velikaya Otyechestbyennaya Voina Sovietskogo Soyuza, 1941–1945 (The Great Patriotic War of the Soviet Union, 1941–1945). Moscow: 1985.

Michael Williams, *Map of France showing the partitions under the 1940 Armistice*. September 2007. www.oradour.info/appendix/francez1.htm

ATLASES

Francis Brown, *The War in Maps: An Atlas of The New York Times Maps*. New York: Oxford University Press, 1944.

John Coates, *An Atlas of Australia's Wars*. South Melbourne, Australia: Oxford University Press, 2nd edition, 2006.

Debes-Schlee, *Mittlerer Schulatlas in 72 Kartenseiten*. Leipzig: Verlag von H. Wagner & E. Debes, 1942.

Michael Freeman, *Atlas of Nazi Germany*. London: Croom Helm, 1987.

Thomas E. Griess (series ed.), *The West Point Military History Series, Atlas for the Second World War: Asia and the Pacific*. Wayne, New Jersey: Avery Publishing Group, 1985.

J.F. Horrabin, *An Atlas-History of the Second Great War: Volume 1, September 1939 to January 1940*. London: Thomas Nelson, March 1940.

J.F. Horrabin, *Horrabin's Atlas-History of the Second Great War in Maps & Diagrams with Comment*. 14 Volumes. London: Thomas Nelson, 1940–1945.

David Jordan and Andrew Wiest, *Atlas of World War II*. London: Amber Books, 2007.

Richard Overy (ed.), *The Times Atlas of the 20th Century*. London: Times Books, 1996.

David Smurthwaite, *The Pacific War Atlas, 1941–1945*. London: Mirabel Books, 1995.

Brigadier Peter Young (ed.) and Richard Natkiel (cartographer), *Atlas of the Second World War*. London: Weidenfeld and Nicolson, 1973 (Cassell edition, 1999).

REFERENCE BOOKS

Max Arthur, *Symbol of Courage: A History of the Victoria Cross*. London: Sidgwick and Jackson, 2004.

Stephen Campbell, *Police Battalions of the Third Reich*. Atglen, Pennsylvania: Schiffer Military History, 2007.

Christopher Chant, *The Encyclopedia of Code Names of World War II*. London: Routledge & Kegan Paul, 1986.

Council for the Preservation of Monuments to Resistance and Martyrdom, *Scenes of Fighting and Martyrdom Guide: War Years in Poland, 1939–1945*. Warsaw: Sport I Turystyka, 1968.

I.C.B. Dear and M.R.D. Foot, *The Oxford Companion to World War Two*. Oxford: Oxford University Press, 1995.

Benjamin L. DeWhitt and Jennifer Davis Heaps, *Records Relating to Personal Participation in World War II: American Prisoners of War and Civilian Internees*. Washington DC: National Archives and Records Administration, 1998.

William H. Garzke Jr and Robert O. Dulin Jr, *Battleships: Axis and Neutral Battleships in World War II*. Annapolis: Naval Institute Press, 1985.

Charles Hocking, *Dictionary of Disasters at Sea During the Age of Steam: Including sailing ships and ships of war, 1824–1962*. London: Lloyd's Register of Shipping, 2 volumes (single-volume edition, The London Stamp Exchange, 1989.

Martin Middlebrook and Chris Everitt, *The Bomber Command Diaries: An Operational Reference Book, 1939–1945*. London: Penguin Books, 1985.

Jürgen Rohwer, *Axis Submarine Successes of World War Two: German, Italian and Japanese Submarine Successes, 1939–1945*. London: Greenhill Books, 1999.

Cesare Salmaggi and Alfredo Pallavisini (eds), *2194 Days of War: An illustrated chronology of the Second World War with 620 illustrations and 84 maps*. London: Windward, 1979.

Supreme Headquarters, Allied Expeditionary Force (Evaluation and Dissemination Section G2 (Counter-Intelligence Sub-Division), *KLs (Konzentrationslager) Axis Detention Centres Reported as such in Europe*. No place. No date. Reprinted, Hounslow: World War II Investigator Ltd (no date).

GENERAL HISTORIES

Christopher Chant and others, *World War II: Land, Sea & Air Battles, 1939–1945*. London: Sundial Books, 1977.

Martin Gilbert, *Second World War*. London: Weidenfeld and Nicolson, 1989.

John Ray, *The Daily Telegraph Illustrated History of the Second World War*. London: Weidenfeld and Nicolson, 1999.

H.P. Willmott, *The Second World War in the East*. London: Cassell, 1999. (The Far East and the Pacific.)

BOOKS ON SPECIAL SUBJECTS

Paul Adair, *Hitler's Greatest Defeat: the Collapse of Army Group Centre, June 1944*. London: Cassell, 1994.

Louis Allen, *Burma: The Longest War, 1941–45*. London, J.M. Dent, 1984.

Catherine Andreyev, *Vlasov and the Russian Liberation Movement: Soviet reality and émigré theories*. Cambridge: Cambridge University Press, 1987.

John A. Armstrong (ed.), *Soviet Partisans in World War II*. Madison: University of Wisconsin Press. 1964.

Max Arthur, *Forgotten Voices of World War II: A New History of World War II in the Words of the Men and Women Who Were There*. London: Ebury Press, 2004.

Mark Axworthy, *Third Axis, Fourth Ally: Romanian Armed Forces in the European War, 1941–1945*. London: Arms and Armour Press, 1995.

Anthony Beevor, *Crete: The Battle and the Resistance*. London: John Murray, 1991.

Ralph Bennett, *Intelligence Investigations: How Ultra Changed History, Collected Papers of Ralph Bennett*. London: Frank Cass, 1996.

Moti Lal Bhargava, *Indian National Army: Tokyo Cadets*. New Delhi: Reliance Publishing House, 1986.

Witold Bieganski, *Poles in the Battle of Narvik*. Warsaw: Interpress Publishers, 1969.

Ken Bradley, *Hellfire Pass Memorial: Thai–Burma Railway*. Bangkok: Australian-Thai Chamber of Commerce, 3rd edition (updated by Rod Beattie), 1996.

Clifford Brazier, *XD Operations: Secret British Missions Denying Oil to the Nazis*. Barnsley: Pen & Sword Military, 2004.

Christopher R. Browning, *Ordinary Men: Reserve Police Battalion 101 and the Final Solution in Poland*. New York: HarperCollins, 1992.

David G. Chandler and James Lawton Collins (eds), *The D-Day Encyclopedia*. New York: Simon and Schuster, 1994.

John D. Clarke, *French Eagles, Soviet Heroes: The 'Normandie-Niemen' Squadrons on the Eastern Front*. Stroud: Sutton Publishing, 2005.

Philip Cockrill (ed.), *The War in Malaya and Indonesia, 1941–1945*. London: Philip Cockrill, no date.

John Cooksey, *Operation Chariot: The Raid on St Nazaire*. Barnsley: Pen & Sword Military, 2005.

A.D. Divine, *Dunkirk*. London, Faber & Faber, 1945.

Milovan Djilas, *Wartime*. London: Martin Secker & Warburg, 1977. (The partisan war in Yugoslavia.)

Douglas Dodds-Parker, *Setting Europe Ablaze: Some Accounts of Ungentlemanly Warfare*. Windelsham, Surrey: Springwood Books, 1984.

Trevor Nevitt Dupuy, *Asian and Axis Resistance Movements*. London: Franklin Watts, 1970.

Major L.F. Ellis, *The War in France and Flanders, 1939–1940*. London, Her Majesty's Stationery Office, 1953.

Major L.F. Ellis and others, *Victory in the West, Volume 1, The Battle of Normandy*. London, Her Majesty's Stationery Office, 1962.

Roy Farran, *Winged Dagger: Adventures on Special Service*. London: William Collins, 1948.

M.R.D. Foot, *SOE in France: An Account of the Work of the British Special Operations Executive in France, 1940–1944*. London: Her Majesty's Stationery Office, 1966.

M.R.D. Foot and J.M. Langley, *MI9: Escape and Evasion, 1939–1945*. London: The Bodley Head, 1979.

Roger Ford, *Steel from the Sky: The Jedburgh Raiders, France 1944*. London: Weidenfeld and Nicolson, 2004.

Norman Franks, *The Greatest Air Battle: Dieppe, 19th August 1942*. London: Grub Street, 1992.

Helen Fry, *The King's Most Loyal Enemy Aliens: Germans Who Fought For Britain in the Second World War*. Stroud: Sutton Publishing, 2007.

David Garnett and others, *The Campaign in Greece and Crete*. London: His Majesty's Stationery Office, 1942.

Martin Gilbert, *Winston S. Churchill, Volume 6, Finest Hour, 1939–1941*. London: Heinemann, 1983.

Martin Gilbert, *Winston S. Churchill, Volume 7, Road to Victory, 1941–1945*. London: Heinemann, 1986.

Martin Gilbert, *Second World War*. London: Weidenfeld and Nicolson, 1989.

Martin Gilbert, *D-Day*. New York: Wiley, 1994.

Martin Gilbert, *The Day the War Ended: VE-Day 1945 in Europe and Around the World*. London: HarperCollins, 1995

Teodor Gladkov, *Operation Bagration, 1944*. Moscow: Novosti Press Agency Publishing House, 1980.

Lance Goddard, *Canada and the Liberation of the Netherlands, May 1945*. Toronto: Dundurn Press, 2005.

Philip Henshall, *The Nuclear Axis: Germany, Japan and the Atom Bomb Race, 1939–1945*. Stroud: Sutton Publishing, 2000.

Tonie and Valmai Holt, *Major and Mrs Holt, Battlefield Guide to the Normandy Landing Beaches*. Barnsley: Leo Cooper, 2nd edition, 2000.

Tonie and Valmai Holt, *Major and Mrs Holt, Battlefield Guide to Market-Garden*. Barnsley: Pen & Sword Military, new edition, 2004.

Patrick Howarth, *Undercover: The Men and Women of the Special Operations Executive*. London: Routledge & Kegan Paul, 1980.

Edwin P. Hoyt, *The Death of the U-Boats*. New York: Warner Books, 1988.

T. Jankowski and E. Weese (eds), *Documents on Polish-Soviet Relations, 1939–1945, Volume One, 1939–1945*. London: Heinemann, 1961.

Vladimir Karpov, *Russia at War, 1941–45*. London: Stanley Paul, 1987.

Chris Kempton, 'Loyalty and Honour': The Indian Army, September 1939 – August 1947, Part 1, Divisions. Milton Keynes: The Military Press, 2003.

Ludovic Kennedy, Menace: The Life and Death of the Tirpitz. London: Sidgwick and Jackson, 1978.

Benjamin King and Timothy Kutta, Impact: The History of Germany's V-Weapons in World War II. Staplehurst, Kent: Spellmount Publishers, 1998.

C.M. Kohan, Works and Buildings (History of the Second World War, United Kingdom Civil Series). London: His Majesty's Stationery Office and Longmans, Green, 1952.

Jon Latimer, Burma: The Forgotten War. London: John Murray, 2004.

Peter Leighton-Langer, The King's Own Loyal Enemy Aliens: German and Austrian Refugees in Britain's Armed Forces, 1939–45. London: Vallentine Mitchell, 2006.

George Lepre, Himmler's Bosnian Division: The Waffen-SS Handschar Division, 1943–1945. Atgen, Pennsylvania: Schiffer Publishing, 1997.

Sean Longden, Hitler's Slaves: Allied POWs in Germany, 1939–45. London: Constable, 2005.

Keith Lowe, Inferno: The Fiery Destruction of Hamburg, 1943. New York: Scribner, 2007.

Charles MacDonald, A Time For Trumpets: The Untold Story of the Battle of the Bulge. New York: Bantam Books, 1984.

John Macdonald, Great Battles of World War II. London: Marshall Editions, 1986.

Ben Macintyre, Agent Zigzag: The True Wartime Story of Eddie Chapman: Lover, Traitor, Hero, Spy. London: Bloomsbury, 2007.

Donald Macintyre, The Battle of the Atlantic. London: Pan Books, 1983.

Francis Mackay, Overture to Overlord: Special Operations in Preparation for D-Day. Barnsley: Pen and Sword Military, 2005.

Kenneth Macksey, Commando Strike: The Story of Amphibious Raiding in World War II. London: Secker and Warburg, 1985.

Czeslaw Madajczyk (ed.), Zamojszczyzna: Sonderlaboratorium SS. Warsaw: Ludowa Spóldzielnia Wydawnicza, 1979.

William Manchester, The Arms of Krupp, 1587–1968. Boston: Little, Brown, 1968.

Daniel Marston (editor), The Pacific War Companion: From Pearl Harbor to Hiroshima. Botley, Oxford: Osprey Publishing, 2005.

Ralph G. Martin, The GI War, 1941–1945. Boston: Little, Brown and Company. 1967.

John Masefield, The Nine Days Wonder: The Operation Dynamo. (The Dunkirk evacuation.) London, William Heinemann, 1941.

Evan McGilvray, The Devils' March –A Doomed Odyssey: The 1st Polish Armoured Division, 1939–1945. Solihull: Helion, 2005.

Martin Middlebrook, The Berlin Raids: RAF Bomber Command Winter 1943–44. London: Viking, 1988.

Field Marshal The Viscount Montgomery of Alamein, Normandy to the Baltic. London: Hutchinson, 1946.

Michael Montgomery, Who Sank The Sydney? London: Leo Cooper, 1983.

Gordon Musgrove, Operation Gomorrah: The Hamburg Firestorm Raids. London: Jane's Publishers. 1981.

Michael J. Neufeld, The Rocket and the Reich: Peenemünde and the Coming of the Ballistic Missile Era. New York: The Free Press, 1995.

Samuel J. Newland, Cossacks in the German Army, 1941–1945. London: Frank Cass, 1991.

Office of Assistant Chief of Staff, Intelligence, The AAF in the Invasion of Southern France. Washington DC: Center for Air Force History, 1992.

Alan Palmer, *Northern Shores: A History of the Baltic Sea and its Peoples*. London: John Murray, 2005.

Alfred Price, *Battle of Britain: The Hardest Day, 18 August 1940*. London: Macdonald and Jane's Publishers, 1979.

Henry Probert, *The Forgotten Air Force: The Royal Air Force in the War Against Japan, 1941–1945*. London: Brassey, 1995.

Winston G. Ramsey, *The Blitz: Then and Now, Volume 1, 3 September 1939 – 6 September 1940*. London: After the Battle, 1986.

Graham Rhys-Jones, *The Loss of the Bismarck: An Avoidable Disaster*. London: Cassell, 1999.

Waclaw Jurgielewicz and others, *Polish Women in Combat, 1939–1945*. Warsaw: Rada Narodowa Gospodarka Administracja, 1980.

John Robertson, *Australia at War, 1939–1945*. Melbourne: William Heinemann, 1981.

David Rolf, *The Bloody Road to Tunis: Destruction of the Axis Forces in North Africa, November 1942 – May 1943*. London: Greenhill Books, 2001.

David Rooney, *Wingate and the Chindits: Redressing the Balance*. London: Arms and Armour, 1994

Harrison Salisbury, *The 900 Days: The Siege of Leningrad*. London: Martin Secker &Warburg, 1969.

T.R. Sareen, *Select Documents on Indian National Army*. Delhi: Agam Prakashan, 1988.

Hilary St. George Saunders, *Royal Air Force, 1939–1945: Volume III, The Fight is Won*. London: Her Majesty's Stationary Office, 1954.

T.R. Sareen, *Select Documents on Indian National Army*. Delhi: Agam Prakashan, 1988.

Tim Saunders, *Dieppe Operation Jubilee: Battleground Europe*. Barnsley: Pen and Sword, 2005.

L.A. Sawyer and W.H. Mitchell, *The Liberty Ships: The history of the 'emergency' type cargo ships constructed in the United States during World War II*. Cambridge, Maryland, 1970.

B.B. Schofield, *The Russian Convoys*. London: B.T. Batsford, 1964.

Mark Seaman (introduction), *Operation Foxley: The British Plan to Kill Hitler*. Richmond, Surrey: Public Record Office Publications, 1998.

Hugh Sebag-Montefiore, *Enigma: The Battle for the Code*. London: Weidenfeld and Nicolson, 2000.

Ronald Seth, *Jackals of the Reich: The Story of the British Free Corps*. London: New English Library, 1972.

Christopher Shores, *Duel for the Sky: Ten Crucial Air Battles of World War II Vividly Recreated*. London: Grub Street, 1999.

David Sibley, *The Behar Massacre: The execution of 69 survivors from the British Merchant Ship 'Behar' in 1944 by the Imperial Japanese Navy*. Stockport: A. Lane Publishers, 1997.

Kenneth Slepyan, *Stalin's Guerrillas: Soviet Partisans in World War II*. Lawrence, Kansas: University Press of Kansas, 2006.

Peter Slowe and Richard Woods, *Battlefield Berlin: Siege, Surrender and Occupation, 1945*. London: Robert Hale, 1988.

Colonel C.P. Stacey, *The Canadian Army, 1939–1945: An Official Historical Summary*. Ottawa: Minister of National Defence, 1948.

David Stafford, *Britain and European Resistance, 1940–1945: A Survey of the Special Operations Executive, With Documents*. Toronto: University of Toronto Press, 1980.

Joseph Stalin, *On the Great Patriotic War of the Soviet Union*. Moscow: Foreign Languages Publishing House, 1946 (Collected speeches and Orders of the Day, 3 July 1941 to 3 September 1945.)

Edward R. Stettinius Jr, *Lend-Lease: Weapon for Victory*. New York: The Macmillan Company, 1944.

John Sweetman, *The Dambusters Raid*. London: Cassell, 1999.

Nigel Thomas and Peter Abbott, *Partisan Warfare, 1941–5*. London: Osprey Publishing, 1983.

Julian Thompson, *Victory in Europe Experience: from D-day to the Destruction of the Third Reich*. London, Carlton Books, 2005.

Ian Valentine, *Station 43: Audley End House and SOE's Polish Section*. Stroud: Sutton Publishing, 2004.

Jonathan F. Vance, *Objects of Concern: Canadian Prisoners of War Through the Twentieth Century*. Vancouver: University of British Columbia Press, 1994.

Philip Vickers, *Das Reich: 2nd SS Panzer Division Das Reich – Drive to Normandy, June 1944*. Barnsley: Leo Cooper, 2000.

Brian Lorring Villa, *Unauthorized Action: Mountbatten and the Dieppe Raid*. Oxford: Oxford University Press, 1991.

Philip Warner, *Secret Forces of World War II*. London: Granada, 1985.

Adrian Weir, *The Last Flight of the Luftwaffe: The Suicide Attack on the Eighth Air Force, 7 April 1945*. London: Cassell, 1977.

Charles Whiting, *Britain Under Fire: The Bombing of Britain's Cities, 1940–45*. London: Century Hutchinson, 1986.

George Winter, *Manhay: The Ardennes, Christmas 1944*. Winnipeg: J.J. Fedorowicz Publishing, 1990.

John Winton, *Death of the Scharnhorst*. London: Antony Bird, 1983.

David Wragg, *Second World War Carrier Campaigns*. Barnsley: Pen and Sword Maritime, 2004.

Derrick Wright, *Pacific Victory: Tarawa to Okinawa, 1943–1945*. Stroud: Sutton Publishing, 2005.

Alfred-Maurice de Zayas, *The German Expellees: Victims in War and Peace*. New York: St Martin's Press, 1993.

ARTICLES

Peter Elstob, 'Battle of the Bulge: the Onslaught, Ardennes, Belgium, December 16/19, 1944'. *Purnell's History of the Second World War*, Volume 6, Number 3.

Benjamin B. Fischer, 'The Katyn Controversy: Stalin's Killing Field', *Studies in Intelligence*, Central Intelligence Agency, Winter 1999–2000.

Paul Kennedy, 'The Life and Death of The Tirpitz.' *History of the Second World War*, Volume 5, No.15.

Nataliya Lebedeva, 'The Tragedy of Katyn', *International Affairs*, Moscow, June 1990.

Charles B. MacDonald, 'Slapton Sands: The Cover-up That Never Was', *Army*, Volume 38, No.6, June 1988.

Charles B. MacDonald, 'Battle of the Bulge: The Allied Counterblow, Ardennes, Belgium, December 22, 1944/January 28, 1945, *Purnell's History of the Second World War*, Volume 6, Number 4.

Dr Richard Raiber, 'The Führerhauptquartiere', *After The Battle*, No. 19, 1977.

'Nikolai Baibakov', *The Times*, 8 April 2008 (obituary).

'Lady Sniper' (Lyudmila Pavlichenko), *Time*, 28 September 1942.

Archival sources

Major Tony Hibbert, 'Operation Eclipse: The race to save Denmark from the Russians'. Private monograph, 11 July 2005.

'List of British Air Commonwealth Air Training Plan Facilities in Canada.' Canadian War Museum, Ottawa.

List of Greek villages destroyed or partially destroyed, March–December 1943. National Archives, London: WO 169/15698

Records of World War II Prisoners of War, created 1942–1947, documenting the period 7 December 1941 – 19 November 1946: Record Group 389, The United States Archives and Records Administration, Washington DC.

World War II Prisoners of the Japanese Data File, created April 2005 – February 2006, documenting the period circa 1941 – circa 1945: Collection ADBC, The United States Archives and Records Administration, Washington DC.

Records About Japanese-Americans Relocated During World War II, created 1988–1989, documenting the period 1942–1946: Record Group 219, The United States Archives and Records Administration, Washington DC.

WEBSITES

'Chronology of the Siege of Malta, 1940–43'.
merlinsovermalta.gdenney.co.uk/worldwar2/timeline/

Commonwealth War Graves Commission (cemeteries and individual casualties).
www.cwgc.org

Roger Darlington, 'Czechoslovak Airmen in the Royal Air Force.'
www.rogerdarlington.co.uk/czechsinraf.html

Richard Doody, 'The Grand Duchy of Luxembourg.'
http://worldatwar.net/nations/luxembourg/narrative.html

Karen E. Ebel, 'German-American Internees in the United States during World War II'.
http://www.traces.org/timeline.aftermath.html

'German Firms That Used Slave or Forced Labor During the Nazi Era.'
http://Jewishvirtuallibrary.org/jsource/Holocaust/germancos.html

Dr S.J. Lewis. 'Jedburgh Team Operations in Support of the 12th Army Group, August 1944.' Combat Studies Institute, Combined Arms Research Library, 1991.
http://cgsc.leavenworth.army.mil/carl/resources/csi/lewis/Lewis.asp

Roger Mansell, 'Japanese Camps.' Centre for Research: Allied POWs Under The Japanese. Palo Alto, California.
http://www.mansell.com

Fred Preller, 'Index of 8th AF WWII UK Sites' (United States Eighth Air Force Air Bases in Britain)
http://mighty8thaf.preller.us/

Rick Webb, 'Missions Flown by the 453rd': from February 5, 1944 to April 11, 1945.'
tinpan.fortunecity.com/aprilskies/264/missions.html

Michael Williams, 'Oradour-sur-Glane 10th June 1944.'
www.oradour.info/

'List of Hellship Voyages in Chronological Sequence of Departure Dates.'
http://www.west-point.org/family/Japanese-pow/ShipsNum.htm

'Wartime Memories Project – Prisoner of War Camps.'
http://www.wartimememoriesproject.com/ww2/pow/index.php

'Yugoslav Partisan Air Force: Military Air Bases and Airfields.'
http://www.aeroflight.co.uk/waf/yugo/part/yugo-part-bases.htm

Index

compiled by the author

The Routledge Atlas of the First World War
3rd edition
Martin Gilbert

From its origins to its terrible legacy, the course of the First World War is vividly set out in a series of 173 fascinating maps. Together, these maps form a comprehensive and compelling picture of the war that devastated large parts of Europe, destroying three Empires; these maps illustrate the military, social, political and economic aspects of the war. Starting with the pre-war tensions and war aims, the atlas covers:

- The early months of the war – from the German attack on Belgium and France to the fierce fighting on the Western and Eastern Fronts

- The developing war in Europe and beyond – from the Somme and Verdun to Gallipoli and Mesopotamia, in the Near East and Africa, and in the Pacific

- The war at sea and in the air – from the Zeppelin and air raids to the naval battles, shipping losses and Atlantic convoys

- Life at the front – from the trench system, living underground, the mud of Passchendaele, to the French and Russian mutinies

- Technology and the intensifying war – from phosgene gas to submarines, tanks and aerial bombardment

- The home fronts – war supplies, munitions factories, the air defence of Britain, German food riots, the entry of the United States into the war, the Russian Revolution, and the collapse of the Austro-Hungarian and the Ottoman Empires

- The aftermath – the peace treaties and territorial changes, war debts, war deaths, and the new map of Europe.

This revised edition contains a new section depicting the visual remembrance of the war; a guide to the memorials that commemorate the Battle of the Somme.

ISBN13: 978–0–415–46037–8 (hbk)
ISBN13: 978–0–415–46038–5 (pbk)

For ordering and further information please visit:
www.routledge.com

The Routledge Atlas of the Holocaust
4th edition
Martin Gilbert

'A classic of Holocaust studies. No other single volume quite conveys both the sheer scale of the Holocaust, and the depth of individual tragedy.'

BBC History Magazine

'This book will be an essential part of the teaching of this sad, but sadly recurring chapter of History.'

Andrew Hunt

The harrowing history of the Nazi attempt to destroy the Jews of Europe during the Second World War is illustrated in this series of 333 detailed and graphic maps.

The maps, and the text and photographs that accompany them, vividly depict the fate of the Jews between 1933 and 1945, whilst also setting the chronological story in the wider context of the war itself. The maps include:

- historical background: from the effects of anti-Jewish violence between 1880 and 1933 to the geography of the existing Jewish communities before the advent of the Nazis

- the beginning of the violence – from the destruction of the synagogues in November 1938 to Jewish migrations and deportations, and the establishment of the concentration camps and death camps throughout German-dominated Europe

- the spread of Nazi rule – the fate of the Jews throughout Europe including Germany, Austria, Poland, Greece, Yugoslavia, Bulgaria, Russia, Denmark, Norway, France, Holland, Belgium, Italy, and the Baltic States

- Jewish revolts and resistance; and the work of Christians in saving Jews

- the death marches, the advance of the Allies to the liberation of the camps, the fate of the survivors, and the final death toll.

This revised edition includes a new section which gives an insight into the layout and organisation of some of the most significant places of the Holocaust, including Auschwitz, Treblinka and the Warsaw Ghetto, which will be especially useful to those visiting the sites.

ISBN13: 978–0–415–48481–7 (hbk)
ISBN13: 978–0–415–48486–2 (pbk)

For ordering and further information please visit:
www.routledge.com